The Ultimate Guide to Extraordinary Evildoers Earns High Praise

HOLD THE PRESSES!! ADMIRING WORDS TO FOLLOW!!!

"I wish that *The Supervillain Book* could be required reading so that all the bizarre knowledge that fans like me have on the subject would be shared by everyone."
—Alex Ross, artist of *Kingdom Come* and *Justice*

"Anthropology of the Antisocial! This book dishes all the dirt any fan could ever want."
—Steve Englehart, writer of *Batman: Dark Detective*, *Night Man*, and *The Avengers*

"Sure, Hannibal Lecter was evil, but could he build a time machine out of an old television and a dog whistle? Could Al Capone shoot magnetic beams from his hands? Pikers. *The Supervillain Book* chronicles the origins and schemes of those masked miscreants capable of making even the mighty Superman tremble in his red boots."
—Mark Waid, writer of *Fantastic Four, Superman*, and *Kingdom Come*

"These days, when you sometimes can't tell the difference between the good guys and the bad, it's nice to find a book that tells you straight up who to root for and who you should boo. In the comics the good guys always hog the spotlight, get their names in the title, and certainly get all the press, but a good guy without a really great bad guy is boring. So here's a whole grouping of really great bad guys. Enjoy and tremble at the same time."
—Marv Wolfman, comic-book writer, creator of Blade and Bullseye, and co-creator of the New Teen Titans

"Nothing makes a HERO a TRUE HERO, without a villain that can out-smart him or her at every turn until the end ... a REAL VILLAIN is what makes a REAL HERO EVEN BETTER! *The Supervillain Book* fully embraces this concept and celebrates these characters!"
—Kevin Eastman, Co-creator of the Teenage Mutant Ninja Turtles

"What a welcome addition to the growing list of historical books on the comic-book industry. Gina Misiroglu and Michael Eury have done themselves and the genres of heroes and horror proud! At once, thorough, articulate, and entertaining!"
—Gene Colan, *Captain America, Daredevil*, and *Tomb of Dracula* artist

"What would the light be without the dark? What would the good be without the bad? And what would the hero be without the villain? Much as we love the selfless efforts of popular culture's many supermen and women, it's the twisted and dangerous antics of their anti-thetical opponents that draw us all into the heart of any adventure. Gina Misiroglu, Michael Eury, and their various contributors have culled a definite compendium of the most delightfully horrid characters to ever spin a diabolical scheme. What would the heroes be without their villains? Downright boring."
—Matt Wagner, creator of Grendel and Mage, and writer/artist of *Batman and the Monster Men*

"Super-heroes are fascinating, in and of themselves. But, just as Joe Louis would have been less of a hero without Max Schmelling, super-heroes need a villain worthy of their mettle. A super-villain. And this book catalogs the greatest super-villains of all time."
—Roy Thomas, comic-book writer and editor and Golden Age historian

"A good hero is nothing without a good villain. After all, someone has to devise those incredible obstacles, schemes, and mind-numbing death traps our favorite heroes have to overcome. At long last, Gina Misiroglu and Michael Eury have come forward, in heroic fashion, to tell you everything you need to know about the bad guys who, more than any other, define the good guys!"
—Dan Jurgens, writer and/or artist of *Superman, Thor, Hyperion, City of Heroes*, and *Infinite Crisis Secret Files*

The Supervillain Book

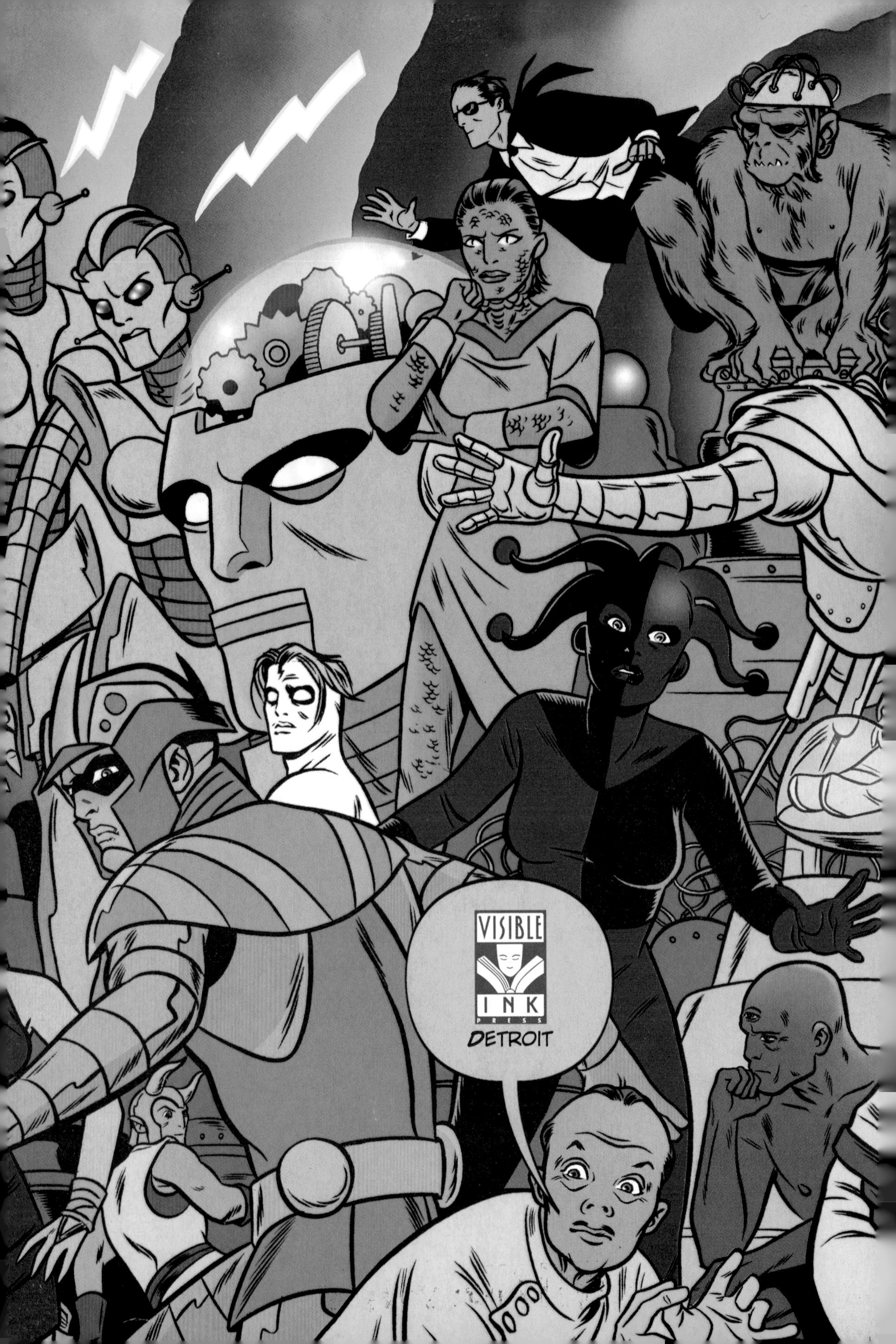
VISIBLE INK PRESS
DETROIT

The Supervillain Book

The Evil Side of Comics and Hollywood

Edited by Gina Misiroglu and Michael Eury

The Supervillain Book: The Evil Side of Comics and Hollywood

© 2006 by Visible Ink Press.

Visible Ink Press®
43311 Joy Rd. #414
Canton, MI 48187-2075
http://www.visibleink.com

Visible Ink Press is a registered trademark of Visible Ink Press LLC.

Art Director: Mary Claire Krzewinski
Typesetting: The Graphix Group

ISBN 10: 0-7808-0977-7

ISBN 13: 978-07808-0977-2

Printed in Singapore

All rights reserved

10 9 8 7 6 5 4 3 2 1

CIP on file with the Library of Congress

Casebound editions published exclusively for Omnigraphics

info@omnigraphics.com
1-800-875-1340
Editorial Office: 615 Griswold St.
Detroit, MI 48226
www.omnigraphics.com

Contents

A Word from Stan Lee   xi
Those Who Worship Evil's Might: An Introduction   xiii
The People We Would Like to Thank: The Acknowledgments   xix
The People Who Helped Make the Book: The Contributors   xxi

Contents

Contents

A Word from Stan Lee

Hi, Heroes!

Here's a quick quiz for you …

Who's the one character you absolutely must have in a superhero series? If you answered "the superhero," go to the head of the class. But wait; it gets tricky.

The next question is, who are the most important *characters* in a superhero series? Come on now, the title of this book oughta give you a clue. That's it! You're right! The most important characters in any superhero series are, and always have been, the super*villains*!

Want proof? Let's take just one example. Where would Spider-Man be without the Green Goblin, Doc Ock, the Lizard, the Sandman, the Kingpin, or any of his other splendidly savage and sinister supervillains?

Sure, you always need the hero, but ask yourself this: how eager would you be to read about a superhero who fought litterbugs, jaywalkers, or income-tax evaders? I somehow suspect you wouldn't be racing to the comic-book store to grab every new issue about that particular do-gooder.

In fact, think about most of the great action movies you've seen. I'll bet the Joker's makeup kit that the ones you liked best, the ones that stick in your memory the longest, are inevitably the ones with the most unique, colorful, and dangerous villains.

So, although you certainly can't have a superhero saga without a superhero, the series would soon be history without a steady stream of scary supervillains to keep it going.

Of course, like everything else in life, supervillains keep changing in style and substance. As superhero comics keep evolving, the stories tend to get darker and edgier, and, just as the tales grow ever heavier, the supervillains, too, tend to get darker, meaner, and more macabre. And y'know something? The scarier and more menacing they become, the more the public (and that's you, Charlie!) can't get enough of them.

So let's face it. Gina Misiroglu and Michael Eury's beautifully written and illustrated *Supervillain Book* is just what superhero fans have been waiting for. It gives us exciting insights into the lives, powers, and motivations of the greatest supervillains in all of comicdom, film, and television.

Naturally there's a lot more I could say about this terrific book, but I don't wanna keep you from all the fun and excitement on the pages ahead. Anyway, it's not as though we're leaving each other, because you can bet I'll be eagerly reading right along with you.

Excelsior!

Stan

Those Who Worship Evil's Might: An Introduction

"These days, the racks at your local comic store read like a lineup on *America's Most Wanted*," reported *Wizard* magazine not long ago. The industry fanzine also noted that the litany of supervillain-centric comic books available today is unprecedented, with their numbers projected to rise. As we pen these words, joining perennial favorite *Catwoman* (star of her own monthly series) are DC's *Lex Luthor: Man of Steel* and Marvel's *Fantastic Four: Foes* and *Books of* [Dr.] *Doom*, all miniseries that examine the psyches of some of comics' most sinister figures; Ra's al Ghul and the Scarecrow "Year One" miniseries; the *House of M* crossover, depicting a Magneto-controlled Marvel Universe; the Secret Society of Super-Villains' onslaught against the Justice League; recent *Deadshot* and *Thanos* miniseries; supervillain free-for-alls in DC's *Villains United*, Marvel's *Spider-Man: Breakout!*, and Image's *Spawn* #150, the latter of which gathered Spawn's enemies in hell; and Ben Raab's *Living in Infamy* (Ludovico Technique, 2005–2006), featuring a suburban witness-protection program of reformed supervillains.

With this in mind, an encyclopedic study of the supervillain archetype—pop culture's most malevolent costumed criminals, sinister societies, and destructive dominators that have battled super- and other fictional heroes—could not be more timely or useful. Drawing from sources in comic books, film, live-action and animated television, newspaper strips, Japanese manga and anime, and toys, this definitive A-to-Z guide to evil masterminds, sinister megalomaniacs, world-class menaces, and marauding mutants is the follow-up to the critically acclaimed *Superhero Book*. In *The Supervillain Book* you will learn about each character's origin, costumes, weapons and gadgetry, secret hideouts, and chief henchmen, as well as the history behind the creation of the character and enough trivia tidbits to make you a walking encyclopedia. Because *The Supervillain Book* is as much a reference on modern mythology as it is a chronicle of the extremely wicked, the book discusses the cultural phenomenon of each character and its various incarnations in the popular culture. Splashing the pages are exciting film stills and comic-book images of villains in action, plus sidebars galore.

Why this attraction to supervillainy? The bigger-than-ordinary-life antagonist is just plain interesting and fun. The fall from grace is a devastating tumble, the need for revenge eternal and recognizably *human*. Supervillains pique our interest in the yin-yang relationship of good and evil. We rally behind superheroes because they devote themselves to saving the world (and often, along the way, have to overcome character flaws and personal doubt), but the supervillains' attempts to do just the opposite cater to our darkest desires.

Comic books have a long history of interpreting the news, ranging from superhero battles with Hitler and Nazi soliders to 9/11-type disasters. Just as comic-book villains represented our fears of nuclear annihilation during the cold war, today's breed are proxy evildoers displacing modern anxiety: terrorists operating outside any moral code we can understand, disease epidemics of unimaginable scale, the steady crumbling of the environment, and the usurping of jobs, security, and the American way of life by internal and external forces. Once again, after a very brief respite, we live in chaotic and uncertain times, fearing phantom-like supervillains able to thwart and taunt the mightiest power on Earth. Sound familiar?

Drawing inspiration from today's headlines, the comic universe pits the battle between good and evil in recognizable settings and with sentiments easily understood by readers. These battles *matter*. One of the better examples of the comic-book mirror is Marvel's *Civil War,* a seven-issue limited monthly series examining the current conflict between security and freedom, with familiar storylines featuring superheroes participating in a reality television show, embedded reporters on the front lines of war, a search for weapons of mass destruction, enemy combatants, and an attack on civil liberties that divides superheroes into warring camps. Many of the best-known Marvel characters take sides and are sorely tested, including Spider-Man, Captain America, the Fantastic Four, and Iron Man.

No theme in popular culture has been exploited like that of good versus evil. From the earliest epic tales like *Beowulf* to the latest video games, evil is personified as the *villain*, or in more extreme cases, the *supervillain*, an exaggerated character basking in self-indulgence. Extraordinary men, women, or beings of an entirely different genesis, they possess a level of ambition consistent with the desire to be the world's greatest menace. They are dedicated to acquiring great wealth, spreading hate and fear, accomplishing stupendous evil, corrupting humanity, conquering Earth, and/or becoming the most powerful entity in the universe. And they display a certain tendency toward showing off, basking in media attention, and creating mass hysteria. In today's celebrity-saturated world, the exaggerated swagger of the supervillain is the stuff of superstardom. Consider the declaration of infamous Silver Age Superman foe Jax-Ur: "Who wants to be a hero? I'd rather be notorious!"

While we root for the hero, let's be *honest*: we can't take our eyes off of the bad guy, girl, beast, or alien, whatever the case might be. Like a showbiz diva, supervillains always make a grand entrance and steal the scene. Performance art and thievery are part of their raffish charm. Supervillains possess pizzazz, spout blood-curdling dialogue, and are stunningly resourceful—just when you think they're down for the count, up they pop, unleashing yet another powerful blow, from a debilitating stun blast to a disorienting remark like, "Luke, I am your father." They are the characters we love to hate, who challenge the social order and our beloved superheroes, who create grave peril for the world at large. In short, a supervillain is our worst nightmare—a really bad actor lacking any social inhibitions and armed with very powerful bad stuff. The words of the great Stan

Lee ring true: "The most important characters in any superhero series are, and always have been, the super*villains*!"

Fans may identify with the villain for his or her distinctive qualities of rebelliousness, individuality, and antisocial leanings. Some of today's supervillains possess a degree of moral relativism—where ethical judgments and notions of right and wrong are up for interpretation—that strikes an empathic chord with their audience, from Ra's al Ghul's attempts to "cleanse" the world of the "blight" of humanity to Magneto's agenda of elevating his mutant species to supremacy. And that audience has expanded dramatically. Supervillains have not only taken control of comics, they are holding Hollywood and the gaming worlds hostage; think about the casting frenzy over which villains would battle with the hero in *Spider-Man 3.* Ultimately Sandman and Venom were chosen, but earlier rumors involved everyone from the Chameleon to Kraven the Hunter to Electro. Powerful, often supernatural horror haunts the prime-time television schedule, while public curiosity about the modus operandi of criminals has inspired forensic science–based reality and dramatic television shows like CBs's *C.S.I.* franchise. News programming is filled with terrorists and religious extremists grabbing headlines and holding our attention. We are at once threatened and fascinated by what makes the villain tick.

With dozens of villains for every hero, the supervillain field is ripe for harvesting—even though the criminals themselves are rotten to the core. *The Supervillain Book* takes a definitive look at the bad-guy mentality, exposing hundreds of sinister super-foils for all their worth, chronicling the histories of the most evil and wretchedly ruthless, the most brutal and coldly cunning, and the cruelest and coolest fictional characters of popular culture.

With such an expansive mission statement as this, we needed to be discerning with regard to which villains to include. How does one distinguish a supervillain from a run-of-the-mill rogue? A thug or bandit relies upon a weapon—a gun, a knife, a sword, a baseball bat, brass knuckles, or a fist—to intimidate a (usually weaker) victim. The goals of the average bad guy are small and often forged in desperation: knock over a convenience store, rip off a purse. And the mundane crook *reacts*—runs and hides when there's trouble, and nervously shoots, scratches, or screams when cornered.

The supervillain has a larger worldview. He or she may, and probably does, employ weapons, but they are ones of mass destruction—a thermonuclear warhead, a disintegration beam, a deadly virus, or a shrinking ray. Thinking big is a characteristic of the trade. The goals of a villain are far-reaching: aim a nuke at the San Andreas Fault to sink California, control the weather with a satellite, or subjugate all earthlings. And the supervillain is *proactive*—committing crimes, from contaminating cosmetics with a nerve toxin to reconstructing reality, that are the result of cold, calculated, sociopathic, or megalomaniacal cunning. As the superhero risks life to protect others, the supervillain chooses to perpetrate evil, acting on his or her innermost desires. Ego often dictates that these maniacs and miscreants flaunt their twisted psyches, weapons arsenals, hidden laboratories, unique paraphernalia, and motivations for world domination.

Pop-culture scholar Dr. Peter Coogan has spent the better part of his adult life studying villains and heroes. In his book *Superhero: The Secret History of a Genre*, Coogan describes the supervillainous archetypes: the monster, the enemy commander, the mad scientist, the criminal mastermind, and the inverted-superhero supervillain. Although other subtypes emerge, such as alien, evil god, femme fatale, and super-henchman, these types always have a primary identification as one of the main types—while Darkseid is an evil god, he's primarily an enemy commander; though the Skrulls are aliens, they're mainly monsters. According to Coogan, the simplest definition of the supervillain is "a villain who is *super*, that is, someone who commits villainous or evil acts and does so in a superior way or at a magnified level."

The following seven criteria apply to the supervillain:

1. The supervillain has a selfish, antisocial mission. The supervillain seeks something—typically wealth or power, but often fame or infamy in addition—that will serve his interests and not those of others or the larger culture.

2. Supervillains are superior to the ordinary authorities. They have cunning, genius, resources, powers, or extraordinary abilities that render the ordinary agents of the social order helpless to stop them, or at least put the authorities at a distinct disadvantage.

3. The supervillain's dream reaches far beyond the acquisitive scheme of the ordinary crook. The supervillain is an artist whose medium is crime.

4. The supervillain's mania is what raises him above the common person and above the common criminal. It is this mania that permits the supervillain to view the epic criminal acts as art or as analogous to great accomplishments in other fields and also to accomplish (or nearly accomplish, as he is almost always stopped by the hero) his great scheme.

5. The supervillain's selfishness is absolute, solipsistic. He sees himself as the center of existence.

6. This self-aggrandizement arises from a sense of victimhood, from a wound that the supervillain never recovers from.

7. The supervillain's wound prompts him to monologue, to sit the hero down—whether to dinner or in a death trap—and tell his story.

Operating outside the law and any moral conventions, the supervillain is extremely obsessive, powerful, and enduring. And as with any other profession, there is an elite. *The Supervillain Book* spotlights the "MVPs"—the "Most Villainous Players"—those major-league malcontents one would expect to find in such a volume, including Blofeld, Darth Vader, Dr. Doom, Green Goblin, the Joker, Lex Luthor, Lord Voldemort, Ming the Merciless, the Penguin, and the Riddler.

Also on hand are biographies of some characters that may not be as well known but are yet remarkably intriguing, such as the Absorbing Man, Bizarro, Galactus, Harley Quinn, the Kingpin, Loki, Mr. Mxyzptlk, Ocean Master, Mystique, and the Violator.

Supervillain teams, from the Brotherhood of Evil Mutants to the Injustice Society, from the Monster Society of Evil to the Sinister Six, are found inside.

Unique supervillains who have, at one time or another, made an impact upon popular culture are profiled, including Agent Smith, the Claw, Dr. Evil (*both* versions), Dr. Zin, Khan, the Phantom Blot, and Rasputin.

Atlas, *Dragon Ball* Villains, and Sesshomaru are among the entries tailored toward the manga and anime aficionado, while contemporary comics readers will find villains from such hit series as *Astro City*, *Powers*, and *Tom Strong* herein. We follow the Cartoon Network's *Teen Titans*, *Powerpuff Girls*, and *Justice League Unlimited* animated shows, in which supervillains wreak havoc within the reflective world of television (especially *JLU*, which reintroduced the Legion of Doom in 2005).

Entries covering oddball supervillains such as Wonder Woman's egg-shaped enemy Egg Fu, the 1970s Saturday-morning star Dr. Shrinker, and the bizarre bad guys from those fondly remembered Hostess Twinkies and Cupcakes comic-book ads remind us that not all supervillains must strike fear into our hearts.

And thematic entries, a unique feature of this ultimate resource, explore supervillainous trends, with a range of captivating subjects including Alien Invaders, the Criminal Economy, Evil Twins, Monster Supervillains, and Supervillain Team-Ups.

Comic-book aficionados, graphic-novel readers, pop-culture lovers, students of fairy tales and myths, superheroes and their supporters, crime enthusiasts and common criminals, seekers of great disasters, fans of giant calamity, and the intellectually gifted, as well as the economically flush and the reasonably attired, come celebrate the supervillain with us, as these notable nasties—in all their color, psychosis, and idiosyncrasies—run amok.

—Gina Misiroglu, Los Angeles
—Michael Eury, Portland
2006

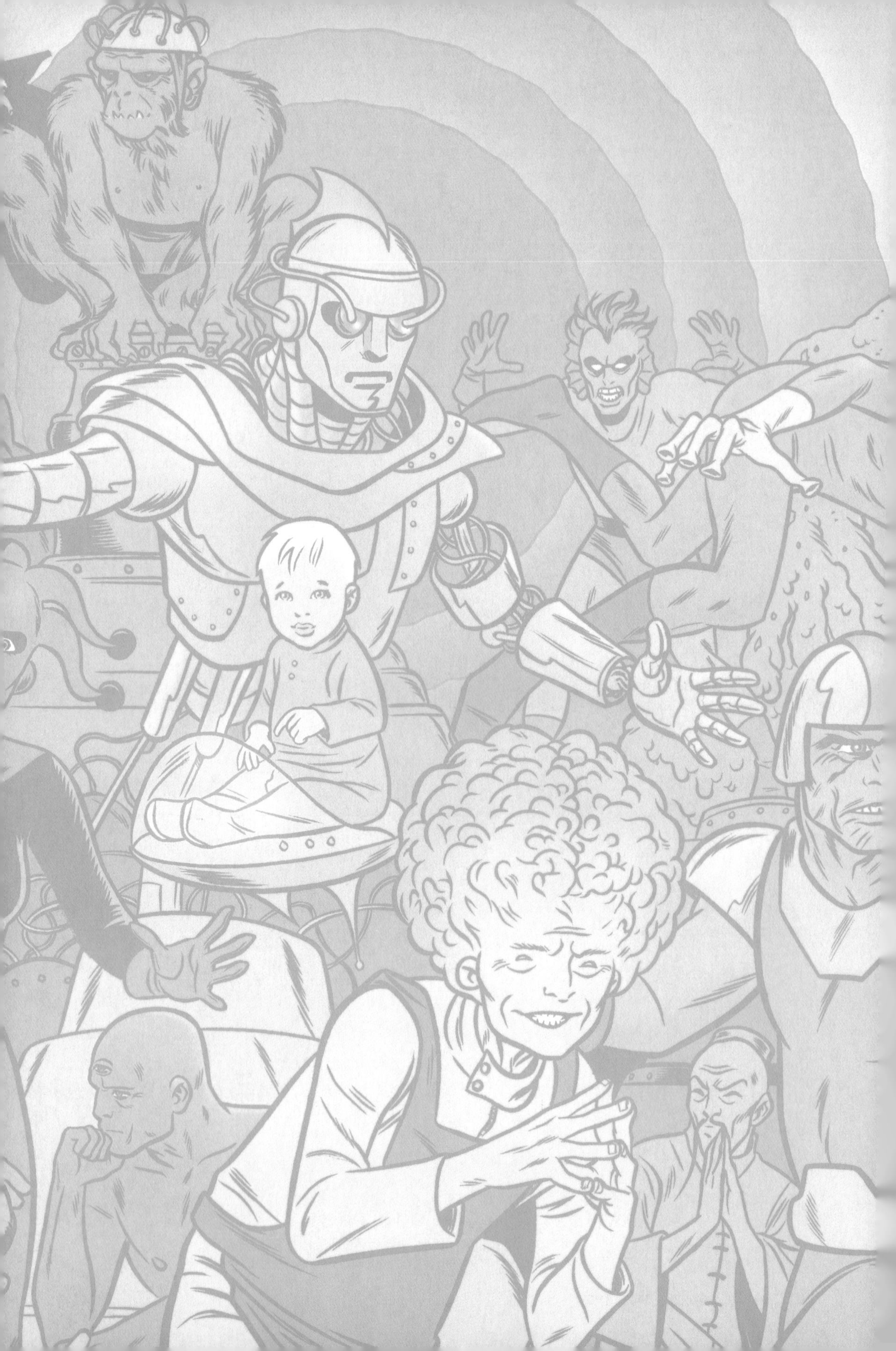

The People We Would Like to Thank: The Acknowledgments

The list of people who made this book possible is too long to reproduce here. Regardless, we are indebted to the following professionals for their energy, time, and expertise: Scott Allie, Brian Bolland, John Carbonaro, ComicSmash! (www.comicsmash.com), Peter Coogan, Kevin Eastman, Rich J. Fowlks, Heritage Comics (heritagecomics.com), Amy Huey, Erik Larsen, Stan Lee, Mike Manley, Dave Marshall, Todd McFarlane, Mike Mignola, Gary Richardson, Rose Rummel-Eury, Steve Saffel, Gail Simone, Joe Staton, Matt Wagner, Mark Waid, Bill Walko of Titanstower.com, and David Weiner. Contributing writers Mike W. Barr, Alex Boney, Heidi MacDonald, Andy Mangels, Mike Martin, Marc McKenzie, Peter Sanderson, and J. C. Vaughn went beyond the call of duty with their research and writing skills and overall gusto for the project. Some of the contributors provided images as well, making this truly a collaborative effort. Extra-special thank yous go to Mike and Laura Allred for their enthusiasm and wonderful cover art, and to our team at Visible Ink Press, without whom this encyclopedic volume would not have been possible: publisher Martin Connors, project manager Terri Schell, editor Christa Gainor, acquisitions editor Roger Matuz, indexer Anne Johnson, preproduction guru Bob Huffman, art director Mary Claire Krzewinski, typesetter Jake Di Vita, marketing director Mary Beth Perrot, and president Roger Jänecke.

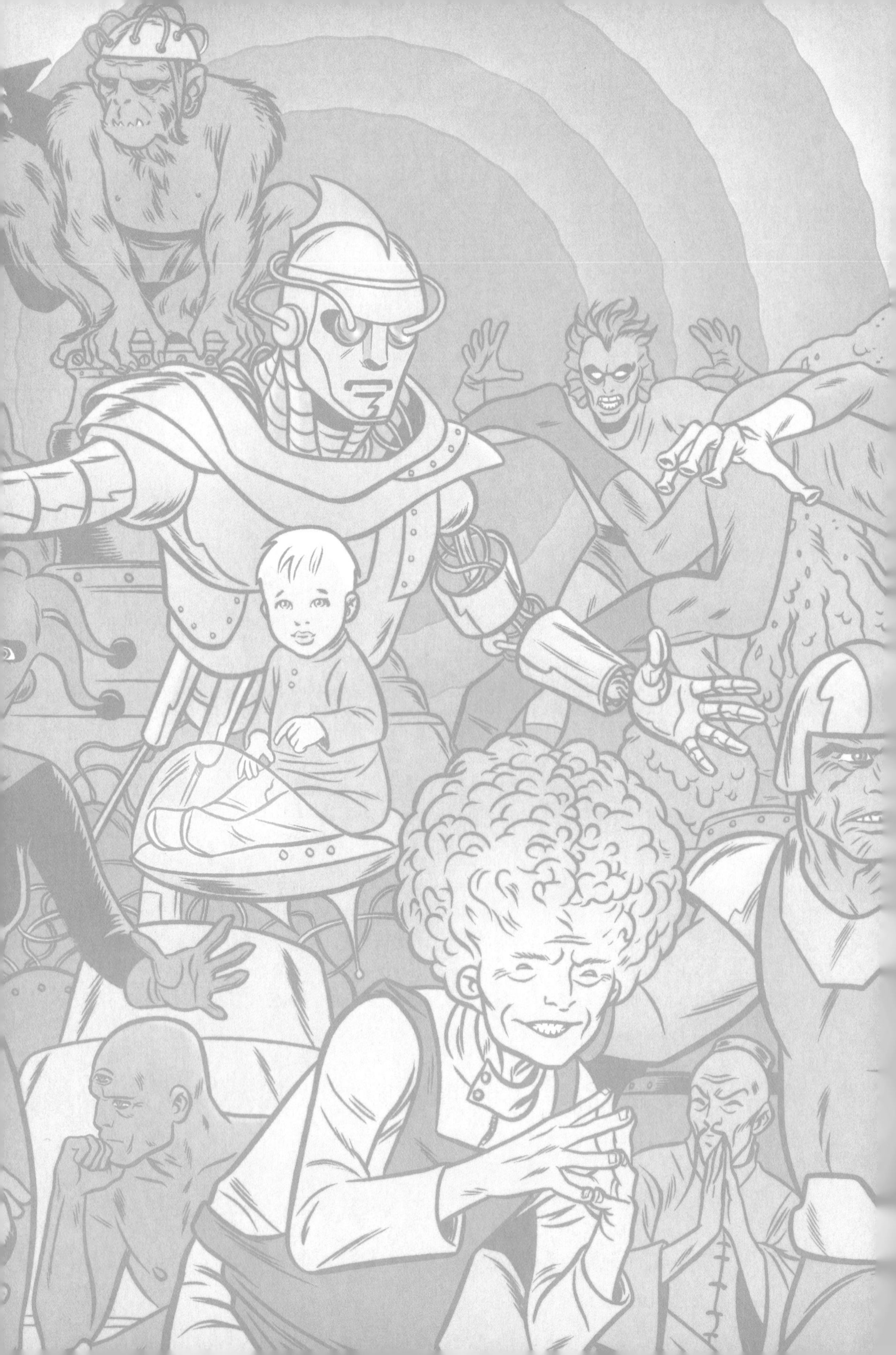

The People Who Helped Make the Book: The Contributors

Editors

Gina Misiroglu (GM), aka the Taskmistress, has cracked the deadline whip on this book's contributors with an efficiency that would give even Catwoman pause. Misiroglu is the editor of Visible Ink Press's critically acclaimed *Super-hero Book: The Ultimate Encyclopedia of Comic-Book Icons and Hollywood Heroes* (2004). Passionate about the world of comics, she began her serious study of heroes and villains during her tenure at Warner Bros. Studios. There she production-managed and edited books based on popular Warner Bros., Hanna-Barbera, and Cartoon Network properties, including Scooby-Doo, *Dexter's Lab*, the Looney Tunes, Animaniacs, *Mars Attacks!*, *Babylon 5*, *Friends*, and *ER*. Firmly situated on the West Coast, Misiroglu has also authored and/or edited several dozen pop-culture trade titles, including *Imagine: The Spirit of Twentieth-Century American Heroes* (1999) and *Space Jammin': Bugs and Michael Hit the Big Screen* (1997).

Michael Eury (ME) is a reformed supervillain, having spent several years banished to the Phantom Zone for tearing off pesky "do not remove under penalty of law" pillow tags. He now toils for truth, justice, and several other virtues that look good on his résumé as the editor of *BACK ISSUE* magazine and an advisor to *The Overstreet Comic Book Price Guide*. A former editor for DC Comics and Dark Horse Comics, Eury has authored for TwoMorrows Publishing the books *The Justice League Companion* (2005); *Dick Giordano: Changing Comics, One Day at a Time* (2003); and *Captain Action: The Original Super-Hero Action Figure* (2002). He was a contributing writer to Visible Ink Press's *The Superhero Book* (2004). Additionally, he has written cartoons, comics, and copy for Nike, Toys R Us, Warner Bros. Worldwide Publishing, MSN, *Cracked*, and Bowen Designs.

Foreword Writer

Stan Lee, chairman emeritus of Marvel Enterprises, Inc., is among the comic-book medium's most influential personalities. He co-created the Fantastic Four, Spider-Man, the Incredible Hulk, the X-Men, Iron Man, and Daredevil, as well as some of the most memorable and menacing supervillains of all time, including Dr. Doom, the Green Goblin, Dr. Octopus, and Magneto. Lee's flair for pithy prose and his mastery of fun-spirited hyperbole catapulted Marvel Comics from a 1960s cult favorite into marketplace dominance. He ultimately ventured to Hollywood to help bring Marvel's characters to television, film, and the Internet, and was recruited in the early 2000s to produce his own alternate-reality versions of competitor DC Comics' characters. For Marvel fans, however, Stan Lee will always be "the Man."

Contributing Writers

Mike W. Barr (MWB) made his first professional sale to *Ellery Queen's Mystery Magazine*. He has worked in comic books for over two decades, writing such best-selling titles as *Camelot 3000*, an Arthurian sequel; *The Maze Agency*, an Eisner- and Harvey Award–nominated whodunit detective series revived in 2005 by IDW; "Batman: Year Two," which was adapted into the movie *Batman: Mask of the Phantasm*; and the first *Batman* graphic novel, 1987's *Batman: Son of the Demon*. For the Malibu Ultraverse he created and wrote the best-selling title *Mantra*. He has written Internet comics for Stan Lee Media and Icebox; a popular Internet fantasy comic strip, *Sorcerer of Fortune*; manga for TokyoPop; and many *Star Trek* comics for DC and Malibu. Returning to his first medium, prose, Mike wrote *Gemini*, a *Star Trek* novel, published in February 2003, and has contributed short stories to anthologies and magazines, including *Noir*; *Hot Blood*; *Path of the Bold*, which won the 2005 Origin Award (presented by the Academy of Adventure Gaming Arts and Design) for "Best Fiction Publication"; *Star Wars Insider*; and *Kolchak: The Night Stalker Chronicles*, an anthology based on the 1970s cult TV show.

Alex Boney (AB) received his master of arts degree from Ohio State University and is pursuing his doctorate in English literature. His dissertation, titled *Modernist League of America: Modernist American Fiction and the Origins of Superhero Comics* (2006), explores the intersections between American literature and popular culture. Currently, Boney teaches writing and literature courses at Ohio State and Ohio Dominican University in Columbus. He has presented on comics and modernist literature at several conferences, including the Comics Arts Conference in San Diego, California, and the Bloomsday 100 International James Joyce Symposium in Dublin, Ireland. His essay about James Joyce and Chris Ware, titled "From Modern Novel to Graphic Novel: What Joyce Taught Us About Contemporary Epic Narrative," was published in the latter conference's proceedings in 2005.

Dr. Peter Coogan (PC) has been reading comics since his mother let him buy a *Captain America* comic book on a family trip when he was eight. He earned a Ph.D. in American studies at Michigan State University with his dissertation, *The Secret Origin of the Superhero: The Origin and Evolution of the Superhero Genre in America* (2002). Coogan has been the co-chair of the Comics Arts Conference, which is held at the San Diego Comic-Con International, since co-founding it in 1992 as a graduate student. He is a contributor to *Myths of the Modern Age* (2005) and the author of *Superhero: Secret Origin of a Genre* (2006) as well as numerous online articles in the parascholarly discipline of Wold-Newtonry, including an English/Mangani dictionary. He works as a writing specialist at Fontbonne University in St. Louis, Missouri.

Heidi MacDonald (HM)'s writings about comics have appeared in *Publishers Weekly, The Comics Journal, The Comics Buyer's Guide, LA Weekly,* and *The Pulse.* She is currently the writer of *The Beat,* the premiere newsblog of comics culture (http://www.comicon.com/thebeat). She has worked as a senior editor at *Disney Adventures* magazine, and as an editor at DC Comics.

Andy Mangels (AM) is a best-selling author and co-author of more than a dozen books, including *Star Trek* and *Roswell* novels, and the books *Animation on DVD: The Ultimate Guide* (2003) and *Star Wars: The Essential Guide to Characters* (1995). He is an award-winning comic-book anthology editor, and has written comics for almost two decades. He has also written thousands of articles for entertainment and lifestyle magazines and newspapers in the United States, England, and Italy, mostly about film and television. Mangels has provided Special Features content and has scripted and directed a series of sixteen half-hour DVD documentaries for BCI Eclipse, on *He-Man and the Masters of the Universe.* Although his favorite character is Wonder Woman, Mangels owns a life-size mannequin of *Star Wars* villain Boba Fett, and he bears a Boba Fett tattoo. Mangels resides in Portland, Oregon.

Rocketed to Earth from his home planet moments before its destruction, **Michael A. Martin (MAM)** has enjoyed a lifelong obsession with comic-book heroes and villains. Years after this origin tale, Martin schlepped the funnies to the direct-sales market, first for Marvel Comics and later for Dark Horse Comics. In 1996, he began collaborating with Andy Mangels on scripts for Marvel's *Star Trek: Deep Space 9* comics. That same year, Martin's solo original short fiction began appearing in *The Magazine of Fantasy & Science Fiction,* and he has also co-authored (also with Andy Mangels) several *Star Trek* novels and shorter pieces of *Star Trek* fiction for Pocket Books, as well as a trio of novels based on the late, lamented *Roswell* television series. He has written for *Star Trek Monthly,* Atlas Editions, *Dreamwatch,* Grolier Books, WildStorm, Platinum Studios, *Gobshite Quarterly, The Oregonian,* and Gareth Stevens, Inc., for whom he has penned six *World Almanac Library of the States* nonfiction books.

A long-time comic-book fan, **Marc McKenzie (MM)** became interested in Japanese animation after watching *Robotech* in the late 1980s. At the same time, the first English translations of Japanese manga were starting to appear in America, and McKenzie quickly took an interest in such titles as Masaomi Kanzaki's *Heavy Metal Warrior Xenon*; Kazuya Kudo and Ryoichi Ikegami's *Mai, the Psychic Girl*; Kaoru Shintani's *Area 88*; Yoshihisa Tagami's *Grey*; and Masamune Shirow's *Appleseed.* After earning a degree in biology from St. Peter's College in Jersey City, New Jersey, he went on to study computer animation at the Art Institute of Philadelphia. Now a freelance artist and writer, McKenzie has written for the web sites of the Slush Factory and Silver Bullet Comic Books, and he has created artwork for the 2003 Otakon anime convention.

Peter Sanderson (PS) is a comics critic and historian who holds three degrees in English literature from Columbia University. He began teaching the course "Comics as Literature" at New York University in 2004, and he is a graphic novel reviewer for *Publishers Weekly.* Sanderson has been interviewed about cartoon art on *CBS Sunday Morning* and regularly speaks about graphic novels at New York's Museum of Comic and Cartoon Art. Sanderson was the first official archivist at Marvel Comics, and he is the author of the books *Marvel Universe* (1996) and *The Ultimate Guide to the X-Men* (2000). Sanderson was also one of the principal writers for the original four versions of *The Official Handbook of the Marvel Universe* and DC Comics' *Who's Who*. A frequent contributor to magazines about comics, Sanderson has written for *BACK ISSUE*, *Comic Buyer's Guide*, *The Comics Journal*, and *Wizard*. Sanderson writes the online column "Comics in Context," a weekly series of essays on comic and cartoon art, for IGN Comics (http://comics.ign.com/).

J. C. Vaughn (JCV) is the executive editor of Gemstone Publishing, where he has worked on *The Official Overstreet Comic Book Price Guide*, *Hake's Price Guide to Character Toys*, *The Official Price Guide to Disney Character Collectibles*, *The Overstreet Comic Book Companion*, and other projects. He is the author of more than 2,000 articles, reviews, interviews, and columns in the collectibles field. He's also the co-writer of the comics *24* (based on the Fox TV show) and *Shi*.

Cover Artist

Michael "Doc" Allred grew up in the 1960s and 1970s and was constantly surrounded by the best in pop culture and a steady diet of music, movies, and comic books. So it should come as no surprise that he keeps a hand in film (he's currently finishing a screenplay for a live-action *Madman* movie for Robert Rodriguez) and music (he's lead singer and guitarist for the Gear), but comic books have been a seminal source of joy for Mike, and that joy remains the primary ingredient in most of his work. Other than *Madman* and his freelance work for Marvel and DC Comics, he wrote and drew the sci-fi/rock 'n' roll history/adventure series *Red Rocket 7* and *The Atomics* (a *Madman* spin-off), and he's illustrating the entire *Book of Mormon* with his wife, award-winning colorist Laura Allred, in a project called *The Golden Plates*. They live big on the Oregon coast with their offspring.

The Abomination

Picture a gamma-spawned monstrosity mightier and more hideous than the Incredible Hulk—this is the Abomination. In *Tales to Astonish* #90 (1967), in the story "The Abomination!" by Stan Lee and Gil Kane, Slavic spy Emil Blonsky infiltrates a U.S. military base to filch the technology that transformed scientist Bruce Banner into the Hulk. He activates Banner's gamma device and is immersed in radiation, instantly transmogrifying into an emerald-hued grotesquerie capable of heaving 100 tons, shrugging off artillery fire, and hurdling two miles in a single bound.

The Abomination is much more than the Hulk's evil twin. Banner's Hulk transformations are triggered by rage, after which he returns to his human self, but Blonsky's metamorphosis is permanent. While Banner's intelligence fades when he morphs into the Hulk, Blonsky's faculties are fully intact, although his judgment is routinely clouded by his unbridled hatred of his jade-jawed foe. The most discernable difference between the two is the supervillain's appearance: with his repulsive reptilian hide, Blonsky is unmistakably an Abomination.

The supervillain's appellation was greeted with trepidation amid the Marvel Comics Bullpen, Stan Lee recalled in the trade paperback *Bring on the Bad Guys* (1976). "The Abomination is a lousy name for a villain!" scoffed one staffer. Lee stuck by his guns; "I had had it up to here with names like The Purple Potato or The Living Bedspread," he wrote. In the character's debut, the behemoth's name was coined by Banner's girlfriend (and later, wife) Betty Ross, daughter of Hulk-hunter General "Thunderbolt" Ross, who gasped, "Who ... or *what* ... can that *abomination* be?"

Fueled by ego and ire, the Abomination has repeatedly gone monster-to-monster with the Hulk. His menace has not been relegated solely to Earth: during a series of intergalactic adventures, the Abomination left such a trail of annihilation in his wake that he was dubbed "the Ravager of Worlds." The Hulk's *private* world was ravaged by the Abomination's most decisive coup: his murder of Betty Ross Banner by gamma-radiation poisoning. The rancor between green-skinned goliaths has intensified over the years, with Banner engaging in a tryst with Blonsky's estranged wife, Nadia. The acrimonious Abomination's acclaim in the 2000s includes his own miniseries, deceptively titled *Hulk: Destruction* (2005), written by popular *Hulk* scribe Peter David.

The Abomination's grudge match with "Ol' Greenskin" has also burst into non-comics venues. Voiced by Richard Moll of *Night Court* fame, the supervillain appeared in UPN's *The Incredible Hulk* animated series (1996–1999) and has been converted into action figures by Toy Biz. The young-adult

From *Tales to Astonish* #90 ©1967 Marvel Comics.
ART BY GIL KANE.

novel *The Incredible Hulk: Abominations* by Jason Henderson (1997) features Blonsky, as does Game Boy Advance's *The Incredible Hulk* (2003). The Abomination is the rumored villain to appear in the sequel to the 2003 live-action *Hulk* movie. No matter the medium in which the Abomination/Hulk battles take place, heaven help the person—or *city*—that stands in their path when these titans clash. —*ME*

Abra Kadabra

You've got to hand it to the thievish mage Abra Kadabra—a *big hand*, that is. In "The Case of the Real-Gone Flash" in *The Flash* #128 (1962), writer John Broome and artist Carmine Infantino introduce Citizen Abra, a refugee from Earth's sixty-fourth century, a time when individuality is not tolerated. A fanatical narcissist, Abra travels to the late twentieth century and uses his era's sophisticated technology to feign magic, commanding observers to applaud his acts. Encountering the second Flash (Barry Allen) in Central City, the techno-sorcerer immodestly calling himself Abra Kadabra makes the Flash vanish—leaving behind only his empty costume—but the fleet-footed hero outsmarts the egotistic villain, earning Abra's scorn.

Abra Kadabra materialized time and time again, often brandishing a magic wand and displaying science-based teleportation, telekinesis, telepathy, and mind over matter to pester the Flash. Some of his most popular tricks included transforming the Scarlet Speedster into a life-sized marionette, making the hero unable to see to crimes committed around him, and exiling him into "Cartoon-Land." After the Flash perished in *Crisis on Infinite Earths* #8 (1985), Abra cast his spells on the hero's lightning-fast successor, Wally West. The magician was disfigured in an explosion caused by a malfunction of his technology, cracking his already-fragile psyche. Abra Kadabra's hatred for the third Flash is as intense as the villain's ego, and after receiving authentic occult abilities from the demon Neron, he is committed to conjure the final curtain for his foe. —*ME*

The Absorbing Man

Carl "Crusher" Creel was bad news before he joined the ranks of supervillainy as the

Opposite: *Marvel Knights: Spider-Man* #15 ©2005 Marvel Comics.
COVER ART BY STEVE McNIVEN.

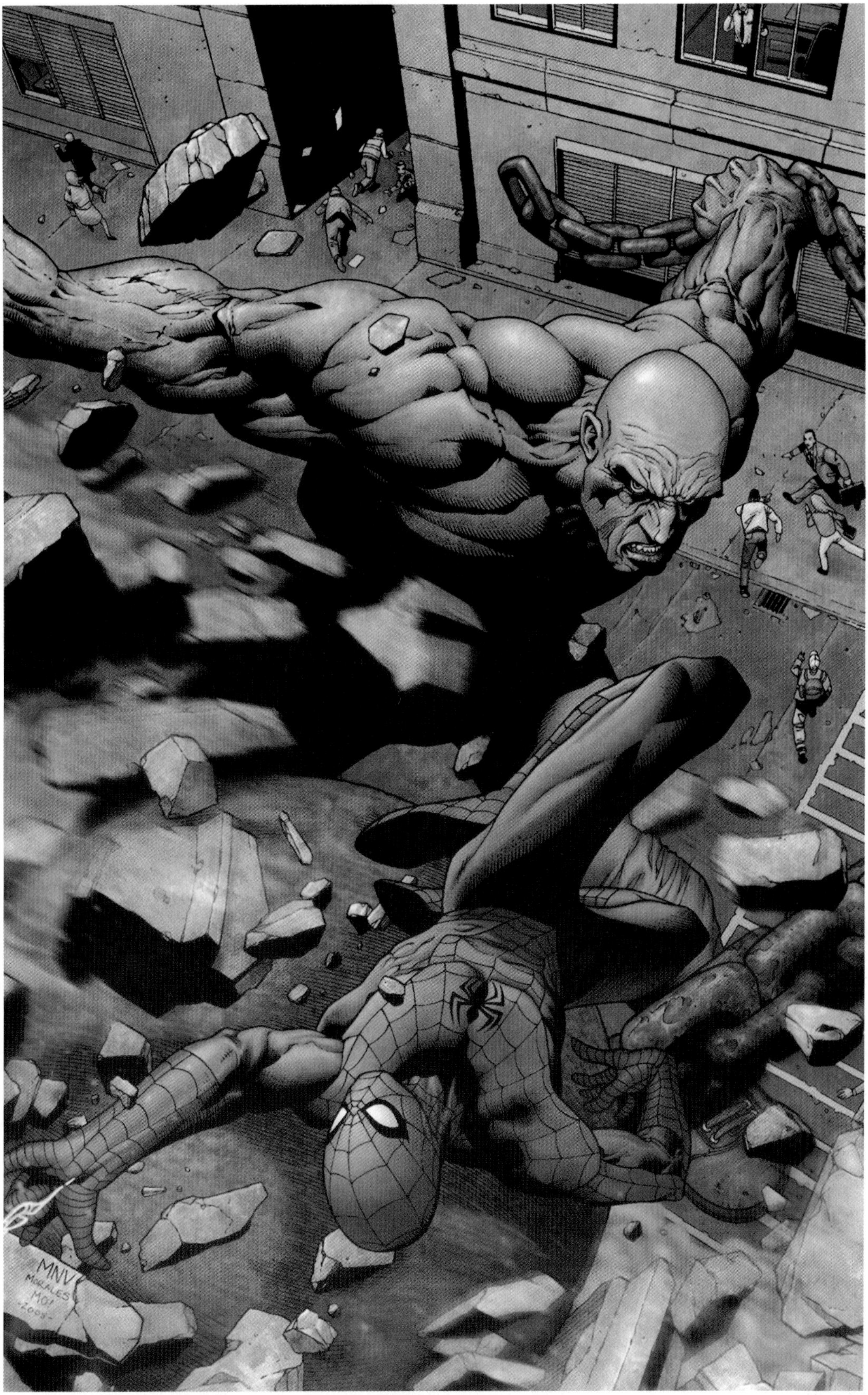

Absorbing Man. When first seen in Stan Lee and Jack Kirby's "The Stronger I Am, the Sooner I Die" in *Journey into Mystery* #114 (1965), this kneecap-busting ruffian is serving a well-deserved stretch in the pokey. The Asgardian god of mischief Loki spikes Creel's drinking water with an herbal potion, imbuing the man-mountain with the ability to duplicate the physical assets of any object he touches. Smashing out of the slammer clad in nothing more than his prison-issue pants and a ball and chain, the Absorbing Man is manipulated by Loki into fighting Thor, and comes close to crowning the thunder god by replicating the might of both Thor and his enchanted hammer Mjolnir. Thor outwits Creel, however, as brainpower is the one attribute the pugnacious villain cannot seem to absorb.

The Absorbing Man soon returned for a rematch with Thor, but was discharged into outer space by the deity-hero's father, the almighty Odin. Hightailing it back to Earth on a comet, Creel clashed with the Hulk in *The Incredible Hulk* #125 (1970): "I can add your might ... to my own! And nobody can beat somebody who's always just a little bit stronger than they are ... *nobody!*" he grunted. One of Marvel Comics' most durable supervillains, the Absorbing Man has frequently fought with Thor and the Hulk, and tried to squash almost every superhero from the Avengers to Spider-Man.

The Absorbing Man prefers to mimic solids, most often pummeling heroes by becoming steel or stone. He can assimilate the properties of non-solids, but many of those transformations—water, snow, gasses, light, and even cosmic energy—are unstable and beyond his control. His power has its limits: while Creel has expanded to skyscraper size, his attempt to engulf all of Earth's energy caused him to detonate (he got better).

The Absorbing Man never strays too far from the old ball and chain. His jailhouse "souvenirs" share his absorption capacities, and Creel wields them like a club. He similarly stays close to his wife, the supervillainess Titania, whom he met in the maxiseries *Marvel Super Heroes Secret Wars* (1984–1985). After a crime-based courtship the couple wed in *Avengers Unplugged* #4 (1996), their ceremony crashed by She-Hulk and other heroes who misinterpreted the reason for their gathering.

Mr. and Mrs. Creel have flirted with a life of lawfulness, but they find evil too beguiling to ignore.

Jim Cummings voiced the Absorbing Man in the animated television series *The Incredible Hulk* (1996–1999), and several action figures of the villain have been produced. Nick Nolte's character of David Banner transmogrified into an unidentified Absorbing Man in the climax of the live-action blockbuster *The Hulk* (2003). —*ME*

Agent Smith

Not all supervillains wear gaudy costumes, maintain high-tech subterranean lairs, or display any of the other conventional trappings of the archetypal comic-book arch-foe; some *uber*–bad guys instead don the livery of duly-instituted law and order. In the eponymous virtual world of the stylish cyberpunk/martial-arts films *The Matrix* (1999), *The Matrix Reloaded* (2003), and *The Matrix Revolutions* (2003), Agent Smith—played to vicious perfection by Hugo Weaving—is cast in the mold of a dour Secret Service agent, complete with a *Men in Black*–style suit and an ear-mounted radio wire.

Agent Smith represents legitimate-appearing authority carried to tyrannical extremes, and he is the diametric philosophical opposite of the *Matrix* franchise's youthful, freedom-loving cyber-hero Thomas A. Anderson (Keanu Reeves)—better known by his electronic moniker "Neo." While Neo symbolizes the freewheeling informational anarchy of the late 1990s Internet, Smith is his antithesis, one of many all-but-unstoppable intelligent software programs whose function is to purge the online virtual world of the Matrix of all sources of disorder, including the thousands of free spirits who have fled the Matrix to live in the off-line "real world" community called Zion. Besides Neo, Smith's other prime targets include Trinity (Neo's girlfriend, played by Carrie-Anne Moss) and Morpheus (Laurence Fishburne), one of Zion's leaders.

Smith is motivated both by a built-in deference to the strict rules that enable the Matrix to function, and by a profound hatred of unconstrained, frailty-prone humanity. "Human beings are a disease," Smith declares in the first film. "A cancer of this planet. You are a plague, and we are the cure." Smith discovers that his ability to "rewrite" other cyber-entities into submission won't work on Neo, cementing the mutually antagonistic relationship between the agent and the young hero.

Despite his devotion to order, Smith himself grows to feel constrained by the rules that govern the Matrix; he yearns to be free and sees the destruction of Zion as his only chance to achieve that freedom. Although his campaign against Zion fails, *The Matrix Reloaded* finds Smith separated from his fellow agents and possessed of the ability to create an apparently infinite number of copies of himself. And although Smith attributes his liberation to Neo, Smith is ill-equipped to deal successfully with freedom; during a series of martial arts battles of ever-escalating savagery, Smith demonstrates that his hatred of the anarchy Neo represents hasn't diminished. All the while, Smith's power over the Matrix grows, to the point that he threatens both the virtual world and Zion, where he attacks Neo and Trinity by "possessing" a flesh-and-blood human named Bane. "There's nowhere I can't go," Smith gloats to his prey, speaking through Bane. "There is nowhere I won't find you."

Thanks in part to the wisdom of a cyber-entity known as the Oracle, Neo comes to understand Smith's philosophical nature, as well as the extreme severity of the threat the rogue agent poses to the existence of both the Matrix and Zion. "He won't stop until there's nothing left at all," the Oracle reveals to Neo in *The Matrix Revolutions*. "He is you. Your opposite, your negative. The result of the equation trying to balance itself out."

During his climactic final, flying, twirling, chop-sockey showdown with Neo, Smith is both intrigued and enraged by his exhausted opponent's obstinate refusal to surrender, even in the face of apparently certain defeat. Smith harangues his battered foe, revealing a core of nihilism in the former agent's soul: "Do you believe you're fighting *for* something? For more than your survival? Can you tell me what it is? Do you even *know*? Is it freedom, or truth? Perhaps peace? Could it be for love? Illusions, Mr. Anderson. Vagaries of perception. Temporary constructs of a feeble human intellect trying desperately to justify an existence that is without meaning or purpose!"

In typical supervillain fashion, Smith appears to defeat Neo when he "rewrites" Neo's cyber-persona, transforming the hero into yet another copy of Smith—only to discover that Neo has actually co-opted Smith's own software, causing the agent and his army of duplicates to vanish in a spectacular light show. Neo disappears in this conflagration as hero and villain cancel each other out like colliding antiparticles, recalling Sherlock Holmes and Moriarty plunging to their deaths over the Reichenbach Falls. Smith's ultimate defeat, which ensures the continued survival and autonomy of Zion, represents the triumph of optimism over nihilism, hope's conquest of despair. Whether or not Smith and Neo return from the grave for a rematch—as Holmes and Moriarty did in Arthur Conan Doyle's post-1893 Sherlock Holmes prequels—remains to be seen. —*MAM*

A.I.M.

A spin-off of Marvel Comics' Hydra, Advanced Idea Mechanics (A.I.M.) is an organization whose mission is to foment global revolution via high-tech weaponry—while at the same time turning a tidy profit by selling that selfsame gadgetry to rogue nations and lawless individuals determined to wreak havoc around the world. A.I.M. is a coterie of technocratic anarchists—brilliant but amoral scientists and their hired henchmen—bent on overthrowing every government on Earth through super-technological means.

Headquartered on the remote island of Boca Caliente, A.I.M. boasts a global network of some 1,500 operatives, strategically placed to create trouble for a list of adversaries that includes Captain America, S.H.I.E.L.D., Iron Man, Quasar, the first Ms. Marvel, and even the Incredible Hulk. Among A.I.M.'s membership requirements are a master's degree or Ph.D. in the sciences or business, along with a fervent belief in the ideology of global technocracy.

During the debut appearance of A.I.M. in *Strange Tales* vol. 1 #146 (1966), writer Stan Lee and illustrators Jack Kirby and Don Heck gave the world its first glimpse of A.I.M.'s techno-villains, whose initial preoccupation is android-building and whose bucket-headed yellow uniforms evoke images of Chernobyl beekeepers. A.I.M.'s origins remained vague at first, but eventually stood revealed as stretching back to Nazi Germany, where the group's founder Baron Wolfgang von Strucker used the organization as the legitimate business front for Hydra, an umbrella organization that was forced underground at the end of World War II. Operating more or less in plain sight as an international technology merchant—developing everything from advanced lasers to space vehicles—A.I.M. kept its subversive goals concealed for decades as its scientists pushed the boundaries of numerous scientific disciplines, such as bioengineering, bionics, physics, and robotics. All the while, A.I.M. functioned as the covert research division of Hydra, its equally covert parent organization, and even managed to become an important contractor of the U.S. government. A.I.M.'s nefarious nature was finally exposed after its plot to disgrace S.H.I.E.L.D. director Nick Fury, thereby forcing him from his job, backfired.

Being thoroughgoing fanatics, A.I.M.'s members generally prefer death to capture. The group's leader, known as the Scientist Supreme, transformed one such rank-and-file A.I.M. member into MODOK (Mental Organism Designed Only for Killing), a mutated creature with an atrophied body and a giant brain capable of various psionic feats, including telekinesis. MODOK soon killed the Scientist Supreme, taking his place, and established A.I.M.'s independence from the already-vanquished Hydra. A.I.M.'s other seminal superscientific creations include the Super-Adaptoid, an android capable of mimicking both the appearance and abilities of its costumed adversaries, and the Cosmic Cube, a "wishing" machine able to rewrite reality itself.

During later years, A.I.M. splintered into multiple power blocs, a development that led to MODOK's eventual ouster from the group, with the assistance of an allied evil organization, the snake-themed Serpent Squad. The sundered A.I.M. factions eventually reconciled, with MODOK taken prisoner and conditioned to obey the wishes of A.I.M.'s board of directors. Following a major defeat at the hands of Iron Man and turncoat A.I.M. member Clytemnestra Erwin, A.I.M. employed MODOK more as a CEO than as an iron-fisted technoconqueror; realizing that supervillainous tactics can be all but fruitless in a twenty-first-century milieu in which cor-

porate power has become the coin of the realm, MODOK has set A.I.M.'s sights on becoming the next Microsoft. While A.I.M. has by no means "gone legit," its leaders now consult the *Wall Street Journal* as often as they crack their supervillain handbooks. —*MAM*

Aku

A ku, the merciless shapeshifter who describes himself as "the Master of Masters, the Deliverer of Darkness, the Shogun of Sorrow," was created by animator Genndy Tartakovsky (who also developed the animated hit *Dexter's Laboratory*) in "The Beginning" (original airdate: August 10, 2001), the premiere installment of the Cartoon Network's *Samurai Jack* (2001–2004).

Eons ago, a consortium of deities—Odin, Ra, and Rama—narrowly subdues a primeval entity of absolute malevolence. Yet a vestige of this amorphous evil survives, creeping like a virus across the globe, the eradication of the dinosaurs among its atrocities. Millennia later, after slaughtering countless Japanese warriors, the demonic force is wounded by a magic arrow but does not die, instead taking the form of Aku. After being imprisoned by an emperor who brandishes a supernatural sword, Aku escapes years later: "Once again, I am free to smite the world as I did in days long past." He is challenged by the magic sword–wielding Samurai Jack, who has trained his whole life for the eventuality of Aku's return, but the shapeshifting menace banishes the young nomad to the future, "where my evil is law." And thus Samurai Jack roams the Aku-ruled future Earth, with its dangerous robots, aliens, and Aku's minions (with sinister names like Demongo), seeking a chronal gateway to return to the past to defeat the Deliverer of Darkness before his global empire is built. (Tartakovsky initially drew fire for plagiarizing Frank Miller's similarly themed DC Comics 1983–1984 miniseries *Ronin*; nonetheless, *Samurai Jack* quickly established and maintained its own identity throughout its celebrated 52-episode run.)

This colorful villain, a Kabuki horror emerging from hellfire, was bloodcurdlingly voiced by Japanese actor Mako, whose numerous film credits include *The Sand Pebbles* (1966), *Conan the Barbarian* (1982), and *Bulletproof Monk* (2003). Aku's malevolence inspired the video game *Samurai Jack: The Shadow of Aku* (2004), plus a "Flame Blade Aku" action figure and a 12-inch maquette. While *Samurai Jack* has been relegated to DVD collections and an occasional Cartoon Network rerun, its brave hero still battles Aku in the far-flung era. —*ME*

Alien Invaders

All the many tales of extraterrestrial invaders in twentieth- and twenty-first-century popular culture derive from a single common ancestor, the first great work on this theme, H. G. Wells' 1898 novel, *The War of the Worlds*.

Whereas Wells wrote about Martians invading Victorian England and leveling London, various later adapters of his work have updated and altered its setting to reflect the concerns of their own time. Only a year before the start of World War II, Orson Welles' 1938 radio adaptation included fake news bulletins about the Martians landing in New Jersey; thinking the reports were real, many Americans panicked. Animator George Pal produced the 1953 film version, which reflected the tensions of the cold war. Steven Spielberg's 2005 blockbuster adaptation, which, like Welles', focuses on New Jersey, includes allusions to the September 11, 2001, terrorist attacks. Wells' *War of the Worlds* has also been adapted into comics, including a memorable issue of *Classics Illustrated* (#124, 1955).

Writer Roy Thomas and artist Neal Adams conceived the basic ideas for Marvel's *War of the Worlds* series that debuted in *Amazing Adventures* #18 (1973). According to this series, Wells' Martians returned and conquered Earth in 2001. Like a futuristic Spartacus, Killraven, a warrior raised to fight as a gladiator, led a band of freedom fighters in battling the Martians. The series, soon retitled *Killraven*, is best remembered for the remarkable work by writer Don McGregor and artist P. Craig Russell.

In the second volume of their comics series *The League of Extraordinary Gentlemen* (2002–2003), the British duo of writer Alan Moore and artist Kevin O'Neill depict their team of late Victorian heroes playing a role in Wells' *War of the Worlds*.

But Wells' intelligent, octopus-like aliens are hardly the only kind of Martians in popular culture. Indeed, *League* includes appearances by Martian races from other authors' books, including Edgar Rice Burroughs' *John Carter, Warlord of Mars* series (1917–1943).

DC Comics even has a Martian superhero, J'onn J'onzz, the Martian Manhunter, who debuted in *Detective Comics* #225 (1955) and appears regularly on Cartoon Network's *Justice League* (2001–2004) and *Justice League Unlimited* (2004–present). In both the original and contemporary backstories for the Martian Manhunter, there were a race of green-skinned Martians, to which J'onn belonged, and his enemies, the warlike White Martians. In the original continuity, the White Martians devastated their planet, and the surviving Martians abandoned their native world, later making an unsuccessful effort to invade Earth. In the revised continuity, most Green Martians perished ages ago, but the White Martians survived in another dimension. In 1997 and 2000 the White Martians twice attempted to conquer Earth; Superman subsequently banished them into the Phantom Zone.

There are even comedic versions of Martian invaders, including the gnomish creatures in Tim Burton's film *Mars Attacks!* (1996) and Chuck Jones's Marvin the Martian, nemesis of Bugs Bunny and Daffy Duck (in his *Duck Dodgers* persona).

Aliens also invaded the movies, including the creature from Howard Hawks' film *The Thing from Another World* (1951), the righteous Klaatu from *The Day the Earth Stood Still* (1951), the "pod people" from *Invasion of the Body Snatchers* (first filmed in 1956; remade in 1976 and 1993), the title creatures from Twentieth Century Fox's *Alien* franchise (starting in 1979), and the unnamed race of alien invaders in director Roland Emmerich's *Independence Day* (1996). In television's *The Invaders* (1967–1968) and *The X-Files* (1993–2002), the heroes attempt in vain to warn the populace about the alien invaders in their midst. In the original *Battlestar Galactica* (1978–1979) and its 2003 revival, both set in the future, the alien Cylons seek to wipe out the remaining humans in the galaxy.

In its many incarnations (beginning in 1966), *Star Trek* has introduced numerous alien races

The Martians are coming! From producer George Pal's *The War of the Worlds* (1953).

that have opposed Earth, including the Klingons, Romulans, Cardassians, and the Dominion. The most formidable of these races is the Borg, which actually consists of members of many humanoid races, all of whom have been converted into half-robotic cyborgs, thereby forcibly "assimilated" into a collective with a group mind, bent on conquest.

Another comedy treatment of the alien invader theme is *Men in Black*, which originated as a comic book (1990) before being adapted into movies (1997, 2002) and television animation of the same name (1997–2001). Here "alien" invaders from space are presented as if they were alien immigrants from abroad: most of them are peacefully trying to assimilate into American society, while a few prove to be threats to national— and planetary—security.

Stan Lee and Jack Kirby co-created two great galactic empires for the Marvel Universe. The first is that of the Skrulls, reptilian shapeshifters who first appeared in *Fantastic Four* #2 (1962). Like aliens in

many other works, such as *The X-Files*, the Skrulls can impersonate human beings and thereby infiltrate Earth's population. The other empire is that of the Kree, humanoids whose skin color is either blue or pink, resembling Earth's Caucasians. The Fantastic Four first ran afoul of the Kree when they defeated a giant robot Sentry, which the Kree had stationed on Earth (*Fantastic Four* #64, July 1967). In retaliation, the Supreme Intelligence, a composite of the greatest minds in Kree history, dispatched his chief enforcer, Ronan the Accuser, to punish them (*Fantastic Four* #65, August 1967), but the Fantastic Four overcame him. Then the Kree sent a military officer, Captain Mar-Vell, created by Lee and artist Gene Colan in *Marvel Super-Heroes* #12 (December 1967), to spy on Earth, but this new "Captain Mar-vell" ended up siding with the Earthlings.

Writer Roy Thomas then staged a war between the two empires, with Earth and its superheroes caught in the middle. Primarily illustrated by Neal Adams, the Kree-Skrull War (in *Avengers* #89–#97,

1971–1972) remains one of the greatest epics in Marvel history.

Other malevolent Marvel aliens include the reptile-like Badoon (introduced in *Silver Surfer* #2, 1968), the insect-like Brood (who debuted in *Uncanny X-Men* #155, 1982), and the Borg-like Phalanx (who first appeared in *Uncanny X-Men* #311, 1994).

The DC Universe also has an assortment of dangerous aliens. The Weaponers of Qward, created by John Broome and Gil Kane in *Green Lantern* #2 (1960), inhabited an antimatter universe; their warriors hurled energy weapons resembling golden thunderbolts. Inspired by the 1940s superhero created by Joe Simon and Jack Kirby, the Manhunters (from *First Issue Special* #5, 1975) are androids created by the benevolent Guardians of the Universe to battle injustice; after the Manhunters rebelled, the Guardians instituted the Green Lantern Corps instead. The Dominators (from *Adventure Comics* #361, 1967) are cunning strategists, the Gordanians (from *Green Lantern* #142, 1981) are infamous slavers, the militaristic Khunds (from *Adventure Comics* #346, 1966) build their culture around warfare, and the Psions (who originated, oddly, in *Witching Hour* #13, 1971) perform amoral scientific experiments.

There have been some particularly unusual twists on the alien invasion theme. In both an episode of television's *The Outer Limits* (1963–1965) and comics' *Watchmen* (1986–1987), an alien invasion is faked to prevent a nuclear war on Earth. Alien invaders also haunted many episodes of television's original *Twilight Zone* (1959–1964), but one episode, "The Invaders," demonstrates that from the perspective of the denizens of other worlds, humankind are the alien invaders. —PS

Alternate-Reality Supervillains

In their comic-book stories, Marvel Comics and DC Comics each depict a "mainstream" version of the universe in which its principal fictional characters dwell. But over the decades Marvel and DC

have also published series that take place in alternate realities of various kinds. For example, they portray parallel Earths that exist in other dimensions, and alternate timelines in which familiar characters lead different lives than they do in mainstream reality.

In *The Avengers* #85 (1971), writer Roy Thomas co-created the Squadron Supreme, a superhero team of a parallel Earth, who were semi-satiric versions of the members of DC's Justice League of America. (The characters appeared previously as the Squadron Sinister in *Avengers* #70, 1969.) Subsequently, Don and Maggie Thompson co-created Emil Burbank, a bearded, long-haired counterpart for Lex Luthor, in *Thor* #280 (1979). In his *Squadron Supreme* maxiseries, writer Mark Gruenwald gave Burbank an armored battlesuit and dubbed him Master Menace, thereby also making him an analog to Dr. Doom.

In *Squadron* #5 (1986), Gruenwald introduced the Institute of Evil, including Ape X, Dr. Decibel, Foxfire, Lamprey, Quagmire, and the Shape. Gruenwald also co-created three nemeses for Nighthawk, the Squadron's version of Batman: Remnant, Puffin, and the Mink, who paralleled the Joker, the Penguin, and Catwoman, respectively (debuting in *Squadron Supreme* #6, 1986).

Editor in chief Jim Shooter conceived of Marvel's "New Universe" series, set in their own "reality," as a more realistic approach to superheroes: hence, he disdained putting its "paranormal" villains, such as Mindwolf (from *Psi-Force* #1, 1986), in costumes.

Perhaps the New Universe's leading villain is Philip Nolan Voigt, alias Overshadow, created by Gruenwald and artist Paul Ryan in *D. P. 7* #1 (1986). Having gained the power to duplicate and augment within himself any paranormal's power, Voigt secretly used his Clinic for Paranormal Research to organize an army of paranormals. Voigt even became president of the United States.

The "Marvel 2099" line of comics was set at the end of an alternate version of the twenty-first century and presented futuristic counterparts to present-day heroes, such as *Spider-Man 2099*. Foremost among its villains is the title character of *Doom 2099* (1993–1996), who may or may not be the original Dr. Doom, thrust into the future, where he quickly mastered late-twenty-first-century science and began a new quest for political power.

Another memorable 2099 menace is Jordan Boone, who became the mad shapeshifter Halloween Jack (in *X-Men 2099* #16, 1995), a criminal trickster in the tradition of the Joker.

Writer Peter David and artist Rick Leonardi created the mysterious menace Thanatos in *Spider-Man 2099* #11 (1993). In a 2002 *Captain Marvel* story, David brought Thanatos back, revealing that he is an alternate timeline version of long-time supporting character Rick Jones. As Thanatos he retains the immense superpowers Jones gained during the Kree-Skrull War, an intergalactic conflict that pitted two alien empires against each other.

In the early 1990s Malibu Comics commissioned leading comics professionals to create new series for its "Ultraverse," which were bought by Marvel in 1994. Among the Ultraverse characters was Barry Windsor-Smith's Rune, who first appeared in *Sludge* #1 (1993) and starred in several comics series. Originating on an alien world ages ago, Rune is a winged sorcerer who feeds vampirically on the blood of others. He has battled Thor, Adam Warlock, the Silver Surfer, and even Conan.

Perhaps the most imaginatively conceived Ultraverse villain is Lord Pumpkin, who debuted in *Sludge* #3 (1993) and also starred in his own series (*Lord Pumpkin* #0, 1994, *Lord Pumpkin/Necromantra* #1–#4, 1995). An evil, sentient plant creature with a head like a Jack o' Lantern, Lord Pumpkin can be regarded as a sinister counterpart to DC's Swamp Thing.

In the late 1990s former Marvel editor in chief Tom DeFalco masterminded Marvel's "MC2" line of titles, set in an alternate future a decade and a half hence. The only "MC2" series being published in 2006 is DeFalco's *Spider-Girl*, a book about Spider-Man's teenage daughter. In co-creating its huge rogues' gallery, DeFalco seeks to recapture the spirit of Stan Lee and Steve Ditko's classic *Spider-Man* foes. Hence, paralleling Lee and Ditko's Sinister Six team, DeFalco organized *Spider-Girl* villains into the Savage Six: Dragon King (a human turned into a dragon), Funny Face (who

dresses as a clown), Killerwatt (who has electrical powers), Mr. Abnormal (whose body stretches), Raptor (who has wings), and Sabreclaw (Wolverine's son). Other *Spider-Girl* villains include Crazy Eight (who throws 8-balls containing weapons), Mr. Nobody (a teleporter), and a new Green Goblin, the grandson of the original.

In *Kingdom Come* (1996) writer Mark Waid and artist Alex Ross created a vast array of new characters for their alternate future version of the DC Universe. Among the most notable is Ra's al Ghul's successor, Ibn al Xu'ffasch, the son of Batman and Talia. Many of their new superheroes seemed more like supervillains, recklessly fighting criminals and each other. The foremost of this "new breed" was the biblically named Magog, who killed the Joker and inadvertently caused the nuclear obliteration of Kansas. A similar character, Gog (who debuted in *Gog* #1, 1998), has battled the Superman of mainstream DC continuity. Even though *Crisis on Infinite Earths* (1985–1986) supposedly got rid of DC's parallel worlds and alternate realities, series like *Kingdom Come*, other *Elseworlds*, and Mark Waid's "Hypertime" concept seem to have brought them back. —PS

Amazo

"I am the most powerful creature in the universe!" boasted the barrel-chested, towering android—Amazo—in the Justice League of America's third appearance, *The Brave and the Bold* #30 (1960). On individual missions, JLA members the Flash, Green Lantern, Wonder Woman, Aquaman, and Martian Manhunter withstand evanescent losses of their superpowers. Their extraordinary abilities are being siphoned by the rogue scientist Professor Ivo to empower his synthetic serf, Amazo. One by one, the dumbstruck Justice Leaguers fall victim to the arrogant automaton who plies their own awesome faculties and weapons against them. Green Lantern's quick thinking enables him to outwit Amazo, who, in a dormant state, is relegated to souvenir status in the League's Secret Sanctuary.

The JLA had no choice but to revive Amazo to combat the inexorable alien "I" in *Justice League* of America #27 (1964). In subsequent reactivations, including several late-1970s skirmishes with Superman, Ivo's upgrades of Amazo's "absorption cells" have made this "One-Man Justice League" virtually unstoppable. Amazo's replication of the might of the League's entire roster, including reservists, in *JLA* #27 (1999) would have resulted in the deaths of an army of superheroes had Superman not disbanded the team to crash the android's programming.

The rogues' gallery of the Cartoon Network's animated *Justice League* series and its expanded-cast continuation, *Justice League Unlimited* (2004–present), includes a redesigned Amazo voiced by Robert Picardo. Both the television and comics versions of the supervillain have been immortalized as action figures. —*ME*

Amos Fortune

On Mike Sekowsky and Murphy Anderson's cover to *Justice League of America* #6 (1961)—a recreation of the Justice Society cover to *All Star Comics* #42 (1948)—the Flash, Green Lantern, Green Arrow, Aquaman, Martian Manhunter, and Wonder Woman are strapped to a spinning "Wheel of Misfortune," furiously spun by a robed, plump figure with a receding hairline. This is Professor Amos Fortune, a loony genius who mixes superstition with super-science. With his "Stimoluck" device, which incites the Justice League's "bad-luck glands" (!), Fortune maneuvers the heroes into embarrassing mishaps as he tests his chance-altering abilities. The professor is no megalomaniac, but instead an opportunist garnering wealth though his mastery of odds. Fortune finds himself in conflict with the JLA, trapping them on his wheel and cursing them with perpetual bad luck to keep them from thwarting his gambits. The one thing Amos Fortune doesn't anticipate, however, is the Martian Manhunter's alien physiology's immunity to his glandular stimulation, and Fortune's luck runs out.

Professor Fortune returned to perturb the JLA on several occasions during the 1960s, masquerading as "Mr. Memory" in the Atom's first adventure with the League (issue #14, 1962), then as the "Ace of Clubs," the organizer of the

roguish Royal Flush Gang. He eventually left the Gang and returned to his solo probability crimes, but each time he resurfaces, Fortune always finds the deck stacked against him. —*ME*

Anarky

Gotham City's corrupt CEOs and drug peddlers may look over their shoulders for the winged shadow of the Batman, but it is Anarky they truly fear. An extreme activist consumed by leftist political convictions, Anarky first strikes against social injustices in *Detective Comics* #608–#609 (1989) by writer Alan Grant and artist Norm Breyfogle. A tall, gangly figure cloaked in crimson and hiding his face behind a golden mask, Anarky wields intimidation, property destruction, and murder in a campaign against amoral land developers and corporate polluters, leaving behind spray-painted "A" warnings in the wake of his actions. He makes headlines after electrocuting the dope-dealing rock star Johnny Vomit, attracting Batman's cowled eye. Warding off Anarky's walking-staff taser, gas bombs, and martial artistry, Batman is startled once he uncovers the terrorist's secret: beneath the red garb is *13-year-old* Lonnie Machin.

After a brief stint in a juvenile jail, Machin—who once bankrupted dishonest businessmen as the computer hacker Moneyspider—amplified his intellect after commandeering a Green Lantern power ring. Upon discovering that he was adopted, Machin was traumatized when he learned the apparent identity of his father: the Joker. Anarky's ethical motivations and his youth have made Batman and his ally Robin sympathetic toward him, and despite his violent propensities Anarky has on several occasions aided numerous superheroes. Still, Anarky remains dedicated to initiating a global revolution in the hopes of making the world a better place. —*ME*

Anime Evil Masterminds

Whether endowed with superpowers or not, many memorable villains do not always carry out their dirty deeds single-handedly. Most of them employ henchmen and/or are backed by a massive secret organization that they use to wage their evil campaigns. These villains move beyond one-man operations to become "masterminds." Despite this elaborate network of evil, some masterminds do, at times, personally face off against the heroes. These masterminds are major threats to our heroes—and the very existence of the world itself. While such villains are staples of American comics, they also exist in *anime* (the Japanese word for "animation"); many popular anime characters are based on popular manga (Japanese comics), and some eventually reach America (albeit in an edited form). Generally, at the end of the series, whether in manga or anime, the evil mastermind is defeated, but the price of victory is often great to the heroes.

One mastermind from the early years of television anime was Dr. Spectra from *Eighth Man*. The U.S. TV series—based on the 1963 manga created by Kazumasa Hirai and Jiro Kuwata—followed the adventures of the android hero Tobor, the Eighth Man, who had been given the mind of a murdered special agent. Dr. Spectra, introduced in the episode titled simply "Dr. Spectra," became perhaps the deadliest enemy of Eighth Man. Driven by his unrelenting desire to acquire the means to construct an army of androids based on Eighth Man, Spectra eventually learned the whole truth about his foe's origins. This soon placed everyone that Tobor knew and cared about at risk.

In 1963 Shotaro Ishinomori's manga *Cyborg 009* began. It introduced the world not only to nine superpowered cyborgs (perhaps manga's first "superteam") but also to the terrorist organization that created them: Black Ghost. The organization's leader was also named Black Ghost, and he resembled a dark figure wearing a skull-like helmet or mask. The nine cyborg heroes rejected the organization and waged constant battles against their creators. Black Ghost responded by sending various cyborgs and war machines to stop their wayward creations. *Cyborg 009* became an animated series in Japan

in 1968, and an animated film was released in Japan in 1980. A heavily edited version of the film was released in America in the mid-1980s. A new animated series titled *Cyborg 009* aired in Japan in 2001 and ran on Cartoon Network in 2003 with its original title intact.

In 1972 the anime *Science Ninja Team Gatchaman* premiered in Japan, and it was brought to the United States in the late 1970s under the title *Battle of the Planets*. The mastermind of this series was Zoltar (in *Gatchaman*, Berg Katse), a tall man wearing a purple outfit with cape and cowl, and with red lips. As the military leader of Spectra (a malevolent empire whose planet faced depletion of its resources), Zoltar sought to conquer Earth and its allied planets to gain their resources. A highly skilled military leader, Zoltar was also a master of deception and lies. He would send Spectra's armies and robotic monsters into action, but would usually find some way to escape to fight another day. Opposing Zoltar and his plans was G-Force, five teens with superpowers and advanced weaponry developed by their guardian, Chief Anderson. Yet even Zoltar was a loyal soldier to the Luminous One, a spectral figure who was the real power behind Spectra.

Of course, things were rather different in *Gatchaman*: Berg Katse was the leader of Galactor, a terrorist organization that was actually a front for an alien force bent of invading Earth. Katse, however, was revealed to be a hermaphroditic mutant; at the end of *Gatchaman*, he committed suicide by throwing him/herself into a lava pit. This story point was cut from *Battle of the Planets*.

So influential was *Gatchaman* in Japan that in the thirty-plus years since its debut, other anime have had villains in the mold of (but not necessarily resembling) Berg Katse. Also, not every mastermind is male: Sister Jill from Go Nagai's *Cutey Honey* (1971) and Queen Beryl of Naoko Takeuchi's *Sailor Moon* (1992) prove that female masterminds can be just as cold and cruel—and as popular—as their male counterparts.

One of the most unusual masterminds in anime would prove true the adage "size matters

Opposite: Zoltar. From *Battle of the Planets Artbook* vol. 1 #1 ©2004 Top Cow Productions.
ART BY ALEX ROSS.

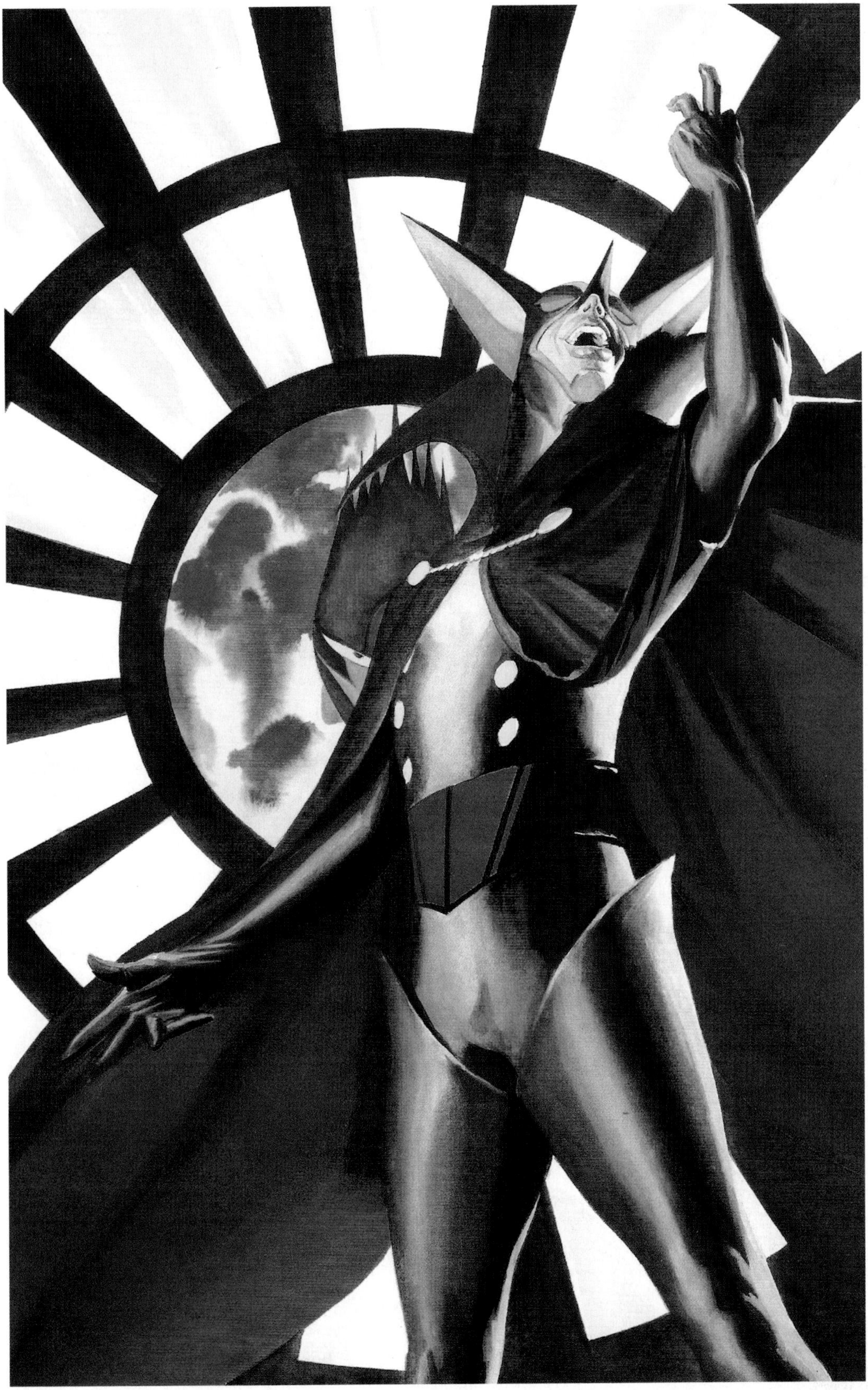

not." That was Colonel MacDougal from the 1990 manga *Spriggan,* created by Hiroshi Takashige and Ryoji Minagawa (the manga was released in America in 1992 by Viz under the title *Striker: The Armored Warrior*). MacDougal was introduced in the "Noah's Ark" storyline (which was the basis for the animated *Spriggan* film released in 2000) as the head of the Machine Corps, a renegade branch of the Pentagon. The Machine Corps sought to gain the technology left by an ancient advanced civilization; many of these artifacts were held by the group Arcam.

Arcam had just discovered Noah's Ark—and it was *not* the ship described in the Bible, but much more. Assisting MacDougal to capture the Ark were an army of soldiers, including the supersoldiers Little Boy and Fatman, named after the two atomic bombs dropped on Hiroshima and Nagasaki. The only person capable of standing up to MacDougal was Yu Ominae, Arcam's top supersoldier, or "Spriggan."

MacDougal's appearance was of a young boy between eight and ten years of age wearing jeans, athletic shoes, a jacket, and a baseball cap, but he had the personality of an adult. What made MacDougal a truly formidable villain were his powerful telekinetic abilities, which allowed him to manipulate objects (or twist bones and flesh) with his mind, or to create an impervious psychic shield. These powers were the result of a device implanted in his brain, but the device would give him massive, painful headaches—and it was slowly killing him. MacDougal wanted to gain the Ark because of its true purpose: it was an ancient weather control station, as well as a genetic laboratory. The Ark had affected the evolution of life on Earth, and MacDougal wanted that power for himself. After a bloody battle with Yu Ominae, MacDougal was stopped; refusing to admit defeat, he activated the Ark's self-destruct system, and he was destroyed along with it. —*MM*

Annihilus

The Fantastic Four had assumed that the antimatter universe called the Negative Zone could produce no creature more abominable than Blastaar, the Living Bomb-Burst.

They were wrong.

In the extraordinary tale "Let There Be Life!" in *Fantastic Four Annual* #6 (1968), written by Stan Lee and illustrated by Jack Kirby and Joe Sinnott, Marvel Comics' super-family stands on the threshold of its most joyous moment: the impending birth of Reed (Mr. Fantastic) and Sue (Invisible Girl, later Woman) Richards' first child. Difficulties with Sue's pregnancy compel Reed and his teammates, the Thing and the Human Torch, to venture into the hazardous Negative Zone to obtain the only device known to man that will spare the lives of Sue and her unborn child. The authoritarian lord of much of the Zone, Annihilus—once an insect/humanoid mutated into a cosmically powered conqueror after discovering a helmet possessing the hoarded knowledge of the intellectually superior Tyannan race—stands in their way. Only the bond of familial love empowers the heroes to succeed and escape Annihilus' wrath, returning to Earth just in time to help Sue bring young Franklin Richards into the world.

Protected by an astonishingly sophisticated exoskeleton, Annihilus can withstand the Thing's mightiest blows and the Torch's blazing heat. His metallic wings whisk him through the voids of the Negative Zone, and his weapon of choice—the Cosmic Control Rod, worn upon his collarbone and capable of projecting inestimable force—allows Annihilus to swarm like a lethal locust. He has occasionally allied with Blastaar to attack the Fantastic Four, but their Negative Zone turf wars and Blastaar's efforts at acquiring the Cosmic Control Rod have made them more foes than friends. Pushed to the brink of madness by his quest to destroy, Annihilus has infested Earth on several occasions. A 2005 encounter with the FF, in the miniseries *Fantastic Four: Foes* #2, permitted readers a better understanding of the twisted intellect that drives Annihilus on his unending path of extermination.

In the pages of Marvel Comics' reimagination of the FF, *Ultimate Fantastic Four* (2004–present), Annihilus exists in the altered form of Nihil, an alien with a lengthy lifespan who schemes to abandon his ancient universe of the N-Zone for the greener pastures of the Ultimate FF's Earth. Veteran animation voice actor Clyde Kusatsu played the traditional Marvel version of Annihilus in the "Behold the Negative Zone" episode of the third *Fantastic Four* cartoon (1994–1996); an Annihilus action figure was merchandized as a tie-in to the show. —*ME*

The Anti-Monitor

First seen in *Crisis on Infinite Earths* #2 (1985), the Anti-Monitor, an ebon-armored eradicator boasting unfathomable cosmic power, was DC Comics' most notorious mass-murderer.

DC's "multiverse" was a science-fiction plot device borrowed to allow the publishers' Golden Age (1938–1954) and Silver Age (1956–1969) versions of characters to coexist on alternate worlds (i.e., the Earth-One Flash and Earth-Two Flash). Throughout the 1970s, more parallel worlds were introduced as DC purchased characters from defunct companies, and by the 1980s the publisher felt that its expanded universes should be streamlined into one. To achieve this goal, writer Marv Wolfman and artist George Pérez produced the epic *Crisis on Infinite Earths* (1985–1986), a twelve-issue series featuring the cosmos-quaking conflict between two omnipotent beings: the Monitor, a benevolent surveyor of manifold realities, and his bloodthirsty doppelgänger from the anti-matter world of Qward, the Anti-Monitor.

Abetted by his destructive shadow demons, the Anti-Monitor augmented his might by annihilating and absorbing myriad realities, killing billions and threatening to extinguish life in all eras and universes. The Monitor drafted DC's greatest superheroes from various timelines—as well as some supervillains—to stand against the Anti-Monitor in a multi-chaptered clash that resulted in the deaths of the Silver Age Supergirl and Flash, plus some outmoded DC characters beyond salvaging. *Crisis* #11 (1986), the series' penultimate chapter, pitted the towering Anti-Monitor in deadly battle with a leviathan-sized Spectre at the dawn of time, but in the final issue, it took the combined might of virtually every DC champion to destroy this mightiest of supervillains. —*ME*

Apocalypse

The idea of the "superman" goes back to nineteenth-century philosopher Friedrich Nietzsche's concept of the *ubermensch*, a superior individual whom he considered to be "beyond good and evil." The American superhero adapts this idea to democratic society; the superhero is a member of the community, helping them but not ruling them. Nazi ideologues adapted Nietszche's concepts differently, creating their philosophy of a "master race" dominating or supplanting weaker races.

Marvel's mutant villain Apocalypse embodies the dark side of the *ubermensch* concept. His name means "the end of the world" as depicted in the last book of the New Testament, the Book of Revelation, often referred to as the Book of the Apocalypse. Apocalypse's philosophy is an extreme version of social Darwinism: he believes in the survival of the fittest, that the strong deserve to rule, and even to destroy, the weak. Since he is one of Earth's most powerful mutants, Apocalypse believes it is his destiny to rule the planet.

Apocalypse first appeared in shadow in *X-Factor* #5 (1986), written by Bob Layton and drawn by Jackson "Butch" Guice, but he emerged into full view in *X-Factor* #6, drawn by Guice and written by Louise Simonson. The character has continued to appear in Marvel's *X-Men* and related titles.

One of the first known superhuman mutants in the history of Marvel's fictional Earth, Apocalypse has mental control over his body's molecular structure, enabling him to change shape at will. By absorbing energy from outside sources, he can augment his superhuman strength without any known limit. He can also absorb mass in order to increase his size. Apocalypse has mastered methods of genetic engineering that are advanced far beyond conventional science.

Apocalypse's origin was revealed in the miniseries *The Rise of Apocalypse* #1–#4 (1996–1997), written by Terry Kavanagh and drawn by Adam Pollina, depicting him as an evil kind of Messiah. He was born nearly five thousand years ago in Egypt. Believed to be a demon, the grotesque infant was abandoned in the desert to die. But he was found by a band of raiders, whose leader, Baal, sensed the infant's latent power. Baal named the infant "En Sabah Nur" (which signifies "The First One") and raised him as his son. It was Baal who taught En Sabah Nur his philosophy of the survival of the fittest.

When En Sabah Nur was seventeen, Baal brought him into a sacred cave, where they became entrapped. There Baal told Nur that he believed the youth was a prophesied conqueror who was destined to overthrow Egypt's ruler, Pharaoh Rama-Tut, who years before had massacred much of their tribe and enslaved the survivors. (Rama-Tut was actually a time traveler from the far future, who had come to ancient Egypt to find Apocalypse as a child and raise him to serve him.) Baal starved to death in the cave, but the mutant Nur made his way back to the surface.

Biding his time, En Sabah Nur labored as a slave. Eventually he came face to face with Rama-Tut, who offered to make him his heir. When Nur refused, Rama-Tut ordered him killed. But the superhumanly powerful Nur defeated Rama-Tut's warlord Ozymandias, and Rama-Tut fled into the future, where he became the Avengers' arch-nemesis, Kang the Conqueror.

Spurned by Nephri, the woman he loved, Nur dedicated his life to conquest. For thousands of years, Nur traveled the planet, worshipped as a god by ancient civilizations. Implementing his philosophy, Nur manipulated nations into fighting wars in order to determine which country's people would prove to be the stronger.

As recorded in the comics miniseries *The Further Adventures of Cyclops and Phoenix* (1996), in AD 1859 Apocalypse encountered Dr. Nathaniel Essex, a scientist who believed he could create a superhuman "master race" through selective breeding. Apocalypse transformed Essex into the superhuman being Mr. Sinister. But the time-traveling Cyclops and Phoenix (Jean Grey) of the X-Men thwarted Apocalypse's plot to assassinate Queen Victoria.

More than a century later, Apocalypse believed that the newly emerging race of superhuman mutants were the "strong" who were destined to conquer the weak "normal" humans. Apocalypse first clashed with the original X-Factor, a team comprised of members of the original X-Men, including Cyclops.

Apocalypse used his advanced science to genetically alter the Angel, one of X-Factor's members, into the blue-skinned Archangel, giving him new wings, hard like metal. Apocalypse intended Archangel to serve as one of his "Four Horsemen," named after the figures of War, Death, Famine, and Pestilence in the Bible's Book of Revelation. But Archangel rebelled and rejoined X-Factor.

Apocalypse later infected Cyclops' infant son, Nathan Summers, with a lethal "techno-organic" virus. Nathan was transported to the far future by the Askani, a cult of freedom fighters, who saved his life. In that alternate future, Apocalypse ruled Earth, but he had to keep transferring his mind and powers into new host bodies to survive. Apocalypse raised Stryfe, a clone of Nathan, intending to make him his new host. But the teenage Nathan slew Apocalypse (as seen in the comics miniseries *The Adventures of Cyclops and Phoenix* in 1994) and grew up to become the warrior Cable. (The adult Cable journeyed back to the X-Men's time in the hope of changing future history by defeating Apocalypse back then.)

In the recent past, Cyclops thwarted Apocalypse's attempt to transfer his consciousness into the body of Nate Grey, the mutant called X-Man. Instead, Apocalypse merged with Cyclops. Jean Grey later used her powers to exorcise Apocalypse from Cyclops' body, and Cable seemingly destroyed Apocalypse's astral form (as seen in *X-Men: The Search for Cyclops* #4, 2001). But can even this defeat stop a being capable of possessing other people's bodies?

In 1995 Marvel introduced "The Age of Apocalypse," an alternate timeline in which Apocalypse had conquered North America and undertook genetic "cleansing" of humanity, slaughtering those he deemed unfit to live, until he was killed by Magneto. "The Age of Apocalypse" made the connection between Apocalypse's philosophy and the Nazis' master race ideology clear.

Apocalypse has appeared on television as a major villain in *X-Men: The Animated Series* (1992–1997) and the animated *X-Men: Evolution* (2000–2003). He has also appeared in the 1990s computer arcade games *X-Men vs. Street Fighter* and *Marvel Super Heroes vs. Street Fighter* and in the video games *X-Men: Reign of Apocalypse* (2001) and *X-Men Legends II: Rise of Apocalypse* (2005). —*PS*

Aquatic Supervillains

In the tradition of real-life pirates Captain Kidd and Blackbeard and fictional cutthroats Long John Silver and Captain Hook, many comic-book supervillains have roiled the seas for profit.

Mr. Crabb, a crimson-skinned energy baron, tried to commandeer the Gulf Coast's oil market from a domed underwater lair until Blue Beetle pulled the plug on his operation in 1965. Captain Whale, appearing only once in Dell Comics' aqua-superhero series *Nukla* #3 (1966), was a thinly veiled version of Jules Verne's Captain Nemo who nearly stirred up World War III in his high-tech sub the Killer Whale. Dr. Fang, one of a gushing torrent of "Yellow Peril" Asian masterminds, and his water-breathing subordinates, the Lemurians, dreamed of global conquest—above and below the sea—but were opposed by U.N.D.E.R.S.E.A. operative Lt. Davey Jones in Tower Comics' *Undersea Agent* #1 (1966).

DC Comics' Aquaman, monarch of the legendary sunken continent of Atlantis, has frequently battled the Black Manta, the Ocean Master, and the Shark, but earlier in his crime-fighting career protected both sea and land from mundane smugglers and crooks. One of his first costumed foes was a former champion swimmer who, with a glider-winged uniform, evaded the hero by taking to the air as the Human Flying Fish in a 1960 tale. The Fisherman, the yellow-hooded, adversarial angler in a purple scuba suit, premiered in *Aquaman* vol. 1 #21 (1965), hooking ill-gotten gain from ships with his titanium fishing rod.

The amphibious terrorist Charybdis originally fought Aquaman in 1994 and bested the hero, leaving him to a school of piranhas that feasted upon the Sea King's left hand. Gamemnae, an outcast Atlantean sorceress born 3,000 years ago, skirmished with Aquaman and his Justice League in both the past and the present. The most monstrous of Aquaman's foes was the Thirst, the mud-golem that premiered in 2003; consuming both aquatic deities and water itself, the Thirst briefly amalgamated with Aquaman into a single, hideous form

Dr. Fang. *Undersea Agent* #1 1966. © & ™ John Carbonaro.
COVER ART BY RAY BAILEY.

before the golem was apparently destroyed—but Aquaman wondered if such a creature can truly die.

Marvel Comics' Atlantis is governed by Prince Namor, the Sub-Mariner. His throne has been contested by water-breathing warriors Attuma and Krang, aided by co-conspirators including Namor's own cousin, Byrrah. The blue-skinned vixen Llyra first splashed into Namor's life in *Sub-Mariner* vol. 2 #32 (1970) and was responsible for the death of his betrothed Lady Dorma. A behind-the-scenes player in Atlantis' power struggle was Dr. Lemuel Dorcas, a twisted genius responsible for unholy experiments upon sea-dwellers. He produced the blue-skinned powerhouse solider named Orca; the Piranha, a fish mutated into a fish-man; and Piranha's school of monstrosities called Men-Fish.

Tiger Shark was another of Dorcas' creations. The doctor's "morphotron" genetically imprinted former Olympic swimmer Todd Arliss with DNA from both a shark and Namor in *Sub-Mariner* vol. 2 #5 (1968). With the strength, amphibian agility, and avarice of his namesake, Tiger Shark has frequently fought Sub-Mariner and has also taken his menace landside, joining the Masters of Evil and encountering the Thunderbolts (he also appeared in a 1999 *Avengers* television cartoon).

U-Man, a former subject of Namor, was an amphibious agent of the Third Reich introduced in 1975's issue #3 of *The Invaders*, Marvel's superteam series set during World War II. This blue-skinned Atlantean was not the only costumed Nazi in multi-colored tights—Killer Shark, a superhumanly strong Nazi general, struggled with the aerial Allies known as the Blackhawks beginning in 1952; a second version of Killer Shark, a costumed scalawag, battled the piloting paragons in a mid-1980s *Blackhawk* revival.

The dismal waters of the planet Apokolips are protected by the overlord Darkseid's amphibious agents Slig, Gole, Kurin, Jaffer, Trok, and Shaligo—the Deep Six. Created by Jack Kirby in *New Gods* vol. 1 #2 (1971), the Six, or members thereof, have occasionally appeared since.

Perhaps the oddest aquatic supervillains appeared in *The Sea Devils*, the *Sea Hunt*–meets–*Challengers of the Unknown* DC Comics series created by writer Robert Kanigher and artist Russ Heath. In virtually every one of *Sea Devils*' thirty-five issues (1961–1967), the underwater adventurers battled a mega-sized monster with a descriptive name, including the Octopus Man, the Human Tidal Wave, the Flame-Headed Watchman, the Magnetic Menace, and the Manosaur.

With vile creatures such as these occupying the murky depths, one can certainly understand why most superheroes prefer to be landlubbers! —*ME*

Arachnid Adversaries

Fascinating to some, frightening to others, arachnids, named for the Greek mythological weaver Arachne, have captivated writers, artists, and fans.

Some readers felt stung when Quality Comics' Golden Age (1938–1954) pulp-like hero the Spider was retroactively remade into a supervillain in the 1990s in the pages of *Starman* vol. 2, from publisher DC Comics, which had purchased Quality's characters. *Starman* scribe James Robinson revealed that the Spider's superheroics secretly shielded his behind-the-scenes involvement in Keystone City's underworld. The Shade, a supervillain with unpredictable motivations, ended the Spider's web of deceptions—permanently.

Archie Comics' Spider Spry (aka the Spider), created by Joe Simon and Jack Kirby in *The Adventures of the Fly* #1 (1959), was a dumpy crook who used his technological wizardry to pull heists with his web-shooting device and giant robotic scorpions.

DC's Spider-Girl, aka Sussa Paka from thirtieth-century Earth, could, like Marvel's Medusa, control her malleable hair; her first brush with the Legion of Super-Heroes took place in *Adventure Comics* #323 (1964). Spider-Woman is an often recycled name for Marvel superheroines, but a 1966 Space Ghost villainess misappropriated that alias for *underwater* capers, trapping the spectral hero in an aquarium as an intended snack for a three-headed shark. In the Man of Steel's first live-action screen appearance, the Columbia Pictures movie serial *Superman* (1948), he battled the Spider Lady, a bland crime queen who spent most of the serial's fifteen chapters radioing orders to her lackeys.

Spider Lady actress Carol Forman portrayed another arachnid-based femme fatale in the thirteen-chapter serial *The Black Widow* (1947); there she was a "Yellow Peril" atomic saboteur who became entangled with investigator Steve Colt. Marvel Comics' Black Widow, when first seen in the Iron Man adventure in *Tales of Suspense* #52 (1964), was a Soviet spy who soon switched camps and signed up as an agent of S.H.I.E.L.D. and later, as a member of the Avengers. Batman's web-swinging enemy Black Spider, who debuted in *Detective Comics* #463 (1976), was DC Comics' first African-American supervillain.

Three Tarantulas have scampered through Spider-Man's life: South American terrorist Anton

Miguel Rodriguez was the first, starting his career in *The Amazing Spider-Man* vol. 1 #134 (1974) by taking pleasure cruisers hostage. This spike-booted Tarantula was later mutated into an eight-legged monster-man, and died in a hail of police bullets. He was succeeded by Luis Alvarez in *Web of Spider-Man* #36 (1988), who took a variation of Captain America's Super-Soldier Serum to become the vengeful Tarantula II, but eventually, like his predecessor, died violently. Then came Argentinan Carlos LaMuerto, aka Black Tarantula, whose crime connections brought him into a Manhattan Mafia gang war in *Amazing Spider-Man* #419 (1997). Sort of a counterpart to Batman's foe Bane, Black Tarantula is considerably stronger than Spidey and can heal wounds.

It should come as no surprise that the amazing Spider-Man has been plagued with enough spidery enemies to give even the wall-crawler a case of arachnophobia. One of his most powerful nemeses is Venom, his dark counterpart, from which Venom's gory offspring Carnage sprung (and from Carnage came the next in this lethal lineage, Toxin). The 1992 crossover *Infinity War* gave birth to a grotesque, eight-armed distortion of Spider-Man appropriately called Doppelganger. In 1993, superhero wannabe Brian Kornfeld made a pact with Dwarf, an agent of the demon Chthon, for Spider-Man-like powers conjured through the magical book *The Darkhold*, transmogrifying into the loathsome insectoid Spider-X before being fried in a battle with the electrical beast Zzzax. Clones of Spidey's alter ego, Peter Parker, were altered by the Jackal into the supervillains Kaine (first seen in *Web of Spider-Man* #119, 1994), an assassin with many of Spidey's powers and the ability to burn "the mark of Kaine" into his victims; and the Venom-esque shapeshifter Spidercide, briefly seen in a 1995 storyline. Alien abductors spliced Peter Parker's DNA with their own to create the monstrous Spider-Hybrid in 2000.

One of Spider-Man's most persistent and nastiest foes is the Scorpion, the green-costumed villain with the 7-foot mechanical tail who has frequently attempted to wipe out the web-slinger since 1965's *Amazing Spider-Man* #20 (and who inspired the short-lived career of DC's Stingaree, in *Metamorpho* #10, 1967). "The Scorpion" has been a popular name for film and pulp villains, a noted example being the criminal identity of the dastardly Professor Bentley, who, from behind a black hood and robe adorned with white scorpion applications, created malice with his scorpion-shaped disintegrator in the twelve-chapter movie serial *The Adventures of Captain Marvel* (1941).

Death-Web was the name taken by Dr. Sylvie Yaqua, Theo, and Hashi Noto in *Avengers West Coast* #82 (1992) when spider-venom injections transformed them into Arachne (able to emit toxins and webs from her wrists), Therak (a six-armed strongman), and Antro (a teleporter). And in 1982, Marvel's original Spider-Woman met the weirdest arachnid supervillain of all: Daddy Longlegs, a dancer whose exposure to Giant-Man's growth formula transformed him into a 13-foot supervillain who was light on his feet. —*ME*

Arcade

Arcade, the master escape artist who delights in illusion and has been caught and jailed only on occasion, first appeared in *Marvel Team-Up* vol. 1 #65 (1978), written by Chris Claremont and drawn by John Byrne. Arcade has told his own backstory, so any details he alleges about his past are questionable. Nevertheless, Arcade, whose real name is unrevealed, insists he was born into a wealthy family in Beverly Hills (or Texas, depending upon the version), growing up with a silver spoon in his mouth. When his father cut him off, Arcade murdered him, amassing his vast fortune. He traveled the world as a hired killer, eventually discovering his *real* calling as the eccentric host of a chamber of horrors–like amusement park he designed with his robotics and mechanical engineering expertise: Murderworld.

With the help of his assistants Miss Locke and Mr. Chambers, Arcane lured his victims into Murderworld, taunting and torturing them in a variety of deathtraps, twisted games, and demented plottings, customized (for the price of $1 million) to exploit the weaknesses of his human targets. The carnival hitman first attempted to outdo Spider-Man and Captain Britain, but has since tried to set up (and take down) almost every major hero in the Marvel Universe, usually in pairs, including Gambit

Original color guide to *X-Men* vol. 1 #122, page 30 ©1979 Marvel Comics.
ART BY JOHN BYRNE AND TERRY AUSTIN.

style costume and accoutrements are as intentionally mock-trendy as the Joker's zoot suit was in the 1940s.

In the 2000s, Arcade resurfaced in the *Ultimate X-Men* series as a gaming prodigy who invented a first-person shooter. When the *Ultimate* Universe version of Longshot was found guilty of murdering a Genoshan politician, he was sentenced to participate in a reality TV show in which he was stranded on an island and hunted by Arcade.

Similarly, the animated TV series *X-Men: Evolution* (2000–2003) reimagined Arcade as a high-school gamer named Webber Torque (who called himself Arcade), tricked by a disguised Mystique into believing that the X-Men's mansion security console was an elaborate video game and used it to attack the X-Men, who he believed to be game characters. Despite nearly killing the X-Men, this version of Arcade was not evil, and he apologized for having played the "video game" without permission. —*GM*

and Wolverine, Colossus and Shadowcat, and Iceman and Angel. He has also battled major hero groups, such as the X-Men and Alpha Flight, and takes particular delight in trying to undo the villainous, including the Green Goblin.

A long-running villain still alive and kicking today, Claremont and Byrne created Arcade in the tradition of DC trickster villains like the Toyman, the Trickster, and even the Joker, who turns children's toys into lethal weapons. Arcade's disco-

Arcane

Created by Len Wein and Bernie Wrightson, Anton Arcane debuted in *Swamp Thing* vol. 1 #2 (1972–1973). He appears as a spindly scientist and amateur occultist from a Balkan nation who is obsessed by two desires: the achievement of power and eternal life. During World War II, he mistakenly allies himself with the Nazis, including the Führer himself, only to venture deeper into the world of sorcery and debauchery, along the way creating creatures such as the horrific, artificial life forms the Un-Men and the Patchwork Man, assembled from decaying body parts.

Although Arcane became immortal, his human body aged. Seeking out the Swamp Thing, Arcane offered him humanity in exchange for using his powerful plant body for himself. Swamp Thing agreed and was magically transformed into Alec Holland. However, when Holland realized that Arcane would use Swamp Thing's monstrous body to make himself ruler of the world, he quickly reverted the process. Arcane fled, seemingly plum-meting to his death.

The encounter was not the death of Arcane, nor was it the last time Arcane and Swamp Thing would go head to head. Arcane has assumed many forms over the years, including the body of an Un-Men, an insectoid creature, and the body of his niece Abigail's husband, Matthew Cable, during which Arcane developed strong telekinetic powers. Arcane died in one of his last Swamp Thing encoun-ters and was damned to a life in hell. After years of underworld punishment, he was made a minor demon in Beelzebub's ranks and emerged as a 12-feet-tall, 2,000-pound, deformed, gargoyle-like eye-sore with amazing strength and quick-footedness (as disclosed in *Swamp Thing* vol. 2 #96, 1990). Later, Arcane redeemed himself, but he was even-tually (perhaps inevitably) cast out of heaven and back into hell. He returned to Louisiana intent on appropriating Swamp Thing's body as a permanent earthly vessel for his soul, but was defeated and returned to hell to suffer eternal torment yet again. A quote from one of his demon lovers who returned to Earth with him put it thusly: "And when they write about Arcane, they should say that he dragged Hell in his wake" (*Swamp Thing* vol. 4 #11, 2005).

Anton Arcane has enjoyed many forays into the media world outside of comics' pages. Por-trayed by Louis Jourdan, Arcane can be seen in the Wes Craven–directed feature film *Swamp Thing* (1982) and the Jim Wynorski–directed sequel *Return of the Swamp Thing* (1989). He regularly appeared (portrayed by Mark Lindsay Chapman) in FOX's live-action television series *Swamp Thing* (1990–1993), as well as the FOX animated *Swamp Thing* television series (1990), voiced by Don Francks. Based on the Swamp Thing toy line by Kenner and inspired by the success of the *Swamp*

Thing comic book and films, the animated show chronicled Swamp Thing's battle with Arcane and the Un-Men. The series, which lasted only five episodes, was produced by DIC. —*GM*

Arkham Asylum: *See* **Supervillain Prisons**

Astro City Supervillains

Created by writer Kurt Busiek, penciler Brent Anderson, and cover artist Alex Ross, Astro City is a fictional metropolis as full of super-heroes—and supervillains—as Marvel Comics' version of New York. Its saga began in Image Comics' *Kurt Busiek's Astro City* vol. 1 #1 (1995) and continues to be published by DC Comics.

In 2002 Busiek told the comics website Newsarama that *Astro City* was "about what it would be like if that kind of world was real." He pointed out that "we don't follow any one particular character or even a team. We tell stories from a variety of view-points." A story could be told from the perspective of the hero, or "an innocent bystander" or even "a villain wanting to prove himself."

In *Astro City* Busiek intentionally fashions new heroes and villains upon familiar archetypes in the superhero genre.

The *Astro City* story arc that most focuses on supervillains is "The Tarnished Angel" (*Kurt Bus-iek's Astro City* vol. 2 #14–#20, 1998–2000). Its protagonist is Carl Donewicz, alias Steeljack, a for-mer supervillain with metallic skin (like that of the X-Men's Colossus), portrayed as a look-alike of actor Robert Mitchum. Like a modern *film noir*, Busiek's storyline presents Steeljack as an ex-convict attempting to go straight, who investigates the murders of other supercriminals by the "Black Mask Killer." The culprit is the Conquistador, who was formerly El Hombre, a costumed hero (reminis-cent of Zorro) who fell from grace and was out to discredit other superheroes.

A continual stream of new villains has poured from Busiek's imagination. The Brass Monkey (vol. 1 #3, 1995), a living statue with human intelligence, and the Gorilla Swarm (vol. 2 #2, 1996) are in the tradition of such super-simians as Grodd (*The Flash*) and Monsieur Mallah (of *Doom Patrol*'s Brotherhood of Evil). The Chessmen (vol. 1 #3, 1995) model their criminal personas after chess pieces as the Royal Flush Gang (in *Justice League*) do after playing cards. The Deacon (vol. 1 #3, 1995), who dresses like a clergyman, is the head of Astro City's largest criminal organization, yet he has never been convicted. Hence, he not only resembles villains like the Kingpin (*Daredevil*), who pose as honest businessmen, but also fits the archetype of the religious hypocrite. Dr. Saturday (vol. 1 #1, 1995), who devises giant robots resembling Saturday morning cartoon characters, is another of the villains who turn childhood playthings to lethal ends, like the Toyman (*Superman*).

The Junkman (vol. 2 #10, 1997), one of Busiek's "viewpoint" characters, is Hiram Potterstone, an elderly villain (like Spider-Man's Vulture) who believes that society discards the old; hence he builds his weaponry out of discarded junk. The Living Nightmare (vol. 1 #1, 1995) was created by a psychiatrist in a Jekyll-like experiment to eradicate fear. Instead he gave fear a physical form, which lashes out in mindless rage at whoever threatens it (rather like the Hulk). Lord Volcanus (vol. 2 #3, 1996) rules a subterranean race, much like Marvel's Mole Man and Tyrannus. The Middleman (vol. 1 #3, 1995), who gets hold of villains' weaponry and sells it to other criminals, provides Astro City's example of supervillains' underground "criminal economy." The Mock Turtle (vol. 2 #17, 1999), another "viewpoint" character, was once Dr. Martin Chefwick, an Englishman who invented an armored battlesuit, and borrowed his alias from Lewis Carroll, like Batman's Mad Hatter. The Mock Turtle naively got in over his head as a criminal and was finally murdered by the Black Mask Killer.

PYRAMID (vol. 1 #1, 1995), a global subversive organization seeking world domination, is Busiek's answer to similar cabals like Hydra, which themselves were inspired by SPECTRE from the James Bond canon. PYRAMID's claim to date back to ancient Egypt suggests similarities with the Illuminati and even the Freemasons. The Silver Brain (vol. 2 #2, 1996) is Sergei Vlataroff, a scientist who became "pure brain" and seeks world con-

quest, evokes villains who exist as bodiless brains, including the Brain (*Doom Patrol*) and Dr. Sun (*Tomb of Dracula*). The Time-Keeper (vol. 2 #1/2, 1996) is Busiek's counterpart to the various villains who seek to master time, like Kang (*Avengers*) and Per Degaton (from Justice Society stories). The Unholy Alliance (vol. 1 #4, 1995) is a supervillain team like Marvel's Masters of Evil. It includes Demolitia (who carries a wrecking ball), Flamethrower, Glowworm, the monstrous Slamburger, and Spice.

In 2005 Busiek launched his longest *Astro City* story arc to date with *Astro City: The Dark Age* #1, which began with another villain, the L. S. Deviant, creating worldwide panic by using his powers to alter reality all over the planet. —*PS*

Atlas

Osamu Tezuka's Astro Boy, the first anime (Japanese animation) hero to appear on American television in 1963, has had quite the rogues' gallery of villains. Despite going up against dozens of villains, the cute little boy robot found Atlas a particularly troublesome foe. The super-robot first appeared in Tezuka's *Tetsuwan Atom* (the original Japanese title for *Astro Boy*) manga in March 1956 during *Astro*'s serialization in *Shonen* magazine.

A tall, barrel-chested robot with super-strength and the ability to fly, Atlas was created by the scientist Dr. Ran to take revenge on the human race. Atlas was fitted with the "Omega Factor," a device that gave him the ability to be evil. His attempt to destroy a village with a lava flow from an erupting volcano was halted by Astro, but Ran sent Atlas out to rob a bank while wearing a false Astro head, thus causing Astro a whole lot of trouble! Atlas would eventually turn on Ran, but he was destroyed following a fierce battle with Astro.

Atlas returned in the 1980 *Astro Boy* series, but with a different look and origin; originally a boy robot like Astro, he used to commit crimes but was destroyed, only to be rebuilt as a tall, bronzed robot, equipped with a robot horse and a "lightning saber." He also had the Omega Factor, which gave him a conscience, although he was still evil. His companion, the beautiful female robot Livian, was not evil—and even leaked information on Atlas and his plans to Astro. She would discover the truth that Atlas and Astro were created from the same plans, making them essentially brothers.

In the 2003 *Astro Boy* series, Atlas again returned, and in a new form. This time, he was a robot created to replace Daichi, the deceased son of a millionaire. But he became rebellious, and he lacked Astro's ability to feel compassion. He was destroyed during his second confrontation with Astro, but not before saving his father's life. —*MM*

Attuma

W hat threat could unite staunch enemies the Fantastic Four and the vengeful Sub-Mariner? The aquatic nomad Attuma, as Marvel Comics readers discovered in 1964 in *Fantastic Four* #33's "Side-by-Side with Sub-Mariner!" by Stan Lee and Jack Kirby. This blue-skinned savage, chieftain of a tribe of water-breathing warriors (Homo mermanus) long since departed from the sunken civilization of Atlantis, attacks the under-sea kingdom, convinced that he is fulfilling prophecy by claiming his rightful throne from Prince Namor (Sub-Mariner). With a bloodthirsty army under his command and an arsenal including a hydro-powered battering ram and an ionic ray, Attuma almost seizes Atlantis until the FF—fearing that Attuma would next invade the surface world—helps Sub-Mariner defend his kingdom. Pummeling Attuma to his knees, Namor rebukes, "No barbarian shall wrest from me my crown and scepter!"

This defeat did not settle well with Attuma, who enlisted the aid of other supervillains—including Krang, Dr. Dorcas, Tiger Shark, and even Dr. Doom—in his later efforts to obtain the Atlantean throne and wreak malice across the globe. Casting a startling image in his serpent-skull helmet and wielding his trident-sword with unnerving accuracy, Attuma, who sometimes wages war in his battle-crafts called Octo-Meks, finally usurped Namor's crown in 2001, forcing the Sub-Mariner to once again seek help—from the superhero "non-team" the Defenders—to vanquish Attuma's forces.

The original Attuma story was adapted for animation in 1967 as the "Danger in the Depths"

Barbarian Supervillains

Savage in appearance and intent, these supervillains have wreaked havoc with sinew, swords, and superpowers:

· **King Kull** (no relation to Robert E. Howard's barbarian hero), the Lord of the Beast-Men, first fought the original Captain Marvel in 1951. Through suspended animation Kull became the sole survivor of an ancient warrior race and waged a cold-blooded war against the civilized humans of the "modern" day. A member of the Golden Age (1938–1954) Monster Society of Evil, the skull-helmeted Kull's most ambitious scheme was his organization of an army of supervillains to attempt to destroy life on three multiple Earths (*Justice League of America* #135–#137, 1976).

· **IBAC** (sometimes Ibac), who premiered in *Captain Marvel Adventures* #8 (1942), was skinny "Stinky" Printwhistle, a lackey of Mr. Mind, who made a deal with the devil (actually, "Prince Lucifer") to become a hulkish supervillain. By saying "IBAC," an acronym of the first letters of the names of four masters of evil (Ivan the Terrible, Cesare Borgia, Atilla the Hun, and Caligula), Stinky was transformed in a wall of green flame into the barbaric Captain Marvel enemy who dared not say his own name aloud, else he would revert to his puny original identity.

· **Arkon the Imperion**, the superhumanly strong warrior supreme from a culture of combatants, attacked Earth in *The Avengers* #75 (1970) when humankind's nuclear tests were jeopardizing his interdimensional world of Polemachus. Hurling lightning bolts powerful enough to stop the mighty Thor, Arkon has returned to Earth on several occasions, sometimes as a foe, other times as a friend.

· **Thulsa Doom** used sorcery to imbue his emerald-hued sword to siphon his opponents' strength. Created in 1967 by Robert E. Howard as an adversary for King Kull (the hero), Thulsa Doom is best known from the first film adaptation of another of Howard's heroes, Conan; James Earl Jones, the voice of *Star Wars*' Darth Vader, played the barbarian supervillain in *Conan the Barbarian* (1982), in which Thulsa Doom held dominion over serpents and possessed the superpower to transform into a giant snake.

episode of Hanna-Barbera's *Fantastic Four* series, with a character named "Prince Triton" (not the member of the Inhumans) replacing Sub-Mariner, who was unavailable due to another licensing agreement. Toy Biz produced an Attuma action figure—with "sword-slashing action!"—in 1996. *—ME*

The Authority Rogues' Gallery

*T*he *Authority*, created by Warren Ellis and Bryan Hitch for WildStorm Comics in 1999, is a superhero team that grew out of the ashes of *Stormwatch*, another team book published by WildStorm in the 1990s. After Stormwatch was destroyed and many of its members killed, team member Jenny Sparks assembled the remaining heroes and recruited a few new members to form a group named the Authority. Unaffiliated with any particular nation, the Authority's primary mission is to protect Earth from large-scale threats. Ellis reimagined superhero team books that changed expectations of the genre.

In the book's first three storylines, the Authority faces a global danger, an interdimensional danger, and a cosmic danger in the form of God himself. The first villain the Authority fights is actually a throwback to the first decade of superhero comics villains. Kaizen Gamorra, the tyrannical ruler of an island nation in Southeast Asia, recalls the stereotypical portrayals of Japanese characters in World War II–era comics. Sporting the familiar Cheshire grin and long pointed fingernails, Gamorra and his superpowered strike force pose an extensive threat to major cities across the globe. Even before September 11, 2001, Gamorra demonstrated the type of threat most likely to strike the global community in the twenty-first century: "Terror is the blood of life and its guiding principle. I have no politics to espouse through my terror, no ideals to force through. Terror is its own reward" (*The Authority* vol. 1 #1). Gamorra's "reward" is cut short when Authority member Midnighter runs the team's giant ship (called the Carrier) through his headquarters and crushes him.

The next villain the Authority faces is from an interdimensional alien/human hybrid race led by a despotic, demonic alien named Regis, but the rogue from Ellis' third and final arc defines the full extent of *The Authority*'s reach. In issues #9–#12 (2000), God—in the form of a gargantuan floating pyramid—returns to Earth, discovers that his home has been overrun by humans, and tries to transform the planet into what it was when he left it millions of years ago. The threat is averted when the Authority drives the Carrier into God's bloodstream and Jenny Sparks sacrifices herself by releasing all her energy into God's brain.

When writer Mark Millar took over the book after Warren Ellis' departure, he adopted and actually enhanced *The Authority*'s unique tone and subject matter. The first line of his issue is, "Why do super-people never go after the *real* bastards?" (vol. 1 #13, 2000). Millar answers this question by turning the Authority's attention to "real-world" political and corporate corruption. After the team begins imposing its heavy-handed moral authority on the nations of Earth, former government operative and science genius Jacob Krigstein unleashes a cold war–era secret unit of superhumans called "the Americans" on the Authority. The Americans are repelled, and Krigstein is eventually recruited to help the Authority in its mission of making a finer world.

The Authority is a political book, and Mark Millar and subsequent writer Robbie Morrison use the book to address a slew of real-world issues such as oppression, third-world poverty, nuclear tension, and popular religion. In a storyline called "Godhead" (vol. 2 #6–#9, 2003–2004), a preacher named Rev. John Clay tries to turn the world's populace against the Authority by preaching the potential of humanity (not superhumanity). Clay eventually reveals his own corruption, but only after exposing the hypocrisy of morally questionable heroes deciding what's best for humanity.

Ultimately, the significance of *The Authority* lies not in endless hero/villain fights and resolutions, but in the epic human issues the book raises. In one of the most memorable speeches of the series, new team leader Jack Hawksmoor tells the president of the United States, "We're not some comic book super-team who participate in

Henry Bendix. *The Authority: Revolution* #9 ©2005
WildStorm Productions/DC Comics.
COVER ART BY DUSTIN NGUYEN.

pointless fights with pointless super-criminals every month to preserve the status quo. This has to be a world worth saving if my colleagues and I are going to be out there risking our lives on the front line" (vol. 1 #13). *The Authority* is a fully postmodern superhero book that reflects the subjectivity and ambiguity of the contemporary world. Embracing the authoritarian overtones of all superhero comics, *The Authority* changed the mission of superheroes.

While the Authority consider themselves benevolent leaders on a crusade for freedom and justice, others see them as "commie dictators." Sometimes the team seems more tyrannical and villainous than the rogues they fight. After the U.S. government triggers an interdimensional conflict, the Authority seizes control of the government in order to impose meaningful, lasting change (*The Authority: Coup D' Etat,* 2004). But as Jack Hawksmoor conceded just before the Authority recently disbanded, "Progress forced at the end of a gun may not be perceived as change for the better at all" (*The Authority: Revolution* #5, 2005). The team often learns as much from their failures as they do from their victories. The Authority's most recent villain bears this pattern out.

Henry Bendix, a "cyberneticist" who actually created Stormwatch and eventually wanted the team to become a fascist corporate structure, supposedly died during the events that led to Stormwatch's collapse. After secretly organizing the dismantlement of the Authority during the *Revolution* series, Bendix emerges once again to destroy the team's disparate members and seize control of Earth. Writer Ed Brubaker thus uses Bendix, a significant threat with ties to the Authority's origins, to explore the team's fundamental components and reset it for the years and threats to come. —AB

Bane

Bane, a 350-pound behemoth who looks as if he stepped out of the Mexican wrestling arena, was first seen in *Batman: Vengeance of Bane* #1 (1993). His real name is unknown but his past is legend. Bane was raised behind bars in the rueful Pena Duro, serving a life sentence in subrogation for his insurrectionist father. Slaughtering an inmate at the "tender" age of eight, Bane matured into the prison's most feared felon and was roped into being a guinea pig for the strength-enhancing chemical Venom. In the serialized DC Comics storyline "Knightfall" (1993), Bane engineers a bloody jailbreak, migrates to Gotham City, and releases the supervillains of Arkham Asylum. Their crime rampage so fatigues their mutual foe Batman that when the Venom-propelled Bane goes one-on-one with the hero, he snaps Batman's spine in a brutal body slam, forcing the Dark Knight into recuperation.

Batman's stand-in Azrael later humbled Bane, but the villain resurfaced to terrorize Gotham both alone and in an alliance with Ra's al Ghul. After discovering the identity of the father who abandoned him—the crimelord King Snake—Bane re-created himself in one of Ra's' regenerating Lazurus Pits, but Batman suspects his foe's new leaf may wilt.

Bane has often tormented Batman in cartoons: Henry Silva voiced the villain in *Batman:*

Batman #497 ©1993 DC Comics.
COVER ART BY KELLEY JONES.

The Animated Series (1992–1995), followed by Hector Elizondo in the direct-to-video film *Batman: Mystery of the Batwoman* (2003) and Joaquim de Almeida in the animated TV series *The Batman* (2004–present). Real-life wrestler Jeep Swenson played the man-monster in director Joel Schumacher's *Batman & Robin* (1997), and Bane was featured in the 2003 video game *Batman: Rise of Sin Tzu*. Kenner and DC Direct have produced a number of Bane action figures in the 1990s and 2000s. —*ME*

Baron Karza

"**B**ring on the deathtank! Let the games begin!" This heinous command was barked by the insidious autocrat Baron Karza in Marvel Comics' *Micronauts* vol. 1 #1 (1979), based upon a popular Mego toy line (originating in 1976 as "Micromen" from Japanese manufacturer Takara) of interchangeable, miniature warriors that dominated toy shelves from 1976 through 1980. Mego's Micronauts figures generated over $300 million in sales during its run, making it second only to Kenner's *Star Wars* line during the late 1970s.

Baron Karza, the toy, was unmistakably evil, molded in black "armor" with red highlights and outfitted with (rubber-tipped) chest missiles and firing fists. Some fans familiar with Karza only through the Marvel comic have assumed that his resemblance to Darth Vader was an attempt to cash in on the *Star Wars* phenomenon, but Karza predated Vader, and reportedly was inspired by a character in the Japanese anime *Kotetsu jeeg* (1975–1976). The Baron's name was coined as the result of an in-joke at Mego, "Karza" being the surname of an employee, Azrak, spelled backwards.

In Marvel's *Micronauts*, writer Bill Mantlo and artist Michael Golden built upon the encapsulated backstory provided on toy packaging and made Karza utterly diabolical. Originally a human scientist, power-hungry Karza melded with his armor via sorcery and technology, allowing him to transform at will into a centaur (achieved in the toy world by interlocking Karza's torso with the equestrian body of the Andromeda figure). Karza proffered immortality to the people of Homeworld, existing within

The Micronauts vol. 1 #1 ©1979 Marvel Comics.
COVER ART BY DAVE COCKRUM AND AL MILGROM.

the subatomic Microverse, in exchange for their subservience—with "an otherwise inevitable death" being the price for their refusal. Aided by the loyal soldier Prince Shaitan and attack robots, Baron Karza ruled Homeworld with an iron fist and performed acts of "perverted science" in his Body Banks, challenged only by the Micronauts' Royal Family led by Commander Arcturus Rann. This premise compelled Marvel's series for 59 issues (1979–1984) and a 20-issue second volume (1984–1986), and was successful enough to warrant a 4-issue crossover miniseries, *X-Men and the Micronauts* (1984), in which Baron Karza was forced to ally with his Micronaut nemeses to fight a common foe, the Entity.

Baron Karza and the Micronauts have found new life in the 2000s, stimulated by adult visionaries who grew up on the Mego toys of the 1970s. Palisades Toys reissued the Micronauts in 2002, and both Image Comics and Devil's Due Publishing released new *Micronauts* comic books, including Image's four-issue *Micronauts: Karza* (2003), starring the villain. Emmett/Furla Films announced in 2004 their development of a Micronauts feature film, and in July 2005 Eagle One Media repackaged artwork from the Devil's Due comics series as *Micronauts: Revolution*, a DVD digital comic. —ME

Baron Mordo

Transylvania-nobleman-cum-sorcerer Karl Amadeus Mordo, otherwise known as Baron Mordo, was the apprentice to the exalted sorcerer called the Ancient One, who helped transform destitute neurosurgeon Stephen Strange into the Master of the Mystic Arts, Dr. Strange. Created by writer-editor Stan Lee and artist Steve Ditko for Marvel Comics' *Strange Tales* #111 (1963), Mordo's pride and lust for power have made him a loner for much of his villainous career. From the beginning he has been obsessed with destroying Dr. Strange, and little has changed during their long rivalry.

The megalomaniac Baron Mordo is considered among the most powerful Earth-born sorcerers operating in the Marvel Universe. Mordo derives his magic from three major sources: personal powers of the mind and body (affording him mesmerism, astral projection, and thought-casting abilities); powers gained by amassing the universe's ambient magical energy (employed for effects such as teleportation and energy projection); and powers gained through invoking entities or objects of power residing in mystical dimensions. Mordo is an expert at invoking spells, whether original or those found in various mystic texts. He has been known to call on otherworldly powers whenever he needs a little boost, including the most demonic of the Marvel Universe, Dormammu and Satannish.

Years of rage finally took a toll on Mordo, who developed "terminal cancer" and (temporarily) disappeared from comics' pages in 1996 (*Dr. Strange* #87). However, the occultist left behind an equally destructive force to be reckoned with: his daughter, Astrid. Baron Mordo unexpectedly turned up alive to attack Dr. Strange once more in *The Amaz-*

From *Strange Tales* #117 ©1964 Marvel Comics.
ART BY STEVE DITKO.

ing Spider-Man #500 (2003), written by J. Michael Straczynski, who also penned a revised version of Dr. Strange's origin, featuring Mordo, in the miniseries *Strange* (2004–2005).

In television animation, Baron Mordo (voiced by Tony Jay) appeared in the *Spider-Man* series that ran from 1994 to 1998. —GM

Baron Wolfgang von Strucker: *See* **A.I.M.** *and* **Hydra**

Baron Zemo

Though Baron Heinrich Zemo was one of Adolf Hitler's most brilliant scientists, his main infamy comes from having slain Bucky Barnes, aide to the World War II superhero Captain America in a story penned by Stan Lee and rendered by Jack Kirby (*Avengers* #4, 1964). Zemo's research for

Hitler yielded a "death ray" that was a precursor to today's laser beam, which was destroyed in a raid by Sergeant Nick Fury's Howling Commandos (*Sgt. Fury and His Howling Commandos* #8, 1964). After this, Zemo often wore a red hood in an attempt to hide his identity, even from the Germans.

However, Zemo's most notorious achievement was "Adhesive X," a glue so strong that no force known to man could dissolve it. Late in the war, the Allies' super-agent Captain America and his aide Bucky were sent to destroy Zemo's research. They were captured during the ensuing battle, but not before Zemo was doused with "Adhesive X," causing his hood to adhere permanently to his face. Late in the war, Zemo was ordered to London to steal a top-secret drone rocket being developed by the Allies. Captain America and Bucky were overcome by Zemo's forces when they tried to stop him, and were tied to the plane as Zemo stole it. The resulting explosion killed Bucky, though Captain America escaped.

Decades later, Zemo, who had relocated to South America, again met Captain America when he realized the original "Cap" had not perished. Driven by fervent hatred of the man who trapped him under the hood that still clung to his face, Zemo first assembled a group of costumed acrobats to attempt to kill the Star-Spangled Avenger (*Tales of Suspense* #60, 1964). When this failed, Zemo united a group of supervillains under the name the Masters of Evil in an attempt to occupy the attentions of the Avengers, whom Cap had joined, while Zemo unsuccessfully attempted, to kill Captain America. Zemo later kidnapped Rick Jones, Cap's new partner, to lure the Avenger to his death. Captain America freed Jones, but Zemo was killed in a landslide of his own creation (*Avengers* #15, 1965).

A later attempt to blackmail the world with a "solar ray" from an orbiting satellite was thought to have been staged by Zemo, but was actually the plot of the slain Baron's pilot, under Zemo's name.

Besides Adhesive X, Baron Zemo's personal arsenal consisted of a disintegrator gun—possibly a smaller application of his "death-ray"—and a cadre of androids which he used as bodyguards and combat troops. He was also a formidable hand-to-hand combatant.

In recent years, the Baron's son, Helmut, the thirteenth Baron Zemo, has assumed his father's title and tried to take revenge upon Captain America for his father's death. This plot failed, though the new Baron Zemo escaped and constitutes a threat to the world at large. —*MWB*

Batman TV Villains

Holy Casting Call, Batman! When ABC's live-action *Batman* exploded onto television on Wednesday, January 12, 1966, "Batmania" devoured America—and Hollywood. "People [actors] would call up, or they would send their agents around, saying, can't so and so be on?" recalled executive producer William Dozier in a 1980s interview. Comic-book carryovers Riddler, Joker, Mr. Freeze, Mad Hatter, Catwoman, and Penguin only went so far: the series' twice-weekly production schedule demanded fresh, fiendish faces to fight Batman and Robin. So Dozier and his writers brainstormed a bevy of bad guys to ensure that viewers kept tuning in at the "same Bat-time, same Bat-channel."

In the two-part opener, 1960s sex-kitten Jill St. John cheekily hijacked the camera from *Batman*'s most manic and memorable villain, Frank Gorshin's Riddler. As Molly the Moll, she seduced the Caped Crusader into a discotheque "Batusi" dance and suckered him with her impersonation of Robin the *Boy* Wonder. Julie Newmar's kinky Catwoman may be celebrated for elevating the blood pressures of male viewers, but Jill St. John first charted that tantalizing territory.

Oscar-winner Anne Baxter beat out contenders Zsa Zsa Gabor and Bette Davis to play reluctant criminal escape artist ("All I ever wanted to be was a poor, honest magician") Zelda the Great in a pair of episodes loosely adapting writer John Broome's "Batman's Inescapable Doom-Trap!" from *Detective Comics* #346 (1965). The partner of larcenist Eivol Ekdal (Jack Kruschen), a little-known felon transplanted from Broome's story, Zelda was a substitute for that issue's Carnado when Dozier mandated, "Let's remember we must work dames into these scripts."

"Not even his mother will recognize the actor playing False Face" touted a February 2, 1966, ABC press release promoting the two episodes adapting a minor villain from *Batman* #113 (1958). The uncredited performer behind the many masks of master-of-disguise False Face was Malachi Throne, whose career of five decades has included fare as diverse as *Perry Mason*, *The Six Million Dollar Man*, and *Catch Me if You Can*. Throne returned to Gotham City by voicing Fingers the Gorilla in a 2000 episode of *Batman Beyond*.

Corpulent character actor Victor Buono donned a scarab-adorned headdress as King Tut, a Yale professor turned ruler of the Nile via a knock on the noggin. Tut attempted to re-create ancient Thebes in Gotham City, surrounding himself with costumed lackeys who never quite shared his compulsion ("How many times must I tell you? Queens consume nectars and ambrosia, not hot dogs"). The first major TV Bat-villain who did not originate in the comics, King Tut was featured in a total of ten episodes during the show's three-season run. Prior to Tut's debut, *TV Guide* erroneously reported that Robert Morley would portray the character.

Best known for his *Planet of the Apes* roles, former child star Roddy McDowall played season one's last non-comics villain, the Bookworm, a voracious reader whose book-related crimes engaged Batman in a contest of wits.

Season two followed summer 1966's hastily produced *Batman* theatrical movie (featuring Joker, Penguin, Riddler, and Catwoman), an iconic favorite among baby-boomers but a modest performer at the box office. Lorenzo Semple, Jr.'s screenplay was novelized by Winston Lyon as Signet Books' *Batman vs. the Fearsome Foursome*.

The Honeymooners' Art Carney was season two's first new nemesis: the Archer, a Robin Hood knockoff bearing no relation to DC Comics' Archer, the Man of Steel's first costumed foe, from *Superman* #13 (1941). Van Johnson guest starred as the Minstrel, a lute-strumming menace who manipulated the Gotham Stock Exchange, and Shelley Winters played Ma Parker, matriarch of a family of convicts (Legs, Mad Dog, Pretty Boy, and Machine Gun). Winters found *Batman*'s hectic production schedule harrowing, commenting in 1966, "We

didn't even get to read the script or rehearse before shooting."

Clock King was borrowed from Green Arrow's rogues' gallery (actually, Clock King *was* Green Arrow's rogues' gallery), with bushy-browed, tousle-topped Walter Slezak resembling a manic Captain Kangaroo in the role. Clock King and his henchmen (in clock-faced jerseys) nearly drowned the Dynamic Duo in sand in giant hourglass death traps. Veteran horror star Vincent Price hammed it up as Egghead, a hairless crimelord (aided by lackeys named Foo Yung and Benedict) in a suit of (egg) white and (yolk) gold, who schemed to "egg-stract" Bruce Wayne's intellect. Piano virtuoso Liberace sashayed into the role of the insidious ivory-tinkler Chandell, essentially playing himself (and customarily overacting).

The Addams Family's Carolyn Jones was Marsha, Queen of Diamonds, a gem connoisseur who so coveted the Batdiamond (the power source for the Batcave's Batcomputer) that she nearly coerced Batman into matrimony to obtain it. When approached to portray an unspecified Batman villain, actor Cliff Robertson suggested, "It might be kind of fun to play a very, very, very dumb cowboy who took himself very, very seriously." The result was Shame, lampooning the 1953 Alan Ladd Western *Shane*. Maurice Evans (Samantha's father on *Bewitched*) was cast as the Puzzler, confounding the Dynamic Duo with puzzles providing clues to his crimes in a two-parter intended to spotlight the Riddler. When a scheduling conflict made Frank Gorshin unavailable, the script was rewritten to feature a new rogue called "Mr. Conundrum," but later reworked to borrow the name "Puzzler" from a Superman foe.

Returning felons like Newmar's Catwoman, Burgess Meredith's Penguin, and Cesar Romero's Joker added spice to *Batman*'s second season, but a string of derivative do-badders and mediocre performances damaged the show's ratings. Michael Rennie sleepwalked through the role of Dr. Somnambula (aka the Sandman), a European thief whose most distinguishing feature was his mink coat. TV's Gomez Addams, John Astin, was woefully miscast as a substitute Riddler. French dreamboat Jacque Bergerac made stomachs (not

Victor Buono as King Tut, from TV's *Batman* (1966–1968).

seductress played by a pre-*Dynasty* Joan Collins (her henchmen were the melodically named Allegro and Andante); Ethel Merman as (racing) horse thief Lola Lasagne; the cloying Milton Berle as floral-foe Louie the Lilac; Anne Baxter's return in a different role, Olga the Queen of the Bessarovian Cossacks; Rudy Vallee and Glynis Johns as British mist-makers Lord Marmaduke Ffogg and Lady Penelope Peasoup; Barbara Rush as the crooked women's libber Nora Clavicle, abetted by her Ladies' Crime Club; the "entrancing" Dr. Cassandra, an invisible thief played by Ida Lupino (with Howard Duff as her transparent accomplice Cabala); and Zsa Zsa Gabor, who finally made it onto the show as thieving spa-owner Minerva, a role intended for Mae West. Despite the return of Frank Gorshin as the Riddler and the gutsy casting of Eartha Kitt as Catwoman, ratings in the last season continued to erode, and the series was canceled with episode #120, aired March 14, 1968. —*ME*

hearts) flutter as Freddy the Fence, and screen star "Miss" Tallulah Bankhead slobbered her lines in what was to be her final performance as Black Widow, a crime queen with a thing for arachnids. Only Roger C. Carmel's crazed counterfeiter Colonel Gumm sweetened the last cluster of season-two episodes, buoyed by the guest appearances of the Green Hornet and Kato. "I was so bad that it took Batman *and* the Green Hornet to get me," Carmel once joked.

To counter hemorrhaging ratings, Batgirl was introduced in the September 14, 1967, episode season-three opener and *Batman* was demoted to once-weekly status. New villains introduced were the Siren, aka Lorelei Circe, a singing

Bat-Mite

More a bother than a bad guy, the impish Bat-Mite was devised as Batman's answer to Mr. Mxyzptlk. The pint-sized pest first popped into the Caped Crusader's life in 1959 in *Detective Comics* #267's "Batman Meets Bat-Mite" by writer Bill Finger and artist Sheldon Moldoff. "An elf dressed in a crazy-looking Batman costume!" utters Robin the Boy Wonder as this kooky kewpie, standing not-so-tall at just under 3 feet, materializes inside the secret Batcave. A superhero wannabe from another dimension, Bat-Mite's goal is to make the Dynamic Duo a Terrific Trio. He uses his magical powers to fabricate absurdities—from causing a bridge to ripple to animating a giant Batman statue—merely to witness his heroic idol in action. After several scoldings from Batman, Bat-Mite takes a hint and returns home … albeit temporarily, phasing out with a cryptic "Good-bye—for now!"

Nine months later he was back in "The Return of Bat-Mite," in the pages of *Detective* #276 (1960), and returned regularly to bug Batman, Robin, and even Batwoman and the original Bat-Girl. DC Comics first paired him with Mr. Mxyzptlk in *World's Finest Comics* #113 (1960), their union posing a headache for Superman and Batman. On several occasions throughout the 1960s, some of the strangest scenarios encountered by Batman and Superman were mystically manufactured by the troublemaking Bat-Mite/Mr. Mxyzptlk team.

By the late 1960s Bat-Mite was booted into limbo, although he soon found a welcome home on television in Filmation's animated series *The New Adventures of Batman* (1977–1978), reprising his early 1960s comics role as the well-meaning but pesky tag-along. His sole comic-book appearance during that decade occurred in the whimsical "Bat-Mite's New York Adventure" by Bob Rozakis and Michael Golden, appearing in *Detective* #482 (1979), in which the imp made an unappreciated visit to the DC Comics offices.

While mostly a relic of the Silver Age (1956–1969), Bat-Mite still surfaces for a nostalgic romp for readers from time to time. His first appearance in DC's contemporary continuity took place in Alan Grant and Kevin O'Neill's "Legend of the Dark Mite" in *Batman: Legends of the Dark Knight* #38 (1992), in which a hallucinating felon told Batman of his "encounter" with a Bat-dressed troll. Bat-Mite has also been seen in several other noncontinuity stories and as a plush doll, statuette, and action figure from DC Direct. If imitation is indeed the sincerest form of flattery, perhaps Bat-Mite's greatest legacy is his inspiration of Larry, a problematic pixie with a Robin fixation who occasionally appears on the animated series *Teen Titans* (2003–present). —*ME*

Batroc

The Marvel Comics supervillain Batroc (or Batroc the Leaper to friends) plummeted onto the pages of *Tales of Suspense* #75 (1966) in a Captain America story scripted by Stan Lee and drawn by Jack Kirby. A 6-feet-tall, 225-pound French mercenary, Batroc (later named Georges Batroc) specializes in a form of kickboxing known as Savate. Although he is most impressive in size and form—he is an Olympic-level weightlifter capable of bench-pressing 500 pounds and boasts acrobatic-like agility and reflexes—he lacks superpowers of any kind.

Nevertheless, as a great fighter, Batroc greatly respects his number-one adversary, Captain America, as readers see in Lee and Kirby's second Batroc story (in *Tales of Suspense* #85), and later in writers Roger Stern's and Mark Gruenwald's Batroc appearances in *Captain America*. Readers have noted that the Batroc/Captain America fight scene in *Tales of Suspense* #85 is one of the most dynamic battle scenes that Kirby ever drew. Batroc regards "Cap" as a worthy adversary, the rare individual who can fight at his level of expertise.

In part, that is why the supervillain has sometimes joined forces with Cap. The duo teamed up against Hydra in *Tales of Suspense* #85 (1967). Batroc was also horrified enough by Mr. Hyde's mass murder plot in Roger Stern and John Byrne's *Captain America* #251–#252 (1980) that he aided Cap in stopping Hyde. For his part, Cap tends to regard Batroc as a nuisance rather than as evil.

One can almost envision Lee sitting in his office dreaming up character traits for this amusing super-foil: he speaks with a stereotypical French accent ("Batroc ze Leapair") and often spouts random French phrases (such as "*Sacre Bleu!*" and "*Zut Alors!*"); his English is so garbled that Captain America once remarked, "Who gave you your English lessons? Doctor Doom?" His other physical and personality quirks—including his exaggerated Salvador Dali–like mustache—have made him a testimony to Lee's timeless sense of humor. Batroc fans still fondly recite his classic one-liners, such as, "From zis moment on, Batroc shows you no mercy, comprendez-vous?"

Batroc has gone up against many a Marvel hero—he has fought Spider-Man, the Punisher, Deadpool, Hawkeye, Gambit, and Iron Fist—and the honorable rogue continues to make appearances in the twenty-first century, most notably in *Captain America. —GM*

The Beyonder

Hailing from a parallel universe in which he was the only sentient creature, the omnipotent being known as the Beyonder is one of the quintessential outsiders of superhero comics—and possibly one of the silliest and most blatantly commercial. The character was created by Marvel Comics editor in chief Jim Shooter as a jumping-off point for marketing action figures of the various Marvel superheroes and supervillains the Beyonder was to encounter.

The Beyonder was blissfully unaware of the existence of other intelligences until lab worker Owen Reece caused an accident that transformed him into the matter-transmuting Molecule Man—and opened a passage between Earth and the Beyonder's so-called "Beyond-Realm." The Beyonder's first glimpse of Earth triggered a sense of incompleteness and desire that he never before experienced. Desperate to resolve his new feelings, and perplexed by both the behavior and the motivations of humanity, the Beyonder spirited a large group of the Marvel Universe's superheroes and supervillains to a planet called Battleworld (the Beyonder's own creation). Here he observed the ensuing carnage and promised to grant the victors their every wish. But the Beyonder soon found himself rendered powerless, at least temporarily, after Dr. Doom activated a device to siphon off his energies; after regaining his full power, the Beyonder returned his superpowered playthings to Earth, as seen in the maxiseries *Marvel Super Heroes Secret Wars* (1984–1985) and numerous tie-ins.

His sense of existential desire still unsated, the Beyonder subsequently came to Earth, donning and discarding a succession of new human physical forms—his templates included the Molecule Man, Captain America, and finally an unnamed civilian who bore an eerie resemblance to Michael Jackson (circa *Thriller*)—during his peregrinations across the United States. As he traveled, the Beyonder casually bestowed almost unimaginable power upon both ordinary people (like television writer Stewart Cadwall) and superheroes (such as Spider-Man). Confused by the vicissitudes of free will, the Beyonder sought the counsel of heroes and bad guys alike; acting on the dubious advice of a petty crook named "Vinnie," the Beyonder seized complete control of the minds of every human being on Earth, but found no satisfaction in the deed. The Beyonder then tumbled into despair over the apparent futility of life, until the sorcery-wielding Dr. Strange convinced him to devote himself to superheroics, though both Captain America and the Fantastic Four pointed out their fears that humanity may grow dependent upon the Beyonder's beneficent guidance.

The Beyonder then destroyed Death itself, only to undo the deed following a clash with an angry Mephisto—and after reaching the realization that Death is necessary if life is to have any meaning. Sinking into nihilism, the Beyonder decided to restore his earlier emotional equanimity by destroying everything in the multiverse except for his own "Beyond-Realm," only to have to face the massed forces of Earth's superheroes, whom he easily defeated. He even killed the New Mutants, though he restored them to life with his godlike powers and ultimately spared the multiverse.

Still a seeker at heart, the Beyonder briefly became mortal, during which time the Molecule Man apparently killed him, forcing his vast energies into another dimension, where they created an entirely new universe in the *Secret Wars* II miniseries (1985–1986) and numerous tie-ins. But the Beyonder evidently survived this new "Big Bang," going on to explore the cosmos in his newly adopted female identity of Kosmos, along with a young protégé named Kubik, who started life as a reality-altering Cosmic Cube created by A.I.M. (Advanced Idea Mechanics).

In 1997 the Beyonder branched out into the alternate universe of television, appearing as the driving force behind the multipart "Secret Wars" arc in FOX's *Spider-Man* animated series.

Although the Beyonder tends to spread havoc wherever it goes, it does so out of ignorance rather than malice; like a tornado, the Beyonder is more a force of nature than a willfully malevolent adversary. —*MAM*

Bizarro

The history of Bizarro, the defective replica of Superman, is as craggy as the creature's disfigured face. While the layperson or contemporary fan might regard Bizarro as the doppelgänger of the *Man* of Steel, this tragic character first appeared in "the adventures of Superman when he was a *boy*," DC Comics' *Superboy* #68 (1958), written by Otto Binder and illustrated by George Papp. In that tale, Superboy observes the unsuccessful trial run of Smallville scientist Professor Dalton's duplicator. Not only is Dalton a failure as an inventor, he is clumsy, too—he stumbles into his machine, causing it to bathe the Boy of Steel in radiation. And thus is born a (cracked) mirror image of Superboy, a jagged-complexioned, childlike duplicate who dubs himself "Bizarro" after Superboy gasps, "Gosh, that creature is bizarre!" Possessing all of the Boy of Steel's remarkable abilities—except for his grammar (Bizarro substitutes "me" for "I"; "Me am Bizarro" is one of the most famous catchphrases to spring from comics into the American vernacular)—this superpowered cipher blunders through the streets of Smallville looking for acceptance ("Why no one like me?"), inadvertently instigating panic. The unavoidable Superboy-versus-Bizarro clash occurs, and the monster unexpectedly allows itself to be obliterated in an explosion that restores the sight of a blind girl, the only person who befriended this misbegotten soul.

A Bizarro storyline by writer Alvin Schwartz and artist Curt Swan was intended for publication in the *Superman* syndicated newspaper strip prior to the publication of the *Superboy* #68 but was delayed, sparking disagreement among comics historians as to which team—Schwartz and Swan or Binder and Papp—actually created the character. While the definitive answer remains lost to unrecorded history, Binder's prolific résumé as a comics and science-fiction author throws more weight into his corner.

Binder introduced the adult Bizarro as a foe to Superman in *Action Comics* #254–#255 (1959), drawn by Al Plastino. Criminal genius Lex Luthor plagiarized Professor Dalton's duplicating machine and turned it onto the Man of Steel, but by the end of this two-parter, instead of destroying Superman as Luthor had hoped, Bizarro had created a bride—Bizarro Lois—and flown off for an extended honeymoon.

Editor Mort Weisinger quickly realized that Bizarro better served the Superman franchise as a comedic character—and as a Bizarro *society*. With the character's subsequent appearances in various titles, Bizarro used the duplicator ray to produce an expanding civilization of duplicates of his super-self, with the original Bizarro wearing a "Bizarro No. 1" medallion for reader identification (and perhaps out of pride). Before long, Bizarro and his wife Bizarro Lois No. 1 were joined by a son (Bizarro Junior No. 1), more Bizarro Loises, and Bizarro versions of Luthor, Jimmy Olsen, Perry White, Lana Lang, Krypto, and even Batman! This uncanny race resided on the Bizarro World, a square-shaped planet where its inhabitants followed a peculiar code of conduct: "Us do opposite of all earthly things! Us hate beauty! Us love ugliness! Is big crime to make anything perfect on Bizarro World!" Beginning with *Adventure Comics* #285 (1961), "Tales of the Bizarro World" graduated into its own series, with Jerry Siegel, the co-creator of Superman, taking over as writer from Binder and with John Forte as artist, running monthly in the title through issue #299 (1962).

"Camp" comedy became the trend in superhero comics of the mid-1960s, and as many caped crusaders played it for laughs, Bizarro lost much of his uniqueness. By late 1967 he had disappeared from the pages of DC Comics, not appearing again until late 1976. Bizarro No. 1 schlepped through irregular late 1970s and early 1980s appearances, forsaking his humorous past and once again posing a threat to Superman, but the maturing comics market showed little interest in the villain. Children who had discovered DC's superheroes via the various incarnations of TV's *Super Friends* series thought differently: Bizarro was one of the Legion of Doom in *The Challenge of the Super Friends* (1978) and resurfaced in *The Super*

Powers Team: Galactic Guardians (1986), voiced both times by William Callaway.

When writer/artist John Byrne signed on to reboot Superman in the 1986 miniseries *The Man of Steel*, Bizarro was one of the first supervillains to be reintroduced, in issue #5. Byrne's updating borrowed from both the teen and adult Bizarro origins, as Lex Luthor—in the revitalized continuity a vainglorious businessman—tapped geneticist Dr. Teng to clone Superman to use as a superpowered weapon against the real deal. Teng's bio-matrix could not adequately replicate Superman's Kryptonian DNA, and the clone collapsed, soon mutating into a terrifying, chalk-skinned monstrosity with Superman's powers. This darker, more frightening Bizarro lacked the "me" vocabulary and airiness of the original. After operating on residual memories genetically transferred from the Man of Steel and attempting to assimilate into society as a bastardized Clark Kent, the befuddled Bizarro became enraged upon meeting Superman, leading to a climactic conflict that toppled buildings. Once Superman realized that his "ugly friend" was "an artificial being," he shattered the creature into nothingness.

Aside from a second-season episode (featuring actor Barry Meyers) of the syndicated, live-action TV series *Superboy* (1988–1992), Bizarro was not seen again until a serialized DC Comics storyline in 1994, when Luthor's second attempt to clone Superman fared no better than the first. Infatuated with Lois Lane, this Bizarro manufactured a wonky junkyard city—a nod to the 1960s Bizarro World—and, like his comic-book predecessors, died tragically. Also in 1994, ABC's *Lois & Clark: The New Adventures of Superman* (1993–1997) aired the episode "Vatman," a Bizarro homage about a simple-minded Superman duplicate created from a strand of the hero's hair. A Bizarro Superboy, a distorted variation of the contemporary Teen of Steel (who himself is, coincidentally, a Superman clone), debuted in *Superboy Annual* #2 (1995).

A new and unpredictable Bizarro, spawned not by Luthor but by Batman's arch-nemesis the Joker, premiered in *Superman* vol. 2 #160 (2000). When the Joker acquired Mr. Mxyzptlk's reality-warping powers he re-created Earth, with evil supplanting good … and the new, medallion-sporting

Bizarro and Batzarro. *Superman/Batman* #22 ©2005 DC Comics.
COVER ART BY ED McGUINNESS AND DEXTER VINES.

"Bizarro #1" was born. Although the Joker's lunatic world was short-lived, Bizarro survived. Bizarro #1 boasts Superman's most recognizable powers like flight and superstrength, but in true Bizarro-fashion possesses the *opposite* of others (such as freezing vision instead of heat vision)—plus, he is energized by the one substance that weakens Superman, kryptonite. In *Superman/Batman* #22 (2005), Bizarro was joined by a Dark Knight doppelgänger, Batzarro, and was one of the supervillains waging war against DC's superheroes in the crossover *Infinite Crisis* (2005–2006). Bizarro lent his name to a pair of anthologies featuring modish cartoonists' offbeat interpretations of DC superheroes, *Bizarro Comics!* (2001) and *Bizarro World* (2004). He was also seen in the "Bizarro's World" episode in season two of the animated cartoon *Superman*

(1996–2000), and has been produced as action figures in various Superman lines.

Comic books and related merchandising aside, the 1960s version of Bizarro continues to chisel a place in the pop-culture pantheon. In "Klt-pzyym!," an essay in *Give Our Regards to the Atom Smashers!* (Pantheon Books, 2004), a collection of writers' reflections on comic books, author Tom Piazza commented, "I have always had a soft spot in my heart for the original Bizarro, the way one has a soft spot for the monster in *The Bride of Frankenstein*." Bizarro's widest claim to fame was screenwriter David Mandel's "The Bizarro Jerry," an immensely popular episode in season eight of the long-running sitcom *Seinfeld* (1990–1998). While comic-book references were common in the series, Mandel's teleplay was structured around the "reverse image" Bizarro template: Elaine encountered kindhearted counterparts to the spiteful Jerry, George, and Kramer. Jerry's dia-logue expounds the writer's—and actor Jerry Sein-feld's—love for the super-miscreant: "Up is down. Down is up. He says 'hello' when he leaves, 'good-bye' when he arrives." —ME

Black Adam

Black Adam, the deviant doppelgänger of the original Captain Marvel, was in fact the Big Red Cheese's predecessor, as revealed by writer Otto Binder and artist C. C. Beck in Fawcett's *Marvel Family* #1 (1945). Five millennia ago the wizard Shazam selects Teth-Adam to receive the powers of six Egyptian gods and become a juggernaut for justice called the Mighty Adam. By speaking the mage's name, Teth-Adam is imbued with the sta-mina of S̲hu, the swiftness of H̲eru, the strength of A̲mon, the wisdom of Z̲ehuti, the power of A̲ton, and the courage of M̲ehen. He abuses this gift and is exiled in space by Shazam for thousands of years, until returning in 1945 intent upon enslav-ing Earth. When Shazam's new recruits—Captain Marvel, Mary Marvel, and Captain Marvel, Jr.—are vanquished by Adam, only the mortal Uncle Marvel is able to defeat the knave, tricking him into voic-ing "Shazam" and thereby removing his superpow-ers. Black Adam reverts to his true age of over five thousand years and disintegrates into ash.

By 1954 the entire Captain Marvel franchise of titles, once among the best-selling in the comic-book business, also faded from view as the result of a lawsuit with DC Comics over Captain Marvel's supposed similarities to Superman. DC revived the hero in 1973 in the series *Shazam!*, and in issue #28 (1977) Black Adam was resuscitated by the mastermind Dr. Sivana for a clash with the Captain (Black Adam's comic-book return was preceded by a 1976 Shazam! View-Master packet featuring the villain). Black Adam fought Captain Marvel several times in the late 1970s and early 1980s, and appeared in episodes of NBC's animated series, *Kid Super-Power Hour with Shazam!* (1981–1982).

Captain Marvel was rebooted in the mini-series *Legends* (1986–1987), and in the four-issue follow-up series *Shazam!: The New Beginning* (1987), Black Adam was similarly revived in a darker but short-lived interpretation by Roy Thomas and Tom Mandrake.

Writer/artist Jerry Ordway discarded previous continuity and started Captain Marvel afresh in the 1994 graphic novel *The Power of Shazam!*, fol-lowed by a monthly series of the same name (1995–1999), in a version that endures in DC's twenty-first-century continuity. Black Adam's Golden Age backstory remained partially intact, with Teth-Adam transformed by the utterance of the word "Shazam" into "Khem-Adam" (or, in English, Black Adam), serving Prince Khufu (connected to the lore of DC's Hawkman) until turning renegade after the deaths of Adam's family. The wizard Shazam removed Adam's superpowers and placed them inside a scarab-shaped amulet, discovered in the late twentieth century in Pharaoh Rameses' tomb by husband-and-wife archaeologists, the Bat-sons—parents of Billy (Captain Marvel) and Mary (Mary Marvel)—but their cold-blooded aide, Theo Adam (actually introduced in 1991's *War of the Gods* #2), slaughtered them for the trinket, assum-ing Black Adam's phenomenal powers.

Black Adam resurfaced to battle Captain Mar-vel and Shazam on numerous occasions through-out the late 1990s, even teaming with the wizard's bastard offspring Blaze to enchain Shazam. In *JSA* #6 (2000) Adam returned from an intergalactic sojourn to battle the Justice Society of America, a team he fought on several occasions—solo and as one of the Injustice Society—until he reformed and worked with the JSA on a probationary basis (although he was regarded a villain in a 2002 DC Direct action-figure release). Adam ultimately splintered the JSA in the 2004 storyline "Black Reign," leading some of its members on an invasion of his homeland Kahndaq, where Adam established himself as dictator. The trepidation toward Black Adam shared by many JSAers proved founded in 2005 as Teth-Adam joined Lex Luthor's Society—an assemblage of most of the supervillains in the DC Universe—as one of its inner council in the *Villains United* miniseries. —*ME*

Black Manta

T he first recorded clash between DC Comics' Sea King and the enigmatic Black Manta occurred in *Aquaman* vol. 1 #35 (1967). In "Between Two Dooms!" by writer Bob Haney and artist Nick Cardy, the domed, undersea city of Atlantis is endangered by a terrorist clad in a black wetsuit and a silver breathing helmet with glowing visors that resemble fish eyes. This mysterious malefactor's true identity is unknown, but Aquaman intimates at least one previous encounter by identifying him as "my old enemy … Black Manta!" Commanding a school of aggressive mutant Manta-Men that project crackling stun blasts with each flap of their wings, Black Manta, piloting a laser-firing Manta-Ship, makes Atlantis uninhabitable for its water-breathing denizens and kidnaps the Sea King's son "Aquababy" to lure Aquaman into surrendering. As Black Manta draws bead on his nemesis, ready to harpoon him to death, the arrival of another Aqua-foe, the Ocean Master, distracts Manta, allowing Aquaman to save the day.

A scant ten weeks later, after the June 29, 1967, on-sale date of *Aquaman* #35, Black Manta returned, courtesy of the same writer, Bob Haney, but in a different medium: animated television. The premiere Aquaman episode of Filmation's *The Superman/Aquaman Hour of Adventure*, "Menace of the Black Manta" (original airdate: September 9, 1967), featured the villain (in a slightly altered uniform of blue and purple), as well as his Manta-Ship and Manta-Men. Voiced by Ted Knight, also the cartoon's narrator (who later became famous as

befuddled newsman Ted Baxter on *The Mary Tyler Moore Show*), Black Manta appeared in four additional TV episodes. Black Manta's near-contemporaneous comic and cartoon debuts suggest that Haney and the *Aquaman* comic's editor George Kashdan, who also wrote episodes of the TV series, may have co-created the villain for television but absorbed him into the sponge of comic-book continuity.

Black Manta has since been a consistent foe in Aquaman's comic, often battling the Sea King with high-tech weapons. The depth of Black Manta's hatred of the Sea King was explored by writer David Michelinie and artist Jim Aparo in *Adventure Comics* #452 and *Aquaman* #57 (both 1977). Aquababy (by this point more commonly called "Arthur, Jr.," Arthur Curry being Aquaman's real name) was once again in the evildoer's clutches, Manta forcing Aquaman and his sidekick Aqualad into a gladiator-style brawl to spare the child. Aquababy nonetheless perished, a tragedy that haunts the Sea King to this day. The other surprise of this two-part shocker was the disclosure of Black Manta's face: he was revealed to be black—a rarity for comics of the day—becoming DC Comics' second African-American supervillain (after Batman foe Black Spider, who premiered in 1976). Black Manta soon returned to television animation as one of the Legion of Doom in ABC's *Challenge of the Super Friends* (1978–1979), with Ted Cassidy (Lurch of *The Addams Family*) portraying the character.

In subsequent years, Black Manta disappeared and reappeared with the ebb and flow of *Aquaman*'s publication (the title has a long history of cancellations and revivals). A particularly brutal clash between the subsea adversaries transpired in an early 1990s revival, in which Manta nearly gored Aquaman to death. In 1995 Manta sold his soul to the demon Neron and was transmogrified into a gruesome manta-creature, temporarily hiding his affliction inside his classic costume. He briefly became a drug smuggler in the Kevin Smith–scripted *Green Arrow* vol. 3 #3–#4 (2001). In a 2003–2004 *Aquaman* story arc, Aquaman magnanimously used his mystical water-based Healing Hand (bestowed to him by the Lady of the Lake) to restore Black Manta's humanity; Manta

Aquaman vol. 1 #42 ©1968 DC Comics.
COVER ART BY NICK CARDY.

returned Aquaman's kindness by continuing his war against the Sea King, resuming his sinister machinations in 2005 by undergoing water-breathing gene therapy in an effort to become an even greater threat.

Black Manta's popularity in comics and on TV has translated to the collectibles shelves: in the 2000s, he has appeared as Hero Clix gaming miniatures, a Super Friends action figure, a DC Pocket Superheroes figure, and an Alex Ross–designed action figure. —*ME*

Black Mask

"Crazier than the Joker! Deadlier than Ra's al Ghul!"—or so read the cover of *Batman* #386 (1985), introducing Black Mask. Janus Cosmetics falls into the hands of Roman Sionis, heir

to the firm worth millions, once his parents die in a suspicious fire. After he bankrupts the company it is acquired by Bruce (Batman) Wayne, against whom Sionis swears reprisal. Sionis etches an ebon mask from his father's casket lid and, in a pinstripe suit and fedora, becomes Gotham City's newest crime boss, Black Mask, ordering hits on several of Wayne's employees and consequently attracting an investigation by Batman. In a climactic clash, Sionis is critically burned, his mask permanently bonding to his disfigured flesh. (This story unfolded in three chapters, each written by Doug Moench, continuing in *Detective Comics* #553 and *Batman* #387, both 1985; Tom Mandrake drew the *Batman* chapters, and Klaus Janson, the *Detective* installment).

Longtime Batman scribe Moench used Black Mask sporadically over the next ten years, in one case pairing him with fellow felon Black Spider. After Gotham City was partially destroyed by an earthquake in the "No Man's Land" storyline (1999), Black Mask emerged as a major adversary in the Batman family of titles, tangling with (in addition to the Dark Knight) Robin, Nightwing, Batgirl, and Catwoman. Black Mask no longer wears his facial covering, exposing his grotesque, charcoal-like features, which were carved into plastic in a 2005 DC Direct action figure. A master torturer, Black Mask takes psychotic glee in mutilating his foes' faces. He has been presumed dead in the past but has returned to plague Gotham with his sadistically brutal crimes. —*ME*

Black Spider

Black Spider is noteworthy more for his ethnicity than his originality. Swinging into *Detective Comics* #463 (1976), in a tale by writer Gerry Conway and artist Ernie Chua, Black Spider is a self-professed Batman emulator and costumed sniper who puts a bullet through pusher Doc Sugarman, provoking a slugfest with the Caped Crusader. Issue #464 reveals the villain's true identity, Eric Needham—a former junkie who accidentally killed his father, inspiring his sobriety and vendetta against drug peddlers—who happens to be African American. Renowned for his proficiency with his wrist-mounted pistols, Black Spider was Batman's

Detective Comics #463 ©1976 DC Comics.
COVER ART BY ERNIE CHUA.

first black rogue (discounting Eartha Kitt as Catwoman in the alternate reality of the 1966–1968 *Batman* television show) and DC Comics' first black supervillain. A relic of the 1970s, the character was seen only a handful of times before being put out to pasture by the creative team of Alan Grant and Norm Breyfogle in *Batman: Shadow of the Bat* #5 (1992), in which Needham became a suicide bomber to wipe out a narcotics ring.

Receiving his walking papers from hell by Lucifer himself, Needham made cameos in Neil Gaiman's "The Kindly Ones" in *Sandman* vol. 2 #57–#69 (1994–1995), but conversely was shown in hell as Black Spider attempting to broker a deal with the demon Neron in *Underworld Unleashed* #1 (1995).

Narcissistic hitman Johnny LaMonica assumed the Black Spider's costumed identity in *Batman* #518 (1995), contracted to kill Gotham crime boss

Black Mask. Not unlike his predecessor, this Black Spider has maintained a meager status among Batman's rogues, although his inclusion in the miniseries *Villains United* (2005) may hint at a larger profile in the DC Universe's web of evil. —*ME*

Black Tom Cassidy

Like many superheroes, Sean Cassidy, the Irish X-Men member called the Banshee, has an evil brother, Thomas Samuel Eamon Cassidy, better known as Black Tom. Created by writer Chris Claremont and artist Dave Cockrum, Black Tom emerged from the shadows in *X-Men* #101 (1976). A mutant like his brother, Black Tom can generate heat or concussive force, and he employs a wooden Irish shillelagh to focus his blasts. Heir to the Cassidy fortune and castle, Tom lost both in a game of dice to Sean, and turned criminal.

Both brothers were in love with Maeve Rourke, who married Sean. While Sean was on assignment for Interpol, the international police agency, Maeve gave birth to their daughter Theresa. Soon afterward Maeve was killed in an Irish Republican Army bombing, but Tom raised Theresa without ever informing Sean of her existence.

Black Tom formed a partnership with his old friend Cain Marko, the Juggernaut, and together they battled the X-Men and other superheroes, including the original Spider-Woman and X-Force. Black Tom forced Theresa, who had inherited her father's superpowers as the teenage Siryn, to aid him in his crimes, but finally revealed her identity to Sean.

After Black Tom was shot, doctors grafted onto his wounds a substance resembling wood, which spread throughout Tom's body, eventually turning him into a sentient form of plant life that resembled a humanoid made of wood. This gave Black Tom the power to control plants—and even to create plant doppelgängers of himself and other people—but it also drove him insane. (After transforming into a plantlike being, he no longer needed to use the shillelagh.) After Black Tom murdered Marko's friend Sammy Pare, the Juggernaut turned against him. Thus Black Tom Cassidy lost his last friend and final link to his former humanity.

Black Tom has also appeared in *X-Men: The Animated Series* (1992–1997). —*PS*

Blackfire

Created by Marv Wolfman and George Pérez in *The New Teen Titans* #23 (1982), the crimson-haired Blackfire has survived as both a leather-clad villainess and a proud monarch for her people.

Years before adopting the name Blackfire, the first-born daughter of the royal family of the planet Tamaran, Komand'r, was sickly, and she grew up unable to harness the ability of solar-powered flight like the other Tamaraneans. She became insanely jealous of her favored younger sister, Koriand'r, eventually joining the warring Citadel Empire and allying with them to force her sibling's exile. Eventually, both sisters were captured by the alien race known as Psions; the torturous experiments performed on the two women endowed them with massive energy powers.

Komand'r continued her successful rise in the ranks of the Citadel until a clash with Koriand'r, now called Starfire, and her heroic companions, the Teen Titans. Although Blackfire was thought to have been killed, she survived and eventually came to oppose the ideals of the Citadel. Helping to free Tamaran, she became its warrior queen.

When Tamaran was destroyed in a conflict in the Vegan star system, the survivors of their world settled on New Tamaran, but that planet was later eradicated by the Sun-Eater. Thought dead, Komand'r again returned with a vengeance, determined to find a new home for her people, regardless of the cost. Komand'r fought on the side of good in *The Rann-Thanagar War* (2005).

Blackfire appeared in a 2003 episode of the *Teen Titans* cartoon (2003–2006), in which she was wanted for crimes in the Centauri System. Later, she became Grand Ruler of Tamaran until a devious scheme forced her into exile. DC Direct released a Blackfire action figure in 2004. —*AM*

Blacklash: *See* Whiplash

Blastaar

"The Living Bomb-Burst" Blastaar, created by Stan Lee and Jack Kirby, first exploded onto the scene in *Fantastic Four* #62–#63 (1967). As the FF's Reed (Mr. Fantastic) Richards and his ally Triton of the Inhumans scarcely escape the precarious antimatter realm called the Negative Zone, their exodus is viewed by a bestial entity trapped there: Blastaar, the "most deadly of all living beings" (in his own arrogant words, which he shrieks at an ear-piercing volume). Breaking free of an "adhesion suit" fashioned by his own people who rebelled against his brutality, Blastaar trails the heroes to Earth, where he joins forces with the FF's foe the Sandman, who quickly regrets this alliance after witnessing Blastaar's unbridled power. The superhumanly strong Blastaar's fingertips discharge unfathomable force that obliterates buildings and propels him like a rocket through the air. Hell-bent on oppressing Earth, Blastaar storms through New York City, and only *one* of the Fantastic Four's amazing attributes stops him: the intellect of Richards, who slaps an energy-nullifying helmet onto the creature.

Blastaar repeatedly endeavored to gain dominion over Earth, with Richards finding ways to return him to the Negative Zone (or to banish him to other worlds), making the two bitter adversaries. Richards is not alone on Blastaar's enemies list: the Avengers, the X-Men, Thor, and Spider-Man are among the many superheroes he has battled. Blastaar briefly regained control over his race on the world of Baluur, inside the Negative Zone, but mutinous members of the Baluurian army, led by an officer named Tanjaar, overthrew him (*Fantastic Four* #289, 1986). His greatest rival is his fellow Negative Zoner Annihilus, with whom he has skirmished inside and outside of the Zone. The Living Bomb-Burst has been featured in all three of the *Fantastic Four* animated television series (in 1967, 1978, and 1994) and has also been produced as an action figure by manufacturer Toy Biz. —*ME*

Blizzard

The name "Blizzard" refers to several supervillainous characters in the Marvel Universe, all of whom are enemies of Iron Man. He first appeared as the Stark Industries scientist-infiltrator "Jack Frost" in *Tales of Suspense* vol. 1 #45 (1963), and officially adopted the moniker "Blizzard" in his next appearance in *Iron Man* vol. 1 #86 (1976), in a story scripted by Bill Mantlo and penciled by George Tuska. Although Blizzard adopted chilly, ice-based superpowers and donned an icicle-dripping costume, it appears he was killed by the time traveler Iron Man 2020 (Arno Stark, a descendant of Iron Man) in *The Amazing Spider-Man Annual* #20 (1986).

His successor (sometimes referred to as Blizzard II) is Donald "Donny" Gill, whose elemental powers are derived from his Blizzard costume: its high-tech micro-circuitry enables him to manipulate water and ice and to freeze any moisture in the air, creating unusually hard projectiles and shields. Blizzard II resembles human ice, is impervious to sub-zero temperatures, and is capable of shooting small ice bullets with enough force to cut steel. Created by writer David Michelinie, penciler Mark Bright, and co-plotter/inker Bob Layton, this Blizzard first appeared in *Iron Man* #223 (1987). The sub-zero saboteur has occasionally partnered with mischief-makers Beetle, the Melter, Whiplash (also known as Blacklash), and Boomerang, and sometimes befriends other villains in the employ of corrupt multimillionaire Justin Hammer, from whom Blizzard received his costume and for whom he has worked. Although the replacement Iron Man (James Rhodes, later codenamed War Machine) convinced the Blizzard to reform, he eventually returned to a life of crime, which he maintains in the mid-2000s.

After stealing a Blizzard costume from Gill's home, a third Blizzard appeared once in *Marvel Holiday Special* (1992), although he was quickly defeated by Iron Man and has yet to appear in comics again.

Blizzard appeared in the FOX Kids animated television series *Iron Man* (1994–1996). —*GM*

The Blob

When the mutant called the Blob puts his foot down, there's no budging him. Weighing in at 500 pounds, Fred J. Dukes, as seen in Stan Lee and Jack Kirby's *X-Men* vol. 1 #3 (1964), is a carnival attraction—his blubbery belly deflects bullets, his enormous girth makes him immovable, and he's superhumanly strong. "The very molecules of your flesh react to your mental commands and seem to perform any feat you desire!" analyzes Professor Charles Xavier (aka Professor X) upon his invitation to Dukes to join his band of mutant heroes, the X-Men, an offer the grandstanding Blob rejects, instead organizing a posse of sideshow freaks for an unsuccessful hostile takeover of the X-Men's mansion.

When the Blob resurfaced later that year in issue #7, he was in the company of the X-Men's arch-foes the Brotherhood of Evil Mutants. Ironically, the Blob's corpulent invulnerability actually saved the X-Men from a missile attack launched by Brotherhood leader Magneto. From that point the Blob became one of the X-Men's recurring nemeses, sometimes partnering with other rogue mutants including Unus the Untouchable and the Mimic. He has also participated in almost every incarnation of the Brotherhood, including the U.S. government–sponsored Freedom Force, Mystique's version of the group formed in 1985 and charged with policing the Mutant Registration Act. Despite his bravado, the Blob is prone to manipulation by his more intelligent teammates. He has continued to mutate over the years, his powers increasing as his size has ballooned to 8 feet in height and a weight of nearly one-half ton.

The Blob has appeared as a member of the Brotherhood of Evil Mutants on the animated television series *Spider-Man and His Amazing Friends* (1981–1986), *X-Men* (1992–1997), and *X-Men: Evolution* (2000–2003), and Toy Biz has issued Blob action figures in the 1990s and 2000s. —*ME*

Blockbuster

Indisputably inspired by the Incredible Hulk, DC Comics' Blockbuster was a thickset, thickheaded juggernaut who pulverized Batman on several occasions. Debuting in Gardner Fox and Carmine Infantino's "The Blockbuster Invasion of Gotham City" in *Detective Comics* #345 (1965), young scientist

Mark Desmond chemically boosts his feeble form, transforming into Blockbuster ... with his sagacity taking a beating. Manipulated into thievery by his shifty brother Roland, Blockbuster's destructive fury can only be quelled by the face of Bruce Wayne—who once saved Mark from drowning—forcing Batman remove his mask to reveal his Wayne identity to calm the rampaging brute. In later tales, Blockbuster went head-to-head with Solomon Grundy and broke bread with the Secret Society of Super-Villains before being drafted into the Suicide Squad, where he perished fighting Brimstone.

Sibling Roland Desmond hoisted the Blockbuster mantle in *Starman* vol. 1 #9 (1989), pumping up from a super-steroid but, unlike Mark, maintaining his intellect. Blockbuster II strong-armed the underworld in the city of Blüdhaven, developing bitter rivalries with its resident guardian Nightwing and the superhero information broker Oracle. A deal with the demon Neron augmented Blockbuster's brainpower, and the gargantuan genius planned to expand his crime empire into his former digs of Gotham when a bullet fired by anti-hero Tarantula brought an end to his life and to the lethal legacy of the Blockbuster brothers. Yet Blockbuster barrels on, in television's *Justice League Unlimited* (2004–present), voiced by Dee Bradley Baker. —ME

Blofeld

Ernst Stavro Blofeld is the most pertinacious of the supervillains to match wits with British superspy James Bond, having appeared in three Bond novels and seven films. In Ian Fleming's novel *Thunderball* (1961), Blofeld is portrayed as an organizer, not as the tale's principal adversary; *Thunderball*'s prototypical plot regarding stolen nuclear warheads used for extortion is instead propelled by Emilio Largo, one of Blofeld's henchmen. *Thunderball* introduces yet another representative element crucial to spy sagas, the evil organization, in the form of Blofeld's crime network SPECTRE (the Special Executive for Counterintelligence, Terrorism, Revenge, and Extortion).

Blofeld operates from a variety of ultra-sophisticated, expansive laboratories and facilities, popu-

James Bond Supervillains: Nobody Does It Badder

In addition to the resilient Blofeld and the insidious Dr. No, British superspy James Bond has been shaken, not stirred by a multitude of madmen in his popular movie franchise:

- **Auric Goldfinger** (*Goldfinger*, 1964): "The man with the Midas touch," actor Gerb Frobe's bullion broker hoarded gold to cripple the Western economy.
- **Oddjob** (*Goldfinger*, 1964): This silent martial-artist henchman (Harold Sakata) hurled his iron-rimmed bowler at Bond and inspired *Austin Powers*' shoe-throwing Random Task.
- **Emilio Largo** (*Thunderball*, 1964): Eye-patched SPECTRE agent Largo's (Adolfo Celi) penchant for feeding foes to sharks was lampooned by *Austin Powers*' Dr. Evil.
- **Mr. Big** (*Live and Let Die*, 1973): From Harlem hoodlum to heroin-trading crime king, Kananga (Yaphet Kotto), aka Mr. Big, had a thing for alligators, tarot cards, and Jane Seymour.
- **Francisco Scaramanga** (*The Man with the Golden Gun*, 1974): Movie Dracula Christopher Lee played this debonair marksman with the tropical funhouse.
- **Nick Nack** (*The Man with the Golden Gun*, 1974): Herve Villechaize portrayed Scaramanga's peanut-eating, scene-stealing sidekick, preceding his signature second-banana role as *Fantasy Island*'s Tattoo.
- **Karl Stromberg** (*The Spy Who Loved Me*, 1977): A Captain Nemo wannabe, actor Carl Jurgens as billionaire-gone-bad Stromberg plotted nuclear Armageddon to rebuild society from his undersea Atlantis.
- **Jaws** (*The Spy Who Loved Me*, 1977; *Moonraker*, 1979): Seven-foot-two with teeth of steel, Richard Kiel's shark-named lackey was a sinister crowd-pleaser.
- **Hugo Drax** (*Moonraker*, 1979): Bearded and bad-tempered, Michael Lonsdale's megalomaniac in space planned to destroy Earth from his orbiting headquarters.
- **Aristotle Kristatos** (*For Your Eyes Only*, 1981): Patron of ice skating by day, double agent by night, Kristatos (Julian Glover) earned the ire of a crossbow-firing Bond girl.

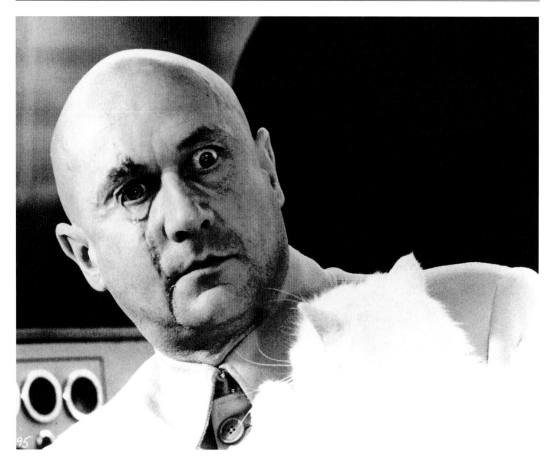

Donald Pleasence as Ernst Stavro Blofeld in *You Only Live Twice* (1967).

lated by mostly nameless accomplices he regards as expendable. His lairs are equipped with secret escape passages and vehicles for his own transport in the always-likely event that Bond will infiltrate and destroy his headquarters. Through SPECTRE, he has attempted such atrocities as goading the superpowers into world war and creating a laser satellite powered by diamonds. His ultimate victory over his arch-foe was his murder of Bond's wife, Tracy.

Blofeld's roots unfolded in Fleming's novels *Thunderball, On Her Majesty's Secret Service* (1963), and *You Only Live Twice* (1964). Born on May 28, 1908 (Fleming's birthdate), in Poland, Blofeld studied science and engineering before working for the Polish government's Ministry of Posts and Telegraphs, where he first engaged in lawlessness via insider trading. Using his government connections he erased all records of his existence

and went underground, selling top-secret information to both sides during World War II, then relocating to South America and setting up SPECTRE.

Fleming regularly altered Blofeld's physical guises in the novels to safeguard his identity, but in the films, beginning with his first screen outing in *From Russia with Love* (1963), his trademarked look was a bald pate (although he had hair in *Diamonds Are Forever*, 1971), a Nehru jacket, and on some occasions a facial scar. Also famous were the teasers in his earliest movie appearances in which Blofeld's face was not revealed, but his hands were shown stroking a white Angora cat and his voice was heard issuing orders (Dr. Claw, nemesis of the 1980s animated hero Inspector Gadget, lampooned this, as did the most blatant of Blofeld parodies, Mike Myers' Dr. Evil from the *Austin Powers* movies).

On the screen, Blofeld has been portrayed by Anthony Dawson (hands) and Eric Pohlman (voice) (*From Russia with Love*, 1963, and *Thunderball*, 1965), Donald Pleasance (replacing the ailing Jan Werich in *You Only Live Twice*, 1967), Telly Savalas (*On Her Majesty's Secret Service*, 1969), Charles Gray (*Diamonds Are Forever*, 1971), John Hollis (uncredited, *For Your Eyes Only*, 1981), and Max von Sydow (*Never Say Never Again*, 1983). Blofeld, whose name was taken from the father of creator Fleming's schoolmate, was also intended for inclusion in the film *The Spy Who Loved Me* (1977) but dropped due to contractual entanglements. —ME

Blood-Sucking Bad Guys (and Gals)

At a gathering of his friends, the poet Lord Byron issued a challenge that they write a tale of the supernatural. The most famous result was Mary Shelley's novel *Frankenstein*, but another response was the first prose story written in English about vampires, John Polidori's "The Vampyre" (1819).

The work that has most influenced the concept of the vampire, in both literature and the popular culture, is Bram Stoker's novel *Dracula* (1897). Director F. W. Murnau presented an unauthorized adaptation of Stoker's novel in his German silent horror film *Nosferatu* (1922). Far more influential on the popular imagination, however, was director Tod Browning's film *Dracula* (1931), based on a stage version, both of which starred Bela Lugosi as a foreign count whose aristocratic manner conceals his vampiric nature.

The character of Dracula has continued to haunt popular culture ever since these early appearances. Britain's Hammer Films produced a long series of movies starring Christopher Lee as the Count, beginning with *Horror of Dracula* (1958). Dracula returned to the best-seller list in Elizabeth Kostova's novel *The Historian* (2005).

Dracula's most notable comics appearances were in Marvel's classic *Tomb of Dracula* series

(1972–1979). Writer Marv Wolfman and artist Gene Colan depicted Dracula as a grand, charismatic figure with a multilayered personality, capable of love and despair as well as rage and murderous violence. In *Tomb* Wolfman and Colan created the vampire hunter Blade, whose arch-foe is Deacon Frost, the vampire who killed his mother. Frost, who could create vampiric dopplegängers of his victims, turned detective Hannibal King into a vampire. Appropriately, Frost became the villain in the first *Blade* film (1998).

Considering they share a bat motif, it is appropriate that one of Batman's earliest foes was a vampire named the Monk (*Detective Comics* #31, 1939). Co-created by writer Gardner Fox, the Monk, garbed in a red robe and hood, tried to turn Bruce Wayne's fiancée Julie Madison into a vampire before Wayne, as Batman, destroyed him.

Producer Dan Curtis introduced a Dracula-like vampire as a villain into his Gothic daytime television serial, *Dark Shadows* (1966–1971). Instead, this character, Barnabas Collins, became the first sympathetic vampire to make a significant impact on popular culture. As played by Jonathan Frid, Barnabas was a "reluctant vampire," a man under a curse, unable to control his addiction to blood. He became the protector of the Collins family against supernatural evils, while guiltily hiding his own secret from them.

Roy Thomas co-created Marvel's own guilt-ridden vampire Morbius (in *Amazing Spider-Man* #101, 1971) as well as the malevolent World War II vampire Baron Blood, who, like Barnabas, posed as a normal member of his family (*The Invaders* #7, 1976). In doing so, Thomas became the first modern Marvel writer to portray vampires as supervillains, pitting them in combat against superheroes.

Over the decades writers have made the sexual connotations of vampirism increasingly explicit. Comics' vampiress Vampirella (who first appeared in *Vampirella* #1, from Warren Publishing, in 1969), was a sex symbol, but not a villainess, and battled other supernatural beings.

In his novel *Salem's Lot* (1975) Stephen King followed the traditional concept of vampires as evil predators. But Anne Rice revolutionized the fictional treatment of vampires with her series of novels,

The Vampire Chronicles, beginning with *Interview with the Vampire* (1976, made into a feature film in 1994). Although they prey on humans, Rice treats her vampires, including her most famous character, the Vampire Lestat, as romantic members of a sub-culture following an alternative lifestyle.

Director Joel Schumacher's cult film *The Lost Boys* (1987) forsakes Dracula's aristocratic trappings, pitting its young heroes against vampires who seem like macho young gang members. It influenced Richard Howell's long-running comics series *Deadbeats* (Claypool Comics), about a New England town plagued by vampires.

In his classic television series *Buffy the Vampire Slayer* (1997–2003) creator Joss Whedon treats vampires more like conventional supervillains: they have superhuman strength and are virtually invulnerable, except to wooden stakes and sunlight. To Whedon, vampires lack souls and hence are disposed toward evil. An exception to this is Angel, a vampire who regained his soul and as a result became tormented with guilt and sought redemption. Angel became the unlikely ally and lover of the series' young heroine, Buffy Summers, and, after they broke up, graduated to his own television series (1999–2004). Occasionally Angel would temporarily lose his soul and revert to his alternate personality, the sadistic Angelus.

Buffy's second season introduced Spike, a British "punk" vampire and his charmingly mad vampire lover Drusilla. Over the following seasons Spike discovered he was in love with Buffy, they had an affair, and Spike underwent a magical ordeal to regain his soul to prove his worth to her. But Buffy was uninterested in a romance with Spike, who moved over to the *Angel* series for its final season.

Whedon's *Buffy* and *Angel* series featured a long line of memorable villains, including the Master (an ancient vampire), Mayor Richard Wilkins (whose banal but ingratiating demeanor masked his lust for power), Faith (a vampire slayer turned rogue, who later reformed), Adam (a modern Frankenstein's monster), Glory (a goddess trapped in mortal form), the Trio (three wannabe supervillains), the First (the shapeshifting embodiment of evil), and the law firm of Wolfram & Hart (whose

practice includes black magic). Whedon's "Buffy-verse" villains have also appeared in Dark Horse's comics and the novels based on the Buffy and Angel television shows. —PS

Boomerang

The freelance assassin known as Boomerang was introduced in an Incredible Hulk feature story in *Tales to Astonish* #81 (1966), scripted by Stan Lee and penciled by Jack Kirby, as major league baseball pitcher "Fred" (he later was given the last name Myers). Although he had an extraordinary arm, Myers was suspended from the league for accepting bribes. Washed up and bitter, he eventually wandered into the Secret Empire, the subversive criminal organization in which he became a special operative code-named Boomerang.

When the Secret Empire disbanded, Boomerang returned to his native Australia, where he honed his natural gift of throwing. As a freelance assassin equipped with weaponry financed by multimillionaire Justin Hammer, Boomerang has primarily fought Spider-Man, although he has taken aim at the Hulk, Iron Fist, Nick Fury, Shang-Chi, the Black Widow, Hawkeye, and the Defenders. He has freelanced for the Kingpin, but has also been affiliated with the Jack O'Lantern–founded team, the Sinister Syndicate (which also included Rhino, Beetle, Hydro-Man, and Speed Demon), and has allied himself with other Marvel villains, such as Viper II, Blizzard II, Silver Samurai, Blacklash, and Hammerhead.

The expert marksman doesn't possess any superpowers to speak of, but his aim is dead on. His primary weapons are his trademark boomerangs, each of which is outfitted for a special purpose: "shatterangs" detonate on impact with explosive power; "gasarangs" release highly concentrated tear gas; "razorangs" slice through almost any material; and "screamerangs" produce a sonic blast. Boomerang can "fly" for several hours at moderate speed thanks to his mentally controlled high-powered boot-jets.

Boomerang's contemporary appearances include moments in *Marvel Knights: Spider-Man* (2005) as a member of Green Goblin's Sinister Twelve. In television animation, Boomerang appeared in a "Hulk" episode of *The Marvel Super-Heroes* series (1966) and in the FOX Kids *Avengers* series (1999–2000). —*GM*

The Brain

The Brain is a genetically enhanced super-genius who is unrelentingly fixated upon global domination.

He is also a laboratory mouse.

Warner Bros. animated stars Pinky and the Brain are white mice living in a research facility called Acme Labs (an homage to the brand name from the *Road Runner* cartoons). With his bulbous head and calculated demeanor, the egocentric, Orson Welles–inspired Brain (voiced by Maurice LaMarche) suffers from delusions of grandeur, always thinking outside of the "box" (in his case, a cage) and concocting elaborate schemes to control the world, abetted by his idiot sidekick Pinky (Rob Paulsen).

Hypnosis through crab meat (the episode "Das Mouse") and dentures ("TV or Not TV"), relocating the masses to his duplicate "Chia Earth" ("It's Only a Paper World"), and becoming a tap dancer to spread subliminal Morse-code mind control ("Mice Don't Dance") are among the Brain's ridiculous efforts to trick, coerce, or sway the populace into obedience. His plots are derailed either by a flaw in his master plan, some unexpected occurrence, or the bumbling interference of Pinky. The Brain's arch-enemy is his old colleague Snowball, now his competitor for world conquest.

Despite his supervillain-esque quest to control the world, the Brain is a sympathetic and likeable protagonist thanks to his tenacity and his semi-altruistic belief, albeit mistaken, that the world will benefit from his leadership. Unshaken from his failures, the Brain formulaically ends each episode by telling Pinky that "tomorrow night" they would do "the same thing we do *every* night—try to take over the world!"

Pinky and the Brain originated in 1993 as a rotating feature on *Animaniacs* (1993–1998) before spinning off into its own 1995–1998 series, which ran 65 episodes including a stint in primetime, and as a short-lived continuation, *Pinky, Elmyra & the Brain* (1998–1999). In 1999 it

received an Emmy Award for "Outstanding Special Class–Animated Program." DC Comics published 27 issues of *Pinky and the Brain* and one Christmas special between 1996 and 1998, and limited merchandising was produced, including miniature toys available with Wendy's kids' meals. A *Pinky and the Brain* DVD collection was released in 2005, keeping the Brain's global "threat" forever alive among fans. —*ME*

Brainiac

Whereas the Lex Luthor/Superman rivalry is a clash of brain versus brawn, the Superman/Brainiac war is one of man versus machine.

A flying saucer buffered by an impenetrable force field arrives on Earth in "The Super-Duel in Space," a Superman tale written by Otto Binder and drawn by Al Plastino in *Action Comics* #242 (1958). Its conceited pilot is a bald, light-green-skinned humanoid, "master of super-scientific forces" Brainiac. With his antennaed space-monkey Koko by his side, Brainiac uses his Shrinking Ray to miniaturize several major Earth cities, depositing them in enormous bottles until he can restore them to full size on an unspecified world that he controls. Examining his bottled civilizations with tongs ("Help! Giant tweezers ripped the George Washington Bridge loose!" screams one tiny New Yorker), Brainiac is challenged by Superman—whom he derides as "Puny-Man"—stalemating the Man of Steel with his technological wizardry. After the shrinking of Metropolis, Superman, also reduced to a minute scale, ultimately saves the day, returning to normal size himself and all of the cities save one—Kandor, the capital of Krypton, which Brainiac had shrunk prior to the planet's demise. The bottle city of Kandor, later kept in Superman's Fortress of Solitude, long remained a bittersweet element in the Superman mythos: it was the Last Son of Krypton's connection to his native people, but a painful reminder of his failure to return them to a normal life.

Curiously, the cover of *Action* #242, illustrated by Curt Swan and Stan Kaye, depicted Brainiac in the form he would soon make famous throughout comics' Silver Age (1956–1969): his pink leotard (with no leggings) and pulsating diodes atop his bald pate; Plastino's interior art, however, depicted the villain in a baggy pink shirt with pink boots and green pants, and with no head-electrodes. Another curiosity is Romado, the Superman comic *strip*'s original version of Brainiac, who briefly appeared in newspapers not long after the villain's *Action* debut; this bearded, bubble-craniumed space brigand possessed a shrunken and jarred Kryptonian city.

After a pair of return engagements, snippets of Brainiac's origin were revealed in *Action* #276 (1961) in a Supergirl story co-starring the Legion of Super-Heroes and introducing the Legionnaire with the "twelfth-level" intellect, Brainiac 5. "Brainy," a blond teen with green skin from the planet Colu (alternately Yod in early texts), was reportedly Brainiac's thirtieth-century descendant. In *Superman* vol. 1 #167 (1964) it was disclosed to readers that Brainiac was an artificial life form, constructed as a spy by the Computer Tyrants of Colu. A lad named Vril Dox was assigned to portray Brainiac's "son" to perpetuate his Coluan guise; Dox, aka Brainiac 2, ultimately spearheaded an uprising against the Computer Tyrants. *Superman* #167 also officially established the network of electrodes on Brainiac's cranium, which consistently became part of his visual design.

For decades Brainiac was one of Superman's most visible foes, thrashing the Man of Tomorrow with an ultra-scientific arsenal. In addition to his Shrinking Ray, which he wielded regularly (even once miniaturizing Superman's friends Lois Lane, Jimmy Olsen, and Perry White as "living trophies") and his force-field belt, able to withstand Superman's mightiest punches, Brainiac attacked the Metropolis Marvel with a red-green kryptonite ray, a space-time craft, a coma-ray, and a thought-caster. A room in Superman's Fortress of Solitude was devoted to the hero's encounters with Brainiac. The fiendish android often joined forces with criminal scientist Lex Luthor, and once teamed with Clayface II to battle Batman and Superman.

Given the importance of Brainiac to the Superman legend, for decades the supervillain's non-comic-book appearances were surprisingly rare. He reduced Metropolis as well as Jimmy and Lois in two 1966 episodes of Filmation's animated *The New*

Adventures of Superman, and he signed up with the Legion of Doom in *Challenge of the Super Friends* (1978–1979); the latter version was parodied on the Cartoon Network decades later in an animated spot in which Brainiac pleaded with Luthor for "a decent pair of pants." While Superman was heavily merchandised throughout the 1960s and 1970s, his villains rarely were: a notable exception was Brainiac's inclusion as one of four hand-painted figurines in a 1967 Superman playset from Canadian manufacturer Multiple Toymakers; a Pocket Super Heroes miniature of the Silver Age Brainiac was released in the early 2000s.

Writer Marv Wolfman and artist Gil Kane redesigned Brainiac in *Action* #544 (1983), the title's 45th anniversary edition. The android abandoned his green-pigmented humanoid body for an imposing robotic form, and with it jettisoned any hint of humanity he once might have possessed. Now an annihilative machine, Brainiac campaigned against Superman in a skull-shaped, tentacled spacecraft. He also appeared in mid-1980s Super Powers–related merchandising, including an action figure, before being unplugged by DC Comics' continuity-revising series *Crisis on Infinite Earths* (1985–1986) and *The Man of Steel* (1986).

In *Adventures of Superman* #438 (1988) the writer/artist team of John Byrne and Jerry Ordway introduced Brainiac into the reconstructed DC Universe. Extrapolating from elements in the previous continuity, Brainiac was now Colu's "scientist prime" Vril Dox, executed during his attempted coup against his world's Computer Tyrants. Just before his death he transmitted his superior intellect across the cosmos to Earth, possessing the mind of "the Amazing Brainiac," a carnival mentalist named Milton Fine who possessed latent psychic powers.

After using Fine's abilities for mind games against Superman, Brainiac partnered with Lex Luthor, who installed a familiar gridwork of circuitry called a "psi-amplifier" onto Brainiac's shaved head to augment his psionic assaults. In *Action* #649 (1990) Brainiac was techno-organically enhanced, emerging from a biochemical pool with a powerful physical form and Coluan green skin. As the decade progressed, Brainiac frequently fought Superman, battled the Justice League and

Action Comics #242 ©1958 DC Comics.
COVER ART BY CURT SWAIN AND STAN KAYE.

the New Gods, and occupied the body of Superman-killer Doomsday.

With the new millennium Brainiac downloaded his Coluan intelligence into an android body, becoming Brainiac 2.5. Another attempt at upgrading his form in the 2000 "Superman: Y2K" story arc resulted in an errant future version of the android called Brainiac 13. Brainiac 13 was banished to the dawn of time, but still managed a 2003 appearance as an action figure. In the mid-2000s Superman, while in the future, skirmished with Brainiac 12, and a digital incarnation of the android infected Barbara Gordon—aka the Oracle, of the Birds of Prey—with Brainiac technology. Brainiac was back in 2005 pushing an angry Superman to the edge of his sanity. With his propensity for upgrades, Brainiac remains a virtually undefeatable Superman foe.

An animated version of Brainiac was introduced in the 1996 "Stolen Memories" episode of *Superman* (1996–2000). Voiced by Corey Burton, Brainiac was originally a computer program on Krypton, surviving the planet's destruction. Traversing the galaxy on a mission emphasizing data collection over sentient life, this blue-skinned Brainiac fought Superman in several episodes and was absorbed into the rogues' gallery of the Cartoon Network's *Justice League* (2001–2004) and *Justice League Unlimited* (2004–present). Brainiac action figures from both series were produced.

Kevin Spacey was considered for the role of Brainiac in the late 1990s in the Tim Burton–helmed movie *Superman Lives*, which was aborted after spiraling pre-production costs and frequent false starts (Sean Connery was rumored to be under consideration for the Brainiac role in an earlier incarnation of the film). Spacey was destined to play a Superman foe, however—Luthor, in Brian Singer's 2006 *Superman Returns*. Brainiac at last made the leap onto the live-action screen in the 2005 season of the WB's *Smallville* (2001–present) when James Masters, a fan favorite from his portrayal of Spike on *Buffy the Vampire Slayer* (1997–2003), was introduced as Brainiac, first seen oozing out of a Kryptonian villains' spaceship that had landed on Earth. Brainiac has assimilated into society as Milton Fine, Clark Kent's college professor, who attempts to persuade the pre-Superman to use his powers against the common good. —*ME*

Brainwave

A world-conquering mad-doctor type from comics' Golden Age (1938–1954), Brainwave (Brain Wave) made his first appearance in *All Star Comics* #15 (1943) in a story written by Gardner Fox and penciled by Joe Gallagher. Introverted psychiatrist Henry King possesses the ability to construct realistic images by projecting his own thoughts. Unsatisfied with his life as a do-good doctor, King establishes an identity as Brainwave and sets about amassing wealth and power.

The crimelord soon turned to truly supervillainous acts, including partnering with several crooks and offering them his unique psychic talents in exchange for proceeds from their criminal activities. One of his first crime-brokering deals was with Professor Elba, who developed with Brainwave an "insanity serum." In an effort to bring about the Justice Society of America's (JSA) demise, Brainwave planted post-hypnotic suggestions into the minds of its members; shrank several members down to 8 inches tall; and—in a bogus identity as dream psychologist Dr. Forest Malone—solicited the team to volunteer for a test of his dream analyzer, nearly driving them mad.

Brainwave appeared throughout the 1940s, during which he battled such heroes as Green Lantern, Starman, Johnny Thunder, and other JSA members, both solo and as a member of the early supervillain team the Injustice Society of the World. Over time his powers became more sophisticated and polished, and have included telepathy, telekinesis, and the ability to generate bolts of raw mental force.

Brainwave was killed in battle with the Ultra-Humanite, but not before passing on his remarkable mental powers to his son, Henry King, Jr., the DC hero Brainwave. —*GM*

some but now loopy Brak (voiced by Andy Merrill) brought on board as a threesome "Paul Shaffer" to Space Ghost's "David Letterman." Brak, a notorious moocher whose pirating was now limited to food raids in the television studio, ultimately wormed his way to co-host status on *Coast to Coast* before landing his own 2000 short-lived variety show, *Brak Presents the Brak Show Starring Brak*, followed by *The Brak Show* (2000–2003), an animated sitcom seen in the Cartoon Network's "Adult Swim" programming block. In this *Space Ghost* prequel, grade-schooler Brak was a supervillain-in-the-making living in suburbia with his human father, bewitching catlike mother, and wind-breaking brother Sisto, and attending class with Zorak and 1960s Hanna-Barbera toon star Wally Gator. The offbeat show's plots involved everything from a putting on a neighborhood musical (with guest-star Charo) to battling Thundercleese, the robot that lived next door. *The Brak Show* merchandising included a 2005 DVD collection and action-figure set; in his *Coast to Coast* incarnation, Brak appeared as an action figure and a maquette. —*ME*

Brak

"Hi, my name is Braaaak!"—not the bloodcurdling introduction one might expect of an interstellar pirate, but with this member of Space Ghost's rogues' gallery, one must expect the unexpected.

First seen in "The Looters," a Space Ghost episode (original airdate: October 22, 1966) of Hanna-Barbera's original *Space Ghost and Dino Boy* series (1966–1968), Brak, voiced by Keye Luke, and his fellow pirates overtake a gold-transport spacecraft with their sleep-inducing gas. Capturing Space Ghost's interloping sidekicks, Brak ultimately wars with the crusading superhero when he comes to their rescue. The saber-toothed space thief who hides his features behind a catlike helmet often wields a ray pistol in his crimes, and he struggled with Space Ghost in animated episodes and in a 1987 *Space Ghost* comic book.

The irreverent cable-TV comedy *Space Ghost: Coast to Coast* (1994–2004) recast the superhero into a talk-show host who interviewed real-life celebrities, with foes Zorak, Moltar, and the formerly fear-

Brimstone

Raining fire and panic upon the scurrying populace who woefully find themselves in his lumbering path, the 50-foot terror called Brimstone is the DC Comics-equivalent of Godzilla—a creature that exists solely to destroy.

Brimstone blazed into the DC Universe in *Legends* #1 (1986), the miniseries in which the evil despot Darkseid of Apokolips attempts to eliminate earthly opposition by eroding the public's confidence in its superheroes. Darkseid's obsequious envoy, the sadistic Desaad, sabotaged a S.T.A.R. Labs nuclear generator to explode, as a result creating Brimstone, a 60,000-pound behemoth possessing some degree of sentience. Programmed with the conviction that it is a fallen angel, Brimstone cuts a swath across the DC Universe with its fiery sword and generation of intense heat.

The Justice League of America, Firestorm the Nuclear Man, and the Suicide Squad have narrowly avoided meltdowns in their conflicts with Brimstone. The creature has on several occasions been eliminated, but is capable of regeneration—and repeated devastation.

Brimstone shambled onto television in the "Initiation" episode of the Cartoon Network's *Justice League Unlimited* (2004–present). In its TV incarnation, the creature was the out-of-control creation of Chinese inventor Chong-Mi, with Justice League recruits including Green Arrow and Captain Atom taking down the fiery beast. —*ME*

Bronze Age Supervillains (1970-1979)

The times, they were a'changin' in the early 1970s, and comics were changing with them. "Relevance" was the buzzword for superheroes, with torn-from-the-headlines social issues inching their way into DC and Marvel stories.

As heroes started to tell it like it is, many of the traditional supervillains weren't with it enough to make the scene. One of the new "villains" that appeared was the real-world threat of drugs. In a letter to Marvel Comics' editor in chief Stan Lee, the U.S. Department of Health, Education, and Welfare "thought it would really be very beneficial if we created a story warning kids about the dangerous effects of drug addiction," Lee remarked in Les Daniels' *Marvel: Five Fabulous Decades of the World's Greatest Comics* (1991). The result was the three-part *The Amazing Spider-Man* vol. 1 #96–#98 (1971), in which Peter (Spider-Man) Parker's roommate Harry Osborn (son of Norman Osborn, the Green Goblin) was hospitalized after a pill addiction. Immediately on its heels came DC Comics' *Green Lantern/Green Arrow* #85–#86, by writer Denny O'Neil and artist Neal Adams, in which Green Arrow's teenage sidekick Speedy was revealed to be a heroin user.

"The Man," counterculture slang for "the establishment" or corrupt authority figures, was another popular "villain." In *Green Lantern/Green Arrow* #76 (1970), the emerald heroes went head-to-head with fatcat Jubal Slade, an oppressive

slumlord, and left-winger Green Arrow delivered an impassioned speech about the "hideous moral cancer" eroding the spirit of America. Connected to "the Man" was his "henchman," pollution, a by-product of corporate gluttony; heroes from the Justice League to their TV counterparts, the Super Friends, battled environmental degradation.

Racial prejudice also became a "villain," the most landmark example being Marvel's Black Panther taking on the Ku Klux Klan (called "the Clan") in a 1976 storyline by Don McGregor and Billy Graham.

Costumed criminals rarely surfaced in DC's superhero titles during the relevance era, with the exception of *The Flash*, in which at least one of the Scarlet Speedster's Rogues' Gallery could be counted upon for an appearance every few issues. Although Wonder Woman had lost her superpowers, she managed a catfight with Catwoman in *Wonder Woman* vol. 1 #201–#202 (1972), and Green Lantern's old enemy Black Hand snuck into a 1971 story. Superman's and Batman's famous foes were at best rarely seen but at worst conspicuously absent. Batman was undergoing a "creature of the night" revamp and mostly encountered ghosts and street-based criminals, with the exceptions of Man-Bat, introduced in 1970, and Ra's al Ghul, first seen in 1971, both of whom fit the hero's new gothic milieu (the Ten-Eyed Man, who "saw" with his fingertips, made the first of a handful of appearances in 1970's *Batman* #226). Superman's powers were temporarily diminished in 1971, and most of his villains were AWOL except for Lex Luthor, who appeared sporadically (bringing with him the alien energy-beast, the Galactic Golem, in 1972)—in fact, no major Superman villain was depicted on the covers of *Action Comics* between issues #389 (June 1970) and #416 (September 1972). Interestingly, during this supervillainous dry spell, neo-DC writer/artist/editor Jack Kirby, fresh from Marvel, introduced Darkseid in 1970, the evil god from Apokolips who would become one of the publisher's major antagonists.

Marvel dabbled in relevant themes in the early 1970s, but not at the expense of their supervillains. Kang, Magneto, Ultron, Green Goblin, Annihilus, and Dr. Doom were among the sinister old-timers returning to battle the heroes of the Marvel Universe, with Thanos (bowing in 1973), Bullseye (first seen in

1976), and Sabretooth (debuting in 1977) among the newcomers joining the pantheon during the decade today known as the Bronze Age of Comics.

Three important Bronze Age stories helped shape the future of comic-book supervillainy: the first occurred in writer Gerry Conway and artist Gil Kane's *Amazing Spider-Man* #121–#122 (June–July 1973), in which Peter Parker's girlfriend Gwen Stacy was killed during a battle between Spidey and his arch-foe, the Green Goblin; the Goblin himself died in this two-parter's climax (although he has since returned from the dead). Earlier superhero-versus-supervillain battles rarely resulted in the deaths of major characters, and Conway's scripted slaughter of Gwen Stacy even startled Stan Lee. The second was the Joker's return from limbo in *Batman* #251's "The Joker's Five-Way Revenge" (September 1973), by O'Neil and Adams. Junkheaped was the wacky Clown Prince of Crime of the 1960s; in his place cackled the homicidal psychotic who relished escalating body counts. This darker interpretation of the Joker led to grimmer overhauls of most of Batman's rogues throughout the decade (and they grew darker yet in later years). The third was Conway and artist Ross Andru's introduction of the Punisher in *Amazing Spider-Man* #129 (February 1974). A villain in this initial story, the Punisher was soon portrayed as an anti-hero, killing in the name of justice and blazing a trail for other similar characters (like Wolverine, who followed later that year) … and blurring the formerly unambiguous division between good and evil.

By the mid-1970s, the relevance trend had passed and DC readily exploited its costumed criminals, spinning off the Joker and Man-Bat into their own titles and launching the bimonthly *The Secret Society of Super-Villains*. Marvel countered with *Super-Villain Team-Up*, joining *The Tomb of Dracula*, the popular comic starring the inarguably evil vampire protagonist, which had been in print since 1972. Vigorous merchandising—Mego action figures, 7-11 Slurpee cups, and Power Records comics among the mix—made supervillains from Mr. Mxyzptlk to the Lizard favorites among children, and various bad guys stormed onto television in animated series starring Marvel and DC heroes.

Not every supervillain seen during the Bronze Age garnered a measure of lasting notoriety. Cultural trends and scientific innovations of the 1970s inspired gaggles of criminals whose careers, like the pet rocks and mood rings of the decade, faded after their fifteen minutes of fame. Consider the motorcycling mayhem-makers Satan's Angels, Stan Lee and Gene Colan's far-from-subtle response to reality's Hell's Angels (as well as the 1969 movie *Easy Rider*), in *Captain America* #128 (1970). Stunt cyclist Evel Knievel's acclaim spawned a 1971 biopic (starring George Hamilton) and a 1972 toy line from Ideal, as well as Marvel's hell-on-wheels hero, the flaming-skulled Ghost Rider. Among the Ghost Rider's two-wheeled foes were Big Daddy Dawson, the Stunt-Master, and the Orb, the latter of whom wore a headpiece resembling a large eyeball.

Another kind of wheels—skateboards—inspired the career of the Rocket Racer, who blazed into *Amazing Spider-Man* #172 (1977) on his jet-powered board. A tech-whiz who turned to crime to help his financially strapped family, Robert Farrell later used his Rocket Racer gear to fight, not perpetuate, crime. Before he gave up supervillainy, though, he became entangled with Big Wheel, aka embezzler Jackson Weele, who rolled into issues #182–#183 (1978) in a gargantuan, weapons-laden steel wheel. Big Wheel's appellation was borrowed from the plastic tricycle that had become a household name by the late 1970s.

Peggy Fleming, the 1968 Olympic Gold medalist, helped popularize figure skating during the 1970s, prompting the Golden Glider, a former ice princess (and the sister of Captain Cold) who skated through the air and into the life of the Fastest Man Alive in *The Flash* vol. 1 #250 (1977). After a number of late 1970s appearances, she was killed in the 1980s.

By the late 1970s, microwave ovens were a fixture in the modern American kitchen, and DC responded by creating Superman's foe the Microwave Man, a has-been thief from the 1950s who used microwave technology to resuscitate his crime career, as seen in *Action* #487 (1978). Three years earlier in *Action* #458 (1975), DC embraced both the TV generation and media fascination with Apollo-retrieved moon rocks with the vil-

E-Man vol. 1 #3 ©1974 Charlton Comics.
COVER ART BY JOE STATON.

Iain Blackrock, who wielded a "power stone" to channel television airwaves into super-energy, riding those waves through the air and using them to fire concussive blasts at the Man of Steel.

The blaxploitation film craze of the 1970s launched the career of Marvel's Shaft-like Luke Cage, Hero for Hire, the first African-American superhero to star in his own magazine. Battling Cage (later dubbed Power Man) were ghetto-hatched supervillains including mob queen Black Mariah, man-mountain Big Ben, costumed assassin Cottonmouth, gangsta-turned-amphibian Mr. Fish, and sharp-toothed tough-guy Piranha Jones. DC's resident African-American hero, Black Lightning, tussled with the black crimelord Tobias Whale, an albino.

Lastly, while there were very few superhero titles published by DC and Marvel's competitors during the Bronze Age, their characters encoun-

tered supervillains all their own. Short-lived mid-1970s publishing house Atlas Comics' villains, like their heroes, imitated better-known characters found elsewhere: Tiger-Man's foe Hypnos mesmerized victims with his monocle, as Ringmaster and the Mad Hatter did with their chapeaus; Doomstalker used Cyclops-like eyebeams to blast the Hulk-esque Brute; and the "burning clutch" of the Destructor's enemy Deathgrip reminded readers of kung-fu fighter Iron Fist. Charlton Comics' witty *E-Man*, by writer Nick Cuti and artist Joe Staton, broke the mold—its villains, like its hero (an energy force turned humanoid hero), were tongue in cheek, from the sibling dangers the Entropy Twins to the power-draining Battery, the latter of whom premiered in a story whose title was inspired by another 1970s "classic": "The Energy Crisis." —ME

The Brood

Introduced by writer Chris Claremont and artist Dave Cockrum in *Uncanny X-Men* #155 (1982), this extraterrestrial race may remind comics readers of the creatures designed by H. R. Giger for Twentieth Century Fox's *Alien* blockbuster film series. The Brood resemble gigantic insects, averaging 8 feet in length, with six legs, and with a tail that ends in two stingers. Their large heads seem more reptilian, with rows of sharp teeth. Their thick carapaces serve as armor, and "warrior" Brood have transparent wings, enabling them to fly. Like ants or bees, the Brood organize themselves into a hive-like society, under a queen, which is far larger than any other Brood and is capable of laying eggs. As with another similar race, *Star Trek*'s Borg, the Queen can communicate telepathically with her subjects.

Fox's Aliens use humans as hosts for their young, which then burst out from their bodies. Claremont's Broodqueens implant eggs into the bodies of humans or other hosts. But when the egg hatches within the host's body, the embryo takes over the host's body from within, genetically transforming the host into an adult member of the Brood. The Brood member can retain the host's form or change back and forth between the host's form and its Brood form. The Brood member will retain any superhuman powers that its host possessed.

No mere animals, the Brood have developed highly advanced science, including the genetic engineering methods they utilized to endow the X-Men's ally Carol Danvers with the superhuman powers she used as Binary to manipulate cosmic energies. The Brood enslave the Acanti, creatures resembling whales that can travel through space, to use them as living starships. Nonetheless, Brood culture seems to have no higher goals than satisfying their needs to feed and to reproduce.

Besides the X-Men, the Brood have also clashed with the Fantastic Four and Ghost Rider. —PS

Brother Blood

A centuries-old murder has led to a savage bloodline and powerful cult led by the charismatic manipulator Brother Blood. First seen in *The New Teen Titans* #21 (1982), in a story by Marv Wolfman and George Pérez, Brother Blood was Brother Sebastian, the leader of the Church of Brother Blood in the European country of Zandia. Sebastian's life was extended and his strength grew with every new member to join his cult.

Unbeknownst to his acolytes, Blood's fearsome costume—red and black with a white cloak and a bony skullcap—was wired with circuitry that allowed him to hurl bolts of energy.

The first Zandian to use the name Brother Blood was a high priest named Sebastian who slew a monk during the Crusades. He took from the dying man a white garment that was purported to have been the prayer shawl of Jesus Christ, now filled with dark magic. Whatever the cloth really was, it gave Sebastian—now calling himself Brother Blood—a form of invulnerability, a slowed aging process, and power derived from the emotions of his followers. The monk cursed Sebastian, telling him that his son would slay him.

Son did kill father and took on the mantle of Blood, and the curse continued through six others. Born in 1941, the seventh Sebastian eventually slew his father and took on the power of the cloak. Building up a worldwide religious cult, Blood placed his minions in positions of power as politicians, prominent businessmen, and media personnel. His needs were taken care of by Mother Mayhem and other perverse followers, even as he plotted eventual world domination.

When a cultist attempted to flee one of the compounds, the Teen Titans came into conflict with Blood for the first time. Their battles would continue over time, with Blood using his media contacts to discredit them. He also brainwashed Robin and used Raven and the "angel" Azrael in "resurrection" schemes to solidify his power base. Eventually, Blood's mind was destroyed, and Mother Mayhem bore a daughter, apparently ending the curse.

But years later, Blood would return to evil, until a young man claiming to be his son slew him and took on the role of cult leader. Blood's acolytes tried to make Raven into the Bride of Blood, but a new group of Teen Titans intervened. They learned that the Church of Blood was founded on the worship the demon Trigon—Raven's father—and that an ancient prophecy foretold Armageddon if Blood and Raven were to wed.

This newest Blood has the power to absorb a man's power through a bite. Although seemingly defeated by the Titans and Deathstroke, Brother Blood has recently returned from an evil dimension, consorting with hordes of demons that resemble Trigon, and swearing vengeance on the young heroes. DC Direct released a modern Brother Blood action figure in 2005.

Although he might seem macabre for a kid's cartoon, Brother Blood appeared on Cartoon Network's *Teen Titans* series (2003–2006) in 2005. As the new headmaster of the HIVE Academy, Blood used his charisma and mental abilities to twist teenage students to evil. He clashed with the Titans multiple times, but was always defeated. —AM

The Brotherhood of Dada: *See* **The Brotherhood of Evil**

The Brotherhood of Evil

A brain in a jar, a talking gorilla, and a plastic woman: anomalies one might expect to see as carnival attractions, this "Brotherhood of Evil" first banded together for the "ultimate mission" of destroying the "World's Strangest Heroes" in DC Comics' *The Doom Patrol* vol. 1 #86 (1964), written by Arnold Drake and illustrated by Bruno Premiani. Masterminded by the Brain, a disembodied genius brain floating in liquid under glass, the Brotherhood—Monsieur Mallah, an intellectually enhanced gorilla (with an IQ of 178), and Madame Rouge, a French beauty with stretching powers, plus their lackey, Mr. Morden, operator of a 100-feet-tall robot called "Rog"—attempt to steal the Statue of Liberty to extort money from the U.S. until the freakish do-gooders the Doom Patrol (DP) stop them.

The Brotherhood was a recurring threat to the DP during 1960s, with the pear-shaped alien Garguax and the undying despot General Immortus occasionally joining its ranks. Never a tight-knit group, the Brotherhood was ultimately undone when the schizophrenic Madame Rouge killed her teammates after confederating with Nazi war criminal Captain Zahl; in this landmark tale in *Doom Patrol* #121 (1968), the DP also perished, at Zahl's hand.

The Brain and Monsieur Mallah survived, however (as did the DP's most popular member, Robotman, who eventually returned in a DP revival with new members), resurfacing in *The New Teen Titans* #14 (1981), courtesy of writer Marv Wolfman and artist George Pérez. Their Brotherhood of Evil added to its ranks the voodoo techno-wizard Houngan, the fear-inducer Phobia, the teleporter Warp, and the protoplasmic creature with the disintegrating touch, Plasmus. The Brain and Mallah regrouped in 1990 as the Society of Sin, joined by the illusionist Trinity.

In *Doom Patrol* vol. 2 #19 (1989), writer Grant Morrison and penciler Richard Case refurbished the DP's arch-enemies. The surrealistic Brotherhood of Dada was organized by the original Brotherhood of Evil wannabe, Mr. Morden, who had been transmogrified into the living abstract Mr. Nobody. Joining him were the cyclonic Frenzy, the superstrong somnambulist Sleepwalk, the cloud-producing Fog, and the Quiz, who could exhibit any superpower one has *never* imagined. Devoted to eliminating the status quo, the Brotherhood of Dada endeavored to expunge Paris via a painting that absorbed matter.

Mr. Nobody later formed another incarnation of this absurd team, featuring Agent "!", Number None, the Toy, and Alias the Blur.

Writer/artist John Byrne rebooted the Doom Patrol in 2004, sidestepping the DP's ties to the Teen Titans, including the Brotherhood of Evil. *Doom Patrol* vol. 3 #14 (2005) sent Robotman through alternate realities that included encounters with the Brain and Monsieur Mallah, Byrne's acknowledgment that these characters are, despite his restart, connected to DP lore.

The Cartoon Network, unencumbered by decades of story contradictions, introduced both the Doom Patrol and the original, three-member Brotherhood of Evil (along with General Immortus) into the 2005 season of its *Teen Titans* series (2003–2006). —*ME*

The Brotherhood of Evil Mutants

It is not just individual superheroes who have evil counterparts; superhero teams have them, too. Hence, the opposite number of Marvel's mutant X-Men is the Brotherhood of Evil Mutants, whose first incarnation was introduced by writer/editor Stan Lee and artist/co-plotter Jack Kirby in *X-Men* #4 (1964). Professor Charles Xavier founded the X-Men to help bring about his dream of peaceful coexistence between mutants and "normal" humans. In contrast, each of the many versions of the Brotherhood has viewed non-superpowered humans as enemies. Though Lee and Kirby did not describe the team this way, each incarnation of the Brotherhood is a band of terrorists; hence, Lee and Kirby's Brotherhood foreshadows the real-life terrorist cells of later decades.

The original Brotherhood of Evil Mutants debuted the same month as the Brotherhood of Evil, the adversaries of DC's Doom Patrol. But there is no evidence that "Doom Patrol" writer Arnold Drake had contact with Lee and Kirby at that time; the similarity is coincidental.

The original Brotherhood of Evil Mutants was headed by Xavier's arch-foe Magneto, who controls magnetism, and included his pathetically submissive flunky, the Toad, who jumps like his namesake; Mastermind, who projects illusions; Quicksilver, who can run at superhuman speed; and his sister the Scarlet Witch, whose mutant "hex power" enables her to alter probability, causing unusual occurrences.

The two siblings, whose real names were Pietro and Wanda Maximoff, aided Magneto because he had once rescued Wanda from a mob who thought she was a real witch. Neither Magneto, Pietro, nor Wanda knew at this time that Magneto was actually Wanda and Pietro's father.

Magneto and this Brotherhood battled the X-Men repeatedly, and even succeeded in temporarily conquering the (fictional) small Latin American nation of Santo Marco.

Magneto finally overreached by attempting to force the Stranger, a superpowered being he assumed was a mutant, to join the Brotherhood. In actuality, the Stranger was a virtually omnipotent extraterrestrial, who turned Mastermind (temporarily) to stone and transported Magneto and the Toad to his homeworld as specimens of Earth mutants. Tired of Magneto's war with humanity, Quicksilver and the Scarlet Witch soon joined a superhero team, the Avengers.

Later, Magneto and the Toad escaped to Earth, where Magneto reenlisted Quicksilver and the Scarlet Witch in his Brotherhood. This time, the Toad finally rebelled against his cruel master, and Quicksilver and the Scarlet Witch eventually returned to the Avengers.

Magneto revived the Brotherhood in *The Defenders* #15–#16 (1974), with Mastermind rejoining. New members included three long-standing foes of the X-Men: the Blob, whose immense mass gives him superhuman strength and virtual invulnerability; Unus the Untouchable, who can surround himself with an impenetrable force field; and Lorelei, whose singing paralyzes the wills of men who hear her.

In *Captain America Annual* #4 (1977), writer/artist Jack Kirby placed Magneto at the head of an otherwise all-new Brotherhood of Evil Mutants. Its roster included Burner, who could induce fires; the super-strong Lifter; Peeper (now

deceased), whose large eyes gave him telescopic vision; Shocker, who emitted electrical blasts; and the reptilian Slither. After Magneto abandoned them, the team called themselves Mutant Force, and later, except for Slither, the Resistants.

The shapeshifting mutant terrorist Mystique then usurped the name of the Brotherhood and organized her own version of the team, which writer Chris Claremont and artist/co-plotter John Byrne introduced in *Uncanny X-Men* #141 (1981). This team included the Blob; the blind Destiny, who could "see" the future; Avalanche, who could induce earthquakes in small areas; and Pyro, who could mentally control flames. In their first public appearance, Mystique's Brotherhood attempted to assassinate Senator Robert Kelly, whom they regarded as a foe of mutant rights, but were thwarted by the X-Men. Mystique brought her protégée Rogue into the Brotherhood, but Rogue soon defected to the X-Men. Under the name "Freedom Force," Mystique's Brotherhood later became special operatives for the U.S. government.

After Freedom Force collapsed, the Toad organized a new criminal Brotherhood, which included the Blob; Pyro; Phantazia, who could disrupt other superhumans' powers; and Sauron, a human transformed into a pterodactyl-like being. This team debuted in *X-Force* #5 (1991).

Since the early 1990s there have been several short-lived Brotherhoods. In *X-Factor* #112 (1995) the Dark Beast founded a Brotherhood that would include Fatale, Random, Ever, and the heroes Aurora, X-Man, and Havok. Professor Xavier unsuccessfully tried to steer another Brotherhood (in *Uncanny X-Men* #363, 1999) including the Toad, the Blob, the Mimic (a nonmutant who could duplicate the superpowers of others), and the super-strong Post toward the straight and narrow.

Then Mystique organized a new terrorist Brotherhood (debuting in *X-Men* #106, 2000) including Avalanche, the Blob, Post, the Toad, Sabretooth, Mastermind II (the original's daughter), and new characters Sabre and Crimson Commando II (who are successors to two former members of Freedom Force). Mystique's new Brotherhood tried again to assassinate Senator Kelly but were thwarted by the dying Pyro.

X-Men vol. 1 #4 ©1964 Marvel Comics.
ART BY JACK KIRBY AND PAUL REINMAN.

There was even a Brotherhood with entirely new members who starred in their own series (*The Brotherhood*, 2001–2002), but all the members were killed.

In *New X-Men* #146 (2003), the mysterious Xorn, who impersonated Magneto, established a Brotherhood, mostly composed of young mutants, but recruited the Toad as well.

Then, in *X-Men* #161 (2004), Black Tom Cassidy and Exodus, a follower of Magneto, set up a Brotherhood including Avalanche, Sabretooth, Mammomax, Nocturne, and another nonmutant, the Juggernaut, who turned against them.

In today's more sophisticated comics, it seems unlikely that Magneto would have referred to Brotherhood members as "evil mutants," unless he was being ironic. In *Ultimate X-Men*, an alternate version of *X-Men* continuity, the team is called the Brotherhood of Mutant Supremacy. In main-stream *X-Men* comics, *X-Men: The Animated Series* (1992–1997), the animated television series *X-Men: Evolution* (2000–2003), and the first *X-Men* (2000) feature film, the group is simply named the Brotherhood of Mutants.

The *X-Men* movie's Brotherhood is led by Magneto and includes Mystique, Sabretooth, and the Toad. In the second film, *X2* (2003), Magneto may well be rebuilding his defeated Brotherhood, since he recruits Pyro to his side. —*PS*

Bug-Based Bad Guys

With over 800,000 species of "Class Insecta" populating the planet, insects are a fertile source of inspiration for supervillains.

The Beetle, the enemy of the Human Torch, Spider-Man, and Daredevil, invaded the pages of Marvel's *Strange Tales* #123 (1964), published the same year the Beatles invaded America on their first U.S. tour. He is actually Abner Jenkins, a former aero-engineer who designed a winged suit of purple-and-green armor with suction-cupped, blast-firing gloves. The Beetle appeared on TV in the 1980s cartoon *Spider-Man and His Amazing Friends* and in 1994 on the animated *Iron Man*. The Scarlet Beetle did not fare as well, proving that even the House of Ideas' master architects Stan Lee and Jack Kirby were occasionally guilty of poor construction. This Ant-Man adversary was an actual beetle given human intelligence and malevolence by atomic radiation. With his telepathic control of insects, the Scarlet Beetle attempted to take over Earth—exactly what Mr. Mind, the bespectacled, super-genius "World's Wickedest Worm" and foe of the original Captain Marvel, has done on several occasions in his career that spans back to 1943. Mr. Mind bears no relation to the Mindworm, the brain-draining mutant that first fought Spider-Man in 1974, or the Earthworm, the little-seen sewer dweller who debuted in an Earth-Two Huntress tale in *Wonder Woman* vol. 1 #309 (1983).

Ancient Egyptians regarded the scarab as sacred, and scarabs have figured prominently in the histories of several comic-book characters, including Captain Marvel and Blue Beetle, and supervillains as well. *Captain America* (1944), the Republic Pictures fifteen-chapter movie serial based upon the Marvel Comics superhero, introduced the mysterious Dr. Maldor (actor Lionel Atwell), a treasure hunter aka the Scarab, whose arsenal included a Thermo-dynamic Vibration Engine, Electronic Firebolts, and a poison called "the Purple Death." The Scarlet Scarab (not to be confused with the aforementioned Scarlet Beetle), an Egyptian archaeologist who controlled the supernatural power source the Ruby Scarab, debuted in Marvel's *The Invaders* vol. 1 #23 (1977). A female Egyptian assassin named Scarab attempted a hit on Batman's junior partner in *Robin* vol. 2 #124 (2004).

Scarab was not the only insect-inspired supervillain driving Batman buggy. No one took Killer Moth (first seen in 1951) seriously until he metamorphosed into the monster Charaxes in 1995 (although he remained the costumed Killer Moth on the Cartoon Network's *Teen Titans*, 2003–2006). The same might be said of Firefly. Introduced by writer France Herron and artist Dick Sprang in *Detective Comics* #184 (1952), he was Garfield Lynns, a lighting-effects expert in the Gotham City theater circuit, who turned to crime in an embarrassingly flashy purple-and-green ensemble with a bug-antenna cowl, blinding Batman and Robin with incandescence. Down-and-out gambler Ted Carson became a different, one-time Firefly in *Batman* #126 (1959), emitting a "deadly glow" beam from his cowl. Firefly was retooled in the 1990s as a warped arsonist who was nearly burned alive in an attempt to incinerate Gotham. He has appeared on the television cartoons *Batman: The Animated Series* (1992–1995) and *The Batman* (2004–present), the latter series inspiring a Firefly action figure. Another arsonist Bat-foe, the Firebug, premiered in 1979 and flickered in and out of the limelight until Firebug II showed up in 2005, having purchased the original villain's gear in an Internet auction.

Winged insect-villains have buzzed through comics' pages for decades. The hypnotic Queen Bee, Zazzala of the bee-world Korll, and her submissive drones have been DC Comics nuisances since 1963, but Harvey Comics' rip-off Queen Bea, with her antennae-topped tiara, appeared only once in a

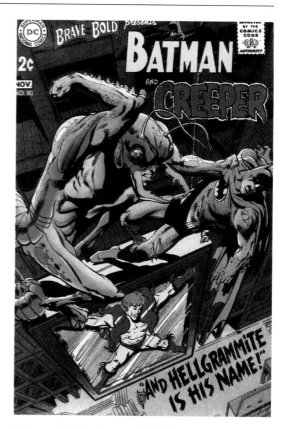

Hellgrammite. *The Brave and the Bold* vol. 1 #80 ©1968 DC Comics.
COVER ART BY NEAL ADAMS.

1967 B-Man adventure. Veronica Dultry, in *X-Men* #94 (1975), gained wings and mesmeric bug eyes from an insect-DNA gene-splicing experiment and became Dragonfly, one of the Ani-Men (and later, the Masters of Evil). Marvel's gossamer-winged Gypsy Moth, first seen in *Spider-Woman* vol. 1 #10 (1978), was originally a loner with little use for others. This telekinetic mutant learned to bond, becoming a team player with the Masters of Evil, the Night Shift, the Femizons, and the Thunderbolts, and in the twenty-first century she is known as Skein. Tiger Moth, Dragon Fly, and Silken Spider were an all-girl rock band that bombed out as supervillainesses after crossing paths with Poison Ivy in Ivy's first adventure in *Batman* #181 (1966). The Yellow Wasp, an ego-driven costumed crook who zipped about on wings and in a Waspmobile, felt the sting of pugilist-hero Wildcat's fists in several 1940s adventures, and the Killer Wasp, reportedly his son, became a foe of the Justice Society in 2000.

Some supervillains have gotten underfoot in ant- and roach-patterned identities. Athlete Eddie Whit performed several dangerous acts of larceny in his pink-hued guise of the Ant in 1966, but as the Teen Titans discovered, he was acting against his will. The Man of Steel once fought an army of giant ants led by his best friend, who under mind control became "King of the Giant Ants" in *Superman's Pal Jimmy Olsen* #54 (1961). Luke Cage's mid-1970s enemy Cockroach Hamilton was an expert brawler and marksman but was a bug only by nickname, unlike the human-sized Cockroach, Howard the Duck's foe (first seen in 1980), who scaled walls, had flesh-stabbing pincers, and evolved other life forms with his Cosmic Key. The cool-headed She-Hulk's fear factor was put to the test in her 1985 graphic novel when she was ambushed by the Cockroaches, a mass of human-consuming insects operating under a shared intelligent mind. His nearly inviolable carapace made the Hellgrammite, the roach-man from *The Brave and the Bold* #80 (1968), a serious threat to the team of Batman and the Creeper; Hellgrammite raided Metropolis in the early 1990s and has posed a threat to Superman several times since.

Locusts, one of the great "supervillains" of the Bible, have also plagued comic books in the form of supervillains. Professor August Hopper is an entomologist in a winged battlesuit who calls himself the Locust. Brandishing high-tech weapons such as a silken snare and a stun ray, the Locust has attacked several Marvel superheroes with insect armies, beginning his crime career in *X-Men* #23 (1966). Tower Comics' *T.H.U.N.D.E.R. Agents* #17 (1967) introduced King Locust, a shakedown artist aided by mechanical grasshoppers. In 2005, Marvel's "Ultimate" Universe introduced "Gah Lak Tus," the Fantastic Four's planet-eating enemy Galactus re-created into a robo-bug pestilence. Swarm, the supervillain first seen in Marvel's *The Champions* #14 (1977), is a living, flying cluster of thousands of insects. Impervious to physical attacks but vulnerable to pesticides, Swarm has fought Spider-Man and the Secret Defenders.

Other bug-based bad guys with labels like the Fly, Bug Man, Humbug, Bug and Byte, Baron Bug, and the Hornet have been swatted into obscurity, but DC's Bug-Eyed Bandit (first seen in *The Atom*

#26, 1966) deserves special mention. One might have thought that Bertram Larvan raided his kitchen for his supervillain uniform: his purple helmet, shaped like a colander, allowed him to direct mechanical insects, and his green, waffle-sized goggles elicited snickers from even the most impressionable young readers. The Bug-Eyed Bandit died unceremoniously in *Crisis on Infinite Earths* #12 (1986), but instead of letting his father rest in peace, Larvan's son adopted the Bandit's preposterous guise. —*ME*

Bullseye

W hile a pen is considered baleful only when it is of the poison variety, in the hands of Bullseye it can be lethal—as can a paper clip, a playing card, or a trashcan lid. "Watch Out for Bullseye— He Never Misses!" warned the title of writer Marv

Daredevil vol. 1 #161 ©1979 Marvel Comics.
COVER ART BY FRANK MILLER AND KLAUS JANSON.

Wolfman's story in *Daredevil* vol. 1 #131 (1976), drawn by Bob Brown and Klaus Janson, introducing Marvel Comics' super-assassin. Bullseye, whose impeccable aim enables him to strike vital areas with deadly accuracy, chucked a potential career as a pro baseball pitcher for the military, acquiring a bloodlust while a solider in Vietnam. After a post-war stint as an African mercenary, he arrives in New York, garbed in a blue-black bodysuit with white concentric bull's-eye circles (a costume designed by John Romita, Sr.), slaughtering a man—with a pen to the neck!—who refused to pay him to spare his life. The blind superhero Daredevil becomes involved, and while the Man without Fear's radar sense allows him to anticipate and counter his foe's maneuvers, Bullseye nonetheless proves a relentless adversary.

Bullseye is wildly psychotic, a condition worsened in earlier appearances by a brain tumor, and obsessively arrogant. His defeats in his first encounters with Daredevil sullied his standing as the premier killer-for-hire, causing his inimical fixation upon the hero.

"A lovely night for a murder, isn't it?" Bullseye smugly asked Daredevil's former girlfriend, the Black Widow, as he attacked her with common household items such as a hairbrush and a hairdryer cord, using her as bait to fish the Man without Fear into conflict, in writer Roger McKenzie and penciler Frank Miller's "In the Hands of Bullseye" in *Daredevil* #160 (1979). It was in Miller's hands that Bullseye would become legend; Miller took over the series as plotter in 1980 and scripter in 1981 for a celebrated writer/artist run. Miller's landmark issue #181 (1982) featured a battle between a scornful Bullseye and Daredevil's love Elektra, who had assumed Bullseye's former role as the crimelord Kingpin's go-to assassin. Bullseye murdered Elektra, skewering her with her own sai, and the ensuing grudge match between the marksman and a retributive Daredevil left Bullseye with a shattered spine.

After recovering, Bullseye's hostility toward Daredevil grew, and their clashes became more brutal. In *Daredevil* vol. 2 #5 (1999), Bullseye struck another blow at his foe by murdering the hero's ex-girlfriend Karen Page—using Daredevil's own weapon, his billy club.

For years, Bullseye's origin and real name were secret, and he preferred it that way, allowing his codename and his reputation to be his calling card, although he had occasionally used the pseudonym "Benjamin Poindexter." Daredevil hinted at his knowledge of Bullseye's past by calling the killer "Lester" in writer Brian Michael Bendis and artist Alex Maleev's *Daredevil* vol. 2 #49 (2003); in that tale, an angry Daredevil knifes a bull's-eye scar into his enemy's forehead, a look paralleling actor Colin Farrell's non-costumed Bullseye from the 2003 live-action *Daredevil* movie (Bullseye has since parroted that look in the comic books). The 2004–2005 miniseries *Bullseye: Greatest Hits* offered more information into the villain's past, including revelations of a former stint as an assassin for the National Security Agency. Bullseye action figures have been produced in the 2000s. —*ME*

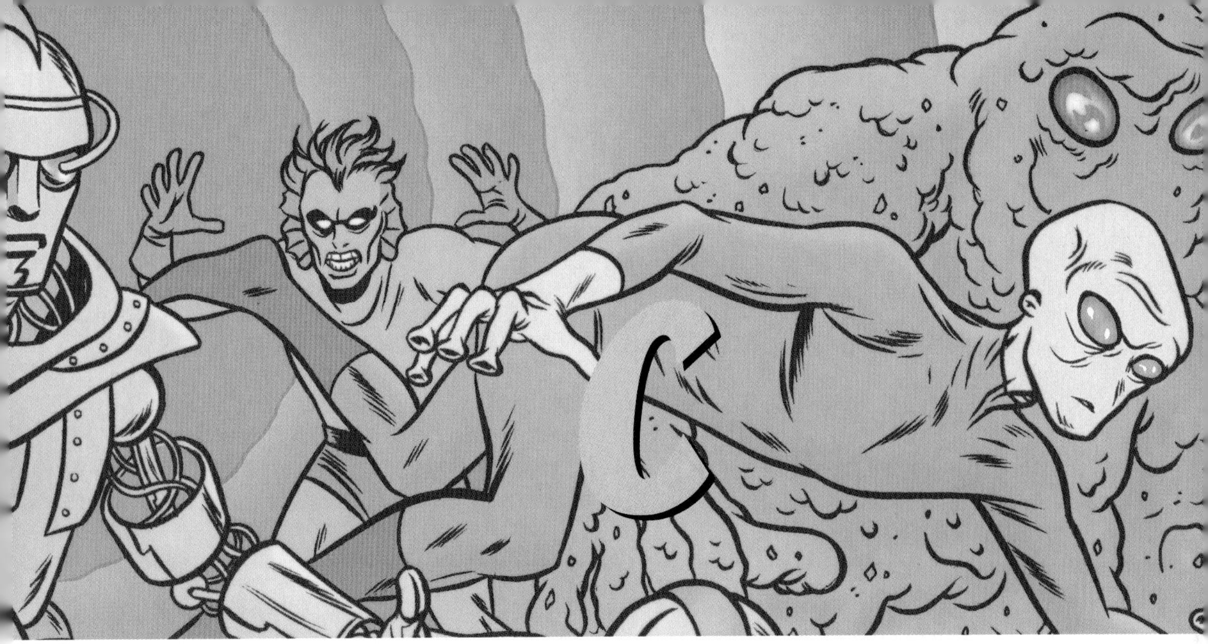
C

The Calculator

The Calculator, DC Comics' master of data accumulation, debuted in *Detective Comics* #463 (1976) in a six-page adventure starring the Atom, "Crimes by Calculation," by writer Bob Rozakis and artist Mike Grell. The villain's vivid uniform (designed by Grell) of purple-and-white tights with an LCD forehead visor and a chest keyboard was more than a bold fashion statement: it housed a computer that allowed its wearer to calculate crucial info, predict attacks, and deduce weaknesses, keeping the Calculator one step ahead of his opponents. In the Atom's burg of Ivy Town, the Calculator plans to pilfer a machine that stops earthquakes. By typing commands into his chestplate keyboard, he emits solid-energy objects through his visor, confounding the Tiny Titan until the Atom finally overcomes this new foe. At story's end, the crafty Calculator is already plotting to challenge another superhero.

The Calculator "started with the idea of a villain who would battle the various back-up [feature] heroes in *Detective*," recalled Rozakis in a 2005 interview in *BACK ISSUE* magazine. For the next four issues the Calculator returned in short stories starring Black Canary, the Elongated Man, and Green Arrow, culminating in issue #468's (1977) full-length tale—written by Rozakis and illustrated by Marshall Rogers and Terry Austin—uniting those "back-up heroes" and the star of *Detective*, Batman. These popular appearances earned the Calculator the number-two position (behind the Joker) in a 1978 DC Comics supervillains poll.

That momentum was ill spent, however, as the Calculator was seen sporadically over the next 25 years, his outings often relegated to skirmishes with minor-league heroes like Air Wave, Blue Beetle, and Hero Hotline. Creator Rozakis had planned to eventually reveal the identity of the man behind the LCD mask, but circumstances prohibited his doing so.

Outside of the occasional walk-on or fan roast, the Calculator slipped into obscurity until he was refurbished in the DC Comics miniseries *Identity Crisis* (2004–2005), scripted by best-selling novelist Brad Meltzer. Retiring his flamboyant costume for an ordinary shirt and tie, the Calculator became the evil equivalent of superhero information-broker Oracle, selling secrets to criminals and supervillains for a fee. Having unmasked the Calculator, Meltzer christened him Noah Kuttler, in actuality the name of one of the author's friends. In the six-issue miniseries *Villains United* (2005), the Calculator joined mega-menaces Lex Luthor, Deathstroke, Talia, Black Adam, and Dr. Psycho in a sinister society dedicated to waging war against DC's crusaders ... and other supervillains. —*ME*

Captain Boomerang

Writer John Broome and artist Carmine Infantino first tossed the rebounding reprobate Captain Boomerang into DC Comics' *The Flash* vol. 1 #117 (1960). He is actually Australian malcontent George "Digger" Harkness, a master boomerang thrower, who is hired by toymaker W. W. Wiggins (in later continuity revealed to be Digger's father) to demonstrate the toy that Wiggins anticipates to be the next big (play)thing: the boomerang. Gallivanting about in a pointed cap and a blue smock adorned with white boomerang logos, Harkness becomes "Captain Boomerang," flamboyantly demonstrating Wiggins' product to a disinterested audience. During a showing in Central City, Captain Boomerang tries his hand as a pickpocket, attracting the attention of the second Flash. Suckering the Scarlet Speedster with a sneak boomerang attack, Harkness gets a taste of supervillainy, but only briefly, as the Flash soon pitches him into custody.

Captain Boomerang spun back quickly, in issue #124 (1961), with a giant boomerang onto which the Flash was strapped and catapulted into the heavens—but with his ability to vibrate at superspeed through most bonds, the Fastest Man Alive was a hard man to hold.

A frequent Flash foe, Captain Boomerang's array of elaborate trick boomerangs included sonic, exploding, metal-piercing, and smokescreen variations. Harkness' physical appearance, in his Silver Age (1956–1969) stories rendered by Infantino, was far from intimidating—with his wild brown mane and receding hairline, he vaguely resembled Larry Fine of the Three Stooges—yet his proficiency with his weapons and his patented immorality made him a substantial threat. He often teamed with other supervillains as one of the Flash's Rogues' Gallery, and during the 1970s he served a stint with the Secret Society of Super-Villains. After the Flash died in 1985's *Crisis on Infinite Earths* #8, Captain Boomerang began to attack the hero's successor, Flash III.

Captain Boomerang, in DC's *Legends* miniseries (1986–1987), was enlisted by the U.S. government into the Suicide Squad, a group of paroled supervillains assigned to life-threatening missions. While an unruly teammate, Captain Boomerang was a valuable asset to the Squad, appearing in most of the 66 issues of the group's own series (1987–1992); during his Squad service, he briefly moonlighted as a criminal, plagiarizing the guise of fellow felon Mirror Master. A streamlined version of the Squad was adapted to animation in the 2005 "Task Force X" episode of the Cartoon Network's *Justice League Unlimited*, with Donal Gibson as Captain Boomerang; Boomerang later returned as one of the series' Legion of Doom.

Like the throwing device from which he derives his name, Captain Boomerang keeps coming back, with death not even slowing him. He was one of several Flash villains who made an unfortunate deal with the demon Neron in the *Underworld Unleashed* crossover (1995), forfeiting his life and pillaging Earth sans soul, although the Flash helped restore his spirit. After more Flash clashes Harkness met his demise in a bloody gun brawl with Jack Drake, father of Batman's ally Robin III (Tim Drake), in *Identity Crisis* #5 (2004). Harkness' long-lost son Owen Mercer then assumed the family mantle as the new Captain Boomerang, the villain with the superspeed throwing arm, inspiring a 2006 action figure. As seen in the "Rogue War" story arc in the pages of *Flash* vol. 2 #220–#225 (2005), efforts by several criminal colleagues to reanimate Harkness' decaying body may signal his return. —*ME*

Captain Cold

Captain Cold, the first major adversary of the Silver Age (1956–1969) Flash, made his chilling debut in *Showcase* #8 (1957), the second tryout issue for the Fastest Man Alive. In "The Coldest Man on Earth!" by writer John Broome and artist Carmine Infantino, "ambitious crook" Leonard "Len" Snart fancies putting Central City's new superhero on ice. Breaking into a nuclear facility under the cloak of night, Snart intends to irradiate a pistol of his own design as an anti-Flash weapon, but is surprised when his weapon instead emits a freezing ray. Fashioning a blue-and-white uniform with a parka and donning snow goggles, he considers the adversarial appellations "Mr. Arctic," "Cold Wave," Sub-Zero," and "Human Icicle" before selecting "Captain Cold." From his Cold Chamber, a sub-freezing hideout, he fuels his Cold Gun with liquid helium and initiates a wintry snap—in July! The fleet-footed Flash is on the skids thanks to Captain Cold's manufactured ice slicks, but he creates a succession of superspeed after-images to confuse his foe, capturing Snart.

With his weapon's ability to produce blustery mirages, slippery slopes, and ice-block prisons, this "Master of Cold" was routinely thawed out to battle the Scarlet Speedster, and occasionally teamed up with his climate antithesis Heat Wave as well as the conniving Trickster. Captain Cold and other Flash felons banded together for the first of many assembled appearances in *The Flash* #155 (1965). In the 1970s he joined the roster of the Secret Society of Super-Villains and was recruited into the Suicide Squad in the late 1980s.

Snart's sister Lisa followed her brother's snowy footprints into crime in *The Flash* #250 (1977), becoming the Golden Glider, with anti-gravity skates that slid upon ice of their own making, but she later perished when her sidekick Chillblaine turned against her. In 1978, Captain Cold made his television debut as one of the Legion of Doom in *Challenge of the Super Friends* (1978), his voice provided by Dick Ryal. Michael Champion played a non-costumed Captain Cold, a hitman who froze his victims, in an episode of the live-action TV series *The Flash* (1990–1991).

When the Silver Age Flash (Barry Allen) died in *Crisis on Infinite Earths* #8 (1986), Snart temporarily mothballed his Captain Cold guise and became a bounty hunter, but he later sold his soul to the demonic Neron for increased powers. Snart returned to villainy, and he remains one of the bitterest opponents of Wally West, the current Flash.

Frosty footnote: while the Golden Age (1938–1954) supervillain the Icicle's 1947 debut predated the similarly themed Captain Cold, the captain premiered before DC Comics' most famous ice-based bad guy, Mr. Freeze, first seen (as Mr. Zero) in *Batman* #121 (1959). —*ME*

Captain Nazi

The embodiment of evils both imaginary and real, "master race" menace Captain Nazi premiered, appropriately, in Fawcett's *Master Comics* #21 (bearing the cryptic cover date of December 1941), in a tale by William Woolfolk and Mac Raboy. The scar-faced Aryan underneath the Swastika-emblazoned green uniform is Albrecht Krieger, son of a German scientist whose astounding "Miracle Food" energizes Albrecht into a superpowered (strength, speed, and endurance) emissary of Adolf Hitler. Captain Nazi is sent to the United States to blitzkrieg Captain Marvel. He next appears mere weeks later in *Whiz Comics* #25, savagely crippling newsboy Freddy Freeman—and inadvertently creating his greatest enemy. Captain Marvel sacrifices a fraction of his astonishing abilities to save Freeman, the boy in turn becoming Captain Marvel, Jr., who would, for the duration of World War II, frequently battled Captain Nazi, their last Fawcett clash occurring in 1944.

Captain Nazi was slow to return after the 1973 revival of Captain Marvel and family in the pages of DC Comics' *Shazam!* series; 1978's issue #34 resurrected the villain, and he was seldom used again until a 1994 Captain Marvel reboot. Captain Nazi was incorporated into contemporary DC continuity by writer Jerry Ordway and artist Peter Krause in *The Power of Shazam!* #6 (1995), in which, as in the Golden Age (1938–1954), his rampage resulted in the creation of Captain Marvel, Jr. Captain Nazi sightings in the twenty-first century have been rare, although he has attempted to resurrect Hitler and has encountered the Joker and the Birds of Prey. Whereas many supervillains' motivations are ambiguous, Captain Nazi is undeniably a force for evil, and his unholy alliance with Lex Luthor's Society in 2005's *Villains United* miniseries proves that he will ally with others to keep the Führer's spirit alive. —*ME*

Captain Planet's Eco-Villains

Toxic terrorists exist who conspire to pollute our skies and waters. The "greenest" of superheroes, Captain Planet, and his teenage aides the Planeteers—seen in the animated television series *Captain Planet and the Planeteers* (1990–1996) and *The New Adventures of Captain Planet* (2003)—fight valiantly to safeguard Earth's environment from these contemptible Eco-Villains:

The sexy but sadistic scientist Dr. Blight, originally a biochemist specializing in chemical weapons, has created destructive bio-beasts and an acrimonious computer named MAL. Meg Ryan—yes, *that* Meg Ryan—was her voice during *Captain Planet*'s initial season.

Duke Nukem knows how to light up a room—with lethal radiation. A living nuclear battery with a red Mohawk and grotesque yellow hide, "the Duke" is sworn to reshape the world into a nuclear wasteland. *Quantum Leap*'s Dean Stockwell was the first actor to play him.

Blissfully profiting by dumping toxic waste where it doesn't belong, Sly Sludge slithers in and out of the law's eye, leaving gunk behind. Decked out in protective coveralls, Sludge, originally voiced by Martin Sheen, is assisted by a bellyaching sidekick named Ooze.

The slovenly Hoggish Greedly, portrayed by Edward Asner, is a human/boar hybrid who pigs out on the planet's natural resources. His voracious appetite is never sated, no matter how many woodlands or species he improvidently engulfs. Greedly is accompanied by a lamebrain lackey named Rigger.

Verminous Skumm is a sewer-spawned monstrosity who schemes to infest the world with pandemonium. A 7-and-a-half-feet-tall rodent-man with a snaking tail, this miscreant dresses in tatters and exudes pestilence. Among the actors playing Skumm was Jeff Goldblum.

The underhanded tempter Zarm is duplicity personified: he can appear as a benign figure or a menacing warlord, whichever best suits his purposes. Zarm often plays the Planeteers against each other through trickery. He has been voiced by a virtual who's who of talent: Sting, David Warner, and Malcolm McDowell.

Looten Plunder, originally performed by James Coburn, helms a global corporate domain erected on the remains of trampled habitats. A reprehen-

sible controller, he puppets a private army led by killer commando Argos Bleak. Always impeccably dressed, Plunder audaciously festoons his jackets with endangered-species pelts.

Most of these Eco-Villains were included in Tiger Toys' 1992 Captain Planet action-figure line. —ME

Carnage

Cletus Kasady was bad news long before becoming Carnage, the Spider-Man foe with the bloodbath M.O. The creation of writer David Michelinie, this convicted mass murderer was first seen in *The Amazing Spider-Man* vol. 1 #344–#345 (1991) as the cellmate of Eddie Brock, the brutish felon who had melded with an alien symbiote to become Venom. Barely in his twenties, Kasady, the product of parental abuse and neglect, is serving hard time for eleven savage murders, including those of his father and several classmates. When the Venom symbiote breaks Brock out of prison to re-bond with its host, this otherworldly entity spawns an offspring that merges with Kasady. In issue #361 (1992) by Michelinie and artist Mark Bagley, the results of that union are evidenced when Spidey faces Kasady in his new, grotesque form: Carnage, the superstrong slaughterer.

Mightier than Spider-Man and Venom combined, the astoundingly lithe Carnage could weave webs, adhere to and climb surfaces, and fashion ejectable and elongating weapons, including blades and snares, from his blood-red costume. While nearly unstoppable, the symbiote that empowered Carnage showed vulnerability to sonic vibrations and extreme heat. After his original 1992 slash-clash with Spider-Man, the supervillain serial killer returned in 1993 in the mega-part "Maximum Carnage" storyline and clawed his way into the web-slinger's life on several other occasions; Spider-Man was forced to ally with others, from the Fantastic Four to Venom himself, to stop Carnage's butchery and return Kasady to the maximum-security Ravencroft Prison.

Carnage met his demise in *New Avengers* #2 (2004), when the no-nonsense superhero Sentry flew the killer into space and ripped him to shreds. Continuing the lineage of the original Venom symbiote is Carnage's own offspring, which overrode the body of ex-cop Pat Mulligan; this supervillain was "born" in the miniseries *Venom vs. Carnage* (2004), then headlined a six-issue 2005 Marvel miniseries bearing his name: *Toxin*.

An alternate incarnation of Carnage was introduced in the 2000s in the pages of *Ultimate Spider-Man*, the reimagining of the wall-crawler's adventures. Ultimate Carnage, co-created by artist Bagley and writer Brian Michael Bendis, is not an alien but rather the genetic creation of Dr. Curt (the Lizard) Connors. In the Ultimate Marvel Universe, Carnage massacred Peter's friend Gwen Stacy.

Scott Cleverdon voiced Carnage in the multi-episode "Sins of the Father" arc in the FOX Kids animated *Spider-Man* series (1994–1998). Carnage has been featured in 1994 and 2000 video games as well as Toy Biz action figures, including a gruesome 2005 Ultimate Carnage figure accompanied by a shriveled corpse of Gwen Stacy. —*ME*

Catman

C atman—no relation to the Golden Age (1938–1954) superhero of the same name—pounced into *Detective Comics* #311 (1963). Writer Bill Finger and artist Jim Mooney present jungle-cat trapper Thomas Blake, who pilfers a Polynesian feline idol and its ceremonial drapery, artifacts that reputedly give their owner nine lives. A blasé Gotham City socialite burdened by gambling debts, Blake entertains the notion of becoming a crime fighter like Batman but instead chooses the path of the Caped Crusader's adversary Catwoman, pulling heists as the "Feline Freebooter," Cat-Man (original spelling).

Prancing in a tawdry orange-and-yellow costume (with a "CM" chest insignia) through a handful of feline-inspired capers riddled with cat-puns and cat-weapons (Cat-Man drove Cat-car, wore cat-clawed gloves, used a catapult, owned a pet panther, and carried a kit-bag instead of a utility belt), Cat-Man's tales often read like lackluster Catwoman stories—without the sexual tension of the Bat/Cat relationship. Interesting, however, was Cat-Man's ability to cheat death, an "invulnerabil-

ity" afforded him by his cape, cut from the Polynesian cloth he discovered in his origin tale.

A 1993 attempt to reinvent the character as a serial killer was ignored by later writers who followed Finger and Mooney's lead. Even the producers of the animated *The Adventures of Batman & Robin* loosely adapted Cat-Man's 1963 origin in "Cult of the Cat," a 1998 episode casting Scott Cleverdon as Blake—but *not* as Cat-Man. By the time Cat-Man crawled out of the litter box of limbo in *Green Arrow* #16–#17 (2002), Blake was a paunchy putz under the Shade's hire, and after a manhandling by the cantankerous bowman, limped away to lick his wounds.

Writer Gail Simone and artist Dale Eaglesham retooled Catman (now spelled without the hyphen) in the six-issue miniseries *Villains United* (2005). Gone was Blake's blubber—the scantily clothed, acutely muscled thief was now an unshaven hottie with rock-star hair and ghastly claw scars on his bare chest, communing with lions in the Medikwe Game Preserve. Blake returned to civilization to join the Secret Six, standing in opposition to a congress of supervillains led by Lex Luthor, against whom Blake harbored a grudge. At odds with fellow Sixer Deadshot, Catman now wears a modified, muted version of his original costume, to which he has added a lethal set of machete-like claws. His cape's former property to grant him nine lives (most of which he had depleted in the previous continuity) is apparently being ignored in the 2000s. —*ME*

Catwoman

P rowling along the back-alley fence dividing good and evil while unpredictably playing both sides to suit her purposes, the slinky, kinky Catwoman—aka the Princess of Plunder, the Feline Fatale, and the Mistress of Malevolence—was envisioned as a copycat of Batman. Remarked Batman's originator and first artist, Bob Kane, of the villainess he co-created with Bill Finger, "We also thought that male readers would appreciate a sensual woman to look at."

Modeling her after actress Hedy Lamarr, Kane's first rendition of the raven-haired vixen—as "the Cat" in *Batman* #1 (1940)—was not in form-

Catwoman: Nine Lives of a Feline Fatale trade paperback
©2004 DC Comics.
COVER ART BY BRIAN BOLLAND.

didn't own what she liked, she'd take it, as Gotham's cat burglar extraordinaire. She scratched her way through a decade's worth of stories before "The Secret Life of Catwoman" in *Batman* #62 (1950) revealed her true stripes. Knocked unconscious while performing the non-villainous act of saving Batman's life, Catwoman came to with no recollection of her past lives as airline stewardess Selina Kyle or Queen of Crime Catwoman. Aiding Batman and Gotham Police Commissioner Gordon in their apprehension her former criminal partner, Kyle was pardoned and tried the straight and narrow as a pet-shop proprietor. Before long, in *Detective Comics* #203 (1954), taunts from the press and the underworld seduced her back into the larcenous nightlife.

Playing off of Batman's bat-inspired arsenal, Catwoman's weaponry included her customized, cat-shaped "kitty car," "catplane," and "catboat"; a crime-escaping "cat-apult"; a throwable "catarang"; and a secret lair called her Catacomb, overrun with enough felines to fill the Gotham Humane Society. While those gimmicks have been litter-boxed in the twenty-first century, Catwoman's signature weapon remains her "cat-o'-nine-tails" whip, which she cracks with painful accuracy—and if that fails, Catwoman is an agile combatant, hissing, punching, kicking, and scraping (with razor-sharp glove claws) her opponents. She has often seemingly perished, only to resurface, making Batman wonder, *Does Catwoman really have nine lives?*

Catwoman's wardrobe would make Mattel's Barbie (or Barbie's real-life counterpart, Paris Hilton) green with envy, with the exception of the appalling full-sized cathead disguise the Princess of Plunder donned in 1940. Her look during most of comics' Golden Age (1938–1954) was a stylish cat-eared cowl, a purple dress, and green cape, felonious fashions she pulled out of her closet for another go during the 1970s and 1980s.

The general public perhaps best recognizes Catwoman in the shimmering, skintight black cat-suit popularized by sex-kitten Julie Newmar on the live-action television series *Batman* (1966–1968). Newmar accepted the Catwoman role at the urging of her college-age brother, who informed her that *Batman* was a huge hit among Harvard students. The show's campus appeal no doubt increased when the gorgeous Newmar

fitting Lycra, as one might expect, but instead in a green gown, her curvaceous shape (presumably) accentuated by a torpedo bra and girdle. "What's the matter? Haven't you ever seen a pretty girl before?" she snaps at Batman as he foils her purloining of Gotham's rich and famous on a luxury yacht. Usually careful not to get too close to his foes—except when delivering a well-deserved haymaker—Batman allows the Cat to embrace him, as she flirtatiously offers half of her ill-gotten gain at the suggestion of a … partnership, a notion that stimulates the hero's libido but repulses his ethics. Yet Batman "accidentally" allows the Cat to escape, much to his sidekick Robin the Boy Wonder's surprise, hoping to encounter her again some day. And thus the cat-and-fledermaus game begins.

For much of her career Catwoman was essentially a pretty girl who liked pretty things. And if she

Halle Berry as the Feline Fatale in *Catwoman* (2004).

teasingly commanded the camera with sensu-
ously cat-like moves that also entranced little
girls hungry for strong female role models, made
little boys squirm with prepubescent stirrings,
and lured daddies into the den for "family viewing
time." "She was the first person I was aware of
that boys wanted to be with and I wanted to be,"
said Suzan Colón, author of the light-hearted history *Catwoman: The Life and Times of a Feline
Fatale* (2003), in a 2005 made-for-DVD documentary (accompanying the DVD release of the 2004
theatrical film *Catwoman*). Newmar's purring of
Rs in her campy dialogue, especially with exaggerated words like "perrrrr-fectly," joined the pop-
culture lexicon.

Newmar's immediate successors to the part,
Lee Meriwether in the theatrical movie *Batman*
(1966) and Eartha Kitt in later episodes of the
television series, each held their own, but it is
Newmar who best defined the role with her
untouchable performance. The casting of African-
American Kitt as Catwoman in *Batman*'s third sea-

son raised eyebrows in the racially charged United
States of the late 1960s, but in later, more enlight-
ened years has become acknowledged as a historically significant move. During the spate of Batman
merchandising inspired by the show, Catwoman
was seen on numerous Batman items, but usually
in her comic-book interpretation, although Newmar's first Catwoman episode was adapted to
handheld "toy" viewing for Batman View-Master
reels and See-a-Show filmstrips.

CBS's *The Batman/Superman Hour*
(1968–1969) and *The Adventures of Batman and
Robin* (1969–1970) brought Catwoman to
Saturday-morning television after the live-action
show was canceled. During this period, comics'
Catwoman slipped into a green-hued version of the
Newmar suit, followed by a skintight blue bodysuit
with a bouncy cat tail; this latter costume was the
basis for 1970s Catwoman figures produced by toy
manufacturer Mego. Meanwhile, the Feline Fatale
returned to the tube in *The New Adventures of Batman* (1977–1978).

Catfights

While Catwoman is the unquestionable queen of catfights—she's mixed it up with everyone from Lois Lane to Batgirl to Sharon Stone!—some of her sinister sisters have sharpened their claws and embraced their inner witches for comics' greatest grudge matches.

- **Cheetah vs. Wonder Woman**: From her early days as a pampered rich girl in feline-spotted "pajamas" to her current incarnation as a werewolf-like cat-woman, the Cheetah has meted out revenge against the Amazon Princess since 1943. With the strength and cunning of a jungle cat, this supervixen even eliminated her competition—a *male* Cheetah—to keep Wonder Woman as her exclusive territory.

- **Deathbird vs. Ms. Marvel/Binary**: Forget claws—Deathbird of Marvel's Shi'Ar Empire has deadly talons, which can slice through glass … plus her 18-foot wingspan and ability to bench press 6 tons makes her one formidable femme. While Deathbird has allied with the X-Men, she has not gotten along with the superheroine Ms. Marvel, their enmity dating back to their first clash in 1977 and continuing on to the do-gooder's later identity of Binary.

- **Blackfire vs. Starfire:** With a name like Komand'r, is it any wonder that Blackfire, a native of Tamaran, became its warrior queen? Blackfire's intense jealousy of her little sister Starfire led to their mutual capture and transformation into super-siblings, and since 1982 these battling sisters have broken nails and bones in their tussles, including an outer-space scuffle in 2006.

- **Titania vs. She-Hulk:** During Marvel's Secret Wars storyline (1984–1985), superstrong Titania beat green giantess She-Hulk into a coma, and ever since it's been duck-and-cover for passersby whenever these two cross paths. One of the most unusual sites for one of their battles was a lingerie shop, where they tangled in 1992.

- **Talia vs. Scandal**: *Villains United* #6 (2005) featured a killer catfight between the offspring of two immortals: Ra's al Ghul's daughter Talia, and Vandal Savage's daughter Scandal. While others "scrabble in the dirt," these two rogues of royalty dueled in honor of their fathers.

In the late 1970s, Batman and Catwoman wed—on "Earth-Two," the parallel reality populated by Golden Age DC Comics characters—and produced a daughter, Helena, who became the superhero the Huntress after the Earth-Two Catwoman was murdered (while the Huntress in twenty-first-century DC continuity is not the daughter of Batman and Catwoman, the Huntress of TV's live-action 2002–2003 series *Birds of Prey* was).

After infrequent 1970s comic-book appearances, Catwoman fared better in the early to mid-1980s, becoming a semi-regular character in *Batman* and *Detective*, often appearing as the reformed Selina Kyle, or fighting alongside Batman as Catwoman. The Joker, unimpressed with Catwoman's change of heart, re-criminalized her in a disturbing experiment in *Detective* #569–#570 (1986–1987)—just in time for Catwoman to get a major reboot.

Frank Miller and David Mazzucchelli's "Batman: Year One" storyline in *Batman* #404–#407 (1987) reintroduced both the Dark Knight and the Feline Fatale. The product of a violent family, Selina Kyle and her sister were sent to a juvenile center after their mother's suicide. Selina ran away to live on the streets during her teens, surviving by any means possible, including prostitution. After witnessing the nascent Batman in action, Kyle was inspired by his disguise and adopted one of her own, donning a gray leather catsuit and whip and becoming the burglar Catwoman, preying upon Gotham's social elite. A 1989 four-issue *Catwoman* miniseries followed.

Cinema once again made Catwoman a household name in 1992 in director Tim Burton's *Batman Returns*. Michelle Pfeiffer portrayed Selina Kyle, a mega-abused headcase who found liberation in death, being reanimated by alleycats that imbued her with a mystical feline spirit and catlike reflexes. Annette Bening was originally cast in the role but dropped out after becoming pregnant, and actress Sean Young, dressed in a cat-costume, made a much-publicized but unsuccessful lobby for the part. Pfeiffer stole the picture in her body-hugging black catsuit, relishing in Catwoman's propensity for toying with her male opponents (after sucker-punching Batman by feigning feminine weakness, she gloated, "I'm a woman and can't be taken for granted. Life's a bitch, now so am I!").

Pfeiffer's Catwoman was softened for kid-friendly television as the Princess of Plunder, in a gray cat-costume and voiced by Adrienne Barbeau, was a recurring character in the acclaimed *Batman: The Animated Series* (1992–1995) and its continuation *The Adventures of Batman & Robin* (1997–1999). Throughout the 1990s, there was no shortage of Catwoman merchandising, based upon the Pfeiffer, animated, and comic-book interpretations of the character, from action figures marketed to boys to dolls and purses targeting girls. DC Comics awarded Catwoman her own monthly series, *Catwoman* vol. 2, which ran 94 issues between 1993 and 2001. She also co-starred in a 1997 crossover with Vampirella and a 1998 miniseries with DC superhero Wildcat, who taught her boxing skills.

Mere months after the cancellation of her series, DC's monthly *Catwoman* vol. 3 was launched with a January 2002 cover date. Catwoman has returned to her black catsuit, albeit with goggles that resemble large cat eyes; her ensemble is also loaded with combative and wall-scaling gear including retractable claws and spring-action boot pistons. In her two monthly comics series, as well as a number of spin-off miniseries and the 2002 graphic novel *Catwoman: Selina's Big Score* (by Darwyn Cooke), Catwoman has become a contemporary Robin Hood. She protects the downtrodden in Gotham's poverty-ridden East End, working with private eye Slam Bradley (a one-time paramour) and Dr. Leslie Thompkins to aid the needy that fall under the radar of police protection. She has become an ally of Batman, and the sexual tension between Cat and Bat continues, although the Dark Knight knows that despite her newfound heroism, this girl's eye can sometimes be distracted by a bright, shiny plaything. Catwoman remains adept at playing both sides: in a 2005 *Catwoman* story arc, she allied with supervillains including the Cheetah, Hush, and Captain Cold to destroy from the inside their aspirations to control the East End.

A *Batman Returns* spin-off *Catwoman* film languished in development for years but finally made it to the screen in 2004. Michelle Pfeiffer turned down the chance to reprise her role; Ashley Judd was at first considered to play Catwoman (as was, reportedly, Nicole Kidman), but Oscar-winner Halle Berry was tapped for the tights. *Catwoman* built upon *Batman Returns* continuity by establishing that a cult of Catwomen had existed for eons (Pfeiffer's Kyle was one). After Berry's character, sheepish advertising artist Patience Phillips, took a fatal spill, she was "breathed" back to life by felines; as Catwoman, she tangled with femme fatale Laurel Hedare (Sharon Stone), a catty businesswoman whose age-defying beauty product had sinister side effects. *Catwoman* suffered from a crippling pre-release backlash from comic-book fans that rejected Berry's streetwalker-like costume (with its abnormally large, helmet-sized catcowl) and the movie's deviation from comic-book mythology. Filmed for an estimated $85 million, *Catwoman* limped through an embarrassing $16 million opening weekend and a total U.S. gross of $40 million.

While the film died at the box office, remember, Catwoman has eight more lives. She strutted onto the tube again in the WB's animated *The Batman* (2004–present), with Gina Gershon playing the part, and continues to tantalize comic-book readers and toy collectors. —ME

Chameleon

The Chameleon is one of Spider-Man's long-standing villains. As his name suggests, he is a master of deceit and disguise and one of Spidey's most illusive enemies. He was introduced in *The Amazing Spider-Man* vol. 1 #1 (1963), penned by Stan Lee and illustrated by Steve Ditko, although the creative team never gave Chameleon an alter ego or explained his background in detail. Years later, writer J. M. DeMatteis established the Chameleon as Russian Dmitri Smerdyakov, after a character in Dostoevsky's *The Brothers Karamazov*, who as a boy was servant and half-brother to the abusive Kraven the Hunter. Eventually, Smerdyakov immigrated to the United States, adopting the Chameleon identity and impersonating Spider-Man during his first crime spree.

Chameleon eventually learned Spider-Man's secret identity and has attacked him through his family and friends, including Parker's wife, Mary Jane Watson.

The Chameleon first wore a blank face-mask to conceal his identity, a stylistic device that was a forerunner to that of the hero the Question created by Ditko for Charlton Comics after his *Amazing Spider-Man* run. Originally, the Chameleon used only makeup and costumes to impersonate his victims. Later, he obtained holographic technology that allowed him to alter his appearance. Later still, the Chameleon ingested an experimental serum that rendered his skin malleable and turned his face virtually featureless, like his original mask. He began wearing costumes made of "memory material" that can be altered by electrical impulses to resemble other people's clothing.

After the suicide of the original Kraven in 1987, the Chameleon sought vengeance on Spider-Man but began losing his sanity. Ultimately the Chameleon attempted to commit suicide by throwing himself off a bridge (in *Webspinners* #12, 1999), somehow surviving and ending up in an insane asylum. Since then he joined the Green Goblin's team of supervillains, the Sinister Twelve (2005). He appeared briefly in TV animation in the "Hulk" episode of the series *The Marvel Super-Heroes* (1966) and in the *Spider-Man* series (1994–1998). Rumors that the Chameleon would appear in the live-action film *Spider-Man 3* swept fandom in mid-2005 but proved unfounded. —*GM*

Charaxes: *See* **Killer Moth**

Cheetah

The most persistent foe of Wonder Woman, the felonious—and feline—Cheetah has plagued DC Comics' heroine for over sixty years. The first Cheetah debuted in the pages of *Wonder Woman* vol. 1 #6 (1943) in a story written by William Moulton Marston (as Charles Moulton) and rendered by Harry G. Peter. Priscilla Rich was a spoiled society girl whose inferiority complex kicked into overdrive when she was upstaged at a charity benefit by Wonder Woman. Rich soon saw in the mirror a ver-

sion of herself clad in a yellow jumpsuit with tan spots, plus cat ears and claws. "I am the real you—the Cheetah—a treacherous relentless huntress!" the figure taunted her.

Over the following four decades, Cheetah faced Wonder Woman time and again in the star-spangled heroine's own title, as well as *Sensation Comics* and even the short-lived *Wonder Woman* newspaper strip (1944–1945). Mostly, Cheetah was trying to kill her rival, while Wonder Woman would return Rich again and again to the Amazons' Reform Island in an attempt to rehabilitate her.

In 1980 wealthy debutante Deborah Domaine was at the deathbed of her reclusive aunt, Priscilla Rich, but the woman was not able to tell her life-long secret before she expired. Domaine was captured by Kobra, who brainwashed her into becoming the next Cheetah. This new Cheetah dressed in a similar costume to her aunt's, complete with steel-cutting razor claws, and set out to on an agenda of radical ecological and animal rights activism/terrorism. This brought her into conflict with Wonder Woman; Cheetah later joined the Secret Society of Super-Villains, and eventually was committed to Arkham Asylum.

When writer/artist George Pérez reinvented the *Wonder Woman* comic-book series in 1987, he quickly brought Cheetah in as an adversary. This time she was Barbara Ann Minerva, a treasure hunter who discovered the secrets of African plant god Urzkartaga and of the ritual that turned her into a feral cat-person whose speed, agility, and strength were heightened, as well as her animal senses. This Cheetah didn't wear a costume but was physically transformed with razor-sharp claws, spotted fur, and a long brown mane. Cheetah was eventually turned into a demon, but Wonder Woman helped exorcize her.

The fourth and most recent Cheetah is Argentinean corporate raider Sébastian Ballesteros, a wealthy man who took on the power of Urzkartaga to become the first male Cheetah. Becoming the lover of ancient witch Circe, the two plotted Wonder Woman's end by transforming her friend Vanessa Kapatellis into the bio-weapon known as the Silver Swan. Barbara Minerva didn't take kindly to the male Cheetah, and the two clashed; it was at her hands that he apparently met his untimely demise (in a continuity retrofit, Minerva also killed the aged Priscilla Rich).

Cheetah has appeared in numerous forms in media and merchandising. She was first animated as one of the members of the Legion of Doom in the *Challenge of the Super Friends* (1978) series. She has since reappeared in the modern *Justice League* (2001–2004) and *Justice League Unlimited* series (2004–present), where, as a biologically fused half-woman half-cat, she continues to claw at Wonder Woman's last nerves. Present in most 1980s merchandising images of DC supervillains, Cheetah finally got her own bookend statue and action figures in the post-millennium years … litter box not included. —AM

Chemo

Chemo, DC Comics' towering engine of destruction, began its startling existence, innocently enough, as a vat of chemicals. Writer Robert Kanigher and artist Ross Andru's *Showcase* #39 (1962), featuring the third appearance of the robotic superheroes the Metal Men, introduces Professor Ramsey Norton, a chemist feverishly determined to eradicate world hunger and disease. Storing the by-products of his failed experiments in a 10-foot humanoid-shaped plastic test tube he nicknames "Chemo," Norton disposes of an organic plant compound into his synthetic mix. Its introduction sparks a chain reaction that imbues Chemo with a primitive sentience. Its toxic contents hissing and gurgling with each of its lumbering steps, Chemo enlarges in size and discharges a lethal chemical spray that kills the professor. The leviathan tromps into the city on a Godzilla-like single-minded mission to eradicate everything in its path. The Metal Men narrowly defeat Chemo by trapping it in a cavernous natural-gas prison.

Boasting the abilities to grow to over 100 feet tall and spew deadly compounds, Chemo has managed to repeatedly return to menace the Metal Men and has even threatened the prodigious Superman. In a 1987 Superman/Metal Men team-up, the Man of Steel was temporarily mutated into a Chemo duplicate after exposure to industrial refuse. The Suicide Squad dispatched

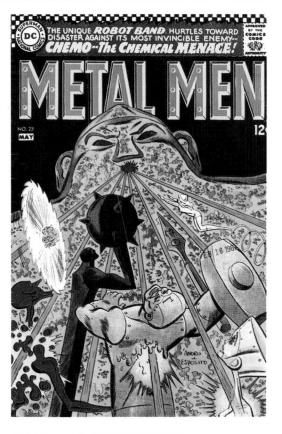

Metal Men vol. 1 #25 ©1967 DC Comics.
COVER ART BY ROSS ANDRU AND MIKE ESPOSITO.

Chemo against the despot Imperiex in the 2001 crossover *Our Worlds at War*, and Chemo was dropped as a living bomb on the city of Blüdhaven in *Batman* #649 (2006). With its uncanny knack for regeneration, however, Chemo may be impossible to permanently defeat. —ME

Cheshire

The highly accomplished international mercenary and assassin Cheshire was introduced in *The New Teen Titans Annual* #2 (1983) in a story written by Marv Wolfman and rendered by George Pérez, as Jade, an orphan of French-Vietnamese heritage who is doomed to a life of slavery until she murders her master and is unofficially adopted by ex-Blackhawk member Wen Ch'ang. Ch'ang teaches Jade the subtler points of the art of guerilla warfare, including skilled hand-to-hand combat. After she couples this talent with an education in mercenary arts and the craft of poison, which she gains from her brief marriage to Kruen Musenda, the Spitting Cobra, Jade emerges as killer-for-hire Cheshire.

The self-determined Cheshire can hold her own in a fight with any hero; as a triple-jointed acrobat she can tangle with—and conquer—the most lithe. She has also been known to conceal poison in her razor-sharp fingernails, giving her that extra edge in combat. She has continually battled the Teen Titans, the all-girl hero group Birds of Prey, and—with fellow vixens the Cheetah and Poison Ivy—Wonder Woman. The wild-haired villainess has led the Ravens, an all-female supervillain team. Never one for maternal instincts, Cheshire gave custody of her daughter Lian to Roy Harper (the hero Arsenal), with whom she had a brief affair.

Although she spent time incarcerated while awaiting a crimes-against-humanity charge for detonating a nuclear device in the Middle Eastern country Qurac, in 2005 Cheshire resurfaced in the DC miniseries *Villains United*, as one of the Secret Six. She had an affair with fellow Sixer Catman and taunted that she might be carrying his child. After betraying her teammates to Lex Luthor's Society, Cheshire took a bullet to the chest courtesy of Deathstroke the Terminator, who remarked, "We don't need any traitors in the Society." —*GM*

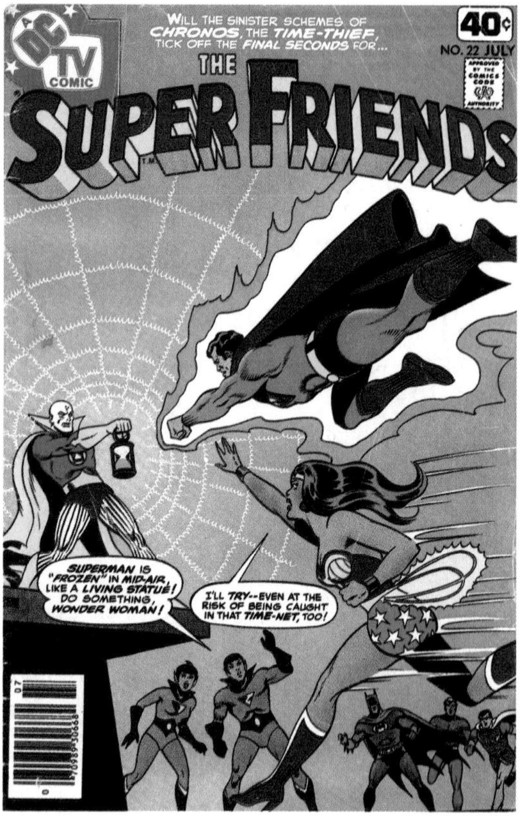
WILL THE SINISTER SCHEMES OF CHRONOS, THE TIME-THIEF, TICK OFF THE FINAL SECONDS FOR...
DC TV COMIC
40¢
NO. 22 JULY
THE SUPER FRIENDS
SUPERMAN IS "FROZEN" IN MID-AIR, LIKE A LIVING STATUE! DO SOMETHING, WONDER WOMAN!
I'LL TRY--EVEN AT THE RISK OF BEING CAUGHT IN THAT TIME-NET, TOO!

Super Friends #22 ©1979 DC Comics.
COVER ART BY RAMONA FRADON.

Chronos

None of the foes of the world's smallest superhero, the Atom, has given him a harder time than Chronos. First seen in Gardner Fox and Gil Kane's "The Time Trap" in *The Atom* #3 (1962), jailed larcenist David Clinton—whose face artist Kane patterned after former U.S. vice president Richard Nixon, who had recently lost a 1960 bid for the U.S. presidency—realizes that inadequate planning has resulted in his failures as a criminal, and zealously studies clock mechanisms in the prison workshop. Upon his reprieve, Clinton festoons himself in one of the most outlandish outfits ever seen in comics—a yellow, red, and green getup with white-and-black vertically striped tights ... and a white cowl with clock hands on the forehead! As Chronos, he takes on the Atom with time-piece weapons, trapping him inside the face of wristwatch and counting the minutes until the hero's execution, but shortly the Tiny Titan cleans Chronos' clock.

Chronos used his alarming arsenal—watches with dart-like hands, sandstorm-generating hourglasses, exploding clocks, and his sundial-shaped hover-board—in frequent battles with the Atom. He occasionally battled other superheroes, mostly through ill-fated alliances with other villains. Chronos ultimately gained limited temporal-manipulation abilities and has become quite rich by using time travel to cheat the stock market. In the 2005 "Crisis of Conscience" storyline in *JLA*, Chronos was reunited with members of the Secret Society of Super-Villains, with whom he fraternized in 1970s comics, for a full-scale assault against the Justice League of America.

Actor Peter MacNicol lent voice to Chronos in the two-part "The Once and Future Thing" episodes on the Cartoon Network's animated *Justice League Unlimited* (2003–present), in which the time thief hopped through different eras, encountering Western anti-heroes Jonah Hex and Bat Lash as well as the futuristic Dark Knight from *Batman Beyond* (1999–2001). —*ME*

The Claw

From the fecund imagination of cartoonist Jack Cole—the comics genius who gave the world Plastic Man, eye-puncturing EC horror tales, and voluptuous *Playboy* vixens—snaked his most appalling concoction, the Claw, the "Oriental demon" described by Cole's biographer (and *Maus* writer/artist) Art Spiegelman as making "Ming the Merciless look like Mother Teresa" (*Jack Cole and Plastic Man: Forms Stretched to Their Limits!*, 2001).

This adversary of the Golden Age (1938–1954) Daredevil (not to be confused with Marvel Comics' blind superhero of the same name), the Claw first terrorized humankind in *Silver Streak Comics* #1 (1939), from publisher Lev Gleason. Born in the Tibetan village ominously named Death's Head, this offspring of an Asian tyrant and a deformed (with tusk-like fangs) Caucasian murderess is orphaned during infancy and raised by villagers, who regret their decision as the boy ages. A misshapen devil with yellow skin, a reptilian-like head, gargantuan fangs, and clawed fingers, throughout his youth the Claw persecutes classmates and teachers—anyone who crosses him— "graduating" from reform school to prison, and then into the world as a warlord. Operating from a skull-shaped castle atop a Tibetan mountain, this "god of hate" sets out to "dominate the universe."

One of the few Golden Age supervillains with actual superpowers, the flame-breathing Claw cast lightning from his fingertips and grew to sky-scraper height when enraged. The Claw invaded America by drilling under the Atlantic Ocean in his boring machine, attacking New York City, where he fought Daredevil for the first time in *Silver Streak* #7 (1941); in this initial battle, the gigantic Claw actually consumed Daredevil, but a throat full of

Silver Streak Comics vol. 1 #6 ©1940 Lev Gleason. COVER ART BY JACK COLE.

dynamite forced him to cough up the hero. They waged an ongoing war for several years, the Claw assaulting Daredevil with a barrage of deathtraps, jeering "Die, swine!" with each deadly strike. The Claw joined forces with the Führer in the landmark *Daredevil* #1 (1941), aka *Daredevil Battles Hitler*.

Continuing his villainy in a solo feature beginning in *Daredevil* #2, the Claw battled a different superhero, the Ghost, for several episodes. After appearing in seven issues of *Silver Streak* and enjoying an unprecedented (for a supervillain strip) four-year run in *Daredevil*, the Claw met his demise at the hands of Daredevil in *Daredevil* #31 (1945). A brief revival attempt (*Boy Comics* #89, 1953) failed, and the Claw has remained dormant since. —*ME*

Clayface

Little did writer Bill Finger and artists Bob Kane and Jerry Robinson imagine that Clayface, the serial killer they conceived as a thinly disguised imitation of horror-movie great Boris Karloff, would over time become a brand name. *Detective Comics* #40 (1940) introduces has-been character actor Basil Karlo, a show-biz pariah due to bad publicity resulting from embarrassing off-screen antics. Infuriated over a different actor being cast in the role that made him famous, the Terror, in a remake of his classic chiller *Dread Castle*, Karlo takes the low road: hiding his identity behind a grisly clay mask and cloaking himself in a purple fedora and coat, Karlo, as Clayface, butchers the cast members one by one. Batman, hanging around the studio in his Bruce Wayne identity while visiting starlet (and then-fiancée) Julie Madison, ultimately stops the slayings. "The Murders of Clayface" was a transitional tale in the Batman canon: it maintained the shadowed moodiness of the Dark Knight's earliest exploits while intermixing the frivolity of the laughing Boy Wonder, with Robin (who bowed in *Detective* #38) marking his third appearance in print.

Scripter Finger borrowed the name of the villain he had created twenty-four years earlier by pitting Batman and Robin against "The Challenge of Clay-Face" (with hyphen) in *Detective* #298 (1961), with art by Sheldon Moldoff and Charles Paris. Karlo was forgotten, despite appearances to the contrary, as a lump-faced, purple-clad figure resembling the 1940 Clayface appeared at the home of a philanthropist. As the wealthy patron handed off a $100,000 Police Benefit Fund donation to intermediaries Batman and Robin, the mysterious figure shucked his trench coat to reveal his ghastly clay-like form (and discretely placed blue swimming trunks), giving Batman the slip by mutating into a giant snake and a living buzz-saw, then soaring away as an eagle, money in talon. This malleable marauder was actually soldier-of-fortune Matt Hagen, whose unexpected splash into a cavern's radioactive pool transmuted him into the shapeshifting super-thief Clay-Face. Batman and Robin were able to overcome Hagen only when his superpowers, which required recharging every forty-eight hours by a repeat dip, expired.

Hagen was back in *Detective* #304 (1962), and by his third outing in issue #312 (1963) the hyphen had been dropped from his name. Readers could count on a Clayface story approximately every six months, with the villain feuding with the Joker and seeping into the pages of *World's Finest Comics*—starring the team of Superman, Batman, and Robin—in which he replicated the Man of Steel and teamed with the evil android Brainiac. By the mid-1960s Clayface was mired in limbo, not seen again in comics until the late 1970s, when he returned for a handful of clashes. Throughout these appearances, readers discovered that Hagen had synthesized the pool's protoplasmic element into a potion, but its life-threatening side effects led him to rarely become Clayface—not that his frequent incarcerations would afford him the luxury of regular supervillainy.

"Clayface is Back!" trumpeted the Marshall Rogers/Terry Austin–drawn cover to *Detective* #478 (1978)—although as Batman was about to discover, this was not your father's transmutating terror. Writer Len Wein's "The Coming of … Clayface III!," illustrated by Rogers and Dick Giordano, unveiled acromegalic Preston Payne, forced into a life of segregation due to the rare disease that made him a modern-day Elephant Man. With no possible cure for his condition, Payne, with the help of convict Matt Hagen, manufactured a new Clayface serum from Hagen's blood, hoping its malleability would afford him normalcy. Instead, Payne became even more the outcast, receiving a touch of death that caused flesh to melt. His own body an unstable wax-like mush, the certifiably insane Payne was forced to wear a containment suit, his unsightly, bubbling face visible through a glass helmet. Clayface III's emergence nullified DC Comics' need to keep Hagen around: Clayface II died in action in the epic maxi-series *Crisis on Infinite Earths* (1985–1986). One of Clayface III's most celebrated stories was "Mortal Clay," by Alan Moore and George Freeman, in *Batman Annual* #11 (1987), in which the whacked-out Bat-baddie wooed a mannequin.

Clayface IV was introduced in *The Outsiders* vol. 1 #21 (1987), in "Strike Force Kobra" by Mike W. Barr and Jim Aparo. Image-conscious Sondra Fuller was unhappy with her looks, and the mastermind Kobra obliged her a makeover, transmogrifying Fuller into an upgraded version of Clayface II. Like Hagen, she appeared as a mud-encrusted humanoid, although her shapely female form was better defined than Clayface II's amorphous body.

Also called "Lady Clay," Clayface IV could mimic any shape she imagined, as well as assuming the abilities of those she aped.

The surviving Clayfaces—including Basil Karlo, who had mustered a return bout with the Dark Knight in *Detective* #496 (1980)—united in 1989 as "the Mud Pack" to attempt to kill Batman, spinning out of *Secret Origins* vol. 2 #44 into *Detective* #604–#607. Karlo obtained blood samples from Payne and Fuller, appropriating their abilities and morphing into the grotesque Ultimate Clayface, not an unexpected appellation from an ego-driven fallen star. Boasting Payne's killer touch and Lady Clay's shape-changing powers, as well as his own innate bloodthirstiness, the Ultimate Clayface has become one of Batman's most dangerous nemeses. Able to convert his hands into deadly weapons or liquefy into a torrent of mud, Karlo is almost unstoppable.

Outcasts Preston Payne and Lady Clay fell in love as a result of their Mud Pack team-up, and *Batman: Shadow of the Bat* #27 (1994) introduced their offspring son Cassius "Clay" Preston. While his name is an obvious Muhammad Ali pun, this lad—Clayface V—is no joke. His developing morphing powers may one day eclipse those of the Ultimate Clayface. Fearing this menace in the making, the U.S. government has taken Cassius away from his parents for safekeeping in a maximum-security facility. During 1999's "No Man's Land" story arc appearing in the various Batman titles, researcher Dr. Peter Malley was mutated into Clayface VI— aka Claything—after coming into contact with a cell sample from Cassius Preston. The Ultimate Clayface returned to battle Wonder Woman in 2000, and was also seen in the best-selling *Batman* storyline "Hush" (2002–2003), by Jeph Loeb and Jim Lee. A brand-new Clayface with a mysterious connection to a murder investigation involving Alfred Pennyworth, Bruce Wayne's butler, slimed into *Batman: Gotham Knights* #69 (2005), evoking the interest of Bat-foe Hush. Regardless of his shape, Clayface can always be counted on to muddy the Dark Knight's world.

Clayface was introduced to a television audience in 1977 in the animated series *The New Adventures of Batman* (1977–1978) from Filmation Studios. He returned to the tube in 1992 in the two-part "Feat of Clay" episode of *Batman: The Animated Series* (*BTAS*). Merging the vocation of Clayface I with the name of version II, *BTAS*'s Clayface was narcissistic actor Matt Hagen (Ron Perlman), whose addiction to the cosmetic "Renu-U" after a disfiguring mishap transformed him into a mud-monster. This Clayface was merchandised in *BTAS* tie-ins, including a Kenner action figure (in the mid-1990s Kenner produced a variant Clayface figure, with "Face Change Force," in its Batman: Legends of the Dark Knight collection). Kirk Baltz guest-starred as Clayface in an episode of the short-lived live-action TV series *Birds of Prey* (2002–2003), joined by a junior counterpart (Ian Reed Kesler). The WB cartoon *The Batman* (2004–present) introduced its own Clayface, coal-colored with glowing green eyes, in the episode "Clayface of Tragedy" (original airdate: May 7, 2005). Like his comic-book predecessors, this Clayface can modify his shape; he was originally Gotham ex-cop Ethan Bennett (Steve Harris), altered into his sinister state after exposure to "Joker Putty." —*ME*

Clown: *See* Violator

Cold War Supervillains

D ark forces conspired against democracy in the decades following World War II, or so paranoid Americans were led to believe. A tentative peace existed between the United States and its allies and the Soviet Union and its bloc of nations, with each side believing that the other had its collective finger on the atomic-bomb button. Pop fiction personified the "Red Scare" through a new breed of Communist spies and cold war supervillains from whom no neighborhood fallout shelter or "duck and cover" classroom drill could offer refuge.

Marvel Comics, searching for a post–Golden Age (1938–1954) trend to cultivate, took the Red Scare seriously. Marvel Boy, a space-age teen titan who in 1950 received his own title for a meager two-issue run, fought various outer-space invaders that substituted for Communists—he even called aliens "Commies" in one story and nuked their desert base. The Star-Spangled Avenger became "Captain America … Commie Smasher!," according to the tagline of *Captain America* #76 (1954), the title's first revived issue after its 1950 cancellation. "Cap" and his sidekick Bucky returned to action with the fervor they had once directed at the Führer (the hero punched Adolf Hitler in the jaw on the cover of his first issue in 1941) now aimed at the Russians, and the Sub-Mariner and the Human Torch, Marvel's other major Golden Age stars, were also revived, all for short runs. Cap fought Electro (no relation to the Spider-Man rogue), a green beast with a pink hammer-and-sickle chest emblem, and the Torch battled Comrade X, an extraterrestrial from the "Red Planet."

Captain America creators Joe Simon and Jack Kirby's *Fighting American* began a seven-issue run in 1954 from Prize Comics. Simon and Kirby bit into the cold war with tongue planted firmly in cheek, creating a Communist rogues' gallery for the hero his young cohort Speedboy featuring over-the-top characters including Russians Gnortz and Bohltz, Poison Ivan and Hotsky Trotski, and Rimsky and Korsikoff.

A real-life cold war supervillain all but toppled comic books in the mid-1950s: psychiatrist Dr. Fredric Wertham, whose 1954 book *Seduction of the Innocent*, a peremptory indictment against "the influence of comic books on today's youth," sparked U.S. Senate subcommittee hearings against the industry. Ensuing negative publicity forced smaller publishers into bankruptcy and neutered the remaining houses, with the content-governing board the Comics Code Authority implemented as a standards watchdog.

The Soviets' October 4, 1957, launch of the Sputnik 1 satellite propelled the Russians and Americans into the "space race," and each nation fired rockets, chimps, and eventually men into orbit in a mad dash for aerospace dominance. With the advent of the Marvel Age of Comics in 1961, as Stan Lee and Jack Kirby's *Fantastic Four* #1 steered the publisher back into the superhero arena, Communist paranoia, the threat of nuclear radiation, and space exploration provided a blue-print for several of the supervillains in the publisher's emerging line.

The Fantastic Four, whose cosmically imbued superpowers came from their own participation in the space race, first met Ivan Kragoff, aka the Red Ghost, in *Fantastic Four* vol. 1 #12 (1963). A Soviet scientist given the power to become a phantom from radiation exposure, the Red Ghost is best known for his unusual "henchmen," his Super-Apes. The Red Ghost also appeared on the 1967 *Fantastic Four* television cartoon. In the vein of the Red Ghost was the Space Phantom, from the planet Phantus, who infiltrated Marvel's mightiest super-team by impersonating some of its members in *The Avengers* #2 (1963).

Since radiation spawned the Incredible Hulk, it should come as no surprise that it also created the Green Goliath's first super-foe: the Gargoyle, the Russian physicist mutated into a pink-skinned, pint-sized monstrosity with a giant cranium in 1962's *The Incredible Hulk* #1. (The Gargoyle's son, the Gremlin, inherited his dad's augmented intelligence and attacked the Hulk with cyborg Super-Troopers eleven years later.) Boris Monguski, the mace-wielding Soviet soldier aka Mongu, took on the monster-hero later in 1962.

The cold war was an integral element to Iron Man's mythos. His Soviet counterpart, the Crimson Dynamo, was introduced in *Tales of Suspense* #46 in 1964 (the same year that saw the premiere of Russian spy Natasha Romanoff, who would later defect to the U.S. and become the superhero Black Widow). Inside Dynamo's jet-booted, arsenal-loaded red armor was scientist Anton Vanko, although other Soviets succeeded him. A *Crimson Dynamo* miniseries, starring discontented Russian teen Gennady Gavrilov, was published in 2003.

After creating the Dynamo's armor, Vanko produced the laser-firing "power horn" worn by Czech Milos Masaryk, a Russian espionage agent, who became the Unicorn in *Tales of Suspense* #69 (1965). The original Titanium Man, first seen in 1965, was Boris Bullski, a Soviet nationalist who defended his country's honor in high-tech metal gear. Also, Spider-Man's master-of-disguise foe the

Chameleon, debuting in 1963, had links to an originally unspecified foreign power that was eventually revealed to be the U.S.S.R.

The Russians did not monopolize all of the cold war villainy in the early years of the Marvel Age. Various Asian soldiers were occasionally depicted as enemies, and the Mandarin, premiering in 1963, became Iron Man's arch-foe. "The bloodthirsty scourge of Asia" General Fang and his army battled the title star of *Hulk* vol. 1 #5 (1963). In Iron Man's origin in *Tales of Suspense* #39 (1963), Vietcong villain Wong-Chu appeared. Chinese expatriate and volunteer guinea pig Dr. Chen Lu underwent radiation immersion treatments in *Journey into Mystery* #93 (1963), becoming the green-skinned human weapon the Radioactive Man.

The popularity of the James Bond theatrical movies, starting with Sean Connery as agent 007 in *Dr. No* (1962), brought the Communist threat—generally depicted as Soviet agents—to pop-culture prominence in the 1960s. Fleming's criminal network SPECTRE paved the way for other evil organizations, whose agents were lurking around every corner, if one trusted television and film. TV's *The Man from U.N.C.L.E.* (1964–1968) featured the crime network T.H.R.U.S.H., with operatives like Comrade Voshnosh, and Marvel Comics' multi-headed organization Hydra took root. John Steed and Emma Peel, of the 1960s British TV spy series *The Avengers*, fought Boris Kartovski, a Russian spy with a mind-transference device. Kooky "Commies" were featured in campy spy spoofs, such as cartoon stars Rocky and Bullwinkle's enemies, Pottsylvanian agents Boris Badenov and Natasha Fatale. Soviet or Soviet-like spies even popped up in prehistoric Bedrock, on *The Flintstones* (1964's "Dr. Sinister" episode, and the 1966 theatrical spin-off *The Man Called Flintstone*), and, of all places, the remote landscape of *Gilligan's Island* (1964–1967).

With its utopian Silver Age (1956–1969) municipalities of Metropolis, Gotham City, and Central City mostly insulated from real-world threats, DC Comics rarely acknowledged the cold war. Notable examples include Egg Fu, Wonder Woman's absurd and politically offensive Asian foe; Batman's Fu Manchu–like enemy Dr. Tzin-Tzin, whose diabolical world threat was first witnessed

in *Detective Comics* #354 (1966); and the original Starfire. *Teen Titans* vol. 1 #18 (1968) introduced superstrong Russian teen Leonid Kovar, aka Starfire, capable of generating white-hot flame. Ideological differences led to his verbal and violent exchanges with Kid Flash, although Starfire eventually became Red Star, an ally of the Titans.

By the 1970s, the certainty of "mutually assured destruction" in a nuclear exchange began to thaw the cold war, even in the Bond movie franchise, which depicted the bedroom détente between 007 (Roger Moore) and Soviet agent Major Anya Amasova (Barbara Bach) in *The Spy Who Loved Me* (1977). Supervillains, being a stubborn sort, refused to concede. Crimson Dynamo, Titanium Man, and Radioactive Man united as the Titanic Three in *Avengers* #130 (1974). The Soviet Super Soldiers, a gathering of previously introduced supervillains Crimson Dynamo, Gremlin, Darkstar (Laynia Petrovna, who created objects from "Darkforce" energies), Ursa Major (Mikhail Ursus, who could transform into an intelligent bear), and Vanguard (the energy-repelling Nicolai Krylenko, armed with a hammer and sickle), first teamed in *Hulk* vol. 2 #258 (1981).

In the 1983 superhero satire *Captain Klutz II*, *MAD* magazine artist Don Martin trotted out a cold war supervillain that might have made *Fighting American*'s Simon and Kirby proud: Comrade Stupidska, from "Soviet Brusha," who tried to drop giant Alka Seltzer tablets into American nuclear power plants' smokestacks.

DC Comics became more reality-minded in its post–*Crisis on Infinite Earths* (1985–1986) universe and frequently acknowledged the cold war. Hammer and Sickle (real names: Boris and Natasha), his-and-her superstrong Russian operatives, and the People's Heroes (superfast Bolshoi, explosive Molotov, and psychic Pravda) premiered in *The Outsiders* vol. 1 #10 (1986). During the 66-issue run of *Suicide Squad* (1987–1992), the Squad occasionally tangled with the Red Shadows, a similar Soviet organization of rogues for hire. Armored super-soldiers the Rocket Red Brigade premiered in *Green Lantern Corps* #208 (1987); while heroes, the Rocket Reds were disliked by some Americans, although one Rocket Red, Dmitri Puskin, eventually became a member of the Justice

League (later appearing on the Cartoon Network's *Justice League Unlimited*, 2004–present). Anatoli Knyazev, the KGBeast, was a Russian super-assassin sent to the United States to execute his country's enemies, including President Ronald Reagan, in *Batman* #417 (1988). His protégé, the NKVDemon, followed the KGBeast's lead in 1990.

After the 1991 dissolution of the Soviet Union marked the end of the cold war, Marvel published a *Soviet Super Soldiers* one-shot in 1992, and the NKVDemon has had two successors. Communist supervillains are usually portrayed satirically in post–cold war appearances, however, such as Boris and Natasha's return in a pair of live-action movies (1992 and 2000), and the Tick's foe the Red Scare. —*ME*

The Composite Superman

While many supervillains of comics' Silver Age (1956–1969) attempted to defeat the valiant team of Superman and Batman, only the Composite Superman succeeded. As shown in *World's Finest Comics* #142 (1964) in a tale by Edmund Hamilton and Curt Swan, former daredevil Joe Meach wrongly blames Superman for ruining his career after rescuing him during a foolhardy high-diving attempt. Shunning the public as the night janitor at—of all places!—Metropolis' Superman Museum, Meach's life is transformed by a freak accident: lightning strikes the museum's statuettes of the Legion of Super-Heroes, inexplicably energizing the petulant Meach with each of the Legionnaires' vast superpowers. He transforms himself into an amalgam of Batman and Superman—with kryptonite-green skin—and as the Composite Superman assaults the heroes (and Batman's ally Robin) with a cache of capabilities that humble even the Man of Steel, bullying the heroes into exile in their alter egos. Were it not for the unexpected disappearance of the villain's powers, the world's finest trio might still be storing their tights in mothballs.

When next seen in 1967, Meach had apparently undergone anger management and held Superman and Batman in the highest regard—until the vengeful extraterrestrial Xan restored him to his rancorous Composite Superman identity. Just as Xan attempted to annihilate Superman and Batman, the Composite Superman's powers faded and Meach sacrificed himself to spare the heroes' lives. Outside of the 1982 emergence of a Composite Superman impersonator, this peculiar but fondly remembered adversary's only other appearance has been as a retro-marketed action figure in 2005. —*ME*

Copperhead

In *The Brave and the Bold* #78 (1968), a Batman/Wonder Woman/Batgirl team-up by Bob Haney and Bob Brown, the Caped Crusader was first perplexed by Copperhead, a contortionist/burglar (whose real name is never disclosed) wearing a snake-skin uniform enabling him to slither through narrow passages. When confronted in his gruesome grotto, Copperhead's "poison mist" is potent enough to render Wonder Woman unconscious, while his headpiece's snake-fangs pack a near-fatal bite for Batman. Batman resolutely expends his "last bit of strength" to clobber Copperhead, while forethoughtful Batgirl saves the hero's life with an anti-venom serum tucked away in her purse.

Copperhead might have permanently crawled under a rock after this villain-of-the-month outing had writer/editor Gerry Conway not tossed him into the pages of *Secret Society of Super-Villains* in 1976. The perfidious rogue was not to be trusted—as if honesty was ever a virtue among this criminal viper pit—and he even snitched on his allies to prison guards to save his own skin. After *Secret Society*'s 1978 cancellation, Copperhead rarely struck until the 1990s, when he returned in various DC Comics titles (*Hawk and Dove*, *Superboy*, etc.) as an assassin-for-hire. He brokered a deal with the demon Neron in 1995's *Underworld Unleashed*, becoming a genuine serpent-man with a venomous touch. Actor Jose Yenque's spine-chilling voice made Copperhead a popular foe on the Cartoon Network's *Justice*

League (2001–2004), hatching the villain's 2004 toy debut as a Justice League figurine distributed at Jack in the Box. —*ME*

Count Nefaria

Count Luchino Nefaria, first appearing in the Stan Lee–scripted and Jack Kirby–illustrated *The Avengers* vol. 1 #13 (1965), is one of the most resilient menaces in the Marvel Universe, having pursued the Avengers, Thor, Captain America, Iron Man, the Thunderbolts, and the X-Men.

During the Silver Age (1956–1969), Count Nefaria had no superpowers. Despite his old-fashioned wardrobe—complete with monocle and opera cape—he utilized highly advanced technology, including a "nightmare machine" with which he could project illusions into sleeping victims' minds, as he did to Iron Man in *Tales of Suspense* #67 (1965). Nefaria clashed with the X-Men when he entrapped Washington, D.C., within an impenetrable dome and attempted to hold the city at ransom in *X-Men* vol. 1 #22–#23 (1966).

An overconfident master planner, Nefaria was the leader of one of the most powerful families within Marvel's Mafia-like Maggia organization, and he has also led several groupings of second-string supervillains to assist him in his evil plottings. His acts involve high levels of intelligence and deception, such as duping the U.S. public into believing that the Avengers were declaring war on America.

Perhaps Count Nefaria's best-remembered appearance took place in *X-Men* #94–#95 (1975), on the heels of the mutant team's *Giant-Size X-Men* #1 revival, in which he captured the NORAD missile base ("Valhalla") at Cheyenne Mountain. The X-Men thwarted him, but at the cost of the life of new X-Men recruit Thunderbird.

In *Avengers* #164–#166 (1977), Nefaria gained superpowers at the hands of Professor Kevin Sturdy during the experiment that gave Wonder Man his ionic abilities, receiving the attributes of laser-like eyebeams, one-hundredfold-multiplied strength, and Hulk-worthy leaping. He is, however, vulnerable to weapons that use that same type of ionic energy. Nefaria destroyed the lab and mortally wounded Professor Sturdy—before he discovered that the experiment possibly went awry, aging rapidly as he attacked the Avengers.

In a later tale, the enfeebled Nefaria was seemingly killed, but was actually in a coma. His "aging" was really his physical body adjusting to the ionic radiation in his body, a process that made the Count immortal and restored him to his prime condition. To maintain his powers he must drain energy from other ionic beings.

Count Nefaria is the father of Whitney Frost, alias Madame Masque, the sometime lover of Iron Man. Though Madame Masque has been Nefaria's ally, they have since become enemies. Count Nefaria appeared in the initial issues of *New Avengers* (2005–present), in which he continued to wreak havoc. —*GM*

The Crime Syndicate of America

Just imagine—a world without superheroes, where five despotic doppelgängers of the most powerful members of the Justice League of America rule with an iron hand. This is the home of the Crime Syndicate of America: Ultraman, Superwoman, Owlman, Johnny Quick, and Power Ring, evil analogs of Superman, Wonder Woman, Batman, the Flash, and Green Lantern, respectively.

In *The Flash* #123 (1961), DC Comics editor Julius Schwartz and writer Gardner Fox borrowed from science fiction the concept of parallel worlds—coexisting alternate realities—in the landmark adventure "Flash of Two Worlds," in which the modern "Earth-One" Flash of the Silver Age (1956–1969) joined forces with the original "Earth-Two" Flash of the Golden Age (1938–1954). Annual team-ups between the JLA and the Golden Age's Justice Society of America soon followed. The second such meeting, in *Justice League of America* #29 and #30 (1964), introduces "Earth-Three," a topsy-turvy planet where American

Christopher Columbus discovered Europe and actor Abe Lincoln shot President John Wilkes Booth. On Earth-Three resides the Crime Syndicate, cavalierly pillaging riches with no one to stop them … leading to their utter *boredom*. Upon discovering Earth-One and its heroes, the Syndicate ventures there for a challenge worthy of its malevolent might, and through trickery overcomes the JLA and soon Earth-Two's JSA. In a climactic rematch, the League narrowly vanquishes the Syndicate, and Green Lantern's power ring imprisons the members in a "dimensional-barrier jail."

Despite their striking costume design by artist Mike Sekowsky, these were supervillains high on concept but low on characterization. Little was offered other than their villainy to differentiate them from the JLA, save for Ultraman's empowerment by (instead of weakness to) kryptonite—he gained a *new* superpower with each exposure!—and Power Ring's revelation that his finger-worn weapon was acquired from a monk named Volthoom (an homage to "Vulthoom," a 1935 fantasy story written by Clark Ashton Smith).

The Crime Syndicate remained in limbo until 1978, resurfacing again in 1982. Ultraman and his criminal cronies were destroyed as multiple worlds perished in the ambitious maxiseries *Crisis on Infinite Earths* (1985–1986); a retroactive rewriting of DC history now ascribed their planet of origin to the antimatter planet of Qward. Writer Grant Morrison resurrected some of the CSA in *Animal Man* #23 and #24 (1990), but their temporary rebirth was the result of the Psycho-Pirate's reality disruptions.

Morrison found this mirror-universe JLA too enticing to ignore. In the graphic novel *JLA: Earth 2* (2000), the writer, with artist Frank Quietly, unveiled a rebooted Crime Syndicate inhabiting a dystopian anti-matter replicate of Earth and operating under the dictum *Cui Bono* ("Who Profits?"). That Earth's *heroic* counterpart to Lex Luthor implored the Justice League to rally to his world's aid. This reimagined CSA has become a major force in DC's twenty-first-century continuity, even dominating eight 2004–2005 issues of *JLA* in the serial "Syndicate Rules," in which they waged war against the Qwardians.

In 2003, DC Direct released a series of action figures based upon the Silver Age Crime Syndicate. —*ME*

The Criminal Economy

"**W**here does he get those wonderful toys?" asks the Joker in director Tim Burton's blockbuster *Batman* (1989). Batman might ask the same of the Joker; his numerous Ha-Haciendas indicate the existence of a network of professional services—a criminal economy—available to the supervillain community, either exclusively criminal or corrupt enough to be willing to work with well-known villains. Evidence of this network is indirect for the most part, but over the years a small portion of the criminal economy has come to light, enough to supply the needs of any supervillain, whether for simple robbery or world conquest.

For the various high-tech murder machines of the trade, turn to Phineas Mason, the Tinkerer, who has supplied the Scorpion's tail, Whirlwind's armor, and even the giant armed-and-armored metal wheel that let Big Wheel crush his enemies. Advanced Idea Mechanics (A.I.M.) is an excellent second choice. Although originally the weapons-design division of Hydra, it broke off on its own to sell advanced weaponry to anyone who could pay the bill, whether supervillain or subversive organization. Check out the trade show A.I.M. stages on its Caribbean island base.

Next a villain needs a spiffy outfit. The best-known tailor to the supervillain set is Paul Gambi, outfitter of the Flash's Rogues' Gallery including the Top, Captain Cold, and Heat Wave. Another possibility is Leo Zelinsky, who has supplied costumes to the Blob, Dr. Doom, and Killshot, as well as the Thing, Spider-Man, and Thor. Be sure to observe his strict policy of seeing heroes on Mondays, Wednesdays, and Saturdays, and villains on Tuesdays and Thursdays to avoid a confrontation with one's arch-nemesis.

Next come henchmen. For professionals trained in everything from picking pockets to cracking safes, check out graduates of "Pockets" Crime School for Boys (*Batman* #3, 1940). For specialists, like an expert dynamiter, a cracksman, or a machine-gunner, see Ivan Kraft for an "artist in villainy" (*Detective*

Comics #84, 1944). For combat thugs, there's no better place than one of the Taskmaster's criminal academies. His "photographic reflexes" let him copy the fighting styles of masters like Captain America and Daredevil, and he puts that knowledge to work in training up the best thugs money can buy.

A lair is a must-have. Unfortunately, builders of hideouts and secret island bases don't advertise in the Yellow Pages. The only lead for a contractor capable of constructing a secret island base—including submarine facilities—is one Mr. Hardin ("The Dreadful Doll," *Jonny Quest*, 1964) last seen in the hands of the authorities thanks to those meddling kids Jonny Quest and Hadji.

Need a consultant? Check in with Metawise, a multinational criminal organization that collects data on superheroes, to get the scoop on your enemies. For a mere 25 percent of the take, Dr. Matthew Thorne's Crime Clinic (*Detective Comics* #77, 1943) will diagnose the weak spots in your scheme and prescribe a fix; for 50 percent, he'll make an outcall and go on the job himself. Need real-time feedback and information? The Calculator does for supervillains what Oracle does for superheroes, brokers information, and he's with you all the way, at least until your credit cards max out.

And then it's time to relax. After fencing with The Shadow, visit the Pink Rat, the Black Ship, or the Club Cadilly—while these places are open to the public, they are patronized almost exclusively by criminals so you'll feel right at home. If you've got a secret identity and you want to relax and network with other supervillains, head to one of the many franchises of the Bar With No Name. But be careful: the Scourge of the Underworld, a vigilante disguise artist, once staged a massacre of eighteen B-list Marvel supervillains at the Bar in Medina County, Ohio, including the Ringer, the Vamp, Cyclone, Rapier, and Steeple Jack II.

On the lam? Hide out in the Shacks, a "crooked row of weather-beaten old houses that serve as a criminal hideout on the edge of the waterfront" (*Detective Comics* #58, 1941), or settle for a cot in a bunker under a gas station from Dick Tracy's villain the Mole in exchange for every bit of cash you have. Caught? Use your one phone call to retain Wolfram & Hart, the law firm that specializes in representing evil. In prison? Make sure your escape insurance is all paid up to the Spook, who built secret escape passages into the Gotham penitentiary while working as an architectural draftsman, although he can help you escape no matter where you're incarcerated. —*PC*

Cyborg Superman

After the Man of Steel died in the mega-selling *Superman* vol. 2 #75 (1993), the Cyborg Superman appeared three issues later as one of four alleged successors of the slain hero (the others being Superboy, Steel, and the Eradicator). Borrowing liberally from James Cameron's *The Terminator*, writer/artist Dan Jurgens' pretender to the Super-throne was a startling amalgam of Superman's cloned organic matter and robotic limbs forged of a Kryptonian alloy.

His story did not begin there, however. *Adventures of Superman* #466 (1990), also by Jurgens, rockets a quartet of astronauts through a cosmic storm in a pastiche of the Fantastic Four's origin. Crew member Hank Henshaw becomes a being of raw energy, and unlike his Marvel Comics counterpart Reed Richards, is none too happy with the transformation, reproaching Superman for the loss of his corporeal form (and his wife).

Possessing the ability to assimilate with electronic circuitry, Henshaw downloaded his essence into the birthing matrix that transported baby Superman to Earth, taking form as the Superman/machine hybrid and posing as the re-created Man of Steel. Seething with hatred of Superman, he deceived many—including Lois Lane—into believing he was the hero reborn, but ultimately was revealed to be in league with Mongul, helping the alien despot execute millions by destroying Coast City. After Superman's resurrection, the hero battled his cybernetic doppelgänger to the death, but the Cyborg Superman—like the Terminator that inspired him—repeatedly returns with newer and deadlier upgrades, a being of uninhibited rage and Kryptonian technology. —*ME*

Dark Lord: *See* **Mordru**

Dark Phoenix

Lord Acton's dictum that absolute power corrupts absolutely is aptly illustrated by the rise and fall of the supremely powerful cosmic being called Dark Phoenix. The creation of the classic writer/artist team of Chris Claremont and John Byrne, Dark Phoenix represents the unrestrained id of Jean Grey, the telepathic/telekinetic superheroine known as Marvel Girl, who had been fairly unassuming since her inception in *X-Men* vol. 1 #1 (1963). While piloting a space shuttle to Earth after a space mission, Grey is lethally irradiated. Fortunately, she also encounters the Phoenix Force, a cosmic entity that apparently revivifies her after a crash-landing in New York's Jamaica Bay. Grey's friends, the outlaw mutant superheroes called the X-Men, fear the worst—until Grey rises from the water in a brilliant blaze of fire shaped like the burned-then-reborn bird of ancient Egyptian legend: the Phoenix. Along with her new super-appellation, Grey acquires a dynamic new costume, an aerobics-instructor-like green catsuit (*X-Men* vol. 1 #99–#100, 1976).

As Phoenix, Grey steadily ascended toward omnipotence while sliding inexorably into amoral, unbridled violence. The cause was the ancient,

immortal Phoenix Force that now possessed her. Exploiting the Phoenix entity's inexperience with human emotions, the mutant villain Mastermind soon manipulated Grey into joining the world-dominating Hellfire Club, thereby blowing out Grey's self-imposed "psychic circuit-breakers," which kept her rising power-levels, along with the Phoenix Force's worst impulses, in check. Grey abruptly became Dark Phoenix, her costume symbolically morphing from placid green to demonic red. Unfettered by conscience, Dark Phoenix psionically struck down Mastermind, then took a savage interstellar "joyride" that extinguished the D'Bari civilization. She then returned to Earth's solar system, where neither the X-Men nor the powerful Shi'ar Empire—whose military was determined to avenge the D'Bari—can stand against her. Fortunately Dark Phoenix retained a spark of Grey's humanity and opted for suicide, apparently ending Grey's life. This fatal denouement for such an integral character was highly unusual for the superhero comics of the day, and it truly caught readers by surprise when it was unleashed in *X-Men* vol. 1 #129–#137 (1980).

The bewitchingly sexy cosmic villainess has proved durably popular, spurring numerous new appearances, including a lengthy run of early 1980s *Uncanny X-Men* comics featuring a replica of Jean Grey named Madeline Pryor, who not only married Grey's teen sweetheart Scott

X-Men vol. 1 #135 ©1980 Marvel Comics.
COVER ART BY JOHN BYRNE AND TERRY AUSTIN.

Dark Phoenix finally reached a mass television audience in the third season of FOX's popular *X-Men* animated series (1992–1997). Voiced by Canadian actress Catherine Disher, the tragic Dark Phoenix of the original 1980 Claremont-Byrne saga survived more or less intact. Back in the comics, the "rebooted" version of the X-Men presented in 2001's ongoing *Ultimate X-Men* series (written by Mark Millar and Chuck Austen and illustrated by Adam Kubert, Chris Bachalo, Esad Ribic, Kaare Andrews, and others) brings the Dark Phoenix saga forward into the new millennium. Like the original Claremont-Byrne iteration, Millar's Dark Phoenix takes Jean Grey on a journey to godhood, though her impulses now appear loftier. "I want to use these gifts to *benefit the world*," Grey declares to her mentor Charles Xavier, ready to use her new powers to literally raise the dead. But after receiving a stern browbeating from Xavier, she backs away from wreaking such well-intended havoc on the world, tamping her vast energies down, at least temporarily (*Ultimate X-Men* #23, 2002). Whether or not Dark Phoenix will motivate Grey into assuming godhood remains to be seen. Her return, however, seems certain. —*MAM*

Darkseid

(Cyclops) Summers, but also served as a vessel for the Phoenix force. Grey herself returned when it came to light that the Dark Phoenix entity that committed suicide had actually been only a duplicate; the *real* Jean Grey was found in suspended animation and revived in *Fantastic Four* #286 (1986). Though many fans regarded Grey's return as a betrayal that undercut her dramatic, Sydney Cartonesque sacrifice, Grey remained a popular character, no doubt owing in part to the possibility that Dark Phoenix might one day run amok once again. Against that possibility, Rachel Summers—the alternate-future daughter of Jean Grey and Scott Summers—eventually became the custodian of the unkillable Phoenix Force in 1992. Dark Phoenix has so far served to supplement Rachel Summers' already-formidable psionic talents, but she has yet to wipe out entire planets.

Jack "King" Kirby quaked the comic-book world in 1970 when he—the co-creator of many of the superhero legends of the Marvel Universe, including the Fantastic Four, the Hulk, and the X-Men—was hired by DC Comics editorial director Carmine Infantino to do for his company what he had done for Marvel: create magic. Writer/artist/editor Kirby produced an interlocking quartet of titles (*Superman's Pal Jimmy Olsen*, *The New Gods*, *The Forever People*, and *Mister Miracle*) called his "Fourth World" saga, a grandiose tapestry of lush history and imaginative characters that was, at heart, a straightforward tale of good versus evil. And "evil," in this case, was Darkseid, the stone-faced, impenitent despot first seen in *Jimmy Olsen* #134 (1970).

Kirby's play on the apocalyptic Norse legend of Ragnarok, the Fourth World's fictional legend began long ago when a holocaust destroyed the "old gods." In its wake arose two warring worlds, one light (New Genesis) and one dark (Apokolips), each occupied by a race of "new gods" divided by their opposing theologies. The hellish Apokolips, described in *New Gods* #1 (1971) as a "dismal, unclean place" by Orion, Darkseid's son "traded" to New Genesis for Scott (Mr. Miracle) Free in the peacekeeping "Pact," is a bleak "armed camp" where "life is the evil here! And death, the great goal!"

Darkseid is Apokolips' undisputed overlord, promising suffering to those who obey and death to those who defy. He ascended to the throne upon his decreed assassination of his mother, Queen Heggra, who was killed by his sycophantic servant Desaad. Darkseid demands not only utter obedience but godlike worship. He is absolutely contemptible and derives perverse pleasure from corrupting the weak and crushing the robust.

Abetted by minions—some obsequious, some fiendish, some barbarous, but all wretched—Darkseid craves intergalactic domination, as well as the acquisition of the means to that end, the all-powerful "Anti-Life Equation." Earth has not escaped his clutches; in his earliest appearances, Darkseid covertly networked in America through his agents, the high-tech mobsters Intergang and media mogul Morgan Edge, and over the years has made direct attempts to invade the planet. This most immoral of gods evinces infinite power, including invulnerability, superstrength, and "Omega Beams," rays fired from his burning crimson eyes that either disintegrate beings upon contact or teleport his targets directly to him—which, in the case of the latter, portends a fate worse than death.

While Darkseid demands loyalty, he rarely offers it, even to his family: in addition to ordering his mother's execution, he abused his wives Suli and Tigra, is demeaning to his boorish son Kalibak, and wars against his heroic son Orion (a third son, Grayven, is lesser known in Fourth World lore). The adversarial relationship between Darkseid and Orion is one of several aspects of Kirby's Fourth World saga that have led many to draw parallels between it and George Lucas' *Star Wars* mythology, which emerged in 1977; other similarities include the Death Star's resemblance to Apokolips, the Fourth World's binding energy, "the Source" (as opposed to *Star Wars*' "Force"), and the pronunciation of Darkseid's name: Dark-side, as in "dark side of the Force."

The Fourth World titles were canceled after nearly two years in print (although *Mister Miracle* ran slightly longer), leaving Kirby unable to conclude the New Genesis–versus–Apokolips/Orion–versus–Darkseid struggle; he briefly revisited the concept in his 1985 graphic novel *The Hunger Dogs*. Prompted by both the appeal of Darkseid as a cosmic supervillain and numerous artists' love for Kirby's characters, DC permanently integrated the Fourth World lore into its superhero continuity after Kirby returned to Marvel in the mid-1970s. Darkseid found it advantageous to ally with the newly formed Secret Society of Super-Villains in 1976, and battled the combined Justice League and Justice Society in 1980. Darkseid's adventures have been chronicled by many popular creators including Mark Evanier, Steve Rude, John Byrne, and Walter Simonson, in various *New Gods* specials and revivals (an incarnation starting in 1989 introduced Darkseid's father Yuga Khan, a character later ignored). Darkseid was the principal protagonist of the 1982 *Legion of Super-Heroes* storyline "The Great Darkness Saga" by Paul Levitz and Keith Giffen; the 1986–1987 crossover miniseries *Legends* (by John Ostrander, Len Wein, and John Byrne), in which his agent Glorious Godfrey defamed Earth's superheroes; and in 1988's *Cosmic Odyssey* (by Jim Starlin and Mike Mignola), in which a squadron of superheroes thwarted his attempt to procure the Anti-Life Equation. In 2001's mega-event "Our Worlds at War," he vied for a toehold on Earth while the planet was under attack by Imperiex.

Many earthly superheroes have been added to his enemies' list. Darkseid's hatred of the Man of Steel rivals his disdain for Orion; in 2004 he attempted to exact revenge against Superman by controlling his Kryptonian cousin Supergirl, and he fought the Man of Tomorrow one-on-one in 2005. Darkseid's enduring stature and diabolism remain the ultimate tribute to the creative brilliance of Jack Kirby.

Darkseid's villainy has not been confined to the comic-book page. The ABC cartoon *The Super Powers Team: Galactic Guardians* (1986–1987) brought Darkseid (voiced by Frank Welker) and many of his aides to television; a Darkseid Super Powers action figure was manufactured by Kenner in 1985 (including the "Darkseid Destroyer" toy vehicle; a 1986 Darkseid playset, the "Tower of

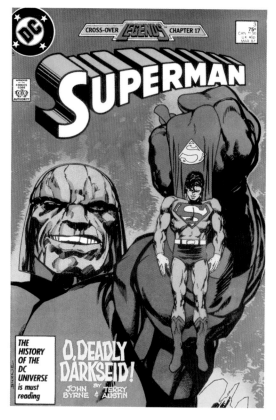

Superman vol. 2 #3 ©1987 DC Comics.
COVER ART BY JOHN BYRNE AND TERRY AUSTIN.

titles, *Superman's Pal Jimmy Olsen*, *The Forever People*, *The New Gods*, and *Mister Miracle*), is populated by downtrodden masses, the "Lowlies," many of whom are refugees from other planets, who cower under the tyranny of the heartless overlord Darkseid. An army of shocktroopers, the airborne Parademons (Para-demons in the original texts), police the streets, ensnaring "para-cables" their primary weapon. (One of the Parademons joined the Secret Six, the supervillain coalition opposing Lex Luthor's Society, in the 2005 miniseries *Villains United*, giving his life to save his teammates in its sixth and final issue.)

An inner circle of inquisitors and warriors introduced in 1971 and 1972, including Darkseid's bestial son Kalibak and armed guard the Female Furies, inflict malice in Darkseid's name. The purple-cloaked, unctuous Desaad, first seen in *Forever People* vol. 1 #1 (1971), is a duplicitous sadist who has created numerous combat weapons and tools of persecution. Darkseid's chief counselor, Desaad has been punished and even murdered (but later revived) by the evil god for his treachery. *Mister Miracle* vol. 1 #2 (1971) introduced the stout matron Granny Goodness, headmistress of Apokolips' forbidding orphanages, hellholes where abuse is a way of life. She delights in torturing her "children" and forces them to beg for more from their "loving" Granny.

The power-mad, insect-like Mantis was the first of Darkseid's agents to swarm to Earth, and with his range of fearsome abilities—an antimatter touch, plus heat and ice generation—he has on occasion challenged Darkseid's authority, only to be chastened by his master. Dr. Bedlam is Apokolips' version of the mad scientist, a terrifying tinkerer known for unspeakable experiments on subjects' minds. He abandoned his physical body long ago to become an energy being, but when it is necessary for him to interact with others he does so by inhabiting one or more of his "animates," faceless androids he can control six at a time. Glorious Godfrey is a handsome, silver-tongued persuader who often seduces victims into Darkseid's corner. During the 1986–1987 crossover *Legends*, he masqueraded as pop psychologist G. Gordon Godfrey and spearheaded a media campaign to impugn the reputation of Earth's superheroes.

Darkness," never made it past the prototype stage), and Darkseid was included in spin-off *Super Powers* DC miniseries in 1985 and 1986 (Kirby, returning to familiar ground, illustrated the 1985 series). Michael Ironside played Darkseid in the animated *Superman* (1996–2000) two-parter "Apokolips … Now!," dedicated to Jack Kirby's memory (he died in 1994), and has continued his portrayal on the Cartoon Network's *Justice League* (2001–2004) and *Justice League Unlimited* (2004–present); related action figures and other merchandise have been issued. —*ME*

Darkseid's Elite

Apokolips, the abominable DC Comics world created in 1970 by writer/artist Jack Kirby for his cosmic "Fourth World" saga (four comic-book

Darkseid, Desaad, and Kalibak vs. Firestorm and Superman. From *Super Friends: The Legendary Super Powers Show* (1984).

Superman writer/artist John Byrne added Godfrey's sister, the equally convictive Amazing Grace, to the Fourth World canon in 1987.

Two of Darkseid's Elite are students of the history of Earth warfare. The officious Virmin Vunderbarr, a strategist who demands nothing short of perfection, is festooned like a nineteenth-century Prussian officer, including a monocle worn more for show than necessity. With sixteenth-century deceivers Lucrezia and Cesare Borgia as his inspiration, the flamboyant Kanto is one of Darkseid's chief assassins. An expert tactician and weapons master, Kanto possesses a deep respect for worthy opponents.

Darkseid's uncle Steppenwolf was born to be wild. One of Apokolips' most brutal military commandants, he has slain opponents in war and for

recreation, using a deadly arsenal including his "electro-ax." Steppenwolf's battle steed is a gargantuan, ferocious dog. He was once killed in battle but was later resurrected by Darkseid.

Other minions, including the aquatic Deep Six, have served Darkseid, and many have been added to the canon in later decades by writers other than Kirby, such as the fire-beast Infernus, the destructive giant Brimstone, the reanimator Necromina, the four-armed fighter Rip Roar, and Mortalla, the woman with the death-touch. Their malignant methods may vary, but all of Darkseid's Elite share one commonality: a fear of their master. As the normally brazen Granny Goodness once quivered, "Darkseid is total power—! He can strike us down or toy with us at will!" (*Mister Miracle* vol. 1 #18, 1974).

Darkseid, Kalibak, and Desaad were chief among the villains in the ABC cartoon *The Super Powers Team: Galactic Guardians* (1986–1987); Kenner's Super Powers toy line included action figures of the trio as well as Steppenwolf, Mantis, and a Parademon. Darkseid's Elite have also appeared on *Superman* (1996–2000), *Justice League* (2001–2004), and *Justice League Unlimited* (2004–present); Rene Auberjonois' serpent-like voice portrayal of Desaad has graced each of these animated programs. —*ME*

Darth Vader

Arguably the most recognizable supervillain in the world, Darth Vader is the creation of film writer/director George Lucas for his sextet of *Star Wars* films. And although Dracula and other monsters may lay claim to centuries of storylines, no single villainous visage has been merchandised as much as Vader's black bell-shaped helmet.

Introduced in the film *Star Wars* (1977), Darth Vader was first seen striding through the smoke-filled, battle-scarred hallways of a Rebel transport, his audible breath chilling, his deep voice commanding, and his prodigious strength evident as he lifted a Rebel soldier and crushed his neck with one hand. Viewers soon learned that Vader was a Dark Lord of the Sith, and the companion to the Galactic Empire's Grand Moff Tarkin, who was planning to use a battle station known as the

Darth Vader (David Prowse) and a defiant Princess Leia (Carrie Fisher) in *Star Wars* (1977).

Death Star to wipe out the Rebel Alliance. Vader captured and tortured Princess Leia Organa and killed Obi-Wan Kenobi, the last of the Jedi Knights and his one-time teacher and friend. As the film ended, Vader's TIE Fighter was struck by lasers and he spun off into space.

Though he continued to appear in novels, comic books, and newspaper comic strips, the "live" Darth Vader next appeared in the film *The Empire Strikes Back* (1980), in which it was revealed that he was second-in-command to the evil Emperor Palpatine … and that he had not killed Luke Skywalker's father (as Obi-Wan had told Luke); he *was* Luke's father! In the third film of the trilogy, *Return of the Jedi* (1983), Luke found out that Leia Organa is his twin sister, and the daughter of Vader. After a lightsaber battle aboard the second Death Star between Luke and Vader, the Sith Lord betrayed the Emperor. Wounded, Vader asked Luke to remove his mask so he might look upon him as his father, Anakin Skywalker, before he died. Anakin's spirit became

one with the light side of the Force, and Luke burned his armor.

In the late 1990s, George Lucas began work on a trilogy of *Star Wars* prequels: *Episode I: The Phantom Menace* (1999), *Episode II: Attack of the Clones* (2002), and *Episode III: Revenge of the Sith* (2005). Set a few decades before *Star Wars* (now known as *Episode IV: A New Hope*), the films first showed nine-year-old Anakin Skywalker—perhaps the result of an immaculate conception—as a slave on the desert planet Tatooine. When Jedi Knights Qui-Gon Jinn and Obi-Wan Kenobi discovered that Anakin had immense powers in the usage of the mystical Force that binds the galaxy together, they took the youngster on as a Padawan apprentice. As Anakin grew, his powers became ever stronger, and the Jedi Council realized that although he might be the prophesized Chosen One who would bring balance to the Force, he also seemed to have a dangerous side to him.

Unfortunately, even as he fought the Clone Wars beside the other Jedi Knights, elements conspired to turn Anakin to the Dark Side of the Force. His mother, Shmi, was killed, and he slaughtered an encampment of Tusken Raiders in revenge. Forbidden to love, Anakin nevertheless embarked on a romance and eventual secret marriage to Senator Padmé Amidala from Naboo. Most worryingly, Anakin was befriended and seduced by Senate Chancellor Palpatine, an ambitious man who—unbeknownst to the Jedi Council—was really the Sith Lord Darth Sidious. Palpatine slowly twisted Anakin to evil, resulting in the young Jedi helping to slaughter members of the Jedi Council and their young initiates.

Anakin faced his mentor in a lightsaber battle on Mustafar, but he fell prey to the superior training of Obi-Wan Kenobi and was badly burned by the molten lava of the planet. Rescued by droids sent by Palpatine, Anakin was reconstructed using cybernetic parts and a suit and helmet that allowed him to breathe and heal. Utterly consumed by the Dark Side of the Force, Anakin was now Darth Vader. He wouldn't find out until decades later that Amidala had died in childbirth, and that Luke and Leia were his children.

In the original *Star Wars* trilogy, Vader was played in the costume by British bodybuilder David Prowse, but his basso voice was provided by James Earl Jones. For the later trilogy, Jake Lloyd played a young Anakin, while Hayden Christensen played the teen Anakin. In one of his many bits of tinkering with his beloved film projects, Lucas digitally inserted Christensen as the ghost of Anakin at the end of the *Return of the Jedi* DVD, though the scene in which Vader is unmasked at his death features actor Sebastian Shaw.

Darth Vader's initial design was by concept artist Ralph McQuarrie, who gave Vader the face-mask as a breathing apparatus to cross between ships in the opening scene of *Star Wars*. Lucas had asked McQuarrie to give Vader a helmet like a medieval samurai and a fluttering cape. Sound designer Ben Burtt created Vader's breathing after many attempts to synthesize eighteen types of human breathing; his solution was to use the sound from a scuba regulator. One element many fans miss is that Vader's breathing is constant, like an iron lung, and is not in tempo with his speaking.

Vader has had many stories told about his life in the novels and comic books spun off from the

Movie Mayhem Makers

As filmmakers have created made-for-movies superheroes, they have also introduced original supervillains to fight them:

- Aided by the metal-eyed liquidator Morovich, **Sergei** (actor Oliver Reed) was a forbidding Soviet spy worthy of a Bond movie—too bad he was stuck in Disney's live-action flop, *Condorman* (1981), starring stage actor Michael Crawford as a ridiculous superhero.

- After playing a scenery-chewing witch in *Mommie Dearest* (1981), Faye Dunaway played a scenery-chewing witch in *Supergirl* (1984), featuring Helen Slater as the Man of Steel's Kryptonian cousin. The Omegahedron, power source of Supergirl's interdimensional home of Argo City, fell into the hands of Dunaway's character, the sorceress **Selena**, giving her enough supernatural powers to banish the Girl of Steel to the Phantom Zone.

- Despite an ample supply of supervillains from which to choose, the producers of *Superman IV: The Quest for Peace* (1987) pitted the Man of Steel against the punk rock–haired, superpowered **Nuclear Man** (portrayed by Mark Pillow), a genetic copy of Superman created by Lex Luthor.

- Run-of-the-mill thug **Dorian Tyrell** (played by Peter Greene) briefly received the wish-fulfillment superpowers of an ancient mask (and a "Heads-Up Dorian" action figure) in *The Mask* (1994), the "Smokin'!" box-office smash starring Jim Carrey. (In a 1995–1997 animated spin-off TV series, Tim Curry voiced the Mask's recurring foe, Pretorius, a big-brained scientist with a detachable head and robotic body.)

- Eccentric mastermind and insane-asylum escapee **Casanova Frankenstein** (actor Geoffrey Rush) and his gang the Disco Boys threatened Champion City with a reality-warping device in the tongue-in-cheek *Mystery Men* (1999), until being stopped by the rag-tag superteam based upon Bob Burden's oddball comics characters.

Star Wars licensing realm—known as the "Expanded Universe" stories— but it was in toy and collectibles licensing that Vader's stories continued in the hands of the fans themselves. Clad in padded black armor and an inky cape and cloak, the two-meter-tall Darth Vader appeared as action figures, puppets, candy dispensers, posters, school supplies, food, clothing, cake pans, costumes, life-size statues, and literally thousands of other items. Lucasfilm licensed the character to appear at autograph tours and Hollywood award functions, and the villain shilled in commercials for soft drinks, candy, and cellular phones.

Although the *Star Wars* films have finished production, Lucas announced in 2005 that more *Star Wars* material, including a television series, is in the works for the future. Set in the time period between the trilogies, it seems likely that fans have not seen the last of Darth Vader, nor heard the last of his thrumming red lightsaber or his tortured breathing. —*AM*

Deadpool

Presumably Marvel Comics' anti-hero Deadpool derived his name from Clint Eastwood's final *Dirty Harry* movie, *The Dead Pool* (1988). But Eastwood's Harry Callahan is a police officer who harshly metes out justice and is a man of severe demeanor and few words. Deadpool, on the other hand, is a mercenary who operates outside the law and has a manic personality, continually rattling off stream-of-consciousness repartee. In this respect Deadpool is like an outlaw Spider-Man on speed, and they even wear similar costumes. Deadpool is often called "the Merc with a Mouth."

Created by artist Rob Liefeld and scripter Fabian Nicieza in *New Mutants* #98 (1991), Deadpool was originally presented as a villain who battled Cable, the original X-Force, and Wolverine. Probably due to his wild sense of humor and panache, Deadpool became so popular that he starred in his own comics miniseries (*Deadpool: The Circle Chase*, 1993, and *Deadpool*, 1994), and graduated to his own regular monthly comic book (*Deadpool*, 1997–2002). Thus Deadpool is another example of the villain who evolves into a hero, or, in his case, anti-hero with emotional depth beneath his banter. Though he remained an

outlaw, Deadpool's stories pit him against considerably more evil opponents.

Deadpool's first name appears to be Jack, but his last name remains unknown. He became a mercenary, and once, when injured, was taken in and nursed back to health by a couple named Wade and Mercedes Wilson. Intending to steal his identity, Jack attacked and seemingly murdered Wade but unintentionally killed Mercedes as well. Guilt over Mercedes' death shook Jack's sanity, and he came to believe he was Wade Wilson.

Eventually "Wilson" contracted terminal cancer and volunteered to be a test subject for the U.S./Canadian "Weapon X" project, the same operation that had experimented on Wolverine. "Wilson" was endowed with a superhuman "healing factor," said to be based on Wolverine's, which halted the progress of his cancer. "Wilson's" healing factor is so powerful that not only can he recover from injuries at superhuman speed, but at its peak capacity his healing factor can regenerate entire body organs, even his heart. The healing factor also enhanced "Wilson's" strength, agility, and reflexes to superhuman levels. However, the interaction of the healing factor with "Wilson's" cancer grotesquely disfigured his face and further worsened his mental stability.

"Wilson" became a special operative for Canada's "Department K," but due to ill health was sent to the Hospice, a medical facility where a Doctor Killebrew secretly experimented on his superhuman patients. These patients held a "deadpool" in which they bet on how long each of them would live. After escaping, "Wilson" adopted the name "Deadpool" and eventually returned to working as a mercenary in his new costumed identity.

Deadpool's most persistent enemy is a rival assassin, T-Ray, who proved not only to be adept at sorcery, but also to be the real Wade Wilson, who magically resurrected Mercedes. In 2004 Deadpool began starring in a new comics series, *Cable/Deadpool*, which teamed him up with his former adversary. —*PS*

Deadshot

No reader in 1950 could have imagined that the rather unremarkable Deadshot, who appeared

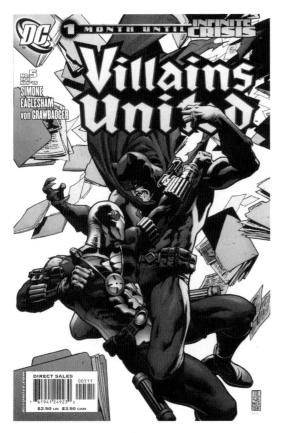

Deadshot vs. Catman. *Villains United* #5 ©2005 DC Comics. COVER ART BY J. G. JONES.

his revised backstory, Floyd Lawton, an emotionally charged hothead with a death wish, fled his dysfunctional family, where his domineering mother nearly manipulated his brother into killing their father. He became the hired assassin Deadshot, his contracts regularly putting him into Batman's sights—and into Belle Reve Prison. Deadshot was reprieved in 1986 to become a core member of the Suicide Squad, the "expendable" task force of villains, diving head-first into the team's hazardous missions but always surviving, when many of his teammates did not. The most popular member of the Squad, Deadshot earned his own 1988 spinoff miniseries.

Later becoming a free agent, the chain-smoking mercenary has since appeared in numerous DC titles, making more enemies than friends. A major player in the best-selling miniseries *Identity Crisis* (2004–2005), Deadshot's profile skyrocketed in 2005. He starred in his second solo miniseries, was one of the Secret Six in the miniseries *Villains United*, received his own DC Direct action figure, and appeared in the "Task Force X" episode of the Cartoon Network's *Justice League Unlimited* (2004–present), with *Smallville*'s Lex Luthor, Michael Rosenbaum, providing his voice. —*ME*

Deathstroke the Terminator

A master tactician and the most deadly mercenary and assassin in the DC Comics universe, Deathstroke the Terminator was inadvertently created by the U.S. government, and he has become the bane of the Teen Titans and other DC characters ever since.

Created by Marv Wolfman and George Pérez in *The New Teen Titans* #2 (1980), and wearing blue-and-black chain-mail armor with orange gloves, boots, shorts, and accents, Deathstroke's most unusual element is his facemask—half of it is black with no eyehole, while the other half is orange with an eyehole—showing adversaries that the Terminator is blind in one eye ... and still kicking their butts! The fact that

with zero fanfare in *Batman* #59, would eventually strike a bull's eye as one of DC Comics' most popular supervillains. In "The Man Who Replaced Batman!" Floyd Lawton is a Gotham City millionaire who plots to steal the Caped Crusader's thunder as the masked, tuxedoed Deadshot, a crack-shot "crime fighter" who shoots to disarm, never to wound or kill. As the decades have shown, no one can replace Batman, and the hero promptly deduces Deadshot's ulterior motive—eliminating Batman to establish himself as the city's new crime boss—playing to Lawton's ego and tricking him into a confession.

Deadshot was reintroduced by writer Steve Englehart and artist Marshall Rogers in *Detective Comics* #474 (1977) in the form in which he is known today: the extraordinary marksman whose fully loaded red-and-white uniform houses an infrared eyepiece and magnum wrist gauntlets. In he often carries a sword, a powered battle staff, explosive grenades, guns, daggers, and other specialized weaponry—and he's highly capable in various forms of combat—might be keys to his battle record. But his origins show another reason for his longevity.

Slade Wilson lied about his age to enter the U.S. Army and became the youngest decorated soldier in the Korean War. Later, while at a special training camp, he met Adeline Kane, a tough instructor who would soon become his wife and the mother of his first son, Grant. Slade went to Vietnam to fight, and volunteered for an army experiment designed to help soldiers combat the effects of truth serum (though it was later revealed the serum was an attempt to create a meta-human soldier). Instead, the serum reacted with Wilson's chemistry to give him superhuman strength and reflexes. It also gave him the ability to use 90 percent of his brain capacity, making him super-intelligent.

Slade returned home to father a second son, Joseph, then disobeyed orders and went back to Vietnam to rescue his POW (prisoner of war) best friend, William Randolph Wintergreen. The army discharged Slade for his actions, but the restless fighter soon became a big-game hunter and mercenary. Even as a mercenary, however, he would only take contracts that didn't conflict with his personal code of ethics. His family didn't know he was the masked mercenary known as Deathstroke the Terminator until the international terrorist known as the Jackal kidnapped Joseph. Slade was seconds too late to save his son, whose vocal chords were severed, leaving him mute. An angry Adeline lashed out at Slade, blinding him in one eye; the pair divorced soon after, and she took the children to raise.

Years later, when Deathstroke turned down a H.I.V.E. (Hierarchy of International Vengeance and Extermination) contract to kill the Teen Titans, a bitter Grant Wilson took it instead. Though he possessed none of his father's altered genetics, Grant called himself the Ravager, but his H.I.V.E.-enhanced abilities weren't enough, and he died in the ensuing fight. To honor his son, Deathstroke took up the contract to bring down the Titans, and he battled them numerous times.

Unbeknownst to them, the Titans were soon infiltrated by Deathstroke's agent, a young socio-pathic girl code-named Terra, who helped him uncover all of their secrets and weaknesses. Even as Deathstroke attacked them on behalf of H.I.V.E., son Joseph—who had gained body-controlling powers due to the chemical agents in his father's blood—joined the Titans as Jericho and helped to stop his father.

Managing to stay ahead of the law, Slade eventually aided the Titans in a case against the Wildebeest Society, and he was forced to thrust his sword into his son's chest, killing Jericho—who had been behind the Wildebeest attacks due to his possession by the Trigon-tainted souls of other-dimensional Azarathians. Despite the fact that Joseph had asked his father to kill him in a moment of lucidity, Slade now felt responsible for both his sons' deaths.

Some time later, Slade learned that he had sired a daughter—Rose—with an exiled Oriental clan princess named Lillian "Sweet Lili" Worth. Rose was kept a secret from Slade until the death of her mother, at which time she was placed in the care of Wintergreen. Gifted with previously untapped powers of her own, Rose even worked alongside the Titans for a while. Then Slade kidnapped her and injected her with the same serum that had been used on him. Rose is now psychotic, and she fights by her father's side as the newest Ravager.

In the pages of his own 65-issue comic-book series, *Deathstroke the Terminator* (1991–1996, including annuals), Slade's career as a mercenary continued, and at times, he even performed heroic deeds and teamed up with other heroes. He was the lover for a time of a former policewoman named Pat Trayce, who became a new version of the Vigilante to fight crime. Deathstroke was also the target of a governmental manhunt when he was framed for supposedly trying to kill the president of the United States, but with the help of Checkmate, he cleared his name. Meanwhile, a new Ravager—eventually revealed as Slade's half-brother Wade DeFarge—killed many of Slade's past associates, and Adeline Kane attacked Deathstroke, now exhibiting extra-human powers due to a blood transfusion from her ex-husband. Deathstroke also learned that he not only had an extra healing factor, but that he was functionally immortal because of it.

Over time, Slade has reverted to a younger age, lost his memory, regained his eye, reverted back to his "regular" genetically enhanced self, and taken on many of the major heroes of the DC Universe. Adeline became the H.I.V.E. mistress and was mortally wounded by Vandal Savage, and Deathstroke learned that the spirit of his son, Jericho, had been hiding within his body in the years since his "death." Controlling his father's body, Jericho decapitated Wintergreen and set out to destroy a new incarnation of the Teen Titans. Back in control of his own body, and working with Rose/Ravager, Deathstroke now intends to stop Jericho and make the Titans' Raven pay for her part in Jericho's madness.

In 2005, Deathstroke began a new relationship, working with Lex Luthor and other major rogues in the DC Universe as part of a new Secret Society of Super-Villains.

Using just the name Slade, Deathstroke appeared as an ongoing villainous character in the *Teen Titans* cartoon (2003–2006). He appeared as an action figure from DC Direct in 2005. —*AM*

Decepticons

The Transformers-Decepticons toy line and resulting media franchise represents one of the first successful examples of Japanese superheroes and supervillains adopted for an American audience. Transformers are intelligent robots (or large humanoids) with the capability to transform themselves, usually into inanimate objects (such as a fighter jet, car, or tank) or animals. The premise of the franchise relies on the age-old struggle between good and evil, with two main factions warring for control of their home planet, Cybertron.

The heroic Autobots (called Cybertrons in the Japanese version) are led by Optimus Prime, and their opponents, the militaristic and brutal Decepticons (Destrons in the Japanese version), are led by Megatron. Megatron was responsible for beginning the Cybertronian Civil War, in which he exterminated Autobots by the millions and earned his claim to fame as the galaxy's most ruthless leader. Other potential world dominators have tried

to usurp Megatron's power, including Astrotrain and Blitzwing, Shockwave, and Galvatron, a Decepticon created from Megatron himself.

Hasbro began the toy line in 1984, which combined the Japanese toy company Takara's successful Diaclone and Micro Change toylines into a new brand for U.S. consumers. The basic backstory of the toy line and subsequent comic books and cartoons were developed by Marvel Comics writers Jim Shooter and Dennis O'Neil. Marvel published several series during the 1980s, even producing a four-issue miniseries, *G.I. Joe and the Transformers* in 1986, followed by later releases from the company in the 1990s.

The animated TV series *Transformers* (1984–1987), created to support the toy franchise, focused on battle after battle as the domineering Decepticons attempted to destroy peace within the galaxy. Subsequent spin-offs, such as *Beast Wars: Transformers* (1996–1999), *Transformers: Robots in Disguise* (2001), and *Transformers: Cybertron* (2005) continued into the 1990s and 2000s. Capitalizing on these shows' high-action content and popularity, the now-defunct Dreamwave Studios published several Transformers comics between 2002 and 2004.

A live-action *Transformers* movie boasts DreamWorks producer Steven Spielberg at the helm. With no less than four writers involved in the project at various points, fans eagerly await leaks regarding the film's development. In mid-2005 writer Alex Kurtzman acknowledged the challenge of developing a the storyline: "It's a movie franchise based on a toy line, so the first question you have to ask yourself is, 'Well, what's the movie?'" In anticipation of the success of the film, IDW Publishing began publishing its line of *Transformers* comics in October 2005, led by the creative team of comics scribe Simon Furman and artist E. J. Su. —*GM*

Desaad: *See* **Darkseid's Elite**

Despero

Is Despero a master strategist with a penchant for chess matches or a brutish hulk capable of pummeling the brawniest Justice Leaguers into submission? *Both*, as this DC Comics supervillain has, since his first appearance, experienced what might be called an extreme makeover.

A squirrelly figure with magenta pigmentation, a scaly fin atop his bald pate, and a freakish third eye upon his forehead, Despero first appeared in *Justice League of America* #1 (1960), the fourth appearance of the JLA (after three try-out issues of *The Brave and the Bold*). The dictatorial ruler of the other-dimensional world of Kalanor, Despero uses his extra orb's hypnotic powers to enslave the heroes except for the Flash, whom he challenges to a rigged chess game with the other Justice Leaguers' fates at stake. With each wrong move, Flash inadvertently sentences his teammates to exile, Despero's "mystic mental powers" expelling them to inescapable planets. The last-minute intervention of JLA mascot Snapper Carr liberates the Leaguers from their deportation.

Many readers assume that Despero was the creation of *JLA* writer Gardner Fox and artist Mike Sekowsky, but in a 2004 interview Murphy Anderson, who drew the cover to *Justice League of America* #1, revealed that he designed the alien's look based upon a brainstorming session with editor Julius Schwartz, who suggested the hero-versus-villain chess concept. That landmark cover has been recreated by other artists on a variety of occasions.

After his capture in *JLA* #1, Despero was returned to his homeworld, where scientists neutralized his powers by surgically amputating his third eye. His eye regenerated, however, as did its mesmerizing attributes, and Despero returned for several additional clashes with the Justice League.

In 1986, *Justice League of America* writer Gerry Conway initiated an evolution of the supervillain that has continued into the twenty-first century. Despero's powers were infinitely magnified upon his entering the Flame of Py'tar. Returning to Earth to exact revenge upon the Justice League, he unleashed a wave of terror including the destruction of the JLA's orbiting satellite headquarters, the torturing of Batman, and the murder of the family of JLAer Gypsy—clearly, this was no longer your father's Despero. In a 1990 battle, Manhattan was partially destroyed as Despero, now a superstrong juggernaut weighing nearly 300

pounds, nearly battered the Martian Manhunter to death. In subsequent adventures Despero has fought Supergirl, the Justice Society, and the junior JLA Young Justice, and his spirit was even exorcised and trapped inside the "Abyssal Plane"—a just fate for a supervillain who in his first outing made the Justice Leaguers intergalactic castaways. Despero remains one of the Justice League's most tenacious and terrifying adversaries, always managing to return from wherever he is banished.

Voiced by Keith David, Despero appeared in the two-part "Hearts and Minds" episode of the Cartoon Network's *Justice League* (2001–2003). In his television incarnation he was purple-skinned with a goatee, but his fin head and third eye remained devilishly intact. —*ME*

Diablo

Stan Lee and Jack Kirby introduced "The Dreaded Diablo!" in *Fantastic Four* #30 (1964). "After all these decades—Diablo is free to walk the earth once more!" cackles the arrogant alchemist who is liberated from a Transylvanian crypt by none other than the FF's ever-lovin' Thing. This is Esteban Corazan Del Diablo, a ninth-century Spanish nobleman kept young by an immortality serum and imprisoned after dabbling in arcane potions. Controlling the Thing via alchemy and the promise of reverting him to his human form, Diablo divides the Fantastic Four, with the Thing serving as his aide as he amasses a fortune selling youth elixirs, plant-growth formulas, and other wonders. When Diablo's potions prove fraudulent, the Thing rejoins the FF to entomb the villain once more. The vengeful Diablo returned a mere five issues later, controlling the winged, fire-spewing beast called Dragon Man.

The horned-cowled Diablo always has something up his sleeve—his paralyzing "somnambumist," an explosive pellet, or the all-powerful Philosopher's Stone, "the quintessential catalyst of (elemental) transmutation." He has battled the FF numerous times over the decades, including the "Diablo" episode of the original *Fantastic Four* animated television series (1967–1970).

Diablo remains a serious threat to the FF in the twenty-first century: The alchemist infiltrated the team's headquarters in *Fantastic Four* #526 (2005) to commandeer Reed (Mr. Fantastic) Richards' time machine and return to the era of the Spanish Inquisition, with revenge on his mind. Richards outsmarted Diablo, however, allowing the unwitting villain to take charge of the FF's interdimensional portal instead. —*ME*

Dr. Alchemy

He's two ... two ... two supervillains in one! In *Showcase* #13 (1958), the third tryout issue of the Silver Age (1956–1969) Flash, writer John Broome and artist Carmine Infantino introduced one of the Scarlet Speedster's earliest costumed foes, Mr. Element. Behind the villain's green jumpsuit and gasmask is Albert Desmond, a chemistry buff turned criminal. Deriding the Flash as he uses element-based gimmicks (such as an undetectable net of gold wire and "elemento," a magnetic light) to thwart the hero's advances, the haughty Mr. Element—accompanied by subservient costumed henchmen named after inert properties like Argon and Xenon—is soon outwitted by the science-savvy Flash. Desmond returns in the very next *Showcase*, issue #14, now calling himself Dr. Alchemy. Cloaked in a green hood with an "A" emblem and wielding the Philosopher's Stone, the legendary tool of transmutation, Dr. Alchemy slows down the racing Flash by turning coins into oily quicksilver and walls into blinding crystal, but the lightning-fast hero whisks the talisman from Desmond's grasp and saves the day.

Vacillating between identities in later clashes with the Flash and the Justice League, this "two-in-one criminal's" motivations evolved beyond the dual-identity gimmick. Desmond was a schizophrenic, the good and evil sides of his personality struggling for dominance. During a period of reformation he buried the Philosopher's Stone, but his "psychic twin" *Alvin* Desmond obtained the talisman in *The Flash* vol. 1 #287 (1980) and became Dr. Alchemy, with the docile Albert Desmond becoming a supporting-cast member in the *Flash* series.

The villain's history has since become as addled as Desmond's mind: *Flash* vol. 2 #41

(1990), starring Wally West, the Silver Age Flash's successor, established that Alvin was the Philosopher's Stone's artificially constructed personification of Albert's dark psyche. The Stone briefly fell into the hands of biochemist Dr. Curtis Engstrom, who used it for supervillainy as the Alchemist. A demented forensic scientist named Alexander Petrov became the new Mr. Element, but his attempt to frame Captain Cold led to his murder at Cold's hands. Albert Desmond has returned to his Dr. Alchemy guise in the 2000s, springing from his cell in Keystone City's supervillain prison Iron Heights into a 2005 stint with the reunited Secret Society of Super-Villains. So long as the schizoid Desmond is within a stone's throw of his elemental weapon, no one in the DC Universe is safe from his transmutations or his evil. —*ME*

Dr. Bedlam: *See* Darkseid's Elite

Dr. Cyclops

Is there any sinister superweapon more popular than the shrinking ray? The study of doll-sized humans has transfixed power-mad maniacs from Brainiac, who collected shrunken cities in bottles, to Dr. Doom, known to reduce his foes upon occasion. But the master of miniaturization was Dr. Cyclops, star of the self-titled 1940 film from Paramount Pictures directed by Ernest B. Schoedsack (a 1940 novelization of the movie was penned by author Will Garth).

Dr. Cyclops is actually Dr. Alexander Thorkel, a stereotypical mad scientist: bald and stocky with thick-lensed, round-framed glasses, toiling from his remote laboratory (in Peru), always clad in a lab coat. Setting up shop in the jungle after the Manhattan science community frowns upon his eccentric methodology, Thorkel taps into a nearby radium reserve and perfects a miniaturization device he tests upon animals. As if his experiments were not already encroaching upon nature's order, he next reduces his housekeeper Mira to the size of a pygmy. She dies, causing Thorkel no compunction—it's merely a minor setback. Some time later, when his former colleagues visit Thorkel's lab upon his invitation, their repulsion at his experiments earns them a ticket to tiny-land, followed by dramatically staged cat-and-mouse chases. Thorkel relishes tyrannizing his minuscule captives, and when one of them smashes a lens of the eyeglasses he depends upon, the squinting, "one-eyed" madman's nom de supervillainy is coined.

Dr. Cyclops was revolutionary for its day, wowing audiences with special effects vastly superior to Schoedsack's better-known earlier effort, *King Kong* (which he co-directed with Merian C. Cooper in 1933), screen marvels magnified by an early use of Technicolor. But actor Albert Dekker as Thorkel makes the film—his forceful presence and mushrooming obsession drive the story. —*ME*

Dr. Doom

Brilliant heroes tend to cast intensely dark shadows, a literary fact illustrated amply by Victor von Doom, the superscience- and magic-wielding nemesis of Marvel's Fantastic Four (FF). Arguably as essential to the success of Stan Lee's and Jack Kirby's quintessential superteam as any of the Fantastic Four's members, Dr. Doom represents the polar opposite of the sunny optimism embodied by the team's leader, Mr. Fantastic. From his first appearance in *Fantastic Four* vol. 1 #5 (1962), Doom's armored visage became a symbol of the horrific side of science and influenced later armored villains, including the Micronauts' Baron Karza and the *Star Wars* franchise's Darth Vader.

Young von Doom's destiny was forged when his native Latveria's tyrannical ruler murdered his father, giving the lad an unquenchable desire for revenge that ultimately leads him to seize Latveria's ruling castle for himself. During his long throneward march, Doom uses a combination of his scientific talents and the collection of mystical herbs and potions left by his late mother, who had been a powerful sorceress. The future Latverian monarch's developing techno-mystical skills soon win him a science scholarship to New York's State University, where he meets Reed Richards, the Fantastic Four's eventual leader. After angrily rejecting Richards' well-intentioned attempt to correct his erroneous calculations in a transdimensional projection experiment—actually Doom's

Fantastic Four Annual #2 ©1964 Marvel Comics.
COVER ART BY JACK KIRBY AND CHIC STONE.

attempt to contact his dead mother—Doom is injured when his apparatus explodes. Echoing the Lex Luthor/Superboy relationship, Doom unfairly blames Richards for the mishap, which scars his face and gets him expelled from school (*Fantastic Four* vol. 1 *Annual* #2, 1964).

Others have subsequently embroidered Doom's origin story, and writer/artist John Byrne's take on the tale is arguably the most compelling. In Byrne's version, Doom's only permanent injury from his accident is one long, thin facial scar. Believing himself to be horribly disfigured, the vain Doom's post-collegiate wanderings take him to Tibet, where an order of monks crafts a special suit of iron armor in which he can hide from his pain. Succumbing to youthful impatience and hubris, Doom permanently sears his entire face when he dons the armor's face-mask while it is still red-hot from the forge (*Fantastic Four* #278, 1985).

Joseph Culp as Dr. Doom in director Oley Sassone's unreleased 1994 film *Fantastic Four*.

tic Four when it suits his purposes. When cosmic ray exposure jeopardized Susan (the Invisible Woman) Storm's pregnancy, Johnny Storm (the Human Torch) called upon Doom to save his sister and her baby after Reed Richards—the child's father—proved incapable. Doom's superscientific expertise rescued both mother and daughter, thereby scoring Doom a major psychological victory over the hated Reed Richards, who had to agree to name the girl after Doom's lost love Valeria. Doom reveled in the fact that Richards will always be reminded of his own shortcomings—and his deep debt to his oldest foe—every time he sees Susan or little Valeria (*Fantastic Four* #483, 2002).

Although he never hesitates to grab power or to launch merciless attacks against adversaries such as Reed Richards, Spider-Man, the Avengers, or the X-Men, there is a good deal more to Victor von Doom than a conqueror's lusts. Although he demands complete obeisance from Latveria's citizenry, Doom governs his subjects with surprising benevolence, filling their every material need. As a head of state, Doom also enjoys diplomatic immunity in most nations, much to the frustration of every superhero who has matched wits with him.

Doom subsequently outfitted his armor with numerous offensive and defensive weapons, including strength-enhancing motors, protective force fields, a jet pack, and projectile and beam weapons; he also equipped his Latverian stronghold with an army of Doom robots (his "Doombot" servants) and even constructed a time machine.

Despite his bitter enmity toward Reed Richards, Dr. Doom will cooperate with the Fantas-

Doom made the jump from comics to television with *The Fantastic Four* (1967), an animated series in which he was voiced by Paul Frees (better known as the voice of Boris Badanov). Doom also appeared in 1981's *Spider-Man and His Amazing Friends*, in which he was voiced by Shepard

Menken; frequented 1994's *Fantastic Four* series, in which Simon Templeman and Neil Ross portrayed the Latverian potentate; and guest-starred in the animated short feature *Spider-Man: Attack of the Octopus* (2002), in which Mark Meer portrayed Doom. In *Fantastic Four*, part of the Marvel *Action Hour* (1994–1996), Lorne Kennedy supplied the voice beneath the armor. From the 1980s forward, Dr. Doom became ubiquitous in toy stores as well as on TV sets, adorning products ranging from Colorforms sets to Halloween costumes to video games to the action-figure lines of Mattel, Toy Biz, and Marvel Legends.

Comic-book reimaginings of Dr. Doom have also continued apace during the past two decades. Under the stewardship of writer John Francis Moore and artist Pat Broderick, the lord of Latveria—or perhaps a facsimile of same—resurfaced near the end of the twenty-first century and immediately began using the original Doom's technology to try to impose order on a chaotic, dystopic future (*Doom 2099*, 1993–1996). In 2003, writer Neil Gaiman and illustrators Andy Kubert and Richard Isanove crafted a comics miniseries titled *Marvel 1602*, which placed many familiar Marvel characters into the Elizabethan era—and presented the nefarious Count Otto von Doom, ruler of Latveria and murderer of Queen Elizabeth.

In 2004, Marvel's acclaimed reimagining of the Fantastic Four (the ongoing *Ultimate Fantastic Four* series, launched in 2004) directly linked the origin of Doom—plausibly rechristened Victor Van Damme—to that of the Fantastic Four by placing Doom in the same transdimensional accident that gave the heroes their powers. In a twist on the original Doom origin story, Van Damme discovered a possible error in Reed's calculations and introduced a correction factor that may have caused the accident. Van Damme's armor, which includes Satanic-looking cloven hooves, is an organic, built-in consequence of the FF's origin mishap, and he has been revealed to be a descendant of the dreaded Vlad Tepes, better known as Dracula. The new Doom lives up to his ancestor's "Impaler" reputation by skewering his enemies on sharpened spikes carried by fast-flying mechanical insects.

Although the 1994 live-action *The Fantastic Four* (produced by Roger Corman and directed by Oley

Sassone) was never released, it anticipated the integration of Doom into the FF's beginnings in *Ultimate Fantastic Four* and in 2005's big-budget *Fantastic Four* feature; in the latter, Doom (portrayed with compelling menace by *Nip/Tuck*'s Julian McMahon) is more boardroom raider than legendary vampire, patterned on Donald Trump rather than on Dracula. —*MAM*

Dr. Evil I

"And so, Captain Action, the contest is over! Soon you will be helplessly in my power!" sneers a ghoulish figure with a pale-blue complexion and an exposed brain as he lords his mind-controlling "hypnotic eye" over his shackled adversary. This is the *original* Dr. Evil (no relation to the *Austin Powers* character), first seen in an advertising campaign for his 1968 release from Ideal Toys. The original supervillain action figure, the poseable, 12-inch Dr. Evil followed in the plastic footsteps of his heroic counterpart, the G.I. Joe–like Captain Action, who premiered two years prior. The Captain could be dressed in an array of costumes (each sold separately) of licensed superheroes from Aquaman to Spider-Man, but his arch-enemy had no such supervillain outfits (although Joker and Red Skull uniforms are rumored to have been in development but never produced). "The sinister invader of Earth," Dr. Evil sported a shimmering blue Nehru jacket and trousers, sandals, and a gold medallion, and was packaged with a "laser gun" and a Caucasian, bearded rubber mask (slipping over the figure's head, concealing his alien face but not his hands or feet), allowing him to assimilate into Earth culture as Dr. Thorpe, "a benign gentleman." A gift set released during Christmas 1968 armed Dr. Evil with an array of "evil, evil things" including a "thought sensor" helmet, a "reducer" shrinking wand, an "ionized hypo," the hypnotic eye, a lab coat, and an additional disguise, the Asian mask of Dr. Ling.

DC Comics readers know of Dr. Evil from two additional sources: a Kurt Schaffenberger–drawn house ad appearing in the publisher's line in 1968 and in issues #3 and #4 (1969) of DC's *Captain Action* series, written and illustrated by *Green Lantern* artist Gil Kane, which posited the bad doc-

Dr. Evil catalog page ©1968 Ideal Toys.

tor as the transmogrified father of Captain Action's late wife. Manufacturer Playing Mantis reissued both Captain Action and Dr. Evil in a short-lived figure line in the late 1990s. With his figural rebirth, Dr. Evil was finally accompanied by licensed supervillain ensembles: Flash Gordon's enemy Ming the Merciless and the Phantom's arch-foe Kabai Singh. —ME

Dr. Evil II

When comedian Mike Myers invented Dr. Evil—a bald, scar-faced Blofeld lampoon, with added mannerisms parodying Myers' *Saturday Night Live* boss, producer Lorne Michaels—for his cinematic spy spoof *Austin Powers: International Man of Mystery* (1997), little did he realize that the greatest menace this wacky world dominator posed to the swinging secret agent was his stealing the film from its title star. (Since Myers played both hero and villain, however, his job security was not threatened.)

As the supervillain discloses in a father-son encounter group, during his childhood he "would sometimes be placed in a burlap bag and beaten with reeds—pretty standard, really." Reared by his prostitute mother and over-achieving Belgian father, a genius with "low-grade narcolepsy and a penchant for buggery" who was prone to "outrageous claims like he invented the question mark," is there any wonder why this doctor—who at age fourteen had his scrotum ritualistically shaved—was destined to become evil? In 1960s England, Dr. Evil built a global crime empire, conducting experiments with his invention, the "laser," and habitually holding the world ransom for one million dollars. To escape capture by Austin Powers he allows himself to be cryogenically frozen, along with his beloved cat Mr. Bigglesworth. Powers is similarly put on ice, and he is resuscitated in 1997 when Dr. Evil thaws himself out to once again terrorize the world. Both Powers and Evil are proverbial fishes out of water, clumsily acclimating themselves to contemporary society.

Striking a comedic chord with audiences and with the actor/screenwriter who portrayed him, Dr. Evil's profile was amplified in the film's continuations *Austin Powers: The Spy Who Shagged Me* (1999) and *Austin Powers in Goldmember* (2002). Fascinated with time travel, Dr. Evil hopped through various decades in both sequels, nabbing Austin's mojo in the second movie and joining forces with the disco-era, roller-boogying scoundrel Goldmember (also portrayed by Myers) in the third.

Sometimes operating from an island base with a Mount Rushmore–sized stone carving of his face, Dr. Evil is aided by a sinister circle: Scott Evil, his son artificially created in a lab during Evil's cryogenic nap; Number Two, the eye-patched front man to Evil's "legitimate" businesses; his loyal Nazi aide (and sometimes lover) Frau Farbissina; and his clone Mini-Me, a diminutive duplicate with whom Dr. Evil formed an unsettling bond. Expendable underlings are at the beck and call of the man who earned the title "doctor" after six years in evil medical school. Despite his intellect, Dr. Evil still has kinks to work out of his weaponry—his "overly elaborate and exotic" death traps are easily escapable, his automated chair never seems to work properly, and instead of

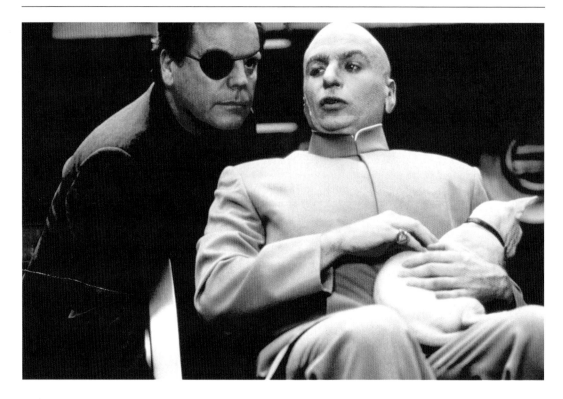

Blofeld parody Dr. Evil (Mike Myers) confides in his aide Number Two (Robert Wagner) in *Austin Powers: International Man of Mystery* (1997).

a tank of sharks with "frickin' laser beams" attached to their heads, the best he can muster are ill-tempered mutated sea bass.

In *Goldmember*, Dr. Evil discovered that he and Austin Powers are actually brothers who were separated as toddlers (and you wondered why they looked so much alike). Dr. Evil reformed, and his heir Scott secretly assumed control of his dastardly domain, should any further sequels develop.

Myers appeared as Dr. Evil at the 2002 MTV Video Music Awards, and his infamous creation has enjoyed a spate of merchandising, from action figures to talking plush dolls to Halloween costumes. —*ME*

Dr. Light

In "The Last Case of the Justice League!" in *Justice League of America* #12 (1962), the irascible illuminator Dr. Light swaggers through the team's Secret Sanctuary, dictating to JLA junior member

Snapper Carr his nefarious tale of the League's defeat. Light has banished the Leaguers to "sidereal worlds" where their environments counter the heroes' superpowers—Aquaman, who requires water every sixty minutes, is trapped on an arid sand planet; Martian Manhunter is incapacitated on a world that spews fire, his weakness; etc. Thanks to the quick thinking of JLA members Superman and Batman, the Leaguers are freed from their interplanetary prisons and return to Earth. The villain's thunderbolts, hard-light and heat beams, blinding flares, and kryptonite ray don't hold a candle to the JLA's teamwork and ingenuity, and it's lights out for Dr. Light!

JLA editor Julius Schwartz took a shine to Dr. Light, having him frequently battle the solo superheroes in his stable. Dr. Light trapped the Atom in a light bulb, pummeled Green Lantern with solid-light shafts, and also lit into the Flash, Batman and Superman, and even the Justice League in return bouts. Despite his grandiose plans of conquest, Light's efforts flickered and he never scored a victory. Lowering his sights in an effort to restore his reputation, Dr. Light challenged the JLA's junior counterparts in *Teen Titans* #44 (1976) … and was unplugged once again.

In *DC Super-Stars* #14's "Secret Origins of Super-Villains" edition (1977), writer Paul Kupperberg and artist Dick Ayers illuminated the rogue's background, revealing his real name, Dr. *Arthur Light*. In an origin that has been amplified in later tales, Light was a physicist employed by S.T.A.R. Labs. His partner Dr. Jacob Finlay created the Dr. Light garb and identity, embarking upon a short-lived superhero career in the guise, but after Finlay's unfortunate demise, Arthur Light nabbed the suit and light-based weaponry and flashed into a crime career.

Dr. Light made occasional appearances in various DC titles over the next few years, losing each battle. Chagrined by his tarnished reputation, in Marv Wolfman and George Pérez's *The New Teen Titans* #3 (1981) the vindictive villain hired a quartet of super-rogues—Psimon, Gizmo, Shimmer, and Mammoth—and as the Fearsome Five blitzed the recently regrouped Titans. Psimon challenged Light for control of the team—"Lousy filth. I should kill him for humiliating me!"—and Dr. Light was ousted from the very team he organized.

The crestfallen criminal temporarily retired and was replaced as Dr. Light by Kimiyo Hoshi in *Crisis on Infinite Earths* #4 (1985), but by 1989 he was back in action alongside the Suicide Squad, the U.S. government–sponsored task force of heroes and villains. Years of defeats had taken their toll, and Dr. Light had become an incessant whiner and an annoyance to those in his circle.

Having exhausted Dr. Light's persecution complex, in 1996 DC Comics began a gradual overhaul of the villain. Light was imprisoned inside Green Lantern's power battery, emerging as a hybrid of flesh and light. He was later recruited by Lex Luthor as a charter member of the Injustice Gang, fighting the Justice League alongside the Joker, Mirror Master, Circe, and the Ocean Master.

Dr. Light was elevated to A-list status in the best-selling miniseries *Identity Crisis* (2004–2005), by writer Brad Meltzer and penciler Rags Morales.

Light was implicated in the grisly murder of the Elongated Man's wife Sue Dibny, and the Justice League's investigation exposed a closeted secret: years ago, Dr. Light had uncovered the League's Achilles heel—the vulnerability of their loved ones. As a safeguard measure, Zatanna magically erased select portions of Light's memories and altered his personality. A cadre of seven Leaguers shielded this from the rest of the team, but Sue's murder unraveled a web of duplicities that made Light aware of what had been done to him.

Now a creature of blind hate, Dr. Light has become utterly lethal. In a rematch with the Teen Titans, in *Teen Titans* vol. 3 #22 (2005) by Geoff Johns and Mike McKone, Light warned the young heroes as they lay prostrate before him, humbled by his blistering light attacks: "You better watch yourselves. If you learn the wrong thing, or maybe if you threaten your mentors sooner than they want to be replaced—they might do it to you. They'll take your mind."

A more light-hearted Dr. Light, voiced by Rodger Bumpass, appeared on television during season one of the Cartoon Network's animated *Teen Titans* (2003–2006). DC Comics' toy division DC Direct has produced a Dr. Light PVC figurine in 2001 and an action figure in 2005. The name "Dr. Light" was first used by DC Comics during the Golden Age (1938–1954) for an adversary of Dr. Mid-Nite. —*ME*

Dr. Loveless

Dr. Miguelito Quixote Loveless was a little man with big plans. As seen in the James Bond–in–the–Old West, "steampunk"-fiction forerunner television series *The Wild Wild West* (1965–1970), the puckish Dr. Loveless, charismatically played by dwarf actor Michael Dunn, was a diminutive mastermind (with an extraordinary singing voice!) often prone to childlike temper tantrums. Regarding civilization as woefully cruel and immoral, he struck out against society with bizarre schemes that, ironically, sometimes employed violence to achieve his goals.

Premiering in the series' third episode, "The Night the Wizard Shook the Earth" (original airdate:

October 1, 1965), Loveless was clearly a scientific genius, having conceived nineteenth-century versions of the automobile, the radio, and the airplane. Surrounded by an unusual "family" including the mute giant Voltaire (played by Richard Kiel, best known as Bond villain Jaws) and fellow crooner Antoinette (actress Phoebe Dorin, with whom Dunn performed in a musical stage act), Loveless believed himself the rightful owner of Southern California. He threatened the United States government with a high-powered explosive in an attempt to reclaim his territory and re-create it into a peaceful sanctuary for society's blameless citizens, its children, before being stopped by U.S. Secret Service agents James West and Artemus Gordon.

The psychotic genius Loveless was featured in an additional nine episodes (Voltaire appeared in a total of three and Antoinette in six; the magician Count Manzeppi, played by Victor Buono, aka King Tut from TV's 1966–1968 *Batman*, was *Wild Wild West*'s only other recurring major villain, seen twice in season two), continuing his efforts to acquire Southern California and, in later episodes, purge the planet of evil. Loveless' inventions included a shrinking powder, a steam-powered robot, a hallucinogen that induced murderous rages, and sound vibrations that transported victims into alternate realities depicted in oil paintings.

The villain's son, Dr. Miguelito Loveless, Jr., played by Paul Williams (later the voice of the Penguin on *Batman: The Animated Series*, 1992–1995), continued the "family business" by building cyborgs and an atomic bomb in *The Wild Wild West Revisited* (1979), a CBS reunion movie; Dunn had since passed away, and the junior Loveless attributed his father's demise to an ulcer caused by his stressful defeats by James West.

Director Barry Sonnenfeld's campy big-budget movie *Wild Wild West* (1999) was a reboot of the TV series, with Will Smith as West and Kevin Kline as Gordon. Kenneth Branagh was cast as Dr. *Arliss* Loveless, a disgruntled Southern super-scientist avenging the recently defeated Confederacy by attacking the United States with, among other weapons, a smoke-spewing, giant mechanical spider. The film included the misguided attempt to make this Loveless "short" by revealing him to be a double amputee. Dr. Loveless merchandising

includes Rittenhouse Archives' trading cards spotlighting the TV series, and a movie-related action figure bearing Branagh's likeness. —*ME*

Dr. No

Dr. Julius No, another of the latter-day Oriental masterminds in the mold of Dr. Fu Manchu, towers over James Bond—literally. He is a good half foot taller than Bond, his excellent posture adding to the impression of height. As described by Ian Fleming in his novel *Dr. No* (1958), "[No's] head was also elongated and tapered from a round, completely bald skull down to a sharp chin so that the impression was of a reversed raindrop—or rather, oildrop, for the skin was of a deep almost translucent yellow." No has, instead of hands, steel pincers; his hands were forcibly

Dr. No adaptation from *Showcase* #43 ©1963 DC Comics. COVER ART BY BOB BROWN.

amputated by one of the Chinese Tongs, from whom No embezzled a million dollars.

From his base on Crab Key Island off Jamaica, where his cover is that of a dealer in bird guano, No sabotages U.S. missile tests for Soviet Russia. Beneath his island, No has constructed a fortress that puts Bond to "a great deal of pain." There Bond is dumped into an electrified tunnel of tortures that includes scalding heat, freezing cold, twenty tarantulas, and a giant squid. His physical nature and his sadistic bent cause No to stand out even among Bond's adversaries and his inevitable death is one of the most abhorrent in the entire Bond canon, but he lives on in the form of a set of trading cards produced for collectors.

Dr. No was the sixth James Bond novel, but the first James Bond film. *Dr. No* (1962), directed by Terence Young, features Joseph Wiseman as No. Given that the cold war has thawed, No is no longer in the pay of the U.S.S.R.; he now works for SPECTRE, a worldwide criminal group whose acronym defines its purpose: Special Executive for Counterintelligence, Terrorism, Revenge, and Extortion. The novel was adapted into a comic strip in Britain in 1960; DC Comics published a comic-book adaptation (*Showcase* #43) of the film in 1963. *—MWB*

Dr. Octopus

Armed and utterly dangerous, Marvel Comics' Dr. Octopus, first seen in Stan Lee and Steve Ditko's *The Amazing Spider-Man* (*ASM*) #3 (1963), was the first supervillain to defeat the web-slinger. Dr. Otto Octavius, "the most brilliant atomic-researcher in our country today," is the creator of a set of four telescoping, mechanical tentacles that allow him to work with radioactive materials from a secure distance. The apparatus, worn around his ample midsection and controlled by rotary dials, earns him the nickname "Dr. Octopus" from his coworkers. A nuclear explosion grafts the robotic arms to his person, and Octavius, now able to manipulate the appendages with his mind—which is criminally corrupted in the mishap—becomes the megalomaniacal Dr. Octopus. As "Doc Ock" takes over the atomic plant that

More James Bond Supervillains: Nobody Does It Badder

When dealing with nuclear-armed nutcases and virtually unstoppable assassins, it's no wonder that 007 has a license to kill!

- **Kamal Khan and General Orlov (*Octopussy*, 1983):** It was double-trouble for 007 when an Indian jewel smuggler (Louis Jourdan) and Russian general (Steven Berkoff) nearly ignited World War III.

- **Max Largo (*Never Say Never Again*, 1983):** Klaus Maria Brandauer played a renamed (originally Emilio Largo) SPECTRE operative in this tepid Thunderball remake.

- **Max Zorin (*A View to a Kill*, 1985):** Christopher Walken's Zorin schemed to trigger the San Andreas fault to level Silicon Valley.

- **May Day (*A View to a Kill*, 1985):** Statuesque Grace Jones' high-kicking "problem eliminator" usurped the limelight from her boss, Zorin.

- **Brad Whitaker (*The Living Daylights*, 1987):** Pudgy Joe Don Baker was walking tall as a half-cocked munitions dealer.

- **Franz Sanchez (*License to Kill*, 1989):** Crater-faced Robert Davi portrayed this ruthless South American druglord.

- **Alec Trevelyan (*Goldeneye*, 1995):** This turncoat British intelligence agent 006, played by Sean Bean, highjacked a satellite-controlled weapons network.

- **Elliot Carver (*Tomorrow Never Dies*, 1997):** Jonathan Pryce's menacing media mogul redefined "ratings war" by trying to trick Britain and China into conflict.

- **Viktor Zokas (*The World Is Not Enough*, 1999):** One of Bond's scariest villains, Zokas (Robert Carlyle), aka Renard, was a psychopathic terrorist unable to feel pain due to a bullet lodged in his brain.

- **Zao and Gustav Graves (*Die Another Day*, 2002):** Zao (Rick Yune) was a Korean criminal with a diamond-studded face, and Graves (Toby Stephens) was an Iceland-based world dominator with a heat-beam-producing satellite mirror.

From *The Amazing Spider-Man* vol. 1 #89
©1970 Marvel Comics.
ART BY GIL KANE AND JOHN ROMITA, SR.

once employed him, he unflinchingly overpowers the brash young Spider-Man with his lightning-fast arms ("He beat me! I—I never had a chance!" ruminates the humbled hero). In a rematch, Spidey blinds Octavius with a well-aimed webbing spurt and kayos "the most dangerous villain I've ever faced." (Curiously, a lettering error—or perhaps an editorial joke—on page eight of that tale has Ock calling his nemesis "*Super*-Man.")

At a mere glance, one might not regard Dr. Octopus as threat. Portly, of meager height, bespectacled (often in goggles), and sporting a bowl cut that should earn the license revocation of his barber, Doc Ock looks remarkably like singer Roy Orbison (a theory that reclusive artist Steve Ditko patterned the character's face after the legendary "Pretty Woman" crooner's has long circulated throughout comics fandom). Normally attired in olive drabs and orange work gloves, Dr. Octopus might even be mistaken for a tradesman—this is to

underestimate Doc Ock is to risk one's life. His telepathic command of his titanium tentacles is uncanny. Normally 6 feet in length, the arms can instantaneously elongate to 25 feet and zoom, either in tandem or autonomously, at 90 miles per second. Each limb posses a three-prong pincer that can delicately caress a grape or forcefully crush a cinderblock. Dr. Octopus frequently walks on two or four of his robotic arms like stilts, and uses them to climb walls … ironically, like a spider.

In Dr. Octopus' return in *ASM* #11–#12 (1964), the madman again trounced Spidey (who was severely weakened by a viral infection) and exposed his Peter Parker identity to the public. Fortunately, it was assumed that Parker was masquerading as the web-slinger to obtain newspaper photos of Doc Ock. A vengeful Dr. Octopus was back in *The Amazing Spider-Man Annual* #1 (1964) with "friends" in tow: fellow Spider-foes Electro, Kraven the Hunter, Sandman, the Vulture, and Mysterio, banding together as the Sinister Six. Ock lost to Spidey in these adventures, his bruised ego deepening his hatred of the arachnid hero.

Spider-Man soon had plenty of reasons to dislike Dr. Octopus: Doc Ock rented a room in the home of gullible, elderly May Parker—Peter's beloved Aunt May—in a four-issue storyline in *ASM* #53–#56 (1967–1968), written by Lee and illustrated by John Romita, Sr. Hiding his mechanical arms under an overcoat, Octavius was unaware that his unassuming suburban hideout was the home of his foe's relative. Later in this serial, Dr. Octopus misled the amnesiac Spidey into becoming his partner in crime, sullying the web-slinger's already-precarious reputation. In 1970, Doc Ock was responsible for the death of police Captain Stacy, father of Peter Parker's girlfriend Gwen. And at no time did Dr. Octopus ever get under Spider-Man's skin more than his attempt to *marry* Aunt May: Gerry Conway and Ross Andru's "My Uncle … My Enemy?" in *ASM* #133 (1974) featured Spidey disrupting their wedding, throwing punches, not rice.

Time and time again, Dr. Octopus has returned to continue his grudge match against Spider-Man, each time more crazed than before. While Spidey has become adept at dodging Ock's tentacles, his defensive spider-sense cannot ready him for the absolute brutality of his opponent's

Alfred Molina as Doc Ock in *Spider-Man 2* (2004).

attacks. Doc Ock has fought other heroes, including the Fantastic Four and Daredevil, but his wall-crawler fixation is unwavering.

As with many characters whose adventures have spanned decades, Dr. Octopus once died. The assassin Kaine offed Ock in 1995's *Spectacular Spider-Man* #221, inspiring not only a posthumous three-issue miniseries (*Spider-Man: Funeral for an Octopus*) but also a replacement. Octavius' scientific protégé Carolyn Trainer, smitten with the twisted genius, accepted the call to arms to become the curvaceous Dr. Octopus II, upgrading the tentacles with lasers and a force field. Otto Octavius soon returned from the dead, reuniting with his robotic arms and resuming his bloodthirsty vendetta against the amazing Spider-Man.

A slightly altered version of Dr. Octopus exists in Marvel's *Ultimate Spider-Man* series (2000–present), a reimagining of the character (and the entire Marvel Universe). Ultimate Doc Ock has morphing arms, is a strapping physical specimen, and is aware of Spider-Man's true identity of Peter Parker.

Dr. Octopus' fame has stretched beyond the pages of Marvel Comics: action figures, newspaper strips, video games, trading cards, a novel (1978's *Mayhem in Manhattan* by Len Wein and Marv Wolf-

man), and even a 7-11 Slurpee cup have sported his ugly mug. Doc Ock has been featured in most of Spider-Man's forays into television animation, portrayed over the years by voice actors Tom Harvey, Stan Jones, Michael Bell, and Efrem Zimbalist, Jr. When *Titanic* and *Terminator* director James Cameron was developing a Spider-Man live-action movie throughout the 1990s, Dr. Octopus was considered as the villain with Arnold Schwarzenegger in the role; Cameron's version never materialized. Alfred Molina, however, finally brought Doc Ock to life in director Sam Raimi's blockbuster *Spider-Man 2* (2004). Instead of a strict reliance upon computer-generated effects for Ock, Raimi often used fiberglass mechanical arms controlled by puppeteers for a more organic effect. —*ME*

Dr. Polaris

Steel girders and tools from a construction site torpedo toward the flying Emerald Crusader on the cover of *Green Lantern* vol. 2 #21 (1962), courtesy of "The Man Who Mastered Magnetism!"—Dr. Polaris, created by writer John Broome and artist Kane. Dr. Neal Emerson is an amiable n' becomes a media darling by ev benefits of polarity, earning him the nickname "Dr. Polaris." Continual exposure to electromagnetism causes Emerson to develop a good/evil split personality, his malevolent side pulling him to crime. Adopting the supervillain guise of Dr. Polaris and wielding a magnetic gun that attracts, repels, and levitates metal objects, Polaris pummels Green Lantern (GL), who luckily beats his new foe by coaxing out Emerson's benign personality.

Emerson's warring psyche made Dr. Polaris an unpredictable enemy. He eventually learned to internally generate his magnetic powers, abandoning his weapon. With each encounter with GL, Polaris became more dangerous. He clobbered the hero with his "magnetic fist" in *Green Lantern* #47 (1966) and funneled flailing innocents into a magnetic field in #135 (1976). As his powers and madness have increased, so has his worldview—thirsting for world domination, Polaris has skirmished with numerous DC Comics superheroes, including the Justice League, the Teen Titans, Steel, the Ray, and the Flash. After years of Jekyll/Hyde personality struggles, Polaris sold Emerson's benevolent soul to the demon Neron in the 1995 crossover *Underworld Unleashed* in exchange for even greater power. Despite his near-infinite power and ability to connect with Earth's magnetic field, Dr. Polaris sought Superman's aid in *Action Comics* #827 (2005) to ward off a new "mistress of magnetism" named Repulse. He was apparently killed during a hero-versus-villain death duel in *Infinite Crisis* #1 (2005), when the superhero the Human Bomb, incensed over the murder of his Freedom Fighters teammate the Phantom Lady, blew Polaris to bits. —*ME*

Dr. Psycho

Writer William Moulton Marston envisioned his creation, Wonder Woman, as perfection personified; one of the Amazon Princess' first foes, Dr. Psycho, represents just the opposite. A wide-eyed dwarf with a bulbous head, this malevolent misogynist created by Marston and artist H. G. Peter in *Wonder Woman* vol. 1 #5 (1943) is conditioned to hate by a society that ridicules him—particularly women, who rebuke his romantic advances. In college, he hypnotizes a co-ed to marry him, but after she turns on him Psycho kills her lover and swears retribution against women. Using ectoplasm from the "spirit world," Dr. Psycho demolishes a World War II munitions plant with a female workforce, earning Wonder Woman's ire.

This "psychopathic madman," attired in a tuxedo and looking like a ventriloquist's dummy gone amok, was drawn with lightning bolts or dotted lines emitting from his bulging eyeballs to convey his hypnosis. Dr. Psycho's brother, the "iron giant" King Ironsides, also fought Wonder Woman during the Golden Age (1938–1954). By the late 1940s Psycho had vanished, returning in issue #160 (1966) for the first of several appearances. He once succeeded in capturing the Amazon with an "electro-atomizer," which separated her soul from her corporeal body, and split her into three Wonder Women, each with a different personality, using his "personality scrambler machine." Psycho was back for another go in 1982, ectoplasmically masquerading as the supervillain Captain Wonder. Both hero and villain were excised from the DC Comics canon once Wonder Woman was rebooted in 1987.

Writer George Pérez and penciler Jill Thompson brought Dr. Psycho into contemporary continuity in *Wonder Woman* vol. 2 #54–#55 (1991). A psychotherapist who stimulates nightmarish visions and delusions through dream manipulation, Dr. Psycho on occasion has gotten into the heroine's head. During his rare incarcerations, an electronic headband has been required to nullify his hallucinatory powers. Dr. Psycho's profile was dramatically increased during the best-selling *Villains United* miniseries of 2005, in which Lex Luthor invited Psycho into his inner circle as one of the six core members of his new Society. Despite this supervillainous union, Dr. Psycho cannot be trusted. He attempted to telepathically control his comrades in *Villains United* #4 ("One can hardly blame the scorpion for its sting," dismissed Luthor). —*ME*

Dr. Shrinker

A supervillain with his own Saturday-morning television program? Who could have thought of such a thing? Sid and Marty Krofft, that's who, the

The ▮▮▮▮▮▮k

prolific producing pair behind some of the splashiest TV offerings of the 1970s, from *H. R. Pufnstuf* to *Donny and Marie*. Their ambitious kid's series *Dr. Shrinker*, one of several live-action shorts sharing space on NBC's offbeat omnibus *The Krofft Supershow* (1976–1978), starred scowl-pussed Jay Robinson—who parlayed his scene-stealing turn as Caligula in *The Robe* (1953) into a successful career as a character actor—as an insane genius flaunting the most popular of sinister superweapons, the shrinking ray, from his creepy laboratory nestled on the most popular of supervillain headquarters, the uncharted island. When a plane containing three teenagers named Brad, Geordie, and B. J. crashes on the eerie isle, Dr. Shrinker now has guinea pigs—his "shrinkies"—making the teens doll-sized and chasing them through sixteen repetitive but endearing episodes. Brad and the gang crawled through colossal-sized props reminiscent of *Land of the Giants*, evading the "madman with an evil mind" (according to the theme song) and working together to thwart his plans to aim his miniaturization device at the rest of the world. To ensure that Dr. Shrinker's machinations weren't *too* gruesome for the kiddies, Billy Barty was on hand for comic relief as the doctor's dwarfish aide Hugo.

A blip of Dr. Shrinker merchandising was produced in 1976 and 1977, including a Halloween costume, a View-Master packet, and a magnifying glass. —*ME*

Dr. Sivana

Dr. Thaddeus Bodog Sivana—a creepy mad-scientist caricature with a bulb-shaped head, Coke-bottle glasses, profound overbite, and white labcoat, premiered in the original Captain Marvel's very first comic book, Fawcett's *Whiz Comics* #2 (1940). An egghead ridiculed for his outrageous inventions, Sivana in retaliation devotes his genius to evil and holds ransom the airwaves by blocking radio broadcasts with his "radio silencer" until "the World's Mightiest Mortal" tunes out his scheme.

Throughout comics' Golden Age (1938–1954), "the World's Wickedest Scientist" barraged Captain Marvel with an eccentric arsenal including coma-

inducing "Suspendium globes," a mind-controlling "hypno ray," a "time-travel device" that enabled him to venture into the past and attempt to prevent newsboy Billy Batson from becoming "the Big Red Cheese," a freezing "cosmic gas," robots forged of the "living" metal "Sivanium," an invisibility-granting "Shazamium bracelet," and a silencing "mute ray" that robbed young Billy of his ability to speak his powers-inducing magic word "Shazam!" Sometimes operating from a lab on Venus, Dr. Sivana was dedicated to global conquest and was a member of Mr. Mind's Monster Society of Evil. He was often aided by his homely adult children, son Sivana, Jr. and daughter Georgia, while his handsome progeny Beautia and Magnificus disapproved of their father's machinations. The Sivanas disappeared in 1954 when Fawcett Comics lost a legal battle with DC Comics over Captain Marvel's alleged semblances to Superman, shutting down the entire "Marvel Family" franchise of titles.

DC resurrected Captain Marvel and company in 1973 in the series *Shazam!*, their twenty-year absence attributed to Sivana's Suspendium. DC's revival maintained the whimsy of the Golden Age tales, an ill fit with the changing climes and reader maturation of the 1970s. Dr. Sivana, by extension, lost his footing, an anachronistic throwback to the scientist-villain of the Great Depression era. He continued to be featured, however, in numerous *Shazam!* tales, and was seen on live-action television in the 1979 campy telefilm *Legends of the Super-Heroes*, in which he was delightfully portrayed by Howard Morris, best known as mountain wildman Ernest T. Bass on *The Andy Griffith Show*. Allan Oppenheimer voiced Sivana on Captain Marvel's NBC's animated series, *Kid Super-Power Hour with Shazam!* (1981–1982).

Despite his television visibility, Dr. Sivana still seemed out of place in the increasingly grimmer DC Universe. A 1987 attempt to make Sivana darker (*Shazam!: The New Beginning*) also connected him to Billy Batson's family, but was excised from continuity in another reboot, 1994's *Power of Shazam!*

In the contemporary DC Universe, Dr. Sivana's technological achievements at one time made him a billionaire, but his underworld connections and implications in the murders of Billy and Mary (Mary

Marvel) Batson's parents ruined his reputation and put him at odds with Captain Marvel. The estranged father of Beautia and Magnificus, Sivana has made scattered appearances in the 1990s and 2000s, partnering with Mr. Mind in 1996 and reviving the Fearsome Five—Psimon, Mammoth, Shimmer, Jinx, and Gizmo, the latter of whom died by the mad doctor's own hand—in a 2004 *Outsiders* storyline. Whether he will one day return to the upper echelon of supervillainy remains something even his heralded "time-travel device" cannot foresee.

While Captain Marvel has been frequently merchandized over the decades, Sivana has rarely accompanied him, a 2003 Pocket Super Heroes miniature from DC Direct being among the rare toy appearances of the villain. —*ME*

Dr. Zin

The treacherous Dr. Zin, arch-nemesis of brilliant inventor Dr. Benton Quest, epitomizes the supervillain mastermind. Sartorially sinister in his lab coat and ascot, this bald, Asian scientist sports a Fu Manchu goatee and a diabolical chuckle. First seen in "Riddle of the Gold," the fourth installment of television's animated *Jonny Quest* (1964–1965), Zin is buffered by soldiers, cutthroats, and servants for whom he has little respect—"You brainless fool, get out!" he derides a dutiful houseboy—yet these minions steadfastly sacrifice themselves for their malicious master.

His past is cloaked in mystery, but one thing about Dr. Zin is clear: his goal of world domination. This insidious intellectual perpetually tinkers with weapons of mass destruction, and what he cannot create, he steals. In his most famous *Jonny Quest* episode, "The Robot Spy," Dr. Zin dispatches a spider-legged, single-eyed automaton to obtain Dr. Quest's experimental weapon, the para-power ray. His efforts foiled by Quest, his son Jonny, Jonny's friend Hadji, and their bodyguard Race Bannon, Zin produces a duplicate of the weapon, his inertia ray, an unperceivable beam capable of downing aircraft.

Dr. Zin, voiced by Vic Perrin, challenged the Quest team in four episodes of the series' original single season, and returned in the 1980s and 1990s in *Jonny Quest* series continuations and made-for-TV animated movies, with Jeffrey Tambor, Clyde Kasatsu, and Frank Welker lending him voice. The doctor's deceitful daughters Anaya and Melana were introduced in 1997, and with them a cybernetic ninja immodestly dubbed a "Zinja." —*ME*

Doomsday

A brawny fist, spiny protrusions shredding the fabric of its glove, hammered through a steel wall in a late 1992 prelude to a Superman storyline. The fist belonged to Doomsday, a 7-foot monstrosity of unknown origin, erupting from a prison pod with wanton destruction on his mind. In DC Comics' landmark "Death of Superman" serial, Doomsday barrels through North America, plowing over the Justice League and attracting the attention of the mighty Man of Steel. Superman and Doomsday's battle evolves over several issues, climaxing in a blood brawl in the highly publicized *Superman* vol. 2 #75 (1993), in which Superman sacrifices his life to stop this behemoth (although the hero was, after much story exploitation, later resurrected).

Doomsday was created by committee. Writers, artists, and editors periodically gathered at "Supersummits" to chart the overlapping events of the franchise of four monthly Superman series, and Doomsday was the group's 1992 attempt to introduce "a foe that Superman could barely defeat," remarked *Superman* #75 artist/writer Dan Jurgens.

The publicity machine behind the "Death of Superman" event triggered international headlines and the brief fashion trend of black "S" armbands. *Superman* #75's release packed millions of new consumers into comics shops, many of whom speculatively purchased multiple copies as future collector's items. The Man of Steel's epic struggle with Doomsday was also chronicled in prose by comics scribe Roger Stern in the best-selling novel *The Death and Life of Superman* (1993).

Eager to revisit this "box-office" bonanza, DC and Jurgens produced the three-issue miniseries *Superman/Doomsday: Hunter/Prey* (1994), revealing Doomsday's origin: eons ago he was genetically engineered on Superman's homeworld of Krypton to be a killing machine capable of regener-

Superman/Doomsday: Hunter/Prey #2 ©1994 DC Comics.
BACK COVER ART BY DAN JURGENS AND BRETT BREEDING.

ation if ever defeated. With the help of a Kryptonian battlesuit, Superman bested Doomsday, but this seemingly unstoppable force continues to occasionally resurface—including television appearances on the Cartoon Network's *Justice League* (2001–2004) and *Justice League Unlimited* (2004–present), with Michael Jai White of *Spawn* fame lending the monster voice. —ME

Dormammu

The Dread Dormammu, the unforgiving arch-foe of Dr. Strange, Master of the Mystic Arts, was created by Marvel Comics visionaries Stan Lee and Steve Ditko. In *Strange Tales* #126–#127 (1964), Dr. Strange is dispatched by the Ancient One into "The Domain of the Dread Dormammu!" to ward off an impending invasion of Earth by the lord of the Dark Dimension. Battling past "unspeakable" men-

aces to reach Dormammu, Dr. Strange goads him into a battle of magic, but the opponents partner to halt an onslaught from the rampaging golems, the Mindless Ones. Grudgingly indebted to the Master of the Mystic Arts for his aid, Dormammu pledges not to attack Earth, but swears, "I shall never rest until I avenge this indignity!"

"Dormammu was probably the first villain we created before the fact," Stan Lee admitted in the reprint collection *Bring on the Bad Guys* (1976), "Dormammu" being an unseen occult entity called upon in many of Dr. Strange's incantations. Had the Sorcerer Supreme known what vile force he was channeling, he might have sought help elsewhere.

Dormammu has no face, but a head engulfed in numinous Faltinian Flame. He is an entity of mystical and cosmic energy, can expand to colossal size, and is capable of traversing dimensions and time.

The autocratic Dormammu is determined to conquer myriad dimensional realms. He and his humanoid sister Umar, first seen in *Strange Tales* #150 (1966), were exiled from their native Faltine realm to the Dark Dimension. Dormammu ascended to overlord, with the realm's denizens slavishly worshipping him. Dr. Strange's lover, Clea, is Umar's daughter, and was enslaved by Dormammu during the Master of the Mystic Arts' first encounter with him in *Strange Tales* #126–#127.

Dormammu has been assisted in his interdimensional conquests by Thor's arch-enemy Loki, the God of Mischief; the sorcerer Baron Mordo; and Umar, although his sister has upon occasion turned against him, eyeing his dark throne. He has been deposed upon occasion, but the near-omnipotent Dormammu has often cheated death and may be impossible to destroy.

Dormammu has battled Dr. Strange's teammates the Defenders, as well as the Avengers and Hellcat. While Dormammu is not a force to be taken lightly, writers Keith Giffen and J. M. DeMatteis and artist Kevin Maguire, best known for their humorous, late 1980s interpretation of DC's *Justice League*, did just that in their 2005 *Defenders* miniseries. This frivolous excursion aside, Dormammu remains one of the most dangerous forces in the Marvel Universe.

Voiced by Ed Gilbert, Dormammu appeared in a 1996 episode of the animated series *Spider-Man* (1994–1998). Toy Biz produced a Dormammu action figure in 2000. —*ME*

Dragon Ball Villains

Akira Toriyama's popular long-running manga (Japanese comics series) *Dragon Ball* (1984–1995) was a loose adaptation of the classic Chinese tale *Journey to the West* (titled *Saiyuki* in Japan). It was not only a phenomenal success in Japan, but was just as popular in America. The anime (Japanese animation) itself was first aired on syndicated television in the United States in the early 1990s before moving to the Cartoon Network, where it runs as of 2006. Toriyama added a strong dose of science fiction and superhero action influenced by American comics. There was also a great deal of destruction from epic battles fought by the characters on Earth and across the universe.

Dragon Ball's hero, Goku, was one of the last survivors of an alien race known as Saiyans, and over the run of the manga—and the anime series adapted from it, which was renamed *Dragon Ball Z* when Goku reached adulthood—he and his allies faced many villains. Toriyama created an amazing variety of characters, each unique in his or her own way, to fill the roles of villains in *Dragon Ball*.

To give a complete overview of every major villain in *Dragon Ball* would require many volumes that would rival the *Encyclopedia Britannica*. However, there are villains whose actions had major consequences on *Dragon Ball*'s characters. Raditz was the first major villain introduced in the first episode of *Dragon Ball Z*, "The Arrival of Raditz" (the original Japanese title "A Sheltered Boy: My Name Is Gohan"). He is Goku's brother, a Saiyan … and he wasn't too happy when his brother refused to join him in conquering the universe. Raditz has superstrength and speed, and like all Saiyans, has the ability to turn into a giant ape-like beast in the light of a full moon. In the battle that followed—which lasted several episodes—Raditz was defeated, but at the cost of Goku's life. These events marked the beginning of the "Saipan Saga," which involved Goku's death, his entrance into the afterlife to further hone his fighting skills, and his resurrection in the world of the living.

Vegeta is another Saiyan who traveled to Earth with his partner Nappa to face off against Goku following a final message broadcast by Raditz. Along the way, the two carved a swath of destruction (destroying the entire planet Arlia, for instance) and engaged in a fierce battle with Goku's allies on Earth. In a no-holds-barred match, Goku and his son Gohan defeated Vegeta, who escaped. Later in the series, Vegeta would become an ally of Goku, but still held within his heart a desire to defeat Goku in combat. Vegeta would eventually marry Bulma, Goku's traveling partner during his teen years, and they would have two children, Trunks and Bra.

Trunks would become a key character in *Dragon Ball Z*, or rather, his older self from the future, called Future Trunks. He was responsible for defeating perhaps the most important villain in *Dragon Ball Z*: Frieza. Introduced during the "Super Saiyan Saga," Frieza is a powerful alien who can take various forms to engage in combat. He nearly wiped out the entire Saiyan race and their home planet, as well as many other worlds across the universe. He also killed Krillin, Goku's close friend, which triggered Goku's transformation into the "Super Saiyan" form. Goku defeated Frieza, literally blowing him to bits, but Frieza's father rebuilt him and, together, both headed to Earth to take revenge on Goku and wipe out the Earth as well. Frieza and his father were stopped by Future Trunks, who arrived and defeated them with ease. Frieza was dispatched by Trunks quite efficiently: not only did Trunks slice the villain into tiny pieces with his sword, but he incinerated them with an energy blast for good measure. —*MM*

The Dragon Lady

Terry and the Pirates, Milton Caniff's popular and long-running adventure comic strip that debuted in the *Chicago Tribune* in 1934, is host to many villainous threats, most notably a femme fatale bar none, the Dragon Lady. The strip was based on "wide-awake

American boy" Terry Lee and his adult sidekick, "two-fisted adventurer" journalist Pat Ryan, who arrive in China in search of a mine that had belonged to Terry's grandfather. Accompanied by their interpreter and guide "Connie," the duo embark on various misadventures throughout the vast Far East.

The Dragon Lady, the head of a band of pirates who operate along China's coast, has been called one of comics' all-time greatest female villains. Fans of the strip immediately recognize the complex and unpredictable relationship the Asian temptress held with the strip's hero. In true fiendish fashion, the exotic bombshell attempted to murder Terry—but she often seduced him, humiliated him, attempted to outwit him, and, interestingly, helped him through the trials and tribulations of puberty.

Although the Dragon Lady joined other villains as a stereotypical Asian foil, other references more accurately reflect America's emergence in World War II. Prohibited by the *Tribune* syndicate from mentioning the Japanese by name, Caniff referred to them as "the invaders," and they soon became the

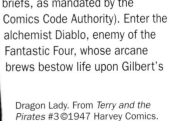

strip's formidable foes. An overtly patriotic Terry joined the U.S. Army, and the Dragon Lady and her pirates were depicted as Chinese guerillas.

The popularity of the strip's exotic characters led to a weekly radio show of the same name, running intermittently from 1937 to 1948, with Agnes Moorehead voicing the show's first Dragon Lady. The *Terry and the Pirates* movie serial was released in 1940, with Sheila Darcy as the Dragon Lady. The 1952 live-action television series featured Gloria Saunders in the Dragon Lady's role. During this period, Whitman Publishing's Little Big Books published a book line based on the characters, and Dell and Charlton both published comic books.

Caniff left the strip in December 1946, but it continued under the creative hand of Associated Press artist George Wunder for another twenty-seven years. In 1986, when graphic-novel publisher NBM's "Flying Buttress" imprint published a twelve-volume set of the comic strip, Caniff's *Terry* became the first major run of an American strip reprinted in its entirety in book form. In 1995, along with several other newspaper comics, *Terry* was featured in a commemorative series of U.S. postage stamps, forever solidifying the strip—and its heroes and villains—in popular culture. —*GM*

Dragon Man

S uper-genius Reed (Mr. Fantastic) Richards wasn't the only big man on campus in *Fantastic Four* #35 (1965)—the 15-foot, 3-ton Dragon Man made the college scene in that issue's tale by Stan Lee and Jack Kirby. While Richards is lecturing students at his alma mater State University, his colleague Professor Gregson Gilbert has created—for some inexplicable reason—a lifeless, gray-skinned dinosaur-man (discreetly wearing briefs, as mandated by the Comics Code Authority). Enter the alchemist Diablo, enemy of the Fantastic Four, whose arcane brews bestow life upon Gilbert's

Dragon Lady. From *Terry and the Pirates* #3 ©1947 Harvey Comics. ART BY MILTON CANIFF.

android and places the beast under the villain's control. Flying on bat-like wings and disgorging flame from its massive jaws, Dragon Man incites "Calamity on the Campus!" (the story's title), but thanks to the intervention of Richards and his FF teammates, the creature and its manipulator plunge into the icy waters of Dead Man's Lake.

Dragon Man returned (as did Diablo) on countless stomp-and-burn rampages, usually as a pawn of some ruthless soul like the Machinesmith, the Dragon Lord, or the evil corporation Roxxon, only to be corralled by the FF, the Avengers, Spider-Man,

She-Hulk, or other heroes. His durable hide can withstand the Thing's blows ("What gives?? When I clobber someone, he's supposed to stay clobbered!"), mortar blasts, and extreme heat and pressure. Dragon Man's 7-feet-long tail thrashes at a dizzying 90 miles per hour. He possesses rudimentary sentience, being about as bright as a dog, and therein lies his appeal—part mutt, part dinosaur, this unorthodox villain has become a favorite of fans and fans turned comics-pros, the latter of whom nostalgically dust off Dragon Man for return engagements. —*ME*

Eclipso

Billed as the "Hero and Villain in One Man," Eclipso debuted in DC Comics' *The House of Secrets* #61 (1963). "The Genius Who Fought Himself!" by Bob Haney and Lee Elias introduced solar physicist Dr. Bruce Gordon, architect of Solar City, a prototypical sun-powered municipality. As a solar eclipse occurs, an ominous pale-blue shadow magically appears over half of the doctor's face, and "that fool Bruce Gordon" transmogrifies into the evil Eclipso. In an ensemble of black and purple with a lunar/solar eclipse emblem, Eclipso, exhibiting superstrength and stamina, decimates Solar City with a devastating dark-light beam projected through a black diamond he holds to his "eclipsed" eye. Possessed of Eclipso's dark spirit from an earlier expedition to Diablo Island in the South Pacific, the heroic Gordon struggled against the demon within in *House of Secrets* for three years, with Gordon's ally Professor Simon Bennett and his daughter Mona (Bruce's girlfriend) returning Eclipso to dormancy by exposing him to his one weakness—light. Eclipso's potency as a villain was often weakened by stories that depicted him succumbing to light sources as bland as camera flashes. Nonetheless, he returned for decades in various DC series, battling Batman, the Justice League, Green Lantern, the Metal Men, the Phantom Stranger, and other heroes.

Eclipso's true nature was revealed in *Eclipso: The Darkness Within* #1 (1992), a giant-sized comic inaugurating a crossover that crept through DC's various summer annuals; a variant edition of issue #1's cover featured a Bart Sears–drawn close-up of Eclipso holding a "real" (plastic) black diamond to his eye. Readers discovered that Eclipso was actually the primeval god of vengeance, a role later served by the Spectre. Eclipso was once imprisoned inside a giant black gem called the Heart of Darkness (a deliberate nod to author Joseph Conrad's tale of the same name), but in the late nineteenth century a jeweler chiseled the stone into a thousand pieces that were dispersed across the globe. Eclipso could corrupt anyone holding one of the diamond fragments once that host succumbed to rage. Throughout the *Darkness Within* crossover, various DC superheroes found themselves "eclipsed" by Eclipso, and the villain spun off into his own monthly series, which ran eighteen issues from 1992 to 1994.

Throughout these and subsequent stories, Eclipso has embarked upon the baleful mission of subjugating Earth into darkness, employing various human and superhuman vessels in his chaotic quest. Bruce Gordon was ultimately freed of Eclipso's influence, and this nocturnal nemesis has become one of the most bloodthirsty menaces in the DC Universe, slaughtering several minor superheroes and countless civilians. For a brief time Eclipso fell under the control of the brother of one of the heroes he murdered, but has since broken free. He once again ascended into prominence in 2005, first possessing Superman, leading to a clash of titans between Captain Marvel and the eclipsed Man of Steel, and later spreading his demonic influence upon Jean Loring, the criminally insane ex-wife of the Atom. As the new Eclipso, Loring allied with the Spectre in the miniseries *Day of Vengeance* (2005), partnering to eliminate magic from Earth. Now a creature of unadulterated evil, Eclipso's roots as the villain who cowered from flashlights are long forgotten. —ME

Egg Fu

Part Fu Manchu, part Humpty Dumpty, the obscure DC Comics supervillain Egg Fu succeeded in slaughtering both Wonder Woman and political correctness. Hatched by writer Robert Kanigher and artists Ross Andru and Mike Esposito in *Wonder Woman* vol. 1 #157–#158 (1965), the "Oriental Egghead" is an observatory-sized, egg-shaped mastermind on the island of Oolong who strikes a blow against democracy for his native Communist China by turning "America's greatest hero" Lt. Steve Trevor, boyfriend of the Amazon Princess, into a living bomb. When Wonder Woman attempts Trevor's rescue, both perish in an explosion, but are reconstructed by Amazonian science. The embodiment of every off-color, World War II–bred Asian stereotype imaginable (including speech, swapping Ls for Rs: "The Amelicans would be warned if the locket were fired at rong range!"), the smirking, orange-skinned Egg Fu next ensnares Wonder Woman and Trevor in his telescoping "mustache trap" before the heroine cracks the villain into tiny pieces with her magic lasso.

In *Wonder Woman* #165 (1966), Kanigher and company served up Egg Fu the Fifth, a smaller version of the villain, closer to human size—but no closer to avoiding the same offensive clichés. Wonder Woman scrambled version five, but Egg Fu managed yet another go-round as a supercomputer

with ties to Darkseid (*Wonder Woman* vol. 2 #129, 1998). —ME

Ego the Living Planet

Larger-than-life characters were a specialty of Stan Lee and Jack Kirby during their construction of Marvel Comics' "House of Ideas," and Ego the Living Planet was certainly one of their largest. The Thunder God discovers this sentient celestial body while on a space sojourn in *Thor* vol. 1 #132 (1966). In a nod to the book of Genesis' creation of woman from man's rib, Ego is producing humanoid drones from its own matter and dispatching them on missions of intergalactic conquest when Thor, with Recorder, his alien companion from Rigel, foils the Living Planet by creating storms on his surface.

Ego resembles Earth's cratered moon, forming an ominous "man in the moon" visage with glowing yellow eyes, a nose, and a mouth (with plantlike "facial hair") when he wishes to communicate with extraterrestrial travelers. He can alter his exterior to appear lush and inviting or bleak and foreboding, and can project rocky tentacles as appendages. Ego can be quite unpredictable—he once allowed refugees from a Galactus-ravaged world to colonize him, then consumed them (life forces provide sustenance for Ego, and his hunger has put him into conflict with numerous heroes including the Silver Surfer and the Fantastic Four). Purportedly born of the Big Bang, Ego hails from the Black Galaxy and has colluded with the cosmic Elders of the Universe, with whom he has warred against Galactus, another of his enemies.

The Living Planet has enjoyed a two significant moments in the sun: a guest appearance on the television cartoon *Fantastic Four* (1994–1996) and a dominant role in the superhero-packed 2000 miniseries *Maximum Security* by Kurt Busiek and Jerry Ordway, which included two accompanying one-shots, *Dangerous Planet* and a *Thor vs. Ego* reprint edition. Ego continues his world-sized threats in the Marvel Universe of the 2000s, including a 2004 attempt to transform the Earth into his "son." —ME

Electro

"All the power of electricity is mine!" cackles New York City's sizzling new supervillain as he loots an armored car by hurling lightning bolts from his hands. This is "The Man Called Electro," making his voltaic debut in *The Amazing Spider-Man* #9 (1964), from the electrifying creative team of author Stan Lee and artist Steve Ditko. Beneath Electro's vibrant green-and-yellow garb is Max Dillon, once an electrical lineman of limited character; in a flashback, he charges a fee from his boss to rescue a fellow worker trapped on a live wire, but in karmic retribution is zapped by lightning. Instead of harming him, however, the bolt energizes Dillon into a living power generator that instinctively recharges itself. Able to expel electrical blasts at the speed of lightning, Electro gives Spider-Man the shock of his nascent career until the wall-crawler short-circuits his foe with a nearby fire hose.

The deviant dynamo returned a mere four months later to battle another superhero, Daredevil, in *Daredevil* #2 (1964), and resurfaced shortly thereafter in *Amazing Spider-Man Annual* #1 (1964) as one of the founding members—with Dr. Octopus, Mysterio, Kraven the Hunter, the Vulture, and Sandman—of the Sinister Six. Although unplugged by DD and Spidey in these tales, Dillon, the formerly self-doubting product of a dysfunctional family, found his confidence sparked by his awesome electrical abilities. Despite his effrontery, however, he still harbored insecurities, often preferring the safety of supervillainous teamwork—Electro attracted Daredevil rogues Stilt-Man, the Matador, the Gladiator, and Frog-Man to become the Emissaries of Evil, and has frequently returned with myriad Sinister Six refurbishments.

Like an AC/DC current, throughout the 1970s Electro switched back and forth between battles with Spider-Man and Daredevil—occasionally jolting other heroes including Captain America and the Defenders—before focusing his ire mostly against Spidey in the ensuing decades. Electro's services are for hire: J. Jonah Jameson once contracted him

The Amazing Spider-Man Pocket Books edition #1 ©1977 Marvel Comics. Artwork originally published in *Amazing Spider-Man Annual* #1 ©1964 Marvel Comics. ART BY STEVE DITKO.

to attempt to defeat Spider-Man ... before a television audience!

At the turn of the millennium, Electro traded his original uniform for blue-and-white togs; while fans had long criticized his gaudy green gear, his new look was universally loathed. Spider-rogue Venom killed the fashion-impaired Electro in 2000, but for an inexplicable reason Dillon zipped through the revolving door separating the corporeal world from the afterlife and, in true comicbook fashion, returned from the dead—in his original costume.

One of Spider-Man's most dangerous foes, Electro can emit arcs of lightning from his fingertips, generate a protective electrical field, psionically con-

Electrical Supervillains

Electro may have claimed the name, but these other high-voltage villains have proved that lightning *does* strike more than once in the same place:

- **Bolt** is a special-effects wizard who fashioned a skull-emblazoned teleportation suit in DC's *Blue Devil* #6 (1984) to become an energy-blasting assassin.
- **Cardiac**, first seen in *Amazing Spider-Man* vol. 1 #344 (1991), has a beta-particle reactor heart and a staff that emits electricity.
- **The Eel** used his insulated outfit to blitz the Human Torch in the early 1960s. He later joined the Serpent Squad, was killed, and was replaced by a new Eel.
- **The Electocutioner** took the law into his voltage-generating hands in *Batman* #331 (1981), executing criminals acquitted by the courts.
- **Livewire**, an acid-tongued radio "shock jock" (voiced by Lori Petty), was transformed into a supervillainess during an electrical storm in late 1990s episodes of the animated *Superman*. She joined the traditional DC Universe in *Action Comics* #835 (2006).
- **The Shocker**'s shtick is vibrations, not voltage, as first displayed in *Amazing Spider-Man* #46 (1967), as well as in *Spider-Man* TV cartoons.
- **Shockwave**, an intelligence agent turned costumed mercenary, jolted the Master of Kung Fu in 1976 before going on to use his electrical-firing armored togs as one of the Masters of Evil.
- **Spark** was a ridiculed performance artist who, through a supernatural ceremony, gained the ability to manipulate electricity and gave Spider-Man a mild shock in the early 1990s.
- **The Stunner**, a mid-1960s supervillain, used his "stun gloves" to attack Archie Comics' superteam the Mighty Crusaders.
- **ZAP!** zips through the air at superspeed and, as ShadowHawk discovered in their first encounter in 2005, he fires lightning from his fingertips.
- **Zzzax**, an enormous, humanoid-shaped electromagnetic field, was called "the thing from the dynamo" in his first battle with the Incredible Hulk in 1973, and he has since managed to snap, crackle, and pop through various Marvel comics.

trol electronic devices, and siphon energy sources (in a 1993 story, he nearly succeeded in blacking out Manhattan). No matter how much power he obtains, Electro is, at heart, a schmuck with a gimmick, and through tenacity and cleverness Spider-Man is always able to turn out his lights.

Electro's supercharged superpowers have made the character a natural for visual media. Tom Harvey voiced the villain on the 1967–1970 *Spider-Man* ABC cartoon; Allan Melvin (best known as the voice of Magilla Gorilla and for playing Sam the Butcher on *The Brady Bunch*) portrayed Electro in episodes of the animated *Spider-Man and His Amazing Friends* (1981–1986); and Ethan Embry was a visually redesigned, nebbish-gone-bad Electro in several episodes of the short-lived MTV *Spider-Man* cartoon in 2003. The Spider-foe co-headlined the 2001 video game *Spider-Man II: Enter Electro*, has been manufactured as an action figure, and was one of the villains rumored to be played by Topher Grace in the movie *Spider-Man 3* before Grace's role as Venom was announced in 2005. —*ME*

Emperor Palpatine

The destruction of the Republic began with the behind-the-scenes machinations of Senator Palpatine of Naboo, leading to a tyrannical new Galactic Empire that was ruled over by the same man. Secretly the Dark Lord of the Sith known as Darth Sidious, Palpatine engineered the destruction of the order of Jedi Knights and began a reign of oppression and terror.

Although he first appeared in the film *The Empire Strikes Back* (1980), Palpatine's chronological screen presence actually came in the trilogy of *Star Wars* prequels: *Episode I: The Phantom Menace* (1999*), Episode II: Attack of the Clones* (2002), and *Episode III: Revenge of the Sith* (2005). In the first film, Senator Palpatine worked with Senator Padmé Amidala to engineer his succession to the role of Chancellor of the Republic; although he promised a return to order and justice, Palpatine was plotting in the background.

Cloaking himself as Darth Sidious, Palpatine trained a pupil named Darth Maul and set him against the Jedi, even as he schemed with the Neimoidians. A decade later, as the Separatist movement led by Count Dooku gained steam, and war against the Republic appeared imminent, no one knew that Dooku was Darth Tyranus, Palpatine's newer apprentice, and that Palpatine actually controlled both sides in the conflict.

During the Clone Wars, Palpatine was granted emergency powers, and eventually shut down the Senate, declaring himself Emperor of the Galactic Empire. Now he was served by his most successful pupil in the arts of the Dark Side of the Force: a promising Jedi he had seduced into evil, Anakin Skywalker, now called Darth Vader.

His body wizened and deformed by use of his Dark Side powers—such as the ability to throw blue lightning from his fingers—Palpatine used a cane and a cloak even as he ruled the Empire with Vader by his side for almost two decades. When the Rebel Alliance began to make headway against the Empire, one of its heroes—Luke Skywalker, the Jedi son of Anakin—became the target of Palpatine's quest for a new pupil. In a battle shown in *Return of the Jedi* (1983), Darth Vader turned on his master to save Luke, and Palpatine was killed in the reactor of his own Death Star weapon.

Emperor Palpatine has reappeared in clone form in *Star Wars* comic books and novels—known as the "Expanded Universe" stories—and has been featured in some licensed collectibles. In the original *Empire Strikes Back*, the hologram of the Emperor was played by an old woman with a chimpanzee's eyes superimposed on her face, and the voice of Clive Revill. For all of his other appearances—and in retrofitted CGI footage in later *Empire* releases—Palpatine was played by Ian McDiarmid. —*AM*

Evil Organizations

T he annals of supervillainy are replete with alliances of amoral individuals who work in concert toward common illicit ends. While such "evil organizations" may employ disparate methods, most share several core characteristics: a rigidly hierarchical network of agents, operatives, and henchmen, led or overseen by one key leader; numerous hideouts and safehouses; a high-tech infrastructure, of which massively destructive weaponry is usually an integral part; and a predilection for world domination, either overt or covert.

Evil organizations frequently derive their names from portentous acronyms. The British superspy James Bond often faced off against operatives of SPECTRE (Special Executive for Counterintelligence, Terrorism, Revenge, and Extortion), a cold war–era criminal order that originated in Ian Fleming's 1961 James Bond novel *Thunderball*, and reprised its world-threatening activities in five more 007 novels and seven Bond feature films. Nuclear blackmail and assassination were among the favorite tactics of SPECTRE, whose diversely international members identified themselves with numeric designations. The group's leader, Ernst Stavro Blofeld, described SPECTRE as "a dedicated fraternity whose strength lies in the absolute integrity of its members."

T.H.R.U.S.H. (Technological Hierarchy for the Removal of Undesirables and the Subjugation of Humanity), a similar acronymic fellowship, bedeviled United Network Command for Law Enforcement agents Napoleon Solo, Illya Kuryakin, and April Dancer in television's *The Man From U.N.C.L.E.* (1964–1968) and *The Girl from U.N.C.L.E.* (1966–1967); U.N.C.L.E.'s agents frequently had to rely on the assistance of ordinary citizens to thwart T.H.R.U.S.H.'s various schemes for global tyranny.

For decades, comic-book superheroes have run afoul of acronymic evil organizations as well, including Marvel Comics' A.I.M. (Advanced Idea Mechanics) and DC Comics' H.I.V.E. (Hierarchy of International Vengeance and Extermination). A.I.M. (which debuted in *Strange Tales* vol. 1 #146, 1966) is initially a legitimate-appearing technology company whose benign inventions long concealed its World War II Nazi origins and provided cover for the machinations of its sinister, bucket-headed operatives and their decades of work toward world conquest; these schemes were routinely thwarted by Captain America and Nick Fury of the cold war–era spy bureau known as S.H.I.E.L.D. (Supreme Headquarters International Espionage Law-Enforcement Division; later, Strategic Hazard Intervention Espionage Logistics Directorate). During the 1980s, Mark Gruenwald's *Captain America* stories showed A.I.M. holding trade shows at which they sold their weaponry to the highest bidder. H.I.V.E. was established in *Superman Family* #205 (1981) by the H.I.V.E. Master, a criminal savant who brought numerous acts of high-tech terrorism to bear against various configurations of the New Teen Titans.

Like most of its ilk, the mission statement of Marvel's Hydra focuses on establishing a new global fascist order by means of space-age technology, which its founder—the Nazi Baron von Strucker—based in part on alien Gnobian technology he discovered in 1944. Hydra, which debuted in *Strange Tales* vol. 1 #135 (1965), differs from most other evil organizations in at least two respects: its name, appropriately enough, derives from the unkillable multiheaded beast from Greek mythology rather than from an acronym, and the group is organized as a cult whose army of masked and costumed foot soldiers treat their leader, whom they address as the Supreme Hydra, as a semi-divine figure. The brainchild of writer Stan Lee and artist Jack Kirby, Hydra reached its creative zenith under the innovative artistic guidance of Jim Steranko in Marvel's original *Nick Fury: Agent of S.H.I.E.L.D.* series (1968–1969).

Other evil organizations have a decidedly more straight-ahead shoot-em-up military bent, as is the case in the action figure–inspired, supersoldier-oriented animated storytelling universe of *G.I. Joe: A Real American Hero*. Since writers tend to design villainous organizations specifically to test the obvious strengths and plumb the hidden weaknesses of their heroes, COBRA and its spin-off group V.E.N.O.M. engage in armed and armored combat and are organized along military lines. The former organization is composed of armed combat operatives, some of whom take snake-suggestive names (Copperhead, Pythona, and Serpentor), and sometimes uses psionic-powered agents in combat; the latter is a cabal of chimeric human-animal hybrids possessed of superhuman fighting skills and inhuman determination (*G.I. Joe: Valor vs. Venom*, 2004). The motiva-

tions of both groups are both vague and irrelevant, since they serve mainly as foils for the *G.I. Joe* combat coterie, giving their cartoony, PG-rated, direct-to-DVD action its raison d' être.

The long-ago, far-away galaxy of George Lucas' *Star Wars* films was governed for centuries by a peaceful and egalitarian Republic—until the rogue Senator Palpatine usurps power, thereby transforming the government into what is arguably the ultimate in evil organizations: the Galactic Empire (*Star Wars: Episode III: Revenge of the Sith*, 2005). Palpatine ascends to the position of emperor, annexing system after system, capitalizing on the terror inspired by his fearsome Imperial Starfleet and its armored, moon-sized Death Star space stations. The Empire's dissolution comes about within decades, because of the actions of stalwart rebels and as a consequence of the poor morale of the overreaching Empire's own punishment-weary minions, as seen in *Star Wars: Episode IV: A New Hope* (1977); *Star Wars: Episode V: The Empire Strikes Back* (1980); and *Star Wars: Episode VI: Return of the Jedi* (1983).

But evil organizations often must employ subtlety rather than brute strength in order to bring their plans of conquest to fruition. Marvel's Secret Empire began as a division of Hydra, but took a substantially different and independent direction years later in the hands of writer Steve Englehart. Englehart's take on the Secret Empire brought Watergate-era politics onto the four-color page, complete with a takeover of the federal government by ruthless agents patterned after members of the Nixon administration. Like Bond's SPECTRE, the Secret Empire assigned numbers to its operatives, and Captain America apparently discovered that the group's leader, the hooded Number One, was actually the president of the United States! Captain America found this insidious intersection of his nation's government with a supervillain organization so demoralizing that he temporarily mothballed his red, white, and blue costume and shield and adopted the stateless superhero identity of Nomad (*Captain America* vol. 1 #175–#183, 1974–1975).

From the 1980s forward, many evil organizations began to adopt the mantle of big-business legitimacy, no doubt encouraged by news stories of real corporate malfeasance, such as the endemic stock market and savings-and-loan scandals of the day. DC's Intergang, originally a Prohibition-era organized crime enterprise in the city of Metropolis, is taken over by broadcasting mogul Morgan Edge, who uses the resources of his legitimate WGBS media empire to abet and conceal Intergang's multifarious acts of supervillainy, which include the development of high-tech weaponry and the use of superpowered "enforcers" who employ paramilitary tactics, poison gas, wall-crawling devices, and quasimagical superweaponry from the Jack Kirby–created planet Apokolips in their endless pursuit of wealth and power (*Forever People* vol. 1 #1, 1971). Intergang's erstwhile "corporate" crime boss, Morgan Edge, has gone on to appear twice in the WB network's *Smallville* series in 2003 (played by Rutger Hauer and Patrick Bergin), in which he serves as a foil to the overlord of yet another "evil corporation": Lionel Luthor, the father of Lex Luthor, a ruthless boardroom raider committed to amassing corporate and supernatural power, as well as to the development of various and sundry high-tech—and often kryptonite-based—weapons.

Because of their obvious silly aspects, evil organizations have made compelling targets for satire and parody for decades. The curiously nonacronymic 1960s evil society known as KAOS, presented goofball cold-war adversaries for the equally nonacronymic CONTROL, and its bumbling American spy Maxwell Smart. *Austin Powers: International Man of Mystery* (1997) began a film trilogy that gave us a SPECTRE-derived parody crime organization that used Starbucks and a Hollywood talent agency as "cover," and whose plans for world domination included a digging device designed to cause global volcanic eruptions, a space-based laser, human organ trafficking, and a Carrot Top movie. FOX's *The Simpsons* has depicted the Republican Party as a secret, world-conquering organization run by both tycoons and vampires who plot global domination in a secret headquarters located in a forbidding mountain keep. Even comic books have gotten into the business of parodying evil organizations. In Bongo's *Simpsons Comics* vol. 1 #3 (1994), Krusty the Clown unsuccessfully pitches a television drama in which his spy bureau K.L.O.W.N. (Keeping Law

& Order With Novelty Items) goes toe to toe with Gabbo, the power-mad ventriloquist's dummy who runs the evil organization known as W.O.O.D. (World Order of Dummies). Just because something threatens the world doesn't mean it can't also be funny. —*MAM*

Evil Twins

"I am but a shadowy reflection of you," observed artifact plunderer Rene Belloq to his nemesis, archaeologist-turned-adventurer Indiana Jones, in the film *Raiders of the Lost Ark* (1981).

Like the Belloq/Jones "reflection," numerous supervillains and superheroes possess similar methods but choose antonymous paths. The Joker and Batman share a yin/yang relationship, each employing violence and dark theatrics to achieve his goals. Venom and Spider-Man, the Reverse-Flash and the Flash, Dr. Doom and Mr. Fantastic, Circe and Wonder Woman, and Sinestro and Green Lantern are among the compatible characters that might have been, or in some cases *were*, friends or colleagues before a decision to bask in evil's light led one party astray.

An evil twin, however, is the hero's exact ethical opposite. He is often the hero's look-alike, albeit with cosmetic or wardrobe differences. He may hail from another world or parallel dimension, or be a clone of the hero gone bad. Through the evil twin, the hero's principles are challenged, and the reader (or the viewer) and the hero are reminded of the codependence of good and evil.

No twins are more codependent than writer Robert Louis Stevenson's Dr. Jekyll and Mr. Hyde, the inspiration for Batman's foe Two-Face, whose morality choices are left to the flip of a coin. DC Comics' Eclipso, who debuted in 1963, was originally dubbed "Hero and Villain in One Man," although that dichotomy was more a gimmick than a psychological study.

Dr. Bruce Banner has at times been separated from his personal "Mr. Hyde," the Incredible Hulk, but fate cruelly reunites them. The Maestro, the brainchild of writer Peter David and artist George Pérez, exists—or *will* exist—as the Hulk's evil twin. First seen in the miniseries *The Incredible Hulk:*

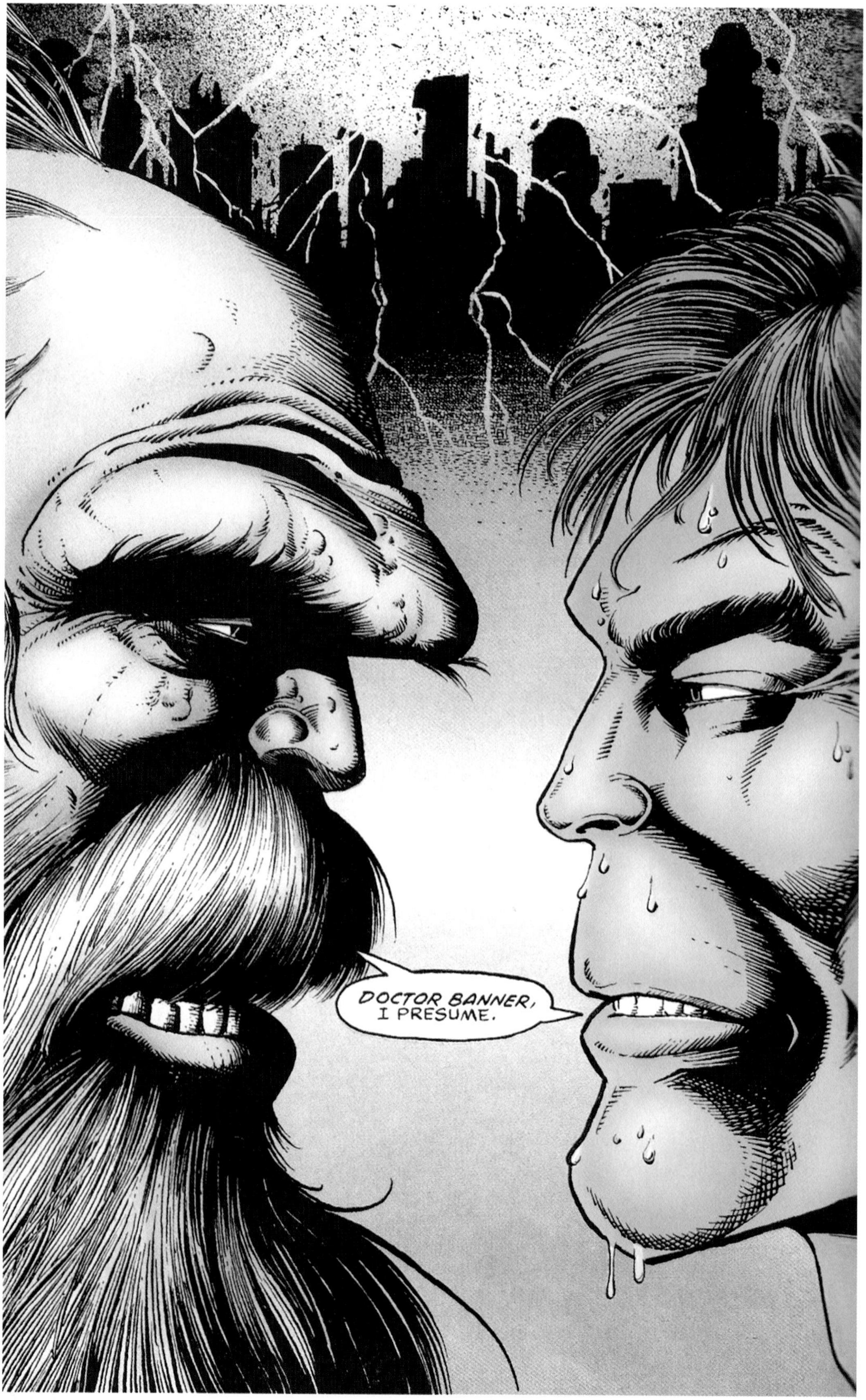
DOCTOR BANNER, I PRESUME.

Future Imperfect (1992), the Maestro lived in an alternate timeline approximately 100 years in Banner's future. A bearded, aged amalgamation of the Hulk's various personalities, the despotic Maestro, abetted by his watchful Gravity Police and their robotic Dogs O'War, turned his future Earth into a dystopia, and the present-day Hulk was forced to face the nightmare he might one day become.

"Mirror, Mirror," screenwriter Jerome Bixby's classic 1967 episode of television's original *Star Trek* (1966–1968), featured several Starship *Enterprise* crewmembers encountering their malicious alternate-reality analogues, including a goatee-adorned Mr. Spock. This episode immortalized facial hair as the defining fashion statement of the evil twin, parodied, among other sources, through goateed doppelgängers of animated characters Cartman (from *South Park*, 1997–present) and the robot Bender (*Futurama*, 1999–2003).

As with *Star Trek*'s "mirror universe," the parallel world is a fertile source for evil twins. *Justice League of America* (JLA) #29 (1964) introduced the Crime Syndicate of America, hailing from an alternate Earth: Ultraman, Owlman, Superwoman, Johnny Quick, and Power Ring, corrupt variations of Superman, Batman, Wonder Woman, the Flash, and Green Lantern. Conversely, that world's Lex Luthor was a superhero, not the criminal scientist known in "our" reality. A different parallel world's Luthor was a hero, along with Clayface, in "Superman and Batman—Outlaws!" in *World's Finest Comics* #148 (1965). Not to be taken quite as seriously were the 1979 *World's Greatest Super Friends* TV episode "Universe of Evil," in which the cartoon version of the Justice League fought its devilish duplicates (including an eye-patched Aquaman, mustached Batman and Robin, and pitchfork-tailed monkey Gleek), and the Power Posse, evil twins of the bargain-basement JLAers, the Super Buddies, in DC's *JLA Classified* #9 (2005). Disney's feathered crime fighter Darkwing Duck tussled with Negaduck, his alternate-Earth duplicate, in the animated series *Darkwing Duck* (1991–1995).

The Teen Titans, He-Man, Prime, and Buffy the Vampire Slayer are among the characters that have met their sinister counterparts, as has Underdog (from the 1964–1973 cartoon), whose evil twin was Overcat. Marvel Comics' Adam Warlock encountered his evil twin in the form of his future-self the Magus, and the X-Men's foe Onslaught is the manifestation of the dark side of Charles (Professor X) Xavier's personality.

Superman has battled no shortage of cracked-mirror replicas of himself, including the Frankenstein-esque Bizarro; the Negative Superman, a negative-energy equivalent (*World's Finest Comics* #126, 1962); and the Sand-Superman, a sand-forged duplicate appearing in an early 1970s storyline. A similar theme has been a war between the Man of Steel and his alter ego, often the result of kryptonite mutations, depicted in such tales as "The Feud Between Superman and Clark Kent" in *Action Comics* #293 (1962) and the live-action movie *Superman III* (1983).

Variations of the evil-twins concept exist. Supervillains have sometimes assumed a superhero's identity through impersonation or mind swapping, a lauded instance being Stan Lee and Jack Kirby's poignant "This Man … This Monster!" from *Fantastic Four* vol. 1 #51 (1966), featuring an unnamed adversary whose jealousy of Reed (Mr. Fantastic) Richards' intellect led him to scientifically transform himself into an "exact replica" of the rock-encrusted hero the Thing. A time-honored tradition in superhero comic books is the hero fighting himself, with covers featuring astonishing images of Spider-Man versus Spider-Man, or Plastic Man versus Plastic Man, sometimes accompanied by "How can this be possible?!"–type blurbs. Usually, these peculiarities are explained away by an imposter, be it friend, foe, robot replicant, or alien, whose reason for masquerading as the hero is revealed by the turn of the last story page. —ME

Evilheart the Great

Reggie Mantle has always been the vain bane of all-American teenager Archie Andrews' exis-

Opposite: From *The Incredible Hulk: Future Imperfect* #1 ©1992 Marvel Comics. ART BY GEORGE PÉREZ.

tence, vying for the heart of vivacious Veronica Lodge by hook or by crook—and briefly, by superpowers. During the superhero boom of the mid-1960s, Archie Comics publisher John Goldwater mandated that their carrot-topped headliner become a superhero, and Pureheart the Powerful was born in *Life with Archie* #42 (1965). Two issues later, in Pureheart's second appearance, Archie's Riverdale High rival Reggie gained a temporary superpower: "the Bloodshot Eye," emitting a "pulverizing beam" from his left eyeball.

Reggie's peculiar alterations were only beginning. In *Life with Archie* #48 (1966) the teen ne'er-do-well is overcome by hostility toward Archie, inexplicably transforming into Evilheart the Great, sporting a flashy green-and-purple caped-and-cowled costume. While his identity is masked, Evilheart scooters about on his *Reggie*cycle, using his enhanced strength and stamina and his "Destructo Ray" to tangle with Pureheart for Veronica's affections—the same modus operandi as "regular" Reggie.

Despite his egocentrism and name, Evilheart was, essentially, a superhero with a bad attitude. He protected Veronica and/or Riverdale from supervillains such as the Bee, who commanded swarms of attack bees; the Rotter, whose ring zapped a ray that caused matter to decay; the sticky-fingered Tar-Man; and the Wishing Weirdo, a gypsy whose wishes became reality. After a couple of years of appearances, Evilheart—along with Pureheart, as well as Betty as Superteen and Jughead as Captain Hero—mothballed his tights when the caped-crusader craze subsided; a mid-1990s revival of these characters in *Archie's Super Teens* failed to catch on. —*ME*

Extant

DC Comics' time-tyrant Extant began his career as a superhero. In *Showcase* #75 (1968), plotter/artist Steve Ditko (with scripter Steve Skeates), motivated by America's political divide over the Vietnam War, introduces Hank and Don Hall, quarrelsome teenage brothers with opposing ideologies. A disembodied voice—later revealed to be the Lords of Chaos and Order—grants the siblings superhuman strength and stamina, with the aggressive Hank and pacifist Don becoming the superheroes Hawk and Dove. They flew in and out of comics for nearly twenty years until Dove was killed in DC's house-cleaning opus *Crisis on Infinite Earths* (1985–1986). Hawk's rage intensified, despite the occasional calming influence of a new, female Dove.

DC announced in 1991 that its crossover *Armageddon 2001* would transform one of its heroes into a villain. Captain Atom was tapped, but a leak to the comics press spoiled the surprise, forcing the supplanting of Hawk as the bad-guy-to-be. In this series, Hawk went insane after a future version of himself killed the new Dove. Donning technologically advanced armor with time-distortion capabilities, Hawk became the despot Monarch and nearly established himself as Earth's sovereign. Three years later he was at it again, with modified raiment and a new name, Extant, in the miniseries *Zero Hour: A Crisis in Time* (1994), in which his chronal manipulations resulted in the deaths of three members of the Justice Society of America. Extant apparently met his demise in a 2000 tussle with the JSA, but with his ability to alter the time stream, his clock may still be ticking. —*ME*

The Fatal Five

The futuristic teen superteam the Legion of Super-Heroes (LSH) meets its match in the Jim Shooter–written/Curt Swan–illustrated *Adventure Comics* #352–#353 (1967) as the vast and virulent galaxy-gulper the Sun-Eater zeroes in on thirtieth-century Earth's sun. When their efforts to repress the Sun-Eater fail, the desperate Legionnaires recruit a quintet of heavy hitters for an assist: Tharok, a cruel, technologically enhanced scientist (Tharok's entire body is vertically halved, his left side, from head to toe, being mechanical); Tharok's obedient charge Validus, a 25-foot mindless, infinitely powerful behemoth that fires lethal psionic bolts; the Emerald Empress, a lime-haired beauty who commands the power totem called the Emerald Eye, a bizarre, floating orb; the Persuader, a husky, iron-masked executioner who wields an atomic ax that slices through any matter or energy field; and Mano, a bubble-helmeted mutant from a toxic world whose right hand—which he normally gloves—can disintegrate any substance. A meeting of minds between Tharok and Legionnaire Brainiac 5 conceives a bomb which must be deposited into the belly of the beast, and valiant Legionnaire Ferro Lad sacrifices his life to deliver the payload. The villains refuse the indebted LSH's offer to pardon their crimes and instead pool their resources as the cacopho-

nous cadre the Fatal Five, hell-bent on conquering the universe they just helped save.

The Fatal Five returned in *Adventure* #365–#366 (1968) as the warlords of the planet Talok VIII; the Legion's headquarters was destroyed in that epic's climactic battle. Throughout the 1970s and 1980s the Fatal Five continued their path of destruction through the pages of Legion stories, perpetrating the death of Legionnaire Invisible Kid and a full-scale assault on the LSH, orchestrated by Tharok's clone the Dark Man.

The reverberations caused by the 1986 revamp of Superman in the *Man of Steel* miniseries rattled Legion lore and caused several subsequent LSH reboots, the trickle-down effect altering the Fatal Five's history. The Fatal Five—boasting the same lethal lineup as the original group—were reintroduced in *Legionnaires* #34 (1996). In this revised continuity, the Legion assembled the Fatal Five at the behest of United Planets' President Chu, who covertly conspired to ignite an intergalactic war via her manipulation of the Sun-Eater threat.

DC Comics readers were puzzled when the Menaces from Tomorrow reappeared in the twenty-first-century adventures of the Man of Tomorrow in *Superman* vol. 2 #171 (2001). "Good characters are good characters," remarked that comic's writer, Jeph Loeb, in a 2001 online interview; "One of the things about using a combined universe should be to combine the characters." The Fatal Fivers pitted against Superman in Loeb and artist Ed McGuiness' tale were actually duplicates created by Brainiac 13. The "real" Fatal Five returned in *The Legion* #16 (2003), and will no doubt perennially plague the current and any future incarnations of the Legion.

A twenty-first-century version of the Persuader, a rebellious Metropolis citizen with an ax to grind, was introduced in *Adventures of Superman* #601 (2002). —*ME*

Fatality

Arch-villain assassin Fatality was bent on slaying Green Lantern during her reign of terror—not just Kyle Rayner, Earth's fifth Green Lantern, but all of the ring-bearing heroes. Co-created by writer Ron Marz and artist Darryl Banks, she first appeared in *Green Lantern* vol. 3 #83 (1997) as Yrra Cynril, the eldest child of a royal family of the planet Xanshi. When the planet is accidentally obliterated by Rayner's predecessor, Green Lantern John Stewart, she swears revenge on the entire Green Lantern Corps, an elite team of super-powered peacekeepers.

As Fatality, the energy-blade-wielding super–martial artist, Cynril traveled the galaxy and defied time and space constraints in search of former Green Lanterns. After murdering them one by one, she arrived on Earth to face off with Rayner. Their battle culminated on a distant planet, where Fatality learned of Stewart's identity and pegged him as the Lantern responsible for her planet's demise. Although she ended up confronting Stewart (who was assisted by Jade, making for an interesting catfight), she presumably died in battle.

Although Fatality's body was never found, that didn't stop her from reappearing in DC Comics' *Villains United* #2 (2005), in which she joined a massive assemblage of villains, part of Lex Luthor's Secret Society, in battle against the Secret Six (a small network of villains who oppose Luthor's grand-scale gathering). And with the resurrection of the Silver Age (1956–1969) Green Lantern, Hal Jordan, from the dead in 2005, she has yet another Emerald Crusader to despise. Although she has sel-

dom appeared outside the comic-book pages, the space-traveling death-dealer was immortalized in a 2002 action figure from DC Direct. —*GM*

The Fearsome Five

When the villainous Dr. Light placed an ad in "The Underworld Star," a newspaper read mostly by the evildoers of the DC Comics' Universe, he wanted to put together a group of supervillains. Those that joined him were known as the Fearsome Five, and they soon became the often-defeated bane of the Teen Titans and Superman.

First appearing in a story by Marv Wolfman and George Pérez in *The New Teen Titans* #3 (1981), the original Fearsome Five membership included Dr. Light, Psimon, Shimmer and her brother Mammoth, and Gizmo. Dr. Light was a scientist named Arthur Light who had gained his light-controlling powers in a scientific accident, and who used them for evil while dressed in a black and white costume replete with cape and finned skullcap. After confrontations with an earlier group of Teen Titans and the Justice League of America, Light had his mind altered by the sorceress Zatanna, and became an ineffectual buffoon the more he tried to be a credible villain.

Psimon was physicist Simon Jones whose experiments led to him gaining almost unlimited psionic powers; he dressed in a brain-exposing cranial dome and magenta robes. Shimmer was Selinda Flinders, an Australian with the power to transmute matter for three minutes; she wore a gold bodysuit with strategically placed cut-outs exposing her skin. Mammoth was her brother Baran, who wore a black bodysuit with yellow boots, gloves, and a harness, and who wielded superstrength. Gizmo was a brilliant midget named Mikron O'Jeneus, who had the power to convert almost any object into a technological weapon; he wore a green military-esque outfit with a hood, and was often bristling with weaponry and a flying backpack.

After run-ins with the Titans, Dr. Light was forced out of the group by Psimon, and the Fearsome Five welcomed East Indian sorceress Jinx into their fold. Later, Superman villain Neutron—whose radioactive punches were as strong as a bomb—also joined the Five. Later still, after the apparent death of Psimon, the Five faced Superman as Mammoth, Gizmo, Shimmer, and new members Charger (who had electrical powers) and Deuce (a low level psychic who could make people believe she was in more than one place at a time).

Psimon was not dead, however, and he eventually tried to kill his ex-teammates, with Shimmer seeming to perish. Later, Dr. Sivana revived the group again, keeping Psimon, a resurrected Shimmer, Mammoth, Jinx, and Gizmo together ... until Sivana killed Gizmo. History shows that the biggest impediment to the Fearsome Five's success is their own behavior toward each other.

In Cartoon Network's *Teen Titans* cartoon (2003–2006), members of the Fearsome Five have appeared regularly, though not as a team. Dr. Light has operated alone, while Gizmo, Jinx, and Mammoth are villainous teenage graduates of the HIVE Academy. Action figures of the animated villains began appearing in 2004 from Bandai, while Dr. Light became an action figure from DC Direct in 2005. —*AM*

Felix Faust

Sorcerer Felix Faust has DC Comics' greatest superheroes at his fingertips in *Justice League of America* #10 (1962). Via finger puppets in the shapes of the JLA members, Faust, who exploits the black arts through incantations learned from the occult bible the *Necronomicon*, persuades the JLA to unearth three artifacts that will grant him governance over the omnipotent demons Abnegazar, Rath, and Ghast. With the Leaguers held motionless by magic spells, Aquaman—commonly regarded as the most useless Justice Leaguer due to his water-dependent superpowers—thwarts Faust's plans by telepathically directing flying fish to kayo the conjurer.

Justice League writer Gardner Fox sampled from a literary cauldron for that tale. Felix Faust idolized his namesake, who "sold his soul to the devil for supernatural powers," a reference to the fifteenth-century fortune teller Faust, whose excursions through Germany earned him a reputation as an actual theurgist and inspired several narratives

(including Johann Wolfgang von Goethe's 1808 poem *Faust*). Legendary horror-fiction scribe H. P. Lovecraft, at one time represented by *JLA* editor Julius Schwartz during Schwartz's pre-comics days as a sci-fi agent, is alluded to in Fox's script in connection to the *Necronomicon*, which appeared in Lovecraft's works.

Writers expanded Felix Faust's backstory in subsequent stories. In 5,000 BC in the African nation of Kor, Faust battled the benevolent wizard Nommo—aka Dr. Mist—for control of the arcane power of the Flame of Life. Exiled into another dimension, he was eventually freed in the twentieth century. Faust has negotiated deals with demons for numinous power and immortality, selling the soul of his son Sebastian (who at one time fought with the Outsiders as the superhero Faust). Felix's reliance upon otherworldly forces and tomes always proves his downfall.

Felix Faust has battled with many of DC's supernatural heroes and has partnered with other rogues, including the Secret Society of Super-Villains. His oddest roles include a position on a villains baseball team in *DC Super-Stars* #10 (1976) and a brief stint as a librarian. After discovering that many of their memories had been "mindwiped" (erased) by the superhero magician Zatanna, Faust and several resentful former members of the Secret Society reunited in 2005 to attack the Justice League. Robert Englund, best known as cinema's Freddy Krueger, has voiced Faust on the Cartoon Network's *Justice League* (2001–2004) and *Justice League Unlimited* (2004–present). —*ME*

The Female Furies

You don't turn your back on the Female Furies. When first seen in *Mister Miracle* vol. 1 #6 (1972), these women warriors—the personal guard of Darkseid—storm to Earth to fetch their former leader Big Barda and return her to Apokolips, her loathsome homeworld she so wisely escaped. Barda, however, has no intentions of going back.

Trained by the dame of depravity, Granny Goodness, each of the Female Furies has a sinister specialty. Lashina is a dominatrix who whips victims with steel bands (she briefly resided on Earth, taking the name Duchess and joining the Suicide Squad); the whirling dervish Mad Harriet packs a painful punch with her spiky fists; the queen-sized Stompa is a foot-stamping stormtropper whose combat boots produce earthquakes; and Bernadeth, twisted sister of Darkseid's two-faced aide Desaad, hacks away with a "fahren-knife" that burns as well as cuts flesh. Leadership squabbles between Bernadeth and Lashina have sometimes weakened their solidarity, but when the Furies attack in tandem they are an imposing force, kicking, slicing, and pummeling their unfortunate opponents (including Hawk and Dove, Supergirl, and Wonder Woman) from all directions in a flurry of motion, unrelentingly savoring the pain they inflict.

Other Female Furies have been added to the group since writer/artist Jack Kirby unleashed them into the pages of DC Comics in 1972: the archer Artemis (not to be confused with the character from *Wonder Woman*), the vampiric Bloody Mary, the fleet-footed Speed Queen, the superstrong Knockout (who, like Barda and Lashina, relocated to Earth, often fighting Superboy), the karate-chopping Gillotina, and the Alice in Wonderland–like Malice Vundabar, whose "pet" is a toothy, devilishly smiling shadow creature named Chessure.

The 1998 "Little Girl Lost" episode of the animated series *Superman* (1996–2000) brought the original Female Furies to television to battle the Man of Steel and Supergirl, with Edward Asner among the voice cast, portraying the Furies' "loving" mentor Granny Goodness. —ME

The Fiddler

While Rome burnt, Emperor Nero fiddled. When the Fiddler fiddles, crime burns the innocent.

When petty thief Isaac Bowin is imprisoned in India, his cellmate, a Hindu fakir, teaches him the secrets of Hindu vibrational mysticism. Bowin learns to hypnotize by utilizing vibrations made by a crude violin, as well as to destroy with sound and to create impassable barriers of noise. He uses his new abilities to escape jail and betray his mentor, then, calling himself the Fiddler, returns to America to attempt to frame his twin brother, the

famed violinist the Maestro Bowin, Although Bowin's scheme was foiled by the Flash in *All-Flash Comics* #32 (1947–1948), in a tale written by Robert Kanigher and illustrated by Lee Elias, it became the first of many encounters between the Fastest Man Alive and his arch-foe. Bowin's reasons for hating his brother are not known.

After several clashes with the Flash, the Fiddler ran afoul of the Justice Society of America when he joined the new Injustice Society. Years later the Fiddler joined forces with the Thinker and the Shade to plunder Keystone City. Their plan was thwarted by the teamwork of two Flashes, Jay Garrick and Barry Allen, the Flash of the other-dimensional planet that was, in the days before the Crisis on Infinite Earths, called Earth-One (*Flash* #123, 1961). Later, the Fiddler, the Wizard, and the Icicle traveled to Earth-One to join Chronos, Dr. Alchemy, and Felix Faust, calling themselves the Crime Champions.

After an alliance with a criminal group titled Injustice Unlimited, the Fiddler seemed to have involuntarily retired, advanced arthritis having rendered him unable to play the violin. However, Bowin (here referred to as "Bowen") was recruited by a mysterious person called "Mockingbird" for the new Secret Six in *Villains United* #1 (2005), in which his seeming incompetence led to Deadshot killing him at Mockingbird's orders. While the malicious melodies of one of the oldest villains in the DC Universe have been silenced, the Fiddler has another string in his bow: his successor, a female violinist named Virtuoso, introduced in *Villains United* #6. —MWB

Fin Fang Foom

In early 1961 Marvel Comics writer/editor Stan Lee was bored: "The various monster stories that made up the bulk of our production at that time were beginning to pale for me," he wrote in his 2002 autobiography *Excelsior!* One of his last creature creations, a collaboration with artist Jack Kirby published one month before their *Fantastic Four* series unleashed what Lee would soon call the "Marvel Age of Comics," would endure throughout Marvel's metamorphosis from monster

From *Strange Tales* vol. 1 #89 ©1961 Marvel Comics.
ART BY JACK KIRBY AND DICK AYERS.

makers to superhero innovators: Fin Fang Foom, the ultimate monster-supervillain.

Strange Tales vol. 1 #89 (1961) takes readers to Red China, where the whispered legend of Fin Fang Foom causes totalitarian strongarms to quake in their boots. When Chan Liuchow, a half-Chinese/half-American insurgent opposed to the Communist regime, stirs Fin Fang Foom from a subterranean slumber with magic herbs, the reason for this beast's infamy are clear. A sentient, egocentric green dragon of Godzilla proportions (and wearing Comics Code–mandated purple briefs), the "mortals"-hating Fin Fang Foom is coaxed by Chan into a rampage that steamrolls over Red Chinese soldiers. Virtually invulnerable and winged for flight, the acid-spewing, talking dragon cracks a section of the Great Wall of China as a bull-whip before Chan tricks him back into his cavern for another snooze.

Over the decades, Fin Fang Foom (or his proxies) has been reanimated to lay waste to the Mar-

vel Universe, with the Fantastic Four and the Hulk mopping up his messes. The dragon has appeared most frequently in the pages of *Iron Man*, sometimes in connection with the Armored Avenger's Far Eastern foe, the Mandarin. It was revealed in 1991 that Fin Fang Foom was an extraterrestrial explorer shipwrecked on Earth centuries ago, and the dragon has—like many other comics characters—perished, only to return for more malice. His name inspired "FOOM" ("Friends Of Ol' Marvel") to be added to the Marvel fandom vernacular; during the 1970s *FOOM* was also the title of a Marvel-published fanzine.

Fin Fang Foom, voiced by Neil Ross, was among the rogues' gallery in the animated *Iron Man* TV series (1994–1996), with a tie-in action figure released. In the 2000s the dragon was sculpted as a collectible mini-bust (in green and red variations), and was featured in the 2005 comic, *Marvel Monsters: Fin Fang Four.* —*ME*

The Flash's Rogues' Gallery

The Flash's Rogues' Gallery first unionized in 1965's John Broome–penned, Carmine Infantino–penciled *The Flash* vol. 1 #155 (while 1962's issue #130 cover-spotlighted five Flash foes, it was a Mirror Master story featuring villain cameos). Six costumed enemies of the Silver Age (1956–1969) Scarlet Speedster (aka Flash II)—Captain Boomerang, Captain Cold, Heat Wave, Mirror Master, Pied Piper, and the Top—steer the Flash into a gauntlet, their gathering secretly coordinated by a seventh villain not depicted on

#155's cover but described in a blurb as "mightier and more dangerous than the other six combined" (Gorilla Grodd). The Flash's assembled foes, despite their petty differences, discover they have much in common: their obvious hatred of (and previous defeats by) the Flash, and a flamboyant fashion sense. "They all even went to the same tailor for their super-villain costumes, a character called Paul Gambi, named after Paul Gambicini, a major fan writer of the day," remarked *Flash* editor Julius Schwartz in *The Flash Archives* vol. 1 (1996).

Unlike Spider-Man's Sinister Six, the disharmonious team that first tried to drub the wall-crawler in 1964, Flash's foes mostly enjoyed each other's company, for the next twenty years occasionally meeting like a criminal coffee klatch in stories so popular they made "Rogues' Gallery" a proper noun. After the Rogues' first adventure, the brilliant Grodd rarely lowered himself to fraternize with these humans, but other villains, from 1960s criminals like the Trickster to 1980s newcomers like the Rainbow Raider, sometimes joined up to make life difficult for the Fastest Man Alive. Even the tailor Gambi continued to thread his way through occasional appearances, including a bizarre team-up between the Flash and a popular comedian in DC Comics' *The Adventures of Jerry Lewis* #112 (1969).

The Flash vol. 1 #174 ©1967 DC Comics.
COVER ART BY CARMINE INFANTINO AND MURPHY ANDERSON.

The Rogues' Gallery ran out of steam when the Flash died in *Crisis on Infinite Earths* #8 (1985). Many reformed, but five Rogues risked eternal damnation for the promise of increased power in the crossover *Underworld Unleashed* (1995), shambling soullessly before regaining their humanity in 1997 courtesy of their enemy's successor, Flash III (formerly sidekick Kid Flash). Some of the Rogues "repaid" the speedster by briefly regrouping, but a 2001 one-shot, *The Flash: Iron Heights*, jump-started a "next generation" of the Rogues' Gallery. Written by Geoff Johns, *Iron Heights*—named after Keystone City's (home of Flash III) penitentiary for malevolent metahumans—featured criminal strategist Blacksmith bringing together some former Rogues, the Teen Titans menace Magenta, and newer villains including the metallic brute Girder and the lurid psycho Murmur.

During his five-year *Flash* run (2000–2005), Johns explored the personalities of the Rogues

through individual stories detailing their roots, their psychoses, and their modus operandi. Captain Cold stepped into the forefront as the organizer of a new Rogues' Gallery, uniting some old teammates and many of their successors, such as the son of Captain Boomerang and the new Trickster. "[Captain Cold] tells the newer Rogues that you don't go out and spill blood just for the sake of it, you only kill somebody when you absolutely have to," observed Johns in a September 2005 *Wizard* magazine interview. Providing the organizational structure that the original Rogues' Gallery lacked—without its camaraderie—Cold has led the criminals into chilling new territory, including a large and lethal assemblage of supervillains in the six-part "Rogue War" *Flash* storyline (2005).

The 2005 "Flash and Substance" episode of the Cartoon Network's *Justice League Unlimited* (2004–present) teamed Captain Cold, the Trickster, and Captain Boomerang in a joint attack against their speedy foe. —ME

The Floronic Man

The Floronic Man, originally called Plant Master (Plant-Master), has a history as long and leguminous as a wisteria. The creature sprouted in *The Atom* #1 (1962) in a story by writer Gardner Fox and artist Gil Kane. Woodrue, a political extremist from an otherworld of wood nymphs and floral spirits, is banished to Earth for punishment for his supremacist activity. Taking on the human identity of botany professor Jason Woodrue, he channels his animosity toward his home planet into research and, in true supervillainous fashion, initiates a "plant-conquest of Earth," an effort fortunately pruned by the Tiny Titan.

Woodrue's propensity for lab experiments and a desire for revenge took him to the extreme of investigating human/plant hybridization. It was during one of these endeavors that student botanist Pamela Isley was turned into Poison Ivy (in director Joel Schumacher's 1997 movie *Batman & Robin*, John Glover played Woodrue in Poison Ivy's origin sequence). Other academic prodigy included Susan Linden (Black Orchid) and Alec Holland (the human template for Swamp Thing).

Woodrue ultimately perfected a serum that allowed him to transform into a plant-based life form, dubbing himself the Floronic Man, complete with pliable, bark-like skin, wooden bones, and green leaves that grow in place of hair. Because he now appeared inhuman, he developed a spray-on synthetic skin that allowed him to masquerade as a human being. This super-strong, red-eyed mutation—whose powers include control over plants and the ability to communicate with them—was a member of the Secret Society of Super-Villains in the late 1970s. He repeatedly tangled with the Atom, as well as the second Green Lantern and—in a celebrated Alan Moore–scripted storyline—Swamp Thing. As Floro, he briefly tried to redeem himself as a member of the New Guardians, an evolved hero team chosen to lead humankind.

The Atom #24 ©1966 DC Comics.
COVER ART BY GIL KANE AND MURPHY ANDERSON.

In the 2005 *JLA* story arc "Crisis of Conscience," he reunited with a cadre of former Secret Society members for a vengeful attack against the Justice League. —GM

The Frightful Four

When the Wizard, the techie terror who whisks through the skies on anti-gravity discs, realized that he and his two new criminal friends—the shapeshifting Sandman and evil epoxier Paste-Pot—could best their mutual enemies the Fantastic Four (FF) by uniting as the heroes' "exact evil counterparts," they formed the Frightful Four in Marvel Comics' *Fantastic Four* #36 (1965). Recruiting Madam Medusa (in her first appearance), the vixen with living hair, the Frightful Four gatecrash the FF's headquarters, the Baxter Building, just as a superhero-packed engagement party for Reed (Mr. Fantastic) Richards and Sue (Invisible Girl) Storm has wound down. In this story by Stan Lee and Jack Kirby, Reed, Sue, and the Thing are sent sailing toward the heavens on the Wizard's discs until the Human Torch nets them. The villains escape to resume their attack another day.

Two issues later, in *FF* #38 (1965), the FF were "Defeated by the Frightful Four!" (a hyperbolic cover blurb screamed, "it had to happen sooner or later!"). With Paste-Pot Pete glue-potting his *nom de guerre* for the moniker the Trapster ("That's a name with dignity … with drama to it!"), the Frightful Four, through teamwork and relentless attacks, got the upper hand, leaving the FF to die in an atomic explosion from which they narrowly escaped.

Perniciously persistent, the Frightful Four, often anchored by its founding trio, have frequently regrouped to attempt to finish what they started. Madam Medusa didn't last long—by 1966 she was revealed to be one of the royal family the Inhumans, her crime career the result of amnesia—and was followed by other members including the sound-master Klaw, the fire-breathing Dragon Man, the female fury Titania, Spider-Man's enemy Electro, the Wonder Woman–like Thundra, the aquatic Hydro-Man, the obstinate Man-Bull, sinister Soviet Red Ghost (and his Super-Apes), and the Thing's counterpart She-Thing. Another FF opposite number was the Frightful Four's hulkish Brute, an alternate-Earth version of Mr. Fantastic. The criminally resourceful teamwork evidenced in the Frightful Four's earliest appearances evaporated after Medusa left the flock; the querulous quartet's disharmony usually accelerates its downfall.

The original Frightful Four story was adapted to television in 1978 for the *Fantastic Four* animated series. —ME

Fu Manchu

Sax Rohmer's *Insidious Dr. Fu Manchu* (1913) introduced what was to become one of the most famous fictional characters of all time, and perhaps the first villain to serve as a series protagonist. His desire was to take over the world and, in a way, he did: "Imagine a person, tall, lean and feline, high-shouldered, with a brow like Shakespeare and a face like Satan, a close-shaven skull, and long, magnetic eyes of the true cat-green. Invest him with all the cruel cunning of an entire Eastern race, accumulated in one giant intellect, with all the resources of science past and present, with all the resources, if you will, of a wealthy government—which, however, already has denied all knowledge of his existence. Imagine that awful being, and you have a mental picture of Dr. Fu-Manchu, the yellow peril incarnate in one man," remarks Denis Nayland Smith to Dr. Petrie in chapter 2 of the novel.

Though he seems to be the personification of the dreaded "Yellow Peril," to attempt to describe the threat Dr. Fu Manchu presents to the world in terms of race hatred is insufficient to sum up his menace. The Devil Doctor will destroy any who stand between him and his goal of destroying the Western world and remake it as an extension of his beloved East … with himself as its absolute ruler.

Beginning with *The Insidious Fu Manchu*, the creation of Sax Rohmer (pseudonym of Arthur Sarsfield Ward, 1883–1959—"Sax Rohmer" is loosely translated as "wandering blade," or "freelance") launched plot after plot at Western civilization, but found his schemes thwarted time and again by Sir Denis Nayland Smith of Scotland Yard and his friend Dr. Petrie. Fu Manchu is aided in his campaigns by the blind loyalty of the Si-Fan cult, by his daughter, Fah Lo Suee, and his own matchless intellect. The Devil Doctor has even conquered age by his Elixir Vitae, which retards the aging process, granting him perpetual life.

Twelve other Fu Manchu novels appeared—*The Return of Dr. Fu Manchu* (1916), *The Hand of Fu Manchu* (1917), *The Daughter of Fu Manchu* (1931), *The Mask of Fu Manchu* (1932), *The Bride of Fu Manchu* (1933), *The Trail of Fu Manchu* (1934), *President Fu Manchu* (1936), *The Drums of Fu Manchu*, (1939), *The Island of Fu Manchu* (1941), *The Shadow of Fu Manchu* (1948), *Re-Enter Fu Manchu* (1957) and *Emperor Fu Manchu* (1959)—and though the Devil Doctor never took over the world, it was not for any lack of imagination. His schemes included falsifying the deaths of scientists, then forcing them to work for him; instilling the murderous skills of Jack the Ripper into his

Si-Fan cultists; and installing a puppet candidate into the office of president of the United States.

The burgeoning medium of radio offered a frequent haven for the Devil Doctor. Fu Manchu first appeared on radio on *The Collier Hour* with adaptations of at least three Rohmer novels (1929–1931). *Fu Manchu* was first broadcast as a series of twelve shows from 1929 to 1930, then from 1932 to 1934 with John C. Daly, then Harold Huber, as the voice of Fu Manchu. A Manchu series starring Frank Cochrane was produced for Radio Luxembourg to compete with the British Broadcasting Company (1936–1937). *The Shadow of Fu Manchu* was syndicated from 1939 to 1940, and starred Ted Osborne as the Devil Doctor. In 1944 *NBC Molle Mystery Theatre* ran a thirty-minute adaptation of *The Insidious Dr. Fu Manchu* in 1944.

The Celestial One has also proven a great favorite of the movies, first appearing on the screen in the fifteen-chapter serial, *The Mystery of Fu Manchu* (1923), with Harry Agar Lyons as Manchu. Agar returned to the role for eight episodes of *The Further Mysteries of Fu Manchu* (1924). In general, the older the production, the more likely it is to rely on Western fear of the "Yellow Peril" and techniques bordering on racism to instill fear for Fu Manchu in the audience. Later productions tend to emphasize the Devil Doctor's scientific accomplishments and his utter ruthlessness in using them to obtain his goals.

Warner Oland stepped into the role for *The Mysterious Dr. Fu Manchu* (1929), and *The Return of Dr. Fu Manchu* (1930). *Daughter of the Dragon* (1931) was Oland's last movie as the Devil Doctor.

In 1940 a fifteen-chapter serial, *Drums of Fu Manchu*, was released; it which was edited to movie length in 1943. A sequel, *Fu Manchu Strikes Back*, was planned, but quashed by the U.S. State Department, reportedly because it would feature the Chinese, America's allies in World War II, in a bad light, though it is certain that many viewers thought of Manchu as Japanese.

The Devil Doctor took a long hiatus from the silver screen, possibly due to worried producers fearing any film treatment would be characterized as "racist," but returned in 1965 in *The Face of Fu Manchu*, the first of a series of five films starring

The Mask of Dr. Fu Manchu ©1951 Avon Publishing. COVER ART BY WALLY WOOD.

Christopher Lee, whose facial features were certainly perfect for depicting an Asian mastermind. Peter Sellers was Manchu in Orion's "hilarious comedy" *The Fiendish Plot of Fu Manchu* (1980), the character's most recent film appearance as of 2006.

Television, which entered virtually every American home in the 1950s, seemed an ideal medium for the Celestial One to disseminate his schemes. Fu Manchu appeared on television in 1952 with *The Zayat Kiss*, starring John Carradine as Fu Manchu. *The Adventures of Fu Manchu,* starring Glen Gordon, lasted thirteen episodes from 1955 to 1956. These shows suffered from low budgets and poor production values, though John Carradine was certainly an inspired casting choice.

Comic books have also proved a popular medium for the Celestial One and his illegitimate offspring, beginning with *Wow, What a Magazine!* in 1936. DC Comics' *Detective Comics* #18 (1938) began the serialization of *The Mysterious Fu Manchu* drawn by Leo O'Mealia. This feature was originally distributed by the Bell Syndicate from 1930 to 1932. Avon released *The Mask of Fu Manchu* in 1951, with art by future great Wally Wood.

The Devil Doctor was doubtless the inspiration for such pulp-magazine villains as *The Mysterious Wu Fang* and *Dr. Yen Sin*. Comic-book villains such as Flash Gordon's Ming the Merciless, the Claw (from the Golden Age *Daredevil* series), the Yellow Claw, and Batman villains such as Dr. Tzin-Tzin and Ra's al Ghul (brought to feature film in 2005's *Batman Begins*) were heavily influenced by Fu Manchu, but his most enduring contribution to comics may be as the father of the Master of Kung Fu.

Marvel Comics, deciding to launch a new character to capitalize on the 1970s kung fu craze, also added Fu Manchu to the mix to prevent rival publisher DC Comics from tying up those rights. In *Marvel Special Edition* #15 (1973), Shang-Chi, the son of Fu Manchu, raised to become a martial arts master and Fu Manchu's chief assassin, would realize his father's evil and turn against him. Created by Steve Englehart, Jim Starlin, and Al Milgrom, the series ran 125 issues, lasting until 1983, with occasional revivals since then. Additional adventures of Shang-Chi, with occasional appearances by his father, appeared in the black-and-white magazine *The Deadly Hands of Kung Fu* (1974–1977). These are his most recent official appearances as of 2006, but it is clearly implied that Fu Manchu is the villain behind the first comic story arc of *The League of Extraordinary Gentlemen* (America's Best Comics, 1999), though not the 2003 film.

Ironically, what is perhaps Fu Manchu's most enduring contribution to the English language was made erroneously. To this day a long, thin mustache is referred to as "a Fu Manchu mustache"— but unlike his depiction in virtually all visual media, Rohmer invariably described the Celestial One as clean-shaven. —*MWB*

Galactus

For three months in 1966, Marvel Comics readers feared the end of the world.

Flames engulf the sky in *Fantastic Four* #48 (1966), blanketing New Yorkers in "the dread grip of panic," followed by a dense sea of space debris choking out the sunlight. As the Fantastic Four (FF) gather to investigate this phenomenon, the Watcher, the otherworldly observer pledged never to interfere with those he surveys, breaks his vow—the astronomical occurrences are *his* creation, he admits, unsuccessful shields to protect Earth. The entrance of the intergalactic scout the Silver Surfer portends a doom that arrives conveniently paced on a last-page reveal in one of comics' greatest cliffhangers. Stepping from a sphere-like spacecraft is a millennia-old, grim, armor-clad giant who might have looked absurd in his winged, coffeemaker-shaped helmet were he not rendered by the king of comics and the king of cosmic, Jack Kirby. Bombastic dialogue by Stan Lee discloses the creature's mission and his name: "This planet shall sustain me until it has been drained of all elemental life! SO SPEAKS GALACTUS!"

Many a kid paced impatiently for the next thirty days waiting for *FF* #49. What those readers discovered has since become legend. Issue #49's "If This Be Doomsday!" was actually act two of

what is now known as the Galactus trilogy (concluding in issue #50).

Mythological gods had long populated the pages of comic books, Marvel's own Norse pantheon in *Thor* among them. But with Galactus, the Devourer of Worlds, readers met not *a* god but *the* "God"—not literally, but by his own admission Lee found inspiration in the angry God of the Old Testament when searching for a bigger, more formidable FF supervillain. Yet the ravenous Galactus does not fancy himself a deity—"Do not the humans themselves slay the lesser beasts for food … for sustenance? Galactus does no less!"—but with his triumphant entrance, his limitless Power Cosmic, his grandiloquence (including his habit of making third-person references), and the Silver Surfer as his shimmering herald, Galactus is omnipotence incarnate. As Galactus methodically readies his "energy converter," the humans buzzing around him are of no significance, until one of them—the Thing's girlfriend, Alicia Masters—appeals to the *man* that was once the Silver Surfer, turning the herald into the fallen angel as he stands against his master, leading the FF on a defiant showdown. The Devourer of Worlds is vanquished by Reed (Mr. Fantastic) Richards, who possesses the Ultimate Nullifier, a weapon powerful enough to stay Galactus' mighty hand. Hence, a truce is negotiated, Galactus vowing never to invade Earth again in exchange for the Nullifier, a pact harkening back to

God's oath to Noah that He would never again flood Earth.

The Galactus trilogy is regarded by many historians and fans as the zenith of Lee and Kirby's fertile collaboration. But their magnum opus raised the cosmic-story bar to an unattainable height. The numerous reappearances of Galactus—he turned away from Earth but found other planets appetizing, as a result combating virtually every Marvel superhero along the way, plus scads of supervillains and alien races—have adequately entertained, but for those who first read the original tales, never quite satisfied.

Yet Galactus has continued to send ripples throughout the Marvel Universe. He is a primary component in the framework of the cosmos, along with other supreme entities such as Eternity, Death, Oblivion, and Infinity. Galactus' intergalactic feeding frenzies have been chronicled in numerous Marvel titles including issues of *Fantastic Four*, *Thor*, *Silver Surfer*, and *Thanos*, plus his own comics, *Super-Villain Classics* #1 (1983), the reprint edition *The Origin of Galactus:* #1 (1996), and *Galactus: The Devourer* #1–#6 (1999–2000). In addition to the Silver Surfer, Galactus' heralds have included Gabriel the Air-Walker, Terrax the Tamer, Firelord, Nova, Morg the Berserker, Red Shift, and Stardust; imbued with a portion of his Power Cosmic, these scouts traverse the galaxy searching for inhabited worlds whose life forces can be drained for Galactus' sustenance. The Devourer of Worlds has been presumably destroyed in some stories, only to later return.

Before he was the Eater of Planets he was Galen (at times, Galan) of the planet Taa, an astronaut engulfed by his universe's implosive "Big Crunch." Cocooning within a "Cosmic Egg," he eventually exited as the cosmic being Galactus, an origin similar to the Fantastic Four's (astronauts given powers by cosmic rays). This parallel was not lost upon the FF's own Johnny (Human Torch) Storm, who, having temporarily assumed the powers of his sister, the Invisible Woman, served as the herald of Galactus in the four-part tale "Rising Storm" (*FF* #520–#523, 2005). Using his newly acquired Power Cosmic, Storm temporarily siphoned Galactus' energies, leaving him the aloof alien Galen, who received firsthand lessons about "the indomitable spirit of the humanoid order." Galen exiled himself to another dimension to contain the swelling Power Cosmic, a redemptive gesture to halt "Galactus' wrath in this universe." It is unlikely, however, that "this universe" has seen the last of Galactus.

In the universe of Marvel's "Ultimate" titles, reimagined versions of its characters, writer Warren Ellis methodically escalated the coming of the Ultimate Galactus in the 2005–2006 miniseries trilogy, *Ultimate Nightmare*, *Ultimate Secret*, and *Ultimate Extinction*. Many of the Ultimate Marvel heroes—including, naturally, the Fantastic Four—united to ward off the impending locust-like plague of "Gah Lak Tus," overhauled to resemble a black metallic skull with pincers.

The original Galactus has occasionally invaded other media. Toy Biz has produced extra-sized action figures of the villain, including an 18-inch 2005 figure boasting 33 articulation points. The Eater of Planets chewed scenery in the animated series *Fantastic Four* (both the 1967 and 1994 incarnations) and *Silver Surfer* (1998–1999). He was parodied in animation as Omnipotus on *The Tick* (1994–1997) and as Lactose the Intolerant on *Sam & Max: Freelance Police* (1997). Galactus, sans face and with altered costume colors, made the cover of the 1969 album "Monster Movie" by the rock group the Can. —ME

Gen 13's Rogues' Gallery

Set in the WildStorm universe originally created by artist Jim Lee in 1992 when he co-founded Image Comics and debuted *WildC.A.T.S* (later simply Wildcats), the young men and women who comprised Gen 13 were the offspring of members of the special ops unit Team 7.

Opposite: Galactus. From *Fantastic Four* #522 ©2005 Marvel Comics.
ART BY MIKE WIERINGO AND KARL KESEL.

"...EVENTUALLY EMERGING AS *GALACTUS*...THE *DEVOURER OF WORLDS!* THE TYRANNY THAT STRIDES THE *STARS,* SHAPED ONLY BY THE ALL-CONSUMING *HUNGER* THAT *TRANSCENDS* OUR PETTY CONCEPTS OF 'GOOD' AND 'EVIL'! HE WHO SIMPLY...*IS!*

"ANNNND... SCENE."

Superweapons of Mass Destruction

From atomic axes to satellite-based lasers, the supervillain's arsenal is an important part of popular fiction—and in *these* cases, the superweapons themselves have taken on an infamy of their own:

- **The Philosopher's Stone** is a fabled ore that affords it holder elemental transmutation and, in some legends, immortality. Heroes as diverse as Harry Potter and Donald Duck have encountered it, and the supervillains Diablo and Dr. Alchemy wield it.

- **The Gamma Bomb** created the Incredible Hulk, and his arch-foe the Leader used it to level an Arizona town in the 1988 "Ground Zero" *Hulk* storyline.

- **Brainiac's Shrinking Ray** has miniaturized intergalactic cities to diminutive size, allowing the evil android to collect civilizations in bottles.

- **The Ultimate Nullifier** is a handheld device of alien origin that can eradicate anything at which it is aimed, a weapon so potentially deadly that even the world-devouring Galactus fears it.

- **The Cosmic Cube**, coveted by Marvel supervillains, fulfills the wishes of its holder, including reality reconstruction. Its DC counterpart in Legion of Super-Heroes continuity was the Miracle Machine.

- **The Anti-Life Equation**'s properties are unknown, but it is the (un)holy grail of Darkseid, from which this overlord of Apokolips hopes to gain mastery over the lives and souls of all beings in the universe.

- **The Infinity Gauntlet** is a golden glove, at one time worn by Marvel's despot Thanos, embroidered with six Infinity Gems endowing its wearer with governance of time, space, power, soul, mind, and reality (a seventh gem permits control over ego).

- **OMACs** (One Man Army Corps, later Omni Mind And Community) evolved from a 1970s superhero concept created by Jack Kirby into a mid-2000s army of cyborgs that overtook the bodies of humans to become assassins of superheroes.

Many of the Team 7 operatives were, in turn, members of Gen 12, or the twelfth generation of test subjects in Project Genesis, an attempt by the clandestine organization International Operations (I.O.) to create "SPBs" or Super-Powered Beings.

The characters and the set-up for the series were revealed in *Gen 13* #1, the first issue of a five-issue miniseries from Image Comics in 1994. The team had first appeared in the second issue of the Image/Valiant crossover series *Deathmate* (1993–1994), though with a substantially altered origin relating to the universe-bending nature of the crossover. The success of the miniseries lead to an ongoing series in 1995.

The villains of the series were frequently centered around various factions of I.O., some of which were directly opposed to each other. While there were some clearcut bad guys and good guys, there were also the stabbed-in-the-back trappings of the espionage world to accompany the traditional superhero rumbles.

The failure of Gen 12 and the resulting ban on Project Genesis didn't stop certain groups from coveting the possibilties of spies and assasains with incredible powers or gifts, so the project was reopened.

An extremely gifted manipulator, Ivana was one of the movers and shakers in the I.O. faction favoring Project Genesis. Her agents brought team members together for testing. Ivana was overtly sexy, favoring form-fitting clothing and impossible poses common in early Image Comics. She worked for Miles Craven, one of the real masterminds of I.O.

Ivana not only had a cadre of regular agents working for her, but she also employed operatives such as Mathew Callahan (Threshold) and Nicole Callahan (Bliss), who were genetically active (superpowered) children of Gen 12 members, too. Like Gen 13's eventual mentor, John (Jack) Lynch, a former Team 7 member, Ivana had no spectacular powers, but relied on her cunning, her treachery, and her ability to command to get things done.

After their escape from Project Genesis, they were tracked by armor-clad I.O. operatives known as Black Hammers (the name of the type of battle suits), met the female warrior descendants of the legendary Amazons in the Codas Citadel (seen previously in *WildC.A.T.S*), and confronted the Pirate King (all in *Gen 13* #5). The team also met Frostbite (with the powers the name implies), the Order of the Cross (the Vatican's superteam), Lord Defile (a Daemonite, the alien species fought be the WildC.A.T.S team), the techno-wizardry of Kaizen, and even the Stupid, Stupid Rat Creatures from cartoonist Jeff Smith's *Bone*.

After the departure of co-creators Brandon Choi and J. Scott Campbell (*Danger Girl*), new foes included the Seven Deadly Sins, Helspont, Tao, and Tindalos. The series ended with the entire team at least appearing to be destroyed by an atomic bomb in *Gen 13* #76 (2002). A follow-up series, from DC Comics' WildStorm imprint, a six-issue *Gen 13* (2003) miniseries, later titled *September Song* in trade-paperback format, featured new characters and a dragon tattoo come to life as a villain. —*JCV*

General Zod

"**Y**ou *will* bow down before me, Jor-El! Both you and then one day, your *heir!*" swears power-mad seditionist General Zod (Terence Stamp) in *Superman: The Movie* (1978) as he and his fellow black-leather-clad insurrectionists are sentenced by Kryptonian scientist Jor-El to an eternity in the otherworldly prison called the Phantom Zone. In *Superman II* (1980), a vindictive Zod and his sub-ordinates Ursa and Non are accidentally freed years later by a nuclear explosion in space. Arriving on Earth, which they first believe to be "Planet Houston" after an ill-fated (for the astronauts) encounter with a moon-walking NASA crew, these cold-hearted conquerors from Krypton—with the same powers as Superman—plow over cities and armies, and even humble the president of the United States before Superman, canoodling with Lois Lane at his arctic Fortress of Solitude during Zod's siege, returns to save the day.

Stamp's General Zod demanded that his subjects kneel and swear eternal allegiance, but even that offered no guarantee that this aspirant deity would not kill them. "It's a joy to play a two-dimensional character for a change," the actor beamed in a *Superman II* promotional interview, surveying

Zod as "brutal, vicious, evil, and corrupt, without any redeeming qualities." Stamp's tour de force was supported by merchandising including action figures of varying sizes from manufacturer Mego. Decades later, his General Zod remains one of cinema's definitive supervillain performances.

General Zod did not originate in the movies, but instead in *Adventure Comics* #283 (1961), in writer Robert Bernstein and artist George Papp's Superboy story that introduced the Phantom Zone to the pages of DC Comics. Originally a Kryptonian army officer/scientist, the egomaniacal Zod, in his purple military uniform and cap, created a militia of Bizarro-like imperfect duplicates in his image and attempted to become the planet's dictator, earning him a one-way ticket to the Zone. He continued to appear in Superboy, Superman, and Supergirl tales until the mid-1980s, usually "seen" in his wraithlike state, conspiring with other Zone prisoners and occasionally breaking free of the ethereal realm to wreak havoc with his superpowers. Once writer/artist John Byrne rebooted Superman in the 1986 miniseries *The Man of Steel*, this version of Zod was retconned into the "Pocket Universe," an alternate timeline shaped by the villainous Time Trapper (but actually created by DC to address continuity inconsistencies between the pre– and post–*Man of Steel* stories involving Superboy and the Legion of Super-Heroes). In a tip of the general's cap to *Superman II*, Zod and fellow fiends Quex-Ul and Zaora escaped from the Phantom Zone for a murder spree until being executed by Superman with green kryptonite in the shocking *Superman* vol. 2 #22 (1988).

Since then, General Zod has resurfaced in different incarnations. In 2001's "Return to Krypton" storyline, Superman and Lois Lane used the Phantom Zone to travel back in time to the Man of Steel's homeworld, where they met a version of Zod who perished under the collapse of his own machinations. A crimson-cloaked oppressor with abilities similar to Superman's appeared in *Action Comics* #779 (2001), a cold-war baby named Avruskin born to celestially irradiated Soviet cosmonauts. To Superman's surprise, the revengeful life essence of the Pocket Universe Zod had possessed Avruskin, and this new General Zod made life difficult for the hero before dying while fighting

General Zod (Terence Stamp) uses his heat vision to battle the Man of Steel in *Superman II* (1980).

him. Fan-favorite writer/artist team Brian Azzarello and Jim Lee's best-selling "For Tomorrow" *Superman* story arc (2004–2005) unveiled yet another Zod, an ebon-armored refugee from "Metropia," a reality within the Phantom Zone that Superman created as a potential safe haven for his loved ones. Wrestling with the perils he unleashed, the Man of Steel was assaulted physically and psychologically by the diabolical Zod, who laughed at Superman as he refused his helpful hand and slipped into a dimensional rift, apparently to his doom.

Superman suspects what his fans know: that as long as there is a Man of Steel, he will have little rest from his rancorous Kryptonian foe. The 2005 season premiere of television's *Smallville* (2001–present) proves this to be true: two unnamed Kryptonian supervillains were described as "disciples of Zod," revealing Zod's existence in *Smallville*'s continuity. —ME

Genoshans

One of the major themes of Marvel's *X-Men* comic-book series is racism, with mutants representing any oppressed minority group. In *Uncanny X-Men* #255 (1988) the mutant team's long-time writer, Chris Claremont, introduced his analogue to South Africa, whose government then followed a policy of apartheid, whereby its black population was reduced to second-class citizens, ruled by the white minority. Claremont created the island nation of Genosha, where mutants were forced to serve as a class of slave laborers.

Located off the eastern coast of Africa, between Madagascar and the Seychelles Islands, Genosha was a haven for pirates for centuries. By the twentieth century its population was almost entirely comprised of Caucasians, apparently of British descent, and English is the nation's official language.

Decades ago, the Sugar Man, a refugee from the alternate timeline called "the Age of Apocalypse," shared his advanced knowledge of genetic engineering with the Genoshan government. As a result, the government established a system whereby it examined all Genoshan teenagers for signs of mutations that would produce superhuman abilities. Adolescents with such mutations were subjected to genetic engineering to augment or change their superhuman powers.

These "mutates" became the government's slaves. No longer allowed to use their names, the mutates were identified by numbers tattooed onto their shaved foreheads. Their uniforms, called "skinsuits," were permanently affixed to their bodies. (The Genoshan slave system also resembles a nightmare version of a military draft.)

Upon the backs of these slave laborers, the Genoshan ruling class built a highly prosperous nation, renowned for its advanced technology.

Eventually the Genoshan militia seized control of the government. As a result, Genosha fell into civil war between mutants and "normal" humans, resembling the 1990s conflict in Bosnia.

The United Nations imposed order on the country by turning it over to the mutant terrorist Magneto, thereby hoping to deter him from waging further war on the human race. Cassandra Nova, the evil twin of Charles Xavier, the X-Men's founder, dispatched Sentinel robots that devastated Genosha. In 2004 Xavier and Magneto joined forces to help the Genoshan survivors rebuild their country.

The nation of Genosha was also depicted in *X-Men: The Animated Series* (1992–1997). —*PS*

The Gentleman Ghost

Nineteenth-century English highwayman James "Gentleman Jim" Craddock swore during his public execution that he would return to haunt those responsible for his demise, including the American West heroes Nighthawk and Cinnamon. At the moment the noose took his life, Craddock slipped through a portal in time and became a ghost of himself, silently walking the modern streets of London.

Created by scripter Robert Kanigher and artist Joe Kubert, the Gentleman Ghost first appeared in *Flash Comics* #88 (1947). In the true spirit of an English gentleman, the Gentleman Ghost dons a white top hat, tails, and an antique flintlock pistol

as he loots the pockets of many innocent victims. Like all ghosts, he is invisible and can move through solid objects. True to his word, he tracked down Nighthawk and Cinnamon, who weren't true Wild West adventurers, but reborn incarnations of ancient Egyptian royals Prince Khufu and his beloved princess Chay-Ara. The spirits of these ancient Egyptians also found their way to Hawkman and Hawkgirl, two heroes that became the Gentleman's key nemeses through much of comics' Golden Age (1938–1954). Like Hawkman, the Gentleman Ghost's soul can never truly die, and so he restlessly wanders the Eearth continually stalking the hero.

Although the phantom villain has resurfaced in Gotham City—where he kidnapped Bruce Wayne's butler Alfred and clashed with Batman—the spirit of the Gentleman Ghost continually returns to haunt his favorite winged hero. —*GM*

Gizmo: *See* **The Fearsome Five**

Glorious Godfrey: *See* **Darkseid's Elite**

Gog

In DC Comics' "Elseworlds" (which embodies the concept of Hypertime, in which various DC realities coexist) miniseries *Kingdom Come* (1996), an atomic blast leveled much of Kansas and brought about the second coming of Superman. A boy named William (his last name was never disclosed) survived the atomic disaster and was rescued by the Man of Steel. As he grew up, William came to believe he was "chosen" to survive the Kansas disaster to establish the Church of Superman and become its first apostle. Superman confronted William and expressed his disapproval of the church, leaving the young man emotionally devastated and without a life purpose—the perfect set-up for a life of villainy. He was soon approached by a group of cosmic gods known as the Quintessence, who bestowed upon him the mantle of Gog.

As described in *Gog* #1 (1998), written by Mark Waid and penciled by Jerry Ordway, the horned, metal-laden, Viking-like Gog possesses superhuman strength, super-durability, and great knowledge. (Interestingly, Gog and Magog are the names of a mysterious biblical land and its people, who feature in apocalyptic prophecy, as written in the books of Ezekiel and Revelation.) Driven to the point of psychosis, he came to believe that Superman was at fault for the Kansas disaster, and searched out Clark Kent and killed him. The villain, complete with his energy beam–radiating staff, traveled back in time, one day at a time, killing Superman again and again until he reached the day when Superman and Wonder Woman's baby was born. Gog kidnapped the newborn, and went back in time to orchestrate an apocalyptic disaster in Kansas. His plan was ultimately thwarted in the *Kingdom Come* saga, as Superman, Batman, and Wonder Woman joined forces against him.

Despite this minor setback, Gog continued to tangle with Superman, committing such atrocities as attacking him with liquid Kryptonite and engaging him in a climactic battle with an army of Gogs from across time. Although Gog came from a possible future history, his appearance in the present makes him part of the DC "reality." —GM

Golden Age Supervillains (1938-1954)

Comic-book superheroes first burst onto the stage of American popular culture in the "Golden Age of Comics," starting with the debut of Superman in *Action Comics* #1 (1938) and closing with the disappearance of most superhero titles in 1951. (Superman, Batman, and Wonder Woman evaded cancellation, so their Golden Age continued into the mid-1950s.)

This was also the period in which the comics supervillain first emerged. But though it may now seem strange, there were surprisingly few supervillains during the Golden Age. The superheroes usually battled more conventional opponents, ranging from bank robbers to Nazi spies or mad scientists. For example, in *Action Comics* #1, Superman con-

tended with a wife-beater, thugs menacing Lois Lane, and a war-mongering political lobbyist.

Yet the appearance of a superhero seems to inspire supervillains to arise to oppose him. A number of Superman's classic foes debuted in the Golden Age, including Lex Luthor, Mr. Mxyzptlk (who then spelled his name "Mxyztplk"), the Toyman, and the Prankster. Superman's first costumed adversary was the Archer (from *Superman* #13, 1941), a former big-game hunter who extorted money from his victims and used his bow and arrow to kill those who refused to pay. Soon afterward, Superman clashed with the Lightning Master, a hooded scientist who threatened to destroy the city of Metropolis with his "lightning machine" (in *Superman* #14, 1942).

In other cases, including that of Luthor, even Superman's supervillains wore conventional clothes rather than costumes. One example is the Puzzler (who debuted in *Action* #49, 1942), a ruthless master criminal who was an expert in puzzles, card games, checkers, and other parlor games.

One of Superman's most frequent Golden Age adversaries, con man J. Wilbur Wolfingham (who first appeared in *Superman* #26, 1944), was bald and wore a monocle but otherwise was the spitting image of W. C. Fields. Thanks to Superman's interventions, Wolfingham's elaborate swindles continually backfired, making his victims rich instead. Superman's strangest Golden Age enemy was Funnyface (from *Superman* #19, 1942), a cartoonist who used a strange ray to bring villains from comic strips to life to commit crimes for him.

Some of the best remembered Golden Age Superman villains never appeared in the comics. The title villains of Max Fleischer's animated *Superman* cartoon "The Bulleteers" (1942) terrorized Metropolis by ramming rocket-powered flying "bullet cars" into buildings at high speed, demolishing them. Atom Man was a super-strong Nazi who gave off Kryptonite radiation in a memorable storyline on the *Superman* radio show in 1945. (Atom Man was belatedly introduced into comics in *World's Finest* #271, 1981.)

More enduring supervillains were created for *Batman* than for other Golden Age series. *Batman* co-creator Bob Kane admired Chester Gould's comic strip *Dick Tracy*, which was famous for its villains with their outsized personalities and distinctive, grotesque looks, such as Flattop and Pruneface. Perhaps Kane wanted to give Batman a similar kind of rogues' gallery. (The Penguin's face even resembles that of a minor *Tracy* villain, Broadway Bates.) Many of Batman's most famous enemies originated in the 1940s, including the Joker and Catwoman.

The first supervillain to menace Batman was Dr. Death (from *Detective Comics* #29, 1939), a criminal scientist who developed a lethal "pollen extract" with which to murder his victims. Identical cousins Deever and Dumfree Tweed, both short, fat, and cherubic-looking, matched wits with Batman as the criminal team of Tweedledee and Tweedledum, starting in *Detective* #74 (1943). Gotham City playboy Mortimer Drake became the Cavalier (in *Detective Comics* #81, 1943), a swashbuckling thief who is costumed as a seventeenth-century musketeer and wields a sword that shoots electrical bolts.

Underworld figures plotting crimes would consulted Dr. Matthew Thorne, "the Crime Surgeon" (starting in *Batman* #18, 1943), who would "prescribed" his recommendations in exchange for a share of the ill-gotten goods. Ironically, Thorne still felt bound by the Hippocratic oath and even once operated on Robin to save his life. Though the original Crime Surgeon died, DC later introduced the modern version, Dr. Bradford Thorne, the Crime Doctor, practicing in the twenty-first century in the miniseries *Villains United* (2005).

Floyd Ventris, alias Mirror-Man, employed mirrors in his robberies, starting in *Detective* #213 (1954). Using an "X-ray mirror" Mirror-Man saw through Batman's mask, but Batman ultimately succeeded in persuading Ventris he was not Bruce Wayne. Criminal Phil Cobb adopted two different costumed identities: first, he became the Signalman, who took signs and signals as his theme (in *Batman* #112, 1957), and later he became the Blue Bowman, who utilized an array of trick arrows (in *Batman* #139, 1961).

"The Terrible Trio" were a triumvirate of criminal scientists, disguised by animal masks, who invented extraordinary vehicles and advanced weapons with which to commit spectacular robberies, beginning in *Detective* #253 (1958). The Fox created devices to be used on land, the Shark specialized in marine vessels, and the Vulture designed advanced aircraft.

During World War II, Wonder Woman frequently battled the Nazis, most notably the ruthless Gestapo agent, Baroness Paula von Gunther (who debuted in *Sensation Comics* #4, 1942). The Nazis were aided by the war god Mars and his subordinate, the Duke of Deception (introduced in *Wonder Woman* #2, 1942), a minor deity who used his powers of illusion to spread deceit.

There was a wackiness to the 1940s *Wonder Woman* comics that manifested itself in some of her villains. Giganta (who debuted in *Wonder Woman* #9, 1944) was originally a large ape who was transformed into a super-strong, savage woman. The oddly titled Minister Blizzard, introduced in *Wonder Woman* #29 (1948), employed cold as a weapon, like the Golden Age Green Lantern's nemesis, the Icicle. Another of Wonder Woman's recurring enemies, the Angle Man (who first appeared in *Wonder Woman* #70, 1954), was a criminal mastermind who always came up with an "angle" to his robberies that made his schemes extraordinary. The Angle Man later acquired a costume and a device called the Angler that enabled him to teleport himself. He perished in *Crisis on Infinite Earths* #10 (1986).

Besides the Fiddler and the Shade, the Golden Age's Flash's most notorious enemy was the Thinker, a district attorney who turned into a brilliant criminal mastermind in *All-Flash* #12 (1943). When he returned in the 1960s, the Thinker had acquired his "thinking cap," which endowed him with telekinetic powers. Yet another Flash adversary was the Rag Doll (introduced in *Flash Comics* #36, 1942), a contortionist with a "triple-jointed skeleton." His son had artificial joints implanted in his body to duplicate his powers, and thus became the Rag Doll who joined the new Secret Six in DC's *Villains United*. Another opponent for the Golden Age Flash was the Turtle (from *All-Flash* #21, 1946), a criminal who moved and talked with excruciating slowness. (A second "Turtle Man" was the first adversary of the Silver Age Flash.)

Besides the monstrous Solomon Grundy, the Golden Age Green Lantern repeatedly battled "Crusher" Crock, a professional athlete turned criminal (who debuted in *All-American Comics* #85, 1947) who later became known as the Sportsmaster, a costumed thief who turns sports equipment into weapons. Other Green Lantern nemeses were the Gambler, a master of disguise (from *Green Lantern* #12, 1944), the Sky Pirate, who used an aircraft to plunder his victims (from *Green Lantern* #27, 1947), and Knodar, a time traveler from the twenty-fifth century (introduced in *Green Lantern* #28, 1947).

Beginning in *Sensation Comics* #68 (1947), the original Huntress attempted to hunt down the costumed crime fighter Wildcat to make him a captive in her private zoo. By the mid-1960s the Huntress had married the Sportsmaster. Wildcat's other leading nemesis was the Yellow Wasp (starting in *Sensation Comics* #20, 1943), a costumed criminal who attacked people with swarms of wasps and even drove a "Waspmobile." The modern supervillain, Killer Wasp, first seen in *JSA* #9 (2000), claims to be the Yellow Wasp's son.

The sorcerer Dr. Fate counted among his leading enemies Ian Karkull, a scientist who turned himself into a living shadow (in *More Fun Comics* #69, 1941) and Mr. Who (from *More Fun Comics* #73, 1941), who used his "Solution Z" to transform himself into a super-strong giant.

Though the Vigilante was a Western gunslinger fighting crime in New York City, his unlikely archenemy was the Dummy (introduced in *Leading Comics* #1, 1941), a diminutive mastermind who looked and dressed like Charlie McCarthy, the famous dummy of 1940s ventriloquist Edgar Bergen.

Joe Simon and Jack Kirby's Boy Commandos were not superheroes, but they encountered a supervillain, Crazy-Quilt, in *Boy Commandos* #15 (1946). After being blinded, Crazy-Quilt underwent an operation that enabled him to see bright colors, and adopted color as the theme of his robberies. He later became an enemy of Batman and Robin.

Simon and Kirby created the mysterious Agent Axis as the Boy Commandos' foe (*Boy Commandos* #1, 1942), but decades later Kirby, perhaps forgetfully, reintroduced him at Marvel as a wartime enemy of Captain America (in *Tales of Suspense* #82, 1966)!

As well as Dr. Sivana, Mr. Mind, and Captain Nazi, Fawcett Publications' Captain Marvel also tangled with the robot Mr. Atom (from *Captain Marvel Adventures* #78, 1947) and the barbarian King Kull (from *Captain Marvel Adventures* #125, 1951, and named after Robert E. Howard's hero). In *Captain Marvel Adventures* #8 (1942), small-time crook "Stinky" Printwhistle made a deal with the devil, enabling him to turn into the super-strong IBAC, empowered by the evil spirits of Ivan the Terrible, Cesare Borgia, Attila the Hun, and Caligula.

Fawcett hero Bulletman counted among his enemies Dr. Riddle (from *Bulletman* #5, 1942), a hunchbacked killer who left riddle clues like the Batman's more famous foe, the Riddler, and the Weeper (from *Master Comics* #23, 1942), a murderer whose characteristic mood was the opposite of the Joker's.

Quality Comics' Plastic Man often battled villains who were as unusual as he was. Among his many one-shot adversaries were "Gargantua, the Phi Beta Gorilla" (from *Police Comics* #81, 1948), a predecessor of Grodd and other super-intelligent apes in comics. Plastic Man also clashed with the Spider, a costumed thief who wore a mask that looked like an actual spider's head and wielded a gun that fired "webbing" made of wire that was stronger than steel. The Spider appeared in *Plastic Man* #46 (1954), only eight years before the debut of Marvel's Spider-Man.

One of the most iconic Golden Age villains was the Claw, artist Jack Cole's variation on Fu Manchu, who debuted in his own series in *Silver Streak Comics* #1 (1939), later published by Lev Gleason Publications, and was repeatedly opposed by the Golden Age Daredevil.

Strangely, Timely Comics, the company that became Marvel in the 1960s, produced few memorable supervillains in the 1940s, with the major exception of Captain America's arch-foe, the Red Skull. Others include the Human Torch's enemy the Asbestos Lady (from *Captain America Comics* #63, 1947), whose asbestos costume afforded her protection from his flames; the Ringmaster of Death (from *Captain America Comics* #5, 1941), a Nazi

Tweedledee and Tweedledum. *Detective Comics* #74
©1943 DC Comics.
COVER ART BY BOB KANE AND GEORGE ROUSSOS.

agent who was the father of Marvel's modern Ring-master; and Byrrah, the Sub-Mariner's malevolent cousin (from *Marvel Mystery Comics* #82, 1947).

Golden Age aficionado Roy Thomas solved the problem of the Timely supervillain shortage by co-creating some of his own for *The Invaders* (1975–1979), a modern Marvel series set during World War II, notably the super-strong Master Man (*Giant-Size Invaders* #1, 1975) and the Nazi vampire Baron Blood (*The Invaders* #7, 1976).

Two alluring women who starred in their own Golden Age series were operatives of the devil. Timely's original Black Widow (who debuted in *Mystic Comics* #4, 1940) killed evildoers to send their souls to her master Satan. Similarly, Madame Satan (who first appeared in MLJ's *Pep Comics* #17, 1941) attempted to seduce men in order to lead them into sin. Madame Satan could kill a man simply by kissing him; the Black Widow needed only to touch her victim's head to slay him.

Finally, another character called the Spider, a costumed archer who first appeared in Quality Comics' *Crack Comics* #1 (1940), was portrayed in the Golden Age as a superhero. But revisionist DC Comics stories have revealed that the Spider actually posed as a superhero to conceal his own activities as a murderer and kidnapper. So one of the earliest superheroes was also one of the first comics supervillains! *—PS*

Gorilla Grodd

He is one of the cruelest supervillains in the DC Universe, thirsty for nothing short of world domination. He can discharge destructive psionic bolts, transfer his psyche into the bodies of others, and telepathically compel victims into blind obedience, all with his formidable "Force of Mind." He is a technological mastermind, the inventor of such insidious devices as the Devolutionizer Ray, and when his vast intellect fails to service him, he is capable of crushing the mightiest of heroes in his bare hands.

And he is an ape.

Born of an era when DC Comics editors (most notably Julius Schwartz) believed that covers featuring super-intelligent gorillas were tantamount to increased sales, Gorilla Grodd first appeared in *The Flash* vol. 1 #106 (1959); contrary to editorial wisdom, however, Grodd was not depicted on the cover. In "Menace of the Super-Gorilla!" by writer John Broome and artist Carmine Infantino, a nuclear-powered "all-purpose craft"—capable of achieving remarkable speeds in flight, underwater, on land, and even while burrowing through the earth—arrives in Central City, home of the Silver Age (1956–1969) Flash. Emerging from the uncanny ship is a talking, genius gorilla—Grodd—seeking "the greatest mind in the world." That mind belongs to fellow primate Solovar, the sovereign of a secret African civilization of scientifically advanced simians, opting to play dumb in a circus cage rather than reveal the existence of his kingdom of Gorilla City. Grodd telepathically usurps Solovar's Force of Mind, intending to use it for conquest, but Flash makes a monkey of Grodd by disorienting him in a superspeed-created whirlwind.

Grodd escaped from a Gorilla City prison in the very next issue (#107, 1959), and was not as

The Flash vol. 1 #172©1967 DC Comics.
COVER ART BY CARMINE INFANTINO AND MURPHY ANDERSON.

easily vanquished by the Flash in their second clash but still beaten once the hero repeatedly punched him in the blink of an eye. By his third appearance—in *Flash* #108 (1959), giving the super-gorilla an impressive three-issue trial run—Grodd was in better control of his Force of Mind, employing the human secret identity of Drew Drowden and uprooting trees as deadly projectiles with his newly honed mind over matter faculty.

Gorilla Grodd was a relentless and consistent threat to the Fastest Man Alive, fighting him solo and orchestrating the first union of the Flash's Rogues' Gallery in *Flash* #155 (1965). Throughout the latter 1970s, Grodd allied with cadres of criminals in *Secret Society of Super-Villains* (1976–1978) and as one of the Legion of Doom in the animated cartoon *Challenge of the Super Friends* (1978–1979); during these uneasy alliances, Grodd held his human and alien partners with low regard and worked with them only to further his personal goals. His popularity during the late 1970s inspired DC Comics to plan a comic book titled *Grodd of Gorilla City*; while the publisher pulled the plug on the title before printing it, the first issue was produced.

Over the decades, Grodd's malevolence has thrust him into conflict with other heroes, including Superman, Hawkman, Blue Devil, Supergirl, Martian Manhunter, the Teen Titans, the Birds of Prey, the Outsiders, and, oddly enough, Swamp Thing. While sometimes succumbing to primate puns in story titles ("Gorilla My Dreams," "Groddspell"), DC Comics writers have, over time, expanded the history of Grodd and Gorilla City. Grodd was married but (not surprisingly) separated, has a son named Gorbzil Mammit, and conflicting reports peg him as either the brother or grandfather of Sam Simeon, the sentient primate cartoonist in DC's offbeat *Angel and the Ape* series. After numerous attempts at wresting control of Gorilla City from Solovar, Grodd orchestrated a coup in the *JLApe: Gorilla Warfare* crossover in DC's 1999 annuals. He had Solovar assassinated, transformed the Justice League into gorillas with his "Gorillabomb," and incited Gorilla City into a war with humans. In the twenty-first century, this super-intelligent simian's bestial side is often displayed, with Grodd even eating his adversaries in the Grant Morrison–penned *JLA: Classified* #1–#3 (2005). With his balance of sentience and savagery, Gorilla Grodd has evolved from a gimmick-spawned villain into one of the deadliest menaces in the DC Universe.

Gorilla Grodd's non-comics appearances include a 2001 action figure and a 2005 Flash-versus-Grodd mini-statue from DC Direct, and appearances on the Cartoon Network's *Justice League* (2001–2004) and *Justice League Unlimited* (2004–present), voiced by Powers Boothe. —*ME*

The Grandmaster

The ultimate "high roller," En Dwi Gast, the Grandmaster, is an alien humanoid who possesses the dangerous combination of vast, godlike powers and an addiction to gambling. Created by writer Roy Thomas and artist Sal Buscema in Marvel's *The Avengers* vol. 1 #69 (1969), the Grandmaster is willing to wager the lives of billions, including his own, in one of his cosmic games of chance.

Like the Collector, the Grandmaster is one of the Elders of the Universe, and hence one of the oldest beings in the Marvel Universe. The Grandmaster belongs to one of the first intelligent races that evolved after the Big Bang. Whereas the rest of his race became extinct ages ago, the Grandmaster somehow became virtually immortal.

His extraordinary psionic powers enable him to mentally manipulate and transform matter on a planetary scale. Among his many powers, he possesses superhuman intelligence, can psionically transport himself through time and space, and project bolts of energy. He also holds a limited power over life and death, and can resurrect a mortal who has been dead for a brief time. Like his fellow Elders, the Grandmaster has devoted himself to a particular specialty: in his case, he has become obsessed with games and gambling.

In *Avengers* #69–#71 the Grandmaster engaged in a game with Kang the Conqueror; if Kang lost, the Grandmaster would destroy Earth. The Grandmaster used the Squadron Sinister, a team he had created, as his champions in the game. However, Kang forcibly enlisted the Avengers to compete for him, and they won the game.

In the DC/Marvel crossover series *JLA/Avengers* (2003–2004) the Grandmaster challenged the Green Lantern Corps' enemy Krona to a game involving both superteams to prevent him from destroying the Marvel Universe. The Avengers and Justice League thwarted Krona. Yet the final page revealed that the Grandmaster had imperiled the Marvel and DC Universes in the first place by agreeing to play a game with the New God Metron, who used Krona as a pawn. The Grandmaster is thus willing to risk the end of two entire universes for the sake of a bet. —*PS*

Granny Goodness: *See* **Darkseid's Elite**

Green Goblin

The Green Goblin is, bar none, Spider-Man's greatest nemesis. No one, including his cre-

The Spectacular Spider-Man magazine #2
©1968 Marvel Comics.
COVER ART BY JOHN ROMITA, SR.

ators writer Stan Lee and artist Steve Ditko, could have imagined from the character's first appearance in *The Amazing Spider-Man* vol. 1 #14 (1964) that this grinning gargoyle would spawn a succession of Green Goblins and Hobgoblins, and the Demogoblin, notwithstanding alternate-reality variations. Amid this lethal lineage, one true Goblin reigns supreme: the original, Norman Osborn.

"Gobby is truly the only supervillain who is also a good guy when he's not breaking up Spidey's act," reflected Lee in the 1976 trade paperback *Bring on the Bad Guys*. While calling Osborn a "good guy" might have been a stretch even for Lee, whose wizardry with fun-spirited hyperbole has made the Marvel Comics master a larger-than-life figure as popular as his world-famous co-creations, he was correct in that Osborn, the hard-edged industrialist father of Peter (Spider-Man) Parker's classmate and eventual roommate Harry Osborn, was originally a benefactor to society at large.

Osborn's stature might be comic-book legend, but when the masked Green Goblin stormed into

Spidey's life in *Amazing Spider-Man* #14, his identity was a secret (the Osborn character did not appear until 1966's issue #37). What *was* clear was that this oddly garbed creature could have easily transitioned into hawking for a Halloween costumer given his garish getup of a purple leotard, conical cap, and purse-like satchel. Zipping over Manhattan rooftops on a jet-powered flying broomstick, the Goblin was determined to unite New York's mobs under his leadership (which would eventually be the Kingpin's M.O., although that Spider-foe was still three years away from his debut) and conspired to kill neo-hero Spider-Man to earn a rep among the underworld. Hiring the supervillain team the Enforcers for extra muscle, the Goblin nonetheless failed to destroy the wall-crawler, a defeat his uninhibited ego could not endure.

The Green Goblin soon abandoned his broomstick for his turbine-powered, bat-winged, smoke-spewing Goblin Glider, but since his introduction the villain's arsenal, dangerous weapons of his own design, has remained essentially the same: his pumpkin-shaped goblin grenades, capable of emitting concussive or incendiary blasts, or hallucinogenic gases; plus voltage-zapping gloves.

After issue #14, the Goblin's gangland aspirations unfolded, quite briskly, every few issues, encouraged by what Lee called an "avalanche of mail." Yet it was artist John Romita, Sr. who, as Ditko's replacement on *Amazing Spider-Man*, penciled the Goblin's signature story, in issues #39–#40 (1966). Herein the Goblin dulled Spider-Man's protective spider-sense with a gas he created, allowing him to spy on the hero and discover his alter ego. Kidnapping the flabbergasted Peter Parker, the grandstanding Goblin, in his lair, revealed his own secret identity, as well as his origin, to his helpless, bound enemy: Norman Osborn had framed his business partner Professor Mendel Stromm for embezzlement to grab sole control over their technology corporation (later Osborn Industries, and eventually Oscorp), and hoped to profit from Stromm's notes for "strange-looking formulas." Osborn's attempt to create such a formula produced an explosion; he survived this accident

with enhanced strength and intelligence, but was also made mentally ill, prone to unpredictable outbursts. In a climactic battle with Spider-Man, the Goblin received an electrical shock that erased his memory of his Goblin identity. Spidey chose to hide from Osborn his supervillainy, living with the uncertainty of his foe's memory resurfacing. In later stories, writer Lee seemed to relish toying with readers as Osborn's powderkeg Goblin personality smoldered, occasionally erupting, after which Spidey was barely able to re-induce his arch-foe's amnesia.

In writer Gerry Conway and penciler Gil Kane's *Amazing Spider-Man* #121–#122 (1973), Osborn regained his Goblin memories and struck at the wall-crawler through his lover, Gwen Stacy, tossing her off the George Washington Bridge to her death. In an ensuing fight with Spider-Man, the Goblin was impaled by his own Goblin Glider.

Harry Osborn, who for years was psychologically abused by his overbearing father, assumed the Green Goblin identity in issue #136 (1974) after discovering his roommate Parker's secret identity. The dilemma of battling his unbalanced friend plagued the web-slinger through several clashes with Green Goblin II, leading to a final encounter when Harry was fatally poisoned by his father's Goblin serum in *Spectacular Spider-Man* #200 (1993). (Harry left behind his widow, Liz, and their son, Norman, or "Normie." In the alternate-reality, "next generation" *Spider-Girl* series, 1998–present, Normie is the Green Goblin.)

Before Harry's death, his psychologist, Dr. Bart Hamilton, discovered the Goblin's secrets while treating young Osborn's psychosis with hypnosis. In *Amazing Spider-Man* #176–#180 (1978), Hamilton became the Green Goblin III, warring with the crime czar Silvermane before meeting his demise in a grudge match with Goblin II. The first of several criminals to plunder New York as the Hobgoblin debuted in 1983, eventually followed by the demon/human hybrid Demogoblin in 1992. A fourth Green Goblin, Phil Urich, nephew of reporter Ben Urich (a supporting-cast player in *Spider-Man* and *Daredevil*), happened across Harry Osborn's

Opposite: The Green Goblin (Willem Dafoe) terrorizes New York City in Spider-Man *(2002).*

The Supervillain Book

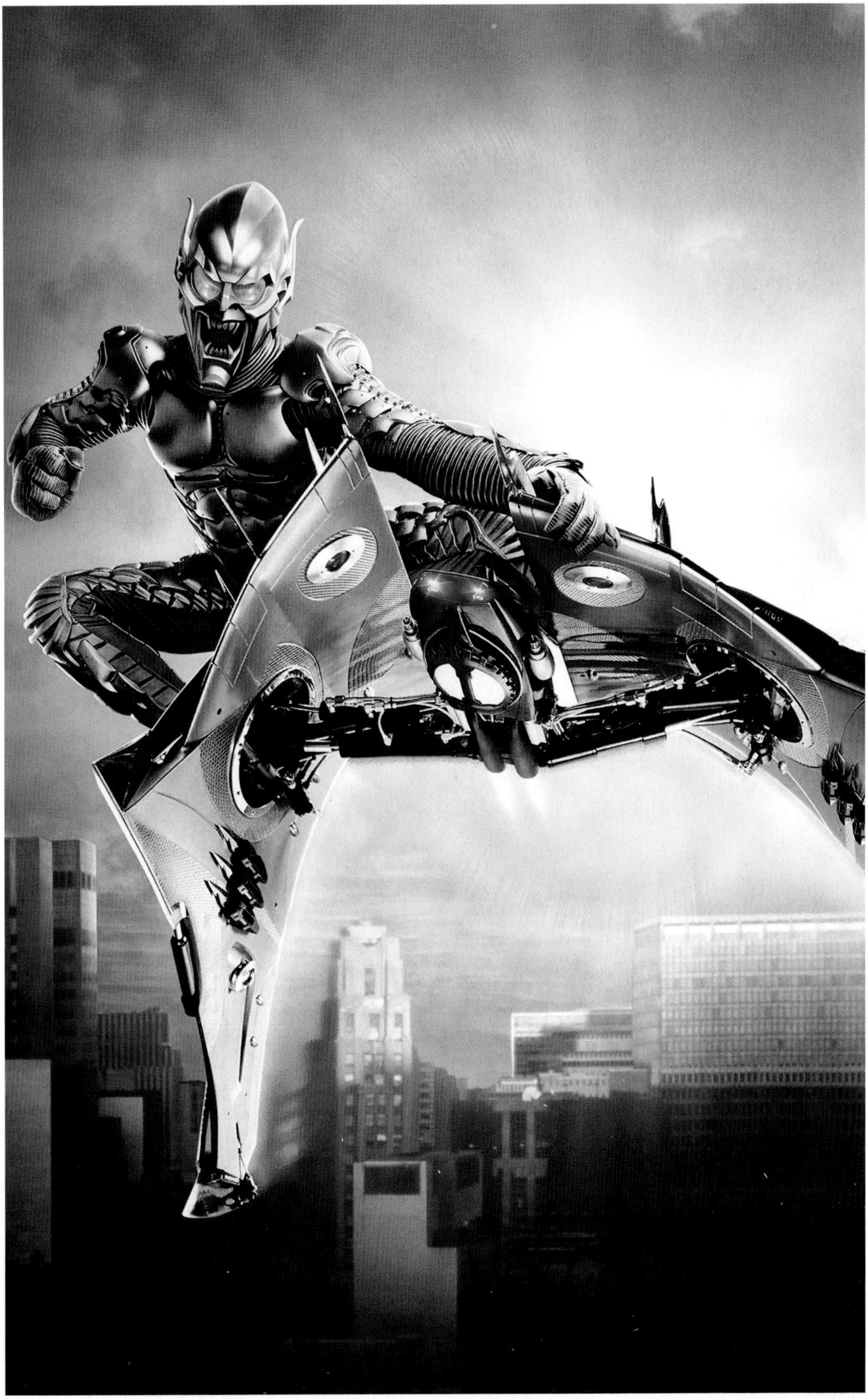

headquarters and became the Green Goblin IV in *Web of Spider-Man* #125 (1995). Urich became an anti-hero in the guise, winging through the sky in an updated version of the Goblin outfit and headlining his own thirteen-issue title, *Green Goblin* (1995–1996). Haunted by the specter of those preceding him, Goblin IV soon hung up his tights.

A world without a Green Goblin might be Spider-Man's preference, but it was not Marvel Comics'. The four-part storyline "Revelations," serialized through the various *Spider-Man* titles in 1996, returned Norman Osborn from limbo (and retroactively amended some of Spidey's continuity). It was disclosed that his Goblin formula had allowed his body to heal his once-fatal wound. After awakening on a morgue slab, Osborn went into hiding for years with the underground cabal called the Scriers. The death of his son Harry brought Osborn out into the open to renew his assaults against his arch-foe, which included his manipulation of the Jackal's efforts to clone Spider-Man, the slaughter of Parker's clone Ben Reilly, and the death of Parker's Aunt May (later revealed as a sick hoax). In the 2000 miniseries *Spider-Man: Revenge of the Green Goblin*, Osborn drugged and brainwashed Parker, attempting to groom him to become the next Goblin.

None of the reborn Green Goblin's storylines shocked—or *enraged*—fans more than the introduction of the Stacy Twins in the J. Michael Straczynski–written/Mike Deodato–penciled "Sins Past" in *Amazing Spider-Man* #509–#514 (2004–2005). Years ago, the charismatic Osborn seduced young Gwen Stacy into an affair, impregnating her, then shunting her off to Europe to secretly give birth to twins. Aging rapidly due to their father's Goblin serum-tainted blood, the super-agile Gabriel and Sarah Stacy, when physiologically aged to their late teens, confronted Spider-Man, thinking him to be their father. Upon learning of his true parentage, Gabriel became the Gray Goblin, continuing the warped legacy of Spider-Man's deadliest foe.

The Ultimate Green Goblin, from Marvel's reimagined *Ultimate Spider-Man* series (2001–present), is a hulkish, mutated goblin-man, a transformation originating during Osborn's failed attempt to recreate the accident that turned teenage Peter Parker into the Ultimate Spider-Man.

The Green Goblin appeared in the 1967, 1981, and 1994 *Spider-Man* animated series, the 1981 *Spider-Man and His Amazing Friends* cartoon, and the 1999 *Spider-Man Unlimited* show. Over the decades, the Green Goblin has been featured on Spidey-related board games, toy viewers, action figures of various sizes, and video games, among other licensed items, but no mass-media presentation is more famous than director Sam Raimi's live-action blockbuster *Spider-Man* (2002). Willem Dafoe was perfectly cast as Norman Osborn, who, like his comics counterpart, was driven to madness as his strength-enhancing experiment went awry, but comic-book diehards disliked the design of the Green Goblin's high-tech, body-armored costume, particularly its faceplate mask, which obstructed Dafoe's own sinisterly expressive features (the Goblin has adopted a similar appearance, sans the iron mask, in the comics since the film). The movie's climax adapted the bridge-top battle royal of *Amazing Spider-Man* #121–#122, with Mary Jane Watson replacing Gwen Stacy, but surviving the ordeal. Dafoe's Goblin died in a similar Glider accident, compelling events in the sequels toward Harry Osborn's (James Franco) eventual ascension into his father's footsteps. —*ME*

Gremlin

The super-scientist known as the Gremlin, a formidable foe of the Hulk and Iron Man, first appeared in the Steve Englehart–scripted, Herb Trimpe–drawn *The Incredible Hulk* vol. 2 #163 (1973). A misshapen boy genius who inherited augmented brainpower from his Soviet mastermind father, the radiation-mutated Gargoyle (the Hulk's first adversary from the hero's 1963 first issue), the Gremlin—whose grotesque, balloon-headed appearance came from his father's altered genes—operated from his secret base in a frozen Russian wasteland. Following in his father's footsteps, the Gremlin, funded by the Soviet government, designed the high-tech armor worn by his strike force, the Super-Troopers, who proved a worthy threat to the superstrong behemoth Hulk.

The Gremlin's principal weapon was his damage-resistant battlesuit of titanium armor—hence his alternate name, Titanium Man (though not to be confused with the original Titanium Man)—which magnified his strength to superhuman levels, enabled him to fly, and from which he could project devastating energy blasts. At the end of his comic-book run, the Gremlin was attacked by Iron Man, who believed that the Gremlin's Titanium Man armor incorporated some of the stolen designs for Iron Man's own metal gear. In a battle with Iron Man, Titanium Man/Gremlin died when his armor jets ignited and exploded (*Iron Man* #229, 1988).

Although the Gremlin hasn't appeared on TV, the Gargoyle, renamed "the Gorgon," was seen in a "Hulk" episode of the 1966 *The Marvel Super-Heroes* animated series. Under the name the Gargoyle he was also in *The Incredible Hulk* animated series (1996–1999). —*GM*

Grey Gargoyle

T he Marvel supervillain the Grey Gargoyle first appeared in the Thor story in *Journey into Mystery* #107 (1964), scripted by Stan Lee and illustrated by Jack Kirby. While working in the lab, French chemist Paul Pierre Duval accidentally encounters a substance that turns his hand to living stone. Duval soon learns that he can transform his entire body into the rock-like material simply by rubbing his hand over himself. Any matter he touches also turns to stone, although it is incapable of movement. (The Grey Gargoyle's transformations last for about an hour, after which time the objects revert to their normal state.) Duval decides to exploit his unique power for personal gain, and as the Grey Gargoyle embarks on a life of crime and hero bashing.

A former ally of the evil organization A.I.M. (Advance Idea Mechanics), former captain of the starship *Bird of Prey*, and all-around bad guy, the Grey Gargoyle has fought such Marvel heroes as Thor, from whom he tried to wrest the secret of immortality; Captain America, the Falcon, and Nick Fury, as he attempted to capture the deadly compound "Element X"; the Hulk; the Avengers; and the Fantastic Four, whose member the Thing he attempted to turn into nonliving stone (were the

Thing's woeful existence as a rock-skinned mutation not already bad enough).

The 750-pound Grey Gargoyle possesses superhuman strength while in his rock-solid persona, with the ability to lift almost a dozen tons. Despite his weight and mass, his powerful legs enable him jump up to about 20 feet. The Gargoyle prevents unwanted use of his power by wearing a specially treated glove, which has a small area in the palm that is usually left open to allow the use of his power at any time.

The Grey Gargoyle appeared in a "Thor" episode of the 1966 *Marvel Super-Heroes* animated TV series, as well as on the cartoon *Iron Man* (1994–1996). —*GM*

Griffith

G riffith was one of the major heroes of Kentaro Miura's popular ongoing medieval fantasy *Berzerk* (1989–present), but the hand of fate would cast him into the depths of evil, shedding his humanity in the process.

First introduced in 1992 in vol. 3 of the manga, Griffith was the handsome and charismatic leader of the mercenary army the Band of the Hawks. Little was known of his past, other than he was a commoner, not of noble birth. An excellent warrior, highly regarded by all, Griffith even recruits the fierce warrior Guts, much to the shock of his men (and Casca, the only women in the Hawks). Over the next several years, the Hawks—now employed by the Kingdom of Midland—become a force to be reckoned with.

As the reputation of the Hawks grows, so do Griffith's ambitions for power. Behind the scenes, this calm, unruffled young man orchestrates the deaths of his enemies in the Royal House. But when total power is within his grasp, everything shatters when Guts leaves the Hawks. Things spiral downward quickly for Griffith; one year later, he is locked away in a dungeon. Guts and the remaining Hawks rescue Griffith, but madness has taken their old commander. With the help of a special talisman, Griffith unleashes the Godhand upon the land. This vicious demonic army wipes out the Hawks and transforms Griffith into the being

Griffith as Femto. From *Berserk* vol. 3 ©1991, 2004 Kentaro Miura. Published by Dark Horse Comics (2004).
ART BY KENTARO MIURA.

enemy: Guts, now called the Black Swordsman. —*MM*

The Grim Reaper

As a child, "bad" Eric Williams never lived up to the example set by his "good" brother, Simon. This dysfunctional family dynamic established a lifetime of conflict between the siblings: Eric, who becomes the villainous Grim Reaper, and Simon, who becomes Avengers team member Wonder Man. Although Eric both loved and resented Simon, when Simon "died" as Wonder Man (*The Avengers* vol. 1 #9, 1964), Eric was consumed by a desire for vengeance, blaming the Marvel Comics superteam, and taking the identity of the Grim Reaper to punish them.

Dressed in a blue bodysuit with a skull and crossbones, and accompanying red cape, the Grim Reaper possesses no superhuman powers, but wields a scythe fused to his right hand. The Reaper's virtually indestructible blade is a superweapon, housing a force blaster, cerebral stunner (inducing paralysis in its victims), and a spinner (which allows the scythe to function like a buzz saw). Since his introduction in scribe Roy Thomas and artist John Buscema's *Avengers* #52 (1968), in which he revealed his backstory to the team as he attacked them, the Reaper has spent his entire criminal career battling the Avengers, even briefly forming the villainous Lethal Legion in an attempt to defeat them.

Femto. Only Guts and Casca escape the horror, but not unscathed.

Griffith's embrace of the Godhand brought him the power he desired, but the result was the emergence of demons upon the human world, a new dark age. The only challenge to this would come from Griffith's old friend and comrade—now his sworn

In a detailed 1986 storyline, the Reaper died, and then returned from death as a living zombie. Although he was invulnerable to the effects of heat, cold, radiation, and disease, he needed to sustain his undead state by killing victims with his scythe. He murdered his lover Nekra, the Mandrill, and countless others until Wonder Man halted his brother's reign of terror. Afterward, the Grim Reaper allied himself with demonic forces, but was seemingly killed by his evil masters ... until he was resurrected once again to join the evil crime family, the Maggia. Thanks to Scarlet Witch's magic, the Grim Reaper is fully human once more, and has appeared battling the Avengers, this time on behalf of his employer, Count Nefaria. —*GM*

The Hand

Although the way of the ninja dawned more than 800 years ago in feudal Japan, comics scribe Frank Miller created an elite group of ninja warriors, the Hand, during his *Daredevil* run during the 1980s. Miller introduced the Hand in *Daredevil* vol. 1 #168 (1981) as a highly trained band of ninja fighters, specializing in espionage and assassination.

Unlike other ninja cells, which ply their skills as mercenaries and are content merely to survive, the Hand is driven by a desire for supremacy and domination. Refusing to be governed by any one leader, the Hand ninja roam the world with two goals: the elimination of their enemies or the acquisition of power. From early in their history, the Hand ninja depended on dark magic—imparted by their demonic master, the Beast (no relation to the furry member of the X-Men)—to supplement their honed skills. One spell turns a ninja Hand's body to dust shortly after his death, in order to prevent another being from looking upon his countenance. The Hand has loose parallels with DC Comics' League of Assassins, an elite band of ninja warriors that came to the screen as the League of Shadows in *Batman Begins* (2005).

Despite such highly coveted skills and merciless ambitions, the Hand has its adversary in a clan of warriors, the Chaste, once led my martial-arts master Stick, who trained both Matt Murdock (Daredevil) and Elektra Natchios (the Greek assassin Elektra). With Stick dead, the Hand has consistently attempted to eliminate the Chaste in an effort to weaken Daredevil's allies. As such, Hand members have often found themselves in heated battle with Daredevil and/or Elektra and Black Widow—both in Daredevil's hometown of New York City and on their home turf. The Hand has also attempted to eliminate the remnants of Stick's ninja order to prevent any one of its members from locating the newborn child that is to be Stick reincarnated, and will no doubt continue to rise up against the Man without Fear.

The Hand appeared in the live-action film *Elektra* (2005). Moreover, the Foot, an organization of evil ninjas in *Teenage Mutant Ninja Turtles* (first the comics, then on TV and in film), was created as a parody of the Hand of Miller's *Daredevil*. —GM

The Harlequin

The Harlequin—not to be confused with the Teen Titan named Harlequin (aka "the Joker's Daughter") or Batman foe Harley Quinn—is a court jester–like villainess who originated during comics' Golden Age (1938–1954). She leapt into an early Green Lantern (GL) story written by Robert Kanigher and penciled by Irwin Hasen in *All-American Comics*

#89 (1947) as tomboy secretary Molly Mayne, who worked at Gotham City radio station WXYZ and fantasized about dating GL. As part of its *Green Lantern* radio serial, the station invented a recurring villain called "the Harlequin" to taunt the hero on air. Trying to attract the attention of the real-life GL (whose alter ego, Alan Scott, was a WXYZ broadcaster), Mayne created a costume and nimbly leaped over Gotham rooftops as the Harlequin.

After locating a pair of special glasses and a flying car from a secret source, Harlequin formed her own crime gang. Her cat-eyeglasses projected realistic illusions and were rigged to give anyone but Mayne a strong electrical shock if touched. With Olympic-level athleticism and a heavy wooden mandolin that doubled as a club, she was Green Lantern's first female adversary—and one of a long list of comics' femme fatales. While robbing banks and committing petty crimes, Harlequin often battled GL; her efforts not to hurt the dreamy do-gooder inadvertently caused mishaps that landed the clumsy crime queen on the hit lists of Gotham gangsters. When it was later disclosed that the Harlequin was doing double duty as an FBI agent, she and the Green Lantern teamed up to capture super-criminals like the Wraith, the Sportsmaster, and assorted Communist agents.

While the Harlequin virtually disappeared from comics pages in 1949, she was seen briefly in the 1980s as an aging villainess who, after disclosing her secret identity, married long-time crush Alan Scott. —*GM*

Harley Quinn

H arley Quinn, the breakaway character from *Batman: The Animated Series* (1992–1997), is at heart just a girl who's head over heels for a guy—but in Harley's case, she's "hopelessly in love with a murderous psychopathic clown": the Joker.

She wasn't always a jester-clad, chalk-faced, superhumanly agile moll. Behind the makeup is—actually, *was*, since her original identity has been lost to her certifiable lunacy—Dr. Harleen Quinzel, a psychiatrist at Arkham Asylum for the Criminally Insane, where Gotham City's malicious madmen are penned and padded-celled after being appre-

hended by Batman. Quinzel studied the incarcerated Joker's psychotic mind, and was mesmerized by his homicidal tendencies and warped sense of humor. After lending the Joker a helping hand in escaping Arkham, she next lent him her heart, joining her "Puddin'" as the pining princess of plunder, Harley Quinn. You can't blame a girl for falling for the Joker's seductive smile and wicked wit; as Harley says of "Mr. J," in the voice of actress Arleen Sorkin, "Gee, boss, you really know how to put the fun in funeral."

"Originally, Harley was only supposed to be in one episode," remarked *Batman: The Animated Series* (BTAS) writer Paul Dini in a 1994 *Cinefantastique* interview, "but she was very appealing and she added this other dimension to the Joker; most of his henchpeople are pretty expendable." Not that the mercurial Clown Prince of Crime hasn't tried to dump her. He's given her the slip, and the slap, and even strapped her to a rocket for a "final" send-off, but she keeps returning for more—or he calls her back (but usually for an ulterior motive), making the Joker and Harley Quinn the ultimate codependent supervillain couple.

After her intended one-time outing in *BTAS*'s episode seven, "Joker's Favor" (original airdate: September 11, 1992), Harley kept popping up on the show with and without Mr. J, and has followed him through a variety of subsequent animated series: *Superman* (1996–2000), *The Adventures of Batman & Robin* (1997–1999), *Static Shock!* (2000–2004), and *Justice League* (2001–2004), as well as the made-for-video animated movie *Batman Beyond: Return of the Joker* (2000). Harley even rode the Clown Prince of Crime's purple coattails into comic books, first in DC Comics' *BTAS* tie-ins written and drawn in the "animated" style and later in the darker "real" DC Universe, beginning with the 1999 one-shot *Batman: Harley Quinn*, then continuing with her own monthly series *Harley Quinn*, which ran 38 issues from 2000 through 2004.

Harley enjoys a Thelma and Louise–like friendship with fellow Bat-rogue Poison Ivy, from whom she received an herbal application that makes her immune to toxins, and adores her pet hyenas, which she affectionately calls her "babies." She has been the subject of action figures, statues, and even a

Harley Quinn #3 ©2001 DC Comics.
COVER ART BY TERRY AND RACHEL DODSON.

2005 limited edition (1,007 produced) hand-painted marionette retailing at $290.95! Not bad for a down-home gal with a wild streak ("Trouble? Don't mind if I do!") and a dream of one day settling down and raising (demented) kids with her Puddin'.

Mia Sara played Dr. Harleen Quinzel in the live-action TV series *Birds of Prey* (2002–2003). In the concluding moments of season one's final episode she appeared in a modified Harley Quinn costume, but the series' cancellation stalled Sara's Harley. —*ME*

Heat Wave

Resembling a HAZMAT worker, volatile villain Heat Wave first blazed into DC Comics in *The Flash* #140 (1963), written by John Broome and penciled by Carmine Infantino. The man behind the white asbestos suit and goggles is pyromaniac Mick Rory, who has suffered from cryophobia since a traumatic childhood incident when he was trapped inside a freezer. With his self-designed Heat Gun, a flame-throwing pistol also capable of generating extreme temperatures, Rory ignites a crime career in Central City as Heat Wave. In his first outing he encounters his climate doppel-gänger, Captain Cold, and the two weather rivals team up against the city's protector, the Flash.

Not the most original supervillain, Heat Wave worked better with Captain Cold and the collected Flash's Rogues' Gallery than on his own. Long troubled by his obsession with fire, he hung up his flame-retardant togs and reformed, even becoming the Flash's friend. In the *Underworld Unleashed* crossover (1995), Rory was one of several criminals lured to hell and offered tremendous power by the demon Neron, who deposited him back onto Earth sans his soul. Rory's spirit was later returned and he was morally altered by his harrowing experience, taking a job with the FBI as Heat Wave, charged with apprehending superpowered felons. Writer Geoff Johns penned a sympathetic examination of Rory's pyromania in *Flash* vol. 2 #218 (2005), but as of issue #222, Flash foe the Top was mentally rekindling Heat Wave's villainous tendencies.

Lex Lang, an actor whose resonant baritone often graces movie trailers (including *The Matrix*), played Heat Wave in a 2005 episode of the Cartoon Network's *Justice League Unlimited*. —*ME*

Hector Hammond

While the world of supervillains has no shortage of swelled heads, the term truly applies to Hector Hammond. Writer John Broome and artist Gil Kane introduce Hammond in *Green Lantern* (GL) vol. 2 #5 (1961) as smooth-talking shyster who encounters a meteor fragment that triggers evolutionary advancement. He abducts a quartet of scientists and alters them into future-men, their brains accelerated but their resolve dampened, and coerces them to invent technologically superior gadgets for which he takes credit and gains celebrity. The scientists construct a device that attracts (like a magnet) Green

From *Thor* vol. 1 #190 ©1971 Marvel Comics.
ART BY JOHN BUSCEMA AND JOE SINNOTT.

meteor's radiation, ultimately paying an unexpected price: he now boasts a highly developed mind—and a gigantic, distorted head—with stupefying telekinetic and telepathic abilities, but has become physically inert, applying his machinations from a chair. Hammond's enmity against GL has engulfed those in Jordan's circle. Directing the bestial Shaggy Man to attack the Justice League, spearheading a new version of the Royal Flush Gang, attempting to control GL Guy Gardner, and faking the death of original GL Alan Scott's friend Doiby Dickles are just some of head games Hammond has played. With Jordan's resurrection from the dead in 2005, Hammond has reemerged, determined to return his power-ringed foe to the grave. —*ME*

Hela

In the Marvel Universe, Hela, Goddess of Death, is known to the citizens of Asgard, although she is generally believed to be a mythological character by the people of Earth. Allegedly born to the Asgardian god of mischief Loki and the sorceress Angrboda in the land of Jotunheim, Hela was introduced in *Journey into Mystery* #102 (1964), in a story scripted by Stan Lee and illustrated by Jack Kirby. As goddess and ruler of the spirits of the Asgardian dead, Hela watches over the otherworldly realms of Hel and Niffleheim, two of the nine worlds of Norse mythology.

Hela's principal desire is to bring more Asgardian souls under her control, and she longs to possess the souls of Odin and his son Thor. Like all

Lantern's power ring, which Hammond does not realize is actually the hero's spare, and with it he wages war against Green Lantern (Hal Jordan), Hammond being trounced when his ring loses its twenty-four-hour charge.

After a brief prison stint, the spiteful Hammond exposed himself to the meteor's rays, reappearing in *Justice League of America* #14 (1962) with an enlarged cranium and mind-over-matter powers. His obsession with mental amplification led Hammond to continually self-administer the

Asgardian gods and goddesses, she is extremely long-lived (although not immortal like the Olympians), possesses superhuman strength, is immune to all diseases, and is resistant to injury. The 500-pound goddess, capable of lifting 100 tons and standing up against superhumans like Thor, can generate great mystical power within her hand, enabling it to strike a blow that can twist even the strongest Asgardian flesh. She calls this power her "hand of glory." To these superpowers she also adds levitation, casting illusions, disguise, and mental control.

Interestingly, Hela's costume—her cloak, cowl, and headdress—preserve her physical vitality. Legend has it that, without her cloak, Hela would be unable to leave the realm of the dead.

During Thor's initial popularity throughout the 1960s and early 1970s, Hela was a staple of the Marvel Universe. In the 1980s, she was a particular favorite of writer/artist Walter Simonson, who established the power of her cloak. Her current status in the mid-2000s is unclear since the Asgardian gods seemingly all perished in Ragnarok (the twilight of the gods) at the end of the *Thor* vol. 2 series (2004). Presumably when Marvel inevitably revives *Thor*, Hela will sooner or later return as well. —GM

The Hellfire Club

S ince the dawn of civilization, various elites have used their power and resources to sway human destiny, and the era of the radiation-spawned mutant is no exception. The Hellfire Club, obliquely introduced by writer Chris Claremont and artist Dave Cockrum in 1976 (*Uncanny X-Men* vol. 1 #100), is one such influential clique of the privileged. Established in the mid–eighteenth century as a cabal of the wealthiest, most powerful people in England, the Hellfire Club not only catered to the decadent tastes of its wealthy roster—upper-crust bordellos called Hellfire Clubs actually existed during Victorian times—it also furthered the expansion and consolidation of its members' economic and political influence. A decade or so after the Hellfire Club's inception, several of its members emigrated to New York City to establish the American Hellfire Club, which they based in an abandoned church on Fifth Avenue, a short distance away from the eventual location of the Avengers' Manhattan headquarters. Former British Parliament member Sir Patrick Clemens, along with his mistress, the famous actress Diana Knight, held the respective titles of Black King and Black Queen in the new Hellfire Club's chess-themed leadership structure, which also included white and black bishops, knights, rooks, and pawns (*X-Men: The Hellfire Club* miniseries, 2000).

More than two centuries on, the Hellfire Club has become more powerful than ever before, and considerably more dangerous, its leadership (known as the Lords Cardinal of the Inner Circle, or the Council of the Chosen) comprised of superpowered mutants. As with its early predecessors, this latter-day cabal confers membership by invitation only; such offers are rare, sought-after, and almost never declined. As far as the general public knows, the Hellfire Club is merely an exclusive upper-class social fraternity, a country club in the heart of America's premiere city; in reality—and unknown even to most Hellfire Club members (which include the parents of the X-Men's Angel)—the group's Inner Circle pursues a clandestine agenda of total domination of the global political-economic stage. The modern Hellfire Club maintains a London branch, which has boasted Union Jack and Captain Britain among its members, as well as subsidiaries in such cities as Hong Kong, Moscow, Rio de Janeiro, Tokyo, and Venice.

With their vast financial holdings, their command of high technology, and their army of blue-and-red-garbed masked mercenaries, the Hellfire Club's leaders are well positioned to take over the world, both overtly and while acting from behind the scenes. They even used heavily armed, vaguely humanoid robots known as Sentinels in a failed attempt to neutralize other mutants who might oppose them, making it clear that only powerful mutants of good will, such as the students of Professor Charles Xavier (aka the X-Men), have any hope of thwarting their plans of global conquest. Visually inspired by the Hellfire Club depicted on the classic 1960s television spy series *The Avengers*, the members of the Hellfire Club's Inner Circle distinguish themselves from other supervillains by affecting a strange blend of Enlightenment-era dress, complete with cravats, waistcoats, and breeches for the men and Frederick's of Hollywood–evocative lingerie for the women.

In the hands of the writer/artist team of Chris Claremont and John Byrne in *X-Men* vol. 1 #129–#135 (1979 and 1980), the Hellfire Club reached full flower. Led by Black King Sebastian Shaw and White Queen Emma Frost, the Hellfire Club's Inner Circle—and its never-ending pursuit of power, influence, and money—severely complicated the lives of the X-Men. Anticipating the real-world corporate raiders of the go-go 1980s, both Shaw and Frost were revealed to be the heads of major corporations, with the enterprising Ms. Frost also serving as the headmistress of the Massachusetts Academy, an elite prep school whose student body included the youthful superpowered mutant team known as the Hellions.

Like most of the Inner Circle, Shaw and Frost also possessed powerful mutant abilities (kinetic energy-absorption powers and psionic talents, respectively), and brought all of their metahuman might, as well as all their vast financial resources, to bear against the X-Men, the only other superpowered group apparently able to undo the Hellfire Club's schemes. To those ends, Shaw's company (Shaw Industries) acquired a secret contract to construct a new generation of Sentinel robots for Project Wideawake, a paranoid, Reagan-era U.S. government effort aimed at subduing, studying, and ultimately controlling and exterminating superpowered mutants. Meanwhile, the particularly devious Hellfire Club member Jason Wyngarde (aka the telepathic mutant Mastermind) mentally influenced the X-Men's Jean Grey (aka Marvel Girl, aka Phoenix) into willingly becoming the Inner Circle's Black Queen. But Wyngarde's psionic persuasions had a deadly unintended effect: they precipitated Grey's transformation into an evil, world-destroying entity called Dark Phoenix, who left Wyngarde temporarily catatonic before laying waste to an entire inhabited planet (not Earth, thankfully); in a momentary flash of lucidity and love for her fiancé Scott (Cyclops) Summers, Grey subsequently immolated herself, dying (temporarily, at least) in a spectacular cosmic conflagration.

Like many groups of the powerful and arrogant, the Inner Circle of the Hellfire Club faces as much peril from within its ranks as from without; while they have clashed repeatedly with such "good guy" mutant teams as the X-Men and the New Mutants, they are also prone to quarrel amongst themselves, vying for control of the Hellfire Club's vast resources. Notable examples include: Magneto, who briefly became a member of the Inner Circle and seized power long enough to rescue the New Mutants from the Hellfire Club's clutches; White Bishop Donald Pierce, a cyborg who tried to take command of the Inner Circle at the expense of his scheming mutant colleagues; and Black Queen Selene, a powerful sorceress-vampire and *soi-disant* goddess who orchestrated her own power-grab conspiracy within the Inner Circle. The Inner Circle itself was eventually overthrown and replaced (however temporarily) by younger mutants known as the Upstarts, a group led by Shinobi Shaw, Sebastian Shaw's son.

An alternate version of the Hellfire Club debuted in *Ultimate X-Men* #18–#19 (2003), dressed in modern tuxedoes and gowns in order to pose as "thoughtful billionaires investing in the future." Once again led by Sebastian Shaw, this almost completely reimagined, updated iteration of the Hellfire Club stood revealed as the secret financiers of Professor Charles Xavier, the mentor and leader of an equally rebooted X-Men team. But this Hellfire Club proved just as malevolently power-mad as the Claremont-Byrne version, summoning dark eldritch forces that could only be held at bay by an inexperienced eighteen-year-old telepath named Jean Grey—and which apparently wiped the Hellfire Club itself out of existence. Given the Hellfire Club's deep roots in the Marvel Universe, however, as well as the apparent unwillingness of deceased superheroes and supervillains alike to remain dead, the group's eventual return appears to be all but a certainty. —*MAM*

Henchmen, Minions, and Underlings

Supervillains need more than garish costumes, formidable powers or weapons, and egomaniacal monologuing to bring their schemes to fruition:

they require grunt labor as well. Although such low-echelon bad guys (and gals) very often do not satisfy many of the criteria for supervillainy themselves, the machinations of a great many supervillains and evil organizations are hugely dependent on the efforts of their faithful followers.

Almost always ranking at a level considerably below that of a supervillain's team partners (such as members of the Frightful Four or the Injustice Gang) or sidekicks (such as the Joker's junior crony Harley Quinn), the motivations of supervillainous aides-de-camp vary. For many, including the campy, crooked-camera-angle stooges of ABC's *Batman* television series (1966–1968), henchmanship is a means of sharing in a particular supervillain's profits. For others, like the uniformed paramilitary goons employed by industrialized, weapon-happy world-beaters like G.I. Joe's Cobra Commander or the Blofeld-esque Dr. Evil (who debuted in 1997's *Austin Powers: International Man of Mystery*), the henchman game appears to be simply a paycheck job that includes medical benefits and perhaps even compulsory union membership. The masked, rifle-toting, blue-and-red clenched henchmen of Chris Claremont and John Byrne's Hellfire Club are disinclined to give their last full measure of devotion to their mutant bosses for a mere paycheck; when confronted with Wolverine's razor-sharp adamantium claws, one such flunky not only disarmed, he also answered all the hero's questions about his employers (*X-Men* vol. 1 #133, 1980).

Very rarely, a flunky will prove to be highly "upwardly mobile" in a given evil organization, and this usually happens more because of happenstance than innate skill on the part of the henchmen (otherwise, he would likely have pursued a different trade in the first place). A good example of an underling's accidental rise to prominence is the faceless stooge of Advanced Idea Mechanics (A.I.M.) who is experimentally transformed into the large-brained entity known as MODOK (Mental Organism Designed Only for Killing), whose newly activated psionic powers quickly landed him in the organization's driver's seat (*Tales of Suspense* vol. 1 #93–#94, 1967; *Captain America* vol. 1 #133, 1971).

By contrast, henchmen who might be better characterized as minions or underlings—such as the uniformed acolytes of Marvel's Hydra, the off-the-rack Nazis of comics' Golden Age (1938–1954) and the Indiana Jones movies, or the genetically enhanced followers of *Star Trek*'s Khan—fill out the bottom ranks of a supervillain's hierarchies out of a quasi-religious devotion to their charismatic-yet-nefarious leader. "Hired" henchmen, by contrast, are far less inclined to blithely throw their lives away defending a supervillain; superspy Nigel Powers (played by Michael Caine in *Austin Powers in Goldmember,* 2002) even manages to convince one of Dr. Evil's armed guards to lie down on the floor rather than force Powers to kill him. "Do you have any idea how many anonymous henchmen I've killed over the years?" asks the suave secret agent of the compliant hireling.

Henchmen are permitted varying degrees of autonomy in pursuit of their superiors' criminal objectives. Most of these, like the battle droids and stormtroopers of the *Star Wars* movies, serve merely as the arms and legs of their super-patron's whims, annexing territory and defending the villain's headquarters from interlopers, very often at the cost of their own lives. These faceless, and usually hapless, goons have no decision-making authority and are generally no more than supernumeraries, however essential their contributions may be to a given supervillain's cause. Others, such as the assassins, terrorists, and rogue scientists of SPECTRE—the organization that bedeviled James Bond throughout the cold war—function more or less independently. Organized into cells, these operatives identify themselves using code numbers and answer only to SPECTRE's highest-ranking members, such as Ernst Stavro Blofeld or his one-eyed successor, the nuclear terrorist Emilio Largo. But SPECTRE's underlings are a cautious lot—their leaders punish all discipline breaches with summary execution.

Henchmen everywhere share several characteristics, which are frequently and justifiably lampooned. Detention-cell guards tend to stare intently in one direction and to be far too easily distracted by the sounds pebbles thrown by captured (and soon-to-be-escaping) heroes; paramilitary henchmen, such as the stormtroopers of *Star Wars*, are notoriously poor marksmen, incapable of hitting even the most stationary and distracted of heroes; and ninja assassins tend to attack heroes in single-file lines, rather than simply surrounding and overwhelming them. This appalling lack of quality control is easily understandable, however, in the light of labor economics. Even though heroes continuously create new openings for all manner of henchmen, minions, and underlings, supervillains have no paucity of recruits; in the world of professional henchmen, it is clearly an employer's market. —*MAM*

The High Evolutionary

T he bizarre genetic mutations of the High Evolutionary, Stan Lee and Jack Kirby's cosmic version of H. G. Wells' Dr. Moreau, were first revealed to Marvel Comics readers in *Thor* vol. 1 #134–#135 (1966). The Thunder God goes not to a Moreau-esque island but to a baroque citadel on Transia's "forbidden" Wundagore Mountain, deftly guarded by the Knights of Wundagore on their airborne "atomic steeds." Thor hammers through these sentries but is astounded to discover that they are actually "New-Men," beasts anthropomorphically endowed by the lordly High Evolutionary. More an obsessed scientist than a malefactor, the High Evolutionary nonetheless displays a "warning sign" of his impending supervillainy—a flair for monologuing—overdramatically lamenting to Thor the woes of his phylogenic experiments and blathering the story of his origin. Behind his purple helmet (interestingly, its sharp-browed faceplate vaguely resembles the craggy visage of Darkseid, the DC Comics supervillain Kirby would create four years later) is Herbert Edgar Wyndham, a geneticist from the 1930s elevated to artificial godhood by his scientific experiments. Fearing "the death knell of the entire human race" when one of his creations, the wicked Man-Beast, runs amok, the High Evolutionary rockets away from Earth in Wundagore—which is actually a spacecraft—to find a new home.

That home was Counter-Earth, a duplicate he created on the opposite side of the sun (his mutated Knights were entrusted with a world of their own, Wundagore II), which in the 1970s

became the residence of the superhero Adam Warlock. Regarding himself the deity of his manufactured world, the High Evolutionary's actions have been deemed amoral by many, particularly the Avengers, who halted the High Evolutionary's most ambitious effort, the Evolutionary War, via which the would-be god endeavored to rapidly evolve humankind, attempting the extermination of certain races including mutants (as seen in Marvel's 1988 annuals). Mr. Sinister, the X-Men foe who is actually a nineteenth-century evolutionist, is a former colleague of Wyndham's.

The High Evolutionary appeared in a 1996 episode of the animated series *X-Men* (1992–1997), and was a principal character in the poorly received cartoon *Spider-Man Unlimited* (1999–2001), a series set on Counter-Earth. —*ME*

Hobgoblin

C alculating, cackling, and cold-blooded, the Hobgoblin, a familiar yet dangerously different threat to the friendly neighborhood Spider-Man, first appeared in *The Amazing Spider-Man* vol. 1 #238 (1983). When escaping bank robber George Hill discovers one of the Green Goblin's abandoned lairs, complete with a cache of the Goblin's weapons—electrical blast-firing gloves, goblin grenades, exploding jack-o-lanterns, batwinged aerial Goblin Gliders, and a strength-enhancing formula—he calls an unidentified crime associate to whom he intends to sell this equipment. Hill's mystery contact kills him, keeping the arsenal for himself, modifying the supervillain's uniform to become the Hobgoblin, Spider-Man's newest challenge.

The Hobgoblin challenged Marvel Comics readers as well. The character's co-creator, writer Roger Stern, countered the expectations to introduce a new Green Goblin to follow the original, Norman Osborn, and his successors, his son Harry Osborn and Bart Hamilton, by inventing an all-new character. As Stan Lee and Steve Ditko did two decades earlier with the identity of the Green Goblin, Stern and penciler Ron Frenz kept Hobgoblin's true identity a secret, tantalizing fans who speculated over the libertine's alter ego.

The Amazing Spider-Man vol. 1 #312 ©1989 Marvel Comics.
COVER ART BY TODD McFARLANE.

Hobgoblin's identity had yet to be disclosed when Stern vacated the title in 1984. Over the course of several years and in the hands of several writers, unmasked and/or revealed as the Hobgoblin were financier Roderick Kingsley, goon-for-hire Arnold "Lefty" Donovan, *Daily Bugle* reporter Ned Leeds (whose body was found in a Hobgoblin uniform, leaving readers assuming for some time that he was the villain), and the former Jack O'Lantern Jason Macendale (the incarnation of the Hobgoblin that appeared on the 1994–1998 *Spider-Man* animated television cartoon, voiced by Mark Hamill); even long-time Spider-Man supporting-cast member Flash Thompson was discovered doped up and dressed as Hobgoblin. Confusing matters even more were the introductions of the Demogoblin in *Web of Spider-Man #86* (1992)—N'Astirh, an otherwordly fiend that at first used Macendale's body as an earthly host then split into a separate Demogoblin form—and a fourth, *superhero* Green Goblin, Phil Urich, in 1995.

What had originally seemed like a good idea had spiraled out of control with too many twists and red herrings, and Stern and Frenz reunited for the miniseries *Spider-Man: Hobgoblin Lives* (1997) to establish that Kingsley, Stern's original choice, was the real Hobgoblin. In the "Goblins at the Gate" storyline in *Spectacular Spider-Man #259–#261* (1998), the original Green Goblin, Norman Osborn, who had recently returned from the dead, clashed with Hobgoblin. Kingsley retreated to the Caribbean, and the Hobgoblin has since remained in retirement, other than an occasional appearance as a collector-targeted mini-bust or action figure.

The Ultimate Hobgoblin was part of the *Ultimate Spider-Man*'s (2000–present) reimagining of the web-slinger. In this continuity, instead of succeeding his father as Green Goblin II, Norman Osborn's son Harry underwent a fiery transformation into a monstrous Hobgoblin, beginning in *Ultimate Spider-Man #75–#76* (2005). —ME

Hostess Supervillains

A sinister subculture of malicious marauders and global subjugators once plagued humankind, their twisted taste for evil vulnerable to only one weakness: sugar cravings. No matter their insidious plans, this baleful breed—Battleaxe, Icemaster, Monotony Man, Killer Bee and Son, Professor Sneer, Jet-Set Jessie, the Magpies, the Laughing Gas Bandits, the Mink Marauder, Professor Plutonium, and the Robot Master among their number—could be instantly vanquished at the mere sight of Hostess Twinkies, Cupcakes, or Fruit Pies.

From the mid-1970s through the early 1980s, comics' most popular superheroes added "salesman" to their résumés, starring in a series of 148 one-page Hostess advertisements appearing in Marvel and DC comic books (Archie and Harvey Comics also produced their own Hostess ads), written and illustrated in comic-book style by the creative flavors of the day (including Ross Andru, Sal Buscema, Dave Cockrum, Dick Giordano, Gil Kane, Bob Rozakis, Joe Sinnott, Curt Swan, Herb

Supervillains Only a Mother Could Love

Although they put their best foot forward, these underachieving supervillains failed to make the A- (or B-) list:

- **Dr. Bong**, Howard the Duck's arch-foe first seen in 1977, borrowed a page from Dr. Moreau's playbook in boosting lower-ordered beings up the evolutionary ladder—including Howard, whom he turned into a human. When Dr. Bong rang his bell-helmeted head with his ball-handled gauntlet, the resulting sonic vibrations created concussive waves or induced paralysis.
- Dr. Bong's stylistic predecessor, Archie Comics' **Ironfist,** had a steel cannonball for a hand, and in 1966 tried to whack the superhero called the Web.
- **The Eraser**, a lanky larcenist with a rubber-topped headpiece and pencil-sharp pointed loafers, nearly rubbed out Batman and Robin in *Batman* #188 (1966).
- **The Living Eraser**, first seen in 1963, used his handheld "Dimensionizer" to teleport the Hulk and other heroes to another dimension by "erasing" them with a few strokes.
- **Mouse Man**, a tiny villain in a rodent-like costume complete with mouse ears, whiskers, and a tail, pestered Wonder Woman during the mid-1960s.
- **The Man-Elephant** was a hydraulics engineer in an elephant-headed supersuit who stampeded in and out of *The Savage She-Hulk* #17 (1981).
- **The Porcupine**, a weapons designer who used his quill-covered battlesuit for crime, began his career fighting Ant-Man and the Wasp in *Tales to Astonish* #48 (1963). His original costume resembled a straw-covered potbellied stove, but was later streamlined into a spiny yellow uniform.
- **Father Nature**, an orange-skinned, yellow-haired alien wielding an alchemical "power prong" staff, tried to give Earth an environmental makeover in *Superman* vol. 1 #358 (1981).
- Even with his hypnotic powers, **Dr. Tzin-Tzin**, the Asian international criminal who fought Batman for the first time in *Detective Comics* #354 (1966), seems little more than a Fu Manchu clone.

Trimpe, and George Tuska). Directed never to depict the superheroes actually *eating* the baked goods (spandex shows no mercy after a crime fighter's pastry binge), writers instead used Hostess treats as a delectable *deus ex machina* to spoil an adversary's appetite for crime.

Hostess' yummy baked goods were known to quell riots, and Twinkies conquered the taste buds of the time-displaced Julius Caesar. A nosey reporter ferreting through the Superman suits in Clark Kent's closet found Hostess treats a more appetizing headline, and Captain America discovered that Fruit Pies easily deter green-skinned alien warriors.

Several established comic-book supervillains made Hostess appearances, fighting heroes from Batman to Daredevil, among them the Cheetah, Mirror Master, the Trapster, the Abomination and Wendigo (tag-teaming the Hulk), Catman, and the League of Assassins. Aquaman's foes the Manta Men, seen in comics and animation as the mutated henchmen (Manta-Men) of Black Manta, were reconfigured as underwater crooks wearing absurd headgear. The Joker and the Penguin were popular enough to star in their own Hostess ads, and even the wish-providing weapon the Cosmic Cube took a shine to Twinkies.

A campy cadre of cookie-cutter criminals was specifically created for the ads, including the Roller Disco Devils, Home Wrecker, Human Computer ("I'm programmed to love this chocolaty cake"), June Jitsu, Photoman, Legal Eagle, Chairman (who turned people into ambulatory chairs), Pigeon Person, Sore Sir's Apprentices, Mad Deserter, the Bureauc-rat, and Dr. Sorcery (with his Philosopher's Stone, perhaps on loan from Diablo or Dr. Alchemy). Other one-shot Hostess supervillains were Torgo the Ultimate Weapon, Impercepto, Goldigger, Flame Thrower, the Corsair of Crime, amphibian-man Slud-Jak, Triclops, Topsy-Turvy Man, the Stony-Eyed Medusa ("I shouldn't have taken my eyes off of you, Flash, but Hostess Fruit Pies are too good to ignore!"), the Beverly Hillbillies–like Ding-a-Ling Family, Cousin Betsy the Plant Lady (and her criminal gang of giant monster plants, including a choking artichoke), and the Godzilla-sized Green Frog.

The next time a contemporary superhero is cornered by a frothing serial killer or an omnipotent warlord capable of rearranging the timeline with a belch, he or she would do well to remember the halcyon days of the "Hostess Universe," where a savory snack could save the day. —ME

Hugo Strange

B atman had barely been in print for a year when Professor Hugo Strange reared his ugly head in writer Bill Finger and artist Bob Kane's *Detective Comics* #36 (1940). Typifying the stereotypical mad scientist with his egg-headed bald pate and thick-lensed, round-framed eyeglasses—and a creepy beard to boot—Strange's diabolical reputation is renowned, although little is actually known of him—Bruce (Batman) Wayne calls him "the most dangerous man in the world!" Strange proves just that as he chokes Gotham City with artificially manufactured fog so that his henchmen may pillage under its veil. No stranger to the dark, Batman becomes involved, and he is apprehended and even savagely lashed with a bullwhip by Strange before breaking free. In two other appearances during comics' Golden Age (1938–1954), Professor Strange mutates asylum patients into zombies and attempts to seize control of the United States with his "fear dust," but falls to his presumed death in 1940, the victim of DC Comics' softening of Batman's original foreboding tone.

Publishing climes were darker in 1977 when the creative team of Steve Englehart and Marshall Rogers resurrected Hugo Strange in *Detective* #471–#472. Running a private hospital catering to wealthy patients, Strange discovered Batman's true identity when an injured Bruce Wayne checked in. The professor planned to auction this information to other villains but took the secret to his grave when Boss Rupert Thorne tried to torture the info from him—although Strange's ghost lingered long enough to give Thorne nightmares.

Strange was reintroduced in *Batman: Legends of the Dark Knight* #11–#15 (1990-1991), penned by Doug Moench and penciled by Paul Gulacy. "Prey," a five-issue story arc in set early in Batman's career, presented Strange as a psychologist hired to advise a Gotham police task force on the methodology of the Dark Knight, then considered a vigilante. Strange ferreted out Batman's Wayne identity, but instead of aiding in his apprehension became obsessed with the hero, even masquerading as Batman.

In subsequent appearances, Hugo Strange has been engulfed by a psychotic fixation upon Batman, desiring nothing short of "becoming" the Masked Manhunter, and even, as has been his pattern since his inception, regularly returning from the dead to attempt his goal. In a 2000 encounter Wayne resorted to hypnotizing himself to forget his Batman identity to dupe the mad professor. "Over the years, Hugo Strange has developed into much more than his initial 'mad scientist' roots," observes Matt Wagner, writer/artist of *Batman and the Monster Men*, a 2005 miniseries set early in Batman's career ("I jokingly call it 'Batman Year 1.5," adds Wagner). "As one of only a handful of his enemies to have ever deduced Batman's secret identity, he represents an intellectual threat far removed from and, in a way, far deadlier than some of his flashier counterparts." Weary of alliances with Batman's other "flashier" enemies, Professor Hugo Strange prefers to work alone, the wheels of his demented mind always turning, even when he is imprisoned in Arkham Asylum, to concoct new ways of overthrowing Batman.

Ray Buktenica voiced Hugo Strange in the episode "The Strange Secret of Bruce Wayne" (original airdate: October 19, 1992) of *Batman: The Animated Series* (1992–1997), loosely adapting the 1977 comic story. Strange has cameoed in the *Justice League Unlimited* (2004–present) and was seen in a heftier and hairier incarnation in the "Strange Minds" episode of the WB's *The Batman* (2004–present), with 1960s TV Riddler Frank Gorshin lending him voice. —ME

Hush

W hen Batman saved a youngster from Killer Croc, Catwoman appeared and grabbed the ransom money for herself. Both Croc and Catwoman, though, were under the influence of Poison Ivy, who in turn had been hired by a mysterious new villain. Completely wrapped in bandages, this strange, strong figure quoted poetry and alluded to detailed information of Batman's and Bruce Wayne's past. Chasing Catwoman, Batman suffered a nearly fatal fall. Dr. Thomas Elliot, Bruce's childhood friend and a noted surgeon, saved his life, and opened a fascinating chapter in the history of Caped Crusader.

Batman #608 (2003) saw the first appearance of this fresh criminal mastermind in the debut of the creative team of Jeph Loeb and Jim Lee on the best-selling story arc bearing the new villain's name: "Hush." Possessing no apparent superpowers, Hush quickly framed the Joker for Tommy Elliot's murder and became a central conversation point in Batman-related discussions.

Unlike many of Batman's other recurring foes, the question of Hush's identity is at least as important to the story as what he's going to do. There have be numerous "revelations" of his identity that didn't stand up, including during the first arc when he identified himself as Jason Todd, the late, former Robin. While the ending of the first major Hush story left it somewhat ambiguous, many believed it was Elliot himself, who turned out to be not so dead. Subsequent appearances, though, have shown Elliot still alive but in the same room with Hush. Other readers have suggested that Hush is Paul Sloan, an actor hired by Batman's rogues to play the role of Two-Face. Regardless of his true identity, Hush joined the upper echelons of Batman's rogues' gallery when he appeared as an action figure from DC Direct. —JCV

Hydra

"**C**ut off a limb and two more shall take its place!" This boast is perhaps the most emblematic of Marvel Comics' Hydra, a subversive organization of truly global scope. Named after the durable, many-headed beast that challenged Hercules in Greek mythology, Hydra has risen from apparent defeat several times since its founding in 1944 by Nazi Baron von Strucker, who used extraterrestrial Gnobian technology to create a high-tech infrastructure for worldwide fascist revolution. Patterned on the Nazi hierarchy—Hydra operatives greet one another with shouts of "Hail Hydra!"—Hydra quickly became a militant cult of world conquest.

Created by Stan Lee and Jack Kirby during the height of the 1960s spy craze, when James Bond, Flint, John Steed and Emma Peel, the men from U.N.C.L.E, and even Maxwell Smart gained huge audiences, Hydra quickly became Marvel's embodiment of justifiable cold-war paranoia. During his indoctrination into S.H.I.E.L.D. (Supreme Headquarters, International Espionage, Law-Enforcement Division), Colonel Nick Fury learns that "our enemies are the most deadly, dangerous fanatics the world has ever known! They call themselves Hydra—and their sole objective is the complete and unchallenged mastery of the world!" Indeed, a S.H.I.E.L.D. raid on a Hydra outpost, mentioned during the group's debut (Strange Tales vol. 1 #135, 1965), yielded a large globe of Earth caught in the grip of a multi-tentacled creature capped with the green-hooded, red-goggled head of a Hydra operative.

Though based primarily on the remote Pacific Ocean locale known as Hydra island, Hydra maintains a worldwide network of agents and safehouses. Hydra's tactics include assassination, high-tech sabotage, and nuclear- and biological-weapons blackmail. Thanks to its covert subsidiary A.I.M. (Advanced Idea Mechanics), Hydra has long enjoyed a seemingly inexhaustible supply of cutting-edge vehicles, killer androids, and other weapons; devices such as the Betatron Bomb, the Death Spore Bomb, the Overkill Horn, and the Satan Claw number among Hydra's most notable near-successes.

Hydra's early leadership structure is strictly hierarchical, with the operative known as the Supreme Hydra (sometimes addressed as "the Master" or "the Imperial Hydra") chairing a central ruling committee, which in turn oversees the division chiefs who command Hydra's green-garbed rank-and-file operatives. The Supreme Hydra is treated almost as a divine figure, and maintains discipline with harsh efficiency; no matter how loyal a Hydra agent may profess to be, failure is punishable by summary execution, though operatives may redeem themselves by overcoming their would-be replacements in mortal combat. In the words of one of Hydra's hooded Masters, "No member of Hydra lives to fail a second time!" During its early decades, only males could join Hydra, though exceptions were made later for brain-washed S.H.I.E.L.D. agent Laura Brown, daughter of Imperial Hydra Arnold Brown, Madame Hydra (aka Viper), and even Jessica Drew (the original Spider-Woman), who briefly trained with Hydra but dropped out when she proved unable to assassinate Nick Fury. Like the SPECTRE agents from the James Bond milieu, early Hydra operatives addressed each other using code numbers rather than names, and even remained masked in each other's presence.

During its decades of cyclic defeats and comebacks, Hydra's kudzu-like limbs have endured pruning at the hands of many heroes, including Captain Simon Savage and his Leatherneck Raiders, the Avengers, the Black Widow, G. W. Bridge, Captain America, the Fantastic Four, the Hulk, Iron Man, the second Madame Masque, Magneto, the Punisher, the Samurai Squad, Silver Sable, Spider-Man, Jessica Drew (formerly Spider-Woman), the Thunderiders (aka Team America), the Wild Pack, Wolverine, and Professor Charles Xavier. Hydra's power declines sharply following the apparent incineration of Strucker and S.H.I.E.L.D.'s sinking of Hydra Island; Hydra's surviving remnants subsequently remain active—even managing to strike back at S.H.I.E.L.D. hard enough to kill off an entire graduating class of cadets—but are weakened by a series of turf wars involving such villains as the Grim Reaper, Madame Hydra, the Red Skull, and even the gangsters known as Silvermane, the Kingpin, and his son Richard Fisk (aka the Schemer). S.H.I.E.L.D. later takes down most of these factions, while subsidiary groups such as A.I.M. and the Secret Empire (the latter of which had made strong inroads into the U.S. government) become autonomous entities, operating independently of Hydra.

Another worldwide Hydra organization has emerged, though it is doubtful that the late Baron Strucker would recognize much about it other than the traditional green-hooded uniforms. Though still committed to world domination, Hydra has adopted a more corporate style, offering its operatives attractive salaries and generous medical benefits. In the twenty-first century, women now hold influential positions within the organization, agents no longer conceal their names from their colleagues, and Strucker's Hitlerian "leader cult" is no more. The identity of the Supreme Hydra remains a closely guarded secret, however, and failure remains a capital crime.

The current postmodern, boardroom version of Hydra has made little progress toward its goal of world domination, though the free market for terror appears to be profitable enough to support not only Hydra but also competing spin-off groups such as A.I.M., Fenris, and Hydra's breakaway Pearl Sect (youthful "Strucker purists" who debuted in 1995). With Hydra's glory days clearly behind it, it might one day find itself vulnerable to a hostile takeover by Strucker himself, who has refused to remain dead. —*MAM*

Hydro-Man

Spider-Man's hard-to-hold foe, Hydro-Man, dove into the Marvel Universe in the pages of *The Amazing Spider-Man* vol. 1 #212 (1981). The creation of writer Dennis O'Neil and artist John Romita, Jr., this aquatic antagonist is actually Morris "Morrie" Bench, a cargo ship swab who is inadvertently tossed overboard by Spidey during the testing of an experimental generator. One splashy disaster later, Bench undergoes cellular reconstruction and surfaces as Hydro-Man, able to transform himself into living liquid. Predictably peeved at Spidey for the loss of his humanity, Hydro-Man attacks the wall-crawler, turning his arms into geysers and evading Spider-Man's grasp by simply slipping through his fingers. Spidey prevails by splattering Hydro-Man over such a distance that the villain evaporates before being able to reassemble his dispersed molecules.

Drably dressed in a black T-shirt and jeans, Hydro-Man has never risen above B-level status in Spider-Man's rogues' gallery, but his water-based powers have provided some interesting challenges for the hero—traveling through water sources, transforming into tsunamis, and firing himself like a water cannon are among Bench's superpowers. Hydro-Man once teamed with Sandman to tackle Spidey, and has also joined forces with the Frightful

Four and Sinister Syndicate. In addition to numerous encounters with Spider-Man, he has fought the Fantastic Four, Captain America, and other heroes.

Rob Paulsen voiced Hydro-Man on FOX's *Spider-Man* animated series (1994–1998), while Brad Garrett of *Everybody Loves Raymond* fame voiced the villain in a 1995 episode of the *Fantastic Four* cartoon (1994–1996). Hydro-Man is one of the supervillains "seen" in the 3-D "The Amazing Adventures of Spider-Man" ride at Universal Orlando's Marvel Super Hero Island, soaking riders who narrowly elude his grasp. —ME

The Icicle

Dr. Joar Mahkent began his life as a criminal by faking his own death in a story in *All-American Comics* #90 (1947). He then kills the man who tries to steal his "cold ray gun" invention, taking his victim's place after plastic surgery. Beginning a long criminal career calling himself "the Icicle," Mahkent often fought the Golden Age (1938–1954) Green Lantern (Alan Scott), and joined the second Injustice Society. Mahkent, more than most such criminals, frequently worked as a villain for hire, implementing the schemes of those who employed him, implying that his motivation was financial rather than ideological.

Mahkent later retired, but emerged from retirement to fight the reformed Justice Society of America as one of the Crime Champions during the battle that has become known as "Crisis on Earth-One" and "Crisis on Earth-Two" (*Justice League of America* #21–#22, 1963). Finally he returned to his initial career as an inventor and achieved wealth. Mahkent died during the *Crisis on Infinite Earths* storyline of 1986, but his son Cameron assumed the identity of the Icicle, and joined the current Injustice Society (*JSA* #10, 2000), joining forces with Shiv, Geomancer, Count Vertigo, Killer Wasp, Blackbriar Thorn, and Tigress under the leadership of Johnny Sorrow. Though they were

defeated by Wildcat, Johnny Sorrow teleported them away before they could be incarcerated. Given that his own father shunned his condition as an albino, which the younger Mahkent blames on the JSA, his reasons for becoming the Icicle are probably not fully understood, even by him. In the 2000s he appeared in *JSA* #37 (2002), in the continuity titled "Stealing Thunder" by David Goyer & Geoff Jones, Leonard Kirk, and Keith Champagne, in which he was offered the chance to reform, but refused.

The original Icicle wielded his creation, the cold ray gun, which was capable of generating extremely low temperatures with great speed. The current Icicle has somehow become imbued with a biological version of the sub-zero capabilities of his father's cold-ray gun, and can freeze objects with a touch. —MWB

Imperiex

The cosmic destroyer Imperiex tore into the pages of *Superman* vol. 2 #153 (2000) in a story scripted by Jeff Loeb and penciled by Mike McKone. On a quest for ultimate power, this heavily armored monstrosity eradicated countless planets until crossing galaxies with the despot Mongul. When Imperiex destroyed Warworld—Mongul's mega-sized mobile weapon—Mongul's son solicited the aid of one of his father's most power-ful adversaries: Superman.

Superman and Mongul II engaged in a star war with Imperiex's foot soldiers, the Imperiex-Probes. On his unholy mission to reunite the universe in a new Big Bang, Imperiex ordered an army of probes to assault Earth, triggering the Imperiex War (pub-lished by DC Comics in various series under the umbrella title "Our Worlds at War"). Superman united with two of his deadliest foes, Darkseid and Lex Luthor, to stave off Imperiex, but not before the conflict leveled Topeka, Kansas, and Paradise Island. Several heroes—including Aquaman, Max-ima, and Amazonian Queen Hippolyta (Wonder Woman's mother)—were apparently killed, although some have resurfaced. Ultimately, the combined efforts of Superman, et al. defeated Imperiex, who was sent back in time 14 billion years to the original Big Bang, from which Super-man hopes the galaxy monger will never return.

During their struggle, Imperiex provoked an interesting reaction from Superman, who found himself questioning his campaign for truth, justice, and the American way. For a short time the Man of Tomorrow adopted a black background to replace the gold background in his classic "S" chest insignia to commemorate those who died during the Imperiex invasion. —*GM*

The Impossible Man

T he Impossible Man—a not-so-little green man with a cucumber-shaped head—first popped into comics in *Fantastic Four* #11 (1963). Stan Lee and Jack Kirby's story opens with an exuberant extraterrestrial arriving on holiday from the planet Poppup, a hazardous world where its inhabitants rearrange their molecules into any shape imagin-able (making a loud "Pop!" sound in the process). This nameless being ("We Poppupians have no names! We know who we are!") frolics through New York City, impudently morphing to indulge his every whim, breaking laws along the way. The FF responds typically—the Thing punches, the Torch ignites, and Invisible Girl pulls a disappearing

From *Fantastic Four* vol. 1 #11 ©1963 Marvel Comics. ART BY JACK KIRBY AND DICK AYERS.

act—with "the Impossible Man" (as the flustered Thing dubs him) countering their attacks—sprout-ing spikes, turning into a giant water balloon, and clustering the vanishing vixen with flower petals. After perilous transformations into a giant buzz-saw and a bomb elevate the Impossible Man's menace, Mr. Fantastic brainstorms the way to defeat him—by *ignoring* him. Jaded "Impy" rockets away (by becoming a rocket), pledging to tell his fellow Poppupians to avoid the "dull" planet Earth.

Were the FF so lucky. The Impossible Man has occasionally returned over the decades, even demanding that Marvel Comics award him his own title (in *FF* #176, 1976). After Galactus devoured Poppup (welcomed by its dispirited denizens, inci-dentally), the surviving Impy used his race's ability to reproduce by mitosis to fashion a "mate"—the Impossible Woman—followed by offspring. Although the Impossible Man finally got his own comic (two summer one-shots, in 1990 and 1991), to Marvel's credit this oddball character has been used judiciously, never overstaying his welcome. He popped onto the tube for guest shots in the 1978 and 1994 *Fantastic Four* animated programs. —*ME*

The Injustice Society and Beyond

Old habits and inflated egos usually lead supervillains to operate solo, but in *All Star Comics* #37 (1947) a sinful sextet redefined the term "organized crime," pooling their resources to combat DC Comics' Justice Society of America (JSA). Artist Irwin Hasen's cover (which is duplicated inside as the splash page) to this milestone issue depicts a bloodcurdling spectacle: the newly formed *Injustice Society of the World dragging knives through a map of North America, divvying up their shares of the continent, while the mighty members of the JSA are bound helplessly in the background.

Written by Gardner Fox and drawn (in separate chapters) by Hasen, Joe Kubert, Carmine Infantino, and Alex Toth, "The *Injustice Society of the World!*" combines returning JSA rogues the Wizard (acting as team leader), Brain Wave, and Per Degaton with Golden Age (1938–1954) Flash foe the Thinker and Golden Age Green Lantern nemeses the Gambler and Vandal Savage, for an unholy mission intoned by the egg-headed mastermind Brain Wave: "We must vow not to rest until truth and justice are driven from the earth and evil reigns supreme!" Operating from an opulent meeting chamber secreted underground, the Injustice Society manipulates the JSA to split up for individual missions, in which each hero is waylaid by one of the villains. The heroes are placed on trial by their foes, but are reprieved during a surprise attack by Green Lantern.

The Wizard assembled another Injustice Society (alternately called the Injustice "Gang")—the Fiddler, the Icicle, the Sportsmaster, the Huntress I, and the Harlequin—in *All-Star* #41 (1948). The halfhearted-villainess Harlequin joined the group as an undercover operative in an attempt to impress her heartthrob Green Lantern.

When the Justice Society went into limbo at the close of the Golden Age, the Injustice Society retired with them. Once the JSA was reinvented in the Silver Age (1956–1969) as the Justice *League* of America, loosely knit villainous unions became commonplace in the JLA's series, in which insidious plans or happenstance brought together clusters of criminals, only to be vanquished by the League.

Justice League of America #111–#112 (1974) introduced the JLA's version of the Injustice Society: the Injustice Gang of the World, a conglomerate of Silver Age foes: Batman's Poison Ivy and Scarecrow, the Atom's Chronos, the Flash's Mirror Master, Green Lantern's Tattooed Man, and Hawkman's Shadow-Thief. Like the original Injustice Society, the Gang held round-table meetings, in their case under the leadership of the inscrutable villain Libra.

It was not until *Justice League of America* #123–#124 (1975) that the Injustice Society regrouped, in a JLA/JSA crossover. This incarnation was composed of veterans Wizard, Icicle, Sportsmaster, Huntress, and Gambler, plus the Shade and, in a tongue-in-cheek conclusion, *JLA* co-author Cary Bates as the "Plot-Twister." During the mid-1970s revival of *All Star Comics*, the Wizard once again revived the Injustice Society, with the swamp-creature Solomon Grundy lumbering into the roster. The Society returned for the 1980 JLA/JSA team-up, which also involved the New Gods and Darkseid. In *Infinity, Inc.* in 1986, the Wizard pulled out of his hat yet another version of the Injustice Society—Injustice, Unlimited—including several Golden Age villains joined by the Gambler's daughter, the Hazard, and the Huntress' daughter, Artemis.

In the post–*Crisis on Infinite Earths* (1985–1986) DC Comics continuity, iniquitous counterparts to both the Justice League and Society coexist. The first was not to be taken seriously, though: Major Disaster, Multi-Man, Clock King, Cluemaster, Big Sir, and "the Mighty" Bruce comically collided as the Injustice League in *Justice League International* #23 (1989), during the series' light-hearted era by the creative team of Keith Giffen, J. M. DeMatteis, and Kevin Maguire. Lex Luthor organized a new Injustice Gang in *JLA* #9–#10 (1997), a deathly serious incarnation consisting of Dr. Light, the Joker, Mirror Master, and the Ocean Master, plus former hero J'emm, Son of Saturn, under Luthor's control. This group operated from a skull-shaped satellite base constructed by LexCorp's aerospace division and had the stated mission of world domination, but the Joker's lunacy continually interfered with Luthor's plans. Luthor organized the Injustice Gang version 2.0 in 1999, with the Queen Bee abetted by newer JLA menaces the General (formerly Shaggy Man) and Prometheus.

Lastly, the team that started it all, the Injustice Society, was reborn in *JSA* #10 (2000). Coordinated by Johnny Sorrow, its founding lineup was Killer Wasp, the Icicle, Blackbriar Thorn, Geomancer, Count Vertigo, and the Tigress. The "strength in numbers" dictum proved inaccurate when a single superhero—Wildcat—stopped the cadre when they invaded the JSA's headquarters. This group has continued to fight the Justice Society, with Black Adam, the Thinker, and newer characters Shiv and Rival among the ranks.

An animated version of the Injustice Gang, including Luthor, Joker, Cheetah, Star Sapphire, the Ultra-Humanite, Solomon Grundy, and Copperhead, appeared in episodes of the Cartoon Network's *Justice League* (2001–2004). —ME

Intergang

Picture a crime syndicate outfitted with ultra-advanced weaponry. That's exactly what writer/artist Jack Kirby imagined when he created Intergang (originally Inter-Gang) for his unified "Fourth World" titles for DC Comics. The first inkling of this organization's existence is shared in Kirby's *Superman's Pal Jimmy Olsen* #133 (1970), when media mogul Morgan Edge orders a hit on reporter Clark (Superman) Kent, fearing the investigator may be getting too close to Edge's covert criminal connections (the invulnerable Kent is, of course, quite hard to kill). Members of Intergang are first seen in Kirby's *The Forever People* #1

(1971), as a mishmash of Prohibition-style mobsters and uniformed operatives that pack high-tech heat supplied by Darkseid, lord of Apokolips. Readers discover as Kirby's epic unfolds that Intergang is providing Darkseid a toehold on Earth while orchestrating a plethora of street-level and international crimes from its Metropolis headquarters.

Intergang originated in the 1920s under the leadership of Boss Moxie who, like so many other gangsters, was rubbed out by rivals. Morgan Edge revived the organization after Superman established residency in Metropolis, and was succeeded by tough-as-nails Bruno "Ugly" Mannheim; Vincent Edge, Morgan's father, ran Intergang for a while, as did ruthless businessman Lex Luthor in a hostile takeover. Rogue geneticist Dabney Donovan later cloned original Intergang mobsters to run Intergang, including Boss Moxie and strong arms Noose, "Torcher" McGee, and "Machine" Gunn. At various times Intergang has been served by three types of agents—Wall-Crawlers, Shock Troopers, and Gassers—although various superhumans have also been employed by the outfit. Intergang's bizarre *Untouchables*-meets-SPECTRE amalgam has provided a constant threat to Superman and to Metropolis' Special Crimes Unit.

Intergang was spotlighted in the 1997 *Superman* animated episode "Tools of the Trade," written by former Kirby assistant Mark Evanier and starring Bruce Weitz as the voice of Ugly Mannheim. —ME

Iron Maiden

The likeable super-secret superheroes the T.H.U.N.D.E.R. (The Higher United Nations Defense Enforcement Reserves) Agents, who came to prominence during the heyday of comics' Silver Age (1956–1969), encountered their share of adversaries in their efforts to defend the world. Ominously treacherous villains like Andor, Demo, Dynavac, Vibraman, and Dr. Tarantula fought to derail the team's goal of achieving world peace, but one of the Agents' enemies stood above the rest: Iron Maiden.

Iron Maiden originally appeared in the very first issue of *T.H.U.N.D.E.R. Agents* (1965), in a

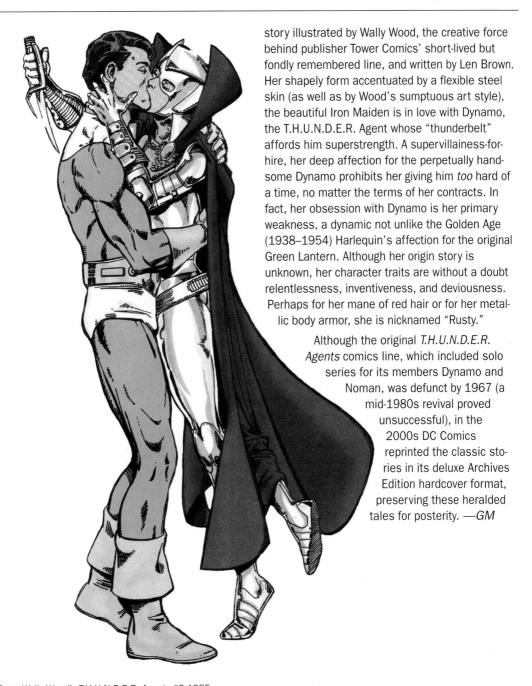

story illustrated by Wally Wood, the creative force behind publisher Tower Comics' short-lived but fondly remembered line, and written by Len Brown. Her shapely form accentuated by a flexible steel skin (as well as by Wood's sumptuous art style), the beautiful Iron Maiden is in love with Dynamo, the T.H.U.N.D.E.R. Agent whose "thunderbelt" affords him superstrength. A supervillainess-for-hire, her deep affection for the perpetually hand-some Dynamo prohibits her giving him *too* hard of a time, no matter the terms of her contracts. In fact, her obsession with Dynamo is her primary weakness, a dynamic not unlike the Golden Age (1938–1954) Harlequin's affection for the original Green Lantern. Although her origin story is unknown, her character traits are without a doubt relentlessness, inventiveness, and deviousness. Perhaps for her mane of red hair or for her metal-lic body armor, she is nicknamed "Rusty."

Although the original *T.H.U.N.D.E.R. Agents* comics line, which included solo series for its members Dynamo and Noman, was defunct by 1967 (a mid-1980s revival proved unsuccessful), in the 2000s DC Comics reprinted the classic sto-ries in its deluxe Archives Edition hardcover format, preserving these heralded tales for posterity. —*GM*

From *Wally Wood's T.H.U.N.D.E.R. Agents* #3 1985.
© & ™ John Carbonaro.
ART BY GEORGE PÉREZ.

Jack O'Lantern

With his "head" ablaze with a traditional jack-o-lantern, the assassin known as Jack O'Lantern has frightened many in the Marvel Universe. The pumpkin-headed terrorist was first introduced in the pages of *Machine Man* #19 (1981) in a story penned by Tom DeFalco and illustrated by Steve Ditko. MIT student Jason Macendale was recruited by the CIA and later became a star marine, but proved too brutal for America's military. He left the service to embark upon a career as an international mercenary.

Underneath Jack O'Lantern's eerie costume—complete with a bulletproof helmet resembling a grotesque carved pumpkin and body armor made of metal-covered, multi-segmented Kevlar panels—Macendale was a highly trained mercenary. His knowledge of hand-to-hand combat, his flexibility, and his martial-arts skills rivaled the most honed Green Beret's. Jack O'Lantern was known for hurling numerous types of custom-designed hand grenades at his targets, including anesthetic, lachrymatory, regurgitant gas, smoke, and concussion grenades. He piloted a glider that resembled a Spanish sombrero, and wore energy blasters on his wrists.

Despite his signature costume and bag of tricks, Jack O'Lantern was defeated by Machine Man, Silver Sable, and Spider-Man on numerous occasions. Growing ever more brutal with each loss, in a lust for power Jack O'Lantern orchestrated the murder of Ned Leeds, whom he believed to be the original Hobgoblin, and assumed that villain's costumed identity, continuing the long and often perplexing lineage of Hobgoblins. In actuality, the original Hobgoblin was Roderick Kingsley, who murdered Macendale years later in the *Spider-Man: Hobgoblin Lives* (1997) series.

Subsequently, yet another Jack O'Lantern appeared, calling himself "Mad Jack." Mad Jack was actually *two* people who took turns using the costume. One was Danny Berkhart, who had once impersonated Spider-Man's enemy, the original Mysterio. The other was Maguire Beck, the original Mysterio's cousin. Eventually Berkhart became a new Mysterio, and Beck became "Mad Jack" full time. —*GM*

Jackal

When writer Stan Lee and artist Steve Ditko introduced Professor Miles Warren in *The Amazing Spider-Man* vol. 1 #31 (1965) as distracted college student Peter (Spider-Man) Parker's biochemistry teacher, they could not have foreseen that a decade later this rather insignificant character would become one of their wall-crawler's most problematic foes.

Fast forward to 1974's *Amazing Spider-Man* #129, valued among comic-book collectors as the first appearance of the Punisher. This tale, by scribe Gerry Conway and artist Ross Andru, also unveils the jeering Jackal, a sprightly figure in a green-furred costume who attacks the web-slinger with drug-tipped and "negatively charged electro-prod" claws, but this new adversary proves just another obstacle for the perennially beleaguered Spidey to overcome.

Yet there was more to the Jackal than met Spider-Man's masked eye. Jackal was actually Professor Warren, who had earlier become infatuated with one of his students, Peter's girlfriend Gwen Stacy. When Gwen was killed the year prior during a battle between the wall-crawler and the Green Goblin, Warren blamed Spidey for her death and targeted the hero out of vengeance.

Warren's preoccupation led to another obsession, this one affecting Spider-Man's scriptwriters: cloning. In a sometimes-confusing 1975 storyline Professor Warren cloned Gwen Stacy, then Spider-Man, and even himself, but each clone appeared to die. Another clone of Warren became the supervillain Carrion in 1978. The Spider-Man clone returned in 1995, surprisingly alive, in a multi-part, reader-disdained storyline, in which questions arose over which Spider-Man was real. Warren genetically altered himself into a mutated Jackal, no longer requiring his gargoyle-like costume, but fell to his doom at the end of this saga. With the impermanence of death in the world of comics, one suspects that the Jackal—or at least another of his clones—may leap into Spider-Man's life once again.

A footnote to the Jackal saga: after Norman Osborn, the original Green Goblin, returned from the dead in 1996, it was revealed via flashbacks that he had manipulated Warren's cloning experiments. —*ME*

The Jester

The Jester is accustomed to bad reviews. First seen in Marvel Comics' *Daredevil* vol. 1 #42

Daredevil vol. 1 #45 ©1968 Marvel Comics.
COVER ART BY GENE COLAN AND FRANK GIACOIA (PHOTO BACKGROUND).

(1968), written by Stan Lee and drawn by Gene Colan, the Jester is secretly thespian Jonathan Powers, whose critically panned stage turn as Cyrano de Bergerac draws the final curtain after a dismal opening-night performance. After a brief stint as a costumed clown on a children's television show, Powers, whose ego far outweighs his talent, hogs the crime spotlight as the hateful harlequin, the Jester. Pummeled by the Jester's pouch of perilous playthings—including a bola yo-yo, knockout gas-spraying flying discs, exploding bouncing balls, a high-voltage artificial hand, and deadly jacks—Daredevil discovers that this mirthful menace is no laughing matter.

Some comics readers have dismissed the Jester as a Joker rip-off. Aside from their visual similarities (and the noir-ish milieus of their adversaries), these criminal clowns share little in common. The Joker's crimes are often rooted in madness, whereas the Jester's vendettas against Daredevil display methodical cunning. His obsession with image has led the Jester to malign Daredevil's reputation through orchestrated media manipulation, and when that fails, the Jester has been known to threaten the Man without Fear with his fencing and gymnastic expertise. Although he has teamed with Daredevil foes Mr. Hyde and Cobra as the Trio of Doom, the Jester is most effective when working alone, as Daredevil has too frequently discovered over the years.

This was the second Marvel supervillain to use the name "Jester," the first being an unrelated character in *Captain America* #65 (1948). Neither of Marvel's Jesters should be confused with the Golden Age (1938–1954) super*hero* of the same name, seen in issues #22–#85 of *Smash Comics*. —ME

Joe Chill

While he may lack the powers, weapons, and/or worldview of the archetypal supervillain, Joe Chill committed one of the most the infamous crimes in the history of popular fiction: the murders of Thomas and Martha Wayne, which their son Bruce avenged by devoting his life to warring against wrongdoers as Batman.

Chill was a nameless mugger with an itchy trigger finger in the earliest texts relating Batman's origin, but was identified in *Batman* #47 (1948) when the Caped Crusader connected Chill to his parents' unsolved murders. A dramatic scene in that Bill Finger/Bob Kane story featured a desperate Batman revealing his Wayne identity to a panicky Chill. Later in that tale Chill met his demise by his own henchmen once they discovered that their boss had "created" their cowled enemy.

Joe Chill has since wandered in and out of the perennially evolving Batman mythos. A 1956 tale portrayed him as a hitman masquerading as a mugger to veil the identity of the crime boss that ordered the Waynes' deaths, and Mike W. Barr and Todd McFarlane presented Chill as Batman's improbable partner in a struggle with a masked vigilante called the Reaper in 1987's "Batman: Year Two" storyline.

Realizing that the apprehension or demise of Joe Chill negates the necessity of Bruce Wayne's continued mission as Batman, DC Comics has, in twenty-first-century Batman continuity, eliminated references to Chill by name, preferring to keep the killer of Wayne's parents unknown. Conversely, the theatrical blockbuster *Batman Begins* (2005) featured Chill (actor Richard Brake) as the Waynes' assassin, later involving him in the film as a mob informant. —ME

Johnny Bates

Toward the end of the Golden Age of comics (1938–1954), the company now called DC Comics sued its rival, Fawcett Publications, claiming that the original Captain Marvel was an imitation of Superman. In 1953 Fawcett settled the suit, agreeing to stop publishing Captain Marvel stories.

This left the company L. Miller & Sons, which had been republishing *Captain Marvel* for the British market, in a bind. So writer/artist Mick Anglo created a similar hero, Mickey Moran, alias Marvelman. Taking the place of Captain Marvel's superpowered sister Mary was Kid Marvelman, who debuted in *Marvelman* #101 (1955). He was really a nine-year-old boy, Johnny Bates, who, upon saying Marvelman's name, gained superhuman strength and speed, near-invulnerability, and the power to fly. The original *Marvelman* series ended in 1963.

In 1982 British comics writer Alan Moore introduced a darker, revisionist version of *Marvelman* in the magazine *Warrior*. When the series was published in the United States, Moore changed the title to *Miracleman* due to a trademark dispute with Marvel Comics. In Moore's version, Bates had remained in his superhuman form for decades, growing into an adult who became the wealthy president of an electronics company. Bates had also gone mad with power and, when Miracleman returned, attempted to destroy him. Bates would have succeeded, had he not inadvertently said Miracleman's name, thereby reverting to his original form, a good-hearted human boy.

Later, while being raped by a bully, the boy Bates desperately transformed back into his evil superpowered form. The insane adult Bates destroyed half of London and murdered 40,000 people. One of Miracleman's allies, the alien Warpsmiths, teleported objects into Bates' body. To escape the intense pain, Bates returned to his innocent human form, and Miracleman sorrowfully killed the boy to ensure he would never again revert to his evil adult persona. —*PS*

Johnny Sorrow

In the days of World War II, Jonathan "Johnny" Sorrow—created by writer Geoff Johns and artist Stephen Sadowski for *Secret Origins of Super-Villains 80-Page Giant* #1 (1999)—was a two-bit crook. Despite his insignificant status, he invented an amazing gadget that allowed him to flit in and out of reality. When the device overloads due to an attack by Sand—a member of the Modern Age Justice Society of America (JSA) and former sidekick to the original Sandman—Sorrow gets sucked into a strange nether dimension called the Subtle Realms. The Realms' inhabitants scheme to use Sorrow as an intermediary into this earthly plane, and disfigure Sorrow's face—which is invisible on the comic-book page—so that anyone who looks upon him dies instantly.

Devilishly dapper in his red suit and gloves, Johnny Sorrow is reminiscent of the classic interpretation of the Invisible Man, but Sorrow's intangible form is hidden behind a red mask instead of bandages. His first attempt to allow the Subtle Realms' god, the King of Tears, to break through into humankind's world was thwarted by the JSA and the Spectre. That didn't stop Sorrow from returning as the brains behind the new Injustice Society of America, sending a team of villains—including Count Vertigo, Tigress, Icicle III, Blackbriar Thorn, Killer Wasp, and Geomancer—into battle against the hero Wildcat while he stole the King of Tears from JSA headquarters. Another effort to unleash the King was opposed by the JSA, who sent Sorrow back to the netherworld.

Sorrow later returned and teamed with Despero against the combined forces of the Justice League of America and the JSA. Whenever Johnny Sorrow shows his face, the JSA can count on trouble. —*GM*

The Joker

Call him what you will—the Clown Prince of Crime, the Harlequin of Hate, the Ace of Knaves, or even "Mr. J"—but Batman's arch-foe the Joker is one of the most recognizable of all supervillains. His chalk-white skin, green hair, rouge-red lips, and toothy, macabre smile are etched into infamy, evoking the clown fears that have traumatized countless children and have lingered in the nightmares of many adults.

When the Joker debuted in *Batman* #1 (1940), he appeared without the benefit of the customary device of an origin, heightening his mystique. In an untitled tale he interrupts a Gotham City radio broadcast to predict in "a toneless voice" the murder of millionaire Henry Claridge and the theft of his priceless Claridge Diamond, to occur at midnight. Despite a police cordon, a panicky Claridge dies laughing at the stroke of twelve, a "repellant, ghastly grin" creeping across his lifeless face. This is calling card of the Joker, the insane serial killer in a purple zoot suit who uses a toxin to cause his victims to, in the words of Jack Nicholson, who played the villain in director Tim Burton's live-action *Batman* (1989), "go with a smile." His other trademark, a Joker playing card, is established in this first tale, luring Batman and Robin onto the Harlequin of Hate's trail. Once cornered, the crackpot, crackshot Joker attempts to ventilate Batman's chest, which is protected by a bulletproof vest, and winds up behind bars, where he diabolically cackles that he will have the last laugh upon his new foe. "The Joker Returns" also appeared in that very multi-story issue, three tales later, and in it he's back to his murderous tricks, wielding an ax at Batman; the Joker almost dies as a knife he attempts to plunge into the hero's chest winds up in his own.

Opposite: Original cover art to *BACK ISSUE* #3 (TwoMorrows Publications, 2004). The Joker ©2004 DC Comics.
ART BY BRIAN BOLLAND.

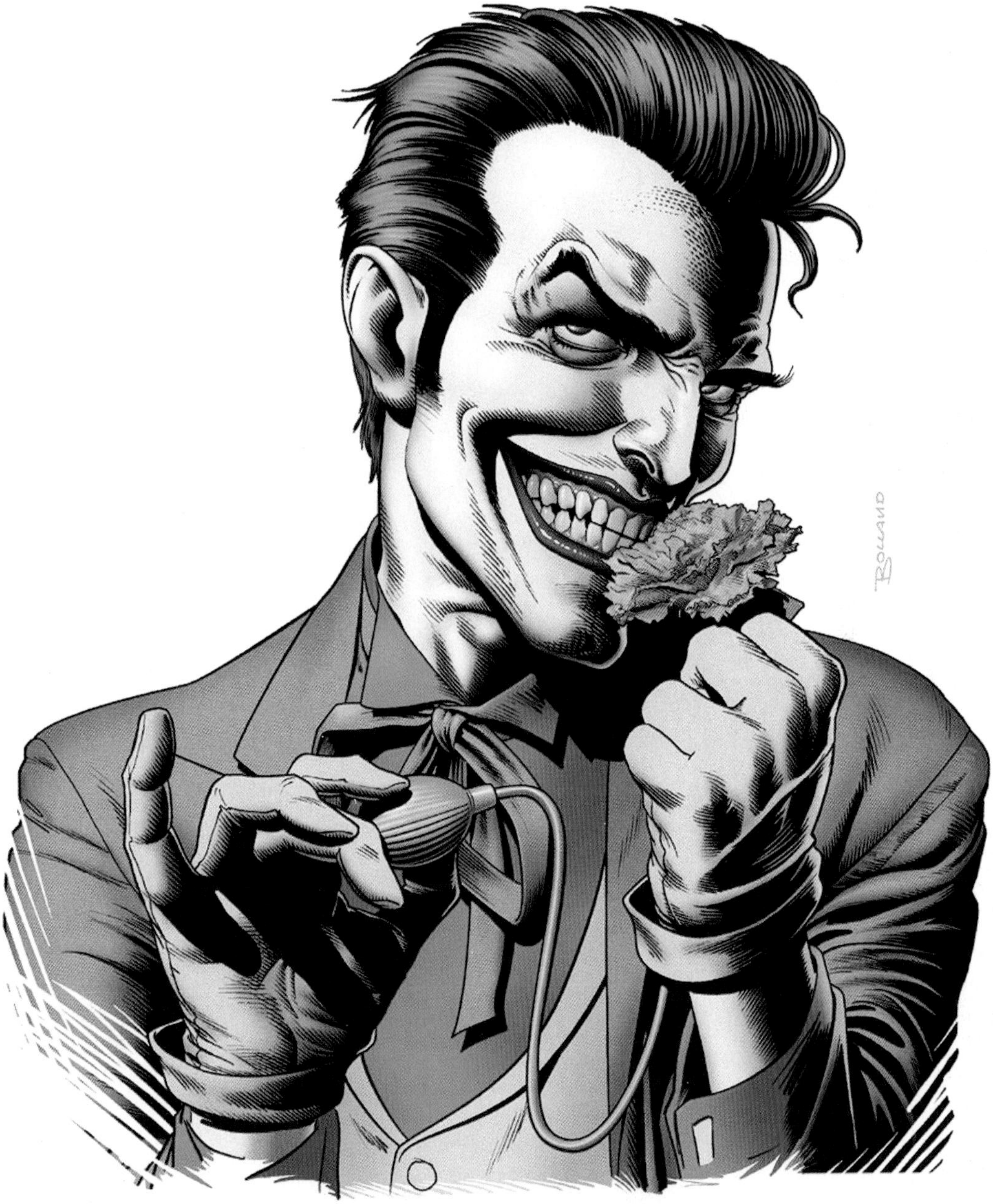
BOLLAND

The Joker's chilling *Batman* #1 premiere succeeded in scaring DC Comics' editors as well as its readers, as the character's homicidal tendencies were jettisoned for practical joke-laced crimes. The Joker became the chaos to the Caped Crusader's order, worming his way into story after story, and soon onto the covers of *Batman* and *Detective Comics* themselves, which had, in Batman and Robin's earliest outings, usually featured generic poses of the heroes rather than story-specific teasers (artist Fred Ray's original cover art to 1942's *Batman* #11, featuring the Joker, fetched an astounding $195,500 in an August 2005 auction from Dallas, Texas' Heritage Comics). He was also seen in newspapers during the mid-1940s, in the *Batman* syndicated strip. By the time "The Joker Follows Suit" was published in *Batman* #37 (1946), the Clown Prince of Crime had been firmly established as Batman's demented doppelgänger, tooling around Gotham around in his Jokermobile, taking to the skies in his Jokergyro, and illuminating the night with his Joker Signal, each dastardly device bearing his smirking face.

The origin of that famous face is marred by controversy, as if the madcap Bat-foe himself orchestrated a cruel joke to disorient historians and fans. Artist Jerry Robinson, originally the assistant to Batman's credited creator and first artist, Bob Kane, is said to have created the Joker, drawing from the obvious playing-card inspiration for the arch-foe's look. Conversely, Kane claimed authorship, in collaboration with Batman's unsung champion, writer Bill Finger. Finger's son Fred cited yet another different source for the Joker's visage: a drawing of a man with a ridiculously wide grin that appeared on advertisements for "the funny place," George C. Tilyou's Steeplechase attraction at Coney Island. Penciler Kane and inker Robinson concurred that when drawing the Joker in *Batman* #1, they based the villain's looks on stills from the silent movie *The Man Who Laughs* (1928), provided to them by Finger, the writer of the first Joker tale. In that film, actor Conrad Veidt portrayed Gwynplaine, a disfigured, rictus-faced character.

The Joker was finally awarded an origin ... of sorts ... in "The Man Behind the Red Hood" in *Detective* #168 (1951). A tuxedoed thief whose features are hidden behind a crimson cowl returned, having evaded Batman early in the hero's crime-fighting career. Batman discovered that the Red Hood was actually the Joker, who, in his original Red Hood adventure, escaped from Batman by swimming through a "pool of chemical wastes" that permanently altered his appearance. His original face was never shown, nor was he named. (A new Red Hood has appeared in 2000s *Batman* continuity.)

Often aided by hapless goons and headquartering from abandoned amusement parks or reconfigured buildings (his lair in some texts has been called his Ha-Ha-Hacienda, even bearing his likeness and deathtraps for uninvited guests), the Joker continued to laugh his way through zany capers throughout the 1950s and into the 1960s, donning his own utility belt, filming his own movies, starting a newspaper, launching a "Crime-of-the-Month Club," and joining forces with Lex Luthor, schemes intended to line his pockets and pester Batman and Robin (and sometimes Superman). While the murderous Joker of *Batman* #1 was a distant memory, his arsenal was still quite hazardous, from electric joy buzzers to acid-spraying boutonnières to exploding vest buttons. During this era, artist Dick Sprang's manic interpretation of the Joker stood out as the villain's signature look.

After editor Julius Schwartz retooled Batman with an updated "new look" in 1964, the Joker flounced into the mainstream as the third villain to be introduced to a television audience in ABC's live-action *Batman* (1966–1968), with screen Latin lover Cesar Romero first appearing as the villain in the two-part episodes "The Joker Is Wild" and "Batman Is Riled" (original airdates: January 22 and 23, 1966). "Jose Ferrer was my first choice for the Joker," series producer William Dozier revealed in a 1986 interview; actor Gig Young was also considered. Ferrer reportedly regretted passing on the role after the show became a runaway success (his son, actor Miguel Ferrer, voiced DC Comics supervillain the Weather Wizard on the animated program *Superman*, 1996–2000). In retrospect, Dozier was ecstatic over the giggling foolishness his old friend

As the Joker, Cesar Romero (with visible mustache) laughed his way through *Batman*'s three TV seasons and one theatrical movie.

ders' mistaken impression that the Joker was a criminal in makeup), an ultra-rare hand puppet available only in a gift set, a mini-comic book distributed in boxes of Pop Tarts, and a paperback collection of his 1950s adventures from Signet Books (*Batman vs. the Joker*, 1966). The Joker was seen in various DC titles, from his home turf of *Batman* and *Detective* to guest shots in other series, and in Batman's syndicated newspaper strip.

After *Batman*'s TV cancellation, the Joker maintained a television presence in animation on CBS's *The Batman/Superman Hour* (1968–1969) and *The Adventures of Batman and Robin* (1969–1970); ABC's *The New Scooby-Doo Movies* (1972–1974); and CBS's *The New Adventures of Batman* (1977–1978). Mego produced Joker action figures in a variety of sizes during the 1970s.

Batman comic books returned the hero to his darker, gothic roots in the early 1970s, and after a few dormant years while the Dark Knight was fighting ghosts and gangsters, "The Joker's Five-Way Revenge" in *Batman* #251 (1973), by writer Denny O'Neil and artist Neal Adams, took the Harlequin of Hate back to square one: serial killer. "Though I wasn't aware of it at the time," O'Neil recounted in a 2004 *BACK ISSUE* interview, "I now know that the Joker is probably the best embodiment of the trickster motif in all of modern fiction, though Hannibal Lecter might be a close second." This was a trickster embodiment with a body count, as the Joker offed his enemies with wild abandon, and came close to doing the same to Batman, even to artist Adams' surprise. "Yes, I wanted to do the Joker, and yes, I wanted him to be bad, but Denny made him real bad," the artist told *BACK ISSUE*. But Adams ultimately jibed

"Butch" Romero brought to the Joker, never regretting going with his second choice: "I was thinking [Ferrer] may have taken himself a little too seriously as an actor to do that." While chuckling through numerous episodes and the 1966 *Batman* spin-off theatrical movie, Romero as the Joker took one thing very seriously—his mustache, which he never shaved for the role, his lip hair visible under the heavy Joker greasepaint.

The Joker was close under Batman's merchandising wing during this era of "Batmania," appearing on Batman lunchboxes, plastic coins, figurines, Topps trading cards (a 1966 series of painted Batman cards featured the Joker with Caucasian ears, artists Bob Powell and Norman Saunwith O'Neil's back-to-brutal-basics approach, elongating the Joker's face to a look that, despite minor variations reflecting artistic preferences, remains canonical in the twenty-first century.

The Joker's rebirth in *Batman* #251 reignited his comics career. He received his own title, *The Joker* (1975–1976), a series that ran out of steam after nine issues as the governing Comics Code Authority required the villain to be apprehended at each issue's end; he also "teamed" with Batman in several issues of *The Brave and the Bold*. Writer Steve Englehart, joined by artist Marshall Rogers, explored the Joker's craziness in *Detective* #475–#476 (1978), in which the Joker ludicrously attempted to copyright freakish "laughing fish" contaminated by his smile toxins. "My sense of it was if you really got to the essence of the Joker, he still had another dimension to go, which was to become insane," Englehart remarked to *BACK ISSUE* in 2004. (The popular Englehart/Rogers team reunited for a 2005 miniseries titled *Batman: Dark Detective*, featuring the Joker's gubernatorial campaign with his persuasive campaign slogan, "Vote for me—or I'll kill you!")

The next milestone in the Joker's career was *Batman: The Dark Knight Returns* (1986), writer/artist Frank Miller's noncontinuity, futuristic vision of a fiftyish Batman grudgingly coming out of retirement to battle, among other things, the Joker. Miller's Joker added a new element to the villain's dichotomous relationship with Batman: homoeroticism, redefining the reasons for the Crime Clown's fixation upon his foe.

Alan Moore and Brian Bolland's 1988 graphic novel *Batman: The Killing Joke*, which *is* part of DC's continuity, built upon the classic "Red Hood" tale by showing the face behind the hood, a nameless working stiff with stand-up comedy aspirations who turned to crime to support his pregnant wife, who died in the story. Since this is an origin told by the Joker, its legitimacy remains uncertain, although events taking place in *Batman: Gotham Knights* #54 (2004) suggest that for once the Joker might not have been pulling readers' legs. *The Killing Joke* is best known for the Joker's kidnapping of Commissioner James Gordon and his debasement and shooting of Gordon's daughter Barbara (the for-

mer Batgirl), which left her confined to a wheelchair. The next year the Joker committed the iniquitous act of killing Jason Todd, the second Robin the Boy Wonder, in the storyline "A Death in the Family" (*Batman* #426–#429, 1989), an execution sanctioned by DC readers who voted for Todd to die in a rather morbid phone-in publicity stunt.

Also that year, the Joker returned to movie houses in the blockbuster *Batman* (1989), with Jack Nicholson cast as mobster Jack Napier, who, while on the lam from the Dark Knight, fell into a vat of chemicals and crawled out of a sewer having been transformed into the Joker. The movie further linked the Joker to Batman by revealing that Napier was the gunman who murdered young Bruce Wayne's parents before the boy's eyes, the tragedy which led him toward his Batman career. Nicholson's Joker, while at times hamfisted with screentime, occasionally displayed Englehart-like moments of mania (not entirely surprising since Englehart was involved with early treatments of the film), and the Joker's grin-inducing toxin received a name, "Smilex" (used for the movie only; in comic books, it is called his "Joker Venom"). Nicholson returned the Joker to merchandising ubiquity: board games, video games, action figures, T-shirts, and a rubber Joker Halloween mask were among the many items bearing his facepainted likeness. Bantam's *The Further Adventures of the Joker*, a collection of prose short stories, was published in early 1990.

The 1990s and 2000s have anchored the Joker's position as a pop-culture figure. He has continued to run amok throughout the DC Universe, becoming more deranged each time he is liberated from his cell in Arkham Asylum. He escaped a death sentence in the graphic novel *The Joker: The Devil's Advocate* (1996), joined the Injustice Gang and fought the JLA in the late 1990s, co-starred with Dark Horse Comics' own grinning goofball in the 2000 *Joker/Mask* crossover, and "Jokerized" criminals in his own image when thinking he was about to die in the miniseries *Joker: Last Laugh* (2001). Despite his gargantuan smile, it is no laughing matter when the Joker shows up, brandishing his pistol that fires a "BANG!" flag (and sometimes spears) or a smiley-face bomb brimming with his deadly Joker Venom.

The Joker has kept television viewers enthralled since 1992. Mark Hamill, having brought another DC supervillain, the Trickster, to life in two episodes of the live-action series *The Flash* (1990–1991), voiced the Joker in *Batman: The Animated Series* (*BTAS*) (1992–1995) and in appearances in *Superman* (1996–2000), *The Adventures of Batman & Robin* (1997–1999), *Static Shock* (2000–2004), the made-for-video animated movie *Batman Beyond: Return of the Joker* (2000), and *Justice League* (2001–2004). Hamill's vocalization became so heavily identified with the Joker that he was hired to provide the villain's voice for the first episode of the live-action *Birds of Prey* (2002–2003) and received an outpouring of fan support to play the Joker in a forthcoming sequel to the live-action box-office hit *Batman Begins* (2005). A Joker playing card left behind at the scene of a crime in *Batman Begins*' epilogue suggested the Clown Prince of Crime's future appearance, and a "casting game" swept fandom and the Internet, with Johnny Depp, Sean Penn, Steve Carell, and Hamill among the names bandied about as Joker candidates.

Hamill's indirect contribution to the Joker canon was the villain's gun moll, Harley Quinn (whose pet names for the Joker are "Puddin'" and "Mr. J."), introduced on *BTAS* and eventually proving so popular that she was incorporated into DC Comics continuity. *The Batman* (2004–present), the animated relaunch of the Batman concept, has introduced a revamped, wild-haired, straight-jacketed martial artist Joker played by Kevin Michael Richardson. A collector could easily fill a bookcase with the Joker action figures and accessories (such as Jokermobiles) produced since the early 1990s to tie in to the various animated and comic-book interpretations of the villain, incluidng a 2005 Red Hood figure, with a removable hood exposing the Joker's sneering face. —*ME*

Judge Death

J udge Dredd, one of comics' most ruthless lawmen and star of the British cult sci-fi comic *2000 AD*, has nothing to fear as judge, jury, and executioner of the post-apocalyptic metropolis

THE CHRONICLES OF **JUDGE DREDD** by John Wagner and Brian Bolland

The Chronicles of Judge Dredd #1 1984. ™ & © Rebellion A/S. COVER ART BY BRIAN BOLLAND.

Mega-City One—except for demented monstrosities like Judge Death.

The brainchild of writer John Wagner and artist Brian Bolland, Judge Death is a supernatural ghoul from another dimension who has come to wreck havoc on Mega-City One. Witnessing the truism that all crime is committed by the living, Judge Death reasoned that life itself is a crime, so he embarked on a personal mission of destroying all life. As such, this super-fiend reaches into the chests of his victims to extract their heart. Although Dredd is forever hunting his rival, Judge Death cannot be killed by ordinary means; once his physical body is destroyed, his spirit moves on to possess another human being. Judge Death frequently operates with his equally horrific brothers Judge Fear, Judge Fire, and Judge Mortis.

Judge Death first appeared in a 1980 issue of *2000 AD*, but has regularly confronted his nemesis in his quest to turn the dystopian Meta-City into a wasteland. Since Dredd's inception in 1977, the character has inspired a *Daily Star* newspaper strip, his own annuals and specials, a monthly "megazine," and a 1995 live-action motion picture (starring Sylvester Stallone in the lead role), the majority of which have included appearances by Judge Death. Dredd and Death are the subjects of several computer games and a host of assorted merchandise. In 2005, the adversaries starred in the DC miniseries *Judge Dredd: Dredd vs. Death.* —GM

Judge Doom

In the spirit of an innovative film comes an innovative villain. Judge Doom (aka Baron von Rotton) is the nemesis of Roger Rabbit, the star of producer Steven Spielberg's four-time Academy Award–winning film *Who Framed Roger Rabbit* (1988), noted in film history for its interaction between live action and animated characters (a film technique that had been previously used, but never so efficiently) and its unprecedented portrayal of Looney Tunes and Disney characters together on one screen.

In a surrealistic noir-esque world of 1947 Los Angeles, where human beings and "Toons" live side by side, Judge Doom (wonderfully portrayed by Christopher Lloyd) is the Nazi-like policer of Toontown, a wacky, animated outcast suburb of Hollywood where all the animated film stars reside. With his self-stated goal to "rein in the insanity" of a world filled with unpredictable cartoon characters, Judge Doom rules Toontown with an iron first, subjecting random, irreverent Toons to "the dip," an oozing green, acid-like liquid composed of turpentine, acetone, and benzene. In torturous fashion, the dip dissolves the Toons in a manner reminiscent of real-life products that were used to clean animation cels in the 1930s and 1940s. Doom is accompanied by his henchmen, the Weasels, scoundrel Toons that aid the villain in his dastardly deeds.

The bespectacled, black-clothed Judge Doom, who shuffles along using a walking stick, suspects zany Maroon Cartoon Studios actor Roger Rabbit (voiced by Charles Fleischer) of the murder of Acme Novelty Co. founder and owner of Toontown, Marvin Acme. Framed for the homicide, Roger solicits the help of boozing private eye Eddie Valiant (Bob Hoskins) to clear his name. Doom's plan of bringing freeways to Los Angeles, thereby bankrupting the existing Pacific & Electric Red Car public transport electric-trolley system (a nod to a real-life scandal), is slowly revealed.

In order to execute his plan, Doom creates an enormous Dip Machine, with "5,000 gallons of heated dip, pumped at enormous velocity through a pressurized water cannon," in an effort to erase Toontown in a matter of minutes. In the film's ending, Doom's true identity as a Toon is revealed and he meets his appropriate death via the dip.

Sprinkled with Looney Tunes–like gags, gadgets, and fight scenes and a femme fatale bar none in the form of celluloid human Jessica Rabbit, *Roger Rabbit* remains an animation classic that celebrates the nuances of the noir thriller genre. —GM

Juggernaut

Sibling rivalry is the source of the Juggernaut's loathing of the X-Men's mentor, Professor Charles Xavier, aka Professor X. And what better name for a hate-filled brother than "Cain"?

Cain Marko, the embittered "irresistible force" under the bullet-helmeted armor of the Juggernaut, plowed into the Marvel Universe in *X-Men* vol. 1 #12 (1965), courtesy of scribe Stan Lee and artist Jack Kirby. Young Cain and Charles become stepbrothers upon the marriage of Kurt Marko and the widowed Sharon Xavier. The undisciplined Cain deeply resents Charles' intellectual superiority and burgeoning telepathy and maltreats him, earning his father's ire. Later, as young men, the stepbrothers are in military service together (the Korean War in the original text, but later retroactively adjusted to more recent conflicts), where Cain deserts under fire, seeking shelter in a hidden temple. There he uncovers an uncanny red ruby, and receives remarkable power upon reading aloud its inscription: "Whosoever touches this gem shall be granted the power of the Crimson Bands of Cyttorak! Henceforth, you who read these words shall become … forevermore … a human juggernaut!"

Imbued with superhuman strength, limitless stamina, and the ability to steamroll at an unstoppable pace, the Juggernaut for years has fought Professor X and his mutant crusaders, the X-Men. His mystical armor's helmet protected him from mental attacks (although the psychic villain Onslaught has penetrated his defenses), and a self-generated force field further buffered him. A belligerent bully, Marko made few friends, although he did for some time partner with Black Tom Cassidy, once even sharing his Cyttorak-spawned power with him; as a duo, they held the World Trade Center hostage (*X-Force* #2–#3, 1991).

One of Marvel's most popular supervillains, the obdurate Juggernaut has barreled through conflicts with almost every Marvel superhero, including Dr. Strange, the Beast, the Hulk, Thor, the Avengers, and Spider-Man—he also went head-to-head with Superman in 1996's *Marvel vs. DC* crossover. *Juggernaut* one-shots were published in 1997 and 1999, and the twelve-issue *J2* series (1998–1999), part of the short-lived, alternate-future "MC2" line, starred Marko's son. Marko's powers were diminished by his patron god Cyttorak in the 1999 "The Eighth Day" storyline, and he has since displayed a heretofore unseen kinder side, even allying with the X-Men and New Excalibur. While the Juggernaut is one of the few X-Men villains who is not a mutant, his "Ultimate" counterpart in Marvel's parallel *Ultimate X-Men* continuity (2001–present) is a survivor of the Weapon X program.

The Juggernaut is no stranger to animated television. He has appeared in the cartoons *Spider-Man and His Amazing Friends* (1981–1986), *X-Men* (1992–1997), *Fantastic Four* (1994–1996), and *X-Men: Evolution* (2000–2003), with scads of video-game and action-figure appearances tying in to those series and to the comics. Soccer jock-turned-movie star Vinnie Jones donned a latex suit—making him tower over his fellow cast members at a whopping 7 feet!—to play the Juggernaut in director Brett Ratner's live-action blockbuster, *X-Men: The Last Stand* (2006). —*ME*

Sinister Siblings

Some superpowered siblings like Juggernaut and Professor X are at odds, but others find supervillainy a family activity:

- **Night and Fog**, or "Nacht und Nebel," were sister-brother Nazis introduced in the 1980s in DC's *All-Star Squadron*, a series set during World War II. Night's hair emitted pitch-black darkness, while Fog could become a living mist.

- **Tweedledee and Tweedledum**, Deever and Dumfree Tweed, might as well have been brothers, as these roly-poly criminal cousins are identical—and equally problematic to Batman since their 1943 debut.

- **The Terror Twins**, Gilbert and Rudy Maroni, were skull-masked teen musicians whose bongo bombs and laser-firing guitars sent Gold Key Comics' the Owl ducking for cover in 1968.

- **Dormammu and his sister Umar** have often teamed to fight Marvel's Sorcerer Supreme Dr. Strange, while DC's Lord Satanus and Blaze, evil offspring of the benevolent wizard Shazam, have imperiled the magic-vulnerable Superman upon occasion.

- **The Brothers Grimm**, Percy and Barton Grimes, donned skeleton-faced supernatural costumes in 1984 and acquired the powers to create storybook-based items out of thin air, attacking Iron Man with nasty novelties like acidic eggs.

- **Nightslayer (aka Night-Thief) and Nocturna** were intimate stepsiblings who battled Batman in the 1980s. Also harmonious are that persuasive brother-sister pair from Apokolips, Glorious Godfrey and Amazing Grace, two of Darkseid's Elite.

- **Bug and Byte**, teens Barney and Blythe Bonner, became enemies of Firestorm in 1984 when an accident that should have electrocuted them instead gave them superpowers: Bug interfaces with computers, while Byte becomes living electricity.

- **Thunder and Lightning**, telepathically linked Vietnamese-American brothers Gan and Tavis with unmanageable weather powers, stormed into the Teen Titans' lives in the early 1980s, and in the 2000s were seen on the Titans' animated TV show.

Kalibak

K alibak the Cruel, the loutish, superstrong savage with the looks of a caveman and the temperament of a barroom brawler, would be any family's black sheep were his father not the merciless Darkseid. Premiering in writer/artist Jack Kirby's *The New Gods* vol. 1 #1 (1971), Darkseid's firstborn is shipped away during his youth to be trained as a warrior after his mother, Suli, is slain by the executive decree of his grandmother, Queen Heggra. Under the tutelage of Darkseid's soldiers, Kalibak matures into the most aggressive and unbeatable bruiser on the wretched planet Apokolips, a reputation that spreads across the galaxy.

Inheriting his father's near-omnipotence but not his intelligence, the obtuse Kalibak deeply resents his heroic half-brother Orion, whom Darkseid favors. He plotted unsuccessfully to murder his sibling, being killed by his father for his perfidy. Darkseid later revived Kalibak, and the barbarous scion remains unshakably faithful to his father, wielding his force-bolt-firing Beta Club in Darkseid's name. Among his few intergalactic enemies who have survived his wrath is Earth's mightiest protector, Superman. Despite his truculence and repugnant form, Kalibak is essentially an insecure "child" aching for a love his soulless father can never provide.

Kalibak appeared on television in the animated series *The Super Powers Team: Galactic Guardians* (1986–1987), *Superman* (1996–2000), *Justice League* (2001–2004), and *Justice League Unlimited* (2004–present). In 1985 Kenner manufactured a Kalibak Super Powers action figure with an accompanying toy vehicle, the rock-catapulting "Kalibak Boulder Bomber." —ME

Kang the Conqueror

L ike many who are discontent with their lot in life, Kang always felt that he had been born in the wrong era. But unlike most people, he had the means to do something about it. The creation of Marvel Comics' prime creative movers Stan Lee and Jack Kirby (*Avengers* vol. 1 #8, 1964), Kang has evolved through an incredibly complex history, owing to his endless peregrinations through the timestream. A possible descendant of both Nathaniel Richards (the father of Mr. Fantastic) and Victor von Doom (whose all-concealing Dr. Doom armor may have inspired Kang's own blue-masked costume) from Earth's thirty-first century, Kang happens upon a functioning time machine and uses it to abandon his own peaceful, prosper-

From *The Avengers* vol. 1 #8 ©1964 Marvel Comics.
ART BY JACK KIRBY AND DICK AYERS.

ous era in favor of an adventurous past that he had always romanticized.

After raiding other eras for weapons and high technology, Kang entered the fortieth century—a time suffering from an evident dearth of superhuman protectors—and subjugated the human race there (as revealed in the "Citizen Kang" saga, serialized in Marvel's 1992 annuals). Still restless, Kang became the ruler of Egypt in 2950 BC, dubbing himself Rama-Tut. Rama-Tut's subsequent defeats at the hands of the Fantastic Four led to a fixation on the late twentieth and early twenty-first centuries, which he invaded and attempted to rule as "Kang the First," only to be stopped by the Avengers, whom he subsequently tried—and failed—to erase from history by using the Hulk to alter the events circa World War I.

Kang's machinations, which mostly centered around seizing power in the present era—as well as restoring life to his beloved, the mortally wounded thirty-first-century Princess Ravonna (aka Terminatrix), and stealing the vast energies of the cosmic being known as the Celestial Madonna—were foiled not only by various configurations of the Avengers, but also, at least in part, by Spider-Man, the Human Torch, and the Inhumans. During a later bid for revenge against the Avengers, and in

the grand melodramatic tradition of comic-book arch-nemeses, Kang died—but only apparently—in *Avengers* vol. 1 #142–#143 (1975–1976).

Throughout the 1970s Kang's existence was marked by a confusing yet compelling succession of multiple identities, the seeds of which were sown early on by writer Roy Thomas, who revealed that the supervillain known as the Scarlet Centurion—who briefly brought to fruition Kang's plans to seize control of Earth—was actually an early version of Kang (*Avengers Annual* vol. 1 #2, 1968). Kang experienced a further renaissance of convolution and complexity under the creative guidance of writer Steve Englehart, who conceived the notion that Kang and Rama-Tut (heretofore separate Lee-Kirby villains) were, in fact, one and the same; Englehart added even greater depth to Kang/Rama-Tut during this period by revealing that Kang will become the evil Immortus (created by Lee and Kirby and debuted in *Avengers* vol. 1 #10, 1964) in his dotage, by which time he will live as an isolated hermit, à la Shakespeare's Prospero, ruling the extradimensional realm known as Limbo, "where things never change." Like Billy Pilgrim, the protagonist of Kurt Vonnegut, Jr.'s novel *Slaughterhouse-Five* (1969), Kang seems to experience his days in almost random order.

By the mid-1980s Kang had reappeared as part of a spandex-clad cast of dozens in the top-selling *Marvel Super Heroes Secret Wars* twelve-issue miniseries (1984–1985); though this project resulted in Kang's immortalization as a Mattel action figure, little of real consequence happened to Kang—until he fell into the hands of writer/artist John Byrne the following year. Byrne explored the inevitable science-fictional consequences of Kang's time-tripping, chronicling the temporal tyrant's interactions with multiple versions of himself in a manner reminiscent of David Gerrold's classic 1973 pretzel-tangled time-travel novel *The Man Who Folded Himself*. Kang's time jaunts not only set into motion countless alternate realities, they also created thousands of Kang doppelgängers, who gathered as a group and ultimately engaged in internecine/suicidal warfare thanks to the manipulations of a mysterious woman known as Nebula; this so-called "Council of Kangs" was eventually winnowed down to a single individual.

Kang achieved marginal TV stardom with guest appearances on the *Fantastic Four* animated series (1967–1970; 1978–1979), as well as on the *Avengers* animated series on FOX Kids in 1999; though this last series, too, failed to make Kang a household name, it brought him into the third dimension a second time with a purple-clad, 6-inch action figure in Toy Biz's *The Avengers: United They Stand* collection.

Writer Mark Gruenwald brought the mighty temporal warlord to his humblest point, allowing him to lose his dominion over time to his former girlfriend Ravonna, who literally stabbed him in the back in a 1993 miniseries. But Kang reappeared alive and well, his destiny shaped by influential *Marvels* writer Kurt Busiek (the *Avengers Forever* twelve-issue miniseries, 1998–2000), and even finally managed to conquer present-day Earth before being defeated yet again; although Kang was prepared to suffer trial, life imprisonment, and even execution at the hands of his greatest adversaries, the Avengers, his son Marcus robbed him of even this small satisfaction by rescuing him. Dishonored by his son's actions, Kang murdered Marcus, leaving himself with neither hope nor a future—but with more time on his hands than any man could ever want. —*MAM*

Kanjar Ro

Extraterrestrial conqueror Kanjar Ro first ventured to Earth in *Justice League of America* #3 (1961), by writer Gardner Fox and artist Mike Sekowsky. Luring the Leaguers to their Secret Sanctuary by manipulating their JLA signal devices, Kanjar Ro traps them in suspended animation by tinkling a golden bell, then immobilizes the entire population of Earth by hammering his Gamma Metal Gong. The "delon" (dictator) of the planet Dhor, Ro will only emancipate the public if the Justice Leaguers contribute their "extraordinary talents" to suppress his intergalactic rivals Hyathis of Alstair, Kromm of Mosteel, and Sayyar of Llarr. Rowing a spacefaring slave ship cosmically powered by Ro's Energi-rod, five JLAers venture to Ro's enemies' homeworlds and capture them. To keep the League at bay, Ro defiantly reneges upon his pledge to free the immotile Earthlings, but the JLA outsmarts the delon and breaks the Gong's spell, exiling Ro and his three adversaries on a habitable Meteor-World.

Kanjar Ro was created not by writer Fox but by editor Julius Schwartz and cover artist Murphy Anderson during a brainstorming session in which *JLA* #3's cover art—Ro forcing the League to row "The Slave Ship of Space!"—was produced first, with the story written around it. Yet Fox's script succeeds in fleshing out this supervillain: Ro is tyrannical, untrustworthy, and armed with an apocalyptic array of gadgets. His Energi-rod cosmically allows him to fly and read minds, communicate through space, transmute matter, and paralyze vocal chords. Based upon looks alone, however, Kanjar Ro might not have been taken seriously: Gaunt and hook-nosed with pink skin and a blue uniform (including briefs with no leggings), he might even appear laughable, like an alien lawn jockey, were it not for his disturbing fly-like eyes and his ubiquitous sneer.

The sequel to "The Slave Ship of Space!" appeared in *Mystery in Space* #75 (1962), in an Adam Strange story guest-starring the JLA. In writer Fox and artists Carmine Infantino and Murphy Anderson's "The Planet That Came to a Standstill!" Kanjar Ro escaped, abandoning his fellow fiends on their penal world: "I swore friendship while a prisoner with you! Now that I'm free—I'm your enemy again! Farewell, fools!" He routed the Justice League on a three-sunned world that tripled his powers, but the intervention of super-spaceman Adam Strange vanquished Ro—and earned his scorn. In later appearances, Ro briefly subjugated Strange's adopted world of Rann and battled both Hawkman and Superman. When he next encountered the League, in *JLA* vol. 2 #78 (2003), Kanjar Ro was almost unrecognizable: Clad in body armor, he had become Minister of Defense of Kylaq, provoking the planet into galactic conflict with neighboring worlds and attracting the attention of the League. While driven from Kylaq by the JLA, Kanjar Ro continues to seek out new worlds to conquer.

Rene Auberjonois portrayed Kanjar Ro, in his original costume, in the two-part episode "In Blackest Night," originally aired in 2001 on the Cartoon Network's *Justice League*, and Ro was one of seven JLA villains featured in a 2001 PVC set. —*ME*

The Key

B orrowing the name of a criminal who fought the Justice Society of America in *All Star Comics* #57 (1951), the Key first tumbled with DC Comics' premier superheroes in *Justice League of America* #41 (1965). Writer Gardner Fox and artist Mike Sekowsky's "The Key-Master of the World!" begins with Superman's startling motion to disband the League—"It's about time!" echoes Wonder Woman. The heroes gleefully toast the team's dissolution while Green Lantern levels their headquarters with his power ring. They are under the influence of the behavior-modifying "psycho-chemical" created by the Key, a mastermind flourishing key-shaped weapons and a key-like headpiece that barely contains his rampant ego. With his costumed Key-Men, the Key unlocks a string of heists under the oblivious noses of the Justice League, until Hawkgirl, not under the drug's control, helps the JLA close the door on the villain. This original incarnation of the Key has twice been captured in plastic, as a 1967 figurine and a 2001 PVC.

While his real name has never been disclosed, the Key is a former Intergang chemist who injected himself with psycho-chemicals to unchain his mind's full potential. He sold his soul to the demon Neron in exchange for a higher state of consciousness—and a gruesome new form. Now with a chalky pallor, glowing red eyes, and a spinal attachment pumping his psycho-chemical into his cerebral cortex, the Key, often abetted by robotic Key-Men, wields a Neural Shock Rifle that dispenses mind-controlling drugs. He once trapped the JLA in an artificial reality, and is concocting new ways to unlock chaos. —*ME*

Khan

E arth's history is replete with conquerors and tyrants whose power, audacity, and charisma arguably qualify them for supervillain status. But once superhuman abilities are added to the mix, supervillainy is all but assured. In the fictional "future historical" backstory established in television's original *Star Trek* series (NBC, 1966–1969), Khan Noonien Singh is one of the world's most influential despots, a man whose extraordinary ambitions had a profound cautionary effect on the development of the show's Utopian United Federation of Planets—which the 1990s spin-off series *Star Trek: Deep Space Nine* depicts as resolutely determined never to allow Khan's crimes to be repeated ("Doctor Bashir, I Presume?" broadcast in 1997).

Created by television scenarists Gene L. Coon and Carey Wilbur for the first-season *Star Trek* episode "Space Seed"—and played to histrionic perfection by Ricardo Montalban—Khan is a Sikh born in India's Punjab region around 1970. Khan is an "Augment," gifted with enhanced strength and intellect—as well as a love for such classic authors as Melville, Milton, and Shakespeare—by Project Chrysalis, a covert human genetic engineering program masterminded by bioscientist Sarina Kaur (his mother). The young Khan becomes absolute ruler of most of Asia by 1992, gaining dominion over roughly one-quarter of Earth's population. Along with hundreds of his fellow DNA-enhanced, power-hungry supermen and superwomen—many of whom violently oppose one another, as well as the world's conventional powers—Khan becomes a central figure in the so-called "Eugenics Wars" of the 1990s, a bloody period that concludes in 1996 with the deaths of most of the Augments.

starship. "There's something inside this man that refuses to accept death," Dr. Leonard H. McCoy (DeForrest Kelley) observes, surprised by Khan's amazing strength and recuperative powers.

Shortly after Kirk discovers Khan's identity, Khan and his people seize the *Enterprise*, thanks to the collaboration of Lieutenant Marla McGivers, the starship's historian, who has become infatuated with the dashing conqueror. After Kirk defeats Khan, prevents him from blowing up the ship, and arrests all the Augments and Lieutenant McGivers, he grants them the dignity of exile on the harsh-but-habitable planet Ceti Alpha V; Kirk has already admitted, after all, to harboring a sneaking admiration for Khan, to the incredulous horror of Commander Spock (Leonard Nimoy), Kirk's first officer and best friend. "It is better to rule in Hell than serve in Heaven," Kirk comments, misquoting John Milton's *Paradise Lost* ("Better to reign in Hell than serve in Heaven") after seeing Khan's eagerness to tame a new world alongside his followers and his new wife (McGivers) ("Space Seed").

Ricardo Montalban reprised his television role as the barrel-chested Khan in the blockbuster film *Star Trek II: The Wrath of Khan* (1982).

Unknown to almost everyone on Earth, Khan and some eighty acolyte Augments agree to go into exile aboard a prototype DY-100 "sleeper ship." Naming the experimental vessel the *S.S. Botany Bay* after the eighteenth-century Australian penal colony, Khan and his people head for the stars in suspended animation, seeking new worlds to conquer. Nearly three centuries later, the crew of the *U.S.S. Enterprise* discovers the *Botany Bay* adrift in the Mutara Sector, and Captain James T. Kirk (William Shatner) brings a revived Khan aboard his

Six months after arriving on Ceti Alpha V, the neighboring world (Ceti Alpha VI) explodes, apparently the victim of a freak singularity encounter. "The shock shifted the orbit of this planet, and everything was *laid waste!*" a gray-haired, vengeance-crazed Khan explains fifteen local years later to Captain Clark Terrell (Paul Winfield) and Commander Pavel A. Chekov (Walter Koenig), who have come seeking a suitable test-site for Project Genesis, a prototype terraforming device with horrific destructive power if misused. Determined to find and kill Kirk (now a Starfleet admiral) for stranding him on the world that took the lives of his beloved wife and most of his people, Khan uses the mind-controlling properties of a local life-form (the madness-inducing Ceti eels) to hijack Terrell's starship, the *U.S.S. Reliant*, then steals the Genesis device, savagely murdering most of the scientists who developed it.

After engaging Kirk in an intense ship-to-ship battle, Khan's superior intellect once again fails to overcome Kirk, a man who has made a career of surviving against impossible odds. His commandeered ship wrecked, his young protégé Joaquim (Judson Scott) dead, Khan quotes the dying words of Herman Melville's Captain Ahab, a man who, like Khan himself, has become defined by his drive for revenge: "From Hell's heart I stab at thee. For hate's sake I spit my last breath at thee." A man fond of grand, fatal gestures—according to Greg Cox's novel *Star Trek: The Eugenics Wars Volume 2: The Rise and Fall of Khan Noonien Singh* (2002), Khan was directly responsible for the creation of the hole in Earth's ozone layer, and once made plans to unleash flesh-eating bacteria as a global doomsday weapon—Khan detonates the Genesis device, vaporizing the *Reliant* and indirectly causing the death of Captain Spock (*Star Trek II: The Wrath of Khan*, 1982).

Fortunately, Spock gets better (*Star Trek III: The Search for Spock*, 1984) and accompanies Kirk and Dr. McCoy back to Ceti Alpha V two years after Khan's death. There they find the remains of the late Lieutenant McGivers, which they give a proper interment, and the journals of both McGivers and Khan; they also discover an anti-Khan splinter group consisting of the offspring of some of the original genetically engineered exiles who had turned away from Khan years earlier. By relocating the surviving second-generation Augments to a suitable new home (a colony of similarly genetically engineered individuals) and reading the diaries, Kirk deals with his own culpability in Khan's latter-day crimes—he never bothered to check on Khan's status after exiling him, after all—and puts Khan's ambitious, tragic spirit at last to rest (*Star Trek: To Reign in Hell—The Exile of Khan Noonien Singh* by Greg Cox, 2005).

Long a favorite villain of *Star Trek* aficionados, Khan moved into the pop-cultural mainstream when Dana Carvey lampooned him in a memorable 1986 *Saturday Night Live* (*SNL*) segment guest-hosted by William Shatner, who played a retired Kirk who has converted the *Enterprise* into a seafood restaurant called "Cap'n Kirk's." A white-haired and wild-eyed Khan (Carvey) is now a visiting health inspector—"There's no sneeze-guard on your salad bar, Kirk!" he snarls in an accent reeking of rich, Corinthian leather—whose desire for vengeance against Kirk remains undiminished. Spoofed by the *SNL* cast, Khan's immortality seems assured. —*MAM*

Killer Croc

Perhaps the most bestial of Batman's enemies, the rampageous reptile-man Killer Croc premiered in *Detective Comics* #523 (1983), by writer Gerry Conway and artist Gene Colan (continued in *Batman* #357, by Conway and Don Newton). Floridian Waylon Jones suffers from a genetic condition that turns his skin into a scaly crocodilian hide. Ostracized by the locals, the minimally educated Jones becomes more reptilian and stronger with age, growing to hate humanity as his disorder separates him from it. After a circus stint as a crocodile wrestler that earns him the nickname "Killer Croc," he slithers into Gotham City to muscle into organized crime, and is soon at odds with Batman.

Early in his comic-book history, Killer Croc had murdered the parents of Jason Todd, the second Robin the Boy Wonder. A continuity revision eliminated Croc's connection to Todd.

Towering over the Dark Knight, Killer Croc is a 7-feet-tall, 686-pound leviathan with prodigious strength, razor-like claws, and sharp-edged teeth, which he wields with both primal fury and combative mastery learned while wrestling. A consistent threat to Batman and Robin, Killer Croc has also encountered Swamp Thing, Man-Bat, and the Creeper. As the Riddler and Penguin will attest, Croc's limited intelligence and loathing of humans make him a poor criminal ally; similarly, the Mad Hatter discovered Killer Croc's ferocity when his plan to drive him mad backfired.

Killer Croc has shown his ugly face on television, in the 1990s on *Batman: The Animated Series* and its continuations, throatily voiced by Aron Kincaid and Brooks Gardner, and on *The Batman* (2004–present), portrayed by *Hellboy*'s Ron Perlman. In the latter series' episode "Swamped" (2005), Croc attempted to submerge Gotham in water to make himself its aquatic crime king. Kenner and DC Direct have produced several Killer Croc action figures, in his various comic-book and animation incarnations. —*ME*

Killer Kane

From the moment futuristic space hero Buck Rogers arrives in the twenty-fifth century, he begins battling colossal villains and alien life forms. Primary is Killer Kane, a "Yellow Peril"–type world dominator who gives the hero a run for his money in the trendsetting science-fiction newspaper strip, *Buck Rogers in the Twenty-Fifth Century* (1929–1968), a popular radio show (1932–1947), and a 1939 movie serial.

Created by Philip Francis Nowlan, Rogers' first appearance was in the story "Armageddon 2419 A.D.," which ran a 1928 issue of the pulp magazine *Amazing Stories*. In a futuristic world threatened by Mongol hordes, Rogers—aided primarily by his sidekick Wilma Deering, his ally Dr. Huer, and his trusty ray gun—battles the super-malevolent Killer Kane. Together, Rogers and Killer Kane represent "the age-old conflict between good and evil; between avari-

Killer Kane. From the *Buck Rogers* newspaper strip of April 8, 1961 ©1961 Dille Family Trust.
ART BY GEORGE TUSKA.

cious self-seekers and peacemakers," notes Robert C. Dille's *The Collected Works of Buck Rogers* (1969). "Kane is no two-dimensional cardboard cutout. He's a believable mixture of motives and traits—most of them rotten … He's endlessly cunning, greedy, revengeful, and resourceful."

The basic premise of Rogers and friends battling all forms of intelligent terror in space worked for the strip, radio show, and assorted Famous Funnies comic books; however, a revised storyline drove the twelve-chapter RKO movie serial. Emerging from a state of suspended animation after 500 years, pilot Rogers (portrayed by Buster Crabbe) and passenger Buddy Wade awaken in the year 2440 to the crude reality of Killer Kane (portrayed by Anthony Warde), an evil gangster who tyrannically rules the world. He is thwarted only by a small resistance effort headquartered from a secret lab run by Dr. Huer. Relying on an arsenal of weapons created in Dr. Huer's lab, Rogers and company solicit the help of Prince Tallen of the planet Saturn. After several encounters with the Zugg men, Buck and Buddy engage in an air battle to wrest control of the universe from the intergalactic ruler. The serial was edited into two feature films, *Planet Outlaws* in 1953 and *Destination Saturn* in 1965.

Killer Kane appeared from 1979 to 1981 in the disco-era television series *Buck Rogers in the Twenty-Fifth Century*, in which Rogers (actor Gil Gerard), an astronaut whose shuttle crash-lands on a nuclear war–ravaged Earth, battled Kane and his minions. Kane was portrayed by two actors, Henry Silva in 1979 and Michael Ansara in 1979–1980. Pamela Hensley appeared as Princess Ardala of Draconia, a would-be world dominator and sometime acquaintance of Kane who also had her sights set on Rogers. —*GM*

Killer Moth

No one took Killer Moth seriously—not his archfoes Batman and Robin, not the other supervillains pillaging Gotham City, and not even the readers of DC Comics. Buzzing into *Batman* #63 (1951), the man behind the moth-shaped mask is racketeer Drury Walker (aka Cameron Van Cleer), who steals a

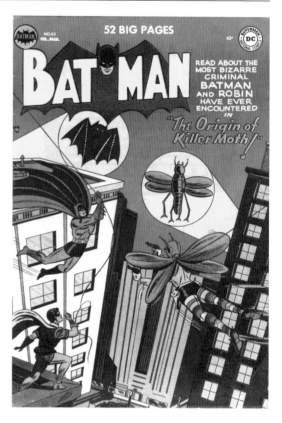

Batman #63 ©1951 DC Comics.
COVER ART BY BOB KANE, LEW SAYRE SCHWARTZ, AND CHARLES PARIS.

page from Batman's playbook: donning a garish purple, orange, and green costume (with insect wings), crawling the streets in a Mothmobile, and shining a Mothsignal into the skies, he takes the name Killer Moth and hires himself out to protect Gotham's gangsters from apprehension. Batman and Robin, however, squash his caper with little effort.

Yet like a pesky gnat, Killer Moth fluttered into comics on numerous occasions, most famously in *Detective Comics* #359 (1967), in which his attempt to kidnap millionaire Bruce (Batman) Wayne was easily swatted by Barbara Gordon in her first appearance as Batgirl. In *Underworld Unleashed* #1 (1995), the ridiculed rogue sold his soul to the demon Neron in exchange for a more formidable identity. Killer Moth metamorphosed into Charaxes, a ghastly humanoid insect with an impervious exoskeleton. Feasting on the bodies of humans, he is no longer a joke, and regularly plagues Robin and sometimes even Batman.

The Killer Moth gang, inane thugs wearing wobbly antenna caps, appeared in the unaired 1967 pilot that introduced Batgirl to the live-action *Batman* series (1966–1968), and the singular Killer Moth, voiced by Thomas Hayden Church, is part of the rogues' gallery on the Cartoon Network's *Teen Titans* (2003–2006). —*ME*

Kingpin

Introduced in Stan Lee and John Romita, Sr.'s frequently imitated "Spider-Man No More!" in *The Amazing Spider-Man* vol. 1 #50 (1967), Marvel Comics' absolute crimelord, the Kingpin, might have been upstaged by that pioneering story's costume-in-the-trash-can scene were it not for Kingpin's matchless ability to fight his way to the top. Taking advantage of Peter Parker's abandonment of his troublesome Spider-Man career, Kingpin initiates "a campaign of crime such as the city as never known," mobilizing his trusty goons in a hostile takeover of New York's underworld. Parker's retirement is short-lived, and when the jovial web-slinger meets his "tubby" opponent in issue #51, he assumes Kingpin to be a pushover until the villain's vise-like grip and surprisingly fast fists wipe the smile from Spidey's masked face.

A bald and brutal man-mountain weighing 450 pounds, the exquisitely dressed Kingpin's appearance owes a nod to the dapper character Kasper Gutman, played by actor Sydney Greenstreet in director John Huston's noir classic *The Maltese Falcon* (1941). Often depicted carrying a diamond-topped cane, which in its earliest appearances emitted laser blasts, Kingpin is a master of all forms of hand-to-hand combat including the size-appropriate art of sumo wrestling, skills he hones through regular "exercise" sessions with unfortunate underlings. A detested, overweight child, Kingpin at an early age disciplined his massive body and his mind, using his bulk to literally muscle his way out of his impoverished roots and into organized crime as a ganglord, masking his myriad rackets under the veil of legitimate businesses (most notably the import of spices from the Far East).

Kingpin was regarded a Spider-Man rogue until *Daredevil* writer/artist Frank Miller appropriated him, beginning with vol. 1 #170 (1981), the issue in which readers finally discovered Kingpin's real name: Wilton Fisk. Kingpin's illegal enterprises gave purpose to Miller's street-level Daredevil, and their relationship evolved from enmity to obsession. In the mid-1980s *Daredevil* storyline "Born Again," Kingpin exposed his foe's weaknesses and left him teetering on the precipice of death. The Man without Fear struck back in "The Fall of the Kingpin" in *Daredevil* #297–#300 (1991), systematically dismantling Fisk's territory and (temporarily) putting the mastermind out of business.

Kingpin's single weakness is his family. When first seen, his wife, Vanessa, an elegant socialite, disapproved of his illegal activities, and upon occasion Kingpin deceived her into believing he had gone straight. During Miller's first *Daredevil* run Vanessa was thought to have been killed, but she later resurfaced. The Schemer, a caped mob czar introduced in *Amazing Spider-Man* #83 (1970), was exposed as Fisk's presumed-dead son Richard, anguished over his father's lawlessness and attempting to bring down Kingpin's empire. Various 1980s and 1990s storylines showed the junior Fisk's love/hate relationship with his father. He covertly maneuvered to destroy Kingpin's organization from within as the masked mobster the Rose, then briefly succeeded his father as Kingpin II, but later struck out against him once again. Vanessa, ever the loyal wife but tainted by her husband's bleak world, executed her traitorous son in *Daredevil* vol. 2 #31 (2002).

Other criminals rose to power when the Kingpin was unseated in the early 1990s, but through cunning and intransigence Fisk regained his underworld stature by the end of the decade. The twenty-first century has provided Fisk with new challenges, including blindness induced by a gunshot to the face and the ascendancy of Daredevil himself as the new Kingpin. By 2005, however, Fisk had begun to claw his way back to supremacy—but where else would one expect to find the Kingpin?

As a testament to the power of writer Lee and artist Romita's original vision of the character, Kingpin appears virtually unaltered in the pages of

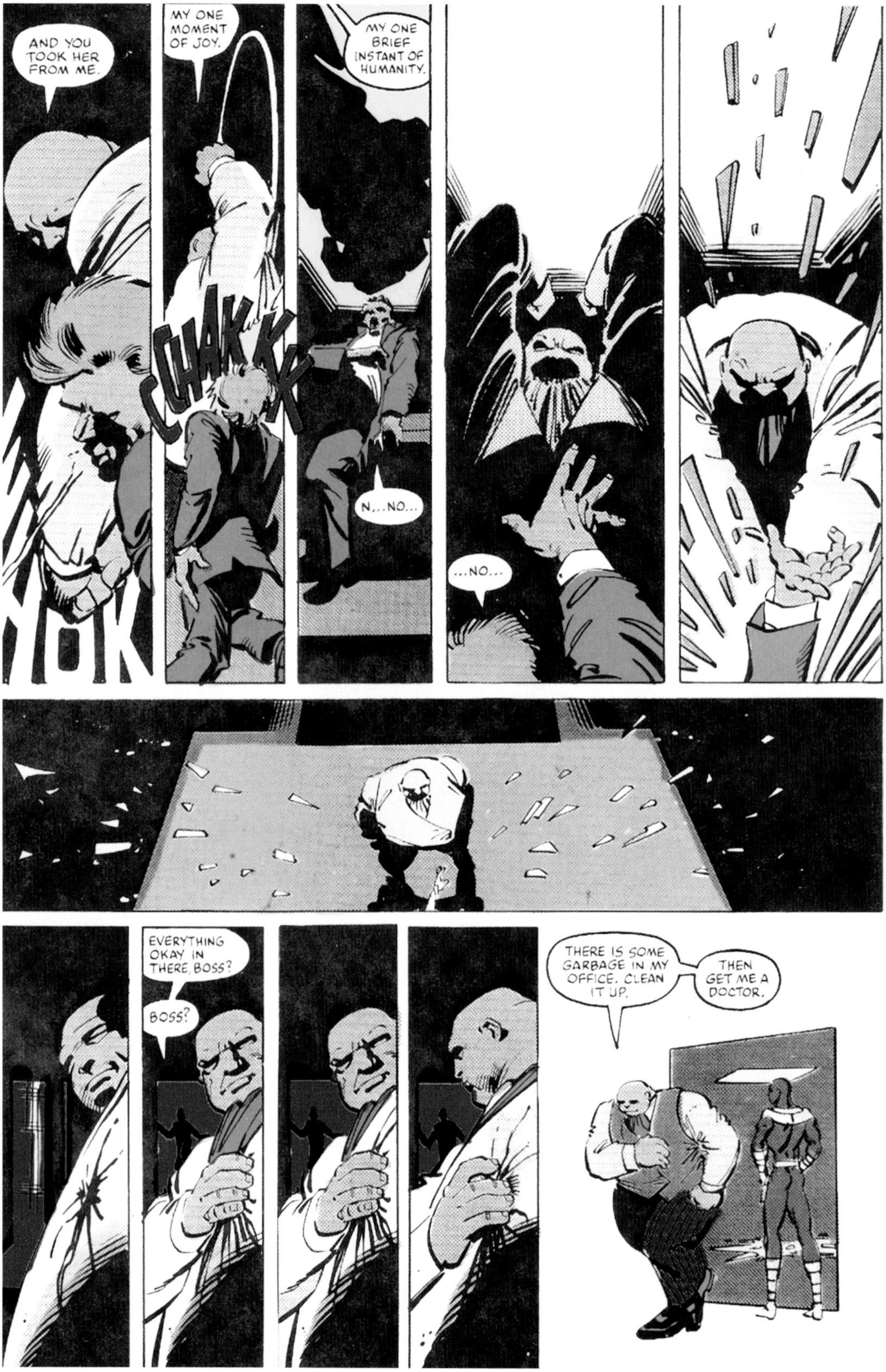
AND YOU TOOK HER FROM ME.
MY ONE MOMENT OF JOY.
CCHAKKK
MY ONE BRIEF INSTANT OF HUMANITY.
N...NO...
...NO...
EVERYTHING OKAY IN THERE, BOSS?
BOSS?
THERE IS SOME GARBAGE IN MY OFFICE. CLEAN IT UP.
THEN GET ME A DOCTOR.

Ultimate Spider-Man (2001–present), Marvel's reimagining of the web-slinger's mythos.

Kingpin has appeared in television animation on the 1967, 1981, 1994, and 2003 incarnations of *Spider-Man* and on *Spider-Woman* (1979–1980). John Rhys-Davies played Fisk in the 1989 live-action TV movie *The Trial of the Incredible Hulk*, while Michael Clarke Duncan portrayed him in the 2003 film *Daredevil*. Several Kingpin action figures and collectible figurines were produced in the 1990s and 2000s. —*ME*

Klarion the Witch Boy

Despite his diminutive size and boylike appearance, Klarion the Witch Boy is a warlock with almost unlimited powers. The 5-feet-tall, 113-pound super-sorcerer came to Earth in DC Comics' *The Demon* vol. 1 #7 (1973), written and illustrated by the legendary Jack Kirby. Most of Klarion's backstory has been told through the mouth of this babe, so it is subject to scrutiny. Nevertheless, he claims he is from the otherdimensional Witch-World, where both he and his parents were persecuted for dabbling in forbidden magic arts. Cast to Earth with the help of a bewitched cat named Teekl, Klarion has a propensity for conjuring spells, wielding magic, and wreaking havoc with his feline accomplice, who can morph into a giant beast at will. Klarion is so ruthless that he even turned his own parents into mice, presumably to feed Teekl. When describing Klarion, reviewer Howard Price said, "Picture Macauley Culkin's role as *The Good Son*, and give him some magic to play with, and you're on the right track."

For years Klarion combated the rhyming supernatural entity known as the Demon Etrigan, which resulted in his banishment from Earth on more than one occasion. Klarion has also teamed with the villainous Contessa to turn groups of superheroes on their heads. In *Young Justice: Sins of Youth* #1 (2000), members of the Justice League of America were turned into adolescent and immature versions of themselves, while the teens of Young Justice became adults!

On the small screen, Klarion unleashed his bag of tricks on Batman in an episode of *The New Batman Adventures*, which aired as part of *The New Batman/Superman Adventures* on the WB network (1997–1999).

In April 2005, Klarion resurfaced as a blue-skinned gothic boy in a Grant Morrison–scripted miniseries, *Seven Soldiers: Klarion the Witch Boy*, in which he is part of Morrison's oddball group of heroes and villains, the Seven Soldiers. Morrison has recast Klarion as one in an underground Puritan-like community of witch people who chooses to rebel; as a defiant protagonist who questions authority, Klarion has been appropriately retooled for the twenty-first century. —*GM*

Klaw

Stan Lee and Jack Kirby's Klaw first struck a chord with readers in *Fantastic Four* #53 (1966). In a flashback, mad scientist Ulysses Klaw safaris into the African nation of Wakanda for its uncommon mineral vibranium, needed to power his "sound transformer." King T'Chaka forbids this interloper access; Klaw responds by ordering his aides to shoot the king before the horrified eyes of his son, T'Challa. The grieving lad defiantly fires Klaw's own weapon at him, destroying the scientist's right hand. Flash forward to the present, as an unforgiving Klaw resurfaces wearing a sonic prosthetic, seeking revenge against the adult T'Challa—now the superhero Black Panther—who, aided by his friends the Fantastic Four, defeats this self-proclaimed Master of Sound. At story's end, Klaw cryptically crawls into the aural vortex of his sound transformer.

Three issues later (#56, 1966), Klaw was back, re-created into a crimson-hued robotic-like being of living sound. With his sonic claw channeling his powers, Klaw pummeled the FF with concussive blasts and near-deafening acoustic surges.

This story was adapted to animation in an episode of Hanna-Barbera's *Fantastic Four* series (1967–1970), in which the villain's name was altered to "Klaws." *FF* #53, Klaw's origin, was retread as "Prey of the Black Panther" in the third cartoon incarnation of *Fantastic Four* (1994–1996). In this version, Klaw, played by Charles Howarton, was a businessman, not a scientist.

After his two initial comic-book outings, Klaw was back in print in 1968 as one of the Masters of Evil, challenging a different super-team, the Avengers. Since then, he has proven one of Marvel Comics' most durable do-badders, continuing his grudge against the Black Panther but also battling Ka-Zar, Quasar, the Thunderbolts, and Captain America, and joining forces with Dr. Doom, the Molecule Man, the Frightful Four, and other villains. —*ME*

Kobra

M aking a villain the protagonist of a series is always a hard sell, but Kobra is never one to take "no" for an answer. Even with his title canceled, he remains a force to be reckoned with in the DC Universe.

The 1976 issue of *Kobra* #1, by Jack Kirby, Steve Sherman, Martin Pasko, and D. Bruce Berry, introduces the man known only as Kobra and his brother, Jason Burr, born "Siamese" (or conjoined) twins. After surgical separation, they are psychically linked: when Burr experiences pain, Kobra also feels it. If one dies, so will the other.

However, the Cobra Cult of India had foretold their birth. One of the twins, destined to be their leader, or "Naja Naja," would guide them through the Kali Yuga, the world's fourth age in which the forces of Order would crumble before those of Chaos. Kobra was kidnapped by the Cult and his training began.

Kobra led the Cult through many schemes, such as trying to assume control of America's "Star Wars" missile defense system and attempting to manipulate the present by tampering with the flow of time. These brought him into conflict with superheroes such as Batman and the Outsiders, Aquaman, Superman, and the Flash. When it was determined that Jason Burr was Kobra's "weakest link,"

Burr was killed during a time when their psychic connection had been temporarily severed.

Kobra endured a similarly tempestuous relationship with a woman known as Eve. Created to give the inhumanly evil character a human aspect and make the character less similar to Marvel's Dr. Doom (another Kirby co-creation), later editorial dictates drove a wedge between Eve and her serpent.

Kobra is a deadly hand-to-hand combatant, and wears battle armor containing lethal weapons such as venom spray that can blind or kill opponents and extendable constrictors that can crush the life from anyone caught in their coils. But his main dangers lie in his scientific genius, his ruthlessness, and his stone-cold ambition.

In the story "Justice Eternity" by David Goyer & Geoff Jones, Leonard Kirk, and Keith Champagne in *JSA* #51 (2003), Kobra appears to have been killed by Black Adam, who yanked Kobra's heart from his body. However, as any herpetologist can tell you, cobras are deadliest when they appear helpless.

Outside of comics, Kobra appeared in Roger Stern's Superman novel *The Never-Ending Battle* (2005). —*MWB*

Krang

T he former warlord of Atlantis Krang—not to be confused with Krang, the super-alien from Dimension X and foe of the Teenage Mutant Ninja Turtles—has frequently gone head-to-head with Namor the Sub-Mariner. Introduced by writer Stan Lee and artist Jack Kirby in *Fantastic Four Annual* #1 (1963), Krang is a member of the water-breathing Homo mermanus of Atlantis who rose through the ranks of the city's militia. He holds a personal grudge against Namor, who exiled him from Atlantis after the villain staged a military coup and tried to seize Atlantis' throne.

Like all members of the Homo mermanus species, Krang exists underwater. Although he possesses a superhumanly strong physiology that enables him to withstand extreme oceanic water-pressure changes and freezing temperatures, the supervillain cannot survive more than ten minutes outside of water without artificial aids. With his domed head, pointy ears, goatee beard, and epi-canthic eyebrows, the usurping tyrant resembles an underwater Ming the Merciless.

Krang rarely operates alone. In order to further his under- and above water schemes, Krang has allied himself with several super-baddies of the Marvel Universe, such as Attuma, Byrrah (Namor's prideful and ambitious cousin), and super-scientist Dr. Lemuel Dorcas. He employed both the criminal Puppet Master and Orka, and has been a member of the Viper's Serpent Squad. He became engaged to Lady Dorma, the Sub-Mariner's true love, and tricked her into complying with his destructive schemes. Krang uses various weaponry and armor built for him by his human and Atlantean allies.

Krang hasn't been seen much since the Sub-Mariner comic was canceled in 1974. His last appearance seems to be in *New Warriors* #36 (1993)—but one may assume that Krang is still out there somewhere plotting a takeover of Atlantis! —*GM*

Kraven the Hunter

S ergei Kravinoff—publicly known as Kraven the Hunter, the world's most renowned animal trapper—swaggers into New York City in *The Amazing Spider-Man* vol. 1 #15 (1964) in pursuit of "the most dangerous game of all": Spider-Man! Ruggedly handsome, mustached, and bursting with machismo, Kravinoff, an overconfident Russian aristocrat exiled from his homeland into Britain, spends much of his youth in Africa, where he gains superhuman strength and stamina from a witch doctor's herbal brews. Able to methodically outmaneuver his prey and overcome any beast with his bare hands, the hunter dubbed "Kraven" is lured to the United States by Spider-Man's first foe, the Chameleon, Kravinoff's "old friend" in the original text but established in later continuity as his half-brother. Kraven comes close to bagging the wall-crawler, but the cunning Spider-Man snares the hunter in a giant web.

Looking every inch the forerunner to circus showmen Siegfried and Roy, Kraven the Hunter was festooned in leopard-print tights, a lion-motif vest with a mane, and a zebra-striped belt dotted with tusks containing tranquilizers, toxins, and strength-augmenting potions. His vest's lion "eyes" emitted "electro-bursts," and he wielded magnetic handcuffs to slow down his prey. Kraven's co-creators, writer Stan Lee and illustrator Steve Ditko, drew inspiration from the character General Zaroff, first seen in Richard Connell's 1924 novel *The Most Dangerous Game* and later translated to film in 1932, 1946, and 1956.

On the heels of his first appearance, Kraven took on Iron Man in *Tales of Suspense* #58, then partnered with five other vanquished Spider-Man enemies—Dr. Octopus, the Vulture, Sandman, Mysterio, and Electro—as the Sinister Six in *The Amazing Spider-Man Annual* #1, both published in 1964. His ego bruised from his ignominious defeats, Kraven sullied Spider-Man's reputation by masquerading as the hero in 1966, his actions goading the real Spidey into a trap, but through unbridled resourcefulness the wall-crawler hammered the hunter once again.

Conceited to a fault, his losses sat poorly with Kraven, and over the next twenty years he frequently returned to attempt to capture Spider-Man, the occasional clash with Ka-Zar, Daredevil, and Man-Wolf aside. Eventually Kraven's sanity was eroded by his defeats and his loss of stature. In an applauded six-part story by writer J. M. DeMatteis and artist Mike Zeck, serialized throughout three different Spider-Man comics series in 1987, Kravinoff executed "Kraven's Last Hunt," finally trapping the wall-crawler—"There's … something in his eyes! This isn't the Kraven I know!" thought a bewildered Spidey—and resorting to firearms, apparently killing the hero. Kraven then usurped the web-slinger's costumed identity, as he did in 1966, on a mad mission of proving his superiority to his fallen foe. Spider-Man was not actually dead, but tranquilized and buried alive, and he escaped from his grave. Satisfied with having bested Spider-Man, Kraven put a shotgun to his mouth and, in a scene chillingly rendered in silhouette by Zeck and inker Bob McLeod, committed suicide.

Kraven's legacy has continued to populate the pages of Marvel Comics in the years after Kravi-

The Amazing Spider-Man vol. 1 #293 ©1987 Marvel Comics.
COVER ART BY MIKE ZECK AND BOB McLEOD.

in MTV's short-lived *Spider-Man* toon of 2003. A 2005 rumor that he would appear in the live-action film *Spider-Man 3* was later dispelled. Never a top-tier Spider-foe, Kraven has sporadically appeared in merchandising in the 1990s and 2000s, including a Toy Biz action figure and collectible mini-busts. —*ME*

The Kryptonite Kid

It must have seemed like a good idea at the time: a supervillain made of Superboy's weakness. After all, the premise proved successful with the hero's adult self, Super*man*, when Lex Luthor temporarily transformed into "The Kryptonite Man!" in *Action Comics* #249 (1959). So in *Superboy* vol. 1 #83 (1960), writer Jerry Siegel and artist George Papp introduce a delinquent teen and his dog from the planet Blor who travel through a curious space cloud, emerging with shimmering green complexions and a Midas-like kryptonite touch. As Kryptonite Kid and Kryptonite Dog, they do what any kryptonite-charged psychotic punk and mutt would do—terrorize Superboy and Krypto the Superdog. Luckily for the Boy of Steel, the magical imp Mr. Mxyzptlk deports the radioactive duo to a dimensional prison, to spare Superboy's life for his *own* tomfoolery.

The problem with the Kryptonite Kid—aside from his preposterous outfit of a magenta shower cap and bathing suit—was his one-dimensional supremacy. Lording his power over the Teen of Steel in several stories, this rare attempt to create a Superboy-specific rogue apparently intimidated writers who realized his limitations. Yet he also mustered a handful of appearances as the adult Kryptonite *Man*, the most noteworthy being *Action Comics* #583 (1986), in which the vengeful rogue poisoned Krypto in an "imaginary" tale by writer Alan Moore and artist Curt Swan. A kryptonite-pigmented clone of the Man of Steel appeared in the contemporary Superman continuity in *Superman* vol. 2 #43 (1990), but the original Kryptonite Kid remains a glowing testament to the wild imagination of comics' Silver Age (1956–1969).

Author Joseph Torchia borrowed the character's name for his 1979 novel *The Kryptonite Kid*, the "real world" story of a boy obsessed with Superman, and

noff's demise. In the mid-1990s his son Vladimir Kravinoff briefly followed his father's footsteps by becoming the "Grim Hunter," but died at the hands of the assassin Kaine, Spider-Man's evil clone. Alyosha Kravinoff, Kraven's illegitimate son first seen in 1997, was obsessed with learning about the father who abandoned him and adopted his Kraven the Hunter identity. After a few clashes with Spider-Man and the Black Panther, Alyosha realized that his gifts were better used for entertainment, adapting to a different type of jungle—Hollywood—as a film producer named "Al Kraven." His adventures in Tinseltown were chronicled in the six-issue miniseries *Get Kraven* (2002)—but between the fickle nature of show business and the supervillainy in his blood, Kraven II may one day resume the hunt.

Gregg Brewer played the original Kraven the Hunter in the animated series *Spider-Man* (1994–1998), and Michael Dorn voiced the villain

Jay Underwood played the villain in an episode of the live-action *Superboy* television series (1988–1992); Underwood later went on to portray another comic-book character, the Human Torch, in the unreleased live-action *Fantastic Four* film of 1994 (not to be confused with 2005's *Fantastic Four*). —ME

Lady Deathstrike

Lady Deathstrike is a cyborg of super proportions. As an assassin and CEO of her father's Oyama Heavy Industries, she has a deep history rooted in Japanese culture, martial arts, and espionage. She was introduced as Yuriko Oyama, the daughter of criminal scientist and Daredevil enemy Lord Dark Wind (once World War II Japanese kamikaze pilot Kenji Oyama) in *Daredevil* vol. 1 #197 (1983), and as Lady Deathstrike in *Alpha Flight* vol. 1 #33 (1985).

Lady Deathstrike is a highly skilled martial artist, who is known for her mastery of art of Ken-jitsu and other samurai warrior skills. She is endowed with superhuman strength, speed, agility, endurance, and reflexes. Her skeleton has been artificially laced with the metal adamantium, making her bones virtually unbreakable. Although Lord Dark Wind developed a process for bonding adamantium to human bone, he did not experiment on his daughter. It was the villain Mojo's accomplice Spiral who had Yuriko converted into a cyborg in his "Body Shoppe." A key opponent of Wolverine, Lady Deathstrike has also gone up against the U.S. government–sponsored Freedom Force team, other members of the X-Men, and Captain America.

Lady Deathstrike's fingers have all been replaced with 12-inch-long adamantium claws, which she is capable of extending to twice their original length, making her a match for Wolverine, whom she has hunted in lands both far and near. She is able to cybernetically interface her consciousness with external computer systems, allowing for direct data access to her brain's memory and granting her the ability to remotely operate such systems. Deathstrike's body also includes an automatic self-repair program. However, the version of Lady Deathstrike in Marvel's *Ultimate X-Men* comic (2001–present) appears to be a mutant rather than a cyborg, and works for the Weapon X program.

Actress Kelly Hu portrayed Lady Deathstrike in *X2: X-Men United* (2004), although in the film the character is referred to only by her real name of Yuriko Oyama. The character also appeared in *X-Men: The Animated Series* (1992–1997). —GM

Lady Shiva

When Sandra Woosan falsely believed that martial artist and spy Richard Dragon had killed her sister, Woosan embarked on a dark and dangerous journey lit by revenge. Becoming a master of many forms of combat, Woosan turned her lust for revenge into a desire for enlightenment and became Lady Shiva, a deadly mercenary with lightning reflexes and a take-no-prisoners attitude. Her

Kelly Hu as Yukiro Oyama, aka Lady Deathstrike, in *X2: X-Men United* (2003).

single-minded passion for martial arts is the trait responsible for turning her skills into an art form.

Introduced in *Richard Dragon, Kung Fu Fighter* #5 (1975–1976) in a story penned by Dennis O'Neil and rendered by Ric Estrada, Lady Shiva is one of the premiere martial artists in the DC Universe. For a time, Lady Shiva fought crime alongside Dragon and martial artist Ben Turner until Dragon temporarily quit the business and Turner was transformed into the hero the Bronze Tiger. She has also shown great respect for Hub City hero Vic Sage (the Question), who has instructed her on the nuances of martial artistry.

Although she has battled Batman, she found her true match in the new Batgirl, Cassandra Cain, who beat her in hand-to-hand combat. Sensing she was holding something back, Shiva agreed to train Batgirl to reach her untapped potential, under the condition that the newly conditioned Batgirl face off with her in a future fight. That she did, and Batgirl triumphed (*Batgirl: A Knight Alone*, 2001).

Well versed in both the healing and combative arts, the coolly intellectual and spiritually calm Shiva continually roams the world seeking perfection as a master of martial arts. Those attributes were put to the test in a 2005 *Batgirl* story arc when she became embroiled in a fracas at Ra's al Ghul's Balkan palace involving the League of Assassins, Mr. Freeze, al Ghul's daughter Nyssa, and an army of the living dead. Who she will run up against next is anybody's guess.

Korean actress Sung Hi Lee portrayed Sandra Wu-San (note change in spelling of last name) and Lady Shiva in a 2002 episode of the live-action television series *Birds of Prey*. —*GM*

The Leader

The Leader followed the Incredible Hulk down a gamma-irradiated path to become one of the Green-Skinned Goliath's arch-foes. Created by the writer/artist duo of Stan Lee and Steve Ditko in

Tales to Astonish #63 (1964, although the Leader was first depicted wearing a helmet, shielding his appearance as a teaser for readers, in issue #62), laborer Samuel Sterns toils in a chemical-research facility when "a one-in-a-million freak accident" triggers the explosion of a gamma-ray cylinder—the type of mishap that, in the real world, would incinerate an individual, but in comics' Marvel Universe instead provides an origin. Sterns emerges with a voracious appetite for reading, but days later, a mutagenesis transpires: his pigmentation turns green and his cranium swells to accommodate his rapidly advancing intellect—but he maintains Sterns' well-groomed mustache—and the Leader, the super-brain with an unquenchable craving to amass knowledge, is born.

The emerald-hued mastermind became preoccupied with studying his superstrong counterpart, the Hulk, dispatching his horde of faceless sythentic beings called Humanoids in an unsuccessful attempt to capture him. Serialized in a storyline that ran for over a year (through *Tales to Astonish* #75, 1966), the Leader's intellectual curiosity quickly flourished into megalomania. From his desert laboratory he employed a network of lackeys (which he later jettisoned for artifically constructed agents) to steal military secrets, allied with the Chameleon and Soviet operatives, developed complex weapons, and pilfered technology from scientist Dr. Bruce Banner (the Hulk's alter ego). While his plans failed, he succeeded at developing enmity with the Incredible Hulk, their war spanning decades of Marvel Comics stories.

In the Leader's advanced mind, he and only he is worthy of controlling the world. No field of science is beyond his mastery, and his strategic and intuitive reasonings are staggering. He possesses total recall and the psionic ability of mind control. Among his android creations are sythentic substitutes for the U.S. president and vice-president, a 500-foot Humanoid, and a Super Humanoid that fired concussive blasts from its fingertips.

During the late 1980s and throughout the 1990s, many of the Leader's malevolent milestones flowed from the mind of writer Peter David, long-time *Incredible Hulk* scribe. In 1987 the Leader temporarily lost his powers, then regained them by siphoning gamma radiation from the

Good Guys, Bad Reputations

Today they may be known as superheroes, but in their earliest adventures these crime fighters faced public-relations nightmares, and rightfully so.

- **Superman** (first seen in *Action Comics* #1, 1938) was the brassy "Champion of the Oppressed" who knocked down walls, slapped wife beaters, and spanked saucy vixens before becoming the personification of "Truth, Justice, and the American Way."

- **Batman** (*Detective Comics* #27, 1939) allowed a killer to fall to his death and heaved adversaries off rooftops, and was regarded a threat to society by his eventual ally Commissioner Gordon—a story element revisited in Dark Knight rebootings.

- **Sub-Mariner** (*Marvel Comics* #1, 1939), Atlantis' "avenging son" Prince Namor, earned his bad rep with his devastating attacks against surface dwellers—which in one landmark tale included the flooding of New York City.

- **Plastic Man** (*Police Comics* #1, 1941) was mobster Eel O'Brian before a chemical mishap transformed him into the Pliable Pretzel. In a classic 1940s storyline, FBI operative "Plas" was assigned to arrest his on-the-lam alter ego!

- **Spider-Man** (*Amazing Fantasy* #15, 1962) was perceived as a menace by the *Daily Bugle*'s blusterous publisher J. Jonah Jameson, whose editorial assaults often turned the law and popular opinion against the web-slinger.

- **The Creeper** (*Showcase* #73, 1968) exploited his freakish appearance and maniacal laugh to make the public think he was a criminal in order to infiltrate the underworld—not unlike the M.O. of the Green Hornet, who debuted in a 1936 radio drama.

- **The Mask** (*Dark Horse Presents* #10, 1987) was, before Jim Carrey mainstreamed him in the 1994 movie *The Mask*, a psychotic Bugs Bunny/Punisher hybrid whose butchering of various lowlife (who had it comin'!) put him on Lt. Kellaway's most-wanted list.

Hulk's friend Rick Jones, who had become Hulk-like himself; in the process the Leader's mutation was worsened, his cranium expanding to monstrous proportions and boils festering across his body. In the 1988 "Ground Zero" storyline the Leader detonated a gamma-bomb that leveled an Arizona town and massacred its 5,000 denizens. Under David's creative control the Leader also reanimated the dead; created an Arctic "utopia" called Freehold, over which he reigned; nearly initiated World War III, blaming a faux terrorists' network; and appeared to die while in a grostequely mutated state. Yet as with many supervillains who perish in a blaze of infamy, criminal flames are difficult to extinguish.

The Leader appeared on television in "Hulk" installments of the animated omnibus *The Marvel Super-Heroes* (1966), voiced by Gillie Fenwick, and in the cartoon *The Incredible Hulk* (1996–1997), with Matt Frewer playing the villain. Toy Biz produced a Leader action figure in 1996 as a TV show tie-in; other merchandising with the character includes the Leader and Gamma Hulk Marvel Mini-Mates action-figure two-pack. —*ME*

The League of Assassins

The League of Assassins, a group of highly trained killers-for-hire, first came to light when Batman saved a wealthy shipping magnate from one of its number in a story penned by Denny O'Neil and rendered by Bob Brown in *Detective Comics* #405 (1970, although oblique references to the organization began, in connection with its agent, the Hook, in *Strange Adventures* #215, 1968). Later its leader, Dr. Ebenezer Darrk, a tall, lean, lantern-jawed figure, kidnapped Talia, the daughter of the criminal mastermind Ra's al Ghul, due to "a falling-out" between the two. Batman foiled Darrk's plan, which inadvertently resulted in the death of Darrk.

Later, Batman learned that al Ghul had been the original leader of the League of Assassins, but that the League had split from his influence when al Ghul and Darrk came to a parting of the ways

(perhaps the "falling-out" cited above). Later the League began to operate solely on its own, under its new leader, the Sensei, a deceptively frail-looking Asian martial artist of indeterminate age. To join the League, a prospective member had to perform a successful assassination. However, if the would-be member failed the test, he would die.

That so many criminals have joined the League and many more wish to, despite this draconian penalty for failure, speaks to the fear—and the respect—the League and its members have achieved in all corners of the world. The League is by definition a secret order, so a complete list of their victims may never be known. Among their more famous kills was Kathy Kane, aka Batwoman.

Over the years, other agents of the League of Assassins have included the Hook, the murderer of Boston Brand, whose spirit became known as Deadman; Ben Turner, aka the Bronze Tiger, a friend of martial-arts master Richard Dragon who was kidnapped by the League and programmed to become one of their operatives (the Tiger later joined the Suicide Squad); Merlyn, a deadly archer who later quit the League and, having failed his assignment to assassinate Batman (*Justice League of America* #94, 1971), was for a time on the run from them; and Kirigi, a supreme martial artist who has become the League of Assassins' trainer. The League's name was used to identify a group of nondescript martial artists appearing in a comic-book advertisement for Hostess baked treats; the ad, starring Batman, was published in the late 1970s.

In comics' pages in the mid-2000s, the League of Assassins can be found, doing their job with their usual efficiency, in *Batgirl*, the series featuring the mute assassin turned Gotham City crime fighter. The League's appearances in the pop-culture limelight include the television cartoon *Batman Beyond* (1999–2001), five episodes of which featured Curaré, an operative of the organization; a Vs. System card game featuring the group, in which players choose or discard a League of Assassins character card from their hand; and inclusion into the subtext of *Batman Begins* (2005, though with a name change, to the League of Shadows), in which viewers learned that Bruce

Wayne's transformation from frustrated victim to hero-in-the-making was thanks in part to training he received from the League. —*MWB*

Legion

In the Bible, spirits possessing a human being declare, "My name is Legion, for I am many." Writer Chris Claremont gave the name Legion to the mutant David Charles Haller, whose psyche had been shattered into multiple personalities. Claremont introduced Legion in Marvel's *The New Mutants* #26 (1985), in which artist Bill Sienkiewicz depicted him as a gangly youth with a tall shock of black hair. Legion was not a true villain, but he proved to be a menace to the entire world.

Legion was the illegitimate son of Charles Xavier, founder of the X-Men, and his former lover Gabrielle Haller. As a small child, David had first used his psionic powers to kill terrorists who had murdered his godfather; the traumatic experience turned David autistic and fragmented his mind into multiple personalities, each of which controlled a different psionic power. When David was a teenager, unable to control his powers, he absorbed the minds of several of Xavier's associates into his own. To rescue them, Xavier and his student Danielle Moonstar projected their astral selves into his mind, which Sienkiewicz depicted as a surreal dreamscape of a war-torn city. There they encountered two of David's personalities, Jack Wayne, who wielded telekinesis, and Cyndi, a pyrokinetic, as well as the terrorist Jemail Karami, whose psyche David had absorbed into his own. Moonstar and Karami cured David's autism and returned the other psyches that he had absorbed to their physical bodies. David was then happily united with his father.

Later, Legion used his powers to go back in time and kill Magneto before he became Xavier's arch-foe. Instead Legion inadvertently killed Xavier, thereby creating the divergent timeline known as the "Age of Apocalypse," in which the evil mutant Apocalypse conquered America. Another X-Men member, Bishop, changed history yet again: this time Xavier survived, and the original timeline was restored, but Legion perished instead. —*PS*

The Legion of Doom

While its title—*Challenge of the Super Friends* (1978–1979)—might lead a viewer to believe that this Hanna-Barbera animated series, the second incarnation of the long-running, frequently reinvented *Super Friends* cartoon, starred the Justice League of America (JLA), it was the *villains* who stole the show (as well as various riches and evil weapons).

"Banded together from remote galaxies are thirteen of the most sinister supervillains of all time!" intoned the voiceover that launched the series each week, flashing frightening clips of a baker's dozen of DC Comics' baddest bad guys—the Legion of Doom—assembled for "a single objective: the conquest of the universe." A lofty goal, granted, but through the show's single season the Legion nearly accomplished its malevolent mission.

Almost every one of the sixteen episodes produced began with a pan across a dismal swamp, with the Legion's dark, domed headquarters, the Hall of Doom, ominously rising from the murky bog. Inside was a meeting table, around which this unholy alliance conspired not only to take over the world, but to destroy the Super Friends in the process.

Four of Superman's arch-nemeses were counted among the Legion's roster. Scientist Lex Luthor (voiced by Stan Jones), in the purple-and-green uniform he donned in the 1970s comics, served as the chairman of this nefarious council, often brainstorming that episode's wicked plan. Green-skinned android Brainiac (Ted Cassidy, best known as Lurch from TV's *Addams Family*) contributed his computerized intellect and shrinking ray to the machinations. Toyman (veteran voice talent Frank Welker), the jester-dressed 1970s reinterpretation of the long-time Super-foe, provided comic relief (although his pernicious playthings like laser-firing toy soldiers were no laughing matter), and show-stealer Bizarro, Superman's backwards duplicate, threateningly pounded the table, his Bizarro-speak uttered by Bill Callaway.

Joining Bizarro in the dunce seats was the pasty-faced swamp monster Solomon Grundy, whose limited vocabulary was perfectly delivered by Jimmy Weldon. Aquaman's enemy Black Manta's metallically hollow voice was, like Brainiac's, courtesy of Ted Cassidy. Vic Perrin, the mouthpiece of numerous animation heavies including Dr. Zin from *Jonny Quest*, added a dash of pomposity to the dialogue of renegade Green Lantern Sinestro. Batman's puzzling clue-master the Riddler (Michael Bell) was, like Toyman, on hand for levity, although the series' other Bat-foe, the fear-mongering Scarecrow, was among the creepiest of the cast, from his horrific mask to Don Messick's bloodcurdling vocalizations.

Messick—one of the vocal superstars behind countless Hanna-Barbera characters including Boo-Boo Bear, Bamm-Bamm, Astro, and Dr. Quest and Bandit—also voiced Captain Cold, the Flash's freeze-gun-toting terror (animated here with an ice-blue complexion). *Challenge*'s other Flash felon was the super-intelligent primate Gorilla Grodd, played by Stanley Ralph Ross, the multi-talented actor/producer/writer who, among his myriad credits, penned thirty-two episodes of ABC's *Batman* (1966–1968). Two Wonder Woman supervillainesses rounded out the cast: the full-figured Giganta (Ruth Forman) and perhaps the weakest of the thirteen villains, Cheetah, whose "purr"-laden dialogue (by Marlene Aragon) suggested that the producers had envisioned this role for Catwoman.

With its lethal array of weapons (most of which were created by Luthor), including the Time Conveyor, the Mental-Matter Ray, the Dream Machine, and the Hypnotic Anger-Ray, the Legion of Doom was always up to no good. Among their nefarious deeds: erasing Superman, Wonder Woman, and Green Lantern from existence by disrupting their origins; obtaining the Monolith of Evil from Earth's core; exiling the Super Friends into the pages of fairy tales; siccing a zombie army on the heroes; and transforming themselves into 100-foot giants. The episode "Super Friends: Rest in Peace" revealed the existence of a *former* member of the Legion of Doom: Dr. Natas, inventor of the lethal element Noxion. Comic-book artist Alex Toth, along with Andre Le Blanc, designed the Legion, cleverly softening their diabolical appearances just enough to pass network censors. In the 2000s, *Challenge of the Super Friends* was the first of the *Super Friends* franchise to be collected as a DVD set, and several of the Legion of Doom were released as Super Friends action figures, accompanying their superhero enemies in two-packs.

The Legion of Doom was reintroduced to a new generation of viewers in the 2005 season premiere of the Cartoon Network's *Justice League Unlimited* (2004–present, a continuation of the 2001–2004 series *Justice League*). This new Legion operates under the leadership of Grodd, but boasts an expanding and varying roster much larger than the original's thirteen. "We kind of took a page with what we did with *Justice League Unlimited*," producer Bruce Timm announced at the 2005 San Diego Comic-Con, "where we opened the ranks of the Justice League to include basically everybody." Some of those "everybodies" include Death Ray (a renamed Black Manta), Killer Frost, Captain Cold, Mirror Master, Giganta, and Silver Banshee.

The classic *Super Friends* Legion of Doom also inspired the supervillain assemblage appearing in the Justice League miniseries *Justice* (2005–2006), by Alex Ross, Jim Krueger, and Doug Braithwaite. —*ME*

The Legion of Super-Villains

"**C**alling the future!" enunciates Superman's most persistent foe into a makeshift communicator from his prison cell. "Arch-criminal (Lex) Luthor from the year 1961 calling the Legion of Super-Villains, in the future! Am imprisoned! Need help! Save me!" As implausible as Luthor's plea may sound, it works, as writer Jerry Siegel and artist Curt Swan disclose in *Superman* vol. 1 #147 (1961). Futuristic weapons materialize inside Luthor's cell, enabling him to escape. He soon convenes with the Legion of Super-Villains, criminal counterparts of the founding members of the thirtieth-century teen-age super-team, the Legion of Super-Heroes, of which Superman was a time-traveling member during his career as Superboy (although in this adventure, the villains appear as adults). Cosmic Boy's doppelgänger is the Venusian master of transmutation, Cosmic King; Lightning Lad's is his older brother Mekt Ranzz, aka Lightning Lord, who shares his sibling's power to generate electricity; and the baleful version of Saturn Girl is Saturn Queen, who professes her passion for outwitting the law with her "super-hypnotism." With advanced science and trickery, Luthor and the evil Legion trap the Man of Steel, but the intervention of three members of the *adult* Legion of Super-Heroes—Cosmic Man, Lightning Man, and Saturn Woman—helps Superman turn the tide.

The adult Legion of Super-Villains encountered the teen Legion of Super-Heroes in 1965, but it was not until *Adventure Comics* #372 (1968) that the team's origin was revealed. "School for Super-Villains" by Jim Shooter and Curt Swan spotlighted Tarik the Mute's academy for malevolent superteens with criminal cadets Radiation Roy, Ron-Karr (Ronn Kar), Spider-Girl, Nemesis Kid, a young Lightning Lord, and others, including Legion "traitor" Colossal Boy, who sold out his heroic teammates to save his parents' lives. (This team would eventually evolve into the adult version depicted in *Superman* #147.) Over time, the teen Legion of Super-Villains recruited Chameleon Chief, Esper Lass, Hunter III, Lazon, Magno Lad, Micro Lad, Mist Master, Neutrax, Ol-Vir, Pharoxx, Silver Slasher, Sun Emperor, Terrus, Tyr (the only member to receive his own action figure, as part of the 1986 Super Powers line from Kenner Toys), and Zymyr.

While a post-*Crisis* rewriting of Legion of Super-Heroes and Superman lore excised the original adult Super-Villain tales, the grown-up Lightning Lord, Cosmic King, and Saturn Queen were seen in writer Jeph Loeb and artist Carlos Pacheco's "Absolute Power" storyline in *Superman/Batman* #14–#18 (2005). These lethal Legionnaires from the future arrived in the late twentieth century at pivotal moments in the origins of Superman and Batman and altered the heroes' histories—and, as a result, the entire DC Universe timeline. As the Man of Steel and Dark Knight's "parents," the Super-Villains raised their "sons" to rule a dystopian Earth with an iron hand. Eventually the World's Finest duo restored the natural order, and the Legion of Super-Villains vanished as the time stream corrected itself. —*ME*

Legion of Super-Villains. *Superman/Batman* #18 ©2005 DC Comics.
COVER ART BY CARLOS PACHECO AND JÉSUS MERINO.

Lex Luthor

Called "the maddest of mad scientists" by writer/artist John Byrne in his introduction to DC Comics' *The Greatest Superman Stories Ever Told* (1987), Superman's arch-enemy Lex Luthor—pronounced "lew-thôr," although "Luther" is a common variation (and at least one diction-challenged lackey has been known to say "lew-tor")—bowed in *Action Comics* #23 (1940), in "Europe at War, Part 2" (continued from issue #22) by Superman's co-creators, writer Jerry Siegel and artist Joe Shuster. A generic, paunchy fellow with a shock of red hair, Luthor's audacious actions compensate for his lackluster looks. He plans to dominate the world by inciting combat, and operates from a sophisticated sky-headquarters kept airborne by a dirigible. In *Superman* vol. 1 #4 (1940), the red-headed rogue now presides over an underwater city from which he assails the planet with an earthquake-producing machine. As Luthor brazenly challenges Superman to engage him, writer Siegel established the defining dynamic between these arch-enemies: mind versus muscle.

Contemporary fans may have a difficult time imagining the famously hairless Luthor with red locks (a colorist's gaff gave the mad scientist gray hair in *Superman* #5, 1940), but in "The Invisible Luthor" in *Superman* #10 (1941), by Siegel and artist Leo Nowak, more than Luthor's body had vanished: he was now bald (although a hairless Luthor had previously appeared in the *Superman* newspaper strip).

In his screen debut, in the fifteen-chapter Columbia Pictures movie serial *Atom Man vs. Superman* (1950), Luthor (Lyle Talbot, who one year earlier played another DC character, Commissioner Gordon, in the serial *Batman and Robin*), aka "Atom Man," imperiled the city of Metropolis with a ground-shaking "Directional Cyclotron" and had perfected teleportation for getaways.

Fantastic weapons were the trademark of "Superman's most inveterate hater" (as he is described in *Action* #47, 1942) who, in the comics, also used electricity to make himself super, then battled Superman for the Powerstone, an artifact that granted limitless might (*Superman* #17, 1942). Luthor was sometimes abetted by "fumbling underlings" (one of whom from Luthor's first adventure was bald and wore a white lab coat, the spitting image of what Luthor himself became) for whom he held little regard, even sacrificing their lives to salvage his plans or to escape capture.

Luthor relied less upon flunkies beginning in the 1950s, but sometimes partnered with other supervillains—the Prankster, Mr. Mxyztplk, the Toyman, and the Joker—motivated by writers' whims to be chummy ("This chance meeting may be the luckiest thing that ever happened!") or crummy ("This is all your fault, you grinning clown!"). The 1950s were unkind to Luthor. He mellowed into a two-dimensional, not-so-mad scientist in a business suit, looking more like a mobster than a mastermind, and was snubbed by producer Whitney Ellsworth from the live-action television series *The Adventures of Superman* (1952–1957); the show's meager budget limited its villains to humdrum hoodlums—which, ironically, is what Luthor had become.

It took Silver Age (1956–1969) Superman editor Mort Weisinger to restore Luthor to prominence as "a character of limitless ambition," as Les Daniels called him in *Superman: The Complete History* (1998). In *Adventure Comics* #271 (1960), the villain's origin was finally told, not in a Superman tale but in "How Luthor Met Superboy," by writer Siegel and artist Al Plastino. Smallville resident Lex Luthor, a teenage scientific prodigy, was friends with the Boy of Steel until Superboy inadvertently caused Lex to permanently lose his hair when using his superbreath to extinguish a fire in Lex's laboratory. Driven mad by the incident, Luthor irrationally accused Superboy of causing the accident out of jealousy over his intellect and dedicated his life, and his science, to proving that he was the Boy of Steel's superior (his humiliated family slithered out of town, changing their name to "Thorul"). The Superboy/young Lex relationship inspired the producers of the WB's live-action television drama *Smallville* (2001–present); the series chronicles the adventures of pre-superhero Clark Kent (Tom Welling), with Michael Rosenbaum as Lex Luthor, the son of callous capitalist Lionel Luthor (John Glover), as Clark's friend and a supervillain-in-the-making.

The adult Luthor chose gray prison drabs as his felonious fashion statement in the 1960s, his reminder of the years of his life wasted behind bars after being arrested by Superman (an action figure of this version of Luthor was produced by DC Direct in 2006). Luthor's loathing knew no bounds. He wished not to merely vanquish the Metropolis Marvel, he aspired to kill him, launching depraved schemes—turning himself into an irradiated "Kryptonite Man," challenging Superman to a death duel under a red sun (under which Superman has no superpowers), creating the backwards-Superman duplicate Bizarro, and teaming with Brainiac among them—to bury his enemy, often working from Luthor's Lair, the name given a variety of sophisticated headquarters secreted in abandoned museums, observatories, and mines, their lead-lined walls shielding the evil scientist from the prying X-ray vision of his arch-foe. In his Lair,

Luthor erected statues of some of history's most infamous figures—including Genghis Khan, Atilla the Hun, Blackbeard, and Benedict Arnold—from whom he drew inspiration. He often kidnapped Superman's friends Lois Lane, Jimmy Olsen, and Perry White to lure the hero into his nefarious traps. This version of Luthor was featured in several episodes of Filmation's animated *The New Adventures of Superman* (1966–1970).

Despite Luthor's malevolence, Superman maintained faith in his former friend, hoping that he would reform and once again devote his genius to the good of humankind. During the Silver Age, snippets of Luthor's humanity emerged. He took great strides to ensure that his younger sister Lena Thorul did not discover that he was her disowned brother, and befriended a beleaguered planet that regarded him a hero; on this world, named Lexor by its grateful inhabitants, Superman was considered a criminal and Luthor had a life separate from his earthly supervillainy, including a wife, Ardora.

While Luthor's modus operandi changed very little during the 1970s, his appearance did; he slimmed down and donned a purple-and-green battlesuit equipped with jet boots and weaponry. This costumed Luthor was popularized on Saturday-morning TV on ABC's *Challenge of the Super Friends* (1978–1979), as the ringleader of the contemptible Legion of Doom.

In December 1978, Oscar-winning actor Gene Hackman brought Luthor to life in director Richard Donner's blockbuster *Superman: The Movie*. More a manipulator than a renegade scientist, Hackman's Luthor was a smooth-talking, scene-stealing deceiver, joined by dimwitted accomplice Otis (Ned Beatty) and voluptuous mistress Miss Techsmacher (Valerie Perrine). Hackman was not required to shave his head to portray Luthor; he wore toupees throughout the movie, only doffing his rug at the movie's end (and revealing a bald wig). Hackman reprised the Luthor role in *Superman II* (1980) and *Superman IV: The Quest for Peace* (1987), the latter film introducing an insipid nephew, Lenny Luthor (Jon Cryer). The comic-book Luthor was mentioned in novels produced in conjunction with the first two movies, *Superman: Last Son of Krypton* (1978) and *Superman: Miracle*

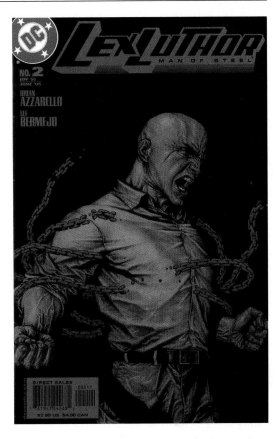

Lex Luthor: Man of Steel #2 ©2005 DC Comics.
COVER ART BY LEE BERMEJO.

Monday (1981), both by Elliot S! Maggin, one of the most prolific writers of Superman comics during the 1970s.

Luthor's uniform was upgraded into a sophisticated "war suit" as part of Superman's 45th anniversary celebration in *Action Comics* #544 (1983). This new look, conceived by artist George Pérez, made Luthor more on par with Superman, but this "robo"-Luthor was short-lived.

Superman was rebooted in 1986's *Man of Steel* miniseries, written and penciled by John Byrne. This new continuity reinvented Luthor into a multi-faceted, constantly evolving figure first seen in a role brainstormed by writer Marv Wolfman: white-collar criminal. The mega-rich tech whiz behind the ubiquitous corporation LexCorp, Luthor was the big man in town until the arrival of Superman (who no longer began his career as Superboy) usurped his position as the *Daily Planet*'s chief headline-maker. A fundamentally unlikable power-broker known for crushing business opponents and coercing female subordinates into sexual relationships, Luthor, untrustworthy of the alien from Krypton who professes to safeguard "his" city, has devoted his wealth and intellect into eliminating this superpowered trespasser.

In the years since *Man of Steel*, Luthor has created the Superman foes Metallo and Bizarro, developed cancer from wearing a kryptonite ring, had his cancer-ravaged hand amputated and replaced with a steel fist, faked his death, transplanted his brain into a younger clone he passed off as his red-headed son, transplanted his brain yet again into another cloned body identical to the original, and organized the anti-Justice League team the Injustice Gang. He has committed various crimes along the way, always stalemating Superman, who was wise to Luthor's machinations.

Luthor's ultimate power play began in 2000 when he was elected president of the DC Universe's United States in a divisive campaign that rivaled the real world's hotly contested Bush v. Gore election (*Superman: President Lex*, 2000). In the story arc "Public Enemies" in *Superman/Batman* #1–#6 (2003–2004), President Lex manipulated public opinion by blaming Superman for a kryptonite asteroid threatening Earth, leading the hero and his ally Batman to work outside of the law to bring down Luthor's presidency. A desperate, near-insane Luthor fought back wearing a battlesuit (a slightly modified version of Pérez's 1983 design), but was ousted from office in disgrace.

In the miniseries *Villains United* (2005) Luthor, sans armor, was seen in full control of his faculties, working underground as the organizer of a supervillain conclave called the Society. Was Luthor a rampaging metal-suited supervillain or a wily criminal strategist? *Villains United* #6 disclosed the startling coexistence of *both* versions: The Society's leader was revealed as an alternate-universe Luthor, while ex-President Lex was exposed as "Mockingbird," the mysterious player behind the Secret Six, the criminal alliance that stood opposed to the Society. This startling revelation created the unusual scenario of Luthor being his own arch-foe, with their struggle unfolding in the continuity-rewrit-

ing crossover *Infinite Crisis* (2005–2006). With duplicity and genius as his guides, Lex Luthor—no matter his form—remains the most dangerous threat to Superman, and to the world.

Voice actor Michael Bell was the first person to play the post-reboot Luthor, in Ruby-Spears' *Superman* cartoon (1988–1989). Luthor has also appeared in each subsequent TV screen adaptation of the Superman legend: the live-action *Superboy* (1988–1992, played by Scott Wells and Sherman Howard), *Lois & Clark: The New Adventures of Superman* (1993–1997, portrayed by John Shea), and *Smallville*; plus the animated *Superman* (1996–2000), *Justice League* (2001–2004), and *Justice League Unlimited* (2004–present), with Clancy Brown voicing him in each. Kevin Spacey brought the bald bad guy to life in Brian Singer's blockbuster movie *Superman Returns* (2006); an earlier, unrealized version of the movie pegged Jack Nicholson for the role. Lex Luthor has been consistently merchandized since the 1978 movie, particularly through a variety of action figures (including a peculiar 1989 version whose "power punch" enabled the toy to hit itself in the eye); the classic mad-scientist Luthor was produced as a mini-bust in the mid-2000s, and in the 1950s through the 1980s was depicted on Superman lunchboxes, puzzles, and board games. —*ME*

Living Laser

Marvel's Living Laser originally derived his name from his weaponry. He was first introduced as Arthur Parks in *The Avengers* vol. 1 #34 (1966) in a story written by Stan Lee and penciled by Don Heck. An experimental scientist, Parks develops miniature laser beams to function as weapons, which he affixes onto his wrists and uses to assume his new identity as the Living Laser.

The Living Laser first found himself in battle with the Avengers after destroying portions of Manhattan in an effort to impress Avengers team member the Wasp, with whom he became infatuated, and then again after he kidnapped her. Although he has worked solo, the Living Laser spent much of his career as a henchman in the employ of Mandarin, Batroc, and the Lethal Legion.

After suffering various defeats, the Living Laser went back to the lab, devising a way to incorporate lasers into his body. With the assistance of underworld scientist Jonas Harrow, the Living Laser implanted miniature laser diodes in his body, enabling him to project laser beams at his mental command. In battle with Iron Man, the Living Laser's diode implants overloaded and exploded, seemingly killing the villain. But the Living Laser did not die: he was re-created into a sentient being composed of photons (particles of light energy, which he can emit as laser beams)—hence, he truly has become a "living laser"! —*GM*

The Lizard

"A super-hero is nothing without a super-villain!" claimed writer Stan Lee's opening caption to Marvel Comics' *The Amazing Spider-Man* vol. 1 #6 (1963), in which Lee and artist Steve Ditko's wall-crawling wonder came "Face-to-Face with … the Lizard!" And while this early addition to Spider-Man's rogues' gallery is one of the hero's deadliest foes, he is also one of his most trusted colleagues.

In the Florida Everglades, hunters and locals are frightened by a truculent half-man, half-reptile who commands "the strength of a dozen bulldozers" and whose scaly skin deflects bullets. Effortlessly snapping a massive tree from its trunk and chucking it at trespassers, the Lizard warns humans to avoid his swampy domain. A *Daily Bugle* publicity stunt lures Spider-Man from New York City to Florida to capture the Lizard, but Spidey soon regrets his involvement when he meets the creature with boundless stamina and a 6-feet-long tail that whips with pile-driver force. The Lizard is actually herpetologist Dr. Curt Connors, an amputee who unlocked the secret of reptiles' limb regeneration, but in tragic turn of events—the stuff from which scientists turned supervillains are made—Connors metamorphoses into the reptilian man-creature. Holing up in an abandoned Spanish fort and protected by alligators that do his bidding, the Lizard plans to repopulate Earth with mutated reptiles, restoring "his" species to their former sovereignty over the planet. Implored not to harm the Lizard by Connors' wife, Martha, and son Billy,

Spider-Man is narrowly able to administer an antidote that reverts the rapscallion to his original human state.

The affable, one-armed Dr. Connors joined Spider-Man's supporting cast in *Amazing Spider-Man* #32 (1966), conducting research in New York and aiding the web-slinger in obtaining a serum to save the life of Aunt May Parker, Peter (Spider-Man) Parker's sole relative, whose blood had become irradiated after a transfusion from Peter. After a few cameos, in issue #43 (1966) Connors assisted Spider-Man in creating an additive to the hero's web fluid that burned through the dense armored hide of the rampaging Rhino.

Before Connors could enjoy his newfound role as Spider-Man's benefactor, tragedy befell him in issue #44 (1967) when, to his dismay, he again transformed into the Lizard. Drawn in this second appearance by Spider-Man's new artist, John Romita, Sr., the single-minded Lizard revived his plan of reseeding the world with reptiles. Spider-Man intervened, but sprained his shoulder in his rematch with the Lizard. The injured web-slinger—ironically now with "one arm," as was Connors before his mutation—struggled through a Lizard-controlled army of snakes and alligators from a city reptile exhibit before deducing his enemy's weakness—extreme cold, "the one thing that will weaken a big, bad, Lacertilian reptile," by luring the Lizard to a train's refrigerator car, where the beast collapses.

The tragic saga of Curt Connors has continued throughout the decades; the scientist's horrific transformations slip into remission and he resumes normalcy with his family, only to have their lives upended by his periodic, uncontrollable alterations. The Lizard has often struck at the most inopportune moments for Spider-Man (as if there were ever a good time for the reptilian rogue to appear), as in the 1971 storyline in which the wall-crawler, cursed with six human arms after his attempt to rid himself of his spider-powers went awry, was battling the living vampire Morbius when the Lizard reared his ugly head. In a 1980 clash, Spider-Man was briefly turned into the Spider-Lizard. But no matter the degree of devastation left in the Lizard's wake, Spider-Man remains dedicated to helping the man beneath the monster.

Usually unable to control his transformations, the superhumanly strong Lizard's tail snakes with a lightning speed that almost defies Spider-Man's protective spider-sense. A network of tiny claws in his hands and feet enable him to scale concrete walls or other sheer surfaces, and he can run and leap at speeds of over 40 mph. The Lizard's coarse skin buffers him from moderate attacks, and he can telepathically exert control over any reptile he encounters. The Lizard is unaware that he is actually Curt Connors, although vestiges of his human memories linger, and the sight of his wife and son have been known to disorient him. Connors must eternally contend with the primordial beast within, hoping that the Lizard will forever remain dormant—but as comic-book history has shown, this lethal Spider-foe cyclically returns every few years for another romp with Spidey.

A basilisk-like alternate version of the Lizard was introduced in 2002 in *Ultimate Marvel Team-Up* #10, part of Marvel's "Ultimate" reimagining of Spider-Man and other characters. In that reality, Dr. Curt Connors was also responsible for creating the Ultimate version of another Spider-foe, Carnage.

The Lizard has frequently slithered out of comics and into television animation, appearing in every one of Spider-Man's cartoon incarnations except for one, *Spider-Man Unlimited* (1999–2001), with Gillie Fenwick, Joseph Campanella, and heavy-metal-rocker-gone-Hollywood Rob Zombie lending their gravelly voices to the supervillain. On the live-action big screen, Dr. Curt Connors was mentioned in the Sam Raimi–directed blockbuster *Spider-Man* (2002) and appeared in *Spider-Man 2* (2004) as a college professor of Peter Parker's, with actor Dylan Baker in the one-armed role; the character's inclusion suggests that the Lizard may eventually emerge in the burgeoning film franchise. In the toy and collectibles market, a cloth-dressed, 8-inch poseable Lizard action figure was released in the mid-1970s in Mego's popular World's Greatest Super-Heroes line, and in the 1990s and 2000s Toy Biz has produced several Lizard figures. Both Bowen Designs and Art Asylum have issued coldcast porcelain mini-busts of the Lizard in the 2000s. —ME

Loki

Many cultures have produced myths of divine tricksters, tempters, and schemers, a fact that may explain why the tale of Loki possesses a universality that translates so naturally into comic-book storytelling. Although more than one comics publisher has used the Norse God of Mischief —Loki's public-domain magicks propelled the exuberant mayhem of the eponymous artifact from Dark Horse's *The Mask* (adapted to feature films in 1994 and 2005)—Marvel Comics has embroidered the legend of Loki far more elaborately than anyone else.

Released into Marvel's superhero pantheon by the seminal storytelling combine of Stan Lee and Jack Kirby in *Journey into Mystery* vol. 1 #85 (1962), long after Loki's much earlier, barely remembered debut pre–Silver Age (1956–1969) era of Marvel/Atlas Comics in *Venus* #6 (1949), Loki is the son of King Laufey, ruler of the frost giants who dwell in the mythical Norse world of Jotunheim, and Queen Farbauti. After Laufey dies in battle against the forces of Odin, ruler of the home of the gods known as Asgard, Odin discovers the infant Loki—whom the frost-giant king had hidden out of shame over the child's decidedly non-giant size—and raises him as his own, alongside the young thunder god Thor.

The Lee/Kirby take on Loki employs a classic dramatic device as old as the tale of Cain and Abel: the sibling rivalry, which also colors a great many other archetypal love-hate relationships between comic-book heroes and villains, such as Dr. Doom and Mr. Fantastic, or Lex Luthor and Superman. True to this pattern, Loki grows up resenting his clearly more-favored adopted brother, dons his sinister trademark green-and-gold ram's-horn-helmeted costume, and thoroughly applies himself to the study of the mystic arts, developing sophisticated powers of hypnotism, illusion-casting, telepathy, and even the ability to change form at will. Determined to destroy the hated Thor, Loki vows to become the most powerful god in Asgard, maturing along the way into the very embodiment of evil and mischief—generally of the sneakiest, most covert variety. Indeed, the Loki of myth is often referred to as the Sly One, among other similar appellations.

From *Marvel's Greatest Superhero Battles'* (1978) reprinting of *The Silver Surfer* vol. 1 ©1969 Marvel Comics.
ART BY JOHN BUSCEMA AND SAL BUSCEMA.

hence, to succumb to the eventual ravages of entropy and final heat-death. And Loki is fated to lead the forces that are to lay waste to Asgard.

Aware of this reality, Odin magically imprisoned Loki within a tree with a spell that could not be broken until someone shed a tear over his plight; by causing a leaf to drop into the eye Heimdall, the guardian of the Bifrost Bridge, Loki brought this circumstance about and escaped. Despite his best efforts to foment chaos, Loki was chagrined early on to discover that he had inadvertently caused a great deal of good. Using his sorcerous powers to cause a train wreck that he blamed on the Hulk, Loki hoped to draw his adopted brother into a fatal battle against the super-strong, gamma-spawned monster. Loki ended up not only temporarily in Thor's custody, but also accidentally caused the formation of the Avengers (*Avengers* vol. 1 #1, 1963). Despite this setback, Loki continued striking against Thor, and grabbing at power by employing surrogates such as the Absorbing Man, whom Loki's magic enables to take on the properties of anything he touches; the magical Asgardian robot known as the Destroyer; the X-Men; and Alpha Flight.

Just as Thor and Odin are embodiments of the forces of order in the universe, Loki represents the eternally countervailing influence of chaos. Like the world-consuming fire-demon Surtur, Loki perpetually threatens to bring about Ragnarok, the long-prophesied end of existence itself. According to the Ragnarok myth, recounted with reasonable accuracy by Lee and Kirby in *Thor* vol. 1 #127 (1966) and by such notable successors as Walter Simonson (*Thor* vol. 1 #337–#382, 1983–1987), Loki's side is fated to win, just as the real universe of planets, stars, and galaxies is destined, billions of years

The Lee/Kirby version of Loki entered the world of (extremely) limited animation in the short-lived *The Marvel Super-Heroes* half-hour series (1966), tangling with his storm-wielding sibling, appropriately enough, every Thursday. Back on the four-color page, Loki's machinations earned him Earthbound exile at the hands of an angry Odin in a 1967–1968 storyline, but the god of mischief was soon able to free himself. He even managed to seize control of Asgard on numerous occasions, but generally fled in characteristically cowardly fashion after enemies such as the monstrous Mangog (the physical manifestation of the anger of an entire race of Asgard's enemies) or the hellfire-spouting Surtur laid siege to the kingdom of the gods.

Like the tricksters of many world legends, Loki often assumes a variety of guises in pursuing his eternal blood-feud against Thor and his never-ending quest for power. He even switches sides when it suits him, as he did when assisting Odin in driving the invader Tyr, Loki's former ally, out of Asgard and when battling Surtur on behalf of Odin and Thor for his own arcane purposes. As part of one bid for power over Asgard, Loki temporarily exchanged bodies with Thor in order to steal Thor's power, thereby making the ultimate transformation. Fortunately, this metamorphosis proved not to be permanent. Loki's reliance on underhanded tactics didn't preclude his taking direct action against his enemies, however. Under Walt Simonson's stewardship, Loki's magic temporarily changed Thor into a frog—a spell that the Frog of Thunder eventually forced Loki to reverse once he laboriously recovered his hammer and his godly powers.

As the years and decades rolled on, Loki's actions became increasingly violent and nasty, no doubt owing to his many frustrating defeats at the hands of his brother. Embittered by the knowledge that his own actions had created the Avengers, Loki finally sought to destroy them by means of assassination; this effort proved to be yet another failure. The Avengers were entirely too canny and well-established to be undone, even by the being whose mischief brought them together in the first place. Loki's escalating viciousness finally forced Thor to execute him (*Thor* vol. 1 #432, 1991), although the trickster's death can't be relied upon to be permanent.

Later in the 1990s, *Thor* writer Warren Ellis offered a unique take on Loki and the other Norse gods, interpreting them with an Arthur C. Clarke–inspired sensibility. Ellis' Norse gods are not deities, but are rather merely supremely powerful alien beings whose technologically created powers are indistinguishable from magic—even to the gods themselves. Under the innovative creative custodianship of British writer Mark Millar and illustrators Bryan Hitch and Paul Neary, Loki has transformed further, becoming a study in existential ambiguity; in *The Ultimates 2*, the second miniseries in Millar's reconceptualization of the Avengers, the very existence of Loki is open to debate. After Thor is arrested and confined by S.H.I.E.L.D. on eco-terrorism charges, is the being who appears to him in his cell—sometimes as a young aide to S.H.I.E.L.D.'s Colonel Nick Fury, sometimes as a talking serpent—really there? Apparently visible only to Thor—whom Millar portrays as a former mental patient as well as a self-styled thunder god and wielder of the storms—the trickster can't resist teasing his imprisoned nemesis about the slippery nature of perception. "What if this *is* just all in your head?" taunts Loki (*The Ultimates* 2 #5, 2005).

Whether constructs of folklore or concrete reality, tricksters such as Loki have endured for countless centuries in human societies, and will doubtless persist as long as people tell tales, on or off the four-color page. —*MAM*

Lord Voldemort

Like any proper villain, Lord Voldemort (or "He-Who-Must-Not-Be-Named" for the more squeamish) quests for immortality and ultimate power. He does not rob banks or hold hostages. He is hell-bent (literally) on world domination and the destruction of everything decent and honorable. Much like epic mythical villains such as the *Lord of the Rings* trilogy's Sauron and real-world megalomaniacs such as Hitler, Voldemort embodies evil incarnate. His only problem is that he doesn't have a body, and his attempt to correct this situation is precisely what guides the events of novelist J. K. Rowling's wildly popular *Harry Potter* series.

Voldemort first appeared in *Harry Potter and the Sorcerer's Stone* (*Philosopher's Stone* in the United Kingdom) in 1997. His origin is clouded and mysterious at first, but Voldemort's sinister history is gradually revealed over the course of the next five books in the series: *The Chamber of Secrets* (1999), *The Prisoner of Azkaban* (1999), *The Goblet of Fire* (2000), *The Order of the Phoenix* (2003), and *The Half-Blood Prince* (2005). Born to a witch mother and a Muggle (non-wizard) father, Tom Riddle was beset with an inferiority complex as a child. Voldemort became a very powerful wizard at an early age, but he compensated for his mixed heritage (perhaps in an attempt to hide it) by using his gifts to torture non-wizards.

Eventually, Voldemort's primary quest became the domination of both the wizard and the Muggle worlds. He became a Master of the Dark Arts and broke all the wizard codes by using the Three Unforgivable Curses to force other wizards to do his will, to inflict pain, and to murder. Like J.R.R. Tolkien's Sauron, Voldemort also sought immortality. Appropriately, his name means "flight from death" in French. He bound parts of his soul to inanimate object called Horcruxes so that he would be able to defy death and return to life as long as the objects remained intact.

At the height of his power, Voldemort initiated a civil war within the wizard community and killed those who refused to join his army. After hearing a prophecy foretelling his downfall and the emergence of a young heroic wizard named Harry Potter, Voldemort decided to kill Potter as an infant. Just prior to the beginning of the first novel in the series, Voldemort killed Harry's parents but failed to kill Harry, who was protected by an older and purer magic. Voldemort cheated death due to the power of his Horcruxes, but the backlash of his attack left him powerless and incorporeal. As Potter grew up an orphan raised in a Muggle household, Voldemort gradually sought to return to power. In each of the books in the series, Potter faces a different manifestation of Voldemort or some evil force the Dark Lord has created to destroy Potter.

Reminiscent of snake figures like the serpent from the biblical Garden of Eden, Voldemort has distinctly reptilian characteristics. Voldemort is one of the few wizards who can speak Parselmouth, or snake language. He has snake-like physical features, the ability to tempt others through sly speech, and the penchant to betray those closest to him for his own personal gain. Over the course of the novels, Potter has become aware of many disturbing similarities between Voldemort and himself. He doesn't know yet what his ultimate destiny

is, but he knows from prophesy and experience that Voldemort is destined to be his nemesis and that, like any proper hero, Potter is destined to stand in his way.

Several years after its creation, the *Harry Potter* series remains a strong presence not just in children's fiction, but in popular culture in general. Four movies have been released based on the first four books in the series. Creator J. K. Rowling has been quite protective of merchandising rights for the *Harry Potter* franchise, but Voldemort has appeared occasionally outside the books and the movies. For example, he has manifested himself twice in plastic form as part of Mattel's action figure line. —*AB*

Lucifer

Although the Lucifer who has battled the X-Men is not the devil, he is appropriately named. When writer Stan Lee and artist Jack Kirby introduced this mysterious masked figure in *X-Men* vol. 1 #9 (1965), they revealed that it was Lucifer who had crippled the team's founder, Professor Charles Xavier, years before, but established virtually nothing else about the character.

Lee's successor as *X-Men* writer, Roy Thomas, explained the mystery in his first two issues (*X-Men* #20–#21, 1966). Lucifer was the advance agent for a race of alien invaders that has been called the Arcane or the Quists, from the planet Quistalium. He looked human, although his mask concealed most of his head. Years ago Lucifer took control of a Tibetan city as his base. The young Xavier aided rebels who forced Lucifer to abandon the city. In revenge, Lucifer dropped a huge slab on Xavier, crushing his legs. Thomas showed how the X-Men stymied Lucifer's attempt to use the Quist computer Dominus to sap the wills of Earth's population, rendering them defenseless.

Furious that the invasion had been thwarted, Quistalium's ruler exiled Lucifer to a "Nameless Dimension" (comparable to the Phantom Zone in *Superman*) in which he somehow acquired the mental ability to manipulate "ionic energy" (*Iron Man* #20, 1969). From this dimension Lucifer could create a psychic link with human hosts on

Earth, endowing them with superhuman abilities. Lucifer intended to use these host bodies to resume his attempt to conquer Earth, but his first host fought off Lucifer's mental domination and his next two hosts perished.

In 1987, the sentient Dominus battled the West Coast Avengers and asserted that Lucifer had been "terminated." Whether Lucifer is indeed dead remains as much an enigma as his true name and his unmasked face. —*PS*

Mad Hatter

The half-cocked haberdasher known as the Mad Hatter owes a tip of the hat for his notoriety to Batman's television appearances.

In *Batman* #49 (1948) writer Bill Finger introduced Jervis Tetch—drawn by artists Bob Kane, Lew Schwartz, and Charles Paris to resemble the Mad Hatter as illustrated by Sir John Tenniel in author Lewis Carroll's children's classic *Alice in Wonderland*—as dwarfish thief who hides dangerous armaments like a gas-gun inside his towering top hat. The Mad Hatter proves little more than a headache for Batman and Robin, however, who quickly capture him.

The Hatter was back, this time as a wild-eyed, wild-haired crackpot obsessed with collecting valuable headgear, in *Detective Comics* #230 (1956), where he nearly obtained Batman's cowl by spraying it with a radioactive chemical, forcing the hero to doff his mask. He returned in *Batman* #161 (1964), attacking the jurors who sent him to prison with an array of trick hats outfitted with weapons. This interpretation of the Mad Hatter and his comic-book appearances were adapted to live-action television as a pair of two-part episodes in ABC's *Batman* (1966–1968), with actor David Wayne in the role of Jervis Tetch.

Wayne's Mad Hatter sported both an odd dialect and a top hat with a hinged lid that opened to reveal a hypnotic device.

The second Mad Hatter was written off as an imposter once an updated version of the *Alice*-inspired villain reemerged in *Detective* #510 (1981). Throughout scarce 1980s sightings in Batman comics, the Mad Hatter employed mind-controlling devices, from chemicals to implanted microchips, for various crimes including extortion and kidnapping, and once nearly beheaded Batman with buzzsaw straw hats.

Television offered the Hatter another shot at wider stardom in *Batman: The Animated Series* (1992–1995). Tetch—voiced by Roddy McDowell and redesigned by artist Kevin Nowlan as a lanky figure with a gargoyle-grin—was an introverted, lovesick scientist who kidnapped his secretary Alice, mentally manipulating her into a perpetual tea party as his fantasy bride. After four additional episodes, the animated Mad Hatter was reconfigured as a shorter, more macabre character for two episodes of *The Adventures of Batman & Robin* (1997–1999) and an installment of the WB's *Superman* cartoon (1996–2000); action figures of both animated incarnations were produced in the 1990s (a comics-inspired Mad Hatter figure was manufactured for the collectors' market in the 2000s).

These various interpretations of the Mad Hatter have blended into the peevishly irrational version populating contemporary DC Comics titles. An expert hypnotist, the Mad Hatter committed one of his most monstrous crimes early in his career. As shown in the miniseries *Robin: Year One* (2000–2001), which retroactively chronicled the history of Dick (the original Robin, later Nightwing) Grayson, Tetch used doctored Walkmans to entrance Grayson's teenage classmates into becoming "Alices," hosting a disturbing tea party. Fortunately the Boy Wonder stopped the Hatter before he could complete phase two of his plan: selling the girls into slavery in Asia. While he remains committed to dastardly haberdashery, the Mad Hatter, thanks to Batman's intervention, always finds Arkham Asylum for the Criminally Insane the perfect place to hang his hat. —*ME*

Mad Mod

The Mad Mod, the Teen Titans' (TTs) most rakish rogue, was cut from the psychedelic cloth of mid-1960s Carnaby Street fashions. The TTs discover in *Teen Titans* vol. 1 #7 (1967) that the smuggling ring they've tailed to London is fronted by Neil Richards, aka the Mad Mod, clothing designer for touring Brit rocker Holley Hip, a patsy whose "loverly" threads secretly conceal contraband. Once the Titans are hip to the Mod's scene, the fiendish fashion plate nearly bags them with a series of deathtraps until the TTs take the Mod to the cleaners.

The brainchild of madcap scribe Bob Haney and illustrator Nick Cardy, the mop-topped Mad Mod was prescient of Austin Powers and Zoolander, decades before those parodies were born. Fads die as quickly as they rise, and after a 1968 return gig at which he stole the Queen's scepter, the Mad Mod, along with mod fashions themselves, peacocked down the runway to limbo, although in a token 1997 appearance the Mod announced that he had reformed. That same year, however, comedian Mike Myers made mod cool again with the soon-to-be-franchised spy spoof *Austin Powers: International Man of Mystery*. On the Italian-leather heels of Powers' third movie in 2002, a Carnaby-conscious public met the Mad

Teen Titans vol. 1 #7 ©1967 DC Comics.
COVER ART BY NICK CARDY.

Mod—"'Ello, Guv'ner!"—on television's anime-like *Teen Titans* (2003–2006).

TV's mind-bending Mad Mod is a brazen bloke who detained the Titans in a brainwashing school ("Mad Mod," original airdate: September 27, 2003), then tried to reclaim New York City as the property of England ("Revolution," October 16, 2004). Rampant pop-culture references dominated both episodes, from *A Hard Day's Night*/*Scooby-Doo*–inspired musically accompanied chase scenes to pastiches of the movie *A Clockwork Orange* (1971), the latter of which starred Malcolm McDowell, the actor who also provided the Mad Mod's cartoon voice. —*ME*

The Mad Thinker

"Another power-mad genius for us to contend with!" sighs the exasperated Invisible Girl as

and even resuscitated the original Human Torch (an android). Dressed in a green jumpsuit, the Thinker was well coiffed in his debut but later sprouted a mop-top. Despite his remarkable mathematical intellect, the Thinker is always stymied by Mr. Fantastic's intuitive brilliance; his perspective in his ongoing war with the FF was chronicled in *Fantastic Four: Foes #1* (2005). While the Thinker refuses to ponder benevolence, his Awesome Android, nicknamed "Awesome Andy," now works as an office assistant at a legal practice that specializes in superhuman law, the firm that also retains She-Hulk. —ME

The Mad Thinker and the Puppet Master. From *Fantastic Four* vol. 1 #28 ©1964 Marvel Comics.
ART BY JACK KIRBY AND CHIC STONE.

she and her teammates are locked out of their headquarters by the Mad Thinker in *Fantastic Four* vol. 1 #15 (1963). Fond of mimicking the contemplative pose of Rodin's famous statue, the Thinker (his "Mad" modifier courtesy of the media) uses computers and his photographic memory to anticipate every probability in committing crimes (a gimmick employed years later by DC Comics' the Calculator). Dispatching the "Awesome Android"—a 15-foot, square-skulled, morphing monstrosity—against the Fantastic Four, the Thinker wields the FF's own weapons against them, but Mr. Fantastic outthinks the Thinker by tripping a circuit breaker to de-power his lab.

Given his unbridled ego, it is odd that the Thinker has revealed little of his past, but his fascination with synthetic beings is no secret. He created Quasimodo (the Quasi-Motivational Destruct Organ) and myriad other assassin automatons,

Madame Masque

The daughter of Count Nefaria, Madame Masque was raised in the United States as Whitney Frost by her wealthy Wall Street foster parents, Byron and Loretta Frost. Her privileged life did not last; Count Nefaria revealed to Whitney that he was her biological father, and that he intended to train her to be his successor as a leader of the infamous Maggia, Marvel Comics' analogue to the Mafia. Shocked and distraught, Whitney refused to follow Nefaria's wishes, but when Count threatened to expose her true identity, she complied. Writer Stan Lee and penciler Gene Colan introduced the villainess in *Tales of Suspense* #98 (1968) as Maggia leader "Big M," her secret identity, and as socialite Whitney Frost in the following issue.

The criminal mastermind has been a former employee of the benevolent millionaire Mordecai Midas, but is mostly identified as the leader of the Nefaria family of the Maggia. Lacking superpowers, Madame Masque is, however, well versed in criminal strategy and the management of underworld operations, and she has excellent combat skills. Her face was severely scarred in a chemical accident, making her self-conscious and at times vulnerable. At the insistence of Midas she wore a gold mask, hence her moniker.

The Kurt Busiek–scripted and George Pérez–penciled *The Avengers* vol. 3 #31–#34 (2000) revealed that the original Madame Masque had been in hiding for years, insanely paranoid after her father's seeming (but accidental) death at the hands of her sometime-lover Iron Man. Convinced she could trust no one, she ran her Maggia family through surrogates, notably "bio-duplicates" (clones) of herself. One defective bio-duplicate became a shapeshifter known as Masque and befriended the Avengers, who eventually located the real Madame Masque and joined forces with her to fight a resurrected Count Nefaria. The real Madame Masque assisted the Avengers and the Thunderbolts in defeating the Count and escaped, a villainess conflicted.

Madame Masque appeared in the *Iron Man* animated television show (1994). *—GM*

Mageddon

B efore the real-world events of September 11, 2001, the comic-book pages unleashed their own weapon of mass destruction: Mageddon, debuting in *JLA* #37 (2000), part of the "World War III" story arc penned by Grant Morrison.

Manufactured by the Old Gods of Urgrund, this enormous squid-like creature ignites feelings of extreme anger and hatred in human beings and amplifies the worst and most hostile threats of a planet's population, triggering global conflicts. To speed up its doomsday mission, Mageddon selects ordinary human beings (or superheroes) on a besieged planet to act as "remote senders": these people manifest a large ectoplasmic eyeball around their upper body to report to the central Mageddon unit. If attacked, senders shoot enormous blasts of energy. Many a villain—including Lex Luthor—fell prey to the influence of Mageddon's probes.

When Mageddon escaped the gravity sink that imprisoned it for 15 billion years, it targeted Earth, setting off random military attacks that resembled the dawn of World War III. Although heroes such as Metron and Orion of the New Gods and members of the Justice League of America tried to stop Mageddon, only Superman was able to thwart its destructive devices when he traveled to the heart of the entity and absorbed the anti-sunlight that empowered it.

Mageddon is known by many names, including the Ultimate Warbringer, the Anti-Sun, the Primordial Annihilator, and Tezcatlipoca. *—GM*

Magneto

M agneto has been the X-Men's foremost nemesis from the very beginning, and one of the greatest supervillains in the Marvel canon. Created by editor/writer Stan Lee and artist/co-plotter Jack Kirby, Magneto debuted in *X-Men* vol. 1 #1 (1963) when he commenced his war on the human race by taking over the American missile base at the fictional Cape Citadel, only to be thwarted by the X-Men in their first public appearance.

One of Earth's most powerful mutants, Magneto has the mental ability to manipulate the forces of magnetism, enabling Magneto to levitate and reshape iron and steel at will, including adamantium, the steel alloy bonded to the skeleton of X-Men member Wolverine. Theoretically Magneto can control all forms of electromagnetic energy, including light. At the height of his abilities, Magneto has proved capable of creating an electromagnetic pulse that paralyzes electronic technology throughout the planet. Some stories even attribute psychic abilities to Magneto, including astral projection. Magneto also possesses advanced knowledge of genetic engineering and has thus artificially created superpowered mutants.

Whereas the X-Men's founder, Professor Charles Xavier, dresses in an ordinary business suit, Magneto in the comics adopts a regal costume including a helmet, apparently adapted by Kirby from those worn by ancient Etruscan warriors. The *X-Men* movies and comics from the 2000s assert that the helmet shields Magneto from Xavier's telepathic powers.

Lee and Kirby established that the longstanding war between Magneto and Xavier's is based in ideological conflict over the strategy that the emerging race of super-powerful mutants should adopt in a world where they are a minority. Xavier pursues his "dream" of peaceful coexistence, but Magneto contends that only through force can mutants will attain freedom from racial oppression. Lee and Kirby created X-Men and Magneto in the early 1960s, during the rise of the African-American civil rights movement, and Bryan Singer, the director of the first two *X-Men* movies (2000, 2003), has compared Xavier to Martin Luther King, Jr., who advocated peaceful demonstrations for civil rights. However, in the first movie, Singer pointedly has Magneto quote another African-American leader, Malcolm X, when he asserts that he will achieve his goals "by any means necessary."

Lee and Kirby were also members of the World War II generation, and they may have conceived Magneto as a neo-fascist reminiscent of the Nazis: Magneto has often maintained that mutants, "Homo superior," are a master race whose superior power proves their worthiness to rule "inferior" humans.

In *X-Men* #4 (1964) Magneto returned as the leader of a team with the unlikely name of the "Brotherhood of Evil Mutants," a sinister counterpart to the X-Men, whose original membership comprised the Toad, Mastermind, and the siblings Quicksilver and the Scarlet Witch. Through the Brotherhood and the subversive organization Hydra, Lee and Kirby foreshadowed the rise of contemporary terrorist organizations, independent of national borders, with Magneto as the charismatic ideological leader.

In *X-Men* #5 (1964) Lee and Kirby created Magneto's original "Asteroid M" base, which orbits Earth as the villain's headquarters. In *X-Men* #11 (1965), the alien Stranger removed Magneto from Earth, supposedly forever, but Magneto escaped to menace the X-Men repeatedly in their series' original run.

Though *X-Men* was canceled in 1970, Magneto continued to appear in other Marvel series, battling the X-Men and other heroes, including the Avengers, the Fantastic Four, and the Defenders. Over the

X-Men vol. 1 #112 ©1978 Marvel Comics.
COVER ART BY GEORGE PÉREZ AND BOB LAYTON.

decades Magneto has guest starred in *Fantastic Four, The Avengers, The Amazing Spider-Man*, and *Captain America*, among other series. At the conclusion of *The Defenders* #16 (1974) a mutant called Alpha reverted Magneto to the form of a helpless infant, and Xavier took him into custody. Shortly after the mid-1970s revival of the *X-Men* comic, Magneto returned to adulthood and renewed his war with Xavier's mutants (*X-Men* #104, 1977).

However, the *X-Men*'s new writer, Chris Claremont, wearied of the traditional depiction of Magneto as irredeemably evil. In various stories, notably *The Uncanny X-Men* #161 (1982), Claremont filled in Magneto's backstory. Magneto's "real" name was Erik Magnus Lehnsherr. (One story established this to be an alias, but Marvel has since ignored this fact.) As a child Magneto was imprisoned in the Nazi concentration camp in Auschwitz, Poland, during World War II; although Clare-

Ian McKellen as Magneto in *X2: X-Men United* (2003).

mont did not make it explicit, the comics and movies have established Magneto as Jewish. (Magneto's ethnicity makes his later embrace of a neo-fascist "master race" philosophy particularly ironic.)

After the war, Lehnsherr and his new wife, Magda, had a daughter named Anya. When a crowd refused to save Anya from dying in a burning building, the enraged Lehnsherr struck out at them with his newly emerged magnetic powers. Horrified, Magda fled from her husband and apparently perished soon after giving birth to twins Pietro and Wanda, who grew up to become Quicksilver and the Scarlet Witch.

Lehnsherr's experiences in Auschwitz made him determined that the emerging mutant race would not suffer a similar fate. (The present-day comics version of Magneto does not look old enough to have been alive in the 1940s. The reason is that when Magneto was restored to adulthood in *X-Men* #104, he became physically far younger than his actual chronological age.)

Under the name "Magnus," he befriended Xavier while both were living in Israel, where they debated the proper course for mutantkind. Ultimately, Magnus decided on preparing for his war against the human race.

In *Uncanny X-Men* #150 (1981), after nearly killing the teenage X-Men member Kitty Pryde, who reminded him of Anya, Magneto suffered a crisis of conscience. Claremont intended to portray Magneto as a terrorist who matures into a statesman, and so Magneto became the X-Men's ally. In fact, when Xavier became incapacitated, he appointed Magneto to take charge of his school for mutants (*Uncanny X-Men* #200, 1985). This Magneto became the New Mutants' headmaster. In the early 1980s Magneto, Quicksilver and the Scarlet Witch finally learned they were father, son, and daughter.

Other Marvel writers and editors have sharply disagreed with Claremont's treatment of Magneto. Eventually, Claremont established that Xavier's colleague Dr. Moira MacTaggert had manipulated Magneto's mind when the latter had reverted to infancy, thereby "brainwashing" him into eventual reform in *X-Men* vol. 2 #1–#3 (1991). With Claremont's departure from Marvel in 1991, editors and writers returned to Lee and Kirby's original characterization. Magneto once again made war on all humanity. Following one of his onslaughts, the United Nations sought to appease Magneto by awarding him the rulership of Genosha, an island nation of mutants. Unsurprisingly, Magneto used his new country as a base from which to launch further attempts at world domination. Eventually Genosha was attacked by robot Sentinels dispatched by Xavier's evil fraternal twin Cassandra Nova.

Perhaps responding to the dangers posed by terrorists of the twenty-first century, writers such as Grant Morrison (in *New X-Men*) and Mark Millar (in *Ultimate X-Men*) have portrayed Magneto as far more ruthless and even bloodthirsty than ever before. In their stories Magneto openly speaks of enslaving or exterminating the human race, or even using them for food. Finally, in *New X-Men* #150 (2004), at the end of Morrison's stint as the series' writer, Wolverine beheaded Magneto with a swipe of his claws.

Or had he? After a decade's absence, Claremont returned to writing books in Marvel's *X-Men* family of titles, and the first issue of Claremont's new version of *Excalibur* (2004) ended with Magneto showing up, alive, to aid Xavier in caring for the mutants left living amid the devastation of Genosha. Morrison's Magneto had apparently been an impostor, and Claremont had brought back his kinder, gentler version of Magneto as the Real McCoy.

So competing interpretations of Magneto in Marvel comics continue, and it remains to be seen which one will eventually prevail.

Magneto has starred in several of his own comics miniseries and has appeared on television in *X-Men: The Animated Series* (1992–1997) and the animated *X-Men: Evolution* (2000–2003). But it was the first *X-Men* movie (2000) through which the character first achieved fame beyond the comic-book audience. Director Bryan Singer persuaded English actor Ian McKellen, with whom he had previously worked in the film *Apt Pupil* (1998), to play the role. Considered by many to be the leading British classical actor of his generation, McKellen gives Magneto intelligence, gravitas, and even a subtle humor that are lacking in the ranting

egotist that so many past comics have depicted. Singer utilized Claremont's backstory that Magneto was an inmate at Auschwitz, but ignored the comic-book Magneto's continuing youthfulness. McKellen, in his sixties, credibly portrays a man who was a child during World War II. In casting another English classical actor, Patrick Stewart, as Xavier, opposite McKellen, Singer helped dramatize Claremont's vision of the two mutant leaders as former colleagues and friends. In the first film Magneto heads a mutant Brotherhood. In the sequel, *X2: X-Men United* (2003), Magneto attempts to bring about the genocide of all non-mutant humans; hence, McKellen's Magneto resembles the most malevolent comic-book versions of the character.

A third *X-Men* movie, including McKellen as Magneto, was released in 2006, and Marvel and Twentieth Century Fox have discussed a *Magneto* spin-off film, dealing with the character's youth. —*PS*

Malebolgia

The devil behind Spawn's creation, Malebolgia, is the conniving ruler of the 8th Circle of Hell, as recounted in both Dante and the canon of Todd McFarlane's long-running *Spawn* comic. Hell-bent on destroying heaven, Malebolgia assembles an army of Hellspawn to aid him in the battle.

Malebolgia created Spawn by making a bargain with the dead spirit of Al Simmons: a chance for Simmons to see his beloved wife Wanda once more in exchange for his fealty as a Hellspawn. In the way of all such bargains with the devil, Malebolgia tricked Spawn by sending him to Earth five years after his death, by which time Wanda had remarried and had a daughter. In the first *Spawn* story (issues #1–#4, 1992), Malebolgia sends the Violator, a minor demon, to watch over Spawn as his "chaperone," but when the Violator fails, Malebolgia reveals himself to them both. Spawn is able to break free of his master, while Malebolgia returns to hell. In issues #51–#53 (1996), drawn by Greg Capullo, Malebolgia returns when Spawn journeys into hell to try to save the life of Terry Fitzgerald, Wanda's new husband. Beset by all manner of hellish threats, Spawn manages to pass all of Malebolgia's tests, and they strike a new bargain: Wanda and Terry will be left alone, but Spawn will once again swear allegiance to his creator.

Malebolgia's third major appearance is in issue #100 (2000). Once again, Wanda's life is in jeopardy, and Spawn goes back to hell for the final battle. This time, Spawn and his devil-fighting ally Angela manage to kill Malebolgia.

Like most McFarlane villains, Malebolgia's central feature is a teeth-filled maw. In the 1997 *Spawn* movie, he was voiced by Frank Welker, and has also appeared as a number of increasingly alarming toys. —HM

Man-Bat

I s he friend or foe? Batman can never be quite sure when the terrifying Man-Bat flutters into view.

"Challenge of the Man-Bat" by writer Frank Robbins and artists Neal Adams and Dick Giordano, in *Detective Comics* #400 (1970), begins with Dr. Kirk Langstrom preparing a "night-creature habitat exhibit" under the auspices of the Gotham [City] Museum of Natural History. He feverishly burns "the midnight oil" on a top-secret project: a bat-gland extract that gives him heightened hearing and self-generated sonar. The zoologist is stunned by his serum's unexpected side effects, as formerly faint sounds are now deafening, and a mere table light is more than his eyes can endure. His woes are only beginning, however—he watches in horror as his hands sprout hair and metamorphose into claws, and his face transforms into a repugnant bat/human hybrid. Aghast, Langstrom intends to find a cure for his mutation, but soon encounters Batman, aiding the hero in battling the Blackout Gang, thieves whose infrared goggles give them night vision. Professing his idolatry of the Caped Crusader—"It was your inspiration … your great fight against criminals of the night—that brought this [transformation] on me!"—Langstrom slips away into the night.

The bat-men again crossed paths two months later in *Detective* #402, when Batman discovered Man-Bat raiding a laboratory for biochemicals needed for his antidote. Appalled after realizing that Man-Bat was *not* wearing a costume as he

had assumed, Batman attempted to help Langstrom, with the aid of the scientist's fiancée, Francine Lee. The growth of bat wings (with a wingspan of more than 13 feet) completed Langstrom's transformation into Man-Bat, his animal instincts overriding his human intelligence. After a climactic battle in the Batcave, where Man-Bat intuitively sought refuge, Batman barely prevailed over this maddened monster. When next seen in *Detective* #407 (1971), Langstrom and Francine married. Being the devoted wife, Francine took her husband's serum and became She-Bat, but a serum created by Batman restored the couple's humanity.

"There's a lot of talk about who created Man-Bat," remarked Julius Schwartz, the editor of *Detective Comics* (and *Batman*) during the 1970s, in Les Daniels' *Batman: The Complete History* (1999), indicating that he brainstormed the character. Conversely, Adams remembers that the idea for Man-Bat was his. In his foreword to *Batman Illustrated by Neal Adams* vol. 2 (2004), Adams recounted that he pitched "Manbat" (no hyphen) to Schwartz: "Manbat is an obvious and great idea … Look, Julie, one day, this same obvious idea is going to occur to someone up at Marvel. They'll giggle first at the idea then they'll do it, just to mess with DC." Adams also wrote that he had constructed the origin story synopsis for Man-Bat, giving it to writer Frank Robbins, who, "along with Milton Caniff, was one of my heroes. It was a gift to a hero, I was glad to do it." Man-Bat's origin story was folded into a sequence of the *Batman* newspaper strip in late 1970, written by E. Nelson Bridwell and illustrated by Al Plastino (who borrowed quite liberally from Adams' originals, swiping several classic poses of the character).

Monster-hero and monster-villain comics were the rage during the 1970s, when the Comic Code Authority lifted its ban on horror characters, and Man-Bat enjoyed frequent appearances in various DC titles. Robbins continued to chronicle Langstrom's saga in *Detective*, also assuming the art chores from Adams (Robbins was known for his long-running *Johnny Hazard* newspaper strip, which he wrote and drew). Man-Bat teamed with Batman in *The Brave and the Bold* #119 (1975), where Batman briefly became a Man-Bat himself, and

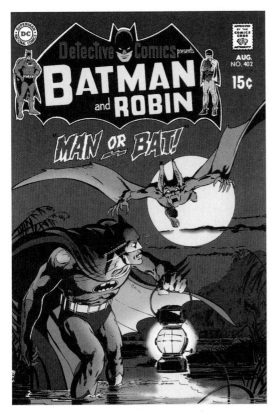

Detective Comics #402 ©1970 DC Comics.
COVER ART BY NEAL ADAMS.

Langstrom graduated into his own series later that year, which ran for two issues. "Robin Meets Man-Bat," a 1976 *Batman* narrated comic book from Power (Peter Pan) Records, featured Neal Adams art (and a partial reprint of *Detective* #402). Man-Bat appeared in solo backup tales in the late 1970s, in both *Detective* and *Batman Family*; emerging fan-favorite artists Marshall Rogers, Howard Chaykin, and Michael Golden were among Man-Bat's artists. As the character's story progressed, Francine temporarily became She-Bat again after being bitten by a vampire bat, and Langstrom improved his serum, gaining control over his conversions and maintaining his intellect as the pseudo-superhero Man-Bat. Mr. and Mrs. Man-Bat had a daughter, Rebecca, in 1978, and into the 1980s Langstrom's mental instability resurfaced during his Man-Bat transformations. In the mid-1980s, a Man-Bat prototype toy was created by Kenner as a possible addition to its Super

Powers action-figure line; the line was discontinued before Man-Bat could be produced.

Man-Bat's tragic tale was first adapted to the screen in "On Leather Wings," a 1992 episode of *Batman: The Animated Series* (*BTAS*). Appropriately, Marc Singer—known to sci-fi fans as the star of *The Beastmaster* (1982)—voiced the bestial Bat-foe. Man-Bat appeared in additional *BTAS* episodes, and Kenner produced an action figure of the softer, kid-friendly cartoon version of the villain. In the years since, additional Man-Bat action figures have been produced bearing the more gruesome visage of the comic's version of the character. In the late 1990s, Man-Bat was rumored to be under consideration, along with the Scarecrow, for what was then being called *Batman 5*, aka *Batman: Darknight* (one word); this version never materialized. Man-Bat returned to television in the animated program *The Batman* (2004–present), portrayed by Peter MacNicol.

DC Comics revamped Man-Bat's origin in *Batman: Legends of the Dark Knight Annual* #5 (1995), as part of a series of "Year One" editions for its characters. In writer Chuck Dixon and illustrator Quique Alcatena's "Wings," Kirk Langstrom was now profoundly hearing impaired, devising his bat-serum as a means to cure his progressive deafness. Subsequent appearances have portrayed Man-Bat more as a monster than a rogue, and the character starred in a 1996 miniseries. Misfortune continues to roost in the Langstrom family cave. The youngest of the brood, Aaron, was born a freakish boy-bat due to his father's tainted cellular structure. To protect Aaron from Gotham's myriad dangers, Francine and Rebecca have become She-Bats. Batman remains sympathetic to this family's peculiar plight, but generally regards Man-Bat as a danger. —*ME*

The Mandarin

In the year when the Beatles' Ringo Starr made fingerwear fashionable, the invincible Iron Man's enemy the Mandarin made them formidable. In *Tales of Suspense* #50 (1964), Iron Man jets to Red China at the behest of the Pentagon to investigate the ruthless "Oriental menace" before whom

From *Tales of Suspense* #50 ©1964 Marvel Comics.
ART BY DON HECK.

obedient servants bow and Communist generals grovel. Plowing through soldiers to enter a fortified castle, the Armored Avenger is smugly greeted by its vainglorious resident, the Mandarin, who paralyzes the high-tech hero with a ray fired from one of his ten rings, and nearly smashes him with a superhumanly strong, steel-splintering karate chop. His armor's energy severely depleted, Iron Man is only able to stall the warlord's attacks before retreating to resume their quarrel another day.

The Mandarin is often regarded as one of the many "Yellow Peril" evildoers, but in his first story, writer Stan Lee and artist Don Heck made gestures to elevate him above Fu Manchu–clone status. While drawn by Heck with the goatee and claw-like fingernails so common among fictional Asian masterminds, the Mandarin wore a green jersey with a shocking-pink cowl, boots, and "M" insignia, clearly categorizing him as a costumed supervillain (on the contrary, the cover by Jack Kirby and George Roussos depicted a stately Mandarin in a jade vestment with purple flourishes; over the years the Mandarin's apparel regularly changed, with robes becoming his standard apparel). Red Chinese armies bent to his will, but the Mandarin, unlike many "Yellow Peril" foes, did not regard physical contact beneath him, crossing swords with Iron Man while boasting of his reputation as

"the greatest karate master the world has ever known." The Mandarin's ten rings, one worn on each finger, appeared ceremonial, yet each possessed a fantastical property: "ice blast," "mento-intensifier" (mind control), "electro blast," "flame blast," "white light" (a laser), "matter rearranger," "impact beam," "vortex beam" (wind control), "disintegration beam," and "black light" (absence of light). His rings' superpowers were aggrandized by his scientific savvy: in some of his numerous battles with Iron Man, the Mandarin commanded the giant robot Ultimo, made "death beam" attacks from a satellite, and programmed nations' weapons to malfunction.

Despite these embellishments, the Mandarin succumbed to "Yellow Peril" trappings. His second story, *Tales of Suspense* #62 (1965), revealed him to be a descendant of Genghis Khan; that tale also disclosed that the Mandarin discovered his rings in a crashed spaceship once guarded by an extraterrestrial dragon (the same race that spawned Fin Fang Foom). The Mandarin perished at the hands of another Asian villain, the Yellow Claw, in 1974, only to be revived three years later when his mind was transferred into a different body. The Mandarin's discord with Iron Man continued for decades in recurring battles until he died, presumably once and for all, at the close of the millennium.

Destiny tapped the Mandarin's son Temugin, who debuted in *Iron Man* vol. 3 #53 (2002), when he received a box containing his father's rings—on the Mandarin's severed hands! Abandoned as an infant by the Mandarin and raised by monks, the princely Temugin continues the legacy of his warlord father, vowing to kill the Armored Avenger, whom he blames for the Mandarin's death. He once humbled Iron Man with his superhuman stamina and martial-arts skills, without the use of the ten rings.

Outside of comics, the Mandarin appeared on television in "Iron Man" episodes of the cartoon anthology *The Marvel Super-Heroes* (1966), and on the *Iron Man* TV series (1994–1996), from which a tie-in action figure was produced. —ME

The Mangog

The 12-foot, 3,500-pound, yellow-skinned creature known as the Mangog growled onto the pages of *Thor* vol. 1 #154 (1968) in a story by superscribe Stan Lee and artist Jack Kirby. Alternatively referred to as a demon, or an "abstract" or "conceptual" being, the superhumanly strong Mangog was created by the magical union of the billions of alien humanoids of a warlike race that Asgardian highfather Odin had defeated and cast into oblivion. After Odin restored the humanoids to life, the Mangog continued to exist, although eventually he shrank to the size of a small rodent.

The Mangog feeds his superstrength from drawing the psionic energies manifested in the hatred and/or vengeance felt by himself or by others. He possesses the power to manipulate magical energies and shows a demigod-like resistance to injury. However, this muscular monstrosity has limitations: the Mangog will shrink or appear to vanish if deprived of his energy sources.

This clawed being has primarily fought Thor and Odin, although he has battled Balder and various Asgardians as well. As part of his plot to stop a death god called Walker, the alien Thanos allied himself with the Mangog. The pair devastated much of the homeworld of the alien Rigellians until they surrendered the "Fire Gem," which Thanos needed to find a woman named Tarene, the Designate. Thanos and the Mangog captured Tarene, but

Thor seemingly destroyed the Mangog and defeated Thanos. History has demonstrated that once he finds a new source of psionic energy, the Mangog will rise yet again. —GM

Mantis: *See* **Darkseid's Elite**

The Master

The Master is the archnemesis of the Doctor, the hero of the British Broadcasting Company's legendary, long-running science fiction series *Doctor Who* (1963–1989, 1996, 2005–present). Like the Doctor, the Master (whose original name is Koschei) is a Time Lord from the planet Gallifrey and travels through time and space in a vehicle called a TARDIS. Yet unlike the benevolent Doctor, the Master is bent on conquering the universe.

The Master debuted in the *Doctor Who* story arc "Terror of the Autons" (1971) and was originally portrayed by actor Roger Delgado, who had an appropriately Mephistophelean look. After Delgado died in an automobile accident, he was succeeded in the role by Peter Pratt, Geoffrey Beevers, Anthony Ainley, Gordon Tipple, and Eric Roberts. A Time Lord is able to stave off death twelve times by regenerating his body. (This is the series' way of justifying recasting the Doctor over the decades.) But the Master (in his Delgado form) had used up all his regenerations, and hence has had to find different methods of extending his existence, including taking possession of host bodies.

Besides his many appearances on the television series, the Master has also been featured in *Doctor Who* novels and audio dramas. As of 2006 the Master's last canonical appearance was in the 1996 *Doctor Who* television movie, in which he was sucked into an artificial "black hole" and seemingly killed. Nevertheless, arch-villains like the Master almost always find a way to survive their apparent destruction. —PS

Mastermind

Looking like a shabby version of Vincent Price, Mastermind debuted in *X-Men* vol. 1 #4 (1964)

as a member of Magneto's Brotherhood of Evil Mutants. Created by writer/editor Stan Lee and co-plotter/artist Jack Kirby, Mastermind had the mutant ability to create illusions.

Mastermind's principal claim to infamy, however, lies in his key role in Chris Claremont and John Byrne's "Dark Phoenix Saga" in *The Uncanny X-Men* (1979–1980). The rather ugly Mastermind used his powers of illusion to make himself appear handsome, and, under his alleged real name, Jason Wyngarde, applied for membership in the ruling Inner Circle of the notorious Hellfire Club. (Claremont and Byrne were inspired by the use of the Hellfire Club in an episode of the British television series *The Avengers*, in which the lead villain was played by actor Peter Wyngarde.) For his initiation test, Mastermind used a device to project his illusions directly into the mind of the X-Men's Phoenix, also known as Jean Grey, drawing out the dark side of her personality. Thus Mastermind brainwashed Phoenix into becoming the Hellfire Club's new Black Queen. But Mastermind had unleashed forces he could not control: she broke free of his mental domination and transformed into the satanic Dark Phoenix.

Years later Mastermind succumbed to the lethal "Legacy Virus," although it's possible that his death may prove to be yet another of his illusions. Mastermind is survived by two daughters: Martinique Jason, alias Mastermind II, and Regan Wyngarde, known as Lady Mastermind. The original Mastermind appeared in *X-Men: The Animated Series* (1992–1997) and the animated *X-Men: Evolution* (2000–2003). —*PS*

The Masters of Evil

A scheming supervillain with a grudge aggregates other costumed criminals to attack Marvel Comics' mightiest superheroes, the Avengers: this successful formula is the basis of each of the numerous iterations of the durable villain team, the Masters of Evil.

Marvel's hitmakers Stan Lee and Jack Kirby devised the formula in *The Avengers* vol. 1 #6 (1964): Nazi scientist Baron Heinrich Zemo so

hates Captain America that when the World War II patriotic paragon is revived by the Avengers after two decades on ice (in suspended animation), Zemo recruits Giant-Man and the Wasp's enemy the Black Knight, Iron Man's nemesis the Melter, and Thor's adversary the Radioactive Man as the first Masters of Evil. The gruesome group paralyzes much of Manhattan with Zemo's "Adhesive X" until being routed by the Avengers.

The implacable Zemo returned in the very next issue, joined by Asgardian deities the Executioner and the Enchantress, unsuccessfully attempting to turn the thunder god Thor against his teammates. Undeterred by defeats, Zemo and his Masters of Evil tried twice more to destroy the Avengers before the Baron met his demise in issue #15 (1965).

The Masters of Evil regrouped in *Avengers* #54 (1968), with returnees Radioactive Man, Black Knight, and the Melter partnering with Klaw and Whirlwind, under the leadership of the enigmatic Crimson Cowl (revealed to be the sinisterly sentient android Ultron). This Masters variation struck at the Avengers through their trusted butler Jarvis. Ultron was dismantled at the end of this extended storyline, but later returned.

A third incarnation of the Masters of Evil rallied in 1982, masterminded by Egghead, the evil scientist with the egg-shaped cranium who had been a foe of Hank (Yellowjacket) Pym's since the size- and costume-changing superhero's Ant-Man days. Whirlwind and Radioactive Man were back, joined by the Beetle, Moonstone, Scorpion, the Shocker, and Tiger Shark. Egghead was killed in the fracas.

Baron Zemo's rancorous son Helmut (Baron Zemo II) gathered a fourth version of the Masters of Evil in 1987, with returning and new members. Zemo bucked tradition by surviving this encounter, but the Avengers nearly did not—the Masters demolished their headquarters and brutalized the heroes. A few years later, Dr. Octopus organized a legion of supervillains as the fifth, easily forgettable version of Masters of Evil.

Lee and Kirby's original blueprint had worn thin, but 1997's sixth variation enlivened the concept. Baron Zemo II, the Beetle, the Fixer, Goliath, Moonstone, and Screaming Mimi masqueraded as super*heroes*—Citizen V, MACH-1, Techno, Atlas, Meteorite, and Songbird, respectively—as the Thunderbolts. Most of the "T-Bolts" actually switched camps, becoming good guys fighting to live down their bad reputations. This reinvigoration of Lee and Kirby's criminal confederation made two subsequent revivals of the Masters of Evil (both spearheaded by a new Crimson Cowl, Justine Hammer) infinitely more interesting, with a rivalry forming between the old Masters (the T-Bolts) and the new.

Outside of comics, Masters of Evil Baron Zemo I, the Melter, and the Radioactive Man teamed with the Red Skull in a "Captain America" installment of the cartoon anthology *The Marvel Super-Heroes* (1966), while Zemo II, the Absorbing Man, Boomerang, Cardinal, Dragonfly, Moonstone, Tiger Shark, and Whirlwind were the Masters of Evil on FOX Kids' animated *The Avengers* (1999–2000). —*ME*

Maximus the Mad

Maximus the Mad is the black sheep of the Royal Family of the Inhumans, the reclusive race given extraordinary abilities by the mutagenic Terrigen Mist. First seen in *Fantastic Four* vol. 1 #47 (1966), in a multi-chapter Stan Lee/Jack Kirby storyline introducing the Inhumans into the Marvel Universe, the wild-eyed "Maximus, the Magnificent" is ruling the Inhumans' "Great Refuge," the city of Attilan, in the absence of its rightful king, Maximus' older brother Black Bolt. Upon the return of the silent monarch Black Bolt, who has been away searching for the amnesiac Inhuman Medusa, readers discover that the "Magnificent" Maximus is quite mad, fanatical in his belief that he, and only he, should govern his people. He steps aside for his sibling to reclaim his crown while conspiring to usurp it, attempting to eradicate humankind with his quake-producing Atmo-Gun so that the Inhumans might "inherit the Earth" under his rule.

Maximus possesses psionic powers, obtained during his infancy from Terrigen exposure. He can influence the behavior of individuals and groups within close proximity, and he can induce memory lapses. Notwithstanding his abrupt mood swings and delusional rants, Maximus is in fact a technological genius who has created a range of diabolical devices to bolster his mental control, including nerve potions, the Nerve Beam, and the Hypno-Gun. Under his thrall are the Alpha Primitives, a subclass of Inhumans, who have aided him in his subsequent schemes—several of which were successful, albeit short-lived—to dominate Attilan.

An Inhumans backup series by Lee and Kirby in *Thor* #146–#152 (1967–1968) revealed Maximus as the second-born son of Attilan geneticists Agon and Rynda. An unsociable teen, he forged a pact with alien warriors the Kree. His older brother Black Bolt intervened by using his ultimate, and forbidden, superpower—his sonic scream—to stop an escaping Kree spacecraft, its ensuing crash tragically killing the siblings' parents. From that moment, Black Bolt realized that he could not trust his younger brother—nor could he trust the force of his own voice.

In addition to his ongoing conflicts with his fellow Inhumans and their friends the Fantastic Four, Maximus' efforts to be proclaimed Emperor Eternal have put him at odds with the Incredible Hulk, the Avengers, X-Factor, and Quicksilver. While he insists on being called Maximus the Magnificent, the egomaniac's reign of atrocities against his own people and others have permanently earned him the title Maximus the Mad.

Mark Hamill, a veteran at voicing cartoon villains, portrayed Maximus in two episodes of the animated series *Fantastic Four* (1994–1996). —*ME*

Maxwell Lord

Maxwell Lord, created by Keith Giffen, J. M. DeMatteis, and Kevin Maguire, pulled a lot of strings to reorganize DC Comics' mightiest superhero team in *Justice League* #1 (1987) and reestablish the League as a global peacekeeping force. "How he does it, no one is quite certain," wrote editor Andrew Helfer in his introduction to a 1989 compilation of the series' first seven issues. "Connections are crossed, mistakes are made, characters enter and leave—and only one thing is certain: Max did it."

Max didn't do it alone. Working in tandem with a sentient computer from the planet New Genesis, Lord, the smiling, smarmy, comic-book equivalent of Donald Trump, was duped by the alien machine, which had an ulterior motive of world domination

(*Justice League International* #12, 1988). The Justice League forgave him.

A "metabomb" detonated by alien invaders (*Invasion!*, 1988–1989) activated Lord's ability to manipulate—or "push"—minds, which Max periodically used to persuade superheroes to join his superteam. The Justice League forgave him.

After several years of hero manipulation, Lord died of a brain tumor and was resurrected as Lord Havok II, a murderous robot, in a mid-1990s storyline. DC Comics executive editor Dan DiDio forgave him.

DiDio announced on the 2005 comics-convention trail, "We thought about that aspect of the story and then asked, 'Did anyone read it?' No. 'Did anyone like the idea?' No. So we moved ahead with Max as being a human." Human with the "metahuman" power of mind-pushing, that is. *Countdown to Infinite Crisis* #1 (2005), a one-shot launching a massive crossover event, disclosed that Lord actually distrusted the superhero community ("All I want is to put Earth's destiny in the hands of humans, not people pretending to be human"), and had used his Justice League connections to learn their weaknesses and conspire against them. When Justice Leaguer Blue Beetle discovered the truth, Lord put a bullet through Beetle's brain. Throughout various DC titles during the summer of 2005, Lord attacked heroes with killer machines called OMACs, and he used his own superpower to "push" Superman into a bloody battle with Batman and Wonder Woman. Wonder Woman did *not* forgive him.

In *Wonder Woman* vol. 2 #219 (2005), the Amazon Princess stopped the power-mad Lord the only way she knew how: by snapping his neck. The menace of Maxwell Lord was over, but repercussions from his machinations will no doubt affect the DC superheroes for years to come.

Tim Matheson played Max Lord (in his pre–*Infinite Crisis* incarnation) in the "Ultimatum" episode (original airdate: December 4, 2004) of the Cartoon Network's *Justice League Unlimited* (2004–present). —*ME*

Mephisto

Sometimes called the Lord of Evil and the Prince of Darkness, Mephisto was created by Stan Lee and John Buscema in *The Silver Surfer* #3 (1968). Viewing worldly events through the iridescent haze of his brazier-spawned "mystic vapors," Mephisto is appalled by the nobility of the irreproachable Silver Surfer, the allegorical fallen angel banished to Earth by his former master Galactus. Fearing the Surfer's attributes ("Your courage—your purity—your lack of malice—pose and intolerable challenge to me—and to all I stand for!"), Mephisto attempts to seduce the Surfer with promises of wealth and power. The Prince of Darkness fails to corrupt the Surfer's indomitable soul, even when using the Surfer's beloved Shalla Bal as a pawn.

Envisioned as the antithesis of the virtuous Silver Surfer, Mephisto is Marvel Comics' proxy for Satan. "I didn't want to hit the reader over the head with religious implications," explained Lee in his book *Bring on the Bad Guys* (1976). Wishing to maintain uncertainty over Mephisto's actual identity, Lee "settled for a name which certainly had the sound of Mephistopheles, but we weren't quite coming out and saying it. Besides, Mephisto is easier to spell."

Mephisto rules the Stygian Deep, his "hell" dimension or "Hades" realm. A demonic, red-skinned figure clad in hellish crimson, he may not be "the" Satan, but he has led many to believe that he is from his first appearance, when he lusted over the triumph he shall reap come Armageddon. Mephisto is virtually indestructible; possesses superhuman strength and stamina; can distort reality; is able to vanish, teleport, fly, and grow to gargantuan height; and can hurl earth-quaking blasts. He covets the souls of others, but can only possess them with the compliance of his victims, which he solicits via temptation and trickery.

Mephisto's genesis is uncertain, although he and others have ascribed various testaments to his roots. Is he connected to the coveted power sources the Infinity Gems? Was he born of a primeval demon? Is he related to the so-called Son of Satan, Daimon Hellstrom? These and other claims, like Mephisto himself, cannot be trusted, and various theories of Mephisto's origins have been discredited.

Mephisto's satanic surrogacy has been exploited by continuity-minded writers and editors, with revelations that various depictions of "the

SO LONG AS I CAN APPEAL TO MAN'S *BASEST* INSTINCTS--

TO HIS *GREED*-- HIS *ENVY*--HIS *HATREDS* AND *AGGRESSION*-- HIS *FEAR* AND *DISTRUST* OF HIS FELLOW MAN--

SO LONG AS MAN TAKES THE *LAW* INTO HIS OWN HANDS --BOTH IN THE *STREETS* --AND ON THE FIELD OF *BATTLE*--

AND, SO LONG AS *CRIME* COVERS THE PLANET LIKE A DEADLY, CREEPING FUNGUS--

THEN, ONLY *MEPHISTO* SHALL REAP THE FINAL, ETERNAL *REWARD!*

From *The Silver Surfer* vol. 1 #3 ©1968 Marvel Comics. ART BY JOHN BUSCEMA AND JOE SINNOTT.

contact with the Silver Surfer or his retrofitted connection to Ghost Rider. He has attempted to control beings as diverse as the thunder god Thor and the omnipotent wanderer the Beyonder. The Lord of Evil succeeded in briefly trapping the spirits of the Richards family (Reed, aka Mr. Fantastic, and Sue, the Invisible Woman, plus their son Franklin) in a 1985 *Fantastic Four* storyline, and created the sorcerer Master Pandemonium, enemy of the West Coast Avengers. He was awarded his own 1987 miniseries, *Mephisto vs ... ,* each issue pitting the chthonian supervillain against of one Marvel's superhero teams (the Fantastic Four, X-Factor, the X-Men, and the Avengers), and he allied with, then fought against, the overlord Thanos in the 1991 miniseries *The Infinity Gauntlet*.

Two pieces of Mephisto's soul that splintered from him during his battle with the Fantastic Four were magically altered into the children of the superheroes the Scarlet Witch and the Vision, unbeknownst to them. When Master Pandemonium reclaimed these soul fragments and returned them to Mephisto in *Avengers West Coast* (formerly titled *West Coast Avengers*) #52 (1989), the children were lost to their parents. The Scarlet Witch eventually went insane from grief and turned against Marvel's heroes, resulting in the crossover events *Avengers Disassembled* (2004) and *House of M* (2005).

Often perched from his stone-carved throne, Mephisto is worshipped and served by lowly demons and netherworldly creatures. He has two

Devil" or "Satan" in some Marvel stories were actually Mephisto in disguise. The most famous instance was the union of the souls of stunt rider Johnny Blaze and the demon Zarathos into the hellspawn motorcyclist Ghost Rider, in *Marvel Spotlight* #5 (1972). Blaze as well as readers assumed this was the work of Satan.

Mephisto's supernatural reach into the Marvel Universe has extended far beyond his initial children, his daughter Mephista and his son Black-heart, both of whom were introduced in the late 1980s. They are by no means a happy family, as Blackheart has attempted to overthrow his father. But such is to be expected of the progeny of the character his own creator, Stan Lee, described as lacking "a single solitary redeeming quality."

Mephisto's perceived connection to Satan has dissuaded television animators and toy manufac-turers from using the villain, although a sculpted mini-bust targeted toward adult collectors, the first three-dimensional depiction of Mephisto, was released for Halloween 2005. —*ME*

Metallo

W riter Robert Bernstein and artist Al Plastino created Metallo, the Man with the Kryptonite Heart, for *Action Comics* #259 (1959), the same issue that debuted the Silver Age (1956–1969) Supergirl. "The Menace of Metallo" opens with unethical journalist John Corben—a dead ringer for Superman (except for Corben's mustache)—gloat-ing as he drives away after committing a murder he staged to appear as a suicide. Critically wounded in an automobile accident, Corben is discovered by motorist Professor Vale. The scientist rebuilds Cor-ben's crushed body and skeleton using a durable, uranium-empowered metal that also gives the rogue tremendous strength. The unstoppable Cor-ben steals uranium from research facilities, hospi-tals, and a U.S. Army base, and the press dubs him "Metallo, the Metal Man." Metallo's discovery that kryptonite—the radioactive mineral lethal to Superman—augments his mechanical power allows him to hold the Man of Steel at bay. The vil-lain ultimately errs by mistakenly inserting into his chest a piece of artificial kryptonite—without the ore's radiation, Metallo suffers the equivalent of a fatal heart attack.

Corben's embittered brother Roger became Metallo II in *Superman* vol. 1 #310 (1977), blam-ing the Man of Steel for his sibling's death. Pub-lished during a period when Earth's kryptonite had been temporarily eradicated due to a bizarre chain reaction (beginning in *Superman* #233, 1971), Roger's cybernetic body, constructed by turncoat

S.T.A.R. Labs scientist Dr. Albert Michaels (aka the Atomic Skull), was fueled by man-made kryptonite. *Superman* #310's cover, by artists José Luis Gar-cia-López and Bob Oksner, presented the new Met-allo in what would be the supervillain's signature pose: opening his shirt and chestplate to reveal his kryptonite heart, waylaying the Man of Steel with its deadly beams. Metallo II soon was dressed in a suit of green-and-orange armor, with a Dr. Doom–like face mask. He assaulted Superman on a handful of occasions, and in one offbeat tale—a Batman/Lois Lane team-up in *The Brave and the Bold* #175 (1981)—brandished a type of manufactured kryptonite that harmed humans.

An all-new Metallo appeared in *Superman* vol. 2 #1 (1987), masterminded by writer/artist John Byrne, following Byrne's continuity-rebooting 1986 *Man of Steel* miniseries. As in the 1959 version, the contemporary Metallo is John Corben, a two-bit criminal whose entire body (including his head) was mangled in a car crash. Professor Emmett (now given a first name) Vale saved Corben by transplanting Corben's brain into a kryptonite-pow-ered robotic body that looked remarkably like the steel assassin in James Cameron's *The Terminator* (1984). Fearing that the newly arrived Superman heralded an impending invasion of Kryptonian super-aliens, Vale created Metallo as Earth's first line of defense and mandated that Corben kill the Man of Tomorrow; he instead murdered Vale. The robotic rogue nonetheless encountered Superman, exposing him to kryptonite for the first time.

His kryptonite heart able to bring the Man of Steel to his knees, the superstrong Metallo has often proved more than a match for the weakened Superman. Metallo received a more powerful body from the demon Neron in 1995, and in 2000 he was temporarily upgraded to giant-robot proportions thanks to Brainiac 13. Utterly merciless and able to interface with any technology, Metallo can also transform, turning parts of his body into weapons. He can be de-powered by removing his kryptonite heart, or by severing his head from his body, but to do either generally requires that Superman partner with other superpowered heroes.

In the story arc "Public Enemies" by writer Jeph Loeb and artist Ed McGuinness, in *Super-man/Batman* #1–#6 (2003–2004), Batman discovered evidence, later shown to be erroneous, that John Corben was the gunman of Thomas and Martha Wayne, parents of the Dark Knight's alter ego Bruce Wayne. A 2005 Metallo action figure was manufactured by DC Direct as part of a special "Public Enemies" collection (a Metallo action figure by Hasbro, part of a Superman versus Metallo two-pack, preceded this toy in the 1990s). Also in the mid-2000s, Hiro Okamura, the teenage tech-whiz known as Toyman (not to be confused with the rotund supervillain of the same name), claimed that Metallo's body was forged of a "metallo" alloy that was the property of his family. To reclaim his "property," Okamura transferred John Corben's psychotic mind into a cloned version of his biological body. Despite Corben's physical rebirth, it is unlikely that the threat of the Man with the Kryptonite Heart will remain dormant for long.

Metallo has been seen on television on several occasions: in live action on the syndicated *Superboy* series (1988–1992), with Michael Callan in the role; in frequent appearances in episodes of the WB's animated *Superman* (1996–2000), voiced by Malcolm McDowell; in the 2003 "Hereafter" episode of the Cartoon Network's *Justice League* (2001–2004), voiced by Corey Burton; and voiced by McDowell again in *Justice League Unlimited* (2004–present).

Long before *Action* #252, a different Metalo (note spelling), a criminal scientist in an ultra-powerful battlesuit, tussled with the Golden Age (1938–1954) Superman in *World's Finest Comics* #6 (1942). Marvel Comics published a story starring its own Metallo, a menace in a giant suit of indestructible armor, in *Tales of Suspense* #16 (1961); this character is regarded as a prototype for the Marvel superhero Iron Man. —*ME*

Mighty Morphin' Power Rangers' Rogues' Gallery

S ince the Power Rangers premiered as TV's hottest karate-kicking defenders of the world, they have been popular with kids across America. In continuing incarnations of the *Mighty Morphin' Power Rangers* show, which first aired on FOX from 1993 to 2001 and thereafter on ABC and its affili-

Paul Freeman as Ivan Ooze in *Mighty Morphin' Power Rangers: The Movie* (1995).

ates, these superpowered teenagers have fought hundreds of adversaries, notably a variety of (often gigantic) witches, demons, monsters, and aliens.

In the early years of the show (1993–1996), the villains were mainly extraterrestrials serving the alien sorceress Rita Repulsa or the self-proclaimed "Emperor of Evil," Lord Zedd. In later seasons, menacing the Power Rangers were demons who served Queen Bansheera; mutant criminals that had traveled back in time with the criminal Ransik; pollution-oriented creatures called Orgs; aliens that served the ninja-master Lothor; servants of the dinosaur-like Mesogog; and Troobians, a warlike space race in the service of Emperor Grumm. Armed with the ancient secrets of martial arts and huge biomechanical machines called Megazords, the Rangers have battled Divatox, Master Org, Dark Spector, Toxica, Jindrax, and dozens of other evil-doers, most of whom have been shrunk to miniatures, thrown in jail, reduced to ooze, or otherwise discarded.

Though *Mighty Morphin' Power Rangers* has been criticized for promoting violence to children, many observers have noted that its heroes exhibit positive traits like camaraderie, teamwork, cultural harmony, and perseverance as they battle progressively stronger villains from season to season.

In the *Mighty Morphin' Power Rangers* live-action film (1995), the Rangers journeyed to outer space to defeat millennia-old villain Ivan Ooze (portrayed by Paul Freeman) in his attempt to take over the world with an army of phlegm creatures.

Often ranked the top action-figure line for boys by licensing and toy trade journals and web sites, Power Ranger toys are perennial favorites. As of 2006, Bandai has produced more than 150 million Power Ranger action figures, playsets, Megazords, vehicles, and role-playing items, with many supervillain products among the mix. —*GM*

Millions Knives

Even though he was not introduced until relatively late in the series, Millions Knives is the primary villain of Yasuhirow Nightow's manga *Trigun* (1995) and its sequel, *Trigun Maximum* (1998–present).

Knives is the twin brother of *Trigun*'s hero, Vash. Though his brother is a pacifist, Knives craves violence and despises humans. Both are genetically engineered beings that appear to be twenty years of age, but are in fact well over one hundred years old. Knives has abilities well above those of a normal human, including use of a powerful energy weapon called the "Angel Arm."

Knives and Vash were "born" during Project SEEDS, a mission involving a fleet of starships carrying colonists fleeing a dying Earth. A woman named Rem Savarem cared for both of them, but while Vash adopted Rem's love for life and pacifism, Knives grew to hate humans and sabotaged the fleet to crash on the targeted planet. Only Rem's sacrificial intervention saved much of the fleet, but not before she ejected Knives and Vash in an escape pod. Years later, Vash encountered Knives, who had murdered any survivors (and their descendants) who had ties to Rem. Knives activated Vash's Angel Arm, but Vash fired, seemingly destroying Knives.

One hundred and thirty years after their birth, Knives pulled Vash into a second confrontation. Using his group of enforcers, the Gung-ho Guns, Knives (who was restoring his damaged body to full strength) set out to inflict pain and suffering on Vash, no matter how many innocents died in the process.

In the *Trigun* anime, which first ran on Cartoon Network in 2003 (and has been released in both VHS and DVD formats in the United States), Vash and Knives' final confrontation occurred in the last episode. Knives was defeated after a fierce firefight, but Vash, true to his beliefs, did not kill his brother. —*MM*

Ming the Merciless

The black-hearted warlord Ming the Merciless was introduced in the opening storyline of the science-fiction comic strip *Flash Gordon*. Co-created by celebrated artist Alex Raymond and writer Don Moore as a Sunday-only feature beginning on January 7, 1934, it became a daily strip in 1940. King Features Syndicate's answer to *Buck Rogers in the*

Max von Sydow as Ming the Merciless in *Flash Gordon* (1980).

Emperor Ming and ultimately halting his threat. Flash remains on Mongo to network with a growing resistance movement to overthrow Ming's oppression, propelling future storylines (drawn in later years by Austin Briggs, Mac Raboy, and Dan Barry).

Emporer Ming embodied many of the physical characteristics of the Fu Manchu–like Asian mastermind (as did Buck Rogers' adversary, the lesser-known Killer Kane), including a widow's peak skull cap, robes, and a goatee. He has no redeeming values and relishes in his evil. His "coldly scientific and ruthless" race has perfected ray-blasting spacecrafts, a "dehumanizing machine" that zaps the wills of his opponents, a "space-graph" surveillance monitor that enables Ming to keep an eye on various ports of call across the universe, a lethal dust called the "Purple Death," and a "paralyzo-ray" that stops attackers dead in their tracks. Ming demands blind obedience and will not tolerate failure—the soldiers in his thrall who fall short in their missions face flogging, dungeon imprisonment, or execution. His daughter, the exquisite Princess Aura, has designs for Gordon, earning her father's scorn. Ming is also an accomplished swordsman.

25th Century (which premiered in 1929), *Flash Gordon* begins with Earth imperiled by the planet Mongo, which is careening toward our world like a comet on a collision course. "Only Miracle Can Save Us" reads a newspaper headline, that miracle being handsome athlete-turned-swashbuckler Gordon—although Flash and his companion by chance, the comely Dale Arden, are "drafted" into heroic duty at gunpoint by the eccentric scientist Dr. Hans Zarkov. In Zarkov's spaceship they take the battle directly to Mongo, encountering its sadistic

Flash Gordon has battled Ming the Merciless in a variety of media. Stern-faced actor Charles Middleton frightened theatergoers as Ming in the movie serials *Flash Gordon* (1936), *Flash Gordon's Trip to Mars* (1938), and *Flash Gordon Conquers the Universe* (1940); these serials were later re-released as full-length features. Ming's quote "Pathetic

Earthlings … Who Can Save You Now?" was the tagline of *Flash Gordon* (1980), a high-octane movie updating of the original comic strip buoyed by Max von Sydow's twisted turn as the Emperor. Screenwriter Stephen Sommers (*The Mummy*, 1999) is returning Ming to the big screen in *Flash Gordon* (in development in 2006). Ming has appeared in numerous original *Flash Gordon* novels, Big Little Books, and comic-book series issued from a variety of publishers, as well as in three television cartoons: 1979's *The New Animated Adventures of Flash Gordon*, 1986's *Defenders of the Earth*, and 1996's *Flash Gordon*. To avoid racial stereotyping, in the latter series Ming was redesigned a pointy-eared reptile-man. Ming action figures tying into the animated series were produced, as was an elaborate Ming outfit for the poseable figure of Captain Action's arch-foe, the original Dr. Evil. —*ME*

Miroku

As the true source of evil in the action fantasy manga *Madara* (1996–1999), Miroku is the one who set the events of the story in motion. Created by Eiji Otsuka (story) and Sho-u Tajima (art), Miroku first appeared to *Madara* readers in the "Tale of the Abandoned Prince" storyline in 1996. However, he is described in the prologue of the first volume of *Madara*.

According to legend, many years earlier, Miroku was the leader of a strange army that claimed to be "descendants of the gods"—meaning he was possibly of extraterrestrial origin. Miroku stood at more than 40 feet tall, and he physically resembled a human being. He also had control over demons called "Moki." Swiftly defeating all enemies, Miroku eventually took over the land, established the Diamond Kingdom, and declared himself emperor.

Yet Miroku's own offspring would become his undoing. When his son was born, Miroku—acting on a prophecy that his son would eventually depose him—sacrificed the infant to the demon lord and divided the body among his eight generals. Only the child's spirit survived, taken away by the wizard Hakutaku. That child is Madara.

Fifteen years later, Madara—his soul now inhabiting a cybernetic (or "gadget") body—began to search for the creatures that possessed the parts of his real body. Each time the boy killed one of Miroku's generals he gained a part of his real body back, as well as the experience needed to defeat his father. Miroku, now alerted to his son's quest, sent out his own army of bizarre and horrific creatures, as well as his demonic henchmen, to destroy Madara. One of his best commanders is Kaos, who later joins with Madara to bring about Miroku's downfall. —*MM*

Mirror Master

Petty crook Sam Scudder learned a trade while in prison. As seen in *The Flash* vol. 1 #105 (1959), Scudder, in the pen's mirror factory, mistakenly applies the incorrect chemical to glass and inadvertently discovers a means of manipulating mirrors into tools for crime. As the high-tech purloiner the Mirror Master, wearing a green cowl and gold bodysuit designed by the tale's artist, Carmine Infantino, Scudder uses his "Image Controller"—writer John Broome's interpretation of a hologram projector—to rob a bank with a mirror-created surrogate of the bank president. The keen-minded Flash, trailing the reflective rogue, is ultimately able to whiz through Mirror Master's deceptive hall of mirrors and gauntlet of holographic grotesqueries to shatter his plans.

Readers witnessed no end to Scudder's mirror-based schemes over the decades. Mirror Master shrunk the Flash to nothingness with a giant mirror, turned the speedster into a mirror-man (which he nearly obliterated into shards), gained superspeed by switching legs with the hero, and second-guessed his foe with his "future-mirror." With each new story, the supervillain's arsenal became more outlandish. He hopped dimensions, produced facsimiles of himself, and even took to the air using mirrors, keeping *Flash* fans guessing as to how the Scarlet Speedster could possibly escape the Mirror Master's traps.

Beginning with *Flash* #155 (1965) Mirror Master signed on as one of the founders of the Flash's Rogues' Gallery, an acrimonious accord that routinely ambushed the Sultan of Speed. He helped organize the Secret Society of Super-Villains in 1976, and on occasion fought the Elongated Man, the Justice League, and Batman. Despite those diversions, Mirror Master remained determined to challenge the Flash, his ardor cracked only by death: first the Flash's, then his own, in issues #8 (1985) and #10 (1986) of the landmark maxiseries *Crisis on Infinite Earths*. Yet the grave could not restrict the Silver Age Mirror Master from media exploitation: former teen heartthrob David Cassidy played a non-costumed Sam Scudder in episode nineteen ("Done with Mirrors," original airdate: April 21, 1991) of CBS's live-action series *The Flash* (1990–1991), and in the 2000s DC Direct merchandized the villain as an action figure and as a pocket-sized miniature.

In the late 1980s, Mirror Master appeared to have returned from the dead, but it was actually fellow Flash rogue Captain Boomerang lifting his identity to commit crimes while a member of the Suicide Squad, a U.S. government–controlled strike force.

A mercenary Scot named Evan McCulloch became the new Mirror Master in *Animal Man* #8 (1989), written by Grant Morrison and drawn by Chas Truog. An orphan whose hardship-filled youth fomented his career as a hired killer, McCulloch was traumatized after learning that one of his hits was actually his biological father. Instead of turning away from evil, he accepted the offer of a corporate/government conclave to use Scudder's original costume and weaponry as a supervillain for hire. McCulloch's troubled past and recurring bouts of substance abuse make this Mirror Master more malignant than Scudder, to the chagrin of the Fastest Man Alive's successor, the Flash III. If the price or incentive is right, the new Mirror Master will ally with others: he joined Lex Luthor's Injustice Gang in 1997, became a regular member of the Flash's Rogues' Gallery, and palled around with Killer Frost in 2005. Mirror Master was added to the burgeoning lineup of the Cartoon Network's *Justice League Unlimited* (2004–present) in 2005, and an action figure was released in conjunction with the show. —*ME*

The Mist

The Mist was an illusive Golden Age (1938–1954) malefactor first introduced in the pages of

The Mist. *The Brave and the Bold* vol. 1 #61 ©1965 DC Comics.
COVER ART BY MURPHY ANDERSON.

Adventure Comics #67 (1941) in a Starman feature story scripted by Alfred Bester and rendered by Jack Burnley. Scientist Kyle (whose last name is never revealed) is adept at creating interesting formulas and devices, most notably an invisibility solution and a matter destabilizer, the rays of which can disintegrate objects. When gangsters attempt to steal the matter destabilizer from the scientist, the invention is turned on him and Kyle transforms into the supervillain the Mist. As a criminal mastermind who is able to convert into an almost-invisible vapor, the Mist battled the Golden Age Starman through most of the 1940s.

The Mist engaged in such diabolical feats as destroying buildings, robbing banks, and taking tourists hostage. Through chronic use of various chemicals or constant manipulation of his physical body, the Mist eventually developed true superpowers, including invisibility and intangibility. At one point, he also possessed the power of weather control. He appeared only once during the Silver Age (1956–1969), in a Starman/Black Canary team-up in *The Brave and the Bold* #61 (1965), adding blackmail to his job description. Eventually, the Mist went insane and sold his soul to the demon Neron, supposedly dying in a nuclear explosion that took the life of the Golden Age Starman.

The Mist's supervillainous legacy continued in his two children: Kyle Jr., who died battling David Knight, the original Starman's son and successor; and his daughter Nash, introduced in the *Starman* series launched in late 1994 and known as the supervillain Mist II. Mist II carried on the work of her father, her powers allowing her to pass through walls and transport herself. Before dying at the hands of her father (who returned from the dead), she conceived a baby with the newest Starman, Jack Night. —*GM*

Mr. Element: *See* **Dr. Alchemy**

Mr. Freeze

The chilling Mr. Freeze may be one of Batman's best-known supervillains, but were it not for a television producer he might have remained in cold storage after his debut. Curt Swan's cover to *Batman* #121 (1959) featured a cookie-cutter criminal (a bald head, a kitschy costume, and a super-weapon) freezing Batman and Robin alive inside giant blocks of ice. The story, "The Ice Crimes of Mister Zero" (yes, Zero) by writer Dave Wood and artist Sheldon Moldoff, begins with Mr. Zero—in green-and-red tights with a protective bubble helmet, looking like a possessed Christmas ornament—pulling a jewelry heist (nabbing "a fortune in 'ice'") with henchmen masquerading as ice cream–truck drivers. During their getaway, Zero's "ice gun" (resembling a pesticide sprayer) slicks the street behind them, sending the pursuing Dynamic Duo flailing. From his "remote mountain" headquarters, Zero discloses that he was once a criminal scientist who was doomed to live in frigid temperatures after an accident with experimental chemicals. Continuing his diamond larceny, he freezes Batman and Robin's Bat-ropes, Whirly-Bat blades, and even the

heroes themselves, until their ingenuity stops—and *cures*—Zero with a steam bath.

When executive producer William Dozier and company scoured comic books for villains for the live-action television series *Batman* (1966–1968), Mr. Zero's story proved enticing. Renamed "Mr. Freeze," he was the fourth Bat-foe introduced in the campy series, bowing on February 2 and 3, 1966, in episodes seven (featuring actress Teri Garr in a bit part) and eight, with George Sanders as the rogue. Much was borrowed from Wood's *Batman* #121 script, including Zero's/Freeze's quick-freeze gun (augmented into an elaborate rifle), his frosty headquarters (with temperature controls to allow henchman access), an ice-cream truck for transportation, and his obsession with stealing diamonds. Freeze's origin was altered to ascribe his transformation to an earlier scuffle with Batman, the hero accidentally spilling Freeze's "Instant Freeze" solution on him; on television the character also donned a NASA-like containment suit instead of the colorful tights seen in the comics. In that two-parter, the industrious Caped Crusader wore Super-Thermo-B Long Underwear beneath his Bat-togs. The villain's ice shtick was popular enough to warrant return engagements without Sanders, whose minimalist performance won him few fans on the over-the-top show; Otto Preminger and Eli Wallach succeeded him in the role.

DC Comics reintroduced the villain as Mr. Freeze in *Detective Comics* #373 (1968). In "Mr. Freeze's Chilling Deathtrap" by Gardner Fox and Chic Stone, Freeze's garb mimicked the television show's (but with green instead of TV's white and silver), and the villain once again immobilized Batman in a block of ice. Afterward DC again retired Mr. Freeze for years. Television, however, regarded the cold-hearted criminal as a major Bat-adversary: Mr. Freeze continued to dog Batman and Robin in their post-live-action series, appearing in animated episodes on *The Batman/Superman Hour* (1968–1969), *The Adventures of Batman and Robin* (1969–1970), and *The New Adventures of Batman* (1977–1978) (the latter program continued to air under various titles until 1981, keeping Mr. Freeze in circulation).

After a minor appearance in a 1977 *Batman* arc featuring a union of the hero's foes, Mr. Freeze

Mr. Freeze, originally Mr. Zero. *Batman* #121
©1959 DC Comics.
COVER ART BY CURT SWAIN AND STAN KAYE.

Bruce Timm, on September 7, 1992. This version of Mr. Freeze was actually Dr. Victor Fries (pronounced "Freeze"), a cryogenics scientist who clandestinely froze his terminally ill wife, Nora, until a cure could be discovered for her condition. A corporate exec ended funding for Fries' research, and an ensuing accident drenched the doctor in his cryogenic solutions, making him unable to exist outside of sub-zero conditions. Damned to life inside a temperature-regulating cybernetic suit, detached from human contact, Fries—now Mr. Freeze—sought vengeance with his cold-producing gun.

Dini, Timm, and series co-creator Eric Radomski hired comic-book artist Mike (*Hellboy*) Mignola to design Mr. Freeze's sleek, simplified animation look. Portraying the villain was Michael Ansara, who struggled to find the right voice. "An actor's first natural instinct is to act," recalled Bruce Timm. "I kept telling him it had to be less, a lot less—like a robot." Ansara's icily heartless performance helped transform Mr. Freeze into arguably the most sympathetic figure in the Dark Knight's rogues' gallery. The frosty foe appeared in several episodes, as well as in the made-for-video animated movie *Batman & Mr. Freeze: SubZero* (1998). DC again followed TV's lead by absorbing this interpretation of Mr. Freeze into the comic-book continuity.

Director Joel Schumacher's big-budget lampoon *Batman & Robin* (1997) starred Arnold Schwarzenegger as Mr. Freeze, spewing a succession of silly one-liners (including "Chill!" and "Cool party!"). While detested by most comics fans, the movie returned Mr. Freeze to the spotlight: action figures and merchandising followed (including a Toys R Us reprint of *Batman* #121), as did two different Six Flags amusement-park attractions based upon the villain.

Clancy Brown was hired to play Mr. Freeze for the animated television series *The Batman* (2004–present), in which the villain has appeared in solo and team-up (with Firefly) episodes. The chilly monstrosity perennially returns to put Batman and Gotham City on ice in various titles, from *Gotham Central* to *Batman: Legends of the Dark Knight*, the latter of which featured Mr. Freeze in a 2005 story arc titled "Snow." —*ME*

was thawed out again—even scoring a Jim Aparo–drawn cover—in "There'll Be a Cold Time in the Old Town Tonight," by Len Wein and John Calnan, in *Batman* #308 (1979). By this point the comic-book version of the villain had taken on a look recognizable to his contemporary fans: a blue-and-white costume, helmet, and crimson goggles. Occasional stories gave Freeze a mid-level profile, and his TV legacy warranted his inclusion in the third series of Kenner's Super Powers action figures (and spin-off comic books) produced in the mid-1980s. An inferior replicate of Kenner's Mr. Freeze figure was produced by then-fledgling manufacturer Toy Biz in 1989.

Leave it to television once again to reinvent Batman's frosty foe. *Batman: The Animated Series*, the long-running "Dark Deco" cartoon that debuted in 1992, first aired "Heart of Ice," an episode written by Paul Dini and directed by

Mr. Glass

Elijah Price (Samuel L. Jackson) believes that comic-book heroes inhabit Earth in writer/director M. Night Shyamalan's thriller *Unbreakable* (2000). Philadelphia security guard David Dunn (Bruce Willis) walks away inscrutably unharmed from a catastrophic rail disaster, its sole survivor. Price, ridiculed as "Mr. Glass" due to a rare condition that makes his bones exceptionally brittle, hopes to find meaning for his lifelong torment. A comics-shop owner and avid collector, Price—slender, unsteady, and often surreally clad in purple leather—attempts to convince Dunn, who has never once been ill or injured, that he is a real-world superhero: "Now that we know who you are, I know who I am," Price contends. "I'm not a mistake."

At first discounting Price's ludicrous theory, Dunn, a misfit whose marriage is troubled, soon finds a path to fulfillment as he, encouraged by his young son, undergoes weight training. Combining his strength and stamina with an intuition that warns him of wrongdoing—a scaled-down version of Spider-Man's spider-sense—he cloaks himself in a poncho and secretly becomes a street-level avenger. Dunn ultimately discovers the unthinkable (*spoiler alert!*): that Price, the obsessive Mr. Glass, engineered not only the train wreck from which Dunn survived but also a host of other accidents, simply to ferret out his paranormal counterpart. "You killed all those people," Dunn gasps. "But I found you," Price retorts. "So many sacrifices just to find you." This climactic revelation from unexpected twist–master Shyamalan and Jackson's subtly seductive portrayal created the haunting "real-world" embodiment of the arch-foe archetype whose impact endures long after the closing credits. —ME

Mr. Hyde

Taking his cue from a classic fictional character, Marvel Comics' Mr. Hyde first appeared in *Journey into Mystery* #99 (1964), in a story scripted by Stan Lee and illustrated by Don Heck. Dr. Calvin Zabo is a medical researcher obsessed with Robert Louis Stevenson's 1886 tale *Dr. Jekyll and Mr. Hyde*. In an effort to duplicate the experiment in Stevenson's book and unleash the essence of humankind's beastlike nature, Zabo creates a formula that allows him to turn into a superstrong creature called Mr. Hyde. The transformation warps Hyde's facial skin, making Zabo unrecognizable.

In his Hyde form, Zabo possesses superhuman strength—a quality he has used to battle longtime adversaries Thor and Daredevil. For a while he held a grudge against Thor because the Thunder God, in his alter ego of Dr. Don Blake, had refused him employment with a company Zabo was attempting to rob. Subsequently Hyde had a long-running partnership with another Thor foe, the Cobra. Mr. Hyde has also battled Captain America, the Falcon, Spider-Man, Ghost Rider, and, as a member of the supergroup the Masters of Evil, the Avengers.

Mr. Hyde has committed numerous cruel crimes, including an attempt to blow up New York City in order to kill his old partner the Cobra. He has been known to commit brutal, prolonged acts of torture, such as those against Avengers butler Edwin Jarvis. In his modern rendering Mr. Hyde looks like a murderous maniac, and has often been compared to the Incredible Hulk in his embodiment of pure rage—not surprising, since the Hulk's co-creators Stan Lee and Jack Kirby envisioned the character as the superhero counterpart to Jekyll and Hyde.

Indeed, Stevenson's tale of personality duplicity also inspired DC Comics' Two-Face. Stevenson's Mr. Hyde served as a member of the title team of Alan Moore and Kevin O'Neill's *The League of Extraordinary Gentlemen* in its first two volumes (1999–2000, 2002–2003), as well as the 2003 movie adaptation. In the tradition of Kirby, O'Neill drew Hyde as a giant, Hulk-like figure.

Marvel's Mr. Hyde has rarely ventured outside of comics' pages, having only appeared in "Thor" episodes of the animated TV series *The Marvel Super-Heroes* (1966). —GM

Mr. Mind

Readers during comics' Golden Age (1938–1954) had to look closely to see Captain Marvel's ultra-intelligent enemy Mr. Mind. He is only "heard" as a broadcasted voice in his first few stories, beginning in Fawcett's *Captain Marvel Adventures* #22 (1943), and four months later in issue #26, writer Otto Binder and artist C. C. Beck disclose this world dominator's secret: he is a *worm*!

Nicknamed "the World's Wickedest Worm," Mr. Mind is the architect behind comics' first supervillain team in the Golden Age's longest-running serial, the 25-chapter, 232-page "Monster Society of Evil" storyline. Hailing from a planet of sentient worms, Mr. Mind boasts staggering telepathic abilities, but his poor eyesight forces him to rely upon round-framed, oversized glasses. A voice amplifier, shaped like a vintage radio and worn around his neck like a medallion, enables the tiny Mind to be heard. During the Monster Society's two-year-long adventure, Mind and his cohorts (myriad villains from Dr. Sivana to Adolf Hitler) destroy property and lives, sending Captain Marvel through a gauntlet of challenges. After the heroic Big Red Cheese crushes the Monster Society in #46 (1945), Mr. Mind is placed on trial for his crimes, which include ordering 186,744 murders, and he receives the electric chair. A taxidermist stuffs the worm's miniscule corpse, which is housed under glass in a museum. Little did the populace realize that Mr. Mind had cheated death— merely stunned by the attempted electrocution, he substituted a surrogate in the museum tomb and cocooned himself into suspended animation.

Mr. Mind emerged almost thirty years later in *Shazam!* #2 (1973), at a new publisher, DC Comics, which had obtained Captain Marvel's publication rights from Fawcett after suing the character out of print in the 1950s. Mr. Mind fought Cap in several innocuous encounters and wiggled onto television in the "Best Seller" episode of NBC's cartoon *Kid Super-Power Hour with Shazam!* (1981–1982). Allan Oppenheimer voiced the villain; episode writer Paul Dini went on to co-create the lauded *Batman: The Animated Series*. Mr. Mind was retroactively inserted into DC's 1940s timeline via an earlier version of the Monster Society in a late 1985 *All-Star Squadron* storyline, but he was excised after DC's continuity-housecleaning series *Crisis on Infinite Earths* (1985–1986).

At the end of *Shazam!: The New Beginning* #4 (1987), a panel depicting a large-eyed worm in a tequila bottle intimated that Roy Thomas, writer of

this Captain Marvel–rebooting miniseries, had intended to revive Mr. Mind in a future story. Yet another Captain Marvel revamp in 1994, this time by Jerry Ordway, squashed Thomas' chances. Ordway introduced a more realistic, fear-provoking version of Mr. Mind in 1996 issues of *The Power of Shazam!*; the worm now originated on Venus, and attempted to populate Fawcett City with members of his species. Mr. Mind returned in 1998, partnering with the robotic Mr. Atom as the new Monster Society and destroying a small town in the process, then was seen again in the 2001 crossover series *The Joker: Last Laugh*. While more underfoot than appreciated in the darker DC Universe of the twenty-first century, Mr. Mind was given another spin by *Bone* cartoonist Jeff Smith in the 2006 miniseries *Shazam!: Monster Society of Evil. —ME*

Mr. Mxyzptlk

T he mischievous magical mite with a mouthful of a name, Mr. Mxyzptlk (pronounced Mix-yez-pitel-ick) first pestered the Man of Steel in *Superman* vol. 1 #30 (1944), in a whimsical tale written by Superman co-creator Jerry Siegel and illustrated by Ira Yarbrough. A derbyed and dapper little man shakes up Metropolis when he is struck by an automobile and apparently killed. Paramedics are puzzled when they are unable to lift the stretcher containing the pulseless victim, but when he springs forth, *alive*—"Confusing, aren't I?"—he steals their ambulance and drives it up the side of a skyscraper! After two more showboating appearances Superman arrives, but the "mad sprite" slips through his steel grip, bends like a rubber band to avoid his punches, and takes to the sky, prompting the dumbfounded Metropolis Marvel to mutter, "I thought *I* was the only man who could fly!" This is Mr. Mxyztplk (note the original spelling), a "court-jester" from another dimension, who exasperates Superman with his "perverted sense of humor" until the hero tricks Mxyztplk into saying his name backwards—"Klptzyxm"—the magic word that returns the nuisance from whence he came.

Siegel's answer to Bugs Bunny, Mr. Mxyztplk (originally pronounced Mix-yizt-pulk, according to former DC Comics editor Alvin Schwartz) was created for *Superman* #30, which went on sale in early July

1944. When DC editorial director Whitney Ellsworth noticed the character pre-publication, however, he was impressed with the character's potential and rushed Mxyztplk into print first in a February 1944 *Superman* newspaper strip sequence.

In *Superman* #30 Mr. Mxyztplk was bent on conquering Earth as its kooky king, but in his frequent reappearances—he popped up on the average twice a year throughout the Golden Age (1938–1954)—the "problem-pixie" seemed content to badger Superman with supernatural pranks like making rivers flow uphill or transmuting stones into rock candy. Despite his boundless magical powers, which were limited only by his writers' imaginations, at each story's conclusion Mxyztplk was formulaically outfoxed by Superman to say his name backwards, thus exorcising him from Earth. In 1946 he teamed with another pest, Lois Lane's niece, the prevaricating moppet Susie Tompkins, and joined Lex Luthor and the Prankster to "declare war on Superman" in 1950.

Elements of Mr. Mxyztplk's mythos fluctuated in earlier texts. His place of origin was cited as a "weird," "unknown," or "other" dimension, the "multi-dimensional world" of Zrfff, and "Topsy-Turvy Land," but by the late 1940s he hailed from the fifth dimension's Land of Zrfff. The duration of his banishment from Earth varied from an undetermined period to a month to 60 days, but it was consistently 90 days as of 1953. His costume was altered from his original purple tux to green permutations to his better-known futuristic orange togs with purple trim (with the derby remaining) by the mid-1950s. A typo inspired the imp's most noteworthy alternation: his name was alternately spelled "Mxyztplk" and "Mxyzptlk" (the letters t and p transposed) in *Action Comics* #208 (1955), and shortly thereafter he was permanently christened Mr. Mxyzptlk. With this change, the backward-spelling of his name became "Kltpzyxm," pronounced Kel-tipz-yex-im. Historians generally regard Mr. Mxyztplk to be the Golden Age version of the character, and Mr. Mxyzptlk, the Silver Age (1956–1969) version; "The Menace of Mr. Mxyzptlk" in *Superman* vol. 1 #131 (1959) is considered the first official Silver Age appearance of the villain, his return from three years in publication limbo.

The constantly expanding Superman family of the Silver Age afforded Mr. Mxyzptlk more characters to annoy. In addition to getting into the Man of Tomorrow's Kryptonian hair with shenanigans such as transforming a steel block into giant alphabet blocks (spelling "Superman is a blockhead") and inciting riots by making money grow on trees, "Mxy" also bothered Supergirl, the Legion of Super-Heroes, Jimmy Olsen, and Lois Lane (of whom he was sometimes enamored). He occasionally partnered with fellow sprite Bat-Mite to bedevil the Superman/Batman/Robin team in *World's Finest Comics*, had an impish girlfriend named Miss Gsptlsnz, and encountered Bizarro and Luthor. Even Superboy could not escape the pest: Mxy was retroactively inserted into Superman's adolescence as "Master Mxyzptlk."

Gil Mack voiced Mr. Mxyzptlk in 1966 in Filmation's animated *The New Adventures of Superman*, Frank Welker played the imp in 1986 on the ABC cartoon *The Super Powers Team: Galactic Guardians*, where his name was pronounced Mixel-plick. During the 1970s Mego Toys produced an 8-inch Mr. Mxyzptlk figure and a 4-inch bendable figurine. "Whatever Happened to the Man of Tomorrow?," the Alan Moore–scripted two-part exodus of the Silver Age version of Superman (*Superman* vol. 1 #423 and *Action* #583, 1986), an "imaginary" tale ("Aren't they all?" asked the author), revealed a homicidal Mr. Mxyzptlk as the catalyst behind a series of events that led to the massacre of most of Superman's friends and foes.

Mr. Mxyzptlk was reintroduced in *Superman* vol. 2 #11 (1987), after Superman's 1986 *Man of Steel* reboot by writer/artist John Byrne, where Mxy, at first calling himself "Ben DeRoy" (Byrne's jab at the Beyonder, the creation of his former Marvel Comics boss Jim Shooter), materializes in Metropolis from, like the previous continuity, Zrfff in the fifth dimension. Challenging Superman to speak, spell, or write his name backwards, Mr. Mxyzptlk flummoxed the hero by turning him into a look-alike of *MAD*'s Alfred E. Neuman, making Lois Lane into a mannequin, and transforming the *Daily Planet* building into an ambulatory skyscraper, his reality-distorting magic fading after he departed Earth.

Mr. Mxyzptlk has remained a recurring Superman foe since the late 1980s. He was taught how

Adventures of Superman #638 ©2005 DC Comics.
COVER ART BY CARLOS MEGLIA.

to lie by Luthor; engineered a race between Superman and the Flash; buddied with Bat-Mite; turned everyone in Metropolis into Mxy-clones; joined forces with Marvel's Impossible Man (*Silver Surfer/Superman*, 1996); lampooned 1992's best-selling "Death of Superman" milestone with a mock Mxy demise; had his powers stolen by the Joker, who used them to create a lunatic Joker-reality; and gave the Man of Steel and his wife Lois a glimpse at what their child might look like. From Superman's perspective, Mxy's visits each 90 days are far too frequent.

Michael J. Pollard played Mr. Mxyzptlk on the live-action *Superboy* series (1988–1992); Howie Mandel portrayed a leprechaun version of Mxyzptlk in a 1996 episode of ABC's *Lois & Clark: The New Adventures of Superman* (1993–1997); comedian Gilbert Godfried voiced Mxy in several episodes of the animated *Superman* (1996–2000), with San-

dra Bernhard as his supermodel-esque wife, Ms. Gsptlsnz; and an exchange student named Mikail Mxyzptlk (Trent Ford) has been spotted on the WB's *Smallville* (2001–present). In the 2000s DC Direct has released a Mr. Mxyzptlk coldcast statue and a plush toy. —ME

Mr. Sinister

When Mr. Sinister first appeared in *Uncanny X-Men* #221 (1987), written by Chris Claremont and drawn by Marc Silvestri, he was quite an enigma. (The name "Mr. Sinister" follows the same formula as "Dr. Doom," but in later stories he has more often simply been called "Sinister.") The issue revealed Sinister to be the employer of the Marauders, a mutant team of assassins who had earlier massacred many of the Morlocks, a community of mutant outcasts dwelling in tunnels beneath Manhattan.

Nearly a decade later, writer Peter Milligan revealed Sinister's origin in the Marvel Comics miniseries *The Further Adventures of Cyclops and Phoenix* (1996), in which the two X-Men traveled back in time to England in 1859. By then Charles Darwin had published *The Origin of Species*, in which he originated the theory of evolution. Using Darwin's theory as a basis, another scientist of that time, Dr. Nathaniel Essex, controversially proposed that human procreation should be controlled in order to produce a genetically superior super-race. One of Essex's motivations appears to be the death of his first son, which was caused by a genetic defect. Not only was the British scientific community horrified by Essex's proposal, but so was his own wife, Rebecca, who died after their second son likewise perished.

Dr. Essex finally met someone who was willing to support his genetic experiments: the long-lived evil mutant Apocalypse, who genetically altered Essex into a superhuman being who seemingly does not age. Essex took as his new name what Rebecca had called him on her deathbed: "Sinister."

The time-traveling Cyclops and Phoenix, Scott Summers and Jean Grey, persuaded Sinister to break off his new alliance with Apocalypse. But as a result of meeting them, Sinister grew fascinated with the Summers and Grey genetic bloodlines.

Over the ensuing hundred years Sinister developed highly advanced methods of genetic engineering, including human cloning. Sinister also worked with Nazi scientists during World War II.

Sinister secretly controlled the orphanage where Scott Summers lived as a boy. Following the apparent death of Jean Grey, Sinister utilized a sample of her genetic material to create her clone, Madelyne Pryor. As Sinister planned, the bereaved Scott fell in love with Madelyne, and they married and had a child named Nathan Summers. Sinister plotted to capture and control this genetically superior child. Jean turned up alive, Madelyne perished in combat with her, and Nathan was transported into the far future, where he became the adult warrior Cable. (The version of Sinister found in the alternate reality known as the "Age of Apocalypse" used genetic material from Summers and Grey to create the young mutant Nate Grey, known as X-Man.)

Through his own experiments, Sinister has endowed himself with an unknown measure of mental control over the molecules of his body. This power enables him to alter his physical appearance and even to render himself invulnerable to various forms of injury.

A leading nemesis of the X-Men in the comics, Sinister also menaced them on television in *X-Men: The Animated Series* (1992–1997). —PS

Mistress Death: *See* Thanos

Modern Age Supervillains
(1980-present)

Early in comics' history, it was much easier to tell the good guys from the bad. Following the tradition of classic Western motion pictures, broad exaggerations of heroes' and villains' characteristics—Boy Scout–like altruism and one-dimensional malevolence—made it as easy to distinguish superhero from supervillain as the cowboy's white hat did from the desperado's black hat.

By the dawn of comics' Modern Age (1980–present), Americans had experienced decades of racial disharmony, the bloody and unpopular Vietnam War, and a U.S. president who resigned in disgrace. The conventional "to the rescue" superhero was now passé to Americans who had buttressed themselves behind a wall of cynicism. To better relate to changing mores and become more believable in a dystopian world, the crime fighter took on traits of the criminal.

Two Marvel Comics characters introduced in the mid-1970s became prototypes for this new wave of anti-hero: the take-no-prisoners vigilante Punisher, who began his career as a Spider-Man villain, and the X-Men's Wolverine, the mutant superhero who struggled to keep his bloodlust in check.

Elekra premiered in late 1980 in writer/artist Frank Miller's *Daredevil*; this sympathetic assassin butchered the type of no-good street scum one might find in a Charles Bronson *Death Wish* movie. From "independent" publishers came hard-edged, killer-protagonists like Mike Baron and Steve Rude's Nexus, a cosmic executioner, and Matt Wagner's Grendel, the personification of vengeance. By the time writer Alan Moore and artist Dave Gibbons deconstructed the good-guy model in their twelve-issue DC Comics masterpiece *Watchmen* (1986–1987), featuring the genocidal super*hero* Ozymandias, "grim and gritty" heroes had so crossed the line that formerly separated them from their opponents that supervillains had no choice but to become grimmer and grittier.

The Joker is a prime example. Frank Miller cast the Clown Prince of Crime as a homoerotic maniac in the futuristic *Batman: The Dark Knight Returns* (1986). Alan Moore and artist Brian Bolland's graphic novel *Batman: The Killing Joke* (1988) depicted the villain shooting, debasing, and voyeuristically photographing Barbara (then the former Batgirl, now Oracle) Gordon and torturing a nude, doggie-collared Commissioner James Gordon. And the "Death in the Family" *Batman* story arc (1989) had the Joker kill the second Robin by the decree of thousands of comics *readers* who gave the Boy Wonder a thumbs-down via a phone-in live-or-die poll.

Not all comic-book supervillains stooped to such depravity during the 1980s. For many, it remained business as usual, although audiences easily distracted by a burgeoning number of entertainment choices required bigger, bolder, and noisier gestures to maintain their attention.

For Marvel and DC readers, the old-fashioned hero-versus-villain story seemed less satisfying. Each company unveiled multi-issue crossovers featuring cosmic threats requiring mass gatherings of superheroes: *Marvel Super Heroes Secret Wars* (1984–1985) took Marvel's mightiest heroes and villains off-planet to Battleworld at the behest of the godlike Beyonder, and DC's *Crisis on Infinite Earths* (1985–1986) assembled heroes and villains from multiple Earths to stand against the Anti-Monitor, an omnipotent being powerful enough to erase reality.

Earthbound machinations of supervillains assumed harsher connotations, reflecting real-life wickedness at an unprecedented level. Mob-related crimes became more graphically depicted, as in the case of Kingpin's bloody war against Daredevil. Corporate corruption was now a common story element, with Lex Luthor's 1986 revamping into a white-collar criminal a famous example. And long before the September 11, 2001, terrorist attacks in the United States, Middle Eastern terrorists replaced the "Yellow Peril" Asian villains of previous generations as the new threat to democracy in comics' pages, with fictionalized nations such as DC's Qurac conspiring to destroy major American cities.

In the 1980s, the sale of comic books shifted from their long-time principal outlet, the newsstand, to the comics or "specialty" shop. New publishers and new titles cropped up during the advent of this "direct sales" marketing, and with those series came a nastier breed of supervillain. Grendel's nemesis was the werewolf Argent, while the DNAgents encountered the monster-maker Verminus and the displaced nineteenth-century rogue Cadaver. Bill Willingham's superteam the Elementals fought such vicious menaces as Ratman, Shapeshifter, the vampire Captain Cadaver (who wore a fanged smiley face on his shirt), Holocaust, and a scripture-obsessed team called the Rapture, including Genesis 6:4 and Exodus 10:21. Lord Weterlackus, empowered by blood sacrifices, and the neo-Nazi ex–Green Beret Hodag, tackled the

psycho-hero Badger. John Gaunt, the city of Cynosure's sword for hire called Grimjack, clashed with gladiators like MacCabre.

Following this trend, "extreme" became the buzzword for comic books of the 1990s. Loose cannons like Wolverine were no longer the fringe—they had become the superhero template. Comics shops were awash in a sea of blood spilled by gung-ho, ultra-violent *heroes* like Cable, Lobo, Spawn, Bloodshot, Firearm, and Barb Wire. Two highly publicized DC storylines in the early 1990s involving almost-unstoppable supervillains turned the bloodbath up a notch: the death of Superman, at the hands of the killing machine called Doomsday, and the breaking of Batman's back, snapped by the drug-enhanced crimelord Bane.

Those events, plus the emergence of superstar artists including Todd McFarlane and Jim Lee (who blossomed in the late 1980s on high-profile Marvel series and then, along with several other hot talents, formed Image Comics in 1992), produced record-setting sales, triggering a speculators' boom that dominated the early to mid-1990s. Upstart and established publishers rushed new and in some cases revived superheroes into print, each with its own universes populated with ultragruesome rogues: Master Darque (from Acclaim Comics' Valiant Universe); Mace Blitzkrieg, Dr. October, and Deathcard (from Dark Horse's Comics' Greatest World); and Primevil, Dr. Vincent Gross, and Maxi-Man (from Malibu's Ultraverse) were among the supervillains who enjoyed a brief shelf life but wandered into extinction after a few years. DC imprint Milestone, featuring the culturally diverse "Dakota Universe," also produced its share of villains, such as Oblivion and Rift, but it is best known for its superhero Static, star of the animated TV series *Static Shock!* (2000–2004). Driven by star power, many of Image's titles bowing during this period remain in print in the 2000s. Spawn's arch-foe the Violator (the Clown) is the most famous supervillain originating in the line, jumping to film in 1997, portrayed by actor John Leguizamo.

Big-budget superhero motion pictures aimed the spotlight on high-profile megastars as supervillains, beginning with Oscar-winner Jack Nicholson's turn as the Joker in *Batman* (1989). Nicholson's Joker wasn't your father's Clown Prince of

From *The Elementals* vol. 1 #2 ©1984 Comico.
ART BY BILL WILLINGHAM AND RICH RANKIN.

Crime, the garish giggler some viewers remembered from the swinging sixties in the pasty-faced form of aging Latin lover Cesar Romero (on TV's *Batman*, 1966–1968). He was a killer, like the homicidal comics version, snickering while slaying, and abruptly turning on his goons at a whim, as he did when he shot point-blank his closest aid Bob the Goon (actor Tracey Walter). The nightmarish Penguin (Danny DeVito) and whacked-out Catwoman (Michelle Pfeiffer) stole the film's sequel, *Batman Returns* (1992), killing enemies and destroying property with wild abandon. These blockbusters cemented the supervillain's stature alongside the superhero. Beginning with *Batman: The Animated Series* (1992–1995), superheroes and supervillains once again aired their grievances on the tube, and shows starring, among others, Spider-Man, the X-Men, Superman, and the Fantastic Four—and with them, Dr. Octopus, Magneto, Lex Luthor, and Dr. Doom—soon filled cable net-

work schedules. Comics-character merchandising became big business, with villains joining heroes on video games, T-shirts, action figures, and breakfast-cereal boxes. Venom also starred in his own comic-book series, as did Eclipso, Catwoman, Magneto, and others.

Writer Mark Waid and illustrator Alex Ross explored the concept of rogue superheroes with supervillain-like disregard for order in their 1996 DC miniseries *Kingdom Come*. Neo-Man of Steel Magog, the Harlequin (aka Joker's Daughter II), and the brute Von Bach were among the superpowered anarchists whose recklessness inspired the reunion of retired old-school superheroes to rout this dangerous new breed, with a messianic Superman appropriately leading the way.

The hope offered by Superman's "second coming" in Waid and Ross' epic seems lost upon the comic-book world of the mid-2000s. While optimistic superhero series have been published since *Kingdom Come*, they have been the minority, and as the long-standing superhero-versus-supervillain struggle steamrolls forward, the body count escalates.

"Our audience is much smarter, much more sophisticated, and not necessarily because it's older," crime novelist-turned-comics author Greg Rucka told the *New York Times* in October 2005, adding, "A 12-year-old 20 years ago and a 12-year-old today are reading at very different levels." His comments were in regard to DC's ongoing revitalization of its characters, most of which were created in the 1940s through the 1960s, and possessing, in the words of DC's executive editor Dan DiDio, "a lot of elements where we've had a disconnect with the reader base of today." To reconnect, DC's mid-2000s storylines featured supervillains who commit rape and superheroes who brainwash their foes. In 2005, DC's supervillains assaulted heroes *en masse* in the pages of the miniseries *Villains United* and *Infinite Crisis*, and throughout related tie-ins. One controversial tale featured Wonder Woman executing mastermind Maxwell Lord to end his mental control over Superman, prompting a "Should Heroes Kill?" debate among readers. Also in the mid-2000s, Marvel's superhero the Scarlet Witch went mad, "disassembling" (i.e., wounding or killing) her fellow Avengers, and the Marvel Universe's reality was reconstructed into a Magneto-ruled, mutant-dominated society in its *House of M* crossover (which led to a related event titled "Decimation").

Amid this climate of mayhem-minded supervillain ubiquity, one must ponder, *With supervillains going to such extremes, how can superheroes remain altruistic in their struggles against them?* That question will be answered by the writers and artists of the new millennium, and the pop-culture historians who will one day examine their efforts. —*ME*

MODOK: *See* A.I.M. and Hydra

Mojo

Rivaling the Blob in obesity, Mojo is unsurpassed in sheer craziness by any other major X-Men villain. Created by writer Ann Nocenti and artist Arthur Adams in Marvel Comics' *Longshot* #3 (1986), Mojo rules Mojoworld, a planet in another dimension. He is one of the Spineless Ones, grotesque beings that are incapable of standing erect; instead, Mojo rides a mechanical platform that can float in the air. Mojo can fire bolts of mystical force from his hands and magically control the minds of others.

Mojo compelled a scientist named Arize to genetically engineer a race of humanoid slaves. One of them, Longshot, led a slave rebellion but was forced to flee to Earth. Mojo pursued him there and began plotting to conquer the planet, only to be defeated by Longshot.

Utilizing Mojo in various *X-Men*–related comics, writer Chris Claremont emphasized that Mojo heads his world's entertainment industry, pacifying the masses through movies and television. Claremont depicted Mojo as a mad producer, continually seeking to ensnare the X-Men into acting in his shows. (Appropriately, Mojo has also appeared in *X-Men: The Animated Series,* 1992–1997.)

Aided by the X-Men, Longshot overthrew and seemingly slew Mojo, who was succeeded by a character known as *Mojo II, the Sequel.* The first Mojo has a look-alike, Mojo V, who lives one hundred years in the future and is the enemy of the 1990s X-Force's Shatterstar. But somehow the original Mojo survived and returned to power, continuing to make trouble for the X-Men.

The *Ultimate X-Men* comic (2001–present), which presents an alternate version of X-Men continuity, has featured a human villain named Mojo Adams, a reality television show host who hates mutants. —*PS*

Mojo Jojo

Many supervillains have battled the pint-sized, preschool superheroines the Powerpuff Girls—including the cross-dressing devil Him; Princess, the spoiled Powerpuff wannabe; the ornery hillbilly Fuzzy Lumpkins; and the Amoeba Boys, three single-celled organisms with barely one brain between them. Yet no foe has made fans go ape more than Mojo Jojo. In the origin of the Powerpuff Girls, mentioned in the animated series' (1998–2004) opener but fully disclosed in the theatrically released *The Powerpuff Girls Movie* (2003), Professor Utonium combines "sugar, spice, and everything nice to create the perfect little girl." When the Professor's playful primate lab assistant Jojo accidentally spills "Chemical X" into the mix, the resulting explosion produces not one but *three* girls—Blossom, Buttercup, and Bubbles, each with superpowers—and transforms Jojo into the megalomaniacal monkey the world would soon know and fear (well, sort of) as Mojo Jojo.

Instead of receiving superpowers like his "sisters," Mojo Jojo's intellect and ego were significantly amplified. He is the master of overstatement, prone to third-person tirades: " ... there is only room enough in this world for one Mojo Jojo. One shall be the number of Mojo Jojos in the world, and the number of Mojo Jojos in the world shall be one. Two Mojo Jojos is too many, and three is right out. So the only Mojo Jojo there is room for in the world shall be me." Lending voice to the simian supervillain was Roger L. Jackson, also known as the telephone caller in the *Scream* movies.

The oft-beleaguered city of Townsville has routinely fallen prey to Mojo Jojo's machinations. Operating from his volcano headquarters, he has turned the populace into dogs, attacked the city with super-monkeys, and engineered the gender-bending Powerpuff Girls counterparts, the Rowdyruff Boys. On one occasion, Mojo even teamed with Him, Fuzzy, and Princess as "the Beat-Alls," but their evil alliance was dissolved when Mojo Jojo broke rank after falling in love with Mojo Ono. His continual defeats at the Girls' tiny hands have fomented his deep hatred of the young superheroines, and Mojo Jojo will stop at *almost* nothing to cause their demise: "I swear that today is the day that I will develop a plan so diabolical and evil that I will crush the Powerpuff Girls. But first … I must attend to the dishes that I have soiled with the food that I have eaten." —*ME*

Mole Man

The Mole Man (originally Moleman) was the first supervillain of the Marvel Age of Comics, originating in the issue that jumpstarted the publisher's new superhero wave, *Fantastic Four* (*FF*) vol. 1 #1 (1961).

Writer Stan Lee and artist Jack Kirby disclosed the Mole Man's tragic tale in *FF* #1. Outcast from society because of his hideousness, an unnamed scientist wanders nomadically ("Even this loneliness is better than the cruelty of my fellow men!") toward the only place he believes he can seek refuge, the center of Earth. Sailing to Monster Isle, he enters a cavern that snakes to a labyrinth to Earth's core. An avalanche robs him of most of his sight, and as the Mole Man, cloaked in green, he dons huge eyeglasses to enhance his weakened vision. The Mole Man dispatches a mindless, subterranean monster to the surface world to destroy nuclear facilities and therefore eliminate power sources, so that he might vengefully storm the globe with his horde of underworld grotesqueries. The Fantastic Four, in their first adventure, rush underground to halt the Mole Man's plan.

Kirby and inker Dick Ayers' oft-imitated cover to *Fantastic Four* #1, pitting the pre-costumed FF against the Mole Man's scaly, clawed leviathan (named "Giganto" in *West Coast Avengers* #54, 1990), straddled the line between the Marvel's forte of the late 1950s, monster comics, and its new territory of the 1960s, superhero comics. The

Mole Man also fit that bill. Looking somewhat like actor Peter Lorre, the creepy Mole Man was distinctly garbed but not flamboyantly costumed, as were supervillains that followed him at Marvel (or preceded him at DC).

As an explosion leveled Monster Isle and sealed off the Mole Man's portal to the outside world at the end of *Fantastic Four* #1, the Invisible Girl remarked, "I just hope we have seen the last of him!" Such was not the case. The Mole Man resurfaced in issue #22 (1964), and has frequently returned with new schemes to muscle control over the civilization that rejected him.

The Mole Man governs his underground kingdom of Subterranea accompanied by innumerous serfs, the bug-eyed, yellowish creatures called Moloids. Like his burrowing namesake, the Mole Man's swollen, squinty eyes are sensitive to light, hence his protective goggles, and he possesses a radar sense. An accomplished combatant, he utilizes a staff, either wooden or a flame-shooting mechanical variety, as his weapon of choice. The Mole Man has created other weapons as well, including lasers and digging machines, employing technology left behind by the subterranean race, the Deviants.

The Mole Man is not the only underground emperor in the Marvel Universe. Tyrannus, created by Lee and Kirby in *The Incredible Hulk* vol. 1 #5 (1963), is a handsome antediluvian wizard who rules a section of the underworld. He and the Mole Man have upon occasion clashed, their rivalry dating back to the Hulk story in *Tales to Astonish* #80 (1966). Kala, first seen in the Iron Man story in *Tales of Suspense* #43 (1963), once ruled the chthonian realm of Netherworld. After feigning affection for the Mole Man in a 1972 *FF* storyline, she later became his unwilling consort after exposure to the surface atmosphere dramatically aged her.

The Mole Man was born Harvey Rupert Elder, although that name is a painful reminder of a life denied him by his repulsiveness. Despite his heartrending past, he once attempted to create an underground utopia for outcast creatures, but the deaths of many of his subjects from industrial drilling renewed his contempt for surface dwellers.

The Mole Man has been a favorite of television animators. He appeared in the *Fantastic Four*

television cartoon series produced in 1967, 1978, and 1994, with a Mole Man action figure (including a miniature Moloid and a "twirling combat staff" accessory) tying in to the 1994 program. In the twenty-first century, coldcast porcelain Mole Man mini-statues and mini-busts have been produced for the discerning collector.

The schizophrenic Dr. Arthur Molekevic is the Mole Man in the pages of *Ultimate Fantastic Four* (2004–present), Marvel Comics' reinvention of the FF. Molekevic, a disturbing, repellent figure nick-named "Moleman" by his students, was ousted from his teaching position at the Baxter Building, a science think tank, for illegal biotech experiments involving the creation of synthetic life. Retreating underground, he became the Ultimate Mole Man, and an enemy of the Ultimate FF. —*ME*

Molecule Man

Uatu the Watcher, an alien whose duty is to study planet Earth, has vowed not to intervene in human affairs. Yet Uatu violated his oath to warn the Fantastic Four about a menace to the entire universe: the Molecule Man, whom editor/writer Stan Lee and artist/co-plotter Jack Kirby introduced in *Fantastic Four* vol. 1 #20 (1963).

This dire threat is Owen Reece, a timid, embittered assistant at an atomic research laboratory. Reece accidentally activates an experimental particle generator, which opens a "pinhole" into another dimension, bombarding him with radiation. The radiation leaves scars resembling lightning bolts on Reece's face, but also activates his latent psionic ability to control matter at the molecular level and manipulate all forms of energy as well. As Molecule Man, Reece decides to use his new powers to take vengeance on the world he believes has mistreated him.

A recurring foe of the Fantastic Four, the Molecule Man was imprisoned in another dimension by the Watcher, although the villain ultimately managed to return to Earth. The all-powerful being called the Beyonder transported Reece to his Battleworld planet to participate in a Secret War involving many of Earth's superheroes and supervillains in the best-selling limited series *Marvel Super*

Subterranean Supervillains

Many writers have imagined vast subterranean civilizations—and where there are humans, there is evil.

- George Reeves first starred as the Man of Steel not on the venerated TV series of the 1950s but in the movie *Superman and the Mole Men* (1951), in which diminutive **Mole Men** "terrorizing" a Midwestern community were merely curious explorers who had crawled out of an oil well.

- **Grottu** (whose name means "Demon"), an ant metamorphosed to giant, super-sentient proportions by a nuclear test in Marvel's *Strange Tales* #73 (1960), tried to dominate Earth several times, fighting heroes from Ant-Man to the Fantastic Four.

- First seen in *X-Men* #41 (1967), the mutant **Grotesk** (sometimes Grotesque) the Sub-Human, the rampaging behemoth from the Gortokian race of Subterraneans, hated surface dwellers much like his aquatic counterpart Namor the Sub-Mariner did.

- Some of Grotesk's Gortokians evolved into the red-skinned tribal clan known as the **Lava Men**, enemies of Thor. Lava-monsters are common adversaries, and have fought heroes as diverse as Space Ghost to DC's 1960s "Inside Earth" explorer Cave Carson.

- **The Deviants**, an ancient, constantly mutating Subterranean race, was introduced by Jack Kirby in *The Eternals* #1 (1976). Their cruel leader, Warlord Kro, has lived for 20,000 years but has kept his longevity a secret from his fellow Deviants.

- Mining engineer Jonathan Darque attacked environmentalists as **Magma**, a supervillain with a lava-shooting gun; from his underground lair he triggered seismological disasters, even taking credit for the Mount St. Helens eruption in his debut in *Marvel Team-Up* #110 (1981).

- **The Mole**, a little-known enemy of the Dark Knight, burrowed into Gotham City in *Batman* #340 (1981).

- The mole-like **Underminer**, who hides his frightful squinty eyes under a lighted spelunker's helmet, is a foe of the Incredibles. In the video game *The Incredibles: Rise of the Underminer* (2005), he attempted to pollute the surface world to govern it from below.

Heroes Secret Wars (1984–1985). There Reece fell in love with fellow supervillain Volcana. Giving up their roles as supervillains, Reece and Volcana returned to Earth to live peaceful lives together.

Reece aided Earth's superheroes in defeating the Beyonder, only to later imbue Volcana with his powers and physically merge with the Beyonder to form a power object called a Cosmic Cube. However, this newly created Cosmic Cube expelled the powerless Reece from its form and evolved into the being called Kosmos. By chance, Volcana encountered Reece and subconsciously returned his powers to him, but Volcana then rejected Reece, who was still in love with her.

Molecule Man appeared briefly in television animation in the Hanna-Barbera–produced *Fantastic Four* cartoon (1967–1970). As of 2006 the Molecule Man remains at large. —*GM and PS*

Moltar

Of the maleficent miscreants in Space Ghost's rogues' gallery—including Creature King, robot master Metallus, Black Widow (Spider-Woman) and her spider monsters, the sleep-inducing bandits Lurker and One-Eye, and Lokar, King of the Killer Locusts—Moltar was handpicked by the star-spanning paragon … to be a talk-show director.

His roots were not behind the camera, but instead were based in unleashing interstellar malice. Premiering in "The Ovens of Moltar" (original airdate: September 10, 1966) on Hanna-Barbera's *Space Ghost and Dino Boy* cartoon (1966–1968), this warped genius (whose face is concealed by a red-and-gray protective helmet) commands troops of lava-men, one of which disables a craft piloted by teenagers Jan and Jace. When their mentor Space Ghost scurries to their aid, the ensuing conflict between the hero and Moltar climaxes with an eruption of the villain's volcanic world.

Whether Moltar is a human mutant or an alien is unknown, but as a molten man he emits blistering temperatures quelled only by his containment suit. After several Space Ghost skirmishes Moltar was incarcerated on Ghost Planet, but he was paroled when the hero changed careers to become the celebrity-interviewing host of the cable comedy

Space Ghost: Coast to Coast (1994–2004), a spoof mixing animation and live action. Moltar, forced into indentured servitude as the show's inattentive director voiced by C. Martin Croker, was usually seen inside the studio's control room, where he preferred watching *CHiPs* reruns over performing his directorial tasks. Moltar appeared as a *Coast to Coast* action figure in the early 2000s. —*ME*

Monarch: *See* Extant

Mongul

Mongul, the abominable lord of the gladiator deathstar Warworld, has battled Superman in three different incarnations. The flaxen-skinned, red-eyed, half-ton titan premiered in *DC Comics Presents* #27 (1980), by writer Len Wein and artist Jim Starlin. Mongul wastes no time in revealing his ruthlessness, pledging on page two to kill Superman's friends unless the hero recovers a key that will allow the villain to regain control of his synthetic planet. After skirmishing with the key's guardian—Martian Manhunter—Superman brawls with Mongul, whose superhuman strength makes him a worthy adversary for the Man of Steel.

Writer/artist Jerry Ordway introduced an all-new Mongul in *The Adventures of Superman* #454 (1989), in which the spacefaring Superman was coerced into Warworld's battle-to-the-death arena, purely for Mongul's amusement. The resolute but compassionate Man of Steel inspired Warworld's combatants to depose their enslaver. Mongul later migrated to Earth, wiping out Coast City and its millions of inhabitants in a malevolent mission of re-creating Warworld. Mongul eventually met his demise at the hands of the demon Neron, who slaughtered him when he declined Neron's offer of power augmentation—at the cost of his soul.

Mongul's son—also named Mongul—first surfaced in *Superman* vol. 2 #151 (1999), imploring the Man of Steel's aid in vanquishing their common foe Imperiex. The deceitful Mongul "Junior" soon betrayed Superman, but the hero defeated him; Mongul II was later killed in an attempt to free the Superman-slayer Doomsday. The Man of Steel's problems with this warrior family are far from over: Mongul II's rancorous sister Mongal has sworn to avenge her father's honor, and Mongul returned from the dead in *Infinite Crisis* #1 (2005), although whether this Mogul is the father or the son is unclear.

The most celebrated of Mongul's appearances was in Alan Moore and Dave Gibbons' "For the Man Who Has Everything" in *Superman Annual* #11 (1985), in which he attacked the hero with an otherworldly plant that cocooned Superman in a nurturing dream state. The story was adapted into an episode of the animated series *Justice League Unlimited* (2004–present). Mongul was voiced by actor Eric Roberts, who also played the villain a few years earlier on the cartoon series *Superman* (1996–2000). —ME

Monologues and Soliloquies

In the middle of listening to Dr. Octopus brag about his power, Spider-Man once asked, "Tell me something, Ock ... are you trying to defeat me by *talking* me to death?!" (*Amazing Spider-Man Annual* #6, 1969). The answer—based upon the propensity of villains to talk, talk, talk—appears to be yes.

Monologuing, coined in *The Incredibles* (2004), refers to supervillains' tendency toward self-absorbed, self-destructive talking; instead of killing the hero, they give a speech about their greatness, the hero's feebleness, and the inevitability of their victory. Ozymanias noted the foolishness of monologuing in *Watchmen* #12 (1987): "I'm not a Republic serial villain. Do you seriously think I'd explain my master stroke if there remained the slightest chance of you affecting its outcome?"

In serials, villains such as Bela Lugosi's Dr. Zorka in *The Phantom Creeps* (1939) and Michael Fox's Dr. Grood in *The Lost Planet* (1953) talk at length about their plans for conquest and domination, creating enough story to fill twelve episodes. The same is true in pulps—writers working for a few cents a word had a great incentive to fill pages with speechifying villains. Ideologically driven supervillains such as Doc Savage's opponents John Sunlight (*The Devil Ghengis,* 1938) and Professor

Homer Randolph (*He Could Stop the World,* 1937) or The Shadow's arch-enemy Shiwan Khan (*The Golden Master,* 1939) are more given to monologuing than crooks driven by avarice, but any criminal mastermind is likely to launch into a half-page of self-aggrandizement. Monologuing also allows writers to recap the storyline and fill the audience in on plot elements they might have missed, so monologuing serves storywriters' purposes well.

But if monologuing were only a tool for the creators, it would not have lasted. Monologuing embodies central aspects of supervillainy. It is a form of hubris that comes out of the villain's belief in his absolute supremacy and the assurance that his plans are unstoppable. Hugo Drax, villain of Ian Fleming's *Moonraker* (1955), conducts a classic death-trap monologue with James Bond bound to a chair in the exhaust pit of a rocket launching pad. Drax says, "You don't know how I have longed for an English audience ... to tell my story." He then tells Bond the story of his life, finishing with the details of his plan to launch a nuclear missile at London, and closes by asking, "What do you think of my story?" Bond dismisses Drax's life as "sad business," which goads the madman into beating Bond and forgetting about a lighter left on his desk. Bond burns off his ropes, escapes certain death, and stops Drax's plan. Drax should have pocketed his lighter, but his desire to reveal himself to Bond and exert his will over the hero overrides his common sense.

Dr. No gives the classic dinner monologue. He feels confident that Bond cannot escape his island, over which he rules absolutely, so he relaxes with 007 over a meal, telling the secret agent, "It is a rare pleasure to have an intelligent listener and I shall enjoy telling you the story of one of the most remarkable men in the world"—himself, of course.

Monologuing seems to put the villain in a state of self-absorption. Auric Goldfinger's eyes go blank and focus inward as he rhapsodizes on his love of gold and its power, "the magic of controlling energy, exacting labor, fulfilling one's every wish and whim, and when need be, purchasing bodies, minds, even souls." For these moments Goldfinger enters a world made of his own words—an expression of his desire to stamp his image on history as the greatest criminal artist who ever lived.

Evil Speak: Ten Bloodcurdling Quotes

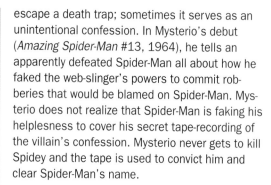

"It may interest you to know that my last coup will be executed in your costume! My last and greatest deed of evil will be to bring dishonor to the name of Captain America!" —**The Red Skull** (*Captain America Comics* #16, 1940)

"I pretended to reform, see? He fell for it, the idiot! Then, when he was off-guard ... wham! ... I fed him killing doses of kryptonite! Bye, bye, Superman! Ha, ha!" —**Lex Luthor** (*Superman* vol. 1 #149, 1961)

"I, Victor von Doom, son of a gypsy and a sorceress, vow that I shall devote my life to becoming the master of all mankind!" —**Dr. Doom** (*Fantastic Four Annual* #2, 1964)

Bond: "Do you expect me to talk?" "No, Mr. Bond, I expect you to die!" —**Auric Goldfinger** (*Goldfinger*, 1964)

"But, I mustn't let the end be too easy for you!... First, you must sit there ... helplessly ... and wonder how I shall strike ... and at what precise instant you'll perish!" —**The Green Goblin** (*The Amazing Spider-Man* vol 1. #40, 1966)

"But I am alive, X-Men. And my one consolation is that when, at last, I bring my plans to fruition—and mankind to its collective knees— you will not be there to interfere!"—**Magneto** (*X-Men* vol. 1 #113, 1978)

"Pathetic earthlings. Hurling your bodies out into the void, without the slightest inkling of who or what is out here. If you had known anything about the true nature of the universe, anything at all, you would've hidden from it in terror." —**Ming the Merciless** (*Flash Gordon*, 1980)

"I win. I always win. Is there no one on this planet to even challenge me?"—**General Zod** (*Superman II*, 1980)

"I now do what other people only dream. I make art until someone dies. I am the world's first fully functioning homicidal artist." —**The Joker** (*Batman*, 1989)

"You owe me a scream." —**Sabretrooth** (*X-Men*, 2000)

escape a death trap; sometimes it serves as an unintentional confession. In Mysterio's debut (*Amazing Spider-Man* #13, 1964), he tells an apparently defeated Spider-Man all about how he faked the web-slinger's powers to commit robberies that would be blamed on Spider-Man. Mysterio does not realize that Spider-Man is faking his helplesness to cover his secret tape-recording of the villain's confession. Mysterio never gets to kill Spidey and the tape is used to convict him and clear Spider-Man's name.

The Silver Age (1956–1969) marked an apex of the classic monologue with stories like "The Fantastic Origin of the Red Skull" (*Tales of Suspense* #66, 1965), in which the Red Skull reminisces about his life to a bound Captain America. The Red Skull discourses for seven pages, at one point slugging Captain America over the head with a pistol into apparent unconsciousness, saying, "And now if I may finish my narrative without any further interruption."

The second form of speechifying, the soliloquy, is performed without an audience or in front of obedient underlings who neither interrupt nor respond to their master's musings. In the soliloquy, the supervillain gives full vent to his ego, proclaiming his greatness and promising vengeance on those who oppose him. In *Amazing Spider-Man* #5 (1963), a solitary Dr. Doom declares, "When one is a master of science, as *I* am, there is nothing which cannot be accomplished! Sooner or later, I shall eliminate all those who dare oppose me!"

But the monologue has great value in conveying the character of a supervillain. In *Spider-Man/Doctor Octopus: Year One* #5 (2005), Octopus holds an apparently defeated Spider-Man in his metal arms and explains that everything— including language—is technology and the "most telling of these technologies is morality ... A device constructed to spur our race to greater things ... the compass by which all actions and advances are judged. Surely, in the age of the atom, we are due for an innovation ... human sentimentalism will be crushed in the wheels of progress." While Octopus monologues, Spider-Man short circuits his metal arms through a feedback loop, rendering Octopus helpless. Had Octavius merely killed Spider-Man instead of holding him aloft and yammer-

Ultimately, though, monologuing is a weakness. It allows a superhero time to recover or ing on about his philosophy of life, Spider-Man could not have beaten him. But the villain's ego demands an audience, and his ego, not the hero's power, brings him down. —*PC*

The Monster Society of Evil

The Monster Society of Evil, created by writer Otto Binder and artist C. C. Beck, holds two distinctions: it was the first supervillain team, and its twenty-five-chapter serialized format was the longest-running storyline produced during the Golden Age of Comics (1938–1954).

Beginning in Fawcett's *Captain Marvel Adventures* #22 (1943), the World's Wickedest Worm, Mr. Mind, declares that he will give Captain Marvel "nightmares" by gathering a gruesome army of the universe's most baleful blackguards. Mr. Mind mobilizes Dr. Sivana, Black Adam, Captain Nazi, Herkimer the Crocodile Man, the hypnotic monster Evil Eye, Jeepers the bat-monster, the robotic Mr. Atom, beast-men King Kull and IBAC, and other nemeses—and real-world despots Hitler, Tojo, and Mussolini—to despoil the globe with attempted atrocities including a second Pearl Harbor bombing and the splitting of Earth into halves. Captain Marvel is busy repressing each of these threats, finally retiring the Monster Society in issue #46's conclusion (1945). This celebrated serial was reprinted in a limited-edition hardcover in 1989.

After DC Comics acquired the Fawcett characters in the early 1970s, Mr. Mind revived the Monster Society of Evil—with much smaller rosters—in 1974 and 1980. *All-Star Squadron* #51–#54 (1985–1986) retroactively offered the first chronological tale of the team, set in the early 1940s. Mr. Mind assembled several of DC's minor Golden Age villains (Mr. Who, the Dummy, Ramulus, Nyola, and Oom) to fight the Justice Society of America (Mr. Mind's role in this tale would later be written out of DC continuity). In the rebooted, post–*Crisis on Infinite Earths* DC Universe, Mr. Mind and Mr. Atom formed a partnership as the Monster Society in a 1998 *The Power of Shazam!* story arc that resulted in the nuclear obliteration of a small town.

Cartoonist Jeff Smith, creator of the critically acclaimed comic *Bone*, produced the miniseries *Shazam!: Monster Society of Evil* in 2006. "It's a classic serial, but it's pretty goofy by today's standards," Smith said. "Giant, out-of-control casts of characters are my specialty." —*ME*

Monster Supervillains

Creatures spawned from mythology and cultural legends—minotaurs, sea beasts, fire-breathing dragons, abominable snowmen, and their ilk—are comic-book and cartoon staples, but several monsters made famous by novels and film have become so engrained as evil in the pop-culture psyche that they are regarded as supervillains.

Frankenstein's Monster, who first appeared in Mary Shelley's 1818 novel *Frankenstein, or The Modern Prometheus*, was the obvious template for Superman's doppelgänger Bizarro, but has also appeared as a supervillain himself. "The X-Men Meet Frankenstein! Nuff Said!" blurbed the cover to *X-Men* #40 (1968), featuring a bolt-necked android bearing more than a passing resemblance to the Boris Karloff version of "the Creature," as the Monster was at times called, in the enduring horror movie classic *Frankenstein* (1931). Superman encountered the Frankenstein Monster on several occasions, including *Superman* vol. 1 #344 (1980), in which the Monster pinned back the Man of Steel's arms while Dracula prepared to feast upon the hero's neck. The sympathetic nature of this man-made monstrosity has also inspired his portrayal in a heroic light in many comic books and animated television cartoons.

The King of Vampires, Count Dracula, is also the king of comic-book monster-supervillains. Marvel's *The Tomb of Dracula* (1972–1979), made famous by writer Marv Wolfman and artist Gene Colan, ran an astounding seventy issues and has enjoyed several revivals. Blending characters from the original source material, Bram Stoker's 1897 novel *Dracula*, with original characters such as Blade the Vampire Slayer and the diabolical scientist Dr. Sun, *Tomb of Dracula* coexisted with other

Marvel Comics series. Wolfman and Colan generally chose not to exploit Dracula's Marvel Universe residency, although issue #50's battle with the Silver Surfer reminded readers of where the Count hung his cape.

Because of their series' success, Dracula has been absorbed into the Marvel's pantheon of villains, combating Spider-Man, Dr. Strange, and the X-Men (Dracula and Spider-Man also clashed in the mid-1970s on TV's *The Electric Company*). Other comics publishers have fallen under Dracula's spell, although unlike the Frankenstein Monster, the King of Vampires has rarely been depicted heroically. Dracula occasionally flutters into the DC Universe, in vehicles such as Doug Moench and Kelley Jones' graphic novel *Batman & Dracula: Red Rain* (1991), in which Batman became a vampire. *The Batman vs. Dracula* (2005) was a made-for-DVD animated movie spin-off of the WB's cartoon series *The Batman* (2004–present). The King of Vampires has fought other famous heroes, including a famous ebon-garbed swashbuckler in Topps Comics' two-issue *Dracula versus Zorro* (1993).

The Wolf Man, the personification of the ancient legend of lycanthropy (humans transformed into wolves), was popularized on the screen by actor Lon Chaney, Jr. in the Universal Pictures horror classic *The Wolf Man* (1941). Werewolves frequently serve as supervillains on the screen, in diverse works from *The Adventures of Jonny Quest* to *Buffy the Vampire Slayer*. Marvel's *Werewolf by Night* title was a 1970s favorite, with its tragic protagonist often regarded a villain by those he met, including Spider-Man and Moon Knight. Readers realized that, like many monsters, the werewolf was merely misunderstood.

A supernatural gem caused astronaut John Jameson (son of *Daily Bugle* publisher J. Jonah Jameson) to mutate into Man-Wolf, another Spider-Man foe who starred in his own short-lived, mid-1970s series (in the title *Creatures on the Loose*). *Superman's Pal Jimmy Olsen* #44 (1960) featured the red-headed cub reporter transmogrified into "The Wolf-Man of Metropolis" after a sip of a strange brew, while Superman and cowboy super-hero the Vigilante tussled with a werewolf in *World's Finest Comics* #214 (1972). Writer Len Wein, with artist Neal Adams, pitted the Caped

Crusader against a werewolf in "Moon of the Wolf" in *Batman* #255 (1974), a story Wein adapted to animation as a 1992 episode of *Batman: The Animated Series* (1992–1995).

Frankenstein, Dracula, and the Wolf Man have occasionally united as a triumvirate of terror. They were played for laughs in the timeless movie classic *Abbott and Costello Meet Frankenstein* (1948), and were only marginally scary in the kid-friendly "The Transylvania Connection" episode of the animated *Spider-Man and His Amazing Friends* (1981–1986). A computer-generated werewolf joined Dracula and Frankenstein as the arch-foes of monster-fighter Hugh Jackman in the 2004 movie *Van Helsing*. Sweet-toothed breakfast-cereal lovers know this trio of monsters in their more palatable incarnations as General Mills' Count Chocula, Frankenberry, and Fruit Brute (along with their fiendish friends Boo Berry the ghost and the Yummy Mummy). Horror comics writer Steve Niles dug up some of these old childhood favorites for the four-issue miniseries *General Mills Massacre* (2005–2006), drawn by Stuart Sayger and published by AFD Press.

Other famous monsters have inspired supervillains in comics and film. Robert Louis Stevenson's 1886 novella *The Strange Case of Dr. Jekyll and Mr. Hyde* and its "monster within the man" struggle gave birth to Batman's enemy Two-Face, whose Jekyll-and-Hyde actions are selected by the flip of a coin. Another Bat-foe, Man-Bat, experienced a similar, sometimes uncontrollable transformation from benevolent scientist to malevolent monster. DC Comics' Eclipso, when created in 1963, was billed as "Hero and Villain in One Man," although his twenty-first century incarnation is exclusively sinister. Mr. Hyde, a researcher turned superhuman, is Marvel's most obvious variation on Stevenson's theme, but when Stan Lee and Jack Kirby co-created the Incredible Hulk in 1962, they did so envisioning their monster-hero as a modern-day Jekyll and Hyde.

Movie monster the Creature from the Black Lagoon inspired the Devil-Fish, a foe in a 1974 Legion of Super-Heroes story, while Marvel baited the same waters in 1975 with Manphibian, seen in the black-and-white magazine *Legion of Monsters* #1. Swamp creatures are comic-book staples,

Count Dracula, Marvel supervillain. *The Tomb of Dracula* vol. 1 #10 ©1973 Marvel Comics.
COVER ART BY GIL KANE AND TOM PALMER.

Hulk—not the incredible green-skinned monster-hero, but the 15-foot furry alien criminal that crash-landed on Earth in *Journey into Mystery* #62 (1960)—was conceived by Lee and Kirby as one of the many one-shot monsters stamping through Marvel's horror anthologies before later being renamed Xemnu the Titan and recast as a Marvel supervillain. Xemnu ultimately became a comic-relief monster, due to John Byrne's less-than-reverent handling of the character in several late 1980s–early 1990s issues of *The Sensational She-Hulk*.

Colossal threat King Kong is a popular supervillain, starring in numerous films and comics, and influencing imitators like Titano the Super-Ape and Konga. Godzilla, also the star of a long-running film franchise, became a Marvel Comics supervillain in a 24-issue run of *Godzilla* (1977–1979), in which the King of Monsters was challenged by numerous heroes including the Fantastic Four and the agents of S.H.I.E.L.D. (concurrently, writer/artist Jack Kirby's unsuccessful *Devil Dinosaur* series was published by Marvel in 1978, lasting only eight issues). Dark Horse Comics picked up the Godzilla license in the late 1980s and published several *Godzilla* series, some of which featured covers and/or interior art by fan-favorite Arthur Adams, a dedicated Godzilla toy collector. Two one-shots pitted the monster against larger-than-life heroes: *Godzilla vs. Barkley* (1993) brought basketball great Charles Barkley to comic books, while *Godzilla vs. Hero Zero* (1995) featured the monster and the size-changing superhero toppling skyscrapers at the San Diego Comic-Con.

Dark Horse has also translated movie monsters the Aliens (the face-hugging breeders first seen in *Alien*, 1979) and the Predators (the human-hunters originating in the film *Predator*, 1987) to comics in numerous series, portraying them as supervillains in several crossovers with DC Comics including *Batman versus Predator* (1991–1992) and *Superman vs. Aliens* (1995); the legendary Ape Man also battled a Predator in the miniseries *Tarzan vs. Predator at the Earth's Core* (1996). These evil extraterrestrials clashed on the big screen in *AVP: Alien vs. Predator* (2004), but in fact their enmity was rooted in Dark Horse stories, beginning with the first Aliens/Predator crossover in *Dark Horse Presents* #34–#36 (1989).

although they, like Frankenstein's Monster, are frequently persecuted innocents just trying to weather another day. Sci-fi author Theodore Sturgeon's 1940 story "It" was an early example of a bog-spawned menace, as were the Heap (first seen in Hillman Publications' *Air Fighter Comics* #3, 1942), the Incredible Hulk's foe the Glob (*Incredible Hulk* vol. 2 #121, 1969), and DC's Swamp Thing and Marvel's Man-Thing, both of which were created in 1971. There is no mistaking the intentions of Solomon Grundy, the maleficent marshman first seen in 1944—he is unquestionably evil.

The Yeti, the primate-like giant rumored to roam the Himalayas, prompted the creation of the 12-foot android the Shaggy Man, who first clobbered DC's heroes in *Justice League of America* #45 (1966). Immoral soldier General Wade Eiling transferred his intellect into the Shaggy Man's shaved synthetic body and attacked the League as "the General" in *JLA* #25 (1999). The Yeti-like

Among the many monster supervillains/anti-heroes introduced by Marvel Comics in the 1970s were the Living Mummy and the Zombie; they, along with Frankenstein, Warwolf, and Vampire by Night, joined forces in the miniseries *Nick Fury's Howling Commandos* (2005–2006), featuring a "shock and awe" covert unit of supernatural operatives. —*ME*

Morbius the Living Vampire

M arvel Comics' macabre Morbius—not to be confused with Morbius the Time Lord from the BBC's adventure series *Doctor Who*—first took wing in *The Amazing Spider-Man* vol. 1 #101 (1971), by writer Roy Thomas and artist Gil Kane. Spider-Man, briefly mutated into a six-armed freak after taking an untested potion intended to eliminate his spider-powers, is attacked by a powerful savage with "inhumanly white" skin and sharp teeth "like an animal's gleaming fangs." This monstrosity, as revealed in issue #102's "Vampire at Large!" is actually Nobel Prize winner Dr. Michael Morbius, a European biochemist who was dying from a blood-cell abnormality. With the aid of his colleague Emil Nikos, Morbius initiated a bizarre therapy involving electroshock treatments and a serum derived from vampire-bat DNA; it bore grisly results, transmogrifying him into a superhumanly strong "living" vampire with an insatiable thirst for human blood. Aghast from his vile compulsion, Morbius attempts to hide from humanity but cannot escape it, encountering Spider-Man. With an unlikely ally in the scaly form of his nemesis the Lizard, Spidey battles Morbius to a stalemate, the bloodsucker swept away in the Hudson River.

Morbius was resurrected in *Marvel Team-Up* vol. 1 #3 (1972), with the Human Torch helping Spidey ward off the vampire. A wave of monster mania swept comics after the Comics Code Authority censorship board lifted its long-time ban on undead characters, and the Living Vampire received his own series, taking over *Adventure into Fear* from Man-Thing, who graduated into his own title. The Uncanny Caretaker, Cat-Demon, and Helleyes were some of the oddball opponents Morbius faced—as well Blade the Vampire

Slayer and CIA operative Simon Stroud—in his series that ran in *Fear* #20–#30 (1974–1975).

During yet another Marvel monster-comic trend, this time in the early 1990s, Morbius again became a star, receiving his own monthly title (*Morbius: The Living Vampire* #1–#32, 1992–1995). The Living Vampire rarely rested in this eventful series. He received psionic and hypnotic abilities through a bogus vampirism cure, momentarily became human during 12-hour intervals (adopting the identity of Dr. Morgan Michaels), vowed to drink only the blood of the wicked, lost his beloved former fiancée, was killed and resurrected, was possessed by the demon Bloodthirst, and went insane. Through battles with dark forces, heroes as sundry as Dr. Strange, She-Hulk, and, of course, Spider-Man regard Morbius as their ally, but do so with trepidation, given his uncontrollable bloodlust.

Nick Jameson voiced Morbius in the FOX *Spider-Man* cartoon (1994–1998), and the supervillain has been sculpted as action figures and cold-cast porcelain mini-busts. —*ME*

Mordru

" C ringe, Legionnaires! Tremble! Flee! Hide!" taunted Mordru the Merciless, the "almost omnipotent" sorcerer who subjugated the planet Zerox, in *Adventure Comics* #369–#370 (1968). And the Legion of Super-Heroes, the teen titans of the thirtieth century, did just that, with engrossed readers fretfully wiping their brows.

To escape Mordru's onslaught, scampering Legionnaires—including the mega-mighty Superboy and Mon-El—time-travel to twentieth-century Smallville, the Boy of Steel's home, seeking refuge in civilian disguises and even self-inducing amnesia. Mordru seizes Smallville with his armies from the future, ferreting out then crushing the Legion and placing them on trial before a jury of thirtieth-century incorrigibles. Conjuring in his hands an energy fireball teeming with "the power to annihilate galaxies," the pitiless mage poises to execute the helpless heroes when the sphere's pulsating force causes the earth around him to cave in, exposing Mordru's sole weakness: airless entombment.

In this era of mostly anemic or buffoonish comic-book supervillains, writer Jim Shooter and artist Curt Swan's Mordru the Merciless cranked up the ten-point evil scale to eleven. Mordru cast a nightmarish figure with his petrifying scowl, claw-like nails, untamed white beard and mane, and eerie wizard's headdress. He grew to leviathan size, probed minds, became intangible, hurled energy bolts, created creeping shadows, cast illusions, manipulated gravity, and incinerated enemies—all in a mere two-part story. And thus this necromancer, also hailed as "the Dark Lord" in Shooter's first script, (arguably) became the superteam's most baneful enemy, with each subsequent wrathful appearance leaving fans wondering if the bountiful Legion would be diminished a hero or two. Yet Mordru was played for laughs in his television debut on the NBC live-action special *Legends of the Super-Heroes* (1979), a spoof starring Adam West as Batman, with actor Gabe Dell as the blustery warlock. That frivolous portrayal was long forgotten by the time Mordru again strayed outside of comics as an action figure in 2002 and a television cartoon villain in 2004 in the *Justice League Unlimited* episode "The Greatest Story Never Told."

Mordru the comic-book character's role has expanded beyond his throne at the apex of the Legion's rogues' gallery. *JSA Secret Files #1* (1999) revealed that the sorcerer now officially called the Dark Lord was timeless—according to legend, he has always existed. In the late twentieth century he slaughtered agents of Order and Chaos in a crusade to obtain the occult powers of Dr. Fate, drawing him into conflict with the Justice Society of America. The Dark Lord allied with his fellow "princes of darkness" Eclipso and Obsidian in a 2003 attempt to thrust the world into eternal night, and struggled with Power Girl in *JSA Classified #2* (2005). For the denizens of the contemporary and future DC Universes, the merciless Mordru poses a gloomy millennia-spanning threat. —ME

Morgan le Fay

In the Arthurian myths, Morgan (sometimes spelled Morgaine) le Fay is often cast in the role of King Arthur's foe. But in many versions of the legend, she is also known as one of the women who will bring about his eventual return.

Next to Queen Guenevere, Morgan le Fay is arguably the most important female figure in the Arthurian myths. In Sir Thomas Malory's *Morte d'Arthur*, Morgan is depicted as Arthur's half sister, the daughter of Arthur's mother Igraine and her first husband, the Duke of Cornwall. Arthur was her half-brother, the child of Igraine and Uther Pendragon. Although Arthur grows to become a formidable warrior and wielder of the mystic blade Excalibur, Morgan possesses a knowledge of mysticism, which she inherited from her mother, that Arthur cannot match. Some sources credit the mother as being the daughter of LeFay, a Welsh sea goddess. (The root of the name "Morgan" means "sea.")

Most modern versions of the Arthurian myths consider Morgan the mother of the evil Mordred (or Modred), fathered by Arthur after Morgan seduced him, though older versions of the myths place Morgan's sister, Morgause, in the role of seductress. Placing Morgan in opposition to Arthur conflicts with older versions of the legend in which Morgan is one of the women who await Arthur on the Isle of Avalon, where he went upon his death, to heal him of his mortal wound while Britain anticipates his return.

In several sources Morgan has nothing against Arthur, but does carry a grudge against some of Arthur's allies and friends. She is depicted as an enemy of Guinevere in the Vulgate *Lancelot,* in which Guinevere puts an end to Morgan's affair with Guiomar, Guinevere's cousin. An angry Morgan becomes determined to expose the queen's infidelity with Lancelot. She attempts this by, among other things, giving Arthur the gift of a magic drinking horn from which only women who are faithful to their husbands can drink without spilling, and attempting to seduce Lancelot herself. From this, it is easy to imagine that authors would fashion enmity between Arthur and Morgan.

The twentieth century brought a renewed interest in Morgan le Fay and her role(s) in the Arthurian legends. Marion Zimmer Bradley brought le Fay to the forefront as the protagonist of her novel *The Mists of Avalon* (1983), reflecting an increased feminist interest in the role of women in the legends. Juliana Margulies played Morgan in the 2001 television adaptation of the same name; Joan Allen played Morgause.

Morgan le Fay has enjoyed a number of interpretations in comic books, though not always in a light in which she might find flattering. For example, the character was portrayed as a matriarchal, but still vital, opponent to King Arthur in Jack Kirby's comic *The Demon* (1972–1974), and is one of the major villains in the DC Comics series *Camelot 3000* (by Mike W. Barr and Brian Bolland, 1982–1985). She has also fought Wonder Woman and other members of the Justice League in an episode ("Kids' Stuff") of the *Justice League Unlimited* cartoon series (2004–present), where she was voiced by Olivia d'Abo.

Morgan le Fay has also appeared in the comic strip *Prince Valiant* by Hal Foster, in the continuity "The Sorceress" (February 26, 1938), and in the Marvel Comics series *Iron Man* by David Michelinie and John Romita, Jr. (1981), *Spider-Woman* by Mark Gruenwald and Carmine Infantino (1981), and *Knights of Pendragon* by Dan Abnett and John Tomlinson, illustrated by various artists (Marvel UK, 1990–1993). She also appears in the Caliber Press revisionist series *Camelot Eternal* by J. Caliafore (1990–1991).

In all these comics series, le Fay is depicted as a villainess, eager to take revenge against the protagonists for some new insult, real or imagined, or to form an alliance with the enemies of King Arthur, to further her own evil schemes. Le Fay is usually depicted as sexually seductive, employing black magic or psychological manipulation, rather than the use of sheer physical power, to achieve her ends. Her frequent ploy is to make a male protagonist fall in love with her, then use him to betray his allies. Borrowing from her Arthurian roots, perhaps some future

series will depict Morgan le Fay not as King Arthur's foe, but as his enigmatic ally. —*MWB*

Morlun

Life was simpler for Peter Parker when he believed that the bite from a radioactive arachnid that transformed him into Spider-Man was a capricious quirk of fate. His discovery of his predestination to become the "totem" of the spider,

The Amazing Spider-Man #526 ©2005 Marvel Comics.
COVER ART BY MIKE DEODATO, JR.

the latest in a cult of insect-powered beings, placed him into the sights of the ancient "totem stalker": Morlun.

Created by writer J. Michael Straczynski and artist John Romita, Jr. in *The Amazing Spider-Man* vol. 2 #30 (2001), Morlun is an energy vampire, a parasitic humanoid that feasts upon totemistic powers rather than blood. Tireless, terrifying, and tremendously strong—much stronger than Spider-Man—the chalk-faced Morlun is the ultimate tracker, able to locate any prey once catching its scent. While Spider-Man is no stranger to vampires and hunters—Morbius the Living Vampire and Kraven the Hunter are among his foes—he finds Morlun inescapable. Weakening with each of the villain's energy-siphoning blows, in this first storyline Spider-Man desperately attempts to poison the vampire by administering to himself a radiation overdose. He nonetheless would have died at Morlun's hands were it not for the intervention of Parker's enigmatic mentor, the fellow spider-man Ezekial, and Dex, the "Renfield" to Morlun's "Dracula," who slays his abusive master.

Like Dracula, Morlun returned from the dead in "The Other," a storyline serialized throughout the Spider-Man comic-book franchise in late 2005 and early 2006. Parker was beaten within an inch of his life by his most lethal enemy, forced to "evolve or die" in this multi-layered adventure that expanded the lore of the spider totems and reset the tone of Spider-Man's adventures.

Should Marvel Comics use the "unstoppable" Morlun judiciously, then he could very well endure in the Spider-Man mythos, but the biggest threat this vampiric villain faces is the publisher's, or an eager writer's, desire to overexpose him. —*ME*

Mud Pack: *See* **Clayface**

Mysterio

"**H**as the amazing Spider-Man turned to crime?" asks writer Stan Lee and artist Steve Ditko's splash page for *The Amazing Spider-Man* vol. 1 #13 (1964), which depicts the web-slinger on the lam with a stolen money bag. This crime is actually committed by Mysterio, aka Quentin Beck, a television special-effects master who disguises himself as Spidey to frame the hero and reap glory—plus a significant reward—by capturing him. Beck longs for more of the spotlight than his behind-the-scenes trade affords, and he attires himself in green with a purple cape and a crystal ball–like one-way helmet (he can see out, but no one can see in) to tackle Spider-Man. Beck's Mysterio uniform is a sartorial warehouse of effects weaponry—he immerses himself in an eerie cloud of fog, leaps prodigiously with sole-mounted springs, and wields a spray that dissolves Spider-Man's webbing—but through stick-to-itiveness Spidey foils Mysterio's plans and exposes him as a supervillain.

In *Amazing Spider-Man Annual* #1 (1964), Mysterio accepted Dr. Octopus' invitation to join the Sinister Six, allying with Electro, Kraven the Hunter, Sandman, and the Vulture in (unsuccessful) gang warfare against Spider-Man; Mysterio remained a Sixer in many revivals of the team. In a classic 1968 clash, Mysterio made Spidey believe that he was trapped inside a miniature model of a danger-filled amusement park, and on more than one occasion he drove the wall-crawler to the brink of insanity. Soured by each defeat, Mysterio continually upgraded his weaponry, over time adding hallucinogenic gasses, holographs, toxins, robots, and even hypnotism and slight-of-hand trickery to his repertoire. With each new encounter, this master of illusions so disoriented Spider-Man that the hero could no longer trust his eyes, learning that nothing with Mysterio was as it seemed.

Nor was Mysterio always *who* he seemed. During a period when the villain had faked his demise, a new Mysterio—Beck's successor Danny Berkhart—made the web-slinger believe that the illusionist had risen from the dead. Berkhart donned the Mysterio guise on several occasions, but Beck later returned to the identity. Eventually Beck discovered that he had developed terminal cancer from repeated exposure to his illusion-casting chemicals (*Daredevil* vol. 2 #7, 1999, by Kevin Smith and Joe Quesada). Targeting a new adversary, Daredevil, for a final hurrah, Mysterio was mortified after failing to defeat the Man without Fear with an elaborate web of deceptions and took his own life. Yet with Mysterio, no one can be fully certain if his death was real. Berkhart resumed the Mysterio mantle, and the miniseries *Spider-Man: The Mysterio Manifesto* (2001) alleviated reader confusion by clarifying which Mysterio appeared in various Spider-Man stories.

One thing with Mysterio is certain: his superpowers translate well to animation. The insidious illusionist (voiced by Chris Wiggins) appeared in two episodes of the original 1967–1970 *Spider-Man* toon, both adapting comics stories, as well as in an episode of Spidey's 1994–1998 series, with Gregg Brewer playing the villain. —*ME*

Mystique

It should come as no surprise that when the mutant shapeshifter Mystique made her first appearance in Marvel Comics' *Ms. Marvel* #16 (April 1978), she was in disguise. Writer Chris Claremont introduced her as a normal-looking woman with shape-changing powers and later identified her as Raven Darkholme, the deputy director of the Defense Advanced Research Planning Agency in the U.S. Defense Department. That may be her real name, but it was not until issue #18 (June 1978) that artist Jim Mooney drew her in her true form, with bright red hair, yellow eyes, and blue-gray skin.

Mystique can psionically manipulate the molecules of her own body and her clothing in order to alter her appearance. Thus she can create new identities for herself or impersonate other people. She cannot increase or decrease her own mass at will; hence, when she once impersonated spymaster Nick Fury, she did not weigh as much as the real Fury. Mystique can fly by giving herself wings. Otherwise, she cannot duplicate the superpowers of people she impersonates.

Among the many identities Mystique has created for herself are billionaire recluse B. Byron Biggs; Mallory Brickman, the wife of a U.S. senator; and supermodel Ronnie Lake. These identities not only enable Mystique to hide from her enemies but also give her positions of influence in society and political circles.

Mystique's mutant power greatly retards her aging, so how long she has lived remains a mystery. Her relationship with the blind precognitive mutant Destiny goes back at least to the 1930s. Though Claremont did not make it explicit, he implied that Mystique and Destiny were lovers. In fact, in the 1930s Mystique adopted a male identity, "Mr. Raven," as Destiny's companion. Mystique loyally remained with Destiny until the latter's death. (Destiny's real name is allegedly Irene Adler, but there is no evidence that she *is* the Irene Adler of Arthur Conan Doyle's Sherlock Holmes stories.)

Yet Mystique has hardly been monogamous. In the 1960s, in her guise as German spy Leni Zauber, she had an affair with the mutant Sabretooth and bore his son, the late Graydon Creed. Ironically, Graydon Creed was not only a "normal" human, but he became a political demagogue attacking the "mutant menace."

Another of her sexual liaisons was with a German count who was actually a demon in human form. When she gave birth to his inhuman-looking son, Nightcrawler, she tried to kill the infant by throwing him over a waterfall. Thus, Mystique's physical resemblance to Nightcrawler of the X-Men is no coincidence.

Mystique and Destiny took in the teenage girl Rogue after she ran away from home upon discovering her mutant power. Rogue came to regard Mystique as her foster mother and joined in her criminal activities. Nonetheless, distraught by her inability to control her power, Rogue eventually abandoned Mystique to seek help from Professor Charles Xavier and joined his mutant team, the X-Men.

Mystique first publicly revealed herself as a mutant when she led her Brotherhood of Evil Mutants (a new version of Magneto's team) in a terrorist attempt to assassinate Senator Robert Kelly, as chronicled in Chris Claremont and John Byrne's classic storyline "Days of Future Past" in *The Uncanny X-Men* #141–#142 (1981). Kelly advocated that the government take action against the potential threat posed by the emerging mutant population; Mystique believed that by killing Kelly she was striking a blow for mutants' freedom. The other members of her Brotherhood included Destiny, the

Rebecca Romijn-Stamos as Mystique in *X2: X-Men United* (2003).

Thus began a continuing pattern in which Mystique alternates between promoting terrorism and (reluctantly) serving the forces of order, reflecting the shifting interpretations of the character by Marvel writers and editors over the years.

Following the collapse of Freedom Force and the death of Destiny in battle, Mystique began losing her sanity and sought help from X-Men member Forge. Later, Forge recruited her into the U.S. government's new team of mutant operatives, X-Force. But Mystique eventually quit X-Force, organized a new Brotherhood, and resumed her terrorist career. She altered the lethal Legacy Virus so that it would affect non-mutant humans, and she blew up most of the Muir Island base of Xavier's colleague Moira MacTaggert, leaving an injured MacTaggert with the virus, which eventually killed her. Mystique led another attempt on Senator Kelly's life and even directed a full-scale terrorist attack on Paris.

Blob, Avalanche, and Pyro. The X-Men thwarted the assassination attempt, in the first of their many clashes with Mystique and her Brotherhood.

As the U.S. government's covert anti-mutant program, "Project: Wideawake," gathered strength, Mystique realized it had become too dangerous for her to continue her terrorist activities. Hence, she offered her services and those of the Brotherhood as special operatives to the federal government. The president accepted Mystique's proposal, and the Brotherhood was renamed Freedom Force. Ironically, this decision gave Mystique the government's blessing to continue battling the X-Men, who were officially regarded as outlaws.

Mystique was eventually captured and jailed, but was sprung from prison by a surprising benefactor: Xavier. Having recently been exposed as the leader of the X-Men, Xavier asked Mystique to become his covert special operative, so that she could take action in situations without the public learning of his involvement. Mystique initially agreed, but, perhaps inevitably, she rebelled, and after an unsuccessful attempt to kill Xavier, she fled.

Marvel awarded Mystique her own comic-book series in 2003, and she has appeared on television in *X-Men: The Animated Series* (1992–1997) and *X-Men: Evolution* (2000–2003). The movie-going public became aware of Mystique when actress Rebecca Romijn-Stamos portrayed her in the films

X-Men (2000), *X2: X-Men United* (2003), and *X-Men: The Last Stand (2006)*. In these movies she is allied with Magneto and gets to impersonate Senator Kelly, her target from the comics. The films ignore the comic-book Mystique's personal connections with Nightcrawler, Rogue, and Sabretooth. As Mystique in her true form, Romijn-Stamos daringly—and memorably—wears no more than a thick application of body makeup, making her skin look like dark blue scales. Hence, the "clothes" that the movie Mystique wears in impersonating others are apparently part of her own flesh. —*PS*

Nightmare

Marvel Comics' Nightmare is a shadowy and ghastly figure, often seen riding a demonic horned steed. A supernatural being with an unrevealed origin, he resides within the dimension of dreams in an outlandish, off-kilter realm visually designed by his co-creator, Steve Ditko. Nightmare might be compared to Neil Gaiman's Morpheus (from *Sandman*), who rules the Dreaming, or to director Wes Craven's Freddy Krueger of the *Nightmare on Elm Street* films, the killer who invades sleepers' dreams.

Debuting in the very first Dr. Strange story in *Strange Tales* #110 (1963), by writer Stan Lee and artist Ditko, Nightmare draws power from the psychic energies of the subconscious minds of dreaming beings, especially those on Earth, controlling their sleeping and drawing from their life essences. Nightmare can also indefinitely trap a sleeper's soul.

In the Marvel Universe, Nightmare has battled Spider-Man, Ghost Rider, the Hulk, Captain America, Excalibur, Deathlok, Thor, and, appropriately, Sleepwalker. He has also tangled with an interdimensional creature called Gulgol, who has the ability to resist Nightmare's spell.

Although he has not made any media appearances, Nightmare once starred in his own comics miniseries titled *Nightmare* (1994–1995). He refuses to slumber, remaining a continuing threat to humanity as long as there are human beings who have nightmares. —*GM*

Nocturna

The Modern Age (1980–present) villainess of the night, Nocturna first appeared in the pages of *Detective Comics* #529 (1983) in a story scripted by Doug Moench and penciled by Gene Colan. At the age of twelve, orphan Natasha encounters the millionaire and closet crimelord Charles Knight, who becomes a father figure to the Gotham City street urchin. After Charles is killed by rivals, Natasha meets her stepbrother Anton, with whom she falls in love. The two soon use up their inheritance, partly due to living a life of luxury and partly due to the expensive medical procedure needed to treat Natasha's sensitivity to sunlight—a disorder that helps perpetuate her identity as an astronomer. When the two run out of money, they take to a life of crime—Anton, clad in a black body suit, robs Gotham's rich as the agile Night-Thief, while Natasha operates behind the scenes as Nocturna, mistress of the night.

Through the years this duo has had several clashes with Batman. During the time that Night-Thief was locked up in prison, Nocturna continued her life of crime with other villainous allies, namely Gotham crook Sturges Hellstrom, aka Nightshade. Still later, she became an intimate friend of both Bruce Wayne and Batman, making her status of foe questionable. Upon his release, Anton—now known as the darker Night-Slayer (*Detective Comics* #544, 1984)—murdered Hellstrom and vowed to kill Nocturna. However, Nocturna disappeared in an accident during DC's *Crisis on Infinite Earths* miniseries and has not been seen in the comic-book pages since. Nocturna was considered for inclusion in *Batman: The Animated Series,* but ultimately FOX Standards nixed the idea of a character with vampire undertones appearing on children's afternoon television. —*GM*

Obsidian

Introduced in *All-Star Squadron* #25 (1983) in a story scripted by Roy Thomas and penciled by Jerry Ordway, the living shadow Obsidian joins the list of heroes who have turned to the dark side.

Unbeknownst to him, Todd Rice was the child of Alan Scott, the original Green Lantern. Raised in Milwaukee by abusive foster parent James Rice, the teenage Todd resolved to become a hero when he discovered both his "shadow powers" and his long-lost twin, Jennie-Lynn Hayden, with whom he can communicate telepathically. Together they became Jade and Obsidian, founding members of the hero group Infinity, Inc., which comprised those heroes who continued the legacy of the Justice Society of America.

Todd can merge his body with his own shadow, becoming either a three-dimensional shadow form or a two-dimensional silhouette. As Obsidian, he possesses superstrength and super-vitality, can float weightlessly, and delights in showing his enemies their own dark side.

Obsidian's connection with the shadow realm (Shadowlands) and his experience of seeing the darkness within the human soul caused him to go gradually insane. After many of his teammates were killed and Infinity, Inc. disbanded, he waged a one-man war against his biological and adoptive fathers. Under the mentorship of Ian Karkull, an age-old Justice Society nemesis, Obsidian has fought numerous heroes, and also partnered with the princes of darkness Dark Lord Mordru and Eclipso. His family and friends remain hopeful that Obsidian will one day reject the evil that has consumed him. —*GM*

Ocean Master

"Aquaman a coward?" queried the cover of DC Comics' *Aquaman* vol. 1 #29 (1966), as the valiant Sea King refused to fight a weirdly garbed marine terrorist cloaked in royal purples, a cape, and a bizarre fish-fin helmet.

"Aquaman, Coward-King of the Seas!" by writer Bob Haney and artist Nick Cardy introduces the Ocean Master, a supercilious pirate who holds the seas hostage. From his golden "Manta-Ship"—bubbling with destructive blasts, an antigravity beam, heat-sensing torpedoes, and a harpoon-firing "killer-craft" mini-sub—he bullies ocean liners and the U.S. Navy. Although Ocean Master repeatedly tries to deep-six Aquaman and his sidekick Aqualad, the Sea King won't allow any harm to befall this brigand, roiling Aqualad to angle an explanation from his mentor: Ocean Master is actually Aquaman's resentful, mortal half-brother Orm Marius. A head injury made Orm forget his

Aquaman vol. 4 #27 ©2005 DC Comics.
COVER ART BY PATRICK GLEASON AND CHRISTIAN ALAMY.

kinship to Aquaman but not his hatred, and with technological devices he became the ominous Ocean Master, affording the Sea King the personal dilemma, "How can I fight a foe who is my own flesh-and-blood?"

The Aquaman/Ocean Master brother-versus-brother conflict floated through years of comics, with other superheroes—including Batman, the Teen Titans, and Superman—netted into the villain's plans. Ocean Master traded technology for sorcery in the four-issue miniseries *Aquaman* vol. 2 (1986), using the Twelve Crystals of the Zodiac in his brotherly war, but he apparently perished in the conflict.

DC's history-heavy miniseries *The Atlantis Chronicles* (1990) altered the Aquaman legend. In the revised continuity, ancient prophecy foretold of two brothers' struggle for the Atlantean throne. Ocean Master was revived by the demon Neron in

the crossover *Underworld Unleashed* (1995) and equipped with a magical trident and the natural ability to breathe water. Orm remains Aquaman's half-brother, the illegitimate offspring of the mage Atlan and an unnamed mother, but the siblings' relationship and destiny only became known to them over time. Ocean Master has also plagued the surface-dwelling world as one of Lex Luthor's insidious Injustice Gang.

Orm temporarily succeeded in usurping his half-brother's crown by magically supplanting Aquaman's life with his own in *Aquaman* vol. 4 #26–#27 (2005). After restoring order Aquaman admonished his wayward brother: "Maybe if you knew anything about being a ruler, you still would." Ocean Master's rage always sinks his plans to dethrone Aquaman, yet that same rage will always compel him to try.

Orm—not called the Ocean Master— attempted to overthrow Aquaman's Atlantean rule in the two-part "The Enemy Below" episode of the Cartoon Network's *Justice League* (2001–2004), with Richard Green voicing the villain. —*ME*

Omega Red

Created by Jim Lee in *X-Men* vol.2 #4 (1992), Omega Red is Arkady Rossovich, a Russian mutant who served the Soviet government as a "super-soldier" decades ago.

Omega Red possesses a "death factor," a mutant ability to generate "death spores," which are special pheromones (kinds of chemicals secreted by the body) that will weaken or even kill people in his immediate proximity. He can drain the life forces of his victims into his own body. Omega Red also possesses superhuman strength and resistance to injury.

Like Wolverine, Omega Red has a "healing factor" that enables him to heal extraordinarily fast from severe injuries. This factor presumably made it possible for Soviet scientists to bond the metal carbonadium to his skeleton; however, this metal is significantly less resistant to damage than the adamantium bonded to Wolverine's bones. The Soviet scientists implanted long carbonadium coils within Omega Red's arms; he can mentally command the coils to emerge from the undersides of his wrists to ensnare his adversaries.

Omega Red's first known clash with Wolverine was in the 1960s. The Soviet government put Omega Red into suspended animation, from which Matsu'o Tsurayaba, a leader of the Hand, revived him many years later. Omega Red has subsequently battled Wolverine, the X-Men, Iron Man, and even Daredevil. Later he became a crime boss in Russia.

Omega Red has appeared on television in *X-Men: The Animated Series* (1992–1997) and the cartoon *X-Men: Evolution* (2000–2003), and has also appeared in Capcom computer arcade games. —*PS*

Onomatopoeia

The black trench coat–wearing assassin Onomatopoeia hurled onto the pages of a Kevin Smith–penned, Phil Hester and Ande Parks–illustrated story in *Green Arrow* vol. 3 #11 (2002). Introduced as a ninja-like murderer of third-string superheroes such as the suburban vigilante Buckeye, Onomatopoeia struck a more well-known superhero, the contemporary Green Arrow, Connor Hawke—an accomplished martial artist himself and son of the original Green Arrow, Oliver Queen. Like his name implies, Onomatopoeia's calling card is that he utters onomatopoeic words—specifically, the sound of the murder weapon he employs during the murder ("Bang!" "Crash!")—just before killing his next victim. While he didn't quite execute Green Arrow, he did manage to hospitalize him by shooting him in the head.

As Green Arrow's arch-nemesis—and by extension, his father's, as the two Emerald Archers fight crime together in Star City—little is known about this evasive, verbally limited supervillain. His face concealed behind a black mask with concentric bull's-eye markings, Onomatopoeia has superpowers that mimic a super–serial killer. He is adept at using guns, swords, knives, and other weaponry, and even goes to such extremes as to bite weapons in two! With behavior that borders on psychotic, the mysterious Onomatopoeia might find a welcome home in the bleaker post–*Infinite Crisis* (2005–2006) DC Universe. —*GM*

Onslaught

Professor Charles Xavier, founder of the X-Men, has devoted his life to his dream of peaceful coexistence between mutants and the rest of humanity. But even this saintly man's subconscious hates "normal" humans who oppress and even try to destroy mutantkind. What if Xavier's dark side took over?

Xavier's shadow self first manifested as a malevolent spirit in *X-Men* vol. 1 #106 (1977), plotted by Bill Mantlo and scripted by Chris Claremont. Xavier's evil side reappeared as a being called the Entity in Mantlo's comics miniseries *X-Men and the Micronauts* (1984). Both times Xavier's evil self was defeated, ending its independent existence.

Years later, Xavier utilized his telepathic powers to shut down arch-rival Magneto's mind, leaving him in a coma. During this psionic contact, the dark side of Magneto's personality fused with the negative aspects of Xavier's own psyche, resulting in the creation of the independent mental entity called Onslaught (which first appeared in *X-Men* vol. 2 #53, 1996).

Eventually, Onslaught took control of Xavier's mind and body, and possessed both Xavier's and Magneto's superpowers. Onslaught captured Franklin Richards, the son of Reed and Susan Richards of the Fantastic Four, in order to utilize the boy's mutant ability to alter reality. Commanding Sentinel robots, Onslaught launched his war on humanity by conquering Manhattan Island. The X-Men, Avengers, and Fantastic Four joined forces to stop him, and Thor rescued Xavier, leaving Onslaught as a being of pure psionic energy. The Fantastic Four and Avengers plunged into Onslaught's form, destroying it from within, seemingly at the cost of their lives. However, Franklin Richards actually transported the heroes to an alternate Earth, from which they eventually all returned safely. —*PS*

The Owl

Called an "ominous overlord of crime," the Owl first appeared in the early days of Marvel's

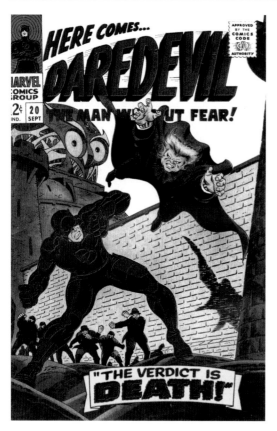

Daredevil vol. 1 #20 ©1966 Marvel Comics.
COVER ART BY JOHN ROMITA, SR. AND FRANK GIACOIA.

serum that gave him the superhuman ability to glide through the air, as if he were an actual bird of prey. (The serum eventually induced a debilitating disease that paralyzed his legs, requiring him to walk using an exoskeleton during his recovery.) Later, the Owl was revealed to have mutations that gave him other owl-like attributes. He has hollow bones, like a bird's, and his fingernails are inch-long, razor-sharp talons. He has extra vertebrae in his neck, enabling to turn his head nearly 180 degrees, and can even rotate his eyes independently of each other, as a real owl can.

In addition to his physical oddities, the Owl is an extraordinary engineer who prides himself in building gigantic flying machines in the shape of owls. He also boasts reclusive city hideouts referred to as his "Aeries."

In addition to Daredevil, the Owl has battled the Black Widow, Spider-Man, Tigra, Shanna the She-Devil, the Black Cat, and Alpha Flight. He butted heads with two fellow villains, the Kingpin and Dr. Octopus, both of whom have tried to do him in on various occasions. Still, the Owl generally operates solo, and has a habit of disappearing and suddenly reappearing in Daredevil's life. *—GM*

Daredevil comic (vol. 1 #3, 1964), in a story written by Stan Lee and penciled by Joe Orlando. He is introduced simply as a ruthless Wall Street financial wizard—whose name was later established as Leland Owlsley—who is a "merciless man ... a man with no friends ... no loved ones ... nothing to connect him with the human race save the fact of his birth!" Although he successfully hides his sketchy business activities by masquerading as a legitimate professional and philanthropist, Owlsley is forced to seek legal counsel when one of his accountants meets a suspicious death. He randomly picks blind attorney Matt Murdock's name from the phone book. Despite believing his client to be a criminal, Murdock is determined to provide a defense. But when Owlsley jumps bail, the lawyer—in his secret identity of Daredevil—refuses to let him get away.

Over the years, the Owl has transformed progressively into an owl-like creature. The Owl took a

Ozymandias

One of the title characters in writer Alan Moore and artist Dave Gibbons' epic superhero series *Watchmen* (DC Comics, 1986–1987), Adrian Veidt adopted the alias Ozymandias, the Greek name for the Egyptian pharaoh Rameses II. Moore was also invoking the poem of that name by the great English Romantic poet Percy Bysshe Shelley (1792–1822), which describes the remains of the arrogant pharaoh's colossal statue, surrounded by the empty desert: its pedestal is inscribed, "Look on my works, ye Mighty, and despair!" Veidt, "the world's smartest man," is based on the Charlton Comics superhero Peter Cannon, aka Thunderbolt, but he also seems inspired by such genius heroes as Mr. Fantastic and Doc Savage.

Born in 1939, Veidt modeled himself after Egypt's conqueror, Alexander the Great, and became a costumed crime fighter. Though Veidt had no actual superpowers, he had trained his body to near physical perfection, and was virtually invincible in hand-to-hand combat.

Nevertheless, in 1975 Veidt retired as a superhero. Instead, like a capitalistic version of Alexander, Veidt built a vast corporate empire, becoming one of the world's wealthiest men. (*Spoiler warning:* Those who do not wish to learn the ending of *Watchmen* should read no further.)

Veidt believed that nuclear war between the United States and the Soviet Union was inevitable unless he implemented an extraordinary scheme. Veidt oversaw a covert project that genetically engineered a monstrous new life form. Veidt planned to teleport the monster into Manhattan, causing it to telepathically slaughter much of the city's population. The world would assume that the creature was from outer space, and the two superpowers would lay aside their differences in order to cooperate in defending themselves against a possible alien invasion.

In 1985 Edward Blake, the superhero known as the Comedian, discovered Veidt's scheme and was horrified. Hence, Veidt went to Blake's apartment, overpowered him, and hurled him to his death. Thus began the murder mystery with which the *Watchmen* series begins. Veidt also manipulated events so as to coerce the world's most powerful being, Dr. Manhattan, into leaving Earth.

The vigilante Rorschach recognized there was a conspiracy afoot. He and the superhero Nite Owl eventually realized that Veidt was behind it and headed to his Antarctic retreat, Karnak. But by the time they finally confronted Veidt, he had already teleported his monster to Manhattan, killing half the population of New York City.

In the aftermath of the September 11, 2001, attack on the World Trade Center, Moore's *Watchmen* scenario seems grimly, unwittingly prophetic. But Veidt's horrific scheme had the effect that he intended, and the United States and Soviet Union backed away from the brink of World War III.

Thus Moore confronts both his superheroes and his readers with this conundrum: was Veidt justified in perpetrating the massacre of millions in order to avert the potential deaths of billions in a nuclear war? In *Watchmen*'s final panel Moore raises the possibility that Veidt's hoax will be exposed, setting the world back on the road to war. So this new Ozymandias' works may also end in despair. —*PS*

Parademon (Parademons):
See **Darkseid's Elite**

Parallax

In a controversial move during the mid-1990s, DC Comics transformed one of its most famous superheroes—Hal Jordan, aka Green Lantern II—into a supervillain. While always a loyal member of the Green Lantern Corps, Jordan had been known to break rank if his personal beliefs conflicted with the tenets of the Corps' governing body, the Guardians of the Universe. When despots Mongul and the Cyborg Superman destroyed Jordan's hometown of Coast City and exterminated its population of millions, the distraught Green Lantern implored the Guardians to use the Corps' energy source, the Central Power Battery, to restore the city and the lives of its deceased. Forbidden by his keepers to alter history, the maddened Jordan arrogantly waged war against the Corps and destroyed the group, killing or scattering its members. Usurping their power rings and the emerald energy of the Central Power Battery, Jordan transformed himself into the megalomaniacal Parallax in *Green Lantern* vol. 3 #50 (1994). This move shocked fans and angered many long-time readers who complained that "fearless" and "honest" Hal Jordan—chosen as Earth's most "deserving" candidate to succeed dying Green Lantern Abin Sur in

Showcase #22 (1959)—would never stoop to such a heinous act.

Partnering with the temporal-villain Extant in the crossover *Zero Hour: Crisis in Time* (1994), Parallax attempted to reconfigure Earth's timeline under his distorted vision of virtue, but was bested by a conclave of heroes. Parallax also teamed with Marvel Comics' Thanos in the DC/Marvel crossover *Green Lantern/Silver Surfer* (1995). Redemption came for Jordan when Parallax valiantly sacrificed himself to stop the stellar-devouring Sun Eater in the miniseries *The Final Night* (1996), living on in the afterlife as the Spirit of Vengeance, the Spectre.

Jordan returned from the dead and resumed his Green Lantern career in the miniseries *Green Lantern: Rebirth* (2004–2005). His transformation into villainy was attributed to his possession by an actual creature called Parallax, a malevolent "cosmic parasite" that influenced his behavior. DC Direct produced an action figure of fallen hero Parallax in 2005. —ME

The Parasite

"Presenting the most dangerous villain Superman has ever faced!" blurbed the cover to *Action Comics* #340 (1966), depicting the Man of Steel being smacked around by the nemesis who "feeds on living energy": the Parasite. Created by writer Jim Shooter, then a teenager who sold hand-drawn scripts to DC Comics editor Mort Weisinger, the Parasite, drawn in his debut by Al Plastino, doesn't look that formidable—with his purple pigmentation and lime briefs, one might imagine him posing for a Fruit of the Loom underwear ad—but he does indeed live up to the cover hype. He is actually Raymond Maxwell Jensen, a sticky-fingered handyman snooping for the secreted payroll in his place of employment, a research lab, and finding instead a container of biohazardous waste. Transmogrified into the Parasite, the irradiated evildoer who absorbs the energies of anyone he touches, he puts the grab on the Metropolis Marvel. After weakening Superman, the Parasite's power play to consume the hero's entire strength backfires as Jensen overloads and is blown to bits. This tale was adapted for television in a 1966 episode of the animated series *The New Adventures of Superman*.

By *Action* #361 (1968) Jensen had reassembled his atoms, returning to drain Superman's energy in more conservative doses. For the next twenty years, the Parasite occasionally surfaced to battle the Man of Tomorrow.

After Superman's 1986 *Man of Steel* reboot, a new, green-skinned version of the Parasite (who later returned to his original purple form) premiered in *The Fury of Firestorm* #58 (1987). In an origin siphoning from the 1966 version, the supervillain was now ne'er-do-well Rudy Jones, a custodian at Pittsburgh's S.T.A.R. Labs, who stuck his hand in the "cookie jar" and was exposed to a radioactive brew concocted by none other than Darkseid. In the grimmer DC Universe of the late 1980s, this reinvented Parasite became a life-force vampire, depleting victims' vigor and discarding their withered husks. Like the 1966 origin, this version was reworked for animation, in the 1996 "Feeding Time" episode of the WB's *Superman* cartoon, with Brion James playing the Parasite; the villain appeared in additional episodes.

The Parasite tussled with Firestorm, the Suicide Squad, and the fifth Starman before encountering Superman in 1991. Drunk with the notion of consuming Superman's vast superpowers, the Parasite was a recurring menace to the Man of Steel,

also challenging Super-allies Superboy, Supergirl, and Steel, and hooking up with the Superman Revenge Squad. In *Action* #715 (1995) the Parasite drained the life essence of Dr. Torval Freeman, retaining not only the scientist's intellect but also remnants of his benevolent personality. Despite consequent crises of conscience, Parasite continued his destructive ways. His absorption of metahuman powers caused him to grow into a behemoth who towered over Superman.

His closest encounter with the Man of Steel occurred in a 1997 story arc in which he kidnapped Clark (Superman) Kent's wife, Lois Lane, using his powers to assume her identity to get within striking distance of the hero. He succeeded, but unknowingly absorbed kryptonite poisoning from the contaminated Man of Steel, perishing as a result (*Superman* vol. 2 #127, 1997). In the 2000s teenage siblings Alex and Alexandra Allston have become Parasites, one green, one purple, guaranteeing that the Parasite legacy will continue to plague Superman—as seen in 2005's *Adventures of Superman* #645, where the energy-vampire was recruited for roguery by Lex Luthor.

A 2005 Parasite action figure from DC Direct presented a new interpretation of the villain designed by artist Alex Ross. The villain, voiced by Marc Worden, appeared in the 2005 season finale of the Cartoon Network's *Justice League Unlimited* (2004–present). *—ME*

The Penguin

"The Man of 1,000 Umbrellas"—the plundering Penguin—belies the stereotype of the fearsome supervillain. He is obese, smokes, dresses as if he's stepping out for a night at the opera, surrounds himself with birds, and wields bumbershoots as weapons. Despite his comical appearance, the Penguin has remained one of the Batman's feistiest foes since his first appearance in DC Comics' *Detective Comics* #58 (1941).

Legend offers conflicting stories behind the creation of this waddling wrongdoer. Batman creator Bob Kane cited the cartoon penguin icon for Kool cigarettes as the villain's inspiration, while Batman's unsung champion, ghostwriter Bill Finger, remarked that he found his felonious muse in emperor penguins, the stately yet stout birds that resemble tuxedoed men. Another contradicting report is the five-page tale "The True Story of Batman and Robin," published in DC's *Real Fact Comics* #5 (1947), which suggests that Kane dreamt up the Penguin upon spying a portly "eccentric fellow" strolling with an unopened umbrella on a blisteringly sunny day. From whichever roost the Penguin hatched, his motivations are clear: to feather his nest with ill-gotten gain, much to the consternation of Gotham City's guardians, Batman and Robin.

To achieve this goal, the Penguin employs an arsenal of trick umbrellas specially outfitted for the cagey bird's menacing brand of fowl play. When cornered in a heist by the meddlesome Dynamic Duo, the Penguin might brandish a pyro-parasol, forcing Batman and Robin to dodge a jet of flame; a machine-gun umbrella, spraying a hail of gunfire at the heroes; or an acid-squirting bumbershoot for a potentially lethal big splash. The tip of the Penguin's umbrella is razor-sharp, and he's not averse to using it when making a point. When all else fails and escape is his only option, some type of getaway umbrella is always at his fingertips, from a spring-coiled "pogo-rella" to a jet-propelled rocket-umbrella to a rotor-blade helicopter-umbrella.

The Penguin's parasol fixation harkens back to his childhood, when, as Oswald Chesterfield Cobblepot, he was forced to carry an umbrella at all times at the behest of his overprotective mother, who worried he might take ill from exposure to the elements. Podgy and beak-nosed, young Cobblepot was egged on by classmates who mercilessly derided him, nicknaming him "Penguin." The ostracized Oswald had no friends, save the feathered ones at his mother's bird shop. From this kinship he was inspired to study ornithology in college, but after the passing of his mother and the bank foreclosure of the family's shop, Cobblepot turned to crime. Motivated by the desire to profit from a society that had rejected him, he becomes the Penguin, Gotham's most dapper and deadly thief.

But not *too* deadly. Despite his perilous umbrella arsenal, during comics' Golden Age (1938–1954) the Penguin was essentially a comic foil to the Dynamic Duo. He was Batman's most gentlemanly adversary, tipping his hat to his caped foe, and he sometimes employed henchmen to do his dirty work. The Penguin toddled through several tales a year in the pages of *Batman*, *Detective*, and *World's Finest Comics*, in mirthful romps with titles like "Four Birds of a Feather" (*Batman* #11, 1942), "The Penguin's Nest" (*Batman* #36, 1946), and "The Umbrellas of Crime" (*Detective* #134, 1948), comfortably predictable crime capers featuring either birds or umbrellas (or both). The cover to *Detective* #67 (1942), depicting "The Man Who Uses Birdlore for Banditry" escaping his Bat-foes by riding an *ostrich*, proved that Penguin stories were not to be taken seriously. By the end the Golden Age, Batman's colorful rogues' gallery was being supplanted by gangsters and alien invaders, and after "The Golden Eggs" in *Batman* #99 (1956), the Penguin migrated into limbo.

Bill Finger, along with artists Sheldon Moldoff and Charles Paris, resurrected the flabby felon in *Batman* #155 (1963) in a story appropriately titled "The Return of the Penguin." Cobblepot, flustered by the scoffs of underworld incorrigibles who regarded him a has-been, emerged from retirement by taking to the skies in his "Penguin's Roc," a penguin-shaped dirigible.

During the superhero boom of the mid-1960s, the Penguin became one of comics' most recognizable supervillains after Burgess Meredith's portrayal of the character in ABC's live-action *Batman* series (1966–1968). Decked out in black tails and a purple top hat, Meredith's fanciful birdlike sway captivated viewers, as did his famous Penguin "quack." That sound, as the actor once revealed in an interview with journalist James H. Burns, was the result of Meredith's allergy to cigarette smoke: "The smoke would get caught in my throat. Since I didn't want to constantly ruin takes by coughing out loud—which the smoke forced me to do—I developed the Penguin's 'quack, quack' to cover it." Meredith's Penguin appeared in more Batman episodes than any other supervillain, and teamed with the Joker, Catwoman, and the Riddler in the motion-picture spin-off of the series, *Batman* (1966). Thanks to this wave of popularity, the Penguin's paunchy puss was plastered onto a bonanza of Batman-related merchandising. He was one of many Bat-villains appearing on trading cards, plastic coins, and board games, but unlike his fellow fiends he was the only Batman villain immortalized as a plastic model kit, courtesy of model-maker Aurora. A flock of Penguin reprints from the 1950s was gathered in *Batman vs. the Penguin* (Signet Books, 1966), the fourth of six quickie paperbacks capitalizing on the Batman craze. The villain also fought Batman and Robin in "The Penguin's Fowl Play," one of a series of sixteen-page *Batman* mini-comic giveaways in 1966 boxes of Kellogg's Pop Tarts.

After the cancellation of the live-action *Batman*, the hero leapt into animation in CBS's *The Batman/Superman Hour* (1968–1969) and *The Adventures of Batman and Robin* (1969–1970), and the Penguin fluttered to his side, appearing in such episodes as "In Again Out Again Penguin" and "Two Penguins Too Many." The Penguin found TV animation a popular perch: he appeared in short *Batman* cartoons running during the premier season (1970) of *Sesame Street*; teamed with the Joker to fight Batman, Robin, and the Scooby-Doo gang in *The New Scooby-Doo Movies* (1972–1974); and was a recurring adversary in *The New Adventures of Batman* (1977–1978), in episodes that would be rebroadcast for several more seasons under various Batman show incarnations. Also during the 1970s, the Penguin was heavily merchandised as action figures (in a variety of sizes) from the Mego Toy Corp., and on sew-on clothing patches, 7-11 Slurpee cups, and Pepsi drinking glasses available at fast-food outlets. He appeared in comic-book ads for Hostess Twinkies, and in 1977— in perhaps the oddest incarnations ever conceived for supervillains—sang and danced with other DC heroes and villains in the traveling stage show *Bugs Bunny Meets the Super-Heroes* and water-skied in Seaworld's *Salute to the DC Super-Heroes*.

The Penguin was not treated as well in his host medium of comics. In the early 1970s DC Comics rejected the campiness of Batman's television heyday and returned the hero to his moody "creature of the night" roots, making the jovial Penguin an uncomfortable fit in this noir-ish world. He still surfaced for a token, nostalgic appearance from time to time throughout the 1970s and 1980s, even returning to television in 1985 as a villain on *The Super Powers Team: Galactic Guardians*, a tie-in to Kenner Toys' Super Powers action-figure line, which included a Penguin figure.

Batman #169 ©1965 DC Comics.
COVER ART BY CARMINE INFANTINO AND JOE GIELLA.

In "The Killing Peck" in *Secret Origins Special* #1 (1989), the Penguin was given a harsher edge, his brutality spawned by repressed hatred for those who tormented him during his youth. Three years later, director Tim Burton's *Batman Returns* (1992) thrust the Penguin back into the media spotlight in a horrifying interpretation portrayed by Danny DeVito. A sewer-dwelling freak of nature, DeVito's gruesome, sludge-slobbering Penguin reportedly frightened young filmgoers and enraged their mothers—much to the chagrin of McDonald's, which had licensed the villain for Happy Meals toys. The darker tone of *Batman Returns* aside, the movie managed to borrow two bits from the live-action *Batman* series (the Penguin running for mayor and stealing the Batmobile), but nearly lost its footing with its absurd climax featuring thousands of penguins armed with missiles.

The Burton Penguin was softened for the fall 1992 debut of the long-running *Batman: The Animated Series*, with Paul Williams voicing the debonair racketeer. The Penguin was back on the tube in a new animated series, the WB's *The Batman* (2004—present), with actor Tom Kenny in the role.

In the 1999 multi-part story "No Man's Land," serialized through DC's Batman family of titles, Gotham City was devastated by an earthquake, allowing the opportunistic Penguin to reap obscene profits by gouging citizens and criminals alike on grossly overpriced necessities. In the 2000s the Penguin operates a covert crime cartel under the auspices of his legitimate business ventures, including the Gotham hotspot the Iceberg Lounge. Batman, however, knows that the Penguin cannot be trusted and forever keeps the Man of 1,000 Umbrellas under his watchful eye. —*ME*

Phantasm

A n "Angel of Death" appears in Gotham City, a shrouded executioner with a skull-like face-plate, slicing through crimelords with a wrist-mounted scythe, then vanishing supernaturally into a wisp of fog. Batman is blamed for the murders, placing the Dark Knight in double jeopardy as he hunts down this vexing vigilante while evading an unremitting police force. Complicating his life is the return of Andrea Beaumont, the first love of the man behind the Bat-mask, Bruce Wayne. And thus begins one of Batman's most personal stories, his heart torn asunder by a flame that still flickers, and his flesh endangered by the blade of the merciless supervillain known as Phantasm.

This most poignant of Batman stories ... is a cartoon.

Batman: Mask of the Phantasm, a 76-minute animated film directed by Eric Radomski and Bruce Timm, was released theatrically on Christmas Day 1993. A spin-off of television's *Batman: The Animated Series* (1992–1995), *Phantasm* was envisioned as a made-for-video feature but was upgraded to theatrical status shortly into its production (to producer Warner Bros.' chagrin; the movie performed poorly at the box office, but it later became a home-video favorite).

Phantasm, from the animated theatrical release *Batman: Mask of the Phantasm* (1993).

Disney Supervillains

Although the name "Walt Disney" is synonymous with wholesome family entertainment, "Disney Supervillains" is *not* an oxymoron. Among Disney's animated feature films one can find dozens of superbly rendered and malevolently mouthed mischief-makers:

· **Maleficent**: *Sleeping Beauty*'s (1959) horn-headed enchantress—whose name derives from the words "malice" and "malevolent"—raises the bar for all fairy-tale spell casters as she seeks to destroy Princess Aurora and the benevolent kingdom.

· **The Evil Queen**: The beauty-coveting queen—so jealous of her "fairest" stepdaughter that she wants her heart in a box—endures as one of Hollywood's most memorable murderesses since her debut in *Snow White and the Seven Dwarfs* (1937).

· **Captain Hook**: One of Disney's first attempts at a purely comical villain, the revenge-seeking, seafaring scoundrel is master bully beyond compare in the whimsical *Peter Pan* (1953).

· **Hades**: Named after the king of the dead in Greek mythology, the *Hercules* (1997) "Lord of the Underworld" is a neurotic negotiator, brokering deals with mere mortals with their souls as collateral. Eager to usurp Zeus' Olympic throne, irascible, faming-blue-haired Hades and his henchmen, Pain and Panic, will stop at nothing to take over the universe.

· **Cruella De Vil**: This diabolical dog-snatcher—best known for her animated role in *101 Dalmatians* (1961) and Glenn Close's portrayal in the live-action adaptation and its sequel (1996 and 2000)—gives PETA its *raison d'etre*.

· **The Horned King**: This spine-tingling supernatural skeleton takes center stage in the dark fantasy *The Black Cauldron* (1985) as he summons an army of dead soldiers to aid in his gaining possession of the magical black cauldron.

· **Chernabog**: Created by Ukrainian animator Bill Tytla, the demonic Chernabog need not utter a word to be an imposing presence in *Fantasia*'s (1940) "Night on Bald Mountain" sequence. Possessing almost limitless powers, Chernabog's only weakness is the rising sun.

Phantasm was inspired by the Reaper, the slayer in DC Comics' 1987 "Batman: Year Two" storyline. While not as graphic as comics' Reaper (to maintain the film's PG rating), Phantasm's screen presence was buttressed by atmospheric moodiness—the villain's emergence from and disappearance into the fog, plus eerie orchestral nuances by soundtrack composer Shirley Walker—that might have escaped the character had Phantasm originated on the comic-book page. Although the film's revelation (*spoiler warning!*) that Wayne's love interest Andrea (Dana Delany) was actually Phantasm surprised only the acutely naive (as well as a few little boys who bought the tie-in Phantasm action figure, removed its forbidding cloak, and gasped, "Hey, it's a girl!"), the exceptionally well-made, Art Deco-esque *Mask of the Phantasm* was, until the release of 2005's live-action *Batman Begins*, regarded by many Dark Knight devotees as the best Batman movie ever produced. —*ME*

The Phantom Blot

He's not your ordinary phantom—in fact, he's not a phantom at all. Yet this character is often called one of the classic "phantoms" of comics.

Created by long-time *Mickey Mouse* comic-strip writer/artist Floyd Gottfredson, the Phantom Blot first appeared in Mickey's daily strip in 1939. Disguised as a menacing, ghostlike figure in a black cowl and cloak, the Phantom Blot is a criminal mastermind of the craftiest order. Because he is draped in black, he takes on the appearance of a human-shaped inkblot, hence his moniker.

Subsequent writers and artists have elaborated upon Gottfredson's one-time depiction of the Blot. This classic Disney supervillain was spun off into his own Gold Key comic book, *The Phantom Blot*, which ran seven issues from 1964 to 1966 (1965's #2 introduced dim-bulb dog Goofy as Super Goof in a story where the red-long-johned caped crusader went after the Blot).

Whether he is confiscating diamonds, forging famous works of art, or venturing into outer space, the Phantom Blot specializes in derailing Mickey and friends—including Minnie Mouse, Donald Duck, Scrooge McDuck, and Chief O'Hara—but the slippery scoundrel always manages to escape unscathed, leaving behind at the scene of a crime his calling card: a piece of paper, "signed" with an inkblot.

Over the years the Blot has managed to amass large sums of money, which he uses to finance his diabolical plots. His passion for increased wealth and power is only surpassed by his desire to be immortalized in the "annals of crime." While essentially an egotistic loner, the Blot is occasionally aided by fellow baddies the Beagle Boys, Idgit the Midget, Mad Madam Mim, and the Mysterious Mister X.

The Phantom Blot ventured into cartoons in a 1987 episode of *Duck Tales*, and in the mid-2000s appears on Toon Disney's *House of Mouse*. His heroic counterpart, Blotman, was created in a one-shot comic from Disney and Gemstone Publishing in 2005. —*GM*

Phantom Zone Supervillains

Most Superman fans discovered the eerie "twilight dimension" called the Phantom Zone in the pages of DC Comics or in the first two *Superman* live-action movies starring Christopher Reeve (1978, 1980). The Zone in fact entered the Man of Steel's mythos in the 1950 movie serial *Atom Man vs. Superman*, where a diabolical hooded scientist (revealed to be Lex Luthor) located this ghostly realm. The Phantom Zone materialized into print in a Superboy tale by writer Robert Bernstein in *Adventure Comics* #283 (1961) that also introduced its most famous immaterial inmate, General Zod.

Kryptonians did not condone capital punishment—instead, they exiled their hardened law-breakers into a state of suspended animation inside orbiting space capsules. (The malevolent Mala—a Superman look-alike—and his brothers U-Ban and Kizo broke out of their capsules in *Superman* #65, 1950, and rumbled with the Man of Steel as the "Three Supermen from Krypton!") This form of punishment was abandoned when scientist Jor-El, father of Kal-El (Superman), detected the ethereal Phantom Zone and constructed a Phantom Zone Projector to transmit felons into imprisonment for (mostly) finite sentences.

Existing as ageless wraiths able to telepathically communicate with one another and observe, but not participate in, actions in the corporeal realm, the Phantom Zone villains lusted for freedom, and once the son of Jor-El began his superheroics on Earth as Superboy, and later as Superman, they conspired to escape—and occasionally succeeded, perpetrating chaos with a full range of superpowers, just like Superman's. Superman often kept tabs on them with his Phantom Zone Viewer (which included a Zone-ophone). On rare occasions, non-violent offenders would be liberated by the Kandorian Phantom Zone Parole Board and allowed to live in the bottle city of Kandor, the Kryptonian burg miniaturized by Brainiac.

Aside from Zod, perhaps the best-known Phantom Zone criminal was Jax-Ur, first seen in *Adventure* #289 (1961). A renegade scientist turned mass murderer after his atomic-missile decimation of the inhabited Kryptonian moon Wegthor, the remorseless Jax-Ur got "life" in the Zone (although his sentence was noted as thirty years in the Krypton-themed *Superman Annual* #5, 1962). Were it not for his mustache and futuristic fashions he would have been dead ringer for the 1960s Luthor, and he similarly regarded the Boy and Man of Steel with acrimony.

Other noteworthy Phantom Zone rogues were biochemist Professor Vakox (Va-Kox), whose bizarre evolutionary experiments imperiled the populace; Faora Hu-Ul, a seductive man-hater who sadistically tortured males; Dr. Xadu (Xa-Du), whose stasis experiments cursed human guinea pigs into perpetual slumber; Jor-El's black-sheep cousin Kru-El, developer of weapons of mass destruction; Az-Rel and Nadira, exiled from the planet Bokos, who used pyro- and psycho-kinesis to torment Kryptonians; and Quex-El, an innocent wrongly sentenced to the Zone and later reprieved by Superman, who stripped him of his powers and memory and established for him the Earth identity of Charlie Kweskill. Other criminals were shown either inhabiting or being sentenced to the Phantom Zone—including Gaz-Or, Ras-Krom, and Ral-En—but the realm's only superhero was teenager Mon-El, Superboy's superpowered friend from

Daxam who spent 1,000 years as a specter until a cure for his vulnerability to lead was found.

Superman entered the Zone upon occasion, and was tricked into it (along with Kweskill) in the four-issue miniseries *The Phantom Zone* (1982) as *all* of its supervillains fled the Zone and pillaged Earth. Written by Steve Gerber and illustrated by Gene Colan, this horrific tale depicted the super-rogues tossing the Justice League satellite out of orbit, ransacking the Fortress of Solitude, overpowering Green Lantern and Supergirl, and nearly triggering World War III. Predating the miniseries and coinciding with the theatrical release of *Superman II* (featuring three Phantom Zone supervillains) was *Superman in "The Phantom Zone Connection"* (1980), a kid-friendly Big Little Book by E. Nelson Bridwell.

In current Superman continuity, the Phantom Zone is a netherdimension identified long ago by Superman's ancestor Kem-L. The Man of Steel maintains a Phantom Zone Projector that has enabled him to venture into Krypton's past; he used the Projector to trap the inimical White Martians in this ghostly realm. The *Superman* storyline "For Tomorrow" (2004–2005) introduced a new Zod who emerged from "Metropia," a plane that Superman created within the Zone.

Phantom Zone supervillains appearing outside of comic books include General Zod (Terence Stamp) and his underlings Ursa (Sarah Douglas) and Non (Jack O'Halloran) in *Superman: The Movie* (1978) and *Superman II* (1980); a conclave of Zoners who endangered the Man of Steel in "The Hunter," an episode of Ruby-Spears' *Superman* cartoon (1988–1989); and Jax-Ur (Ron Perlman) and a revised, female Mala (Leslie Easterbrook, and later Sarah Douglas), seen in episodes of the WB's *Superman* animated series (1996–2000). Two Kryptonian criminals, referred to as "the disciples of Zod," were introduced on the 2005 season opener of the WB's *Smallville* (2001–present) and banished into the Phantom Zone by young Clark Kent. —*ME*

Pied Piper

The Fastest Man Alive first faced the music of the Pied Piper in *The Flash* vol. 1 #106 (1959), by writer John Broome and artist Carmine Infan-

tino. This "Master of Sound"—wearing a green jerkin with white polka dots and a minstrel's cap—parades into Central City, tooting a Super-Sonic Flute that emits mind-controlling tones. Acoustically manipulating vibratory fields with his melodies, the Pied Piper stops the Scarlet Speedster dead in his tracks and buries him in an earthly fissure before the Flash whirlwinds to victory.

Although enigmatic in his first outing, more was revealed about the Pied Piper in his reappearances. The felonious flutist is actually Hartley Rathaway, a spoiled rich kid who was born deaf but surgically cured of his affliction, sparking his fascination with sound. Developing his knack for hypnotism through music, the Piper's crime career was fostered out of boredom, not economic necessity, and he occasionally waltzed with the speedster alone and while partnered with other rogues. The Flash's death in *Crisis on Infinite Earths* #8 (1986) took the wind out of Rathaway, who became a costumed social advocate and an ally of the Flash's speedy successor Wally West.

The Piper surprised his fast friend in *Flash* vol. 2 #53 (1991) by revealing his homosexuality, becoming one of the few comic-book characters of the era to be openly gay. In the 2000s his life has been anything but melodious. Rathaway was framed for his parents' murder and escaped from the supervillain penitentiary Iron Heights before being able to prove his innocence. His sanity has since wavered, and his mental manipulation by the villainous Top in the "Rogue War" *Flash* storyline (2005) has left the Flash wondering if the Pied Piper will soon resume his sinister songs.

A one-hit wonder Batman villain called the Pied Piper—"the man of 1,000 pipes"—pulled pipe-related crimes (involving everything from smoking pipes to sewer pipes) in *Detective Comics* #143 (1949). —*ME*

Plant Master: *See* The Floronic Man

Poison Ivy

The botanical beauty Poison Ivy has a habit of getting into the Masked Manhunter's blood. A curvaceous, auburn-haired knockout dressed in a foliage-motif bathing suit with tights—picture a pinup girl attired by the Jolly Green Giant's tailor— she struts into *Batman* #181 (1966), stealing the limelight from Dragon Fly, Silken Spider, and Tiger Moth, three costumed femme fatales "starring" in a Gotham City pop-art exhibit. Soon Poison Ivy is stealing jewelry, aided by non-descript henchmen, and Batman's price for trying to stop her is … a kiss. Ivy's lipstick contains a "chloroform base" that makes the Caped Crusader open to her suggestion, and the hero is at her beck and call ("You can't resist me—once you've had a touch of Poison Ivy!"), aiding her in her crime wave, to Robin the Boy Wonder's dismay. In this tale's conclusion (two issues later in *Batman* #183), the Gotham Guardian shakes off the effects of Poison Ivy's toxin and prunes the career of the "contagious villainess."

Readers were not as smitten with Poison Ivy as was Batman, and the character withered away after her two-part debut—there was only room for one Batman bad girl in the boy-dominated comic-book market of the 1960s, and Catwoman had filled that slot since 1940. Poison Ivy's creator, writer Robert Kanigher (Sheldon Moldoff and Joe Giella drew Ivy's original two-part adventure), tried again to cultivate interest in the villainess by featuring Ivy in a 1977 "Rose and the Thorn" short story, to no avail. From the 1970s through the late 1980s Poison Ivy occasionally sprung up but failed to take root, and when seen she was usually in the company of other costumed criminals (the Injustice Gang, the Secret Society of Super-Villains, and the Suicide Squad). Through these stories buds of information sprouted, like her real name (Pamela Isley) and her pre-criminal past (a botanist gone bad because of a treacherous boyfriend). Writer Neil Gaiman, in the three-issue *Black Orchid* miniseries (1988–1989) painted by Dave McKean, then planted the seeds that allowed Poison Ivy to thrive:

Poison Ivy was originally Pamela Lillian Isley, an unattractive, acquiescent (yes, a shrinking violet) botanist. Her mentor, Dr. Jason Woodrue—who would one day become one of the Atom's arch-foes, the Floronic Man—made her the subject of flora/fauna hybridization experiment by injecting plant toxins into her bloodstream. Blossoming into a virtual Venus with pale green skin, Isley gained immunity to natural poisons, from bacteria to fungi, and the control over plant life (varying texts have ascribed this power to telepathy, others to the seed pods she dispensed). Able to secrete pheromones through her skin in order to drive men wild, Poison Ivy often exerts this control via a kiss, just as Kanigher imagined back in 1966.

Early in her career Poison Ivy relocated from the lush Pacific Northwest to the tenebrous Gotham City, where she poisoned the city's wealthiest citizens with toxic plant spores, extorting millions before relinquishing an antidote (*Shadow of the Bat Annual* #5, 1995)—a caper snipped by Batman in their first kiss-and-kick battle. She often resorts to eco-terrorism to protect the green, funding her efforts by stealing. Ivy has germinated different areas of Gotham into jungles. A noted example occurred during the 1999 multi-part Batman serial "No Man's Land," in which she remade Robinson Park (named for legendary Batman artist Jerry Robinson) into a modern-day Eden where, showing rare compassion for humans, she cared for children orphaned by an earthquake that crippled the city.

Ivy's other soft spot is Harley Quinn, the Joker's sometime-lover/sometime-sidekick, with whom she has become friends and occasional partners in crime. Their relationship originated on television, in *Batman: The Animated Series* (1992–1995), and later pollinated comics. In "Harley and Ivy" and other episodes of *Batman*, Poison Ivy was a softer, more seductive character, blueprinted by artist Lynne Naylor. Series co-creator Bruce Timm redesigned the animated Ivy, paling her skin and neutering her voluptuousness, when the series was revamped into *The Adventures of Batman & Robin* (1997–1999). Diane Pershing voiced the character on both series, as well as Poison Ivy's guest appearances in *Static Shock* (2000–2004) and *Justice League* (2001–2004). Poison Ivy and Harley Quinn have co-starred in DC Comics miniseries in both the "animated" and traditional styles.

Poison Ivy's origin was modified, connecting Pamela Isley with future Batgirl Barbara Gordon, in the WB's reinvention of the Batman cartoon, *The Batman* (2004–present); Piera Coppola provided her voice. The supervillainess' other media appear-

Uma Thurman as a campy Poison Ivy in *Batman & Robin* (1997).

ance, director Joel Schumacher's *Batman & Robin* (1997), cast Uma Thurman in the role (Demi Moore and Julia Roberts were considered), teaming her with Arnold Schwarzenegger as Mr. Freeze. The movie Poison Ivy borrowed heavily from the comic-book mythos (Jason Woodrue even appeared), but Thurman's campy-vampy, Mae West–inspired portrayal was one of several over-the-top performances in the movie critically lambasted by Bat-buffs.

Her occasional protection of children aside, Poison Ivy's comic-book persona leaves no margin for frivolity. At times she has used a vine whip and a crossbow, but her pheromonal control remains her most potent weapon—even the mighty Superman succumbed to her charms in the best-selling 2003 *Batman* storyline "Hush," by writer Jeph Loeb and artist Jim Lee. She apparently perished in that serial, but by the mid-2000s had bloomed once again.

Beginning with *Batman: The Animated Series* tie-ins in the 1990s, Poison Ivy has been produced as action figures and dolls, and in other merchandise. For the discerning collector, superstar artist Adam Hughes designed and John G. Mathews sculpted an exquisite Poison Ivy "Women of the DC Universe" coldcast porcelain bust, a 2006 release from DC Direct. —*ME*

Powers Villains

*P*owers, created by Brian Michael Bendis and Michael Avon Oeming in 2000, is an amalgam of superhero and crime comics. Bendis, *Powers'* writer, has often cited playwright David Mamet (*Glengarry Glen Ross*, *American Buffalo*) as one of his major influences. Mamet's work is saturated with morally ambiguous characters, many of whom are difficult to pinpoint on the hero/villain spectrum. In much of Bendis' work, as in Mamet's, everyone has the potential to be heroic or villainous. Ultimately, the characters in *Powers* are not inherently good or evil: they are potentially both and are ultimately defined by the choices they make.

Powers follows Detectives Christian Walker and Deena Pilgrim, cops assigned to investigate homicides among the superpowered citizens ("Powers") of an unnamed city. Over time, it becomes clear that Walker himself was once a Power named Diamond. The story arc "Forever" (vol. 1 #31–#37, 2003) reveals that Walker is a near-immortal being who has been alive since prehistoric times.

Although *Powers* is steeped in crime fiction and film noir, the book pulls from a wide range of supervillain types—from the archetypal nemesis to the modern "relevant" villain. Walker's arch-nemesis, a villain type patterned on recognizable antagonists such as Sherlock Holmes' Moriarty, is another Power known as Haemon—a sadistic, demonic figure who is compelled to fight Walker throughout time. Walker and Haemon battle as Neanderthals, then in ancient Greece, and then again in 1930s Chicago, where Haemon gruesomely murders Walker's wife and manages to escape. In 1986, Walker engages in a climactic battle with Haemon. After losing his powers and going to prison, Haemon eventually gets his powers back and escapes again, only to be killed at last by Walker.

Another major villain in *Powers* actually begins as a superhero. A mysterious being with "Level Nine" abilities, Supershock gradually loses touch with humanity and begins to think himself a god. Repulsed by a sordid sex tape made by a supposed superhero, Supershock goes on a rampage and destroys Utah, the Vatican, the Gaza Strip, and Baghdad in order to rid the world of religious hypocrisy. Eventually, Ultrabright, Supershock's lover and the mother of his son, persuades him to kill himself. Supershock's attack has lasting effects, however, as the world's governments collectively decide to outlaw all Powers. Supershock, a complex character who reflects contemporary political and social concerns, recalls similarly relevant characters such as Batman villain/eco-terrorist Ra's al Ghul and DC's superpowered group of anti-heroes known as the Elite. —*HM and AB*

The Prankster

One of Superman's original costumed foes, the mirthful miscreant known as the Prankster first pulled the Man of Steel's leg in *Action Comics* #51 (1942), in a story by writer Jerry Siegel and artist John Sikela. When egocentric comedian Oswald Loomis' career goes bust he turns to crime, with an M.O. of taking practical jokes to near-lethal limits. Accompanied by his posse of hoodlums he storms into two Metropolis banks, giving away (illgotten) money instead of stealing it. Welcomed with open arms in a third bank, the Prankster turns the tables by robbing it, but when pursued by Superman he seeks refuge underground and apparently dies in a cave-in.

The Prankster survived, bouncing back for consistent appearances throughout the Golden Age (1938–1954), mocking Superman with devilish glee. A throwback to Vaudevillian slapstick comedians with his straw hat, bow tie, gap-toothed smirk, and spherical body, the Prankster was intended for comic relief, not surprising since Siegel and his Superman co-creator Joe Shuster once had aspirations to produce a humor strip (in 1947 the collaborated on a short-lived comic book starring a comedic superhero named Funnyman). Padded with an array of gag-weapons that would make the Joker jealous—teargas peashooters, a squirting label pin, and laughing gas, to name a few—the Prankster perpetrated gaggles of gimmicks that irritated the Man of Steel, including copyrighting the alphabet and extorting money for its use. Sometimes using asinine aliases like P. R. Ankster and Mr. Van Prank, Loomis occasionally teamed with other supervillains—Lex Luthor, the Toyman, and Mr. Mxyptlk—but like a bad standup whose shtick wore thin, was booked into limbo during later decades.

Then came the reboot in *Superman* vol. 2 #16 (1987). The new Loomis, the star of Metropolis' long-running kid's program *The Uncle Oswald Show*, went mad after his series was canceled by station exec Morgan Edge. Terrorizing and nearly killing Edge as well as kidnapping Lois Lane, the Prankster's deadly gags attracted Superman's ire. In *Adventures of Superman* #579 (2000) Loomis received a slimmer new body from the dark deity Lord Satanus, and he occasionally rolls into Metropolis to attempt to kill Edge or merely annoy Superman with his nanotechnologically enhanced novelties.

The Prankster appeared as one of the supervillain team "A.P.E" (Allied Perpetrators of

Evil) in a 1966 episode of Filmation's animated *The New Adventures of Superman*, in the "Triple-Play" episode of Ruby-Spears' *Superman* cartoon (1988–1989), and in two episodes of ABC's live-action *Lois & Clark: The New Adventures of Superman* (1993–1997), with Bronson Pinchot starring as a reworked Prankster named Kyle Griffen. —*ME*

Professor Zoom: *See* **The Reverse-Flash**

Prometheus

The hero hunter Prometheus blazed onto the page of his self-titled one-shot comic book in early 1998 in a story penned by Grant Morrison. According to the villain himself, he is the son of a Bonnie and Clyde–like couple who travels with his parents on a crime spree through America until they are cornered and killed by the police. Interestingly, he shares the same history as billionaire industrialist Bruce (Batman) Wayne—who also witnessed his parents die mercilessly at the hands of others—but instead of becoming an agent for good, the young boy (whose name is not revealed in his origin story) vows to dedicate his life to opposing the forces of justice.

At sixteen he traveled to the legendary city of Shamballa, where he was trained by monks and given the so-called Cosmic Key that allows him access to the Ghost Zone, a realm of nothingness that also doubles as the arch-assassin's headquarters. He then built a high-tech suit of armor and weapons arsenal with which he could download the fighting techniques of the world's most highly skilled martial artists—including Batman—into his own neural system. As Prometheus, he infiltrated the Justice League of America (JLA)'s Watchtower headquarters and took out most of the team before being defeated by Catwoman. The villain later returned as a member of Lex Luthor's Injustice Gang during the Mageddon War, and defeated several Justice Leaguers before being stopped by Batman and the Huntress. Obsessed with plotting a death trap for every member of the JLA, Prometheus is certain to remain a recurring threat to the heroes. —*GM*

Psycho-Pirate

The Psycho-Pirate is the man who knew too much. In *Showcase* #56 (1965), written by Gardner Fox and illustrated by Murphy Anderson, Dr. Fate and Hourman meet a pillager in a red-and-black harlequin costume who manipulates human emotions with the Medusa Masks, prized relics he has stolen. But this Psycho-Pirate is not the emotion-master of the same name who originally fought the heroes' Justice Society of America (JSA) teammates during comics' Golden Age (1938–1954)—that villain, a mousey, mustached typesetter named Charles Halstead, was jailed by the JSA, and behind bars he blabbed the secrets of the Medusa Masks to his cellmate, wastrel Roger Hayden. Upon his release Hayden became the new Psycho-Pirate, able to bombard victims with uncontrollable outbursts by expressing an emotion on his own face.

Fusing the Medusa Masks into a single face-plate, Hayden occasionally committed crimes as the Psycho-Pirate, but did not foresee the pitfalls of manipulating human feelings—he became both consumed and maddened by these experiences. The Anti-Monitor, the despot who engineered the Crisis on Infinite Earths in the 1985–1986 maxiseries of the same name, manipulated the Psycho-Pirate in the world-altering affair. After the Crisis, which merged several parallel realities into one (and streamlined DC Comics' multiple continuities into one universe), Hayden was the only Earthling who remembered the worlds as they originally were. Knowledge of these dissonant realities drove him insane—and into a straitjacket.

The Psycho-Pirate has become a pawn yet again, this time of writers wishing to dabble in pre-*Crisis* lore in post-*Crisis* continuity. Grant Morrison used Hayden to distort reality and temporarily revive old DC characters in *Animal Man* #23 and #24 (1990), and Geoff Johns found the villain a useful tool to unravel the confusing origins of Power Girl in the miniseries *JSA Classified* (2005)—as well as to set into motion the events of DC's Earths-altering crossover *Infinite Crisis* (2005–2006).

DC Direct released a Psycho-Pirate action figure in its 2005 Crisis on Infinite Earths toy line. —*ME*

The Puke

Mike Allred's off-kilter superhero Madman took on retro science-fiction villains with an air of goofiness that came off as satirical but was really a throwback to the more innocent days of super-hero comics. Fittingly, he often fought bad guys who were based on the basic villain archetypes—evil scientists, robots, and muck monsters.

Such a character is the Puke, introduced in Dark Horse's *Madman Comics* #8 (1995) as an innocent man named Terrence who is transformed into, well, you guessed it … a giant pile of puke. In the grand tradition of comics' blob and mud mon-sters, Madman must battle the Puke through the halls of a hospital. The Puke's high acidic content proves deadly to many cannon fodder security guards, eliciting cries of "Aagh! I'm burning!" from

Madman Comics #8 ™ & ©1995 Mike Allred.
COVER ART BY MIKE ALLRED AND DAVE COOPER.

his victims. To defeat his foe, Madman attacks the monster with Alka-Seltzer (a practical choice), borax chloride, and, in desperation, popcorn. Although the Puke is almost invulnerable, he's eventually shrunk down to a size where Madman can stuff him into a beaker—with a toilet plunger. (The same reducing substance used against the Puke returned in issue #9, shrinking Madman into Mini-Madman!)

Not surprisingly, the story comes off as more amusing than disgusting, given Allred's pop-art influences. While an inarticulate muck monster to the end, the Puke proved iconic enough to end up on a magnet and—who knows—he could even appear in the long-rumored *Madman* movie. —HM

Pulp Supervillains

Early inexpensive magazines, printed on cheap "pulp" paper, became known by the term "pulps." The adventure pulps, containing tales of high excite-ment and fantastic heroes, were the predecessors of the comic-book industry that soon followed, and the ancestry of comic-book supervillains can be found in the villains of pulp magazines and syndicated comic strips. The larger-than-life actions of the heroes and villains of the pulp magazines served as a template for the writers of early comic books and comic strips, who had to supply stories even more quickly than the authors of pulp magazines.

One of the most enduring pulp villains was Shiwan Khan, the evil Oriental inspired by Fu Manchu, and the most formidable adversary faced by the pulp hero The Shadow: "Wide at the fore-head, his face tapered toward a pointed chin. The center of that triangular visage was a straight-marked nose … His eyebrows were thin curves of black that ran almost to his temples. His lips formed a thin, straight streak of brown, set against a saffron background. There were also a thin mus-tache and a dab of chin whisker. … Most amazing of all his features were his eyes. They were green, cat-like in their glow … "

Like his forebear, Genghis Khan, Shiwan Khan dreamed of ruling the world. In the novel "The Golden Master" (*Shadow*, September 15, 1939) by Maxwell Grant (Walter Gibson), Khan first demonstrated his combat mastery, skill at hypnosis, and mental illusions. He fought The Shadow a record four times, three encounters more than most villains lasted against the Master of Darkness.

Khan also appeared in the 1990s comic book *The Shadow Strikes!* John Lone portrayed a Shiwan Khan in the feature film *The Shadow* (1994), which somewhat differed from the character's pulp and comic incarnations, but preserved the character's atmosphere and menace.

Comic-strip villain Kabai Singh inherited the mantle of leadership of the pirate band known as the Singh Brotherhood and led the Brotherhood in many battles against the early comic strip hero the Phantom, the jungle lord also called "the Ghost Who Walks." Singh pirates murdered the father of the boy who would become the first Phantom in 1525 when plundering a merchant ship, causing the boy to devote his life to the fight against piracy and injustice. This initiated an enmity between the Phantom and the Singh Brotherhood that would span centuries, beginning with the *Phantom* comic strip on February 17, 1936, by Lee Falk and Ray Moore. The Brotherhood would eventually slay the father of the current Phantom, assuring no end of ill will between them and the Ghost Who Walks.

Cary-Hiroyuki Tagawa portrayed Kabai Singh in the film *The Phantom* (1996). This appearance, together with the importance of the Singh Brotherhood in the ongoing *Phantom* comic strip, engendered enough notoriety for Kabai Singh to merchandise him as a costume for Dr. Evil, the nemesis of action figure Captain Action, in 1999.

The pulp villain John Sunlight was the only mastermind ever to battle Doc Savage twice. He first appeared in the novel *The Fortress of Solitude* by Kenneth Robeson (Lester Dent), printed in the pulp magazine *Doc Savage* (October 1938), in which he took over Savage's arctic headquarters and proceeded to sell the experimental weapons stored there to the highest bidder. Sunlight was thought dead at the end of this adventure, but later was found to have survived in *The Devil Genghis* (December 1938), at the end of which he was hacked to death by his angry victims.

Sunlight considered himself a uniter rather than a conqueror, feeling that humankind would benefit by having one ruler, rather than being divided into hundreds of warring nations. He preferred to wear clothing of all one color, although the actual color was of no matter. Wrote Robeson: "[Sunlight] resembled a gentle poet, with his great shock of dark hair, his remarkably high forehead, his hollow burning eyes set in a starved face. His body was very long, very thin. His … fingers being almost the length of an ordinary man's whole hand." In the 1980s Sunlight appeared in *Doc Savage* comic books published by DC Comics, and in the 1990s in Millennium Comics' *Doc Savage* series, in which his treatment was consonant with his pulp origins.

Although Will Eisner's comic-strip hero the Spirit—the masked identity assumed by Central City criminologist Denny Colt after his alleged death on June 2, 1940—is considered an unorthodox crime fighter, his enemies are no less strange. Most of the Spirit's major enemies appeared after World War II; however, some of his more colorful foes debuted before the war. These include Dr. Cobra, who tried to kill Denny Colt but created the Spirit; Orang, "the ape that is human"; and the Black Queen, a former defense lawyer turned villainess. Eisner's femme fatales became his trademark in the postwar years, a bevy of gorgeous women who couldn't decide if they wanted to kill the Spirit or seduce him. Among these were Sand Saref, his childhood friend; Plaster of Paris; and, best of all, P'Gell, the sensuous beauty who accumulated husbands like matches—and disposed of them nearly as quickly.

Also causing the Spirit no end of grief were Carrion, an undertaker gone bad, and his buzzard Julia. But in the forefront of this unique group stands the criminal mastermind the Octopus, perhaps the only villain whose criminal name is less bizarre than his actual name, Zithbath Zark. Though the Octopus first appeared in the "Spirit" Sunday comic section in 1946, his full origin was unknown until told in *The Spirit #2* (1966). Though his face is never seen, he can be recognized by his purple gloves with three yellow stripes.

Though comic books, strips, and popular fiction have made great strides toward sophistication, many of the villains still take their cues from their pulp forebears. —*MWB*

Punch and Jewelee

Picture two off-the-hook court jester–like "reformed" criminals who frequent suburbia and try to raise baby amongst backyard barbeques and car pools, and you've envisioned the ex–Suicide Squad villains known as Punch and Jewelee. These two Coney Island puppeteers turned petty criminals were birthed in the pages of Charlton Comics' *Captain Atom* #85 (1967), in a story scripted by David Kaler and penciled by Steve Ditko.

Amoral, whimsical, and outright unpredictable, Punch and Jewelee are minding their own business as thieves on Coney Island, until one day Punch finds a small box of alien technology abandoned by extraterrestrial passers-by. The couple uses the discarded weaponry to build an elaborate underground headquarters from which they operate as Brooklyn's baddest villains, often exacting random acts of violence on the most unsuspecting.

With their bags of tricks and Vaudevillian props—such as Jewelee's illusion-creating "hypno-jewel" and Punch's gun that blasts "sting strings"—the demented duo often bumped up against Central Bureau of Intelligence agent Nightshade and her partner King Faraday. The couple was eventually adopted into the Suicide Squad, a volatile team of supervillains recruited into service for the U.S. government, but—unbeknownst to them—they were soon considered loose cannons and a serious liability. When Jewelee became pregnant the couple defected to Middle America, where husband and wife chose to live quiet lives as borderline-psychotic parents who flirt with returning to a life of crime. Although they haven't been heard from in years, just like a grotesque jack-in-the-box, there's no telling where they might pop up next. —*GM*

The Puppet Master

For a man who plays with dolls, the Puppet Master is one of the most dangerous enemies of the Fantastic Four (FF). He first pulls the group's strings in *Fantastic Four* vol. 1 #8 (1962), when writer Stan Lee and artist Jack Kirby show him taking control of the FF's strongest member, the Thing, via a miniature proxy he forges of radioactive clay, and psionically maneuvering him into combat against his teammates. Detached from humanity but determined to control it, the Puppet Master endeavors to establish himself as a global king, with the FF as his slaves. His blind stepdaughter Alicia intervenes, appalled by his megalomaniacal rants, accidentally making him drop a puppet he has made in his own likeness—which, in a karmic twist of fate, causes the Puppet Master to fall out a window to his death.

But death and supervillains rarely walk hand in hand. The Puppet Master soon resurfaced, determined to control the FF, plying his puppetry alone and often as the partner of the Mad Thinker; he has even allied with Dr. Doom.

In his original design for the character, artist Kirby fashioned the Puppet Master's face after that of a ventriloquist dummy—he is bald, with a Cheshire Cat–like toothy smile, pronounced lips, and exaggerated eyelashes. These features give the Puppet Master an androgynous appearance that widens the chasm between the paternal father figure he should be and his actual personality as a self-absorbed madman.

Marvel Team-Up vol. 1 #6 (1973) offered a peek into his past, where the Puppet Master—actually Philip Masters—was an alienated youth reared in a Balkan nation appropriately named for a man with no allegiance to others: Transia. He is responsible for the accident that blinded his stepdaughter, and through Alicia Masters readers have occasionally witnessed what little compassion the Puppet Master possesses. Prone to emotional flare-ups, the Puppet Master is essentially a coward who relies upon manipulation for personal empowerment. He has appeared on television cartoons in a 1982 episode of *The Incredible Hulk* and a 1994 episode of *Fantastic Four*. A scene deleted from the live-action movie *Fantastic Four* (2005) acknowledged the Puppet Master's existence; this deleted scene's inclusion in the film's European DVD edition placed the Puppet Master into contention as a villain in the movie's sequel, planned for a 2007 release. —*ME*

The Purple Man

Born in Yugoslavia, Zebediah Killgrave was once a spy who attempted to steal an experimental chemical from the U.S. Army. A guard fired at Killgrave and missed, hitting a canister of the chemical, dousing the spy. Not only did the chemical permanently dye Killgrave's skin and hair purple, but it also altered his physiology: now Killgrave's body gives off psychoactive chemicals comparable to pheromones that weaken the willpower of people in his vicinity. Killgrave can simply ask a person to do something, no matter how ridiculous or horrific, and the victim will feel obliged to obey.

Only a relatively few people have the strength of will to resist the Purple Man's power, including his foremost nemesis Daredevil, who defeated Killgrave in the latter's first appearance, in Marvel Comics' *Daredevil* vol. 1 #4 (1964), written by Stan Lee and drawn by Joe Orlando. Although the Purple Man built a criminal empire and even considered ruling the world, he eventually gave up both ambitions, since he could have anything he wanted simply by asking for it.

Whereas Frank Miller portrayed the Purple Man as a humorous prankster in *Marvel Team-Up Annual* #3 (1980), in 2003 Brian Michael Bendis depicted Killgrave as a sadistic figure who mentally enslaved Jessica Jones, the former superhero of the Marvel series *Alias*.

Kara Killgrave, alias the Purple Girl or Persuasion, a character from *Alpha Flight*, has purple skin and powers similar to Zebediah Killgrave's, and believes him to be her father. Oddly, the Purple

Man's only appearance on screen is in an episode of *X-Men: The Animated Series* (1992–1997). —*PS*

Pyro

First appearing as a member of Mystique's Brotherhood of Evil Mutants, Pyro was created by writer Chris Claremont and penciler/co-plotter John Byrne for *Uncanny X-Men* #141–#142 (1981). In those issues Pyro participated in Mystique's first attempt to assassinate Senator Robert Kelly.

Pyro has the mutant ability to mentally control fire: he can increase its size and intensity and even manipulate its shape. For example, he can cause a fire to take the form of a living creature, and then direct it to attack an opponent. Pyro's power does not enable him to create flames, so he wears a flamethrower as part of his costume. Once Pyro has taken psionic control of a fire, he is invulnerable to it.

Claremont revealed Pyro's backstory for *The Official Handbook of the Marvel Universe* (1983–1984). He was Australian St. John Allerdyce, and he worked as a journalist and novelist before allying himself with Mystique.

Eventually Pyro fell victim to the Legacy Virus, which distorted his powers, causing flames in his vicinity to rage uncontrollably. Facing his mortality caused Pyro to reevaluate his life. His final act was to prevent Mystique's minion post from killing Kelly, and Pyro died in the senator's arms.

But Pyro still lives onscreen. Played by Aaron Stanford, Pyro was introduced in *X2: X-Men United* (2003) as American teenager John Allerdyce, a student at Professor Xavier's school for mutants who ends up allying himself with the terrorist Magneto instead. Pyro has also appeared in *X-Men: The Last Stand* (2006). —*PS*

Q

The being known only as "Q" was first encountered by the crew of the *U.S.S. Enterprise-D* in the year 2364 near the outer space station called Farpoint. Although he appeared as a human male in a 1987 TV episode of *Star Trek: The Next Generation* (played by actor John DeLancie, who also voiced the character in the computer game, *Star Trek: Borg*), Q claimed to be a member of a race called the "Q," immortal beings possessing nearly omnipotent powers, residing in the Q Continuum. Other members of the Q also appear humanoid, with varying features of either gender, though they are actually noncorporeal beings. The Q feel immensely superior to human beings; Q considers humankind "grievously savage," and takes great delight in testing the nerve and will of these inferior beings. Q also made the mechanized, hive-like collective called the "Borg" aware of the existence of humanity, initiating a series of attempts by the Borg to subjugate and assimilate humankind. Despite this, the Q seem to have an unending curiosity about humankind, and, at times, even a concern for the welfare of the species, though this is never couched in such amiable terms. Q once suggested that eventually the humankind might advance beyond the level of the Q.

The episode "Death Wish" of *Star Trek: Voyager* (1995–2001) features the first recorded visit by outsiders to the Q Continuum, and in "The Q and the Grey," Q proclaims his desire to have a child with *U.S.S. Voyager* Captain Katherine Janeway.

Q also appeared in a handful of episodes of *Star Trek: Deep Space Nine* (1993–1999), including "Q-Less," in which Commander Benjamin Sisko punches Q in the face, an experience both Picard and Janeway must have envied.

Q has also appeared in a number of novels including *Encounter at Farpoint* (by David Gerrold, 1987), a novelization of the first episode of *Star Trek: The Next Generation*; and original titles such as *Q-in-Law* (1991) and *Q-Squared* (1993), both by Peter David, *I,Q* by John DeLancie and Peter David (2000), and the *Q Continuum* trilogy: *Q-Space, Q-Zone* and *Q-Strike*, all by Greg Cox in 1998. Q is the narrator of *Q's Guide to the Continuum*, by Michael Jan Friedman and Robert Greenberger (1998). In 1999, Alien Voices, a producer of audio books, released *Spock vs. Q*, in which actors Leonard Nimoy and John DeLancie, respectively, played their famous *Star Trek* characters in their first meeting. This project was followed up in 2000 with the release of *Spock vs. Q: The Sequel*, with the same cast. —*MWB*

Queen Bee

The dazzling dominatrix Queen Bee—aka Zazzala of the insect-like world of Korll—forced DC

Comics' mightiest superheroes to toil as obedient drones in *Justice League of America* #23 (1963), by Gardner Fox and Mike Sekowsky. With fluttering Bee-Men at her thrall, the winged Zazzala, wearing an orange-and-black horizontally striped bathing suit, threatens to demolish Earth unless the Leaguers obtain for her three vials that will afford her immortality.

Queen Bee was outfoxed by the JLA in that initial tale, but when next seen in issue #60 (1968), she has achieved everlasting life, with an unexpected side effect—immobility. With her "magno-nuclear rod" she shrunk six JLAers and guest-star Batgirl into tiny winged slaves and dispatched them to find the antidote for her "living death." Queen Bee befuddled the League, Wonder Woman, and Superman in several return appearances, and was included in a 2001 PVC set of classic JLA villains.

In the sticky honeycomb of DC's evolving continuity, a different Queen Bee, a hypnotist, buzzed into power in the nation of Bialya in a late 1980s story arc in *Justice League International*, but was executed by that country's General Sumaan Harjavti. Beginning in *JLA* vol. 2 #34 (1999), writer Grant Morrison and artist Howard Porter unveiled a reimagined, world-subjugating Zazzala. Like the original, this new Queen Bee hailed from the densely populated hive-planet Korll and lorded over Bee-Troopers, but her appearance was radically altered, with more entomological attributes than her predecessor, most noticeably intricate, bug-like eyes. Attracted to Earth by Lex Luthor to join his Injustice Gang, Zazzala enslaved New York City with her "hypno-pollen," establishing her Royal Egg-Matrix in the heart of Manhattan. She was swatted by the League, but will not be satisfied until all of Earth falls under her authority.

Another Queen Bee, Tazzala, reportedly the sister of Zazzala, was part of an alien alliance sworn to dominate Earth in the eight-issue series *Creature Commandos* (2000). —*ME*

Ra's al Ghul

Thirty years before Osama bin Laden and al Qaeda occupied the public consciousness, the first mention (in *Detective Comics* #411, 1971) of the international eco-terrorist Ra's al Ghul (pronounced "raish al gool") warranted an explanatory caption from editor Julius Schwartz defining the villain's name (which Schwartz himself coined): "Editor's note: in Arabic, 'the Demon's Head'! Literally, al Ghul signifies a mischief-maker, and appears as the ghoul of the Arabian Nights!"

Batman first meets al Ghul in—off all places!—his secret Batcave, as the calm yet intense figure with "an icy, penetrating voice," guarded by his Herculean manservant Ubu, slips out of the shadows in *Batman* #232 (1971). He explains to the dismayed Dark Knight that his own deductions and the subsequent investigation by his "organization" ferreted out Batman's identity and the location of his headquarters. Both al Ghul's fetching daughter Talia, whom Batman recently met, and the hero's own "son," his ward and partner Robin, have been kidnapped by the same unidentified party, prompting al Ghul's enlistment of the aid of the masked man he calls "detective" to help find them. After a transcontinental liberation effort with enough exotic settings, leopard attacks, sniper assaults, and martial-arts skirmishes to fill a

Batman #232 ©1971 DC Comics.
COVER ART BY NEAL ADAMS.

James Bond movie, Batman discerns that the dual abduction is a hoax. The astute hero is flabber-

The duplicitous Henri Ducard (Liam Neeson) and Ra's al Ghul (Ken Watanabe) from *Batman Begins* (2005).

gasted, however, by the reason for the subterfuge—"My darling Talia loves you!" admits papa al Ghul, who orchestrated this entire exercise as a test of Batman's mettle and personally anoints the "detective" as worthy of assuming his crime empire and his daughter's hand in marriage.

In subsequent tales transpiring intermittently over the next few years, more about al Ghul unfolded, courtesy of writer Denny O'Neil, who co-created the villain. Al Ghul had lived for centuries, periodically rejuvenating himself by dips into his restorative Lazurus Pit. His egressions from the Pit were accompanied by brief periods of insanity, with superhumanly augmented strength. He was a master fighter and swordsman, and he controlled the clandestine League of Assassins. Al Ghul believed himself a messiah, conspiring to purge the planet of the blight of humanity (often through releasing deadly viruses) and repopulate it anew, with himself at its fore. In pursuit of his vision, he sequestered himself in vast strongholds nestled in the most remote corners of the globe.

O'Neil conceived the character along with artist Neal Adams, penciler of *Batman* #232, when editor Schwartz was looking for new villains for a new, post-television *Batman* age. "We didn't want just another street thug with a costume and a fancy name," O'Neil recalled in a 2005 *BACK ISSUE* interview; "We were going for grandeur." In his visual designs, Adams intentionally afforded al Ghul a pronounced brow, to suggest conceit: "I wanted to get across the idea that he was what he was, and he was confident in it, not ashamed or embarrassed like some teenager or matinee idol," commented the artist in *BACK ISSUE*. Adams also gave Ra's al Ghul recessed eyes that, while not paranormal, appeared to glow supernaturally, increasing the character's mystique, a look exaggerated by his absence of eyebrows.

With the creation of Batman's *uber*-villain, a character that, with minimal adaptations, could exist in the real world, Ra's al Ghul helped the hero transition from the corny Caped Crusader of the 1960s to the grim-and-gritty Dark Knight known by contemporary audiences. Over the years Batman and al Ghul have occasionally clashed, with Talia—a forbidden fruit Batman finds appealing, but can never truly "taste" due to their ideological divide—being the connecting corner in a compelling personal triangle that has long outlasted the original O'Neil/Adams adventures of the early 1970s. Talia's toehold in both characters' lives illustrates that Batman and Ra's are, in many ways, flip sides of the same proverbial coin: they each use violence in their quests to forge a nonviolent world, al Ghul trumping Batman with a marked advantage—patience, a virtue acquired from his Lazarus Pit–spawned immortality.

While al Ghul's turgid worldview has put him into conflict with the Justice League ("Tower of Babel," *JLA* #43–#46, 2000) and other heroes, he seemed to prefer his entanglements with the "detective," although at one point he estranged himself from Talia at his insistence that Bane substitute for Batman as her mate.

In the nine-issue series *Batman: Death and the Maidens* (2003–2004), writer Greg Rucka and artist Klaus Janson introduced another of al Ghul's daughters, Nyssa, a fellow immortal who, during the eighteenth century, renounced her father and rose up against him in the current day. Al Ghul set up Nyssa and Talia as duel heads of the League of Assassins, but Nyssa ultimately murdered her father. Ra's al Ghul's propensity for extending his life, however, suggests that his death may be far from permanent.

The messianic Ra's al Ghul has upon occasion escaped the confines of comic books for screen depictions. David Warner voiced the villain in several episodes of *Batman: The Animated Series* (1992–1995), and reprised the role in the "future Batman" cartoon series, *Batman Beyond* (1999–2001), as well as an episode of the animated *Superman* (1996–2000). In this "animated" continuity, al Ghul also has a malicious son, Arkady. In *Batman Beyond*, he appeared in a different form: the body of Talia, which he had possessed.

Ra's al Ghul's widest claim to fame was his inclusion in director Christopher Nolan's relaunch of the Batman movie franchise, *Batman Begins* (2005). A cryptic figure named Henri Ducard (Liam

Neeson; Viggo Mortenssen had turned down the role, and Daniel Day-Lewis was also considered) recruited Batman-in-training Bruce Wayne (Christian Bale) to study with the League of Shadows (the movie version of the League of Assassins), led by the aloof, unblinking Ra's al Ghul (Ra's pronounced "ros" throughout the movie). The casting of Japanese-born Ken Watanabe, previously seen in *The Last Samurai* (2003), as al Ghul surprised comic-book purists expecting an actor of Middle-Eastern descent in the role—even *MAD* magazine took a swipe at his ethnicity in its parody, "Battyman Begone" (*MAD* #455, 2005)—but fans were surprised even more when (*spoiler warning!*) he was revealed to be a surrogate, with Ducard actually being al Ghul. Neeson's al Ghul was presumably killed in an elevated train crash in the movie's climax, but circumstances surrounding his death were vague enough to suggest a return in a future movie (perhaps joined by Talia, conspicuously absent from the film). Ra's al Ghul action figures were produced to coincide with both *Batman: The Animated Series* and *Batman Begins*. —ME

Rasputin

Long a staple of occult lore, Grigori Rasputin, the Mad Monk of Russian history, appears as a villain in Mike Mignola's *Hellboy* comics. In Mignola's version, Rasputin has real powers of immortality, and appears as a bald, imposing magician with powerful multi-dimensional sorcerous abilities.

According to the tale in *Hellboy: Seed of Destruction* (1994), after escaping the ruins of the Revolution, Rasputin holed up for a while in Italy before teaming with the occult-obsessed Nazis for more mystical experimentation. Rasputin became involved in a Nazi plan called "Ragna Rok," which would result in a demonic invasion of Earth. A trip to the North Sea in 1944 to summon a demon resulted in the birth of Hellboy, but an English mystic intercepted the summoning, and Hellboy ended up being raised by Professor Bruttenholm, who trained the young demon to become the world's greatest paranormal investigator.

Forty years later, Rasputin returned, having awoken a demon from beyond named Sadu-Hem,

I WAS CHOSEN BY THE DRAGON, OGDRU JAHAD, TO DELIVER HIM FROM HIS PRISON AND BRING ABOUT THE END OF THE WORLD, TO MAKE WAY FOR A NEW WORLD. AND I...I *ALONE* WILL BE LORD OVER *THAT!*

FROM CAVENDISH HALL I SHOOK THE DRAGON AND SOON ENOUGH I WILL BREAK HIS CHAINS AND SET HIM FREE!

Rasputin. From the epilogue to the trade-paperback edition of *Hellboy: Conqueror Worm* ©2002 Mike Mignola. ART BY MIKE MIGNOLA.

and planned to use the pyrokinetic powers of Hellboy's teammate Liz Sherman to breach the walls of our dimension to unleash a horde of monsters upon Earth. In the final battle, Rasputin tried to use his role as Hellboy's creator to bring him to the dark side. "If you kill me you will never know who you are," Rasputin taunted. Hellboy resisted temptation and fought to save Liz, sending Rasputin to parts unknown, doubtless to regroup for another assault on Earth.

In the 2004 film *Hellboy*, Rasputin is the main villain, played by Karl Roden. Among the movie's merchandising tie-ins were Mezco's 8-inch Rasputin action figure (with a smaller baby Hellboy figure) and a Hellboy-Rasputin "Mtz-Itz" two-pack of mini-figures.

Although the origin story in which he appears isn't the best Hellboy yarn, Rasputin's fabled reputation makes him fit right in to Mignola's spooky, supernatural world. —*HM*

Red Skull

He was the man Hitler was afraid of.

Johann Schmidt's origins in Marvel Comics' *Tales of Suspense* #66 (1966) give no clue as to his eventual fate. His father, upon learning that his wife had died in childbirth, tries to drown the child, before committing suicide. Schmidt runs away from home and fends for himself on the streets of his native Germany, eventually meeting a young Jewish girl who shows him kindness, which he misinterprets. When she rejects his advances, he murders her. Drifting from job to job in the impoverished Germany between wars, Schmidt eventually encounters the man who is to change his life: Adolf Hitler.

Schmidt was working as a bellboy when Hitler, a guest in the hotel, claimed to his subordinates that he could train even "that bellboy" to do a better job than they. Hitler saw, in Schmidt's eyes, the same hatred of humanity that Hitler himself felt, and took the bellboy under his wing. At first Hitler's men tried to make Schmidt into a typical Nazi soldier, but Hitler personally took charge of Schmidt's training, giving him the crimson skull mask that would achieve him worldwide notoriety and the name of the Red Skull.

The Red Skull answered only to Hitler himself, operating on top-secret projects vital to Germany's wartime interests. The Red Skull was a master schemer and a superb hand-to-hand combatant. He also employed a deadly spray he called his "dust of death" to murder his enemies. In his early appearances the Red Skull often played or whistled Chopin's funeral march when disposing of his victims, an affectation he later abandoned.

It was to combat the Red Skull's campaigns that the Allies created an agent of their own, the patriotic war hero Captain America. To co-creator Jack Kirby, Captain America and the Red Skull symbolized the battle epitomized by the Nazis and the Allies. "Captain America represents patriotism," Kirby told interviewer Mark Evanier in 1986. "Patriotism is an endless and valid state of mind. It will never leave the human being, just as love and anger will never leave us. I think our great characters stem from those feelings … People related to Captain America."

The Red Skull and Captain America first met before America had officially entered World War II, in a Joe Simon–written and Kirby-rendered story in the pages of *Captain America Comics* #1 (1941). Eventually, the Red Skull's malignant influence expanded to such a degree that even Hitler was afraid of the impoverished bellhop he had plucked from obscurity, but it was too late to stop the Red Skull's rise to power, as the Red Skull was already acting secretly to create his own power base within the Third Reich.

It was the Red Skull who sent Baron Wolfgang von Strucker, a Nazi agent who had fallen out of favor with Hitler, to Japan to create an organization that would eventually become Hydra. It is a back-handed tribute to Strucker's traitorous nature that he eventually threw off the Red Skull's influence and took over the organization, building it into one of the most feared terrorist organizations in the world and a major threat to international peace in the postwar era.

During World War II the Red Skull assumed increasingly greater power over many of Hitler's other agents, such as Baron Heinrich Zemo and scientist Arnim Zola. He would continue such actions after the war, briefly aligning himself with the Hate-Monger, a clone of Adolf Hitler, before betraying him.

Late in the war, when the Nazi cause was lost, the Red Skull supervised the construction of a series of destructive machines called Sleepers that would destroy the world should the Nazis lose the war.

In the last days of the war, the Red Skull was tracked to his hidden bunker lair by Captain America. As the two fought, the bunker was damaged by the bombs of an Allied air raid. Captain America escaped, but the Red Skull was trapped in the bunker that filled with an experimental suspended-animation gas that had been released during the Red Skull's clash with Captain America. The Red Skull slept through the late 1940s and 1950s, prevented from aging by the gas.

During the 1950s, during Marvel Comics' short-lived revival of *Captain America*, the Russians used an agent of their own posing as the Red Skull, hoping to capitalize on the notoriety and fear inspired by the original.

The true Red Skull was released from suspended animation by a search team sent by the organization known as T.H.E.M., which was eventually revealed to be an arm of Hydra. Unleashed upon the world anew, the Red Skull eventually had the 1950s-era imposter murdered by an agent known as Scourge, and continued in his campaign to further the Nazi cause and overthrow the forces of democracy. His schemes included trying to use the long-forgotten Sleepers in his own failed bid to rule the world, as well as using the nearly omnipotent weapon designated the Cosmic Cube, which he stole from a criminal organization designated Advanced Idea Mechanics (A.I.M.), to transfer his mind to the body of Captain America, and vice versa, to continue his campaign of terrorism under the guise of freedom's greatest champion. The Red Skull was aided in many of these attempts by a band of former Nazi agents called the Exiles, who had spent the postwar years in hiding on a secret base, Exile Island. Here the Red Skull resided in a mansion he called Skull House and fathered, by a common washerwoman, a daughter who later became known as Mother Superior, whom he had scientifically aged to adulthood and given superhuman abilities. The child's mother

Captain America #103 ©1968 Marvel Comics.
COVER ART BY JACK KIRBY AND SYD SHORES.

had died giving birth, a grim reminder of the Red Skull's own origins.

Eventually, however, the Red Skull's past caught with him. By the 1980s, the gas that had prevented him from aging in his years of enforced slumber began to reverse its effects on his metabolism, slowly advancing him to his true physical age. After a failed attempt to take his mortal enemy, Captain America, to the grave with him, his Nazi ally, the scientist Arnim Zola, transferred the Red Skull's mind into a clone of Captain America, after which the Red Skull began to experiment with other philosophies and strategies to destroy America, proclaiming Nazism to be a bankrupt ideology. Working behind the scenes the Red Skull controlled a senate committee, compelling them to strip Steve Rogers of the title of Captain America and replace him with an operative referred to as the U.S. Agent. In a confrontation with Steve Rogers, the Red Skull acciden-

tally exposed himself with his "dust of death," which gave him a permanent skull-like appearance and tinted his skin crimson. The same death's-head visage he had imposed on so many of his victims over the years now became his permanent face.

In 2000 the Red Skull obtained another Cosmic Cube, which he internalized, making it part of his very being, but was seemingly tricked by Captain America into destroying himself. However, it seems unlikely that, after surviving death so many times, the threat of the Red Skull is truly ended. —*MWB*

Reinvented Supervillains

In the early twenty-first century, Marvel and DC Comics still utilize classic supervillains who have been created as long ago as 1940, when the Joker and Lex Luthor first appeared. How can comics creators keep these characters vital after so many years and previous stories?

In many cases, editors, writers, and artists have felt it necessary to give the villains a conceptual makeover. That process can take different forms.

From the 1930s into the early 1960s, neither creators nor readers cared about continuity, and changes could be made without explanation. Hence, when Superman first encountered Luthor in 1940, the latter had a full head of red hair, but in 1941 Luthor abruptly became bald. Moreover, in the early 1960s editor Mort Weisinger established that their enmity began when they were adolescents, ignoring the stories from 1940.

Sometimes an earlier villain's name is recycled for a different character. The 1940 version of Clayface (*Detective Comics* #40) was Basil Karlo, a horror movie actor who was adept at makeup. But in 1961 (*Detective* #298), the name Clayface was reused for Matt Hagen, who could actually change shape.

An old villain can be killed off, and a new character will subsequently take his place. The original Mirror Master, a foe of the Silver Age (1956–1969) Flash, perished in *Crisis on Infinite Earths* (1985–1986). A Scots mercenary named Evan McCulloch adopted the deceased rogue's costume and mirror weaponry (in *Animal Man* #8, 1989) and has been the new Mirror Master ever since.

Frequently the dead villain's successor is his own son. After the apparent demise of Norman Osborn, the original Green Goblin, his son Harry took over his costumed identity (starting in *Amazing Spider-Man* #136, 1974). In strange story twists in the comics, Harry himself later died, and ultimately Norman turned up alive, succeeding his own son as the Green Goblin!

The original Captain Boomerang was killed in *Identity Crisis* (2004–2005), and his son has taken over his title. The son is an "improved" version, since, unlike his father, he can throw boomerangs at superspeed.

A new villain can represent a variation on the concept underlying an older one. Realizing that much of the Green Goblin's original appeal lay in the mystery of his true identity, writer Roger Stern co-created the Hobgoblin (in *Amazing Spider-Man* #238, 1983), who modified Norman Osborn's costume and equipment but was a wholly different character, whose identity remained secret for years.

In some cases a forgotten supervillain simply needs an editor and writer to return him to the spotlight. The Riddler made two comics appearances in 1948 and then vanished until new *Batman* editor Julius Schwartz and writer Gardner Fox brought him back in 1965 (*Batman* #171). The next year the Riddler was the first villain featured on the *Batman* television show, which made him enduringly famous.

Introduced by writer Mike Friedrich and artist Neal Adams in *Justice League of America* #94 (1971), Merlyn the Archer (not to be confused with the Arthurian wizard) was a rival of Green Arrow and, as a member of the League of Assassins, an enemy of Batman. Thereafter Merlyn rarely appeared until 2004, when he achieved high visibility in DC's *Identity Crisis*.

Similarly, the *Batman* villain Cat-Man (from *Detective* #311, 1963), once a pale imitation of Catwoman, suddenly became a leading character as a member of the new Secret Six in DC's *Villains United* (2005).

Writers may also update a veteran villain's costume and modus operandi. The Calculator (introduced in *Detective* #463, 1976) began as a thief whose costume contained a gimmick that was ahead of its time: a personal computer. In *Identity*

Crisis novelist Brad Meltzer remodeled the Calculator into a plain-clothes information broker for other villains, a role tailored to the new Internet Age.

Having updated Deadshot in *Detective* #474 (1977), writer Steve Englehart and artist Marshall Rogers gave a makeover to another forgotten villain in the miniseries *Batman: Dark Detective* (2005): Dr. X, who was created by writer Dave Wood and artist Sheldon Moldoff in *Detective* #261 (1958) but had not been featured in a story since 1963. In his first stories this criminal scientist had created a powerful duplicate of himself out of pure energy, called Dr. Double X. In Englehart's updated version, the scientist calls himself Dr. Double X, and has found a new outlet in contemporary science for his interest in duality: he creates clones.

Writers can also update a villain from more innocent times by remodeling his personality to fit the "grim and gritty" mode of contemporary comics. Created by writer Bill Finger and artist Sheldon Moldoff in *Detective* #259 (1958), the Calendar Man was a thief named Julian Day who patterned his crimes on the theme of dates or times of the year. For example, in his initial appearance Day based each of his crimes on a different season, such as summer or winter, wearing a different costume to symbolize each one.

In *Batman: The Long Halloween* (1996–1997) writer Jeph Loeb turned Day into a madman like Hannibal Lecter, doling out clues from his asylum cell to Batman about the "Holiday" killer. Later, in *Batman 80-Page Giant* #3 (2000), writer Chuck Dixon portrayed the Calendar Man as an insane terrorist who caused a jet plane to crash and tried to blow up a nuclear power plant.

The most popular contemporary method of making over supervillains and superheroes is by rebooting their series: all past continuity is declared null and void, and the series starts over from the beginning. The pattern was set when DC Comics hired writer/artist John Byrne to reboot Superman in the comics miniseries *The Man of Steel* (1986). Although Marvel has traditionally attempted to keep its continuity intact since 1961, reboots have become common at DC.

The *Superman* reboot produced perhaps the best example of rebooting a villain. Traditionally Lex Luthor was portrayed as a criminal scientific genius who was continually breaking out of jail to battle Superman. Working from a suggestion by Marv Wolfman, in *Man of Steel*, Byrne reintroduced Luthor as the widely respected but secretly unscrupulous billionaire head of LexCorp. Byrne and Wolfman's Luthor has been nearly universally accepted, including by the television series *Lois and Clark* (1993–1997), the animated *Superman* (1997–2000), and *Smallville* (2001–present).

The makers of movies and television series almost never adhere to the strict letter of comics continuity, and hence they are continually rebooting characters from the comics. For example, *Batman: The Animated Series* (1992–1995) combined two comics versions of Clayface into one, introducing the shapeshifting Matt Hagen as a former movie star. The later animated series *The Batman* (2004–present) went further, making an entirely different person, policeman Ethan Bennett, into Clayface.

Finally, sometimes revitalizing a classic supervillain requires no more than realizing what made the character work in the first place. In the first Joker story (*Batman #1*, 1940), writer Bill Finger portrayed this villain as a sinister serial killer. Over the next three decades, though the Joker tried to kill Batman, his life of crime otherwise consisted of robbing banks and pulling pranks. In their landmark story "The Joker's Five-Way Revenge" (*Batman #251*, 1973), writer Denny O'Neil and artist Neal Adams returned the Joker to his roots, making him a murderer once more. Virtually everyone who has used the Joker since in comics, television, and film has followed their lead. Thus through the different paths they have taken to reinvention, Lex Luthor and the Joker, two of comics' oldest villains, remain vital and contemporary even in the early twenty-first century. —*PS*

Reverse-Flash

The Reverse-Flash, the Scarlet Speedster's opposite in both costume (the yellows and reds are inverted) and morality, zoomed into the DC Universe in *The Flash* vol. 1 #139 (1963), written by John Broome and illustrated by Carmine Infantino. A resident of the twenty-fifth century, demented genius Eobard Thawne (aka Professor Zoom) is fixated

upon the twentieth-century Flash (secretly police scientist Barry Allen). Discovering one of the hero's original uniforms in a time capsule, Zoom scientifically boosts its original wearer's residual superspeed energies (defined in later texts as the "Speed Force") and infuses the suit, which he dyes, with the ability to enable him to run at superhuman velocities. Becoming the Fastest Man Alive of the future, he zips through a crime wave until the Flash, on a time-traveling mission in Zoom's era, trips him up.

Zoom's Flash fixation ultimately became a fatal attraction: he regularly whisked to the twentieth century to torment the Scarlet Speedster, becoming obsessed with Allen's wife, Iris, and eventually murdering her after she spurned his advances. Later, when Allen had fallen in love with another woman, Fiona Webb, the Reverse-Flash struck again, attempting to kill her—but in an ensuing struggle to save Fiona's life, the Flash accidentally broke Zoom's neck in *Flash #324* (1983), initiating a lengthy "Trial of the Flash" storyline that would dominate the hero's title for over two years.

Once the Flash died in *Crisis on Infinite Earths #8* (1985), his former sidekick Kid Flash (Wally West) took his place, but was shocked to behold "The Return of Barry Allen" in *Flash* vol. 2 #74–#79 (1993). As writer Mark Waid and penciler Greg LaRocque disclosed, the supposedly revived Allen/Flash was actually a disguised Professor Zoom, having traveled from the twenty-fifth century during a time *before* his death in the 1983 comic. This paradox aside, the Reverse-Flash was still dead.

"When I was going over the Rogues early on," admitted *Flash* scribe Geoff Johns in a 2005 *Wizard* magazine interview, "I said how I wished Professor Zoom wasn't dead, and [Editor] Joey [Cavalieri] casually suggested, 'So make a new one.'" With artist Scott Kolins, Johns did just that in *Flash* vol. 2 #197 (2003). The new Reverse-Flash is actually Hunter Zolomon (first seen in *Flash Secret Files #3*, 2001), a former police profiler in the Flash's burg of Keystone City, who was left a paraplegic after a confrontation with Gorilla Grodd. Morose over his disability, Zolomon jury-rigged Flash's time-travel apparatus, the Cosmic Treadmill, in a foolhardy attempt to trek to the past and prevent his injury, instead causing an accident that propelled him into a sped-up timeline that gave him superspeed but distorted his perspective of reality. The new Professor Zoom's nothing-to-lose vehemence makes him among the most dangerous of the Flash's Rogues.

What little Professor Zoom merchandising exists includes Pocket Super Hero and Heroclix mini-figurines. —*ME*

Rhino

The thick-skinned, thick-skulled Rhino first charged into the Marvel Universe in *The Amazing Spider-Man* #41 (1966), by writer Stan Lee and artist John Romita, Sr. This double-tusked terror unyieldingly stomps across the U.S.A. toward New York City. Cosseted from head to toe (except for his blunt-nosed face) in gray garb resembling a rhinoceros hide, the Rhino shrugs off bullets fired by flabbergasted law-enforcement agents and plows through stone barricades in his path. Arriving in Manhattan, he kidnaps astronaut John Jameson, son of *Daily Bugle* publisher J. Jonah Jameson, to ransom him to Eastern enemies hungry for space-race dominance. Spider-Man intervenes, and after scarcely dodging the Rhino's blows, defeats the lummox by fatiguing him. As the authorities remove the unconscious miscreant from the premises, Spider-Man ponders, "How are they gonna keep the Rhino in jail after they get him there?"

Not easily, as the next issue revealed when, after regaining consciousness, the Rhino smashed free of a corrections hospital—"Hah! How can anything halt the Rhino's charge?!!"—until taken down by tranquilizing gas. The Rhino

was running amok again in the next month's issue #43, in which readers discovered his origin. The Rhino was originally an unnamed, dim-witted thug-for-hire goaded by foreign agents into a perverse chemical/radiation experiment. After arduous months of treatments, this human guinea pig's strength and stamina were augmented, and he was outfitted with skin-tight armor forged of a near-impervious polymer. Envisioned by his handlers as "the perfect assassin! Brainless—obedient—invin-

Original cover artwork to *The Amazing Spider-Man* vol. 1 #41 ©1966 Marvel Comics. COVER ART BY JOHN ROMITA, SR. AND MIKE ESPOSITO.

cible," the Rhino scoffed at their plans and razed their laboratory, lumbering off as a free agent. In their rematch, Spider-Man was only able to stop the menacing man-mountain by adding an acidic compound to his web fluid that caused the Rhino's hide to melt from his body.

The Rhino received new armor from the very spies who had created him in *The Incredible Hulk* (*Hulk*) vol. 2 #104 (1968), his strength enhanced by gamma radiation and his retooled hide now made acid-resistant. After unsuccessfully butting heads with the Green Goliath, the Rhino was manipulated by the Hulk's gamma-irradiated foe the Leader, through whose machinations the Rhino's uniform was permanently bonded to his skin. He was eventually separated from his rhino-hide, after which time he commissioned a new suit from criminal industrialist Justin Hammer.

The Rhino's limited intelligence usually steers him toward singular goals—raise money for his Eastern European family, fund the removal of his suit, or vengefully trample Spider-Man. While a regular foe of both Spidey and the Hulk, over the years he has locked horns with Iron Man, Ka-Zar, the Thunderbolts, Deadpool, the Defenders, and She-Hulk, among others. Even neo-hero Gravity had a run-in with the Rhino in the second issue of his comic book (2005). A slightly modified version of the Rhino exists in the alternate reality of Marvel's *Ultimate Spider-Man* series.

Despite his massive weight of 700 pounds, the Rhino can stampede up to nearly 100 mph and is virtually tireless. He is difficult to incarcerate—he has been kept under constant sedation, locked up in the high-security Omega Block of the supervillain prison the Vault, and miniaturized in the paranormal penitentiary the Big House. After nearly thirty years of being known simply as "the Rhino," he was given an alter ego by writer Peter David in *Hulk* #435 (1995): Alex O'Hirn (his surname is an anagram of "Rhino"). The Rhino's intelligence was temporarily heightened in "Flowers for Rhino" in *Spider-Man's Tangled Web* #5–#6 (2001). He has fought Spider-Man in numerous animated-television and video-game appearances, with Ed McNamara, Dee Bradly Baker, and John DiMaggio among the actors portraying the Rhino; and he has been featured in numerous Spider-Man merchandising from board games to action figures. —*ME*

The Riddler

Riddle me this: what is the first appearance of the Prince of Puzzlers, the Riddler? The answer: *Detective Comics* #140 (1948), by writer Bill Finger and artist Dick Sprang.

In his Finger/Sprang origin, adolescent Edward Nigma—or E. Nigma—painstakingly studies the pieces of a jigsaw puzzle he later dishonestly pretends to have mastered as he cheats his way to a classroom puzzle-assembling victory, earning a reputation as an expert at solving challenges. As an adult, he parlays his obsession into a career as a sideshow attraction ("Match Wits with E. Nigma, the Puzzle King"). Bored by the carnival's "small pickings," he becomes the Riddler, in the question mark-studded, lime-green tights and purple domino mask recognized by millions, and plays head games with Gotham City's Batman through a series of Byzantine riddles forewarning of his impending crimes. Batman, himself a master of solving the unsolvable, and his ally Robin the Boy Wonder wade through the Riddler's crime clues and trap the lawbreaker at the end of his bomb-rigged maze on a waterfront pier. The Riddler presumably drowns, but a floating question mark left behind at the scene of his "demise" makes the Dynamic Duo wonder if this trickster might not return.

Two issues later, the Riddler was back with another chain of conundrums to confound the Caped Crusader, but after this tale, he did not stage another speedy comeback. It wasn't until *Batman* #171 (1965) that the Riddler was seen again, cackling his way back into print at a time early into Batman's "new look," a revitalization of the hero. In "Remarkable Ruse of the Riddler!" by writer Gardner Fox and artists Sheldon Moldoff and Joe Giella (all ghosting "as" Bob Kane, due to DC Comics' contractual agreement with Kane, Batman's credited creator), E. Nigma had spent his jail sentence strategizing a rematch with Batman. Nigma pretended to have reformed to help the Dynamic Duo corral their current crime headache, the Molehill Mob, simply so he could have Bat-

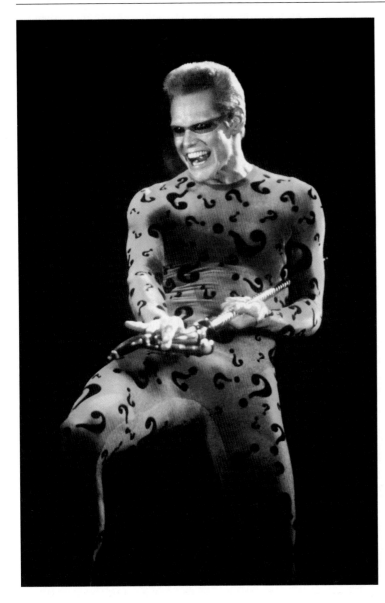

Jim Carrey as the Riddler in *Batman Forever* (1995).

the reader to witness Batman's intellect in action. The Riddler's puzzles were two-tiered, an easier initial answer hinting at a more complex meaning that connected the clue to the crime.

On January 12 and 13, 1966, ABC's live-action *Batman* (1966–1968), the twice-weekly adventure-fest starring Adam West and Burt Ward as the Dynamic Duo, premiered with a loose adaptation of "Remarkable Ruse of the Riddler!" as the two-part "Hi Diddle Riddle" and "Smack in the Middle." A much-told tale in comic-book circles contends that television producer William Dozier conceived the idea for the *Batman* show after unexpectedly spying a copy of *Batman* #171 while on an airplane, but in his book *Batman: The Complete History* (1999), author Les Daniels debunked that myth, writing that Dozier recalled that his in-flight reading of the issue transpired "because ABC had already acquired the rights to the character." While it may not have inspired the TV show, *Batman* #171's importance in comics history as the reintroduction of the Riddler into the Silver Age (1956–1969) was saluted in 2005 by DC Direct's release of a "1st Appearance" action figure of the Riddler, complete with a miniature reprint of *Batman* #171.

man's full attention for his own capers. And thus the gray-matter struggles resumed, with the Riddler frequently reappearing.

At face value the King of Conundrums seemed a negligible threat—his obsessive compulsiveness provided more cerebral than physical challenges for Batman. But given the Caped Crusader's crime-solving roots—he *did* originate in *Detective Comics*, after all—the Riddler's puzzles allowed

Impressionist Frank Gorshin, a former Vegas headliner with a smattering of TV guest credits, sprung to instant stardom in an unrestrained portrayal of the Riddler fondly remembered for the actor's infectious but dangerous chortle. "I developed the Riddler's fiendish laugh at Hollywood parties," Gorshin revealed in a May 1, 1966, *New*

York Times interview. "I came to realize that it wasn't so much how I laughed as what I laughed at that created a sense of menace." Gorshin, in both a simplified version of the comics' Riddler unitard and a question mark–pocked green jacket and bowler, reprised the role in numerous episodes (often aided by costumed henchmen) and in the 1966 *Batman* theatrical movie. John Astin, aka Gomez of TV's *The Addams Family*, took an infamous turn as the Riddler in a February 1967 *Batman* two-parter when Gorshin was unavailable; Gorshin had so defined the role that audiences rejected the talented but miscast Astin, leading producers to coerce Gorshin back for a single third-season episode. (Gorshin also appeared in the 2003 Batman reunion TV movie, *Return to the Batcave: The Misadventures of Adam and Burt*.)

Once *Batman* went off the air in 1968, the Riddler maintained a mass-market presence for a dozen years predicated upon his Gorshin-generated clout, on TV cartoons (*The Batman/Superman Hour*, 1968–1969, and as one of the Legion of Doom on *Challenge of the Super Friends*, 1978–1979), 7-11 Slurpee cups, Mego action figures, even sew-on clothing patches. As Batman's comic-book mythology grew grimmer and more gothic throughout the 1970s and 1980s, however, the Prince of Puzzlers seemed too cheery, and perhaps too goofy, a fixture for more than occasional token romps.

After a lighthearted Neil Gaiman/Bernie Mireault retelling of Nigma's roots in *Secret Origins Special* #1 (1989), various DC Comics writers began adapting the analytical Riddler into the graphic, noir-ish Gotham City of the 1990s and 2000s, although in earlier stories, Nigma himself lamented how gruesome his once-bright reality had become. His puzzle-generating modus operandi has remained intact, but his intellect usually steers him from violent exchanges; to navigate Gotham's tough streets, he often dispatches uniformed goons—sporting variations of his own question-marked tights—to handle the rough stuff, with female agents named Query and Echo offering a nod to the 1960s TV *Batman* days.

Writer Jeph Loeb and artist Jim Lee employed the Riddler as a central figure in their popular "Hush" *Batman* storyline in 2003–2004. Nigma, having deduced the answer to the ultimate riddle—"Who is

Batman?"—used his knowledge of the Dark Knight's Bruce Wayne identity to attempt to eliminate his foe. He failed, but maintains Batman's secret, concocting his next puzzle from his Arkham Asylum cell.

Jim Carrey's exaggerated, Gorshin-channeling performance as the Riddler in director Joel Schumacher's movie *Batman Forever* (1995) attracted huge box office (Robin Williams was rumored to have been offered the role before Carrey); scads of merchandising with neon-green question marks accompanied the film's release. The Riddler has also appeared in *Batman: The Animated Series* (1992–1995) and its continuations throughout the 1990s, voiced by John Glover; and in *The Batman* (2004–present), in which he was given a new, rock star–like look and played by Robert Englund. —ME

The Ringmaster and the Circus of Crime

Maynard Tiboldt—aka the grandstanding Ringmaster—really knows how to mesmerize an audience. Stepping into the arena in *The Incredible Hulk* vol. 1 #3 (1962), courtesy of Marvel Comics' own ringmasters, writer Stan Lee and artist Jack Kirby, Tiboldt wears a top hat that sends out psionic waves (drawn as concentric circles for the reader's benefit) that allow him to control minds. As the Ringmaster, he fronts a traveling circus whose performers—including the pick-pocketing Clown, the sticky-fingered Teena the Fat Lady, the safe-hoisting strongman Bruto, and cat-burglar acrobats the Great Gambinos (Gambonnos in later texts)—steal from spellbound carnival-goers. Tiboldt entrances the Incredible Hulk, passing him off as a crowd-luring attraction, until the arrival of the Hulk's teenage sidekick Rick Jones breaks the Ringmaster's spell.

It's unlikely that many of the readers who plunked down their 12 cents for that *Hulk* comic knew that the Ringmaster was actually a second-generation supervillain. Two decades earlier, Kirby, with his partner Joe Simon, introduced "The Ringmaster of Death" in *Captain America Comics* #5

(1941). Austrian Fritz Tiboldt starred in Tiboldt's Circus, a group of Nazi sympathizers using performances in America to masquerade their espionage, which included political assassinations. After Captain America pulled the curtain on their act, Fritz and his wife were murdered by obdurate Nazis. Their son Maynard modified his father's hypnotic apparatus, the "nullatron," a weapon developed by German scientists, and adapted it to his hat to become the Ringmaster of Crime.

The Ringmaster and the Circus of Crime (with a streamlined membership) returned in *The Amazing Spider-Man* vol. 1 #16, up to its old tricks; Spidey fell under Tiboldt's enchantment, but the blind superhero Daredevil, immune to the Ringmaster's optically induced mind control, sent the Circus packing their tents. In later appearances, the Circus booted out the Ringmaster, branding him a bungler, with the caustic Clown taking charge (and the group calling itself the Masters of Menace), but Tiboldt later resumed leadership. The Circus of Crime's roster has included the Human Cannonball, Princess Python, Blackwing, Ulik, and Live Wire. The team's basic premise—a carnival with a criminal ulterior motive, with the Ringmaster in the center ring—has been adapted to animation in a "Hulk" episode of *The Marvel Super-Heroes* (1966), on *The Amazing Spider-Man* (1981–1982), and on *The Avengers* (1999–2000).

As carnivals faded from mass popularity in the late twentieth century, the Crime Circus came to town with diminishing frequency. The Ringmaster has fared better as a solo villain: after a hiatus in the early 2000s he returned, jockeying to salvage his rep, in the "Ring of the Master" storyline in *Marvel Team-Up* vol. 3 #7–#10 (2005), and will no doubt continue his flamboyant brand of mind control ... until the fat lady sings. —*ME*

Robotic Supervillains

Reflecting both the anxieties of the nuclear age and fears of Soviet Communism, the robot-as-conquering-menace proliferated in the print, film, and television media of the post–World War II era. Jack Williamson's classic story "With Folded

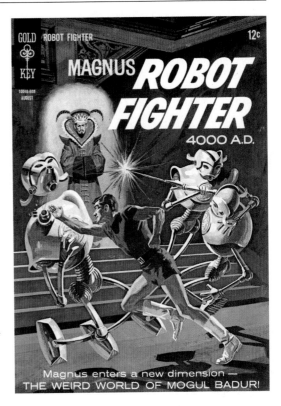

Magnus Robot Fighter vol. 1 #15 ©1966 Gold Key Comics. COVER ART BY RUSS MANNING.

Hands" is a seminal example, portraying a human race tranquilized into sedentary helplessness by their industrious, overprotective robot slaves-cum-caretakers. Throughout the 1950s, robots are often portrayed as fearsome killers or as laughably over-the-top threats in such campy films as *Robot Monster* (1953), in which an actor in a gorilla suit topped with an antennae-festooned diving helmet tries to carry off a human woman. Even Gort (Lock Martin), the giant, gleaming robotic servant of the alien Klaatu (Michael Rennie) in Robert Wise's landmark film *The Day the Earth Stood Still* (1951) qualifies for villain status by threatening Earth with annihilation unless humanity abandons its warlike ways.

Robot villains abounded in the comics of the 1950s and 1960s. The team of robot heroes called the Metal Men (created by writer and editor Robert Kanigher and illustrators Ross Andru and Mike Esposito for DC's *Showcase* #37, 1962) faced its own cadre of cybernetic scoundrels, including a group whose members, like the Metal Men themselves, embodied the chemical properties of particular metallic elements (the Metal Men, whose powers, appearance, and names were based on iron, gold, lead, tin, mercury, and platinum went up against robotic villains crafted from aluminum, barium, calcium, zirconium, sodium, and plutonium). Far from being indicators of pop culture technophobia, these robotic villains—and the Metal Men themselves—existed mainly to deliver chemistry lessons to DC's young readership.

While the Metal Men were built by a scientist named Will Magnus, another Magnus engaged in mortal combat against an endless array of killer automata: Gold Key Comics' *Magnus, Robot Fighter, 4000 AD* (1963–1977), whose title character protected the futuristic city of North Am from marauding automata. The creation of writer/artist Russ Manning, Magnus was trained from childhood by the benevolent Robot 1A, who honed Magnus' martial abilities until he could take on any robot barehanded, and equipped him with implanted robot eavesdropping devices. Resurrected by Valiant/Acclaim (*Magnus, Robot Fighter* #1, 1992), Magnus faced grittier mechanical menaces than Manning's, including vampire-like robots that fed on human life-energy.

Since human comic-book villains have been known occasionally to "go straight," it is unsurprising that "evil robots" also occasionally cross the aisle to become superheroes. While the 1960s incarnations of DC's Red Tornado and Marvel's Vision began their four-color careers as nemeses, respectively, of the Justice League of America and the Avengers, both weathered existential crises that resulted in their joining their former foes (*Justice League of America* #64, 1968; *Avengers* vol. 1 #57–#58, 1968).

Like the comics, the toy industry has made a number of significant contributions to the annals of robotic villainy. Among these are the Decepticons, created in the 1980s as foils for the Transformers, a line of Japanese-style robot toys that can be reconfigured with a few Rubik's Cube–style moves into various cars and trucks; the evil Decepticons, created purely to wage war against the good Autobot Transformers of the planet Cybertron, subsequently made their way onto the pages of comic books published

by Marvel (1984–1991), Blackthorne (1987–1988), and Dreamwave (2002–2004). Lego has introduced a successful line of robots known as Bionicle, whose perpetually clashing villains and heroes come not only with intricate back stories rife with internecine mechanical conflicts, and have also generated collectible card games, CDs, comics, a video game, and three popular animated DVD features: *Bionicle: Mask of Light* (2003), *Bionicle 2: Legends of Metru Nui* (2004), and *Bionicle 3: Web of Shadows* (2005).

As literary science fiction became increasingly sophisticated in the 1960s and 1970s, so-called "killer robots" migrated steadily into film and television. Being creations of the mass media, many of these robot stories naturally dealt with the evergreen working-class anxiety over advancing mechanization, as the implacably murder-minded, wheeled tin-can Dalek armies of the BBC's *Doctor Who* (1963–1996) and the conquest-bent, techno-organic drones of the Borg Collective demonstrate (*Star Trek: The Next Generation*, 1987–1994; *Star Trek: First Contact*, 1996). The original *Star Trek* television series (1966–1969) pitted the crew of the *Enterprise* against robot adversaries on several occasions as well, including: Dr. Roger Korby, who made a failed attempt to replace Captain James Kirk, as well as other influential humans, with android duplicates (in the episode titled "What Are Little Girls Made Of?"); the planet-destroying space probe known as Nomad, which Kirk persuaded to commit suicide ("The Changeling"); an automated, solar-system-devouring berserker weapon built eons ago by aliens ("The Doomsday Machine"); and a multitude of Jack Williamson–esque androids whose attempt to conquer humanity through kindness fails in the face of Captain Kirk's deliberately orchestrated operetta of android-slaying illogic ("I, Mudd"). Even the kindly Lieutenant Commander Data of *Star Trek: The Next Generation* had a dark opposite number—his android "brother" Lore, an earlier creation of Dr. Noonien Soong who routinely violated Asimov's Laws and had to be deactivated because of his paranoia and aggression ("Datalore"; "Brothers"; and "Descent, Parts I and II").

ABC's *The Six Million Dollar Man* (1973–1978) featured android assassins intended to pass themselves off either as the title character (the superstrong bionic hero Col. Steve Austin, played by Lee

Majors) or as various supporting cast members or guest stars. These implacable killers (dubbed collectively as "Maskatron" by the show's action-figure licensees) were all but indistinguishable from their human templates until their lifelike face-masks were dislodged, revealing the blinking, inhuman circuitry that lay beneath the skin. Col. Austin also faced numerous "Fembots"—female android killers—as did the campy 1960s-era British superspy Austin D. Powers (*Austin Powers: International Man of Mystery*, 1997), who not only was tricked into marrying a Fembot, but also nearly succumbed to the lethal effects of her "machine-gun jubblies" (breast-mounted automatic weaponry) in *Austin Powers: The Spy Who Shagged Me* (1999). The androids of *Westworld* (1973) and its film and television sequels—such as the kill-crazed android cowboy gunfighter portrayed by the steely-eyed Yul Brynner—are cut from far more frightening cloth; these amusements turned assassins anticipated the self-emancipating, human-exterminating robots as seen in the *Terminator* film franchise, and on television's *Battlestar Galactica* (1978–1979) and its spin-offs, including the Sci-Fi Channel's *Galactica* reboot (2003–present).

The android-as-antagonist received an ambiguous, discomfiting veneer of humanity in Philip K. Dick's novel *Do Androids Dream of Electric Sheep?* (1968) and its film adaptation, Ridley Scott's *Blade Runner* (1982). Though the two works differed in many respects, both focused on the sometimes blurry line between humans and robots (or "replicants"), making the story's murderous android bad guy Roy Batty (played by Rutger Hauer) arguably at least as sympathetic as the former policeman Rick Deckard (Harrison Ford) who was tasked with assassinating ("retiring") him.

The historic ambivalence with which storytellers treat the ethical capabilities of robots continues to this day. The servile humanoid robots from the film version of Isaac Asimov's *I, Robot* (2004) are constrained by Asimov's famous Laws that prevent robots from harming humans—until the sentient computer that governs robot design and manufacture (V.I.K.I., the Virtual Interactive Kinetic Intelligence) decides to set a horde of robots free of their behavioral constraints, enabling a robot named

Sonny (Alan Tudyk) to make a moral decision that might save the human race from cybernetic anarchy. By contrast, *Star Wars Episode III: Revenge of the Sith* (2005) shows Obi-Wan Kenobi (Ewan McGregor) slaying the aggressive cyborg General Grievous, who is presented as a thoroughgoing villain despite his many doubtless legitimate grievances against the treatment of his fellow droids by the Galactic Republic. Like the often deceptive boundary between mankind and her technological offspring, the line between heroism and villainy can be as difficult to see among robots as it is among humans. —*MAM*

Rodak

"From the far reaches of outer space … comes a threat to planet Earth!"—Rodak, an alien conqueror who covets the third rock from the sun, "the most beautiful of all planets," but who bafflingly dispatches a legion of monsters (actors in rubber suits) to lay waste to it.

Rodak was the recurring nemesis on *Ambassador Magma*, a low-budget, live-action *Mighty Morphin' Power Rangers* forerunner produced in Japan from 1966–1967. Poorly  dubbed into English in 1972 as *Space Avenger*, by the late 1970s the half-hour program was syndicated internationally as *Space Giants* and gobbled up by "Superstation" TBS mogul Ted Turner during the infancy of 24-hour cable-television networks. TBS aired *Space Giants* on weekday afternoons during the late 1970s and early

Rodak. From *The Space Giants* #1 ©1993 Pat Gabriele.
ART BY PAT GABRIELE AND JEFF NEWMAN

1980s to an entranced audience of eager-eyed children, sci-fi buffs, and stoners glued to afternoon TV.

The "Giants" were a family of transforming super-robots (Goldar, Silvar, and Gam the Rocket Boy) residing in a volcano, brought to Earth by a wizard to repel Rodak's invasion. Hovering over the planet in a domed, bat-shaped spaceship, Rodak was served by a loyal army of Lugo Men, black-cloaked emissaries who oozed into oatmeal-like goo whenever blasted by the forces of good. Foaming with disdain for Earth's denizens ("You Earthlings are so stupid, you can't even cure the common cold!"), Rodak's glittery mask, not unlike a giant Mardi Gras head, bore only one expression, a constant grimace, and his bowl-cut hair and droopy fangs elicited chuckles. While *Space Giants* has not been aired domestically in decades, Rodak and company appeared in original American comic books in 1979 and 1993. —*ME*

The Royal Flush Gang

E ach time the players of the card-garbed Royal Flush Gang change hands, the Justice League can bet on raw deal. First seen in *Justice League of America* #43 (1966), the King of Clubs, Queen of Clubs, Jack of Clubs, and Ten of Clubs are costumed crooks gathered under the leadership of the Ace of Clubs, actually Professor Amos Fortune, a foe of the JLA. Using Fortune's astrological power of "stellaration" to negatively influence the League's luck, this Royal Flush Gang nearly trumps the heroes until JLA mascot Snapper Carr rushes to their aid as a jester-clad "Joker," helping them shuffle free of the Gang's control.

When next seen in issue #54 (1967), the Gang plied bizarre superpowers afforded by newly acquired historical costumes; they later traded Clubs for Spades as their vestmental suit. Ever-evolving rosters of the Royal Flush Gang—each with playing card–inspired weaponry such as explosive Spades and disorienting Diamonds—have appeared over the years, at various times working under the orchestration of Hector Hammond and the Gambler, fighting the Justice League, the Teen Titans, and other heroes. In *Superman: The Man of Steel* #21 (2002), the Royal Flush Gang expanded into a network of 52 operatives.

The Royal Flush Gang has been a favorite of television animators, with different incarnations of the team appearing on *Super Powers Team: Galactic Guardians* (1986–1987), *Batman Beyond* (1999–2001), and *Justice League* (2001–2004). In comics and on TV, the Gang has worked with and against the Clown Prince of Crime, the Joker. —*ME*

Sabretooth

Wolverine's archenemy Sabretooth first appeared not in Marvel Comics' *X-Men* but in *Iron Fist* #14 (1977), battling the title character, a martial-arts superhero. But Sabretooth's creators, writer Chris Claremont and artist John Byrne, already had his *X-Men* connection in mind. Sabretooth looks like a bigger, even more ferocious version of Wolverine, but with blond hair. In contrast with Wolverine's claws that emerge from the back of his hands, Sabretooth's fingernails are like razor-sharp talons. Sabretooth proved to have the same mutant powers as Wolverine, including superhumanly acute senses and a "fast healing" ability that enables him to recover with superhuman quickness from virtually any injury. Though they never made it explicit in a story, in a 2004 interview for *BACK ISSUE* magazine Byrne and Claremont stated that they intended Sabretooth to be Wolverine's father; however, the *Wolverine: Origin* series (2001–2002) seems to disprove this.

Nevertheless, Wolverine and Sabretooth have a long-standing personal enmity, which seems appropriate for two characters that are simultaneously so much alike and so very different. Each of them has a bestial side to his psyche, capable of berserker madness and savage violence. But, as Claremont has stated in interviews, Wolverine aspires to humanity and self-control, whereas Sabretooth has abandoned his humanity to surrender to the beast within himself. In 2004 Claremont told *BACK ISSUE*, "The difference between him [Wolverine, aka Logan] and Sabretooth is that Logan is governed by a moral center and Sabretooth is not. Sabretooth is a creature solely and completely of appetite: he wants something, he takes it. There's no regret, no redemption, no mercy, no nothing. It is a total amorality, almost animal amorality." Wolverine and Sabretooth see within each other that which each despises about himself.

Sabretooth's healing ability also greatly slows his aging so, like Wolverine, he may be over a century old. Sabretooth's real name appears to be Victor Creed. Even as a child he possessed fang-like teeth and claws. Sabretooth recalls being locked in a basement by his father, who considered him a "freak."

In the 1960s Creed, code-named Sabretooth, was a Central Intelligence Agency (CIA) special operative partnered with Logan, alias Wolverine. It was in this period that Creed had a sexual liaison with the German spy Leni Zauber, who was actually the mutant Mystique. (Their son was Graydon Creed, the anti-mutant politician, now deceased.) Sometime later, the CIA's Weapon X program altered Victor Creed's memories in an attempt to turn him into a "super-soldier."

Sabretooth first clashed with the X-Men when, as a member of the Marauders, he helped carry out the massacre of the Morlocks, an underground community of mutants. He continually battles Wolverine, both with and without the latter's X-Men allies.

Once, the X-Men's founder, Charles Xavier, held Sabretooth prisoner, seeking in vain to cure his madness. The U.S. government forcibly inducted Sabretooth into its official team of mutant operatives, X-Factor, but he rebelled and escaped.

Subsequently, Sabretooth's skeleton was laced with molecules of adamantium, a (fictional) nearly indestructible steel alloy, just as Wolverine's was. The mutant Apocalypse drew the adamantium out of Sabretooth's body. However, the revived Weapon X project captured Sabretooth and again bonded adamantium to his skeleton, making it virtually unbreakable.

In addition to appearing in *X-Men: The Animated Series* (1992–1997) and the animated TV series *X-Men: Evolution* (2000–2003) Sabretooth appeared in the first *X-Men* movie (2000) as a member of Magneto's mutant Brotherhood, and was played by former wrestler Tyler Mane. With the merchandising might of the X-Men, Sabretooth has appeared in three-dimensional form as action figures and collectible mini-busts. —PS

Sandman

It was no day at the beach for Marvel Comics' wise-cracking web-slinger when the shapeshifting Sandman sludged into *The Amazing Spider-Man* vol. 1 #4 (1963). Career hoodlum William Baker, aka Flint Marko, is on the lam after escaping from an island prison, swearing "never to be recaptured alive." Baker ducks a dragnet by hiding out in an off-limits coastal nuclear-testing facility, and one surprise atomic reaction later, his irradiated body coalesces with beach sand. He becomes a living Sandman, able to reconstruct his body from a glissading stream of granules to a torrent of quicksand to granite-hard weapons. Spider-Man finds Sandman hard to hold until he outsmarts the supervillain by vacuuming him while in his "sand-grain form." This classic Spidey adventure, written by Stan Lee and rendered by Steve Ditko, was adapted to animated television as the "Sands of Crime" episode of ABC's animated *Spider-Man*

(1967–1970), with Tom Harvey offering his gravelly voice as the Sandman.

Stan Lee was taken with the Sandman's pliable powers and made him one of the Marvel Universe's all-purpose supervillains, sliding the reprobate from one superhero's series to another. Four months after his debut, Sandman tried to douse the Human Torch in *Strange Tales* #115 (1963) before making two 1964 return bouts with Spidey, including his co-founding of the Sinister Six (with Dr. Octopus, Mysterio, Kraven, Electro, and the Vulture). He signed up with another supervillain team in 1965—the Frightful Four—joining the Wizard, the Trapster (formerly Paste-Pot Pete), and the soon-to-be-reformed Medusa to tackle the Fantastic Four, in whose series he stuck around for regular encounters (including a foolhardy federation with the Negative Zone outcast Blastaar the Living-Bomb in 1967). Sandman also nearly overpowered the Incredible Hulk in 1969.

After Lee left the day-to-day writer/editor grind in the 1970s for Marvel executive and Hollywood duties, Sandman blew into other writers' hands, who for decades have dusted off the shapeshifter for routine routs against Spider-Man and the Fantastic Four.

The Sandman shifted sides in the early 1990s, briefly reforming and fighting crime with Silver Sable and the Wild Pack, as well as the Avengers, but a device created by his ex–Frightful Four partner the Wizard rekindled Sandman's villainy. In 2000 Sandman was bitten by Spider-rogue Venom, provoking a biochemical reaction that caused his body to break apart, but he has since reconstructed his sandy form and his position as one of Marvel's most dangerous desperadoes.

An alternate version of the Sandman exists in Marvel's *Ultimate Spider-Man* series, an out-of-traditional-continuity comic that started in 2001, which spun off an *Ultimate Six* miniseries (a Sinister Six reworking) in 2003–2004 with Sandman in the team's roster.

In addition to his 1967 television appearance, Sandman was featured in the animated cartoons *The New Fantastic Four* (1978–1979), *Spider-Man and His Amazing Friends* (1981–1986), and *Spider-Man* (1981–1987). Once actor Thomas Haden Church was tapped in early 2005 to play an unspecified villain in *Spider-Man 3*, Sandman was one of the rumored candidates, as was the Chameleon; Church's role of Sandman was confirmed in the fall of 2005. Toy Biz has produced Sandman action figures in the 1990s and 2000s. —*ME*

Santa Claus as a Supervillain

He sees you when you're sleeping. He knows when you're awake.

Thank goodness Santa Claus is on our side!

Or *is* he? The jolly, jumbo gift-giver has occasionally been portrayed as naughty, not nice, by writers, artists, and filmmakers. Casting aspersions upon Santa's character is his long list of aliases, Saint Nicholas, St. Nick, Kris Kringle, Father Christmas, and Papá Noel among them. Perhaps we should ask ourselves, *Is Santa Claus sliding down our chimney a welcomed sight?*

DC Comics' Star-Spangled Kid and Stripesy were puzzled by the "Mystery of the Santa Claus Pirate!" in *Leading Comics* #2 (1942). Sailing the seven seas in a skull-and-crossboned galleon, the Santa Claus Pirate was actually corpulent sea-thief Captain Bigg in disguise, tricking pleasure cruisers into lowering their guards so that he and his band of cutthroats could steal from them.

Writer Denny O'Neil and penciler Frank Miller's "Wanted: Santa Claus, Dead or Alive!" from *DC Special Series* #21 (1980) was future *Dark Knight* auteur Miller's first Batman story. Boomer Katz was its Santa, a second-story-man struggling to go straight as a department-store St. Nick, until coerced by two former crime associates into robbing his employer. Marvel Comics' *Spectacular Spider-Man* vol. 1 #112 (1986) concerned a shopping-mall Santa who used his disguise to trick innocent children into letting him into their homes, which he would burglarize. Billy Bob Thornton ran a similar con as the hard-boozing, sexually promiscuous *Bad Santa* in director Terry Zwigoff's irreverent 2003 film, and Ben Affleck played a hapless ex-con suckered into a casino heist with Santa-disguised robbers in the action movie *Reindeer Games* (2000).

The supervillain Multiple Santa was created when a crook on the lam ducked the law by masquerading as Kris Kringle; an electrical jolt allowed him to replicate into Santa-clones, creating a nightmare for the Tick and his sidekick Arthur in a 1995 episode of the animated series *The Tick* (1994–1997). Stanley Ipkiss' ancient faceplate fell into the hands of his banker friend Charlie Schumacher, who commercialized Christmas as the Santa-garbed "Ma$k" in the Dark Horse comic *Adventures of the Mask* #11 (1996).

Devilish stand-in Santas are a common theme. Horror novelist Dean Koontz's 1996 children's book *Santa's Twin* featured Santa's errant sibling Bob Claus stealing his brother's sleigh and delivering mud pies and cat feces to unsuspecting kiddies. Director Tim Burton's animated holiday film *The Nightmare Before Christmas* (1993) starred pumpkin king Jack Skellington holding Santa hostage and usurping his identity. The sourpuss Grinch ("whose heart is two sizes too small"), as a bogus Santa, tried to rob the happy people of Whoville of their holiday in Dr. Seuss' 1957 classic story *How the Grinch Stole Christmas!* (immortalized in animation in 1966 and as a live-action movie in 2000). None of Santa's doppelgängers was more insidious than the Anti-Claus, from Marvel's offbeat omnibus *Bizarre Adventures* #34 (1983). The Anti-Claus stormed into the North Pole in a skull-embossed sleigh pulled by warthogs and killed Santa, paving the way for the Son of Santa to take over.

At times Santa Claus has been cast in the role of brawler. *Incredible Hulk* vol. 2 #378 (1991) featured the thick-skinned supervillain the Rhino dressed as Kris Kringle, going head-to-head with the Hulk. DC's Lobo was hired by the Easter Bunny to off St. Nick in the ultra-gory, Santa-versus-Lobo clash *The Lobo Paramilitary Christmas Special* (1991); this one-shot was translated to celluloid in a 2002 fan film. Maximum Press' *Santa the Barbarian* #1 (1996) featured St. Nick with an attitude, riled over the growing number of naughty kids.

Nothing slaughtered St. Nick's reputation more than the low-budget slasher flicks *Christmas Evil*, aka *You Better Watch Out* (1980), and *Silent Night, Deadly Night* (1984), each with ax-wielding psychos in Santa suits chopping up victims (the latter film

Adventures of the Mask #11 ©1996 Dark Horse Comics.
COVER ART BY MARC CAMPOS.

became a franchise of five movies). Not to be out-done, artist Bill Sienkiewicz illustrated the eerie cover to *Batman* #596 (2001), depicting a hatchet-hoisting Santa sneaking up on the crouching Caped Crusader; this was the serial killer Santa Klaus, who appeared in the DC Comics crossover *Joker: Last Laugh.* Continuing this tradition is the demon-as-Santa horror/comedy film *Santa's Slay* (2005).

Fortunately for those with visions of sugar plums dancing in their heads, most pop-culture portrayals of Santa Claus are kind, and at times, heroic. They can even be *super*heroic: Santa assisted the title star of *Nick Fury, Agent of S.H.I.E.L.D.* vol. 1 #10 (1969) in thwarting the Hate-Monger's plan to nuke New York City, teamed up with Superman to bag the Toyman in *DC Comics Presents* #67 (1984), and even saved the entire world in the 1964 movie, *Santa Claus Conquers the Martians! —ME*

Satana

Both villainess and heroine, Satana Hellstrom is the daughter of a human woman and a demon called Marduk Kurios, who posed as the biblical Satan. She is the sister of Daimon Hellstrom, the occult-based Marvel Comics superhero best known as the Son of Satan. Created by writer Roy Thomas and artist John Romita, Sr., Satana made her debut in Marvel's black-and-white comics maga-zine *Vampire Tales* #2 (1973).

Satana's father turned her into a succubus who requires the draining of male souls to survive. In order to access them, she usually kisses her victim as she draws forth his soul, causing his body to shrivel. The soul then takes the form of a butterfly-like being, which she promptly crushes with her fingers, thereby absorbing its psionic energy. After she feeds on this soul power, the spirit is cast down into her father's realm of hell. Satana's other powers include levitation and superhuman strength. She can cast magical spells and project bolts of "soulfire," which do not physi-cally burn but cause pain to a victim's life-force.

Marduk Kurios also bonded Satana to an immensely powerful demon called the Basilisk. Satana could release the Basilisk from her body to do her bidding, but her control over it lessened each time she did so.

When Satana refused to consume the soul of a former priest who had once saved her life, Mar-duk Kurios became her enemy and banished her from the hell dimension he ruled. Satana came to value her friendships with humans and became a leading foe of the N'garai, an ancient demonic race that sought to conquer humankind.

When the soul of Earth's sorcerer supreme, Dr. Strange, was captured by demons, Satana went to his rescue. Satana saved Strange's soul, but a demon used a mystical weapon to mortally wound her. The Basilisk then turned on her, but it perished when she died in *Marvel Team-Up* vol. 1 #81 (1979).

In *Hellstorm* #8 (1993), a series starring Satana's brother Daimon, a minister named Rev-erend Joshua Crow resurrected Satana, who consumed his soul. A villainess once more, she began preying on other men to gain enough power to take over hell, but this scheme came to nothing.

In the *Witches* miniseries (2004), Dr. Strange brought Satana back to Earth to team up with the sorceress Jennifer Kale and the empath Topaz against a menace called the Hellphyr. Satana discovered that her father was behind the threat, and Marduk Kurios offered to let Satana rule his hell dimension alongside him. But Satana refused her father's offer and aided Kale and Topaz in destroying the Hellphyr. With her demonic heritage, however, a path of permanent benevolence for Satana is, at best, dubious. —PS

Saturday-Morning Supervillains

In the era before 24/7 cable television and on-demand videos and DVDs—the 1950s through the 1970s—Saturday morning was a magical time when kids ruled the airwaves. Aside from tantalizing commercials for sugar-coated cereals and the newest toy that *must* be added to every child's Christmas wish list, only one thing disrupted the lives of TV's beloved animated heroes: supervillains. This criminal ilk attacked indiscriminately— whether you were a superhero, a wacky racer, or a moose or a squirrel, you'd never know when a bad guy would show up!

A popular cartoon supervillain archetype was rooted in, of all places, *Uncle Tom's Cabin*, abolitionist author Harriet Beecher Stowe's 1852 novel that introduced readers to the abusive slave owner Simon Legree. From Legree sprung an archetype of patently corrupt villains, often clad in black capes, that snarled onto screen in the silent films of the early twentieth century, chewing scenery in wildly exaggerated performances to clearly convey evil to a then-naive viewing audience. Snidley Whiplash, arch-foe of the befuddled Royal Canadian Mountie Dudley Do-Right (a staple of 1960s and early 1970s TV), best exemplifies this type of villain, with his handlebar mustache, ebon top hat, and propensity for tying the kidnap-prone Nell Fenwick to railroad tracks. Whiplash, wonderfully but sinis-

terly voiced by Hans Conried in animation, was brought to life in the live-action comedy *Dudley Do-Right* (1999) by none other than Alfred Molina, whose better-known supervillain movie role was Dr. Octopus in *Spider-Man 2* (2004).

Paul Winchell was the voice of the similarly nasty Dick Dastardly, an inept, Wile E. Coyote–inspired troublemaker whose machinations always went awry, much to the amusement of his snickering canine sidekick Muttley (Don Messick). Dastardly was first seen in 1968 in Hanna-Barbera's *Wacky Races*, which earned him a 1969 spin-off, *Dastardly and Muttley in Their Flying Machines*. Dastardly is not to be confused with the money-grabbing Sylvester Sneekly, aka the Hooded Claw, from a second *Wacky Races* spin-off, 1969's *The Perils of Penelope Pitstop*. Sneekly/Claw was performed by Paul Lynde, who declined a screen credit reportedly due to his belief that TV toons were beneath him. Other dark and diabolical cartoon criminals in this vein are long-time cartoon favorite Mighty Mouse's enemy Oil Can Harry, and Dishonest John, who roiled the waters for Beany and Cecil the Seasick Sea Serpent in their 1960s show. An old-style brute whose infamy has achieved supervillain status is the bully Bluto, sometimes called Brutus, arch-enemy of Popeye the Sailor Man (who has also been bothered by the sorceress Sea Hag).

And could any black-clad cold-war spies be more devious than Boris Badenov and Natasha Fatale? The brainchildren of animator Jay Ward (who also created Dudley Do-Right and several other eccentric cartoons), the pint-sized Boris and his slinky accomplice Natasha, hailing from the spiteful nation of Pottsylvania, were dispatched by their Fearless Leader on democracy-busting missions in the U.S. Luckily, their plans were always thwarted by offbeat heroes Rocket J. Squirrel, aka Rocky the flying squirrel, and his dopey friend Bullwinkle J. Moose. Ward's characters premiered in 1959 in the syndicated *Rocky and His Friends* before segueing to network TV with Bullwinkle usurping the show's title for a lengthy run, through 1973. The thick-accented Boris and Natasha were voiced by Paul Frees and June Foray (Foray was also the voice of Rocky), and were twice adapted to the live-action screen: Dave Thomas and Sally Kellerman played the pair in *Boris and Natasha* (1992), as did Jason Alexander and Rene Russo in *The Adventures of Rocky and Bullwinkle* (2000, which also featured Robert DeNiro as Fearless Leader).

Mad scientists, the reliable villainous archetype from early movies, pulp magazines, and comic books, migrated to Saturday-morning TV in huge numbers. Felix the Cat ("the wonderful, wonderful cat," beginning a long syndicated run in 1960) held tight his magic bag of tricks, as it was coveted by the bushy-mustached mastermind called the Professor, whose bulldog lackey Rock Bottom could be relied upon for muscle. Simon Bar Sinister was the evil genius who was the bane of the existence of Underdog in the floppy-eared superhero's 1964–1973 series. Allen Swift played Bar Sinister, master of dangerous superweapons like the shrinking ray (a favorite of mad scientists), who announced his attacks by uttering, "Simon Says." Swift also voiced Underdog's other major adversary, canine crime boss Riff Raff. A summer 2005 announcement that Walt Disney Pictures and Spyglass Entertainment would bring Underdog to the big screen in 2007 in a live-action movie, starring a CGI-enhanced *real* dog, bodes well for Simon Bar Sinister making his movie debut.

No mad scientist is madder than Lex Luthor, Superman's most persistent enemy, who was a regular nemesis in episodes of Filmation's *The New Adventures of Superman*, which started on CBS in 1966 and endured several seasons and two title changes. Joining Luthor on TV were comic-book transplants Brainiac, Toyman, Mr. Mxyzptlk, the Parasite, and the Prankster, as well as all-new (but uninspired) villains created for the series like Merlin, the Sorcerer, the Warlock, Satana and her Plasto-men, the fire-breathing Robot of Riga, Mr. Suji and his Japanese Sandman, and the mysterious Mr. Mist.

Similarly, superheroes Batman and Spider-Man, each boasting enormous casts of costumed criminals, saw their rogues' galleries amplified with made-for-TV menaces. Newcomer Simon the Pieman fought Batman and Robin in their 1968 cartoon series, and when the Dynamic Duo returned to Saturday morning in 1977, Moonman, Sweet Tooth, Prof. Bubbles, and the alien Zarbor were there to fight them. On the tube Spider-Man

wrestled with his comic-book enemies Dr. Octopus, the Rhino, and Green Goblin, among other popular foes, but in *Spider-Man and His Amazing Friends* (1981–1984) the Fantastic Mr. Frump, Video Man, Lightwave, and the Gamesman also stirred up trouble, continuing a pattern established in Spidey's 1967 cartoon debut with Saturday-morning-only supervillains such as the Flying Dutchman, the Fifth Avenue Phantom, the Imposter, Parafino, Dr. Noah Boddy, Dr. Zap, Dr. Dumpty, and Dr. Von Schlick fighting the hero.

It is widely known that in cartoon land, falling anvils and dynamite are readily available, but so were doctorate degrees for supercriminals. In addition to Spider-Man's diabolical doctors, also seen on Saturday morning were Dr. Destructo (enemy of the late 1950s space hero Colonel Bleep; another villain with the same name fought the Lone Ranger in 1966), Dr. Gizmo (Super Chicken), Dr. Flood (Johnny Cypher), Dr. Who (no relation to the British hero of the *Doctor Who* TV series; this Who was after King Kong in the giant ape's 1966–1969 series), Dr. Millennium and Dr. Freezoids (Birdman), and Dr. Dome (Plastic Man, who also fought a villain whose name somehow squeaked past 1979 censors: the Weed). While there was no shortage of doctors, copyright attorneys were scarce, as numerous TV heroes fought supervillains whose names, and often their powers, were lifted from established comic-book characters: Batman tussled with Electro and the Chameleon (chief executive-turned-superhero Super President, star of a 1967 series, also fought a Chameleon all his own); the Lone Ranger and Tonto tackled Western-era foes appropriating the names the Trickster, Quicksilver, Puppetmaster, Black Knight, and Queen Bee; and different villains named the Ringmaster each battled Birdman, the Impossibles, and Superstretch and Microwoman.

Hanna-Barbera Productions was one of the giants of television animation, creating vast universes of superheroes that stood ready to protect planet Earth, or the universe, against myriad monsters and malcontents. In the mid-1960s, boy adventurer Jonny Quest and his family (who started in prime time in 1964 before jumping to Saturday morning) were imperiled by would-be world dominator Dr. Zin and the living mummy Anubis; the rock-star heroes the Impossibles took on the Satanic Surfer, the Sinister Speck, and the Spinner; while Frankenstein, Jr. fought the Colossal Junk Master, the Shocking Electrical Monster, and the Spyder Man, the latter of which could not have emerged in the litigious twenty-first century. Birdman flew into combat against X the Eliminator, Vulturo the Mind Taker, and Reducto, while his series mates the Galaxy Trio struggled against Computron, Titan the Titanium Man, and the Moltens of Meterous; and caped caveman Mighty Mightor was opposed by prehistoric supervillains Storm King and Tyrannor. The trend continued in the 1970s, as Lowbrow, the Queen Hornet, the Red Vulture, and the Injustice League of America were enemies of Dynomutt and Blue Falcon; and basketball heroes the Super Globetrotters slam-dunked do-badders Museum Man, the Facelift, Tattoo Man, and Bwana Bob.

Not all Saturday-morning supervillains were animated. Producers Sid and Marty Krofft unleashed a spate of live-action kid shows in the 1970s featuring over-the-top rogues such as Dr. Shrinker, the cackling Witchiepoo (from the trippy 1969–1970 *H. R. Pufnstuf*, which inspired a 1970 *Pufnstuf* movie also featuring the villainess), Horatio J. Hoodoo (Lidsville), and the rogues' gallery of mid-1970s superheroines ElecraWoman and Dyna-Girl: the Spider Lady, Ali Baba, the Pharoah, the Sorcerer and Miss Dazzle, and Glitter Rock. *Shazam!* and *Isis*, two live-action superhero shows of the mid-1970s, were tailor made for supervillains but opted instead for heavy-handed morality plays featuring wayward teens and preteens.

Lastly, one of the greatest supervillains of Saturday morning originated in movie theaters. Spaced-out Marvin the Martian, the diminutive intergalactic conqueror armored like the Roman god of war Mars (albeit with white sneakers), startled Bugs Bunny when the wascally wabbit stepped foot on the moon in the short *Haredevil Hare* (1948). Marvin and his dog K-9 appeared in four subsequent space-themed toons, the most famous of which was *Duck Dodgers in the 24 1/2th Century* (1953), in which Daffy Duck, as the Buck Rogers–parody star, warred with Marvin over Planet X. Marvin became a sleeper sensation: he wasn't named in his theatrical appearances and was

ignored for years in Looney Tunes–related merchandising, but developed a cult TV following through endless cartoon repeats. *The Bugs Bunny/Road Runner Movie* (1979), a compilation of shorts, finally gave him the name "Marvin Martian" in an image gallery ("the" was added shortly thereafter), and from subsequent film and TV cartoons, Marvin the Martian became a mega-star. Marvin (along with the supervillain the Martian Queen) is the recurring adversary on the animated series *Duck Dodgers* (2003–present), aired on the 24-hour cable channel where it's Saturday morning every minute of every day: the Cartoon Network. —ME

Sauron I (*Lord of the Rings*): *See* Sinister Sorcerers and Sorceresses

Sauron II

It may be difficult for contemporary fans to believe, but in the late 1960s, Marvel Comics' *X-Men* was on the cancellation block. So when Neal Adams, rival DC Comics' artistic "It Boy," jumped ship to the House of Ideas and asked editor Stan Lee for a "sandbox" in which he could play unencumbered, *X-Men* landed in his lap. For just under a year, Adams and writer Roy Thomas ran wild with Marvel's mutants, reviving or revitalizing characters like Magneto and the Sentinels, and introducing one of Marvel's most unusual supervillains: the pterodactyl-man Sauron.

Premiering in *X-Men* vol. 1 #60 (1969), Sauron is actually Karl Lykos (first seen in human form in issue #59). Young Lykos, as revealed in a flashback, is mauled by a pterodactyl from the modern-day realm of prehistoric creatures, the Savage Land, and discovers over time that the beast's bites have given him a lust for human life forces. Now an adult psychiatrist, Lykos is charged with the care of the injured X-Man Havok, from whom, in a mad rage, he scientifically siphons "power such as no man has ever known!" This infusion of Havok's mutant energy transforms Lykos into a superhumanly strong, winged, genetic amalgamation of a human being and a pterodactyl. Inspired by "the dark lord who personified evil" from J.R.R. Tolkien's *Lord of the Rings* trilogy,

Identity Crisis: Same-Name Supervillains

When supervillains share the same name, sometimes it's difficult to tell who's who:

- Marvel's obscure assassin **Death-Stroke**, abetted by his black-garbed Terminators, started his career targeting Spider-Woman in 1981. Much more famous is DC's Deathstroke the Terminator, the Teen Titans foe who premiered a year earlier and whose success has included his own 1990s comic book and appearances (as Slade) on TV's animated *Teen Titans*.

- The movie **Predator** (1987) introduced a race of human hunters later seen in various Dark Horse comics—and in crossovers with Batman, Judge Dredd, and other superheroes. An earlier Predator fought Green Lantern in 1984; this clawed, chrome-plated *male* supervillain was the subconscious manifestation of a personality of Carol (Star Sapphire) Ferris, but was later revealed to be an alien parasite.

- DC's **Shockwave** used a high-tech battlesuit in the 1980s as a mercenary until battles with Blue Devil, Superman, and other heroes led to his early retirement. Marvel's Shockwave, an armored criminal who fires electrical blasts, debuted in 1976 and is one of the Masters of Evil.

- Were the Spider-Man mythos not filled with enough **Vultures**, each of them—even the first, the bald-headed Adrian Toomes (first seen in 1963)—owe a thank you to the Golden Age Vulture, the robber in a winged supersuit who debuted in *Doll Man Quarterly* #1 (1941).

- While there's no confusing the Brotherhood of Evil's Brain with the cartoon lab mouse of the same name, or Captain Action's and Austin Powers' Dr. Evils, DC and Marvel each have Scarecrows and Puppet Masters whose similar powers might baffle the novice comics reader. Luckily, the publishers' **Wizards** bear no resemblance beyond their monikers: DC's is a magician in a tux, while Marvel's is an eggshell-helmeted scientist who uses flying disks.

Lykos takes that character's name—Sauron—and like a winged parasite attempts to feast upon the X-Men's life forces.

Sauron has on occasion reverted back to Lykos, but fate always returns him to his reptilian form; during one instance Lykos was mutated into Sauron by the X-Men's enemy the Toad, who recruited him into the Brotherhood of Evil Mutants. Sauron generally resides in the Savage Land, where he has battled the X-Men, Ka-Zar, and Spider-Man. He took a band of superheroes hostage in *New Avengers* #5 (2005), being wounded in the process, but recovered after absorbing Wolverine's healing capacity. With his winged ferocity and ability to hypnotize his enemies, Sauron is one of the Savage Land's greatest dangers.

Robert Bockstael voiced Sauron in the 1994 "Mojovision" episode of the animated *X-Men* series (1992–1997). Sauron and X-Man Angel were produced as an action-figure two-pack by Toy Biz in 1997. —*ME*

The Savage Dragon's Rogues' Gallery

Having put his creative stamp on series such as *The Amazing Spider-Man* and *The Incredible Hulk*, Image Comics co-founder Erik Larsen introduced *The Savage Dragon* three-issue miniseries in 1992, followed by an ongoing monthly series in 1993. The character had originally debuted in *Megaton* #2–#4 (1984) prior to Larsen's success at Marvel and DC Comics, but the creator had never forgotten the Dragon or the seemingly endless supply of supervillains he had conjured up.

Some of these villains were whimsically named or manifested a downright silly appearance, while others were fashioned with a deadly, dramatic sensibility. From the first issue of the original *Savage Dragon* miniseries, though, the villains Dragon came up against contributed as much as the central character and other supporting players in setting the tone, style, and attitude of the series.

The Vicious Circle made their debut in *The Savage Dragon* #1 (1992). Headed by OverLord, the superpowered criminal element in Chicago had supplanted the traditional forces of organized crime with relative ease. With such lieutenants as the shark-like Mako, the blade-wielding HellRazor, and Skullface, a superpowered skeleton with long, red hair, OverLord and the Vicious Circle had run ragged over law enforcement until the Dragon was found unconscious and unharmed in a burning field. Once Dragon became a police officer, it was all-out war between the criminals and the cops. OverLord was revealed as Antonio Seghetti, a former mob chieftain who gained control of the superpowered crowd with a high-tech suit of armor and ruthless willpower. He was not without rivals, though.

CyberFace (*Savage Dragon* #5, 1993), the head of a rival criminal organization known as the Annihilators, was once Sebastian Khan, Seghetti's second-in-command. Khan's reward for helping develop the OverLord armor was betrayal. Revenge, or plans thereof, ensued. CyberFace's powers allowed him to control any mechanical device.

Horde was another early villain (*Savage Dragon* #16, 1995), and he was one of the first elements that tipped Larsen's hand that there was a lot more thought and structure to his world than some of his peers had put into their creations. Horde had originally been the Wicked Worm, a 1940s foe of the hero Mighty Man, Larsen's pastiche of the original Captain Marvel. Inspired by Captain Marvel's enemy Mr. Mind, Wicked Worm had merged with a sorcerer to become a powerful creature that could send out his component leaches and take control of another person's mind.

Larsen never seemed to hesitate to kill off a villain, perhaps because he has never been at a loss for introducing a new one. Such foes as BrainiApe (a gorilla with a brain in a glass bubble; the brain turned out to be Adolf Hitler's) and Powerhouse (who looks like a big, weird chicken pretending to be Superman) are just the tip of the proverbial iceberg. Bad guys such as SkullFace, the Fiend, Cutthroat, UnderMind, Johnny Redbeard, Furious George, Abner Cadaver, Devastator, Darklord, Chelsea Nirvana, Evil Dragon, OpenFace, and even Mister Glum are never far away.

The Dragon's world has been made, unmade, and remade, but the supervillains persist in helping to define the character of the series. Numerous members of his rogues' gallery appeared in the USA Network's *Savage Dragon* cartoon series (1995–1996). —JCV

The Scarecrow

Gotham City's gangly fear-monger made his spine-chilling debut in *World's Finest Comics* #3 (1941), in "Riddle of the Human Scarecrow" by writer Bill Finger and artists Bob Kane, Jerry Robinson, and George Roussos. Underneath the Scarecrow's burlap-bag hood and tattered brown hat and rags is Jonathan Crane, who, as a child, became obsessed with fright after deriving cruel pleasure in terrorizing birds. As a Gotham University psychology professor, the adult Crane, a disheveled recluse nicknamed "Scarecrow" by his colleagues, is an expert on phobias. Adopting the identity of the Scarecrow as a bloodcurdling "symbol of poverty and fear combined!" he extorts money from businessmen and resorts to killing as part of his scheme—but since murder is the last straw in Batman's turf, the Caped Crusader, through detective wizardry, tracks down Crane and captures the Scarecrow.

The Scarecrow returned "by popular demand" (or so said the cover) in *Detective Comics* #73 (1943), orchestrating a string of word-related crimes seemingly out of character for a so-called Master of Fear. His second outing was his last during comics' Golden Age (1938–1954).

Twenty-four years later, *Batman* #189 (1967) resurrected the Scarecrow (with a slightly altered origin) and introduced his modus operandi known to fans and readers today: fear-inducing chemicals. In "Fright of the Scarecrow" by writer Gardner Fox and penciler Sheldon Moldoff, Scarecrow taunted Gotham with hallucinogens powerful enough to turn Batman and Robin into sniveling cowards. A curious omission from the live-action *Batman* (1966–1968) television rogues' gallery (one might picture Jimmy Stewart or Danny Kaye as the Scarecrow, spooking Adam West and Burt Ward's Dynamic Duo), for the next two decades the Scarecrow crept into various DC Comics titles, including a stint with the Injustice

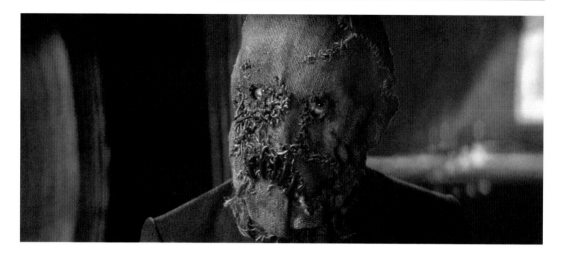

Cilian Murphy as Dr. Jonathan Crane in his Scarecrow guise in *Batman Begins* (2005).

Gang of the World in *Justice League of America* #111 (1974) and a clash with the Clown Prince of Crime in *The Joker* #8 (1976). While *Batman* producer William Dozier overlooked the Scarecrow for TV, animators did not. The Scarecrow appeared on CBS's *The Batman/Superman Hour* (1968–1969) and *The Adventures of Batman and Robin* (1969–1970), and was the most frightening of the Legion of Doom on ABC's *Challenge of the Super Friends* (1978–1979); this *Super Friends* version of Scarecrow was produced as an action figure in a 2003 two-pack with Batman.

A renowned Scarecrow story appeared in *The Brave and the Bold* #197 (1983), an adventure set in the year 1955 on Earth-Two, then DC's parallel-world home for its Golden Age characters. While Alan Brennert and Joe Staton's tale is best remembered for its Batman/Catwoman romance, it was also the third appearance of the Golden Age Scarecrow, and the only time the Earth-Two version of the villain used fear toxins.

In the grim-and-gritty world of Batman that evolved after the mid-1980s classics *Crisis on Infinite Earths* and *Batman: The Dark Knight Returns*, the Scarecrow's fearsomeness was ripe for exploration. Tweaks to Scarecrow's origin revealed that young Crane, a spindly, self-conscious nerd, was persecuted by his classmates, who likened him to both a barnyard scarecrow and *The Legend of Sleepy Hollow*'s Ichabod Crane. Harboring extreme resentment toward his tormentors, Crane studied phobias, as he

did in his 1941 origin, but as an adult college professor his unorthodox classroom techniques so unnerved students that he was fired from the university. Detailed revelations into his background were published in *Batman Annual* #19 (1995) and *Year One: Batman/Scarecrow* #1–#2 (2005).

The Scarecrow's fear gas, which he created, induces paralyzing hallucinations that simulate one's deepest dreads, producing panic attacks so severe that many of his victims have died of cardiac arrest. For added eerie effect, Scarecrow has been known to dispense his compound from an atomizer shaped like a human skull. Posing an additional threat is his bizarre combative style, a turbulent mix of frantic dance and unpredictable flailing movement. The Scarecrow's one weakness is chiropteraphobia, an overwhelming fear of bats, which Batman has used to his advantage during his often psychological clashes with his twisted foe.

Despite his indomitable willpower, Batman has on occasion been debilitated by his personal demons once poisoned by Scarecrow's fear gas, being haunted by the deaths of his parents and of the second Robin the Boy Wonder (Jason Todd). In the best-selling *Batman* storyline "Hush" (2002–2003) by writer Jeph Loeb and artist Jim Lee, the Scarecrow used his toxins on other Batrogues including the Joker and Killer Croc—and even the superheroine the Huntress—to goad them into fighting Batman. (Lee's startling version of the Scarecrow was sculpted as an action figure in

2005). Another *Batman* story arc, 2004's "As the Crow Flies," introduced the Scarebeast, a repellent monstrosity with a secret connection to Scarecrow. Yet no matter how the Scarecrow may attempt to harass Gothamites, the Dark Knight always manages to send the Master of Fear where he belongs—Arkham Asylum for the Criminally Insane.

Throughout the 1990s, the Scarecrow appeared in several episodes of *Batman: The Animated Series* and its continuations, played by voice actors Henry Polic II and Jeffrey Combs; this cartoon interpretation of the character inspired an action figure from Kenner Toys. In the blockbuster motion picture *Batman Begins* (2005), actor Cillian Murphy—who at first auditioned for the Batman role—portrayed Dr. Jonathan Crane, a sicko psychologist who conducted fear-gas experiments on Arkham inmates, sadistic "research" often embellished by his donning of a macabre Scarecrow mask (but no hat or costume); makeup-plastered rocker Marilyn Manson was considered for the part. Murphy's Scarecrow appeared in various *Batman Begins* merchandising, including action figures, an adult-sized latex mask, and a child's Halloween costume. The cinema Scarecrow was lampooned in "Battyman, Begone!," a movie parody in *MAD* magazine #455 (2005), in which the character introduced himself thusly: "I'm Scarycrook, the second-ever *Battyman* movie villain to have a face made out of burlap. The first was Tommy Lee Jones."

Two other supervillainous Scarecrows exist. The first is a minor-league Marvel Comics character named Ebenezer Laughton who premiered in the Iron Man story in *Tales of Suspense* #51 (1964). A contortionist turned superhero, Marvel's Scarecrow soon switched camps and became a criminal, fighting Spider-Man, Captain America, the Falcon, the X-Men, and Ghost Rider. The second Scarecrow is a cartoony crook featured in a 1966 episode of the animated program *The Mighty Heroes*. —*ME*

Scarface: *See* **The Ventriloquist**

Scorpion

Bitter enemies Spider-Man and the Scorpion share one thing in common: a dislike of J.

Jonah Jameson. As shown in Stan Lee and Steve Ditko's *The Amazing Spider-Man* vol. 1 #19 (1964), low-rent P.I. MacDonald "Mac" Gargan is hired by *Daily Bugle* publisher Jameson to shadow photographer Peter Parker to discover how he gets so many photos of Spider-Man. Since Parker *is* Spider-Man, his spider-sense allows him to dodge Gargan's tail, leading Jameson to make another offer in issue #20: for ten grand, Gargan undergoes mutagenic treatments by scientist Farley Stillwell to transform him into the human embodiment of the spider's natural nemesis, the scorpion. With a green ribbed exoskeleton boasting glove pincers and a telepathically controlled, 6-feet-long steel tail he can whip at nearly 100 miles per hour, the Scorpion—driven mad by his transformation—becomes a menace to not only Spider-Man but to the general public as well. Once Jameson attempts to disassociate himself from the rogue he funded, the betrayed Scorpion attacks the newspaper publisher, with Spidey swinging to the rescue.

Genetically conditioned to hate Spider-Man, the Scorpion has become one of the wall-crawler's most consistent foes. He equipped his tail with an energy blaster to fight Spidey and Captain America in *Marvel Team-Up* vol. 1 #106 (1981), and since has added other potentially lethal modifications. The Avengers and Alpha Flight have also felt the Scorpion's sting, but Gargan's sinister focus remains upon Spider-Man, even following the hero into his various television animation incarnations, and into toy stores in the form of action figures manufactured by Toy Biz.

In 2005 Marvel introduced an all-new Scorpion—a teen-age girl with a shady past—as an agent of S.H.I.E.L.D. in the pages of *Amazing Fantasy*. Meanwhile Gargan, after a brief anti-Spider-Man alliance with the Green Goblin, became the new Venom after bonding with the alien Venom symbiote.

The name "Scorpion" has been used on several occasions for other villains, including the nemesis in the film *Blake of Scotland Yard* (1937), Popular Publications' pulp magazine *The Scorpion* #1 (1939), and as a black-robed mastermind in the twelve-chapter movie serial *The Adventures of Captain Marvel* (1941). Atlas/Seaboard Publications produced three issues of a pulp-hero comic book titled *The Scorpion* in 1975. —*ME*

The Secret Society of Super-Villains

"**Y**ou are cordially invited to attend the first bi-monthly meeting of the Secret Society of Super-Villains … Attend or Die!" How could any hero-hating festooned felon refuse a first-issue summons like that?

Teams of supervillains had been around almost as long as their superheroic enemies, but DC Comics' *The Secret Society of Super-Villains* (*SSOSV*), running fifteen issues from 1976 to 1978, was the first major attempt to assemble costumed criminals into an ongoing series with a villainous brand name. A product of "Conway's Corner," the tag given the titles launched by writer/editor Gerry Conway during a company-wide expansion called "the DC Explosion," *SSOSV* #1, by Conway and penciler Pablo Marcos, gathers a criminal confederacy: Captains Boomerang and Cold, Copperhead, Gorilla Grodd, Mirror Master, Shadow-Thief, Sinestro, Star Sapphire, and the Wizard, most of whom are subpoenaed by a mysterious invitation, others liberated from imprisonment. At the fully equipped headquarters the Sinister Citadel, Manhunter appears as team leader, representing a behind-the-scenes organizer he refuses to name. (A different version of *SSOSV* #1 was originally produced by Conway, penciler Ric Estrada, and inker Marcos, featuring a story direction contrary to the vision of then-publisher Carmine Infantino. That tale was shelved but later published in black-and-white in DC's house fanzine, *The Amazing World of DC Comics* #11, 1976.)

It didn't take long for the organizer to reveal himself—the iron hand of Darkseid, overlord of Apokolips, was strongly hinted at in issue #2 and fully disclosed in #3. Nor did it take long for Conway to divest himself of the series, grooming David A. Kraft as co-writer with #2 (Kraft took over with #3), followed by Bob Rozakis (with #5) and then the return of Conway (with #8). Similarly, a variety of cover and interior artists zipped through the book.

The team itself was also unstable—Black Racer, Kalibak, Mantis, Felix Faust, Chronos, Cheetah, the Floronic Man, Hi-Jack (of the Royal Flush Gang), Sinestro, the Reverse-Flash, Bizarro, Captain Stingaree, the Trickster, Lex Luthor, Matter Master, Stan Lee parody Funky Flashman, the Crime Syndicate, Angle Man, Poison Ivy, and Blockbuster were among the characters that appeared, with rancor and treachery common among members. Super*hero* Captain Comet was added in *SSOSV* #2 as the title's continuing good guy, after DC realized that readers needed someone to root for, and Superman, Kid Flash, and the Justice Society were among the heroes stopping by. This chaotic, revolving-door roster provided much of the series' excitement—readers could not anticipate just who might appear, or whether "the world's weirdest hero," the Creeper, who guest-starred in #9 (1977), would side with the good guys or the bad.

Market oversaturation led to 1978's title-axing "DC Implosion," and *SSOSV* was abruptly canceled with issue #15, denying readers the conclusion of a two-part tale (although part two was published in Xerox form in *Cancelled Comic Cavalcade* #2, the second of two compilations of Implosion material issued in extremely limited numbers). Conway resolved the aborted storyline by including the SSOSV in *Justice League of America* #166–#168 (1979), and the Secret Society regrouped again in issues #195–#197 (1981).

Nostalgia triggered the SSOSV's revival in "The Secret Society," a two-part 2003 episode of the Cartoon Network's animated *Justice League* (2001–2004), with Grodd, Sinestro, the Shade, Clayface, and the Parasite appearing. But retribution was behind the group's return in 2005's five-part "Crisis of Conscience" storyline in DC's *JLA*. Incensed over the supervillain "mindwiping" (memory alteration) sanctioned by some Justice Leaguers, Star Sapphire, Chronos, Felix Faust, Floronic Man, and the Wizard, their stolen memories restored by Despero, reunited to assault both the JLA and their loved ones. The "Society" was also the name used by Lex Luthor in the miniseries *Villains United* (2005) to describe his vision of a criminal-controlled world. —*ME*

The Sentinels

"**D**estroy all mutants" may sound like the title of a 1950s science-fiction movie, but it is instead

Rogue battles a Sentinel in the animated TV series *X-Men* (1992–1997).

the mission of the Sentinels, the robotic giants programmed to apprehend or annihilate the X-Men.

As seen in *X-Men* vol. 1 #14 (1965)—by writer Stan Lee, layout artist/co-plotter Jack Kirby, and penciler Werner Roth (using the pseudonym Jay Gavin)—these towering terrors are designed under the auspices of anthropologist Dr. Bolivar Trask, who regards mutants as a threat to Homo sapiens. Attacking during a televised debate between Trask and X-Men founder Charles Xavier (Professor X), the Sentinels kidnap Xavier and take him before the principal Sentinel called Master Mold. Via their artificially constructed logic the Sentinels elect to protect humankind by dominating it, and upon the intervention of the mutant heroes the X-Men, Trask has a change of heart, sacrificing himself to destroy his killer creations.

Mutantdom was not safe for long, however, as the X-Men soon discovered that "The Sentinels Live!" Written by Roy Thomas and penciled by Neal Adams, *X-Men* #57–#59 (1969) introduced the Sentinels Mach II, under the retaliatory command of Trask's son Larry, against whom the automa-

tons turned once discovering that Larry was actually a mutant. The U.S. government later assumed control of the Sentinels, partnering with the Hellfire Club's Sebastian Shaw on Project Wideawake, a means of regulating mutant population.

The Sentinels have consistently attacked the X-Men over the years, but their most dreadful onslaught was their 2001 extermination of the majority of the population of the mutant haven Genosha. Despite the Sentinels' infamy, a twelve-issue *Sentinel* super*hero* series was published in 2003–2004; its *Iron Giant*–like storyline featured a boy who reprogrammed a Sentinel to become a force for good, and its success inspired a 2005–2006 follow-up miniseries.

The Sentinels have also imperiled the X-Men in alternate realities. In 1981's "Days of Future Past" by Chris Claremont and John Byrne, ultrasophisticated Omega-Sentinels ruled the United States, and in a grisly scene incinerated Wolverine. The Sentinels have been a formidable force in the alternate version of the X-Men, *Ultimate X-Men*, since that series' first issue in 2001.

Remotely human in their original appearances, the purple-hued Sentinels, often dispatched under the leadership of a Master Mold, have evolved since Trask first rolled them off his assembly line. Outfitted with mutant-tracking sensors, concussive and disintegrator beams (fired from their palms), telescoping snares, and lasers, the Sentinels can smash through reinforced steel walls and rocket through the air. They speak in steely voices, ordering their mutant prey to surrender or to prepare for extermination. Technological upgrades have produced unending variations: X-Sentinels that duplicate the forms and powers of mutants, microscopic nano-Sentinels, transforming Sentinels, mutant-Sentinel amalgamations, and cyber-organic human-Sentinels. Some Sentinel variants are self-adapting, defensively reprogramming themselves after attacks, making it impossible to use the same offensive strike against them more than once. While their forms may vary, their mission remains singular: the eradication of mutants.

The Sentinels' menace has not been solely relegated to comic books. They appeared in numerous episodes of the animated series *X-Men* (1992–1997) and *X-Men: Evolution* (2000–2003). Computer-generated Sentinels were planned for the live-action film *X2: X-Men United* (2003) but were scrapped because their inclusion would have added $8 million to the movie's budget; Sentinel design sketches were included as extras in *X2*'s DVD release. The Sentinels are popular adversaries in numerous X-Men video games, and collectible mini-busts and toys have been produced, including 2005's "Sentinels Series" from Toy Biz, seven separate pieces of a single Sentinel sold in seven different Marvel superhero action figures, encouraging consumers to purchase them all to build the Sentinel! —*ME*

The Serpent Society

Like the costumed street gangs depicted in Walter Hill's film *The Warriors* (1979), supervillains sometimes adopt group themes; patterned after the snake, a totem of the most atavistic of human fears, Marvel Comics' Serpent Society is emblematic of such "team sport" supervillainy. The Serpent Society's creators—Mark Gruenwald, Ralph Macchio, George Pérez, and Gene Day—also used the snake-like corporate raiders of the 1980s and the organization of the modern corporation itself as satirical source material (*Captain America* vol. 1 #308–#311, #313, 1985–1986; *Captain America Annual* #10, 1991).

A criminal business concern founded and led by the Roxxon oil executive Seth Voelker (aka Sidewinder), the Serpent Society's rank and file initially consists of Anaconda, Asp, Black Mamba, Bushmaster, the Cobra, Cottonmouth, Death Adder, Diamondback, Princess Python, and the Rattler, several of whom are alumni of the precursor Serpent Squad groups. Setting up shop in an abandoned insane asylum (renamed the Serpent Citadel), the Serpent Society evades Captain America while successfully pulling off its first paying criminal job: assassinating MODOK for Advanced Idea Mechanics, the evil high-tech organization that MODOK once led.

Despite this initial success, internal dissension tore at the Serpent Society over Princess Python's sudden departure during the MODOK affair. Next the vigilante called Scourge murdered Death Adder, and Black Racer (not to be confused with the DC Comics character of the same name), Copperhead (not the DC villain), Fer-de-Lance, and Puff Adder joined the Society's membership rolls in 1988. A woman named Viper, a Serpent Squad veteran, soon joined the Serpent Society, manipulating its members into introducing a mutagenic compound into the water supply of Washington, D.C., temporarily turning President Ronald Reagan into a crazed reptilian against whom Captain America reluctantly battled. Several key members of the team assisted Viper in seizing the leadership role, thereby forcing Sidewinder and Diamondback to join forces with Captain America (on whom the female Diamondback had a crush) against the hijacked Serpent Society, touching off a serpentine civil war that ended with Viper's defeat.

Under the mistaken belief that Sidewinder still headed the Serpent Society, the evil priest-lord Ghaur and Lemurian ex-empress Llyra tried to hire him and some former associates to find items necessary for the rebuilding of the Serpent Crown, a magical weapon. Sidewinder eventually performed this mission—and collected the lion's share of the pay—after the Serpent Society, now led by the Cobra, failed in the task.

Despite this setback, the Serpent Society remains one of the more active and prosperous supervillain associations in the business. More mercenary force than outright "evil organization out to rule the world," the group selectively accepts freelance jobs, such as locating the Nazi villain the Red Skull. The Serpent Society also resembles a guild or union; its individual members receive not only plentiful work opportunities and bountiful pay, but also generous health benefits, professional bonhomie, subsidized housing, and even a retirement community, in exchange for modest organizational "dues."

In spite of subsequent defeats by Captain America and the Avengers spin-off superhero team Force Works in the 1990s and 2000s, and even rumors of the snake group's dissolution, the Serpent Society endures today, under the Cobra's guidance. Being both corporate and reptilian, the Serpent Society remains especially relevant in an era plagued by boardroom corruption and Enron-style business scandals. —*MAM*

Sesshomaru

Rumiko Takahashi is perhaps the most popular female manga artist in Japan today. Since the publication of her first major work, *Urusei Yatsura*, in 1977, she has created several popular long-running titles, including *Maison Ikkoku* and the gender-bending martial arts comedy *Ranma 1/2*. Her property, the manga *Inu-Yasha*, began in 1996 as a feature in the magazine *Shonen Sunday*, eventually spawning an animated series (2000–2004; broadcast in 2005 on Cartoon Network), three theatrical films, art books, video games, and other merchandise. Not only is *Inu-Yasha* a popular title in Japan, it has gained many fans in America.

The story revolves around Kagome, a fifteen-year old girl who travels from present-day Japan to the country's feudal period, hundreds of years ago. Kagome frees a mysterious boy pinned to a tree by

an arrow ... and discovers out that he is Inu-Yasha, half-human, half-demon. Shocked by Kagome's resemblance to Kikyo, the woman who pinned him to the tree fifty years earlier, Inu-Yasha travels with Kagome to recover the shards of the Shikon jewel. Along the way, they gain allies, travel through time between feudal Japan and modern Japan, and face many enemies. These foes are both human, and "youkai" (demon).

Perhaps the most popular villain faced by Inu-Yasha and Kagome is Sesshomaru. His conflicts with Inu-Yasha brings new meaning to the term "sibling rivalry." Introduced in the second volume of the manga (1997), Sesshomaru is a tall young man with long white hair, delicate features, gold-colored eyes, and four red stripes—two on each side of his face. Looks can be deceiving, though; he is actually more than seventy years old. There is a purple crescent-shaped mark on his forehead. He wears clothing typical of the feudal period. He is also Inu-Yasha's half-brother. Their father was a demon, but while Inu-Yasha is half-human, Sesshomaru is a full demon. He is able to transform himself into a large dog-like demon, but he can also perform magical attacks.

His personality is cold and calculating, and he dislikes humans. He pursues Inu-Yasha to find out the location of their father's magical sword, the Tetsusaiga. When Sesshomaru discovers that the sword is located in their father's burial temple, he seeks it out ... and the location is in Inu-Yasha's eye. After a fierce battle, Sesshomaru gains the Tetsusaiga—only to discover that he cannot use it. Only Inu-Yasha, due to his half-human nature, can. Sesshomaru is able to briefly use the Tetsusaiga with the help of the demon Naraku, but ends up with the sword's companion, the Tenseiga. However, the sword cannot be used to kill, but to heal. This fact only deepens Sesshomaru's hatred of Inu-Yasha.

Sesshomaru travels with Jaken, a small creature resembling a frog with large eyes; he is Sesshomaru's loyal servant. Later in the series, Sesshomaru gains another traveling companion, a young human girl named Rin. Ironically, Sesshomaru saves her life and takes care of her, and Rin chooses to follow him. —*MM*

The Shade

The criminal motivations of the master of the darkness, the Shade (not to be confused with the superhero Shade, the Changing Man), have been predicated not upon avarice but instead boredom. "The Man Who Commanded the Night" crept into view in *Flash Comics* #33 (1942), courtesy of scribe Gardner Fox and artist Hal Sharp. A slender, top-hat-wearing figure attired in a black, the Shade slinked in and out of the shadows, stealing merely to engage the Fastest Man Alive, the original Flash, in contests just for fun.

Carrying a walking stick that was presumably the conduit of his superpowers, which included the manipulation of "shadowmatter"—creating shapes, weapons, objects, and creatures from the dark— the Shade, whose smirking visage often glowed like a maleficent moon face from within his dark garb, jumped from comics' Golden (1938–1954) to Silver (1956–1969) ages when his co-creator, writer Fox, and penciler Carmine Infantino resurrected the villain in "Flash of Two Worlds!" in *The Flash* vol. 1 #123 (1961), the landmark tale that united the Scarlet Speedsters of two generations and defined DC Comics' multiple-earth concept. For the next three decades the Shade occasionally resurfaced in *Flash* and, along with other Golden Age supervillains, as one of the Injustice Society in *Justice League of America* and *Infinity, Inc.*

The Shade might have wafted into obscurity were it not for writer James Robinson, who transformed the supervillain from a gimmicky felon to a complex ne'er-do-well in the critically acclaimed comic book *Starman* (vol. 2, 1994–2001) and its spin-off four-issue miniseries, *The Shade* (1997). Robinson revealed that the Shade was actually Londoner Richard Swift, an immortal from the nineteenth century, who inexplicably became connected to the dimension known as the Dark Zone along with a dwarfish troublemaker named Simon Culp. Swift and Culp clashed on several occasions, and for a time their personalities shared Swift's body after a bizarre explosion welded their souls together. The Shade's other enemy was Victorian businessman Piers Ludlow, whose descendants continued to assault Swift for decades. His wan-

derlust and agelessness allowed the Shade to meander through the centuries, and over time his motivations have proved ambiguous, as he has on occasion aided some of the superheroes he has also fought against.

The Shade was unmistakably sinister, however, in his adaptation to animation, in "The Secret Society," a two-part 2003 episode of the Cartoon Network's *Justice League* (2001–2004); Stephen McHattie voiced the villain in his television incarnation. DC Direct produced a Shade action figure and a Pocket Super Heroes miniature in 2002. —*ME*

The Shadow-Thief

Billed as "The Shadow-Thief of Midway City!," the fallacious supervillain was introduced in a Silver Age (1956–1969) Hawkman story created by comics greats scripter Gardner Fox and artist Joe Kubert. In *The Brave and the Bold* #36 (1961), two-bit cat burglar Carl Sands' experiments with shadow projection allow him to accidentally contact a creature from an otherworldly dimension. In return for saving the creature's life, Sands is rewarded with a Dimensiometer, enabling him to shift his body into a two-dimensional, intangible "shadow" state, and a pair of ebony gloves, permitting him to hold material objects while in shadow form. With his newly acquired gadgets, Sands embarks on a life of crime as the Shadow-Thief (sometimes Shadow Thief).

The Shadow-Thief can move quickly and quietly across and through most surfaces and materials, while remaining impervious to physical contact and attack. One of the original members of the Secret Society of Super-Villains, the Shadow-Thief has battled many superheroes in the DC Universe but is considered one of Hawkman's major adversaries.

At the hands of scripters John Ostrander and Timothy Truman and artist Graham Nolan, Shadow-Thief was overhauled in *Hawkworld* #5 (1990) to fit his post–*Crisis on Infinite Earths* continuity. The alien Byth hired ninja Carl Sands to steal Hawkman's spaceship and gave him a Thanagarian shadow-field generator for his troubles. The Shadow-Thief continued to battle his favorite rival, Hawkman, but expanded his territory when he murdered Ronnie Raymond, the hero Firestorm, in *Identity Crisis* #5 (2004). Movie bad guy James Remar voiced the villain in his 2005 TV debut as one of the Legion of Doom on *Justice League Unlimited* (2004–present). —*GM*

The Shark

Writer John Broome and artist Gil Kane offered a cautionary tale of the dangers of the atomic age in *Green Lantern* vol. 2 #24 (1963). "The Shark That Hunted Human Prey" was originally a normal tiger shark swimming past an underwater nuclear facility. Radiation evolutionarily accelerates the creature, which mutates into a humanoid with a shark-like head (and a full set of razor-sharp teeth) and psionic and telepathic powers, including matter manipulation and the ability to grow to gigantic size. Despite its intellectual augmentation, this menace—now called the Shark—is driven by its rapacious urges, engorging itself not on flesh but on human psyches. He attempts to induce fear into the mind of Green Lantern II (Hal Jordan), but the hero's indomitable willpower spurs him to victory, and the Shark is devolved to his original state.

The Shark evolved again soon thereafter, but by the mid-1960s had returned to dormancy. Director Steven Spielberg's blockbuster *Jaws* (1975) spawned his return—in combat with Superman—in *Action Comics* #456 (1976), the cover of which, by artist Mike Grell, borrowed heavily from the movie's famous poster. From the 1970s through the 1990s, the Shark occasionally waded into

various DC titles, fighting Aquaman, the Justice League, Black Condor, and his arch-nemesis Green Lantern. At one time he deposed Aquaman from his Atlantean throne, but was bested by the Sea King. Once Hal Jordan returned from the dead in 2005, the Shark—in a grotesque shark-like form—resurfaced to plague the hero in *Green Lantern* vol. 4 #5, inspiring the villain's 2006 to DC Direct's Green Lantern action-figure line.

A different lawbreaker called the Shark predated the mutated Green Lantern foe. This Shark, an evil inventor wearing an oversized shark headpiece, was one of the Terrible Trio (along with the Fox and the Vulture), a minor-league crime team that debuted in the Batman story in *Detective Comics* #253 (1958). —*ME*

Shredder

Brought to life in 1984 in the pages of Kevin Eastman and Peter Laird's self-published black-and-white comic book *Teenage Mutant Ninja Turtles*, the evil crimelord of New York City,

Shredder. From *Teenage Mutant Ninja Turtles* #1 ©1984 Mirage Studios, Inc. ART BY KEVIN EASTMAN AND PETER LAIRD.

Shredder (also variously called "the Shredder") was the formidable foe of the four Turtle brothers and their sensei leader, the oversized rat Splinter.

Shredder, voiced by James Avery, achieved pop-culture infamy in the original animated hit TV show *Teenage Mutant Ninja Turtles* (1987–1996). In most episodes he was portrayed in a menacing suit of spike-covered armor and a metal helmet and mask that covered most of his face, but under that gear was Oroku Saki, a supremely conditioned, middle-aged Japanese ninjitsu master. In the original animated TV series Shredder was often seen with his two incompetent henchmen, Bebop and Rocksteady. Shredder shared a deeply mired connection to the Turtles' main adversary, the mysterious and feared ninja clan known as the Foot (a pastiche of the Hand, from Frank Miller's *Daredevil* series). Shredder was a frequent guest in the spinoff Archie Comics comic-book series *TMNT Adventures* (1988–1995).

Shredder also appeared in two of the three the live-action films; *Teenage Mutant Ninja Turtles: The Movie* (1990), with actor James Saito in the role, and *Teenage Mutant Ninja Turtles II: The Secret of the Ooze* (1991), portrayed by Francois Chau.

An edgier, grimmer Shredder (voiced by Scottie Ray) can be seen in 4Kids Entertainment and Mirage Studios' *Teenage Mutant Ninja Turtles* series (2003–present), accompanied by his mad-scientist henchman, Baxter Stockman. In this new animated series, where the Foot Clan has become a powerful criminal empire in present-day New York City, the Shredder embodies three distinct personas: Oroku Saki, a successful and benevolent Japanese billionaire; the Shredder, the secretive, battle-armored leader of the Foot Clan; and, known to only a select few, the fire-red, cyborg-like Ch'rell, a feared criminal from planet Utrom, fighting a war against the Utroms while residing on Earth. —*GM*

Silver Age Supervillains (1956-1969)

Asking which came first, the superhero or the supervillain, is like asking the same question about the chicken and the egg. The fact remains that every superhero whose career is of any duration has earned the enmity of a stable of do-bad-ders who (to quote another supervillain, Hugo Drax from the film *Moonraker*) "appear with the tedious inevitability of an unloved season."

In the Golden and early Silver ages of comics, the supervillain generally adhered to a pattern: escape from the prison where his nemesis had placed him, establish a variation on the motif around which his villainy was themed (for the Penguin, birds; for the Mirror Master, reflective surfaces; etc.), capture the hero and place him in a deathtrap, then be defeated by the hero and returned to jail. It was a *pas de deux* as intricate and polished as a Kabuki performance. The villain might try to kill the hero, but he would never succeed, and ancillary performers—the hero's girlfriend, sidekick, or police contact—in the play might be endangered, but would rarely die. In fact one of the greatest of all supervillains, the Joker, debuted as a killer in *Batman* #1 (1940), but soon eschewed murder, at the command of DC Comics editor Whitney Ellsworth—and became a much more interesting character as a result.

The Turtle Man has the honor of being the first supervillain of the Silver Age, having been the first costumed foe of the revived Flash, in a story by Robert Kanigher and Carmine Infantino for the Scarlet Speedster's debut in *Showcase* #4 (1956). Naturally slow and stolid, the Turtle Man was the natural contrast to a super-speedster. He returned in later years, using super-scientific devices against his nemesis. The Turtle Man, like the Flash, was also a revision of a Golden Age character.

Another difference between the Golden and Silver ages can be seen in the methods by which superheroes and villains received their unique skills. Though science and magic have always played a part in such origins, magic is much more likely to be found in the origin of a Golden Age character, whether hero or villain. The use of the atomic bomb to end World War II—and America's dual fascination with and repulsion by that device—triggered the supremacy of science as a method for creating super-powered characters; the first generation of Marvel superheroes would not exist were it not for that handy, all-encompassing excuse, atomic radiation. (Of course, it can be argued that the "science" used in most superhero comic books is not much different from magic, but the trappings and the mood of such methods are unquestionably different.) DC editor Julius Schwartz, a former science-fiction agent, used super-science almost exclusively as a venue for Silver Age characters. He retooled Green Lantern from a lone wielder of a mystic power battery to one of 3,600 uniformed cops armed with "power rings" patrolling the galaxy (in a nod, it must be acknowledged, to the Lensman series by E. E. "Doc" Smith), and repositioned the Atom from a guy who was simply short and strong to a scientist who discovered a method to shrink to subatomic sizes and travel through telephone wires.

This method also worked when fashioning supervillains. Byth, who fled from his native planet Thanagar to Earth, was pursued by Thanagarian police officers Katar and Shayera Hol. They had to use all their resources to defeat him—Byth had taken a pill that enabled him to change his shape at will, as seen in *The Brave and the Bold* #34 (1961). After capturing him, the Hols stayed on Earth to study law enforcement techniques, battling crime under the names of Hawkman and Hawkgirl. Byth later broke out of jail and matched wits with the Hawks again. Schwartz's fascination with science is obvious from the many other science-based supervillains introduced in his titles during the Silver Age, including the Justice League of America enemies Xotar the Weapons Master and the Lord of Time, and Green Lantern's foes Sinestro and Black Hand.

The Outsider is a good example of another source of villainy, a friend going bad. Alfred Pennyworth was the trusted butler and confidant of Bruce Wayne, and one of the few who knew Wayne was secretly Batman. Alfred sacrificed his life to save Batman from death at the hands of gangsters in *Detective Comics* #328 (1964, in a story by Bill Finger and Bob Kane), but was later revived by a scientist whose identity remains unknown. The revival effort gave Alfred white skin with odd bumps, as well as superhuman abilities and, for some reason, a virulent hatred of Batman and Robin, according to *Detective* #334 (1964). Calling himself the Outsider, as he regarded himself out-

side the human race, he attacked Batman and Robin at odd intervals until he was defeated and restored to his true identity, at which point he resumed his duties at Wayne Manor, despite the occasional relapse into Batman's dreaded foe. (The true story of the Outsider's origin is far more mundane. After Schwartz was appointed editor of the Batman titles, he decided to kill Alfred to shake up the status quo. But when the *Batman* television show debuted two years later, Alfred was a part of the cast. To make the comics better reflect the television show, Alfred was restored to life. It is not known—and was probably never decided—who the Outsider would have been had not higher powers dictated Alfred's return to life.)

Marvel Comics editor Stan Lee somewhat altered the role the villain played in the superhero comic, as he altered much else in the genre. The Marvel supervillain sprang from an allegedly more naturalistic source, such as human frustration, envy, or misguided love, rather than greed and/or the desire to engage the hero in a battle of wits. This led to many intriguing variations on the classic supervillain, arguably the best of these being Dr. Doom, a supervillain who was so cool he was the king of an entire country!

Although he boasted a flair for innovation, Lee, like Schwartz, found science fiction a rich source for new supervillains, such as Ronan the Accuser. For centuries, the alien race called the Kree thought Earth to be a minor planet of no galactic importance. Then the Kree's robotic monitor on Earth, Sentry 459, was defeated by the Fantastic Four (FF). Ronan was dispatched to Earth by the Kree's Supreme Intelligence to force the FF to answer for their actions, as witnessed in *Fantastic Four* vol. 1 #65 (1967) by Stan Lee and Jack Kirby. Despite his highly technological armor and "universal weapon," which "has the potential to *create* and *destroy* all physical matter," the FF was also able to repel Ronan, which led to ever-greater Kree monitoring of and interference in affairs on the planet Earth. Eventually, Ronan and an ally named Zarek were able to overthrow the Supreme Intelligence, but the Supreme Intelligence was able to regain its position of power.

The Swordsman is an excellent example of how the nature of the supervillain changed in the

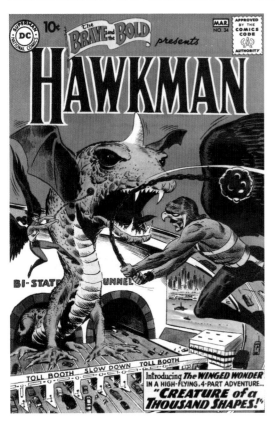

Byth. *The Brave and the Bold* #34 ©1961 DC Comics.
COVER ART BY JOE KUBERT.

late Silver Age (or what a certain company called "the Marvel Age of Comics"). Demonstrably a villain, though not without his own, often labyrinthine, code of ethics, the Swordsman—whose real name may or may not be Jacques Duquesne—was a bundle of contradictions from his first appearance in *The Avengers* vol. 1 #19 (1965). Created by Stan Lee and Don Heck, Duquesne turned out to be the man who had taught a fledging circus performer named Clint Barton everything he knew about edged weapons, then tried to kill the lad when Barton tried to stop him from fleeing with the circus' payroll. It would have taken a lot to stop the Swordsman: his own sword contained a number of offensive weapons such as knockout gas, lightning, and a disintegration beam. These gimmicks, with his purple costume trimmed in magenta, made him as amazing a performer as he was a combatant.

Years later, after Barton had grown up to become the archer Hawkeye, the Swordsman reappeared, applying for Avengers membership, despite a long criminal history in Europe. His request was denied, leading to a long series of conflicts with the Avengers, and an on-again off-again romance with the Scarlet Witch. Eventually, the Swordsman—on the run, unable to find employment, and in the grips of alcoholism—fell in love with a woman named Mantis, who restored his faith in himself and convinced him to reform and make a successful second try at joining the Avengers (though Mantis did not return the Swordsman's affections). It was not until the Swordsman sacrificed himself to save Mantis that she realized she did love him. The Swordsman's body was later restored to life by a member of an alien race called the Cotati; he later married Mantis and departed with her to another plane of existence.

The supervillains from the smaller comics companies hewed to neither the DC nor the Marvel template, but took a little from Column A, and a little from Column B. A good example of this is Gore, the Man-Ape, an adversary faced by Thunderbolt, the superhero identity of journalist Peter Cannon in *Thunderbolt* #52 (1966), published by Charlton Comics. Eric Gore, a bald, monocled scientist, transplanted the right hand of an ape onto his own arm when his own right hand was destroyed in a lab explosion. But the operation had an effect unforeseen by Gore—though probably not by the readers. Gore packs up and travels to an island, determined " ... that the humanity I had sacrificed for, to serve ... *would one day serve me!*" Eventually the wandering Peter Cannon stumbles across Gore's lair and is forced to thwart his plans as Thunderbolt by first facing an arena full of apes, then facing down Gore. When T-Bolt and Gore are trapped in a burning laboratory, Gore's right-hand ape, chooses to save Thunderbolt instead of his evil master.

None of this is particularly original, but the handling of the materiel, by creator, writer and artist Pete A. Morisi, under the pseudonym of P.A.M., added a certain quiet conviction to the story, making it more than just another saga hacked out to meet a deadline. Gore himself is more a Marvel villain than a DC villain, the scientist who tried to master nature and got his come-uppance. Adding to Gore's appeal is the fact that Morisi had the sense to restrict the character to only one appearance, doubtless aware that he had rung every possible change on the villain in this single appearance. Keep in mind that Charlton Comics also gave us the charmingly wacky Punch and Jewelee, a totally contrived pair of villains whose mood and execution were polar opposites from Gore. But the story's ending is classic DC—Cannon, after his harrowing adventure, tries to spend a quiet night watching television, only to find himself watching *King Kong*.

Another Charlton supervillain, the Ghost, crossed paths with Captain Atom and Nightshade, as well as Punch and Jewelee, his civilian identity being one of P&J's first kidnap victims. In a story by Dave Kaler and Steve Ditko (*Captain Atom* #82, 1966), Alec Rois' studies to escape his childhood poverty led to his discovery of teleportation technology. He donned an all-white costume with a cape and full-face mask and began a career of crime, calling himself the Ghost. In their civilian identities, the Ghost, Captain Atom, and Nightshade were friends, unaware of each others' double identities.

In comics today, the slogan "once a villain, always a villain" is no longer true—if it ever was. After all, most villains would argue that villainy—and heroism—are only a point of view, though their victims might beg to differ. —*MWB*

Silver Banshee

Silver Banshee is a relative blip on the map in the world of Superman's arch-enemies, introduced in *Action Comics* #595 (1987) in a story written and illustrated by John Byrne. There it was revealed that, centuries ago, Siobhan McDougal was denied her birthright as the leader of her Gaelic clan because of her gender. While calling upon mystic forces to keep control of the clan out of the hands of her brothers and to claim what is rightfully hers, she is banished to a demonic netherworld where a Crone transforms her into the Silver Banshee—a murderous, silver-haired, skeleton-like being empowered to exact revenge

on the McDougal descendants. Now possessing supernatural strength, speed, and the ability to teleport, Silver Banshee's greatest asset is her eerie wail, which can kill a human within earshot and shred metal. Her search through Metropolis for an ancient magical book thrusts her into conflict with Superman, who, with the help of fellow hero Martian Manhunter, narrowly defeats the wrathful villainess.

Although envisioned by Byrne as one of a new generation of super-rogues, Silver Banshee has appeared infrequently since the late 1980s. In the two-issue limited series *Superman: Silver Banshee* (1998–1999), Siobhan's soul was united with McDougal heir Lacy MacElwain, binding both women together to the Silver Banshee for all of time. In 2005 Silver Banshee made her animated-television debut as one of the Legion of Doom on the Cartoon Network's *Justice League Unlimited* (2004–present). —*GM*

Silver Samurai

The Silver Samurai, one of the first examples of the influence of Japanese culture on American comic books, was created by writer Steve Gerber and artist Bob Brown in *Daredevil* vol. 1 #111 (1974). A superb swordsman and highly skilled martial-arts master, this Japanese warrior can generate a tachyon field of energy around his sword, using the energized blade to slice through any known substance—except the metal adamantium—like a disintegration beam.

Originally his true identity was unknown, but the Silver Samurai was ultimately revealed to be Kenuichio Harada, the mutant son of the deceased Japanese crimelord Shingen Harada. It was writer Chris Claremont who gave him his "real" name and who established his relationship to his father Shingen, a character that Claremont and artist Frank Miller jointly created in 1982 *Wolverine* miniseries. The Samurai is also the half-brother of Wolverine's true love Mariko Yashida, and the cousin of the Japanese mutant superhero Sunfire.

As a boy, Kenuichio was never formally acknowledged as Shingen's son or as a member of

Wolverine vol. 3 #37 ©2005 Marvel Comics.
COVER ART BY KAARE ANDREWS.

Mariko, the Silver Samurai took over leadership of Clan Yashida and attempted to put an end to the clan's criminal connections and restore its honor. The Silver Samurai even became one of the original members of the Japanese superhero team Big Hero 6, as portrayed in the comics miniseries *Sunfire & Big Hero 6* (1998). Subsequently, however, the mutant Blindspot used her powers to erase the Samurai's memories of being a hero, and hence he has returned to his criminal career as head of organized crime in Tokyo.

The Silver Samurai appeared in FOX's animated TV series *X-Men* (1993–1997). He also appears in the Capcom fighting games *Marvel vs. Capcom 2* and *X-Men: Children of the Atom.*

The Silver Samurai's most unusual appearance was in *Marvel Team-Up* vol. 1 #74 (1978), in which Spider-Man met the original cast (the "Not Ready for Prime Time Players") of TV's *Saturday Night Live*. The climax of the story was a sword-fight between the Silver Samurai and John Belushi's samurai character! *—GM*

the Yashida clan of which Shingen was the leader. At an early age, Harada began the study of the fighting methods and code of honor (bushido) of the medieval Japanese samurai warrior-class.

After fulfilling a debt of service to the supervillain the Mandrill, the Silver Samurai bound himself in service to the second Viper, acting as his bodyguard. Later, the Silver Samurai battled Wolverine over the demon-possessed Muramasa sword. Villain and hero banded together to defeat the demon and free Jessica Drew (the original Spider-Woman) from its evil influence. Following the death of

Sinestro

Sinestro, the renegade Green Lantern (GL) created by writer John Broome and artist Gil Kane, first defied the Emerald Crusader in *Green Lantern* vol. 2 #7 (1961). The Guardians of the Universe, overseers of the intergalactic Green Lantern Corps, err when selecting the militant Sinestro of the planet Korugar to obtain their peacekeeping weapon, the power ring, and serve as the GL of space sector 1417. After distinguishing himself among the Corps, Sinestro abuses his power ring and oppresses his homeworld; the Guardians punitively strip him of the weapon and banish him to the antimatter universe of Qward. There he acquires a power ring made of yellow, the color against which the Corps' rings are ineffective, and vindictively spreads malice across the galaxy, placing him into conflict with Earth's Green Lantern, Hal Jordan.

If his name weren't evidence enough, Sinestro's appearance left no question of his villainy. His prodigious cranium intimated his hubris, and his pointed ears, ubiquitous smirk, and red pigmentation suggested his Mephistophelian nature—he was unmistakably the polar opposite of the whitebread, handsome Jordan's knight-in-shining-armor GL.

After five *Green Lantern* appearances between 1961 and 1963, Sinestro's visibility nearly trickled to a standstill until the mid-1970s, when he made a comeback (fighting GL, the Flash, and Superman, and joining the Secret Society of Super-Villains). Soon Sinestro was on television, as one of the Legion of Doom in the cartoon *Challenge of the Super Friends* (1978–1979), and in the live-action comedy special *Legends of the Super-Heroes* (1979), played by wiry, wacky comedian Charlie Callas.

The DC Comics flashback miniseries *Green Lantern: Emerald Dawn II* (1991) disclosed that Sinestro was the GL who tutored neophyte Hal Jordan in the ways of the Green Lantern Corps. Sinestro preached intimidation, in violation of the Guardians' ethics and hinting at his eventual downfall. In the mid-1990s a power-drunk Jordan followed his mentor's footsteps when he rebelled against the Corps and killed several of his colleagues, breaking Sinestro's neck in a death duel. Jordan ultimately sacrificed his life to spare the galaxy in a redemptive epiphany.

Resurrected in 2002, Sinestro resumed his assailment against GL when Jordan returned from the dead in the 2004–2005 miniseries *Green Lantern: Rebirth*. Readers discovered that Sinestro indirectly caused Jordan's fall from grace by freeing the imprisoned fear elemental Parallax, the entity which subliminally corrupted GL; "I made you

Green Lantern: Rebirth #5 ©2005 DC Comics.
COVER ART BY ETHAN VAN SCIVER.

a murderer, Hal Jordan," sneered Sinestro in *Rebirth* #5. With both characters restored to status quo, the Green Lantern-versus-Sinestro enmity is, like the hero and villain themselves, reborn for the new millennium.

Ted Levine voiced Sinestro in episodes of the animated *Superman* (1996–2000), *Static Shock* (2000–2004), and *Justice League* (2001–2004), and John DeLancie, *Star Trek*'s Q, played Sinestro in the "Green Loontern" episode of *Duck Dodgers* (2003–present). Sinestro merchandising includes a Pocket Super Hero miniature, action figures, and a GL-versus-Sinestro coldcast porcelain statue. —*ME*

The Sinister Six

Dr. Octopus was up in arms after a trio of stinging defeats by Marvel Comics' wall-crawler. So in Spider-Man's first giant-sized edition, *The Amaz-*

ing *Spider-Man Annual* #1 (1964), Doc Ock invites each of the supervillains who had battled the web-slinger to join forces as a Spidey-crushing crew. In a 41-page epic written by Stan Lee and illustrated by Steve Ditko, the arrogant Green Goblin and the Fantastic Four–obsessed Dr. Doom decline Dr. Octopus' summons, but Spider-Man's five other foes (this story takes place during the infancy of the hero's rogues' gallery) sign up: Electro, Kraven the Hunter, Mysterio, the Sandman, and the Vulture, joining Ock as the Sinister Six. These villains share two things in common: a hatred of Spidey ... and a dislike of one another. Constant bickering amid the ranks leads Dr. Octopus to rely upon the Six's individual strengths instead of teamwork. Spider-Man is goaded into a gauntlet of supervillains, battling the Sinister Six one at a time, and through sheer will overpowers them.

While various smaller groupings of bad guys fought Spidey after *Annual* #1, it took over twenty years before a new criminal club followed the malevolent footsteps of the Sinister Six. In *Amazing Spider-Man* vol. 1 #280 (1986) Rhino, Hydro-Man, Speed Demon, and Boomerang rallied together under the leadership of the armored Beetle as the Sinister *Syndicate*.

The original Sinister Six—with the Hobgoblin II replacing the deceased Kraven the Hunter—was dusted off for a return bout in 1990. Not to be out-done, the Sinister Syndicate regrouped, commissioned by the mob and comprised of returnees Beetle, Rhino, Speed Demon, and Hydro-Man and recruits Blacklash and Constrictor, in *Deadly Foes of Spider-Man* #1–#4 (1991), a miniseries spotlighting Spidey's enemies. After Dr. Octopus' (temporary) demise at the hands of the assassin Kaine, in 1995 Mysterio assembled the old guard—Vulture, Electro, and Hobgoblin II, along with the Beetle, the Shocker, and Scorpia (a female Scorpion)—as the Sinister *Seven*. The Syndicate was back in 1996, and even the vile Venom got into the team spirit in 1999, bringing together yet another incarnation of the Sinister Six. In the 2000s the group expanded to the Sinister *Twelve* under the leadership of the Green Goblin. As part of its "Ultimate" reimagining of the Marvel Universe, Marvel Comics published an *Ultimate Six* miniseries in 2003–2004, with altered versions of

Sandman, Vulture, Doc Ock, Green Goblin, Electro, and Kraven tackling the sixteen-year-old Ultimate Spidey. No matter the roster, the Sinister Six and its violent variations always spell trouble for Spider-Man.

Outside of comic books, Sinister Six appearances (with varying rosters) include a "Spider-Man and the Sinister Six" action-figure gift pack from Toy Biz; Adam-Troy Castro's novel, *The Gathering of the Sinister Six* (1999); the video game *Spider-Man 2: Sinister Six*; and the "Insidious Six" two-part episode of the 1990s *Spider-Man* cartoon. Inspired by the comic-book supervillains, a Seattle garage band called the Sinister Six made a blip on the music radar in the 1990s. —*ME*

Sinister Sorcerers and Sorceresses

S inister sorcerers and bewitching sorceresses have been a mainstay of storytelling throughout recorded history. There are the pharaoh's court sorcerers in the Bible, the sorceress Circe in Homer's *Odyssey*, and the three witches in William Shakespeare's *Macbeth* (circa 1606). Sorcerers and sorceresses abound in all forms of visual and written arts—be it in ballet, opera, fairy tales, children's literature. novels, comics, television, and film—testifying to their allure and popularity among children and adults alike.

In the twentieth century, fantasy novelists created evildoers who used magic, such as Sauron and his ally, the wizard Saruman, of J.R.R. Tolkien's *The Lord of the Rings* (1954–1955). As the genre's title suggests, malevolent sorcerers continually menace the heroes of sword and sorcery tales. The arch-foes of Robert E. Howard's heroes Conan and King Kull are, respectively, Thoth-Amon, a wizard from Stygia (prehistoric Egypt), and the skull-headed Thulsa Doom. Kulan Gath, the evil wizard co-created by Michael Moorcock in the comic book *Conan the Barbarian* #14 (1972), was resurrected in modern times to plague Spider-Man and the X-Men.

Inspired by fantasy novels and other supernatural tales, superhero comics writers have used sorcerers as villains almost since the genre's inception. In his first published adventure (*More Fun Comics* #55, 1940) the heroic magician Dr. Fate rescued his future wife, Columbia University student Inza Cramer, from the green-skinned sorcerer Wotan (created by writer Gardner Fox and artist Howard Sherman), who would become his recurring antagonist. Having lived for ages in a succession of bodies, Wotan seeks to conquer Earth or, failing that, to destroy it.

One of the leading foes of the avenging spirit known as the Spectre is Kulak (created in *All Star Comics* #2, 1940, by Jerry Siegel and Bernard Baily), high priest of a world called Brztal, who has wiped out numerous civilizations on other worlds and seeks to do the same to Earth's. Kulak directs his mystical powers through his eerie third eye.

In *All-American Comics* #26 (1941) Sargon the Sorcerer debuted as the hero of his own comics series, in which he repeatedly battled a sorceress known as the Blue Lama (who first appeared in *Sensation Comics* #68, 1947). Decades later, Sargon's occult Ruby of Life turned him into a villain, although he ultimately reverted to his true, heroic personality.

The Silver Age Green Lantern, Hal Jordan's predecessor, Abin Sur, captured and shrunk the alien sorcerer Myrwhydden (created by Gardner Fox and artist Gil Kane in *Green Lantern* #26, 1964) and imprisoned him on a tiny world within the power ring that he gave to Jordan, who succeeded him as Myrwhydden's nemesis. Jordan teamed with the magician Zatanna in combating the Warlock of Ys (created by Fox and Kane in *Green Lantern* #42, 1966), the only known denizen of a dimension called the Other Side of the World.

In *Strange Adventures* #187 (1966) June Moore became the Enchantress, who for years used her mystical powers as a champion of humanity, until she turned villainess herself, seeking to conquer the world.

Two leading foes of the enigmatic Phantom Stranger are the seductive sorceress Tala (created by Bob Kanigher and Neal Adams in *The Phantom Stranger* #4, 1969) and her ally Tannarak (introduced by Gerry Conway and Jim Aparo

in *Phantom Stranger* #10, 1970), who seeks to make himself immortal.

Deimos (created by Mike Grell in *First Issue Special* #8, 1975), a high priest who practices black magic in the extradimensional "inner world" of Skartaris, is the foremost enemy of Travis Morgan, the warrior known there as the Warlord.

Ages ago, before the sinking of Atlantis, its Lord High Mage, Arion, defended the realm against his nefarious brother Garn Daanuth (created in *Warlord* #59, in 1982 by writer Paul Kupperberg and artist Jan Duursema), who wielded virtually limitless mystical powers.

Circe, the sorceress from Homer's *Odyssey*, was reintroduced as a foe of DC's Amazon princess in *Wonder Woman* #305 (1983). At Marvel, Jack Kirby portrayed Circe, whose name he spelled "Sersi," into one of the super-powered heroines of his series *The Eternals* (1976–1977).

The Latina sorceress known as La Encantadora (who debuted in *Secret Origins of Super-Villains 80-Page Giant*, 1999) is neither a heroine nor a complete villain. Although she once carried out an assignment to poison Superman with kryptonite radiation, she is strongly attracted to the Man of Steel, and instead helped save his life. Through her enchanted Mists of Ibella, she can perform various mystical feats, which can affect even Superman, who is vulnerable to magic.

In the Marvel Universe, evil magicians have most often been found battling "the Master of the Mystic Arts," Dr. Stephen Strange. Umar, created by Stan Lee and Bill Everett in *Strange Tales* #150 (1966), is the sister of Strange's archenemy, the dread Dormammu, but, unlike him, she has retained her humanoid form. Sometimes Umar is Dormammu's ally, but other times she is his enemy. Nearly equal to her brother in mystical power and villainy, Umar is also the mother of Strange's lover, Clea.

Another Everett co-creation, Kaluu (who debuted in *Strange Tales* #147, 1966), studied the mystical arts side by side with Dr. Strange's mentor, the Ancient One, during the latter's youth, but Kaluu turned to the dark side of sorcery instead.

Another of Dr. Strange's enemies, the magician Xandu, who wields the Wand of Watoomb and was created by Stan Lee and Steve Ditko, actually first appeared in *Amazing Spider-Man Annual* #2 (1965), in which the doctor and the web-slinger teamed up for the first time.

Once a cardinal in the Catholic Church, the man called Silver Dagger (created by Steve Englehart and Frank Brunner in *Doctor Strange* #1, 1974) bears such fanatical hatred of sorcerers like Dr. Strange that he uses black magic himself in his attempts to destroy them.

Another showcase for sinister sorcery is Marvel's *Thor*, especially the malign magic of the Norse thunder god's conniving foster brother Loki. One of his allies is Asgard's leading femme fatale, Amora the Enchantress, a beautiful sorceress who usually operated in partnership with the unusually strong Skurge the Executioner until the latter's demise. Both characters were introduced by Stan Lee and Jack Kirby in *Journey into Mystery* #103 (1964).

Another sensual sorceress created by Lee and Kirby, Karnilla the Norn Queen (in *Journey into Mystery* #107, 1964), sometimes sided with Loki and his forces of evil. But her love for the noble Asgardian god Balder could bring out her better nature, as in Walter Simonson and Sal Buscema's comics miniseries *Balder the Brave* (1985–1986).

Lee and Kirby's Enchanters (from *Thor* #143, 1967) were a triumvirate with vast magical power, the eldest of whom, Forsung, rivaled Odin, King of Asgard, in mystical might.

In the "Tales of Asgard" backup series in *Thor* #137 (1967), Lee and Kirby introduced the tyrannical Mogul of the Mystic Mountain, who, with his powerful "Jinni Devil," was clearly inspired by the *Arabian Nights*.

During his remarkable run as writer and artist on *Thor*, Walter Simonson created Malekith the Accursed in *Thor* #344 (1984), who rules the Dark Elves of the realm of Svartalfheim and possesses various magical abilities, including the ability to transform his appearance.

Among Marvel's other malignant magicians is Zaladane (from *Astonishing Tales* #3, 1970), the high priestess of the Sun People of the prehistoric Savage Land, who is an enemy of Ka-Zar and the X-Men. She claims to be the sister of Lorna Dane, aka Polaris of the X-Men.

The first Black Talon debuted in *Strange Tales* #173 (1974) and, after his death, was succeeded by another, who first appeared in *Avengers* #152 (1976). Both had mastered voodoo, enabling them to raise and command zombies.

Modred the Mystic (from *Marvel Chillers* #1, 1975), a sorcerer from King Arthur's time who was revived from suspended animation in modern times, turned evil when he fell under the control of the primeval demon Chthon.

Dr. Glitternight, from *Werewolf by Night* #27 (1975), was actually a mystical being who was exiled from his native dimension and sought to corrupt the souls of everyone on Earth. Before his apparent demise, he could generate mystical light from his chest in order to perform various magical feats.

The nefarious warlock Nicholas Scratch is the son of Agatha Harkness, the kindly old witch who serves as the Fantastic Four's babysitter. Scratch once headed the secret community of witches and warlocks living in New Salem, Colorado. Scratch's children, now deceased, comprised Salem's Seven, who magically assumed super-powerful forms to combat the Fantastic Four. Scratch and his children debuted in *Fantastic Four* vol. 1 #185–#186 (1977).

Finally, there is the strange case of Wanda Maximoff, the Scarlet Witch, whom Lee and Kirby introduced (in *X-Men* #4, 1964) as a reluctant member of Magneto's Brotherhood of Evil Mutants. She subsequently turned superheroine as a member of the Avengers. Lee asserted that Wanda had a mutant "hex" power to alter the probability of events, but later *Avengers* writer Steve Englehart treated Wanda's power as true magic. Still later, writer Kurt Busiek established that Wanda actually had a mutant ability to tap into and manipulate "chaos magic."

Wanda eventually married her Avengers teammate, the android Vision, whose artificial nature prevented them from having offspring by normal means. Instead, Wanda utilized magic to enable them to conceive children, and she gave birth to twin boys. But Wanda eventually discovered that her "sons" were actually fragments of the spirit of the demon Mephisto. This was the main factor that drove the Scarlet Witch insane, leading her to turn evil and join Magneto in battling the Avengers.

She subsequently recovered, but for years afterward Wanda's subconscious mind was altering reality in an attempt to recreate her children. The result in the "Avengers Disassembled" storyline (2004) was that Wanda suffered a mental breakdown and triggered a series of attacks on the Avengers that seemingly killed several of their members, including the Vision. This set up the *House of M* storyline (2005) in various Marvel series, in which the Scarlet Witch's powers have considerably altered history, radically (and temporarily, in most cases) changing the lives of numerous Marvel characters.

Magical supervillains have also memorably appeared in television and film. In the realm of animated cartoons, cartoonist Carl Barks' sultry sorceress Magica de Spell slithered from the comics into the television series *Duck Tales* (1987–1992) to continue her attempts to steal Scrooge McDuck's lucky "Number One" dime. In Cartoon Network's *Teen Titans* animated series (2003–2006), the title characters have tangled with Mumbo, a retro-style villain in a traditional magician's costume who employs his magic powers to commit otherwise old-fashioned robberies. In another Cartoon Network series, *Samurai Jack* (2001–2004), created by Genndy Tartakovsky, the title character's arch-nemesis is the shapeshifting sorcerer Aku. In Judd Winick's *The Life and Times of Juniper Lee* (2005–present), the title heroine battles various supernatural threats including the witch Auntie Roon.

In live-action TV, producer Dan Curtis' daytime supernatural serial *Dark Shadows* (1967–1971) featured an array of evil sorcerers, most famously Angelique, the beautiful witch who cursed the hero, Barnabas Collins, to become a vampire for spurning her love. For nearly three decades there was no other successful television series that dealt with supernatural villainy until Joss Whedon created *Buffy the Vampire Slayer* (1997–2003). The long-running series included numerous villains who practiced magic, such as Richard Wilkins, the mayor of Buffy's town of Sunnydale, the malevolent occultist Ethan Rayne, and even Buffy's friend Willow, a "good" witch who temporarily became the

evil "Dark Willow" (echoing *X-Men*'s Dark Phoenix). In *Buffy*'s TV spin-off *Angel* (1999–2004), a sinister law firm, Wolfram & Hart, dealt in the practice of black magic. The WB network's series *Charmed* (1998–present) features three sisters who are good witches who battle an array of evil sorcerers and demons.

From their early history movies have also featured evil witches, such as in the Swedish film *Witchcraft through the Ages* (1922). They have also appeared in fantasy films for family audiences, such as the Wicked Witch of the West in *The Wizard of Oz* (1939), Queen Bavmorda in Lucasfilm's *Willow* (1988), the title characters of *The Witches* (1990), Lord Voldemort and his allies in the *Harry Potter* movies (starting in 2001), and the White Witch in *The Chronicles of Narnia: The Lion, the Witch and the Wardrobe* (2005), based on C. S. Lewis' novel. (Oddly, evil male sorcerers appear far less often.)

Throughout the studio's history, many Disney animated features cast magicians as their villains, starting with the Wicked Queen and her other self, the Old Witch, in *Snow White and the Seven Dwarfs* (1937). The most imposing and iconic of Disney's magical villains is the sorceress Maleficent in *Sleeping Beauty* (1959). Other evil Disney magicians include the shapeshifting Madam Mim in *The Sword in the Stone* (1963), the sea witch Ursula in *The Little Mermaid* (1989), and the wizard Jafar in *Aladdin* (1992).

In the twentieth century the mad scientist largely supplanted the role of the evil magician in popular culture. But the enormous success of J. K. Rowling's *Harry Potter* books and the film adaptations of Tolkien's work suggest that in the twenty-first century the sinister sorcerer has made a comeback. —PS

Sinister Syndicate: *See* **The Sinister Six**

Skeletor

Although he never did capture the power of Castle Grayskull and thus control the planet of Eternia and beyond, the villainous Skeletor nevertheless conquered the hearts and imaginations of children of the 1980s. With his bony yellow skeletal face and muscular blue-skinned body, Skeletor was frightening enough, but with added darkly magical powers, an energy-blasting Havoc Staff, and a loyal coterie of villainous followers, Skeletor caused much havoc for Eternia and its main defender, He-Man.

In late 1981, Mattel Toys introduced a line of 5-inch action figures under the umbrella name *Masters of the Universe*. The two stars of the line were Nordic blond-haired barbarian He-Man and the blue-skinned Skeletor. Although mini-comic books were included with the toys, they revealed little about the characters, other than establishing that Skeletor was a tough supervillain for He-Man to defeat.

In 1982, the ultra-popular toy line was developed for a syndicated animated series called *He-Man and the Masters of the Universe* from Filmation, and Skeletor and his minions were more fleshed out. Cruel and fearsome, Skeletor schemed constantly to overtake Castle Grayskull, determined to use its powers to control the universe. His mostly incompetent henchmen included the beauteous-but-cold Evil-Lyn, the orange-furred Beast Man, the amphibious Mer-Man, the mechanical Trap Jaw, and a seemingly endless supply of Robot Knights. Atop his Bone Throne in his lair on Snake Mountain, Skeletor would often caress his pet purple panther, Panthor.

Skeletor exhibited many magical powers over the two-season highly rated 130-episode run of *He-Man and the Masters of the Universe*, and also showed extra strength and a popularity that found

He-Man's arch foe, Skeletor, from *Masters of the Universe*.

him regularly crossing over into the *He-Man* spin-off, *She-Ra, Princess of Power* (1985). His high-pitched voice was provided by Alan Oppenheimer, who tossed off insults toward his minions as often as he threatened the heroes. Later, versatile actor Frank Langella donned a prosthetic makeup application to become Skeletor, battling Dolph Lundgren as He-Man in director Gary Goddard's live-action movie *Masters of the Universe* (1987), a modest box-office success.

Though the toy line faded in popularity, Skeletor returned in a revival of the toys (1989) and cartoon show, *The New Adventures of He-Man* (1990). Here, Skeletor and He-Man were transported to Primus, where Skeletor made a pact with Flogg, the leader of the Evil Mutants of Denebria and the Moon Nordor, and the clash of good and evil was underway again. Skeletor somehow grew eyeballs to go along with a new costume, and a personality that was more crazily comical than dangerous.

In 2002 a new *He-Man and the Masters of the Universe* animated series and toy line debuted, this time based on the original concept, but updated. Now, Skeletor was an evil alchemist named Keldor whose evil magic transformed him into Skeletor. Commanding his evil forces, Skeletor's battles against He-Man and the forces of good to capture the secret of Castle Grayskull raged anew.

In 2005, when BCI Eclipse launched an extensive new DVD line for the classic *He-Man and the Masters of the Universe* cartoon series, the battle lines between Skeletor and He-Man were drawn again, this time for children-of-the-1980s-grown-into-parents to share with their own children. Skeletor's rallying cry of "I'll get you, He-Man!" lives on. —AM

Slade

Although his comic-book sobriquet is the more menacing Deathstroke the Terminator, Slade Wilson uses only his first name as a mysterious mercenary in the animated *Teen Titans* TV series (2003–2006). Wearing a black bodysuit with steel-grey armored parts, the animated Slade also wears a black and orange mask. Extremely athletic and strong, Slade is also possibly enhanced by his suit. His basso voice is provided by actor Ron Perlman, best known as the Beast in the *Beauty and the Beast* TV series (1987–1990) and as the title character in *Hellboy* (2004).

In the first two seasons of *Teen Titans*, Slade mainly acted through other agents he hires, including Jinx, Mammoth, and Gizmo from the HIVE Academy, and through Thunder and Lightning. Apparently in the market for an apprentice, Slade also blackmailed Robin into helping him, until his plans were foiled and Robin and the Titans escaped unscathed.

The second season of *Titans* found Slade recruiting a confused young girl named Terra, who he manipulated into infiltrating and helping break the Titans down. Eventually Terra turned against Slade and helped defeat him, sending him down into a lava pit. Slade appeared to have died, but in season three, Robin learned that somehow, Slade might still be alive!

Slade's resurrection was revealed in 2005's fourth season, wherein Slade targeted Raven, on behalf of her father, the demonic Trigon. Slade now wielded mystical eldritch powers that could burst from the runes on his hands, and the runic Mark of Scath on his forehead. He made a deal to help Trigon bring about the end of the world in exchange for Trigon restoring him to life in a flesh-and-blood body. After Trigon double-crossed him, Slade got his body back from the demonic abyss on his own, and helped the Titans defeat the demon.

Numerous Slade toys and action figures were released by Bandai from 2004 forward. —*AM*

Smallville Villains

When DC Comics gave Jerry Siegel and Joe Shuster's archetypal hero Superman a hith-erto unrevealed career as an adolescent crime fighter in *More Fun Comics* #101 (1944), the character's boyhood town of Smallville had produced few memorable, *bona fide* supervillains other than mainstay arch-rival Lex Luthor. In the WB network's popular teen drama *Smallville* (2001–present), however, adversaries of the Last Son of Krypton are legion. *Smallville*'s eponymous Kansas farm town—the boyhood home of Clark Kent—has been portrayed on the large and small screen before—in short "Superboy" animated features made for *The New Adventures of Superman* (1966–1970), in Richard Donner's 1978 feature *Superman: The Movie*, in Richard Lester's 1983 sequel *Superman III*, in the 1988–1992 *Superboy* syndicated television series, and in ABC's *Lois & Clark: The New Adventures of Superman* (1993–1997)—but no previous television or film drama has ever examined the town and its denizens, superpowered or otherwise, in such in-depth fashion.

Powerful villains abound in Smallville, though most possess no superhuman abilities. These include: Lionel Luthor (cast regular John Glover), the ruthless head of LuthorCorp who murdered his parents to gain access to their fortune; Morgan Edge (played by guest stars Rutger Hauer in "Exile" and Patrick Bergin in "Shattered"), an equally cutthroat Metropolis crimelord with a keen interest in young Clark Kent's amazing Kryptonian abilities; Lex Luthor (series regular Michael Rosenbaum), the ne'er-do-well twentysomething son and successor of Lionel Luthor, who engineers the downfall of his hated father, befriends the teenage Clark Kent for ambiguous and perhaps cynical purposes, appears to be a high-tech/corporate supervillain in training as well as a future U.S. president—and may thereby bring about the apocalypse; and Jor-El, Clark Kent's superpowered Kryptonian father, a disembodied presence who visited Earth some forty years earlier and now tries to force Kal-El to conquer and rule Earth ("Phoenix"; "1961"; "Velocity"; "Legacy"; "Covenant"; "Commencement"). In 2005 the super-intelligent Brainiac, in the person of Clark Kent's college professor Milton Fine (portrayed by James Marsters, who played the ambiguously

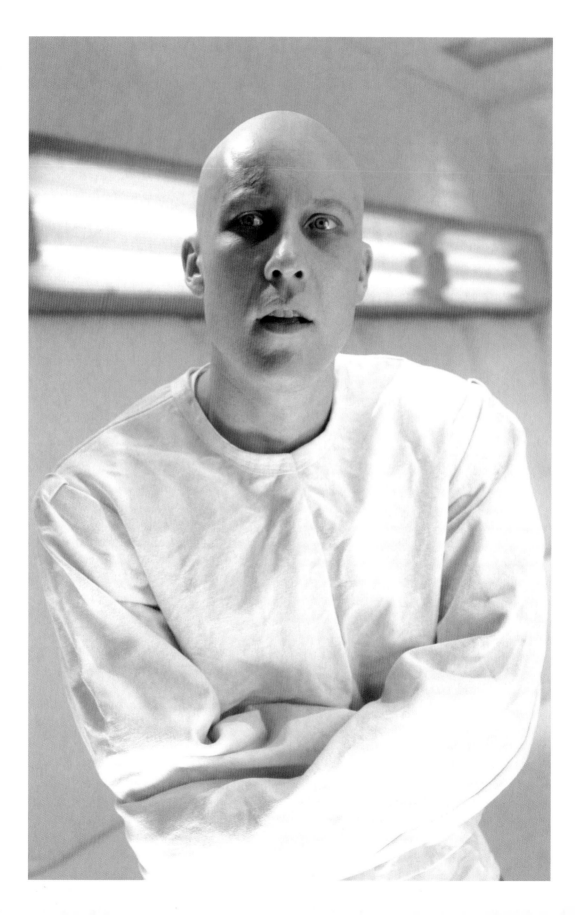

noble vampire Spike on *Buffy the Vampire Slayer* and *Angel*), joined the ever-expanding rogues' gallery of *Smallville's* proto-Superman.

Then come the other, far-more-ubiquitous *Smallville* villains, those who owe their suddenly superpowered existence to the shower of green meteors that devastated the town in 1989. The glowing green kryptonite rocks deposited across Smallville that day constitute the mortal remains of the shattered homeworld of young Kal-El/Clark Kent (played with superb heroic innocence by Tom Welling), whose small spaceship not coincidentally landed in a Smallville cornfield that same day. Those phosphorescent meteor fragments also fuel the all-but-routine supervillainy that proliferates in present-day Smallville; it is no small irony that the same distant, doomed planet that birthed the teen who will be Superman also spawns new adversaries for him on an almost weekly basis some sixteen years later.

Although green kryptonite can kill Kent—the far rarer red variety merely turns him into a brutal, narcissistic teen delinquent ("Red"; "Rush"; "Exile"; "Unsafe")—exposure to the alien material's mutagenic radiation can confer superhuman abilities of various sorts upon ordinary humans, many of whom are adolescents. Indeed, kryptonite-mediated teen metamorphoses are arguably allegorical references to the anxiety stemming from the rapid physical and emotional changes experienced by high school kids. In a nod to the pitfalls of puberty, so many of these kryptonite-powered people prove to be irresponsible with their newfound gifts—powers that include controlling swarms of insects ("Metamorphosis"; "Drone"), telekinesis ("Crush"), teleportation ("Obsession"; "Unsafe"; "Pariah"), the ability to manipulate the laws of probability ("Jinx") and emotions ("Magnetic"), and even the power to turn sexually het-up adolescent boys into hormone-crazed assassins ("Heat")—that Smallville High's student newspaper editor Chloe Sullivan (Allison Mack) has enshrined stories about them on a "Wall of Weird."

Smallville's most serious weakness may be that format and continuity demand that most of

Clark Kent's adversaries—especially those who witness him using his powers—must share one of two possible fates: death or amnesia. Were it otherwise, the (mostly) well-kept secret of Clark's superhuman abilities and extraterrestrial origins would doubtless spread far and wide, thereby ruining the destiny that must someday lead Smallville's callow young Kent to become the protector of Metropolis and the world.

In a modern example of comics imitating live-action imitating comics, *Smallville's* kryptonite-generated villains—along with the likenesses of the show's cast—have spilled back onto DC's sequential art pages in a *Smallville* comic-book series (2003–2005) that featured original stories by writer Mark Verheiden (author of numerous *Smallville* television scripts). Meanwhile, *Smallville's* pageant of kryptonite-powered villains continues. In the pages of the early 1970s comics, every chunk of kryptonite on Earth was once destroyed, a development that turned out to be only temporary. In *Smallville*, only another such unlikely eventuality seems capable of stemming the tide of emergent small-town supervillainy. —*MAM*

Solomon Grundy

"Solomon Grundy, born on Monday, christened on Tuesday, married on Wednesday, took ill on Thursday, worse on Friday, died on Saturday, buried on Sunday, this is the end of Solomon Grundy."

DC Comics' zombie supervillain Solomon Grundy has enjoyed a much longer "life"span than the Grundy in that nineteenth-century nursery rhyme, although sci-fi writer Alfred Bester, who created Grundy for *All-American Comics* #61 (1944), was inspired by the children's poem. With artist Paul Reinman, Bester fishes Solomon Grundy out of Gotham City's Slaughter Swamp as the decades-old skeleton of Cyrus Gold, mired in its murk, is resurrected by an uncanny botanical metamorphosis. Lumbering from the bog is the chalk-skinned, 7-and-a-half-feet-tall Solomon Grundy, an incredibly strong but dim-witted behemoth that is easily coerced into crime after encountering a

Opposite: Michael Rosenbaum as Lex Luthor in TV's *Smallville*.

band of hooligans who use the swamp-man as muscle to rip bank vault doors off their hinges. The Golden Age (1938–1954) Green Lantern (GL) finds Grundy difficult to stop, as the zombie is impervious to the hero's power ring (as well as policemen's bullets), but GL disposes of the beast by tripping him in front of an oncoming train.

It took more than a speeding locomotive to destroy Solomon Grundy; he frequently battled GL, harboring such bitter hostility that the mere sight of the Emerald Crusader drove the simple-minded brute to gutturally snarl, "Hate Green Lantern! Kill Green Lantern!" He was slowed by the end of comics' Golden Age, but during the superhero renaissance of the Silver Age (1956–1969) Grundy returned to feud with Dr. Fate, Hourman, the Justice League and the Justice Society, Superman, Infinity, Inc., Batman, and Green Lantern I *and* II.

Grundy's limitless strength and stamina and his artificially generated lifeforce—he requires neither air, food, nor water—makes him a virtually unstoppable menace. He is difficult to incarcerate: GL has banished Grundy into space by imprisoning him in a power ring–generated sphere, and Superman once dumped him onto a remote planet, yet he still managed to return to Earth to wreak havoc. Grundy has occasionally shown affection to those who have befriended him, including the superheroine Jade (the daughter of his arch-foe GL), and he was briefly a member of the Injustice Gang. He has been destroyed on several occasions but resurrected. No matter the incarnation taking root, one thing is certain: Solomon Grundy is never a welcome presence.

Solomon Grundy, voiced by Jimmy Weldon, was one of the Legion of Doom in ABC's animated *Challenge of the Super Friends* (1978–1979). After being considered for but never appearing on the WB's *Superman* cartoon (1996–2000), Grundy shambled through episodes of the Cartoon Network's *Justice League* (2001–2004) and *Justice League Unlimited* (2004–present) as one of the Injustice Gang, with Mark Hamill as Grundy. Kevin Grevioux portrayed Grundy in a second-season episode of *The Batman* (2004–present), and DC Direct manufactured an action figure and a miniature of the villain in the 2000s. The monster has also been celebrated in music. The Crash Test

Dummies' 1991 "Superman's Song" featured the lyrical bridge, "Superman never made any money, for saving the world from Solomon Grundy." *—ME*

Sonar

Two generations of villains named Sonar have plagued two generations of Green Lanterns.

The first, Bito Wladon of the tiny European country of Modora, was introduced in a 1962 story in *Green Lantern* vol. 2 #14 by John Broome and artist Gil Kane. The apprentice clockmaker wished to make his overlooked nation a world power by supplying it with a "nucleo-sonic bomb." To this end, Wladon embarked for the United States to obtain the technology he needed to realize his theories. His efforts brought him into conflict with Green Lantern, whom he fought with weapons powered by his sonic researches, leading the media to dub him "Sonar." The first Sonar used a "tuning fork gun" to project his sonic energies, which he could use to fly, to project destructive force, and to create mental images to confuse his adversaries. Over the years, he became a regular opponent for Green Lantern and also fought the Elongated Man in the 1992 *Elongated Man* miniseries.

The second criminal to call himself Sonar was introduced in *Green Lantern* vol. 3 #66 (1995) in a story by Ron Marz and Paul Pelletier. He, too, also seems to be a citizen of Modora. His parentage, origin, and true name are unknown, although it has been speculated that he is the son of Bito Wladon. The microcircuits that give him his mastery of sound were originally subcutaneous, although in later appearances much of that circuitry has been exposed, giving him a bizarre appearance. The second Sonar is also able to use local sounds such as noise from traffic as a weapon against his foes. Sonar has attempted to take over the island of Manhattan for his personal kingdom, believing himself to be of royal blood. This attitude gives Sonar an innate sense of entitlement which, combined with his formidable sonic powers, make him a fearsome adversary. He has also fought the team of Green Lantern Kyle Rayner and the third Flash, Wally West, and holds a grudge against them both. *—MWB*

Spellbinder

C reated by writer John Broome and artist Sheldon Moldoff, Spellbinder first mesmerized readers as an op-art-like villain in *Detective Comics* #358 (1966). He was art forger Delbert Billings, who developed optical devices that enabled him to hypnotize others. A second Spellbinder, unrelated to Billings, appeared in 1994 as a green-and-orange-robed mystic who fought the Justice League of America as part of the government-supported Leaguebusters. Billings resumed his Spellbinder guise shortly thereafter, refusing to sell his soul to the demon Neron for enhanced powers (*Underworld Unleashed*, 1995), but was shot to death by his girlfriend Fay Moffit, who was more than willing to accept Neron's offer. Moffit's vertigo inducement is optically generated—her powers are negated when her eyes are covered.

Spellbinder was introduced to a modern audience on the WB's *Batman Beyond* (1999–2001) as Dr. Ira Billings, a high-school guidance counselor for Terry McGinnis, the new Dark Knight of Gotham. He grew tired of advising unappreciative teenagers, and as Spellbinder used his glowing eyeball-like facial feature to project subconscious images directly into his victims' minds, which sent them into a virtual reality.

Spellbinder received greater character depth on the WB network's animated *The Batman* (2004–present) as a three-eyed mystic with the ability to induce hypnotic visions into his victims: "A state of awareness so pure or potent, one could project one's visions into reality," explained Bruce (Batman) Wayne to his butler Alfred. Although *The Batman* Spellbinder has attempted to dupe Gotham's wealthy citizens into giving up their prized possessions—including a rare gem that would strengthen his spells—Batman intervened and used mind over matter to thwart the villain. —GM

Spider-Slayer

O ver the years, Spider-Man has been pursued by a succession of perpetually upgraded robots specifically engineered to counter his arachnid powers and annihilate him, each machine bearing the name "Spider-Slayer."

The Amazing Spider-Man vol. 1 #25 (1965), written by Stan Lee and illustrated by Steve Ditko, introduces Professor Spencer Smythe, a humble inventor who has subscribed to *Daily Bugle* publisher J. Jonah Jameson's media tirade against Spidey by constructing a robot "guaranteed to defeat Spider-Man!" Jameson initially dismisses Smythe as a "crackpot," but *Bugle* photographer Peter Parker—secretly Spider-Man—sophomorically goads J.J.J. into humoring the professor ... and soon regrets his joke, as the robot's sophisticated sensors nearly expose his secret identity. Soon, the robot—bearing Jameson's sneering visage in its video monitor "face," as Jameson helms its controls—pursues Spidey through New York, relentlessly tracking him and nearly overpowering him in a prison of superstrong steel cables. Fortunately, Spidey depowers the Spider-Slayer before Jameson and Smythe arrive on the scene to apprehend him. This comic-book story was adapted to animation as "Captured by J. Jonah Jameson" (original airdate: September 30, 1967) of the late 1960s *Spider-Man* cartoon, with actor Henry Ramer voicing a renamed Henry Smythe.

In the comics, Smythe was soured by the defeat of his robot and slipped into a manic obsession of perfecting his robots and not merely capturing, but actually destroying, Spider-Man. A "bigger, far more powerful, far more deadly" Spider-Slayer Mark II was introduced in *Amazing Spider-Man* #58 (1968), with Jameson again at the "wheel," but it failed to squash the hero. Smythe returned in 1972 with Spider-Slayer Mark III, an eight-armed variation able to shoot synthetic webbing. Realizing Smythe's psychosis, Jameson severed ties with the crazed inventor, earning his ire. Smythe promptly built the tank-sized Spider-Slayer Mark IV, which he operated, nearly crushing Spider-Man until the hero triggered the machine to explode. Smythe was back with a vengeance in 1979 with his "last" Spider-Slayer, and borrowing a cue from Stanley Kramer's 1958 prison-escape movie, *The Defiant Ones*, locked Spidey and Jameson together with techno-handcuffs programmed to detonate within 24 hours. The mad scientist perished, due to radiation poisoning, at the end of this storyline.

His son, Alistair Smythe, resumed the family business beginning in *Amazing Spider-Man Annual*

#19 (1985). Originally financed by crimelord Wilson Fisk, aka the Kingpin, Alistair nearly died in his first vengeful attack against Spidey, returning wheelchair-bound in 1987, operating an upgraded Spider-Slayer in another failed attempt to kill the web-slinger. *Amazing Spider-Man* #368–#373's six-part "Invasion of the Spider-Slayers" (1992–1993) featured Alistair's full-scale assault on Spider-Man with a swarm of mechanical Spider-Slayers equipped with venom-spiked tails and razor-sharp claws; the fanatical son of Smythe surgically enhanced himself into the Ultimate Spider-Slayer, still meeting defeat, yet he tried again in the early 2000s. With his perverted passion for perfecting his father's Spider-Slayer technology and murdering Spider-Man, Alistair Smythe forever remains a threat to the wall-crawler.

The Smythes and their Spider-Slayers appeared frequently in the 1990s animated TV series *Spider-Man* (1994–1998), with Edward Mulhare playing Spencer, succeeded by Maxwell Caulfield as Alistair, the latter of whom was featured in eighteen episodes. This series inspired a 1994 Spider-Slayer action figure from Toy Biz. —*ME*

The Squadron Sinister

The Squadron Sinister was created as part of a game. As revealed by writer Roy Thomas and penciler Sal Buscema in Marvel Comics' *The Avengers* #69–#70 (1969), an immortal extraterrestrial named the Grandmaster, one of the Elders of the Universe, has for eons manipulated beings from across the galaxy into conflicts for his amusement. He and the time-hopping supervillain Kang the Conqueror engage in a contest, with Earth as the arena. The Grandmaster creates evil duplicates of four superheroes he discovers on a parallel world called Counter-Earth, calling his pawns the Squadron Sinister, while Kang manipulates Earth's mightiest superheroes, the Avengers, into the competition. The superhuman powerhouse Hyperion, caped-and-cowled Nighthawk, superspeedster Whizzer, and "Power Prism"–wielding Dr. Spectrum—aka the Squadron Sinister—make worthy opponents, but lose their match to the Avengers.

The comic-book debut of the Squadron Sinister was also created as part of a game. The idea for the Squadron originated at a 1969 party at Thomas' Manhattan apartment, when comics scribe Mike Friedrich suggested that Denny O'Neil, then the writer of DC Comics' *Justice League of America* (*JLA*), and Thomas produce an unofficial crossover between their titles, to be published concurrently. O'Neil's effort was subtle: *JLA* #75 (1969) featured DC heroes fighting evil manifestations of themselves, with Marvel inferences in their actions and dialogue (for example, "evil" Batman threw a trashcan lid at the real Batman, à la Captain America's shield). Thomas' Squadron Sinister, upon closer inspection, was his homage to four JLA members: Hyperion = Superman, Nighthawk = Batman, Whizzer = Flash, and Dr. Spectrum = Green Lantern.

"I took the name 'Hyperion' from a line in *Hamlet*," Thomas revealed in the 2005 book *Justice League Companion*. "Nighthawk" came "from a hoax Richard Kyle pulled on Don and Maggie Thompson's newszine *Newfangles*, in which he referred to a pulp mag named *Nighthawk* with a Batman-like character, and later it turned out that pulp had never existed." Thomas borrowed the name "the Whizzer" from a Golden Age (1938–1954) Marvel superhero, and "'Dr. Spectrum' was a natural name, given Green Lantern's color weakness."

JLA fan Thomas resurrected his Squadron— this time as superheroes, the Squadron Supreme—in *Avengers* #85 (1971). The Counter-Earth JLA counterparts have continued to appear for years with a frequently expanding roster of DC analogs in various comics including a twelve-issue *Squadron Supreme* maxiseries (1985–1986). Sci-fi television scribe J. Michael Straczynski rebooted the Squadron beginning in 2003 in the Marvel series *Supreme Power*. —*ME*

Star Conqueror: *See* **Starro the Conqueror**

Star Sapphire

The illustrious Star Sapphire has had a sparkling career as one of the DC Universe's most menacing supervixens. She was introduced in comics' Golden Age (1938–1954), in a story in *All-Flash*

Green Lantern vol. 2 #16 ©1962 DC Comics.
COVER ART BY GIL KANE AND MURPHY ANDERSON.

gem, allows her to fly and can hurl large blasts of energy—actually defeated the Emerald Crusader in their first meeting. Over much of the Silver Age (1956–1969), Ferris would fall under the Zamarons' hypnotic spell, with Star Sapphire taking control of her form, the supervillainess identity unknown to Ferris. During the mid- to late 1970s she was frequently seen as a member of the Secret Society of Super-Villains. Over the years, Star Sapphire has endured bouts of emotional crisis, split-personality, and the horror of morphing into a male being called the Predator.

In the 2005 "Crisis of Conscience" storyline in *JLA*, Star Sapphire hooked up with her old cronies in the Secret Society of Super-Villains for a full-scale assault against the Justice League of America. The character has appeared on Cartoon Network's *Justice League* (2001–2004), voiced by Olivia d'Abo, in which her streamlined, high-fashion style—designed by superstar artist Bruce Timm—respectfully nods to Kane's original design for the character in the Silver Age *Green Lantern* comics, while contemporizing her for a modern viewership. —*GM*

Starro the Conqueror

In the first published appearance of the Justice League of America in *The Brave and the Bold* #28 (1960), DC Comics' most powerful superheroes were nearly eradicated by … a *starfish*. That oft-reprinted tale, scripted by Gardner Fox and penciled by Mike Sekowsky, begins in the Atlantic Ocean, where a puffer fish telepathically notifies Aquaman of an enormous starfish with a sinister single eye that "traveled across billions of miles of interstellar space" seeking an inhabited world to dominate. This is Starro, an alien oppressor that transmutes Earth marine life into obedient replicas to spread his influence globally. Exercising mind control over the humans it encounters, Starro combats the Justice Leaguers by firing bolts of unfathomable force from its tentacles. Teenager Snapper Carr inadvertently discovers Starro's susceptibility to quicklime, providing the JLA with the key to stopping this otherworldly enslaver.

#32 (1948), as a fish-netted, purple-clad exiled queen of the female warrior race the Zamarons. This original Star Sapphire journeyed to Earth to rule it, and in the process battled the original Flash.

More than a decade later, in the pages of *Green Lantern* vol. 2 #16 (1962), scripted by John Broome and rendered by Gil Kane, the ultra-feminist Zamarons selected career woman Carol Ferris, girlfriend of Hal (Green Lantern) Jordan, as their new ruler, Star Sapphire (sometimes historically referred to as Star Sapphire II). (The original Star Sapphire attempted to eliminate her new rival, but was defeated by the Flashes [Jay Garrick and Barry Allen] and Green Lanterns [Alan Scott and Hal Jordan] of two generations. She disappeared into the Zamarons' 7th Dimension, and has not been seen since.)

Clad in a magenta leotard with matching go-go boots and eyemask and a star emblem on her midriff, Star Sapphire—whose primary weapon, the Green Lantern power ring–like star sapphire

Justice League editor Julius Schwartz named this uncanny supervillain after the title of one of his favorite science-fiction epics, *Tarrano the Conqueror*, a 1925 novel written by Ray Cummings, a former employee of inventor Thomas Alva Edison. While artist Sekowsky concocted Starro's look, the 1956 Japanese horror film *Uchûjin Tokyo ni arawaru*, distributed in the United States as *Warning from Space*, featured extraterrestrial invaders (portrayed by actors in rubber suits) that remarkably resembled Starro's appearance—nearly four years before the character's first comic-book appearance.

Aside from a pair of cameos in issues of *Justice League of America*, Starro next resurfaced for an undersea battle against Aquaman in *Adventure Comics* #451 (1977). In 1981 he returned to attack the entire League, discharging tiny starfish probes that affixed themselves to victims' faces—akin to the "face huggers" in the *Aliens* movie franchise—to exert their master's mental manipulation. He tried once again to overcome the world's greatest superheroes in a 1991 story arc in *Justice League Europe*, in which a Starro-controlled Martian Manhunter nearly made mincemeat of his teammates.

Writer Grant Morrison netted a retooled Starro—now called the "Star Conqueror"—to reassemble the then-disbanded League in *JLA Secret Files* #1 (1997). In that comic, an intergalactic subjugator called "It" dispatched starfish probes to Earth to link with humans' nervous systems. "I am the probe. He is the Conqueror. You are the spaces yet to be taken. Understand that your minds were never your own," muttered the Flash under the Star Conqueror's sway. Another of the Star Conqueror's attempts to lord over Earthlings attracted Morpheus the Sandman, the lord of dreams, and the starfish was quite appropriately banished to incarceration in a numinous fishbowl. It is only a matter of time before the Star Conqueror's swims free of its imprisonment and attempts once again to overpower the Justice League and the planet.

Starro appeared on television in the two-part *Batman Beyond* episode "The Call" (2000). The cover to *The Brave and the Bold* #28 was recreated as a mini-statue by sculptor John G. Matthews in a 2002 release from DC Direct. —*ME*

Steppenwolf: *See* **Darkseid's Elite**

Stilt-Man

O ne must wonder if Stan Lee and Wally Wood, the writer and artist of Marvel Comics' *Daredevil* vol. 1 #8 (1965), believed that their co-creation, the escalating evildoer they called the Stilt-Man (alternately written "Stilt Man" and "Stiltman" in this same issue), would have the legs to survive the decades. Their tale "The Stiltman Cometh" introduces disgruntled Kaxton Industries scientist Wilbur Day, who pockets his employer's new technological achievement, a hydraulic ram, and adapts it to an armored battlesuit with legs that telescope to nearly 300 feet in height. As Manhattan's towering thief, the Stilt-Man takes a spill after encountering the rooftop-swinging Man without Fear, Daredevil.

Stilt-Man's later mid- to late 1960s *Daredevil* appearances were highlighted by the art of Gene Colan, whose inventive upshot and downshot perspectives created a sense of vertigo on the two-dimension comic-book page. Despite the blast– and grenade–firing capabilities of Stilt-Man's armor, however, the David-versus-Goliath-esque Daredevil-versus-Stilt-Man formula wore thin; even grouping the villain with other criminals as the Emissaries of Evil (*Daredevil Annual* #1, 1967) barely helped his stature.

Over the decades, the Stilt-Man nonetheless stepped into scuffles with several Marvel heroes including Captain America, Spider-Man, and Thor, as well as rematches with Daredevil—there was even an obligatory "when giants clash" battle with Black Goliath in 1976. By the time Stilt-Man was featured in writer/artist John Byrne's tongue-in-cheek, fourth wall–breaking satire *The Sensational She-Hulk*, in issue #4's "Tall Dis-Order" (1989), it was clear that the high-stepping supervillain was not to be taken seriously (although he was played straight in a second-season episode of the 1994–1996 television cartoon *Iron Man*). The miniseries *Spider-Man/Daredevil: Unusual Suspects* (2001), published under the edgy "Marvel Knights" imprint, attempted to make Stilt-Man more formidable by darkening his armor and his personality, but *Peter Parker: Spider-Man* #149 (2003) regarded Stilt-Man as a joke, as Spidey overcame him with little effort. In the bleak, ultra-violent comic-book world of the twenty-first century, where supervillains are more bloodthirsty than ever before, perhaps a role as a comic-relief crook is one Stilt-Man will take in stride. —ME

Stryfe

W hen he first appeared in Marvel's *New Mutants* #87 (1990) as a creation of artist Rob Liefeld, Stryfe was a conundrum to readers. This mutant terrorist turned out to be the double of Cable, the New Mutants' new leader. The two also proved to have similar telepathic and telekinetic powers.

Cable was revealed to be Nathan Summers, the son of X-Men member Cyclops (Scott Summers) and Madelyne Pryor, the clone of his true love Jean Grey. The evil mutant Apocalypse had infected the infant Nathan with a "techno-organic" virus; to save his life he was transported two thousand years into an alternate future by an emissary of Mother Askani, another member of the Summers family.

Writer Scott Lobdell continued the story in the comics miniseries *The Adventures of Cyclops and Phoenix* (1994). In case he died, Mother Askani had a clone of the infant Nathan created, free from the techno-organic disease. Still alive in this distant future, Apocalypse abducted the clone and named him Stryfe. So Nathan grew up to become Cable, the leader of the freedom fighters of his future Earth, while Stryfe became his greatest enemy, who even killed Cable's wife, Aliya.

Eventually both Cable and Stryfe traveled back to the X-Men's own time, where they continued their war against each other. Stryfe unleashed the Legacy Virus, which killed many mutants before a cure was found. Though Stryfe's original body was destroyed, his spirit has taken possession of other bodies, even Cable's, to continue his terrorist rampages. —PS

The Suicide Squad

C ongressional aide Amanda Waller knew that desperate times require desperate measures.

A squat but beefy African American bearing more than a passing resemblance to Oprah Winfrey (circa 1986), Waller discovers the classified dossier of "Task Force X," aka the "Suicide Squad," a rag-tag band of operatives led onto dangerous covert missions by team commander Rick Flag (this Squad was first seen in *The Brave and the Bold* vol. 1 #25, 1959). When the despotic Darkseid dispatches the fiery giant Brimstone to Earth in 1987's *Legends* #3 (written by John Ostrander, dialogued by Len Wein, and penciled by John Byrne), Waller realizes that stopping this monster is a suicide mission. And thus she has no choice but to "Send for ... the Suicide Squad," reviving Task Force X as a paranormal patrol. But who would serve on such a foolhardy assignment, of which survival is far from certain? Supervillains with nothing to lose. Waller promises amnesty to Blockbuster, Bronze Tiger, Captain Boomerang, Deadshot, and the Enchantress, and the Suicide Squad, the "expendable" superteam, is born.

Spinning out of *Legends* into its own title, *Suicide Squad* was, during its 66-issue run (1987–1992), one of DC Comics' most daring and least predictable series. Ostrander and co-writer Kim Yale (with pencilers Luke McDonnell, John K. Snyder III, and Geof Isherwood) embraced the cast—largely discarded or underdeveloped adversaries—and gave them the personalities they lacked, with bickering among the ranks the norm. Character backstories were fleshed out, and, in a prophetic pre–September 11, 2001, move, international terrorists were one of the recurring threats requiring the Squad's talents. Of particular note was the Jihad, a superpowered terrorist clan (including Rustam, Djinn, Ravan, Jaculi, and Manticore) from the Iraq-like nation of Qurac that nearly succeeded in destroying Manhattan in 1988; post–September 11, the Jihad has been renamed the Onslaught.

Captain Boomerang and Deadshot were chief among the Suicide Squad's core members, and over the course of the series a legion of lethal luminaries marched in and out of service, some dying in action, including Black Adam, Captain Cold, Chronos, Count Vertigo, Dr. Light, Killer Frost, Nightshade, the Penguin, Plastique, Poison Ivy, and Punch and Jewelee. A few superheroes and anti-heroes such as the Atom, Nemesis, Vixen, and even Batman participated in

Rehabilitated Supervillains

While it took a pardon to encourage the Suicide Squad to fight injustice, a change of heart was enough for these supervillains to abandon their evil origins.

- **Black Canary** (first seen in *Flash Comics* #86, 1947) started her nocturnal fishnetted activities as a high-kicking, Robin Hood–like thief until the smitten Johnny Thunder helped the Blonde Bombshell see the light.
- **The Pied Piper** (*The Flash* #106, 1959) tooted his mind-controlling flute against the Flash for decades until the hero's 1986 death inspired the Piper to become a social crusader and a friend to the new Flash.
- **Hawkeye** (*Tales of Suspense* #57, 1964), the eagle-eyed bowman of the Avengers, was a circus archer lured into lawlessness by the sexy Soviet spy the Black Widow (*Tales of Suspense* #52, 1964). Dangerous encounters with Communists led both to defect to the side of good.
- **The Scarlet Witch and Quicksilver** (*X-Men* #4, 1964), the sister/brother sorceress and super-speedster, aided the Brotherhood of Evil Mutants, not realizing at the time that its leader Magneto was actually their father. They soon followed their natural instincts and reformed, joining the Avengers, but in 2004 an insane Scarlet Witch assaulted her teammates.
- **Medusa** (*Fantastic Four* #36, 1965) wielded her malleable hair as one of the Frightful Four, yet it was amnesia that caused her to be led astray, and once her memory returned she took her heroic place alongside her genetic kinfolk, the Inhumans.
- **The White Queen** (*X-Men* #129, 1980) loyally served the subversive Hellfire Club until the mutant genocide in Genosha motivated her to ply her psionic talents for good. As Emma Frost, she is a member of the team she once conspired against, the X-Men.
- **Lobo** (*Omega Men* #3, 1983), the ultra-violent anti-hero who kicks "bastiches'" butts across the galaxy, has no "heart" to change—he sides with the good guys only when it benefits him.

Suicide Squad cases, and the series afforded the first consistent exposure to former Batgirl Barbara Gordon in her role as information broker Oracle. Waller was the series' most interesting character, using any means necessary, from blackmail to negotiation, to coerce supervillains into her corner.

A 2001–2002 *Suicide Squad* revival by writer Keith Giffen and artist Paco Medina lasted twelve issues and added former Injustice Gang members (including Big Sir, Clock King, and Multi-Man, who were killed in the line of duty) into the mix, with old warhorse Sgt. Rock leading the group. The Suicide Squad blasted onto television in 2005 in the "Task Force X" episode of the Cartoon Network's *Justice League Unlimited* (2004–present), scripted by popular comic-book writer/artist Darwyn Cooke. The animated Squad consisted of Amanda Waller (CCH Pounder), Captain Boomerang (Donal Gibson), Clock King (Alan Rachins), Deadshot (Michael Rosenbaum), Plastique (Juliet Landau), and Rick Flag (Adam Baldwin); their mission: stealing a powerful artifact from the Justice League's headquarters! Waller has continued to appear on *JLU*. —ME

Super-Gorillas

Simians have frequently been characterized in the popular culture possessing a trait most human—malevolence—with four archetypes of evil super-gorillas emerging: super-sentient gorillas, mutant gorillas, colossal gorillas, and man-gorillas.

Orang, "the ape that thinks like a man," bowed in the September 1, 1940, installment of Will Eisner's newspaper comic-book supplement *The Spirit*. While not a gorilla, this orangutan used his scientifically enhanced intellect, afforded him by a Dr. Egel, to adopt humanlike mannerisms—including the worst of the lot, kidnapping and murder—paving the way for later supervillain gorillas like the Flash's foe Grodd and Monsieur Mallah of the Brotherhood of Evil. The Gorilla, an ape with a human brain, premiered shortly thereafter in 1941 in Fox Publications' *Blue Beetle* series, and another brainy primate, Gargantua ("the Phi Beta Gorilla"), fought Plastic Man in 1948.

No publisher went ape over super-sentient gorillas more than DC Comics. "It was a question of trying to find something that sold," long-time DC artist Sheldon Moldoff once reflected, "and if one issue came out and it happened to sell, then immediately they would follow that type of story." Throughout the 1950s intelligent gorillas were staples of editor Julius Schwartz's science-fiction anthologies, particularly *Strange Adventures*, which cover-featured tales including "The Gorilla War Against Earth" and "The Gorilla Who Challenged the World." Jack Schiff, the 1950s Batman editor, occasionally pitted the Dark Knight against primates, most notably "The Gorilla Boss of Gotham City" in *Batman* #75 (1953), featuring crimelord George "Boss" Dyke, whose brain was transplanted into an ape's body. Not to be outdone, Schwartz, who inherited the Batman franchise from Schiff in 1964, armed a gorilla with explosives—the "Living Beast Bomb"—to fight Batman in *Detective Comics* #339 (1965). Schiff, who took over *Strange Adventures* from Schwartz, volleyed in 1967 with Animal-Man's foe the Mod Gorilla Boss, a man mutated into a fashion-conscious gorilla; also that year, Wonder Woman tangled with bubble-helmeted talking gorillas that transformed her into an Amazonian monkey.

Marvel Comics' criminal zoologist Dr. Arthur Nagan, known for Dr. Moreau–like interspecies experiments upon primates, had the tables turned on him in a 1950s horror comic when apes affixed his head onto a gorilla's body, making him the freakish Gorilla-Man (not to be confused with the 1950s Marvel hero of the same name); he was revived in 1975 as the leader of the supervillain team the Headmen (also consisting of Chondu the Mystic, Shrunken Bones, and Ruby Thursday), enemies of the superhero "non-team," the Defenders.

While intelligent gorillas were seldom seen after the early 1970s, with the exception of Gorilla Grodd and 1980s appearances of the Ultra-Humanite, the Golden Age mastermind prone to transferring his intellect into the fearsome form of a white gorilla, in 1995 two super-sentient gorillas were birthed in Image Comics series: BrainiApe, the Savage Dragon foe with a dome-encased super-brain, and the cyborg-simian enemy of Spawn, Cy-Gor (Cy-Gor was also manufactured as an action figure).

Gorilla soldiers, a super-sentient gorilla offshoot, were popularized by Pierre Boulle's novel *Planet of the Apes* (1963) and the film/television franchise and comic-book continuations that followed. Sentient warrior apes were frequent nemeses in Jack Kirby's 1970s DC opus *Kamandi, the Last Boy on Earth*.

Mutant gorillas were also popular during comics' Golden (1938–1954) and Silver (1956–1969) ages. Superboy encountered "The Gorilla with X-Ray Eyes" in *Adventure Comics* #219 (1955), while Superman received a visitor from his homeworld in *Action Comics* #218 (1956): "The Super-Ape from Krypton." An eight-limbed "Octi-Ape" clambered into the pages of *Blackhawk* #152 (1960), while *Fantastic Four* #13 (1963) introduced criminal Soviet scientist the Red Ghost, aided by a trio of irradiated Super-Apes including a superstrong gorilla. *Hawkman* #6 (1965) featured a flying warrior gorilla in a story later reimagined by twenty-first century creators in 2004's *DC Comics Presents: Hawkman* #1, part of a series of tributes to editor Schwartz upon his passing that year. Perhaps the oddest mutant gorilla was the saber-toothed ape/dinosaur hybrid in Gold Key Comics' *Mighty Samson* #10 (1967).

Movie monster King Kong's 1933 theatrical debut spawned innumerable chest-thumping super-sized imitators, most notably Superman's kryptonite-visioned Titano the Super-Ape. *Konga*, a low-budget 1961 *King Kong* clone, inspired a Charlton comics series that ran for nearly two dozen issues. In the 1960s DC's waterlogged superteam the Sea Devils battled an aquatic ape called Monster Gorilla, a name also used by Archie Comics for an enemy of the Fly. Tomahawk, DC's Revolutionary War hero, battled two giant apes—King Colosso and the Gorilla Ranger, the latter of which wore a Native American feathered headband and fired enormous arrows—while the golden gorilla Gorr attacked the Fantastic Four in 1976.

Humans disguised as apes constitute the final super-gorilla archetype. *Daredevil* #10 (1965) introduced the Ani-Men—Ape-Man, Bird-Man, Cat-Man, and Frog-Man—terrorists afforded super-abilities from their animal-inspired uniforms; the agility-enhanced Ape-Man later received Herculean might (Frog-Man eventually left the group, which was renamed the Unholy Three). Wakandan warrior M'Baku cloaked himself in an albino-ape pelt in 1969 and became the superstrong Man-Ape; abetted by his loyal White Gorilla Cult, Man-Ape warred against the Black Panther and his allies, the

DC Comics Presents Hawkman #1 ©2004 DC Comics.
COVER ART BY JOSÉ LUIS GARCIA-LÓPEZ AND KEVIN NOWLAN.

Avengers, and continued to fight the Avengers over the years as one of the Masters of Evil. The Gibbon, first seen in *Amazing Spider-Man* #110 (1972), was an incredibly nimble outcast named Martin Blank who donned a monkey suit he once wore as a circus performer and auditioned to be Spider-Man's partner; after he was spurned by wall-crawler the Gibbon hooked up with the equally vengeful Kraven the Hunter to complicate Spidey's life. —*ME*

Superman Revenge Squad

S howing their sinister solidarity by each plunging a dagger into a Superman emblem, the Superman Revenge Squad is sworn to annihilate the Man of Steel. Superman first meets these extraterres-

trial terrorists in *Action Comics* #287 (1962), when they attack him with red kryptonite in retribution for his preventing their earlier conquest attempts. Uniting as a formidable force, these "Revengers"—with otherworldly names like Dramx, Vlatuu, and Nakox—perpetually plot against the Man of Steel in their Hall of Hate on a desolate planet and wear somber variations of Superman's uniform with emerald insignias that glow like green kryptonite.

Perhaps their most noteworthy adventure occurred in *World's Finest Comics* #175 (1968), which introduced the Batman Revenge Squad (in purple Batman costumes with bat-winged skulls on their chests). This was the first Batman tale illustrated by Neal Adams, who would later distinguish himself as the hero's premier artist of the 1970s; it was also Adams' first pairing with inker and partner-to-be Dick Giordano. A Superboy Revenge Squad briefly appeared in 1982. While a clever story gimmick, the Superman Revenge Squad failed to achieve significant acclaim due to its interchangeable roster of underdeveloped characters.

A 1996 revival of the Squad assembled established Superman villains—the replicating Riot, the human arsenal Barrage, the magician Misa, the "absorbing man" Anomaly, and the spurned superwoman Maxima—who succeeded in defeating Superman, but petty infighting enabled the hero to rise to victory. A later incarnation with Baud and Rock joining returnee Barrage and old-timer the Parasite also failed to overcome the hero. The Superman Revenge Squad made a cameo appearance in the "Hereafter" episode of the TV cartoon *Justice League Unlimited* (2004–present). —*ME*

Super-Nazis and Axis Adversaries

I f the Nazis did not exist, comic books would have had to invent them. In the early days of comics, superheroes fought against corrupt politicians, evil scientists, greedy landlords, and a host of other pseudo real-life menaces that could be defeated with relatively little effort. Writers and publishers began to wonder where they could find a foe worthy of their brainchildren.

Fortunately—for comics, if not comic-book scholarship that would one day study the World War II books in earnest—they had to look no further than their daily newspapers or radio newscasts, from which they learned all about a real-life European madman named Adolf Hitler. Der Führer spoke of a master race that would rule the world, grinding under its hob-nailed boot everyone they deemed inferior, including all members of a religious faith that many comics creators espoused.

Hitler was the perfect arch-villain. Writers and artists could fight the Nazis on the printed page and get paid for it, all before America officially fought in World War II. The cover of *Captain America Comics* #1, dated March 1941, shows a very patriotic "Cap" giving Hitler a sock in the puss months before the attack on Pearl Harbor put America squarely on the map. Nazis and super-Nazis bedeviled superheroes throughout the war as they fought heroes like Captain Flag, the Justice Society of America—christened, for the duration of the war, the Justice Battalion—the Boy Commandos, and many others, in stories that had to do with the unwitting betrayal of military secrets and the necessity of presenting a united front against the Axis powers, unifying all Americans, regardless of race, creed, or gender. Unfortunately, such ringing declarations of American solidarity lasted only until the end of the war, at which time women, Jews, and Negroes were told to return to the back of the bus.

Chronologically, super-Nazis come in two varieties: those who fight in stories set in World War II, and those who continue the bad fight after the war, into the twenty-first century.

Baron Blitzkrieg was introduced in a Wonder Woman story in *World's Finest Comics* #246 (1977) by Gerry Conway and Don Heck. The Baron was a concentration camp commandant whose face was disfigured by acid thrown by a rebellious inmate. Hitler ordered his scientists to try to reconfigure the man's face and, while they were at it, "had his scientists execute a long-developed plan that tapped the commandant's latent psychic powers." He donned golden armor with magenta trim and fought Superman, Wonder Woman, and the All-Star Squadron, among others, and is reportedly active as a terrorist in the twenty-first century, calling himself the Baron.

Baroness Paula Von Gunther, from her first appearance in *Sensation Comics* #4, 1942 (in a Wonder Woman story penned by Charles Moulton and drawn by H. G. Peter), attempted to make American women spy for Nazi Germany through any means: blackmail, torture, or murder. Despite possessing no superpowers, she was one of Wonder Woman's worst enemies until reformed by the Purple Ray on the Amazons' Transformation Island, after which she became a staunch ally of the Amazon. Baroness Von Gunther, portrayed by Christine Belford, appeared in a 1976 episode of the *Wonder Woman* television show, "Wonder Woman Meets Baroness Von Gunther."

Captain Nippon debuted in *Captain Marvel Jr.* #2 (1942), one of the few Japanese super-agents to appear in comics. He was a spy before he was given, by evil sorcerers, enough raw power to go one-on-one with Junior. He wore a loose-fitting soldier's uniform and carried a spiked club, as opposed to another villain also called Captain Nippon, who had a hook in lieu of a right hand and a red sunburst on his forehead, and wore green tights and a cowl. He fought Captain Courageous, who appeared in *Banner Comics* in 1941 by Ace Periodicals.

The Hate Monger, in his first appearance in *Fantastic Four* vol. 1 #21 (1963), by Stan Lee and Jack Kirby, was found, after his death, to be a clone of Adolf Hitler. However, Nazi scientist Arnim Zola gave him the ability to transfer his consciousness to other cloned bodies, so it is virtually impossible for his death to have any permanence. He once used a weapon, the "H-ray," which was capable of stimulating hatred in others and converting other emotions to hate, but now the villain became capable of performing those feats on his own. Following his resurrection by the Cosmic Cube, the Hate Monger essentially became an energy being, capable of regenerating severed limbs. When he has all his limbs he wears a purple jumpsuit and a pointed hood monogrammed with an "H." Though once destroyed, he was resurrected by the Red Skull in the pages of *Captain America*, and continues to spread his poison, sometimes using the civilian name "Adam Hauser."

Per Degaton debuted in *All Star Comics* #35 (1947) in a story by John Broome and Irwin Hasen

YOU UND YOUR VERDAMMT TROOPERS! CAN I HAFF *NO SECRETS* FROM YOU? SINCE I TRAINED YOU TO BE MY OWN PRIVATE VEAPON, YOU HAFF BECOME *TOO* POWERFUL!

YOU NEED NOT WORRY ABOUT ME, MEIN FUEHRER-- *YET!* I CAN AFFORD TO BE--PATIENT.'

From *Tales of Suspense* #67 ©1965 Marvel Comics.
ART BY JACK KIRBY AND FRANK RAY (FRANK GIACOIA).

in a story by Martin Pasko and Jose Delbo, as Nazi Helmut Streicher, a soldier who donned invulnerable body armor and a silver helmet with a swastika and fought Wonder Woman and other members of the JSA in the 1940s. Decades later, a neo-Nazi took the name of the Red Panzer and was slain attacking the modern-day Wonder Woman and the super-heroine Troia. This second Red Panzer's son— who was put up for adoption by his father because he was half black—then took the name and armor, joining Tartarus, a team of villains formed by Vandal Savage, and was killed in combat. Savage offered an operative of the criminal organization H.I.V.E., known only as Justin, the chance to become the fourth Red Panzer and join Tartarus, though he soon quit that organization and relocated to Zandia, where he fought Young Justice. Justin is unique among all Red Panzers; he does not espouse the Nazi philosophy, but is a nihilist.

as an ambitious laboratory assistant of Professor Malachi Zee. He stole Zee's time machine and attempted to conquer the world by altering the past, including the deployment of an army in uniforms that looked suspiciously Nazi-like. Just two issues later, in *All Star* #37, Degaton appeared as a member of the original Injustice Society of the World, wearing the same black outfit with a "D" on the chest. He had red hair and was a little guy, but we all know how troublesome little guys can be. Defeated by the Justice Society of America (JSA), all memories of Degaton's conquests faded from his mind as the true timeline resumed. Dr. Zee was later revealed to be a former member of a group of scientists called the Time Trust, and Degaton would again and again attempt to defeat the JSA, his final plan inadvertently leading to his suicide in *America vs. the Justice Society* #4 (1985). However, since he is a time-traveler, this may not be the last time Per Degaton is heard from.

Red Panzer has had many incarnations. He debuted in *Wonder Woman* vol. 1 #228 (1977),

Nazis continue to serve as villains in popular culture, such as in Steven Spielberg's 1981 film *Raiders of the Lost Ark*, in which the protagonist, Indiana Jones (as portrayed by Harrison Ford), sums up his feelings about the Master Race succinctly: "Nazis. I hate these guys." However, even "fans" of Nazis-as-villains realize they must be used sparingly to retain their effectiveness. *Hellboy* creator Mike Mignola, interviewed in 2001 about his project *The Conqueror Worm,* said: "My feeling is this is that last time I'm going to deal with the whole Nazi thing. It's too easy to use the Nazis now."

But as long as there are comic books, it seems there will be Nazi antagonists; they're just too bad to abandon for good. —*MWB*

Super-Sized Supervillains

Giants have long stomped through legends and mythologies, leaving behind very large footprints and trails of devastation. Goliath in the Old Testament, the giant in the fairy tale *Jack and the Beanstalk*, and Gog and Magog from British lore are among the titans whose towering terrorism has intimidated even the mightiest heroes.

Superman has upon occasion had to "Look! Up in the sky!" at gigantic menaces endangering his beloved Metropolis, including Titano the Super-Ape, the King Kong–sized gorilla with kryptonite vision he first fought in 1959. Superman's pal Jimmy Olsen's disregard of the Man of Steel's warning against fiddling with an enlarging ray led to Jimmy's transmogrification into the mindless Giant Turtle Man, a green-scaled rampaging beast that ripped through suspension bridges in *Superman's Pal Jimmy Olsen* #53 (1961). One of the most dangerous creatures from the Man of Tomorrow's homeworld, Krypton, the bat-winged, fire-spewing Flame-Dragon threatened to destroy Earth in *Superman* vol. 1 #142 (1961), with a second Flame-Dragon hatching in issue #151 (1962). Lex Luthor, in a move worthy of Dr. Frankenstein, created a "pseudo-life" form of cosmic energy called the Galactic Golem in *Superman* #248 (1972); while the Golem stood only a few heads taller than the Man of Steel, his ability to siphon the hero's energy magnified his menace.

Yet none of Superman's foes has used size as a weapon more effectively than Brainiac, whose shrinking ray has reduced the Man of Steel to the height of a doll; the same fate has befallen the Fantastic Four, first shrunken by Dr. Doom in *Fantastic Four* vol. 1 #16 (1963). Batman and Robin were turned into pygmies in several Golden Age (1938–1954) stories, a notable example being *Detective Comics* #148 (1949), in which the miniature Dynamic Duo were trapped under glass by the insane scientist Professor Zero. To Batman's Justice League 6-inch teammate the Atom, the Tiny Titan, virtually any normal-height foe, from an angry thug wielding a shoe to costumed criminals like Chronos, becomes a super-sized enemy. The Golden Age's Doll Man had similar problems with eccentric nemeses such as the Skull and the Mad Hypnotist, as did Marvel Comics' Ant-Man, who, with his pocket-sized heartthrob the Wasp, was nearly trampled by the blob-like Creature from Kosmos and the one-eyed Cyclops in 1960s adventures.

Mega-sized menaces are common in the Marvel Universe—the world-devouring Galactus, Ego the Living Planet, the cosmically imbued mutant the Living Monolith (aka the Living Pharaoh), biocomputer the Supreme Intelligence, the reality-manipulating Shaper of Worlds, and mutant-seeking giant robots the Sentinels have brought superheroes and average Joes and Janes to their knees. The DC Universe has weathered attacks from entities larger than Earth itself: the presence of interdimensional wanderer the Anti-Matter Man almost obliterated the Justice League's Earth-One and the Justice Society's Earth-Two in the teams' fourth crossover (*Justice League of America* #46–#47, 1966), and the gargantuan Anti-Monitor came close to eliminating *all* of DC's parallel worlds in the landmark *Crisis on Infinite Earths* (1985–1986). A prototype for the Anti-Monitor was Shathan, a red-skinned demon that grew to unbelievable proportions and used Earth itself as a weapon to battle the similarly enormous Spectre, in *Showcase* #61 (1966).

The Incredible Hulk, no small threat himself, has gone fist-to-fist with super-sized supervillains. One of his recurring enemies, the Absorbing Man, has often grown to mammoth proportions, and the stone-totem Umbu the Unliving and the Leader's giant android the Super-Adaptoid were among Hulk's early foes. Several of Hulk's larger-than-life adversaries were closer to the Green Goliath's brutish size, such as the Neanderthal-turned-supervillain the Missing Link (first seen in *The Incredible Hulk* vol. 2 #105, 1968), and the "disaster eight miles high," the Bi-Beast (*Hulk* #169, 1973), a twin-faced grotesquerie as strong as the Hulk and as smart as his alter ego Bruce Banner.

In the somber superhero realities of the late twentieth and early twenty-first centuries, super-sized supervillains are usually relegated to cosmic-scale crossovers, like Darkseid's hell-on-Earth minion Brimstone, who blasted DC superheroes in the crossover *Legends* (1986) before doing the same on television in 2004 on *Justice League Unlimited*. Occasionally, however, comics creators can't resist telling a tall tale, as the creative team of Keith Giffen, J. M. DeMatteis, and Kevin Maguire did in *JLA Classified* #9 (2005) by turning the dimwitted canine Green Lantern G'Nort into a Godzilla-sized troublemaker, proving once and for all that size *does* matter! —*ME*

Super-Skrull

P anic sweeps Manhattan in Stan Lee and Jack Kirby's *Fantastic Four* vol. 1 #18 (1963) when a repugnant alien stormtrooper with a furrowed green face and pointy ears touches down in Times Square, claiming Earth for his warrior race of shapeshifters, the Skrulls. Zipping to the scene is the FF, but to their surprise this "Super-Skrull" not only mimics and mixes but *bests* their amazing superpowers—the Thing's superstrength, Mr. Fantastic's elasticity, Invisible Girl's imperceptibility, and the Human Torch's flame! The product of Skrull bioengineering, Super-Skrull bushwhacks the Four with his bonus talent, "the blinding power of irresistible hypnotism." Big brain Mr. Fantastic cobbles together a jamming device that blocks a spaceship-transmitted signal boosting Super-Skrull's energy, and the team seals the weakened extraterrestrial in an island crater.

Super-Skrull—known among his people as Kl'rt—was liberated by the Skrulls and given opportunities to redeem himself in a return match with the FF and a battle with the thunder god Thor, but was routed both times. Yet the disgraced Super-Skrull was conscripted into the Kree/Skrull War, and has been dispatched against or encountered numerous heroes including Captain Marvel, Spider-Man, the Silver Surfer, and the Incredible Hulk. Super-Skrull became a free agent after his homeworld was devoured by Galactus. *Fantastic Four: Foes* #3 (2005) offered his skewed perspective on his ongoing war with the Four. The popular villain has been featured in the 1967, 1978, and 1994 *Fantastic Four* animated television series, and has appeared in several action-figure lines. —*ME*

Supervillain Headquarters

A ny villain worth his bile knows that if he's going to take over the world, he needs a place from which to plot his impending assault. Whether they are scientists, megalomaniacs, or evil geniuses, all supervillains need a home-away-from-prison to hang their hats (or trick umbrellas or labcoats, as the case may be). But not just any location will do. When supervillains set up shop, they try to translate nightmares into architecture. Although villains' headquarters are not as iconic as superheroes' headquarters (Superman's Fortress of Solitude and Batman's Batcave, for example), they do fall into recognizable types and are often as intriguing as the villains themselves.

The traditional supervillain hideout is based on the mad scientist's lab, a workshop away from society in which the villain can plot schemes, mix chemicals, and perform maleficent experiments on living (and sometimes dead) victims. Victor Frankenstein, the protagonist of Mary Shelley's novel *Frankenstein*, set up his laboratory away from the social constraints of friends, family, and colleagues. In his isolation, he lost all sense of moral conscience as he created the monster that would eventually destroy him. In Romantic and Victorian gothic literature, crypts and laboratories were inhabited by mad monks, degenerate royalty, and corrupted geniuses such as Dr. Jekyll. Similar secluded hideouts were presented in pulp novels and film noir of the 1920s and 1930s, and superhero comics seized on this type of headquarters from their very beginnings. Early comics villains such as evil geniuses Lex Luthor and Dr. Sivana (Captain Marvel's nemesis) used laboratories to enhance and focus their villainous designs.

Villains' headquarters have evolved quite a bit since the early years of comics. The following exchange occurs in an episode of the animated TV series *Super Friends* called "History of Doom" (1978):

> *Lex Luthor.* The thirteen of us will form the most powerful and sinister group the world has even seen. From now on we'll be known as the Legion of Doom.

348

Sinestro: But we'll need a headquarters, too.

Black Manta: Yes. And I say it should be at the bottom of the ocean.

Captain Cold: We'll hide it under the ice in the polar cap.

Grodd: Your brain must be frozen, Captain Cold. The jungle is the only logical place.

Luthor: Silence. We'll compromise. Our headquarters will be in the swamp, hidden beneath its murky waters.

Sinestro: Now all we have to do is construct an impenetrable fortress, equipped with the most deadly devices in the universe.

Luthor: Nothing will stop us now. With our combined powers of evil, we must pledge to wipe out the Super Friends.

If a group of supervillains ever built a headquarters that embodied everything a fortress of evil should be, it was the Legion of Doom. The Hall of Doom, which looks like a domed version of Darth Vader's helmet and houses a wide variety of technological tools of terror, is probably the most iconic of all villain headquarters. The base is mobile, but it usually resides in an unspecified swamp—not just *in* the swamp, but *beneath* it.

Many other supervillains have also made their figurative "undergrounds" literal. The first villain the Fantastic Four fought was the Mole Man, the leader of a group of humanoids who live beneath the earth on a remote island. In *Astro City*, a villain named the Junkman operates out of the Astro City Dump and Landfill. The Frightful Four and the Lethal Legion, supervillain groups in the Marvel Universe, both set up their headquarters in subterranean Manhattan. In the Richard Donner–directed *Superman: The Movie* (1978), Lex Luthor constructs an elaborate headquarters—complete with a library and a swimming pool—far beneath the streets of Metropolis. In the 1992 film *Batman Returns*, the Penguin calls the Gotham sewer system his home. One of the deepest locations for supervillains' headquarters, however, is underwater. The Council, a group of villains who once fought Supergirl, set up their base at the bottom of Lake Michigan near Chicago.

Some villains choose to distance themselves from society not by going underground, but by operating outside of the United States. Marvel Comics' villains are particularly international in origin and ambition. Dr. Doom resides (and broods) in an ornate gothic castle in Latveria, an eastern European nation where he is monarch. Baron Heinrich Zemo lives in an exotic castle in the Amazon jungle. For several years, the X-Men villain Magneto ruled an island nation called Genosha before the mutant refuge and most of its inhabitants were destroyed. In the DC Universe, Teen Titans villain Brother Blood operates the Church of Blood out of a country called Zandia.

While most supervillains have managed to spread themselves *across* Earth, some prefer to reside *above* it. To counter the Justice League of America (JLA)'s satellite headquarters, the Injustice Gang launched its own satellite into orbit 22,300 miles above Earth. The Gang's satellite avoided detection by orbiting Earth directly opposite the JLA's base. The Injustice Gang satellite, resurrected in the 2004 miniseries *Identity Crisis*, still serves as a place of recreation and business for the DC Universe's criminal element. To a certain extent, the satellite performs the same function as supervillain gathering places such as the Dark Side Bar (a tavern where many second- and third-tier villains used to congregate) and the Oblivion Bar (a meeting place of many of DC's magical and supernatural characters).

Many supervillains set up their headquarters not on or above Earth, but far away from it. Ming the Merciless, the villain from the 1930s comic strip *Flash Gordon*, rules a city called Mingo on the planet Mongo, where he is worshipped despite his cruel tyranny. In the *Star Wars* saga, the intergalactic Sith Lords Darth Vader and Emperor Palpatine construct the Death Star as a central headquarters that reflects the power and sterility of the Empire itself. Interstellar terrors, along with their magnificent headquarters, also abound in comic books. Darkseid, scourge of the DC Universe, rules a planet of fire pits called Apokolips. Apokolips as a whole represents a hellish nightmare, but Darkseid's palace (the Tower of Rage) concentrates the doom and misery to an even greater extent. Darkseid's matron assistant Granny Goodness operates a school of torture ironically named "Happiness Home" on Apokolips.

As grand as many of the international and intergalactic supervillain bases are, some of the

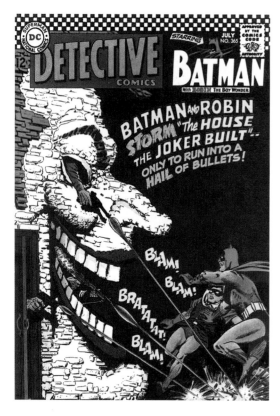

Detective Comics #365 ©1967 DC Comics.
COVER ART BY CARMINE INFANTINO AND MURPHY ANDERSON.

most impressive and frightening headquarters are located out in the open on Earth. Lex Luthor owns much of Metropolis, and his LexCorp building rises above it all as a testament to his realistic *human* power. Similarly, the Kingpin of Crime operates openly in the Hell's Kitchen district of New York City, and Norman Osborn used the resources of Oscorp to facilitate his career as the original Green Goblin. The Brotherhood of Evil, enemies of the original Doom Patrol, actually operated from a Parisian girls' school called École Des Filles, where team member Madame Rouge was headmistress.

Villain headquarters are intriguing because they reflect the aspirations, corruptions, and general style of the people who inhabit them. The Joker's Ha-Ha-Hacienda is as vibrant and as dangerous as the Clown Prince of Crime himself. Lex Luthor's and Dr. Doom's headquarters reflect their hubris and vanity. Supervillain headquarters resonate with audiences because they tap into the

fears and nightmares of haunted houses and dark caverns. This imagination is not limited to the comics page or the screen, though. Several notable villain headquarters have been turned into action figure playsets—most notably the "Tower of Doom" from Mattel's Secret Wars line (1984–1986) and the designed but unproduced "Tower of Darkness" from Kenner's Super Powers line (1984–1986). In 2005 computer game company PlayNC offered players the opportunity to customize their own personal supervillain headquarters when they released their *City of Villains* game (a companion to the popular *City of Heroes*). —AB

Supervillain Prisons

O ne of the most difficult dilemmas in superhero comics is what to do with superpowered criminals once they have been caught. Most supervillain prisons are specifically designed to hold superpowered felons, but supervillains by nature are designed and determined to break out of any conceivable holding facility. This paradox seems to present a hopeless, demoralizing struggle for superheroes, but it actually proves to be a useful and familiar device for readers who expect to see superheroes fighting significant villains on a regular basis. Hence, the prisons' design and security flaws are as variable (and inevitable) as the villains they contain.

Marvel Comics has provided perhaps the most fluid, continuous series of supervillain prisons in superhero comics. Marvel's first supervillain prison was Ryker's Island Prison, a jail patterned after the real Riker's Island in New York City. Like the actual Riker's, Ryker's Prison is situated in the East River between Queens and the Bronx. For many years, prison officials designated one wing of Ryker's as the supervillain wing. Because the prison wasn't designed to accommodate superpowered criminals, it experienced repeated jailbreaks and extensive destruction to the entire facility. U.S. government officials and non-superhuman prisoners who feared for their lives put so much pressure on prison administrators that the superhuman wing was eventually shut down.

The superhuman criminals who had been at Ryker's were then moved to a government research facility called Project: Pegasus, the Marvel equivalent of DC Comics' S.T.A.R. Labs. Many of the inmates were studied at a wing of the Project called "the Compound," which was dedicated to superhuman research. The Project didn't last long, but the information gathered from metahuman research there allowed the government to design a more effective facility dedicated solely to the incarceration of superhuman criminals.

The Vault, the United States government's next and most extensive superhuman prison, was constructed entirely underground in the Rocky Mountain range in Colorado. The compound was heavily fortified and guarded, but supervillains inevitably escaped despite the fact that each cell was customized to neutralize the occupant's superpower. A successor to the Vault is the Raft, a supervillain prison relocated on Ryker's Island. The Raft was built to rectify many of the Vault's weaknesses, but this prison has proven to be just another in a series of porous containment facilities. A major jailbreak at the Vault (*New Avengers* #1–#6, 2004–2005) led the dismantled Avengers to reassemble and pursue a slew of highly dangerous escaped convicts across the planet. Yet another facility for incarcerating Marvel supervillains, the Big House (*She-Hulk* #5, 2004), employed former Ant-Man Hank Pym's shrinking technology to miniaturize felons to action-figure height. A breakout resulted in a stampede of doll-sized villains.

The Slabside Island Maximum Security Facility, located in Antarctica, is the DC Universe's equivalent of Marvel's Raft, *Astro City*'s Biro Island Correctional Facility, and the real world's Alcatraz Island. Designed specifically for metahumans, "the Slab" can hold up to 205 of the most dangerous superhuman criminals on Earth. Like other prisons, the Slab was designed to be escape-proof, but (like other prisons) the Slab has been breached on several occasions—most notably by the intergalactic warlord Mongul, who released a number of supervillains when he escaped (*Green Lantern* vol. 3 #51–#53, 1994). A similar maximum security facility is located at Belle Reve Prison in Terrebonne Parrish, Louisiana. Located on the edge of a swamp, Belle Reve serves both as a prison for many of DC's high-profile villains and as the headquarters for the Suicide Squad—a covert government-organized team of semi-reformed villains trying to earn their freedom.

Besides the Slab and Belle Reve, DC villains are held (however briefly) in several other prisons tied to more specific characters, times, and locations. Many of Superman's superpowered villains are taken to Stryker's Island, a maximum security prison off the shore of Metropolis. Superman also frequently uses the Phantom Zone, an extradimensional abyss, to imprison many of his most dangerous foes. Iron Heights Prison, situated just three miles outside Keystone City, Kansas, is home to many of the Flash's Rogues' Gallery. The one notable escapee from Iron Heights, the Pied Piper, eventually reformed, but he initiated a security (and civil rights) crackdown that led the Flash into frequent conflict with the prison's administration. After the Piper's escape, all superpowered inmates were moved underground to an isolated dungeon-like area called "the Pipeline." One thousand years in the future, the Legion of Super-Heroes uses the prison planet Takron-Galtos to incarcerate intergalactic threats. Another notable DC prison is the Gulag, a prison stronghold built by a number of superheroes in the 1996 Elseworlds series *Kingdom Come*. Intended to lock up out-of-control and dangerous metahumans, the Gulag is a clever visual reflection of the Hall of Doom, the supervillain headquarters in the 1970s animated series *Super Friends*.

While many supervillain prisons are intended to contain and neutralize superpowered criminals, several notable facilities are designed more for mental rehabilitation than incarceration. Unfortunately, this project rarely fares any better than prison containment. Arkham Asylum for the Criminally Insane, probably the most recognizable, distinctive facility in superhero comics, is home to most of the Batman's psychologically troubled rogues. Appropriately, writer Dennis O'Neal named Arkham after a fictional gothic Massachusetts town in H. P. Lovecraft's 1933 story "The Thing On the Doorstep." Arkham's history has been rewritten numerous times, but mid-2000s continuity has the asylum founded in 1921 by Dr. Amadeus Arkham. Amadeus experienced delusions after the death of his mother, but the murder of his wife and daughter pushed him completely over the edge into insanity. He was eventually confined to a cell in his own asylum, where he scratched messages into the walls and floor with his fingernails for the rest of his life.

Arkham Asylum was founded in the midst of psychosis and remains a place of severe psychological trauma for all who go in or near it. As Batman says in the 1989 graphic novel *Arkham Asylum*, "I'm afraid that when I walk through those asylum gates ... when I walk into Arkham and the doors close behind me ... it'll be just like coming home." Even Arkham's employees are susceptible to the ghosts that haunt the building. Former therapist Dr. Harleen Quinzel gradually descended into madness, adopted the name Harley Quinn, and became the Joker's accomplice in crime. Similar rehabilitative failures are experienced frequently at Marvel's equivalent of Arkham, the Ravencroft Institute for the Criminally Insane, where many of Spider-Man's rogues are taken for incarceration and treatment.

Supervillain prisons are familiar and necessary in mainstream comic books, but the conventions associated with them reach into other literary forms as well. One of the most notable prisons in popular literature is Azkaban Prison from the *Harry Potter* novel series. Located on an island in the middle of the North Sea, Azkaban is the holding place for only the very worst offenders of wizard law. The prison is guarded by frightening creatures called Dementors who inflict punishment on prisoners by forcing them to continually relive all of their worst memories. Azkaban is a place of no hope—a place where punishment is valued more than rehabilitation, and where nightmares are used as weapons. The prison also exhibits many recognizable features, from the seclusion of the Slab to the gothic atmosphere of Arkham Asylum. *—AB*

Supervillain Team-Ups

There is safety in numbers, the supervillain community has learned, often rallying together under adversarial appellations like the Masters of Evil, the Secret Society of Super-Villains, and the Sinister Six. These confederacies are usually motivated by a mutual hatred of a hero, and are generally fouled by dissimilarity and deception.

As a rule, supervillains may gang up, but they rarely team up—their selfish motivations and megalomania prohibits cooperation. Yet upon occasion, a pair (or trio) of supervillains will join forces to spell double trouble for their fabled foes, the result of writers' creative inspiration or sales desperation.

Batman #2 (1940) featured an early example, a tale titled "The Joker Meets the Cat-Woman" (Catwoman), although those newly introduced Batrogues were rivals in this adventure. The Joker united with the Penguin in "Knights of Knavery" in *Batman* #25 (1945), sealing their alliance by jointly signing a "Deed of Partnership"; a Joker/Penguin coat of arms hung on the wall of their lair.

In an effort to make the 1966 theatrical spinoff of the live-action series *Batman* (1966–1968) splashier than the small-screen's version, *four* foes—Joker, Penguin, Riddler, and Catwoman—combined forces. Signet Books published a novelization of its screenplay, author Winston Lyon's *Batman vs. the Fearsome Foursome* (1966). That same year, Lyon also penned the original novel *Batman vs. 3 Villains of Doom*, featuring a contest between Penguin, Catwoman, and Joker, while DC Comics' *The Brave and the Bold* #68, a Batman/Metamorpho team-up, also featured Joker, Penguin, and Riddler, chuckling like lunatics as the Caped Crusader was turned into the "Bat-Hulk."

Toward the end of the second season of TV's *Batman*, when the writers were running out of fresh ideas, supervillain team-ups occurred, such as Catwoman and made-for-TV thief Sandman, and Penguin and Marsha, Queen of Diamonds. In this tradition, Batman villain team-ups have become common in Hollywood's interpretations of the Dark Knight. A popular example is the "Harley and Ivy" team—Harley Quinn and Poison Ivy—that was rooted in an episode of *Batman: The Animated Series* (1992–1995) but blossomed into additional episodes and comic-book spin-offs. Batman theatrical movies have continued the team-up trend: Penguin and Catwoman (*Batman Returns*, 1992),

Two-Face and Riddler (*Batman Forever*, 1995), Mr. Freeze and Poison Ivy (*Batman & Robin*, 1997), and Ra's al Ghul and the Scarecrow (*Batman Begins*, 2005). (Following this pattern is the film *Spider-Man 3*, featuring Venom and the Sandman.) The oddest source of a Bat-foes team-up is *The New Scooby-Doo Movies* (1972–1974), the Scooby-Doo-plus-guest-star cartoon in which the Joker and the Penguin united in two episodes featuring the Scooby gang and Batman and Robin.

While the Flash's Rogues' Gallery is perhaps the best-organized team of supervillains, two of its members, Captain Cold and Heat Wave, teamed several times to battle the Fastest Man Alive. In fact, Heat Wave's first appearance occurred in a team-up with his frosty "friend" in *The Flash* vol. 1 #140 (1963).

He may pride himself as being smarter than Superman, but the egocentric Lex Luthor has found it advantageous at times to team up with other villains. As the Joker and Penguin did in 1945, Luthor, the Toyman, and the Prankster contractually inked their alliance as "The Terrible Trio" in *Superman* vol. 1 #88 (1954). During the 1950s, Luthor formed another trio with the Prankster and Mr. Mxyztplk (the original spelling of the villain now known as Mr. Mxyzptlk; "Mxy" later palled around with fellow magical imp Bat-Mite), and hooked up with the Joker to attack Superman and Batman. Luthor and the Joker linked to bedevil Superman and Batman in *World's Finest Comics* #88 (1957) and #129 (1962, in which they formed "Joker-Luthor, Incorporated!"), then waged "The Duel of the Crime-Kings!" in #177 (1968). In post-*Crisis* continuity, their biggest match-up took place in the *World's Finest* miniseries (1990).

During comics' Silver Age (1956–1969), Luthor and the rogue android Brainiac pooled their evil geniuses several times to attempt to kill Superman; in their first team-up, written by Edmond Hamilton (from a plot suggestion by teenage fan Cary Bates, who later became a regular DC Comics writer) and penciler Curt Swan for *Superman* vol. 1 #167 (1964), they imperiled the Man of Steel by removing his superpowers and shrinking him, keeping him in a birdcage while they argued over who should have the "honor" of executing him. Their partnership went sour in writer Alan Moore's "Whatever Happened to the Man of Tomorrow" in *Superman* #423 and *Action Comics* #583 (1986), a two-part "imaginary" tale in which Brainiac took over Luthor's body. Superman's two greatest enemies have occasionally teamed in the years since, in comics and on the animated series *Superman* (1996–2000) and *Justice League Unlimited* (2004–present; in *JLU*, Brainiac telepathically "speaks" to Luthor). Other significant Luthor team-ups include his deceptive subservience to the superpowered General Zod in the movie *Superman II* (1980) and his partnership with Dr. Octopus in DC and Marvel's first superhero crossover, *Superman vs. The Amazing Spider-Man* (1975).

Like Luthor, Marvel's resident mastermind, Dr. Doom, is prone to rampant megalomania but has found coalitions with other supervillains necessary at times. Doom and the vengeful anti-hero the Sub-Mariner wreaked havoc in *Fantastic Four* vol. 1 #6 (1962), and years later, the pair starred in the first thirteen issues of *Super-Villain Team-Up*. That series, running from 1975 through 1980, featured in its later issues Dr. Doom and Magneto, Dr. Doom and the Red Skull, and the Red Skull and the Hate-Monger. Doom and DC's the Parasite paired off against their mutual foes in the Superman/Spider-Man sequel in 1981.

Additional Marvel and DC crossovers, published off and on during the 1980s and 1990s, made strange bedfellows of the Joker and the Shaper of Worlds; Darkseid, Dark Phoenix, and Deathstroke the Terminator; the Joker and Jigsaw; Darkseid and Galactus; Parallax and Thanos; Mr. Mxyzptlk and the Impossible Man; the Joker and the Red Skull; Two-Face and Mr. Hyde; the Kingpin and Ra's al Ghul; Magneto and Darkseid; Galactus and the Cyborg Superman; and Kingpin, Scarecrow, and Catwoman.

Some criminals, like Fantastic Four foes the Mad Thinker and the Puppet Master, have fared better as partners than as solo supervillains. Marvel's shapeshifting Sandman, however, regretted his 1981 anti-Spider-Man team-up with Hydro-Man—their bodies merged into one sopping mess! Golden Age (1938–1954) baddies the Sportsmaster and the Huntress (not to be confused with the superheroine of the same name) enjoyed a much smoother merger—when they came out of retirement to fight Starman and Black Canary in 1965, they surprised the world by announcing their marriage (becoming "Mr. and Mrs. Menace"); Marvel's Absorbing Man and Titania have also tied the knot. Two of Marvel's most malevolent made beautiful music of a different kind—Paul McCartney and Wings' pop tune "Magneto and Titanium Man" hit the charts in 1976, with a third villain joining in on the lyrical bridge, "And the Crimson Dynamo came along for the ride." While supervillain team-ups are rarely this harmonious, they can always be counted on to entertain. —*ME*

Supreme Hydra: *See* **Hydra**

The Supreme Intelligence

The Supreme Intelligence, one of Marvel Comics' many malevolent cosmic beings, is the ultimate group mind. A biocomputer amalgam of the most intelligent scholars of the galactic Kree empire, this entity sometimes called the Supremor made its presence known on Earth by ordering its soldier Ronan the Accuser to attack the interloping title stars of *Fantastic Four* vol. 1 #65 (1967). In its alarming form of an emerald-hued, spud-like organism with tendrils snaking from its head—picture Jabba the Hutt meets the mythological Medusa—the Supreme Intelligence lacks mobility but communicates via projection onto an enormous video monitor.

The Supreme Intelligence was created by the militaristic Kree many millennia ago to aid in their epochal conflict with the shapeshifting Skrulls, but with its collective wisdom supplanted the Kree government, becoming dictator and deity. It has long sought to accelerate Kree evolutionary advancement through a variety of means, including interspecies breeding, the detonation of a "nega-bomb" (which massacred billions), and its use of the Destiny Crystal to spawn the Ruul race. With its mind set upon both governance of the Kree and the domination of other planets, including Earth, the Supreme Intelligence has made many enemies, including the Kree warrior Mar-Vell (Captain Marvel), the Avengers, the Silver Surfer, and Supremor's

own agents, Ronan and Zarek the Imperial Minister, the latter of whom conspired to overthrow the despot. The Supreme Intelligence's tentacles have meandered throughout numerous Marvel titles and onto animated television in the *Silver Surfer* animated television cartoon (1998–1999). —*ME*

Surtur

In *Journey into Mystery* #97 (1963), writer/editor Stan Lee and artist/co-plotter Jack Kirby introduced their version of Surtur, one of the greatest enemies of the gods in Norse mythology. Utilizing traditional imagery of the devil, Kirby drew Surtur as a giant with two immense horns on his forehead, red skin, and a long tail. Lee and Kirby established that Surtur rivaled Odin, king of the Asgardian gods, in power, and that Surtur intended to destroy both Asgard and the universe with his ability to generate intense heat and flame. Following the myths, Lee and Kirby depicted a prophetic vision in which Surtur would set Asgard aflame following the battle of Ragnarok, "the twilight of the gods."

The comics creator who most prominently featured Surtur was writer/artist Walter Simonson in the story arc in *Thor* vol. 1 #337–#353 (1983–1985). Simonson revealed that in ages past Odin and his older brothers Vili and Ve journeyed into Surtur's domain Muspelheim, realm of the fire demons. There the brothers learned that Surtur intended to destroy the Nine Worlds of Norse mythology (including Asgard and Midgard, meaning Earth) with his flaming sword. The brothers broke the sword, but Surtur seemingly slew Vili and Ve. In Simonson's storyline Surtur forged a new sword, Twilight, and was narrowly prevented from destroying the Nine Worlds by Odin and his sons Thor and Loki.

Though Ragnarok took place in the final issues of *Thor* vol. 2 (2004), Surtur may be indestructible and possibly survived even Asgard's (presumably temporary) end. —*PS*

Syndrome

When innocent hero-worship goes unrequited, the consequences can be dire for both the

Syndrome, Mr. Incredible's wannabe sidekick turned bad guy, from *The Incredibles* (2004).

admirer and the admired. Pixar's computer-animated film *The Incredibles* (2004) presents a case in point in one Buddy Pine, a decidedly non-superpowered adolescent with a talent for invention and a stalker-like obsession with the ultrastrong superhero known as Mr. Incredible. After taxing the hero's patience with endless requests for fan-club souvenirs, Buddy follows Mr. Incredible to a robbery scene in the rocket-boot-propelled persona of IncrediBoy and announces his intention to become Mr. Incredible's sidekick. Unimpressed by Buddy's efforts—Buddy's arrival allows the incendiary Francophone thief Bomb Voyage to escape capture, and very nearly gets Buddy killed as well—Mr. Incredible brusquely sends the boy home.

Shortly thereafter, a string of expensive injury lawsuits drives America's superheroes underground, Mr. Incredible included. Meanwhile, the spurned Buddy parlays his developing technological expertise in a full-blown evil empire based on selling high-tech weaponry to dictators and tyrants around the world. Fifteen years after being brushed off by Mr. Incredible, the resentful Buddy Pine has metamorphosed into a self-styled, technologically powered costumed supervillain called Syndrome.

Syndrome's agent, a mysterious and beautiful young woman named Mirage, helps him track down the former Mr. Incredible, whose enforced retirement to a prosaic suburban existence has transformed him into Bob Parr, a fat and depressed family man. Syndrome plans to kill Mr. Incredible using a giant Omnidroid robot, a device whose development expended the lives of a large number of Bob Parr's retired superhero colleagues—Universal Man, Psycwave, Everseer, Macroburst, Phylange, Blazestone, Downburst, Hyper Shock, Apogee, Blazerman, Tradewind, Vectress, Gazerbeam, Stormicide, and Gamma Jack among them.

Syndrome never got over the pain of Mr. Incredible's rejection, and has spent the intervening years using quasimagical technologies such as "Zero Point Energy" to compensate for his lack of superpowers. "Everyone can be super," he says, warning his captured former idol of his eventual plans to sell his technologically simulated powers to one and all. "And when everyone's super … *no one* will be."

After getting even with Parr, Syndrome plans to release his Omnidroid in downtown New York, and then bask in the city's gratitude after appearing to wrestle the metal menace into submission. But in typical power-mad villain fashion, Syndrome overreaches himself by risking Mirage's life when he calls Mr. Incredible's bluff after the captured hero threatens to kill her; Syndrome also ensures his own downfall by threatening the lives of Mr. Incredible's wife Helen Parr (nee Elastigirl) and their two eldest children, Dashiell (the fleet-footed Dash) and Violet (who possesses invisibility and forcefield-casting powers, à la the Fantastic Four's Sue Storm).

Devastated after the Parrs and the ice-powered superhero Frozone end up receiving all the credit for halting the Omnidroid's New York rampage, Syndrome attempts to abduct the Parrs' infant son Jack-Jack with the intent of grooming the child into a sidekick. But the baby's developing flame powers and frightening physical transformations make him literally too hot to handle. Undone by Jack-Jack's sabotage of his rocket boots—and by an automobile hurled at him by an angry Mr. Incredible—Syndrome's own cape drags him into a jet turbine. After fifteen years, Buddy Pine's confused love-hate relationship with Mr. Incredible comes to a tragic, if poetically just, finish.

Visually based on aspects of *The Incredibles* writer-director Brad Bird, animator John Kahres, and animation supervisor Steven Clay Hunter, the young Buddy Pine and his adult supervillain persona are both voiced with a comics fanboy's earnest intensity by Jason Lee, star of Kevin Smith's *Chasing Amy* (1997) and NBC's *My Name Is Earl* (2005–present). Lee's energetic performance gives Syndrome a wounded, sinister-yet-sympathetic quality that makes the character impossible to hate, despite his many reprehensible actions. —*MAM*

T. O. Morrow

Villainous visionary Thomas Oscar Morrow may best be known as a foe of the Justice League of America, but he first appeared in the pages of *The Flash* #143 (1964), in writer John Broome and penciler Carmine Infantino's tale, "Trail of the False Green Lanterns." The inventor of a television that allows him to peer 100 years into the future, Morrow purloins future technology and employs it in contemporary times, producing a duplicate Green Lantern to bedevil the Flash.

In his next appearance, in *Justice League of America* #64 (1968), Morrow constructed cyclone-powered android the Red Tornado to destroy both the Justice League and the Justice Society, but "Reddy" overrode his programming and turned against his designer, provoking a lifelong grudge. With the future as his guide, Morrow occasionally applied his intellect toward stymieing the JLA and the Red Tornado. In a 1973 battle, the criminal scientist divided into two beings, the second being the giant-brained Future Man, in an ill-fated attempt to regain control of his simulacrum.

T. O. Morrow's fascination with artificial life forms led to his partnership with Professor Ivo—creator of Amazo, the android with the powers of the entire League—in *JLA* vol. 2 #5 (1997). This time borrowing from the past instead of the future, Morrow (with Ivo) attempted to eliminate the League via a planted artificial member, Tomorrow Woman, but in a case of history repeating itself the android resisted her encoding and destroyed herself. —ME

Talia

Talia has all the earmarks of a "Bond girl": Beguiling beauty, dubious motivations, an eco-terrorist father, and a pipeline to the hero's libido—only she exists in the world of Batman, not 007.

The beloved daughter of Ra's al Ghul, the international criminal mastermind aka "the Demon's Head," Talia al Ghul (aka Talia Head) first appeared as a damsel in distress in DC Comics' *Detective Comics* #411 (1971), by writer Denny O'Neil and penciler Bob Brown. After being felled by assassins under the command of Dr. Ebenezer Darrk, a severely beaten Batman is unmasked and cared for by Talia, a fellow captive. Forced by the baleful Darrk into a bullfight to save Talia's life, Batman is astonished as the exotic young woman reveals her resourcefulness by shooting Darrk, sending him flailing to his death before an oncoming train. When next seen in *Batman* #232 (1971), by O'Neil and artist Neal Adams, Talia has been kidnapped, along with Batman's teenage aide Robin, and the Caped Crusader is lured by Ra's al

Ghul on a perilous Himalayan rescue mission. The dual abduction is a ruse, a test of Batman's worthiness to marry his daughter, who loves him. As their complex story slowly unfolds over the next few years, the altruistic Batman is offered but refuses al Ghul's throne, but finds Talia irresistible, stealing kisses from her as he upends her father's machinations, forming one of comics' most compelling relationship triangles.

Talia may love Batman, whom she knows to be Bruce Wayne, but her loyalty remains to her father, who raised his daughter single-handedly (not counting al Ghul's surfeit of servants) after her mother died. Under al Ghul's tutelage, Talia became an expert warrior, marksman, and businesswoman (*Batman: Birth of the Demon*, 1992). Her father's contrariety with Batman led al Ghul to encourange a reluctant Talia into coquetry with Bane, the brutish crimelord who temporarily crippled Batman by breaking his back. Talia's business acumen inspired Lex Luthor to tap her as CEO of LexCorp upon his 2000 election to the U.S. presidency, but she proved to truly be her father's daughter by later duplicitly working against Luthor.

Talia discovered the existence of her venomous half-sister Nyssa in *Batman: Death and the Maidens*, the 2003–2004 maxiseries in which her sibling killed her father. Talia resurfaced once again working for Luthor in 2005, this time as one of his inner circle of criminals called the Society in the miniseries *Villains United*. With perfidy as her family credo and a doomed love affair as her heart, Talia can only be trusted to guarantee surprises.

In the 1987 graphic novel *Batman: Son of the Demon* by Mike W. Barr and Jerry Bingham, Talia was revealed to be carrying Batman's child; she claimed to have lost the baby but an epilogue showed the infant in an orphanage. *Son of the Demon* was later deemed out of continuity by DC, but the adult life of the child, named Ibn al Xu'ffasch, has been explored in "Elseworlds" tales.

Movie Supergirl Helen Slater voiced Talia in episodes of *Batman: The Animated Series* (1992–1995); a tie-in action figure followed from Kenner. —*ME*

Talpa

T alpa is the main villain of the 1995 anime *Ronin Warriors*, the English-language adaptation of the Japanese series *Yoroiden Samurai Troopers* (which aired in Japan in 1988). In *Samurai Troopers*, his name is Arago. Talpa was introduced in the first episode "Shadowland," but he was shown as a ghostly visage. Only in later episodes was his true form revealed—a tall figure in a stylized samurai armor with spikes, claws, and a skull-like helmet with white hair (strangely enough, it was never revealed if there was anything *under* that armor!). His exact age is unknown, but it is estimated to be several thousand years old. He is also capable of manipulating dark magic and can bend others' minds to his will.

Talpa was the lord of the evil Dynasty, which existed in another dimension. Over several centuries, he made several attempts to bring his realm to Earth. One thousand years ago, his attempt was foiled by the Ancient One, who represented the forces of good. Not only did the Ancient One prevent Talpa's assault on Earth, he also broke the dark lord's armor into nine pieces. These were later forged into nine mystical suits of armor of great power.

One thousand years later, in modern times, Talpa made another attempt to attack Earth's dimension, with the city of Tokyo as his target— and he actually succeeded. While not at full power, he had regained four of the mystical suits of armor and gave them to four warlords: Anubis, Cale, Sekhmet, and Dais. These four would aid Talpa in his quest to gain the remaining five mystical armors. However, the Ancient One had given these armors to five teen boys; these five—the Ronin Warriors—would oppose Talpa and his warlords. At the conclusion of the series, the five warriors, with the help of Anubis, defeated Talpa, ending the Dynasty's attempt to rule Earth. —*MM*

Task Force X: *See* The Suicide Squad

Taskmaster

T he skull-masked, hooded mimicker known as the Taskmaster first appeared in the pages of

The Avengers vol. 1 #195 (1980), in a story scripted by David Michelinie and penciled by George Pérez. Taskmaster boasts "photographic reflexes" that allow him to duplicate an enemy's movements. He can counter the attack of anyone he's ever studied, either moving like the person's double or instantaneously duplicating his enemy's fighting style to formulate a defense. Taskmaster has been known to carry copies of super-weapons associated with the heroes he mimics—such as Captain America's shield and Hawkeye's arrows—so that he can gain the upper hand in battle.

At first, Taskmaster avoided conflicts with heroes, instead training those who aspired to be professional henchmen. After years of obscurity plying his trade, he was outed by the Avengers and has since become a surprisingly ongoing foe of the superteam. His encounter with the Avengers began a series stand-offs with individual members like Jocasta, Captain America, Ant-Man, and Hawkeye. He has also had run-ins with Spider-Man, Deadpool, and Elektra.

The U.S. government has upon occasion regarded the Taskmaster's uncanny combative skills as crucial to its interests, hiring him to train a man who temporarily substituted for the original Captain America.

Taskmaster was recast by the Udon creative studio as a mercenary in the character's four-issue miniseries, *Taskmaster* (2002). Given an updated appearance and the added ability to duplicate vocal patterns, he held his own against Iron Man. The villain has appeared outside of the comics pages in the *Avengers Assembled!* role-playing game, action figures, and a mini-bust by Bowen Designs. —*GM*

The Tattooed Man

In an era when skin decorations were worn mainly by sailors and bikers, light-fingered seaman Abel Tarrant is exposed to chemicals that allow him to animate tattoos in *Green Lantern* vol. 2 #23 (1963). Adorning his epidermis with tattooed weapons and vicious creatures, this Tattooed Man brings fighter aircrafts, robots, knives, bombs, and other dangers on his skin to "life" merely by touching them, attacking Green Lantern (GL).

Visually modeled after John Wayne by artist Gil Kane and characterized with "sailor speak" by writer Gardner Fox, for the next two decades the Tattooed Man appeared irregularly, tangling with GL and the Justice League of America, and joining other supervillains as the Injustice Gang. Many readers regarded Tarrant's superpower as ridiculous, and in *Green Lantern* #144 (1981) the Tattooed Man was executed after being caught stealing from fellow rogue Goldface.

Changes in fashion ultimately proved that Fox and Kane were decades ahead of their time. In the 1990s, when tattoos had become popular, John Oakes, a former cellmate of Tarrant's who had learned his secrets, starred in *Skin Graft: The Adventures of a Tattooed Man* #1–#4 (1993), in DC Comics' "mature readers" Vertigo imprint. Oakes' supernatural tattoos allowed him to ensnare people by converting them into body embellishments.

It was revealed in the 2000s that the original Tattooed Man was alive, having survived Goldface's assassination attempt. After briefly going straight, Tarrant, whose skin is an elaborate tapestry of tattooed terrors and body piercings, returned to villainy in the pages of *The Outsiders* in 2004. —*ME*

Terra

Although she looked like a gawky, buck-toothed teenage girl, Tara Markov, who joined the Teen Titans as the earth-moving Terra, was not at all what she appeared. Making her debut in DC Comics' *The New Teen Titans* #26 (1982) in a story by Marv Wolfman and George Pérez, Terra wore a tan-and-brown costume with gold trim on the boots and gloves. With powerful control over soil, stone, mud, and lava, Terra could create objects out of the very earth itself, cause earthquakes, and ride clumps of dirt through the air, defying gravity.

The illegitimate daughter of the King of Markovia, Tara Markov was secretly sent to the United States; before she left, a scientist's experiments helped give the girl tremendous powers. At some point in her early teens, the very bitter and sociopathic Tara joined forces with Slade Wilson, aka Deathstroke the Terminator. Together, they hatched a plan via which "poor disadvantaged orphan" Tara first opposed the Titans, then exposed her vulnerability and was invited to join the heroes.

Earning the Titans' confidence, Terra fought bravely alongside them, all the while gathering their secrets and weaknesses. On a mission teaming with the Outsiders, Terra was reunited with her older brother, Brion Markov, now an earth-powered hero known as Geo-Force.

Eventually, in a storyline entitled "The Judas Contract," Terra turned on her teammates and helped Deathstroke capture them and turn them over to H.I.V.E. (Hierarchy of International Vengeance and Extermination) for destruction. But when Nightwing and Jericho managed to help free their friends, Terra lost her slim grip on sanity and brought the cavernous H.I.V.E. complex down on top of her. Teammate Changeling found her dead body, and she was buried as a Titan.

In the years since, another Terra has appeared, fighting alongside the group called Team Titans; it is unknown if this Terra is a clone, a refugee from an alternate timeline, or an amnesiac resurrected Tara Markov. The saga of Terra was also told in 2004's second season of the animated *Teen Titans* (2003–2006), with a similar storyline to "The Judas Contract." The TV Terra sacrificed herself at the end of her storyline, for the good of the city and her fellow Titans.

In 2004 Bandai released the first of several Terra toys and action figures. —*AM*

Terra-Man

Terra-Man, a desperado mixing the old West with super-science, first rode—*flew*, actually, on his Pegasus-like winged steed Nova—into Metropolis in *Superman* vol. 1 #249 (1972), courtesy of writer Cary Bates and the "Swanderson" team of penciler Curt Swan and inker Murphy Anderson. Looking (and sounding) like he stepped out of a Hollywood shoot-'em-up, this "Cosmic Cowboy" sends the Man of Steel a'duckin' for cover with his energy-

blasting six-shooters, remote-controlled lariat, and illusion-casting chewing tobacco! *Superman* #249's backup story, "The Origin of Terra-Man," also scripted by Bates but drawn by Dick Dillin and Neal Adams, divulges that the Man of Steel's newest foe was actually a young outlaw named Toby Manning, born some hundred years ago. Manning's father was accidentally killed by an alien called the Collector, who raised Toby and outfitted him with high-tech weaponry that looked like the guns of his era. Terra-Man and Superman had reg'lar showdowns until the mid-1980s, then the villain galloped off into the sunset of limbo when Superman was reinvented in 1986's *Man of Steel* miniseries.

An all-new Terra-Man, an eco-terrorist co-created by Jerry Ordway and Dan Jurgens, bowed in *Superman* vol. 2 #46 (1990). Like the original, this Terra-Man was named Tobias Manning and had some Wild West overtones (a long Western coat and cowboy-garbed robot aides called Terra-Men), but the comparisons ended there. His extreme environmental convictions allowed him to kill humans who harmed Mother Earth or its fauna, and his armored exoskeleton boosted his strength and enabled him to generate cyclones. Terra-Man II has appeared infrequently since his debut. —*ME*

Thanos

Sometimes a hero and other times a villain, Thanos is a creature of contradictions and extremes. He has repeatedly helped save the universe, but he has also destroyed every living being in it, albeit temporarily. He has striven for the omnipotence of godhood, and yet he has also led the life of a simple farmer. In Marvel Comics' *Thanos: Epiphany* (2004), his frequent ally and foe Adam Warlock said about Thanos, "Lunatic? Monster? Savior? Not my call to make."

Writer/artist Jim Starlin created Thanos and his brother Eros before he started working for Marvel, having been inspired by Sigmund Freud's theories of the death instinct and the sex drive. While writing *Iron Man*, Starlin's friend Mike Friedrich invited him to plot and draw the issue in which Thanos made his debut (*Iron Man* #55, 1973). Later in 1973, Thanos became the major villain in

Marvel's *Captain Marvel* series, on which Starlin and Friedrich collaborated.

Originally Starlin established that Thanos' father, Mentor, was the brother of Zeus, the king of the classical Greek gods. Editor Mark Gruenwald later altered Mentor's backstory, making Mentor the brother of Zuras, the ruler of Jack Kirby's race of Eternals, who greatly resembled Zeus; Starlin went along with the revision. Exiled from Earth, Mentor founded a colony of Eternals on Saturn's moon Titan, where Eros and Thanos were born.

But Thanos was born with Deviant genes (a reference to the demon-like Deviant race in Kirby's *Eternals*) and had grey skin and grotesque facial features. Believing he would never be accepted by the fellow Eternals of Titan, the young Thanos found solace and guidance from his "imaginary friend" who proved to be quite real: Mistress Death. One of the "conceptual beings" of the Marvel Universe, Mistress Death is the embodiment of death itself. Though others may perceive her as a robed skeleton, to Thanos she looks like a beautiful humanoid woman, and over time he fell in love with her. After Thanos conducted a forbidden experiment in which test subjects perished, Mentor exiled Thanos from Titan.

Through bionic means Thanos augmented his superhuman strength and resistance to injury beyond the capacity of any other Eternal. Through meditation and the black arts, Thanos also amplified his natural ability to tap into and mentally manipulate cosmic energies.

Thanos eventually launched a nuclear attack on Titan, killing thousands, including his mother Sui-San; away from Titan at the time, Mentor and Eros survived. Later, Thanos returned to Titan and proclaimed himself ruler.

Obsessively in love with Mistress Death, Thanos sought to prove himself worthy of her. He utilized the Cosmic Cube, which can transform thought into reality, to turn himself into a godlike entity. Instead of destroying his adversary, Captain Mar-Vell, Thanos self-indulgently toyed with him, enabling Mar-Vell to shatter the Cube, returning Thanos to his original state.

This is the first example of a pattern of Thanos always providing the means of his own defeat. Starlin explained in a 2005 interview in *BACK ISSUE* magazine that although Thanos may consciously lust for absolute power, "subconsciously there's a whole different thing going on there ... Every time he's got a hold of ultimate power, he lets it go because he knows it's not what he's going to need." What he really desires out of life, not even Thanos knows.

Abandoned by Mistress Death, Thanos plotted to regain her favor by utilizing the six "Infinity Gems" to destroy all the stars in the universe. Thanos believed that the only threat to his scheme was the Magus, the evil alternate future self of the artificially created superhuman Adam Warlock. Thanos and Warlock joined forces and defeated the Magus in Starlin's 1970s *Warlock* series.

Warlock, Captain Mar-Vell, and the Avengers teamed to stop Thanos' plot to extinguish the stars, and Thanos killed Warlock. But Warlock's spirit transformed Thanos into immobile stone, on the border between life and death.

Mistress Death resurrected Thanos, who captured the six Infinity Gems (in Starlin's *The Thanos Quest* #1–#2, 1990) and affixed them to his glove, "the Infinity Gauntlet," thereby regaining godlike power. In a new attempt to please Mistress Death, Thanos killed half the living beings in the universe. Thanos' alleged granddaughter, the space pirate Nebula, pulled the Infinity Gauntlet from his hand and used it to undo the universe-wide massacre Thanos had just perpetrated. Warlock finally seized control of the Gauntlet (as told in Starlin's *The Infinity Gauntlet* #1–#6, 1991). Claiming that as a result of his three defeats he no longer sought absolute power, Thanos worked as a simple farmer on a distant planet.

Subsequently, Thanos allied himself with Warlock and Earth's superheroes against menaces posed to the universe by the Magus (in Starlin's *The Infinity War*, 1992) and Warlock's female counterpart, the Goddess (in Starlin's *The Infinity Crusade*, 1993).

Over his career Starlin has left and returned to Marvel several times. During his absences, other writers have utilized Thanos, usually presenting him as the nihilistic villain of his early stories. Starlin believes that other writers have ignored his efforts

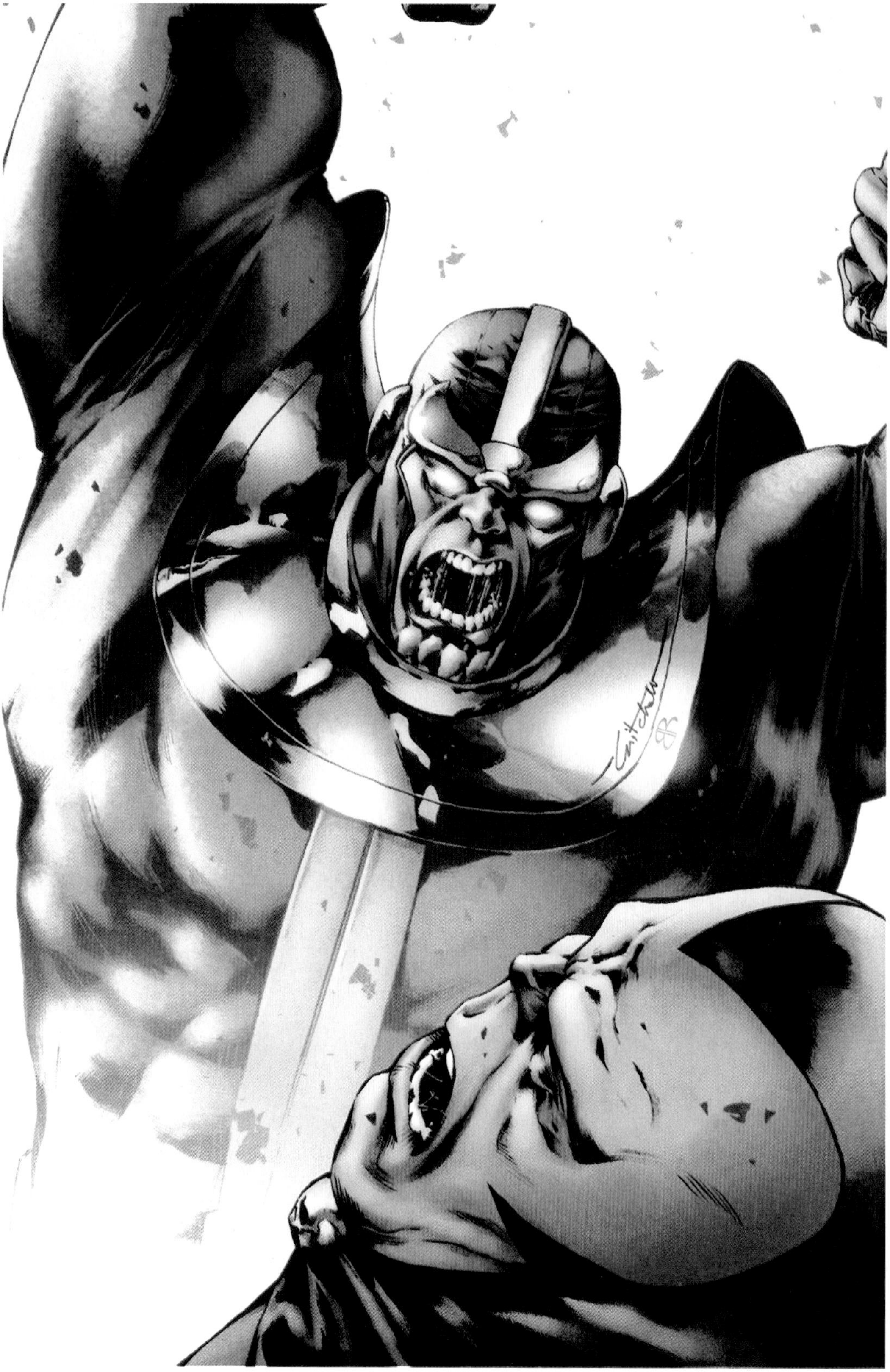

at evolving Thanos' characterization. When Starlin returned to Thanos in *Infinity Abyss* (2002–2003), he revealed that Thanos had created five doppelgängers of himself, who, presumably, had appeared in stories Starlin had not written.

Seeking to protect himself against his past enemies, Thanos achieved godhood again and destroyed the universe in a fit of temper. Realizing he was unsuited for omnipotence, Thanos gave up his new power, thereby restoring the universe's existence (as told in Starlin's *Marvel Universe: The End* #1–#6, 2003). In Thanos's own comics series (2003–2004), Starlin had him seeking redemption for his past crimes. But Starlin admitted that Thanos' new goal would not last long.

Though Thanos physically resembles Jack Kirby's Darkseid, Starlin contends that they are very different characters: whereas Darkseid wanted absolute power over others, Thanos originally wanted not to control them but kill them. Starlin regards Thanos as an unstable sociopath, but one who—in the course of searching for his true role in life—can be a force for great evil or great good. Starlin has said that each time he has returned to Marvel, it has been to do a Thanos story; it remains to be seen where Starlin may take Thanos next.

Voiced by Gary Krawford, Thanos appeared on television in a handful of episodes of the short-lived *Silver Surfer* animated series (1998–1999). A Thanos action figure, with an accompanying Death figure, was produced in 2005, and Thanos mini-busts and miniatures have also been manufactured. —*PS*

The Thorn

The Thorn—not to be confused with the Modern Age anti-hero of the same name—was one of the most bristly babes to shake up the pages of Golden Age (1938–1954) superhero comics. Penned by Robert Kanigher and rendered by Joe Kubert, she first blossomed in *Flash Comics* #89 (1947) as Rose Canton, a botanist student with a latent split personality. While studying the flora of Tashmi Island, Rose discovers that the toxins produced by an indigenous thorn alter her physiology, granting her toughened skin and a limited form of superspeed. The revelation ignites her dormant schizophrenia, sprouting two distinct personalities: the docile Rose (a blonde) and the thunderous Thorn (a redhead).

As a chief antagonist of the Flash, the villainess became the proverbial thorn in the super-speedster's side, often appearing in a whirlwind of green smoke or a tornado of thorns. While wreaking havoc with her plant-based weapons arsenal of explosive and poisonous thorns and her thorn-laden plane or roadster, the Thorn's diabolical plottings were interspersed with the innocent proclamations of Rose—ever convincing the Flash that she was Thorn's "sister" and gaining his trust. The Thorn proved as fickle as she was prickly: after a period of incarceration she lost interest in the Flash and became obsessed with the Golden Age Green Lantern, while Rose, in her new identity of Alyx Florin, developed a crush on the hero's alter ego, Alan Scott. They eventually wed, but when the Thorn reemerged, Rose faked her own demise to spare her husband from her dangerous dual personality. It was disclosed in *Infinity, Inc. Annual* #1 (1985) that at the time of her "death" Rose was pregnant with twins, whom she secreted from the Thorn by putting them up for adoption. Her children—Jennie Lynn Hayden-Scott (Jade of Infinity, Inc., who in 2006 fights with the Outsiders) and Todd Rice-Scott (the living, three-dimensional shadow, Obsidian)—were the villainess' downfall, as Rose committed suicide to prevent Thorn from killing them. —*GM*

Thunderbolts

The Thunderbolts were wolves in sheep's clothing. This super*hero* team, debuting in *The Incredible Hulk* #449 (1997) before spinning off into their own title, was introduced when the Avengers and the Fantastic Four were presumed dead (after the "Onslaught" crossover, building

Opposite: *Drax the Destroyer* #2 ©2005 Marvel Comics. COVER ART BY MITCH BREITWEISER.

toward the ill-received "Heroes Reborn" promotional stunt that reintroduced their titles). In *Thunderbolts* #1 (1997), written by Kurt Busiek and penciled by Mark Bagley, the "T-Bolts"—Citizen V, Meteorite, MACH-1, Songbird, Atlas, and Techno—are welcomed by a world yearning for champions. Readers are in on their secret, however: Earth's newest superheroes are actually some of its most dangerous supervillains, the Masters of Evil—Baron Zemo II, Moonstone, the Beetle, Screaming Mimi, Goliath, and the Fixer, respectively—assuming faux-altruistic identities in strategist Zemo's ruse to manipulate public opinion and eventually dominate the society the "heroes" appear to serve.

As the series progressed, the Thunderbolts battled the Rat Pack, the Wrecking Crew, the Mad Thinker, a new Masters of Evil (Crimson Cowl II, Klaw, Flying Tiger, Tiger Shark, Man-Killer, and Cyclone), and the Elements of Doom, and admitted a new member, Jolt, to the team. But the shrewd Citizen V (Zemo) did not anticipate that most of his co-conspirators would actually *enjoy* being heroes! To maintain a chokehold on the team, Zemo exposed their identities to the government agency S.H.I.E.L.D. in *Thunderbolts* #10 (1998), but the T-Bolts in turn revolted against him.

With Zemo unseated, the outlaw Thunderbolts continued their superheroic careers, although under media and police scrutiny, their series branded "Marvel's Most Wanted." The admission of new characters like Charcoal and established personalities like Hawkeye (the Avengers' archer who began his costumed career as a criminal), plus some of the coolest hardware in comics—V-Wings (hover-boards), the T-Bird flying car, and their ultra-sleek ThunderJet—kept the series fresh through most of its 81-issue run; it was rebooted in 2004 as *New Thunderbolts*. —*ME*

The Tick's Rogues' Gallery

The big blue ball of wonder, the popular 1980s superhero the Tick, is best known for defending "The City" as he bounds over rooftops with his rallying cry of "Spoon!"

Created as a wacky parody of superheroes by cartoonist Ben Edlund, the Tick first appeared in the pages of comic store New England Comics' July–August 1986 newsletter. Since that time, he has segued into various forms of media and merchandise, not the least of which was his animated Saturday-morning cartoon show (1994–1997) that ignited an intense cult following. While fans raved about the Tick, they also embraced the hero's popular rogues' gallery.

Tick villains are not your ordinary supervillians. The debonair and ultra-powerful Chairface Chippendale sports a chair for a head. The deadly Chainsaw Vigilante wants to rid The City of all the superheroes. The Angry Red Herring has machine guns for eyes, and delights in rubbing petroleum jelly on his belly to escape the clutches of heroes. The boy-genius Brainchild is a grade-schooler gone bad—he once captured the Tick and turned him into a two-headed bird that only spoke high-school French. The Deadly Bulb is a man who has a pig for a left leg and a light bulb for a head. Betty, the Ant Queen, commands legions of ants to do her bidding. Other villains include the Evil Midnight Bomber, the Ottoman Empress, the Man-Eating Cow, the Red Scare, Dinosaur Neil, Pineapple Pokopo, the Terror, Omnipotus the Eater of Planets, Thrakkorzog, the Guy with Ears Like Little Raisins, and the Idea Men. Their sheer absurdness made them formidable enemies of the Tick, added to the hero's escalating popularity, and fueled the merchandising effort.

The Tick and his rogues were last seen in the short-lived but critically acclaimed 2001–2002 live-action TV series from FOX. —*GM*

The Time Trapper

Things were much simpler in comics' Silver Age (1956–1969). In those days, Superman began his career during his youth, and as Superboy often broke the time barrier to travel to the thirtieth century, where he was a member of the teenage Legion of Super-Heroes (LSH).

The Time Trapper, one of the Legion's most powerful foes, originated millions of years after the LSH, at the End of Time, where he lived in a portentous citadel. A mysterious figure clad in a tattered purple robe, his face in shadows, the Time Trapper regarded the timeline as one might regard a room: whereas a homeowner reconfigures a room by moving furniture, making it, in essence, an entirely different place, the Time Trapper did the same with pieces of time, affecting the lives, and the histories, of populations across the universe in grandiose gestures of "housecleaning."

With its infinite paradoxes, a crisscrossing timeline might have proved too convoluted a subject for the juvenile readership of 1960s-era comic books had the Time Trapper's creator, science-fiction novelist Edmond Hamilton, and artist John Forte not simplified matters by rendering the timestream as a spectrum of colors labeled with dates (Superboy flew past "1974" ... "1984" ... and so forth, until reaching the future). Hamilton was a master of temporal fiction—his first published novel, *The Time Raider* (1927), involved a figure who snatched beings from the past, a prototype for his Legion villain. Premiering in *Adventure Comics* #321 (1964, although the Trapper was mentioned in issue #317, when the Legion was barricaded from time travel by the Trapper's Iron Curtain of Time), the Time Trapper endeavored to steal the Legion's weapon the Concentrator.

The Time Trapper regularly returned, and the Legion's later writers added story twists (including different identities under the villain's purple cloak) that might have made a bewildered Hamilton scratch his head. A difficult foe to defeat given his ability to reconstruct reality, the Trapper was sidelined as part of DC Comics' own housecleaning event, the maxiseries *Crisis on Infinite Earths* (1985–1986), but was soon summoned to repair a leak in the continuity dam. When Superman was reintroduced, post-*Crisis*, by writer/artist John Byrne in the 1986 *The Man of Steel* miniseries, Superboy was eliminated from the hero's mythos. This damaged Legion lore, as the LSH was founded in honor of the Boy of Steel's legend. DC's editors brainstormed the solution. In *Superman* vol. 2 #8 (1987), readers were informed that the Time Trapper, still alive at the End of Time, had fashioned a "Pocket Universe" containing the Silver Age—or "Earth-One"—versions of Earth and Superboy's homeworld, Krypton. The Legion interacted with the

Time Bandits

Jailed supervillains may have time on their hands, but these chronal criminals have it *in* theirs:

- **Darius Tiko**, created by Jack Kirby for DC Comics in 1958, used a time machine to snatch weapons from the future to plague the Challengers of the Unknown in the present.

- **Xotar the Weapons Master**, the second villain to battle the Justice League of America, was a futuristic criminal genius from the year 11,960 who ducked the Intersolar Police by venturing to 1960 in his time-traveling robot Ilaric.

- **Zarrko the Tomorrow Man**, first seen in 1962, is a militaristic madman who stole twentieth-century weapons such as a cobalt bomb to use in his utopian twenty-third century, fighting Thor on numerous occasions and even waging a time war with Kang the Conqueror. Zarrko appeared on TV in *The Marvel Super Heroes* cartoon (1966) and set himself up as a dictator in the fiftieth century.

- **The Lord of Time**, a long-time foe of the Justice League, first fought the team in 1962 with an army of thieves and incorrigibles recruited from both the past and the future. He joined Calendar Man, Chronos, Clock King, and Lazarium in 1993 as the short-lived villain team the Time Foes.

- **Time Commander** used chronal-controlling weapons during the mid-1960s to twice take on the team of Batman and Green Lantern before his time hopping made him mentally unstable and an even greater threat.

- **The Time-Twisters** are genetic constructs from the End of Time who debuted in the pages of Marvel's *Thor* in 1976. With their abilities to time travel, accelerate or reverse the ages of those they encounter, and extract creatures from any moment in the time stream, they are dangerous temporal terrorists.

- **Timeshadow** is a mutant mercenary who conjured "phase forms" of himself from the near-future to attack X-Factor in 1986.

Superboy of this realm, and the Pocket Universe eventually spawned a heroic Lex Luthor, Phantom Zone villains, and a new Supergirl, before overloaded storylines (including two concurrent versions of the Legion and a new timeline fashioned by the chronal-sorceress Glorith) led to the Time Trapper being eliminated in yet another housecleaning event, *Zero Hour: A Crisis in Time* (1994).

Since *Legion of Super-Heroes* has been rebooted in the 2000s, will the Time Trapper be introduced anew? It's only a matter of time before readers find out. —*ME*

Titania

The Marvel supercriminal Titania, otherwise known as wife of the villain the Absorbing Man, first burst onto the pages of *Marvel Super Heroes Secret Wars* #3 (1984) in a story written by Jim Shooter and penciled by Mike Zeck.

Readers are told very little about the life of Mary "Skeeter" MacPherran before the extradimensional Beyonder transported her suburb of Denver through space to become part of an artificial "heroes-versus-villains" Battleworld he was constructing (as part of the first Secret War storyline, 1984–1985). The supervillain Dr. Doom was fervently building up his arsenal of supervillains to do battle against Battleworld's heroes, and contacted MacPherran and offered her superhuman powers. Doom subjected MacPherran to radiation treatments, augmenting her petite body by several hundred pounds of muscle and giving her superhuman strength and near-invulnerable skin that also gives her resilience to heat, intense cold, and disease.

MacPherran designed a costume for herself and took the name Titania, becoming a highly effective fighter on Doom's team. (She is not to be confused with the professional-wrester-turned-professional-criminal Davida DeVito, sometimes referred to as Titania I, who was murdered by the vigilante Scourge.)

Titania and ten of her fellow criminals escaped the planet of the Beyonder's world when the Molecule Man returned the Denver suburb to Earth. During the first Secret War Titania became attracted to her teammate, "Crusher" Creel, the Absorbing

Man, and they became a couple after they returned home. Titania continued to engage in various criminal activities, most often with the Absorbing Man, although the two often ran afoul of one superhero or another, such as Spider-Man and the Avengers. Titania also had a personal feud with her archenemy, the She-Hulk. Titania and the Absorbing Man have both served in the Masters of Evil, and Titania briefly belonged to the Frightful Four.

Titania and the Absorbing Man finally got married (inviting the grimace-worthy pun from She-Hulk about "Absorbine Jr." being the ideal name for their child) in a ceremony attended by many of their supervillain colleagues. Later, though, Titania contracted cancer. Their old enemy Thor saved Titania's life by arranging for medical help, and Creel publicly thanked his former foe. Mr. and Mrs. Creel entertained a life of lawfulness, but ultimately returned to their villainous ways. —*GM*

Titanium Man

The original Titanium Man was one of Iron Man's greatest enemies, introduced in *Tales of Suspense* #69 (1965) in the story "If I Die, Let It Be with Honor," scripted by Stan Lee and penciled by Don Heck.

An ambitious high official in the Soviet Union, Boris Bullski worked with imprisoned scientists to create a titanium steel battlesuit that was larger, more powerful, and more impenetrable than Iron Man's. The suit provided Bullski with vast superhuman strength and the ability to fly, and was equipped with powerful weapons systems. Titanium Man challenged Iron Man in an effort to prove his superiority physically as an armored man and politically as a Communist (a rivalry he would continue in many return bouts).

Beginning with his second appearance, Titanium Man underwent experiments that nearly doubled his size, donning an even more powerful suit of armor; over the years he has taken on a fully robotic appearance.

During a period when the original Titanium Man was believed to be dead, the Soviet genius called the Gremlin created and wore his own Titanium Man armor. Iron Man traveled to the U.S.S.R.

to combat this new Titanium Man, and in their clash, Iron Man's boot-jet exhaust ignited his opponent's armor, and the Gremlin perished, in *Iron Man* vol. 1 #229 (1988).

After the collapse of the Soviet Union, Bullski returned from limbo. (During this time a Titanium Man worked for the criminal organization A.I.M., but it is unclear if this was Bullski.) Enraged by what he regarded as the fall of Russia, the Titanium Man went on a rampage. Russia's Colonel Valentin Shatalov persuaded Iron Man's alter ego Tony Stark to wear the Crimson Dynamo's battle-suit so it would appear that a Russian hero defeated the Titanium Man. But during the ensuing battle, Shatalov activated the Dynamo's "fusion-caster" weapon by remote control, unleashing a powerful blast that killed the Titanium Man (*Iron Man* #317, 1995).

In *Iron Man* vol. 3 #49 (2002), a mysterious Titanium Man battled Iron Man and destroyed a Stark communications satellite. This Titanium Man returned in 2004, and he turned out to be a Russian agent who calls himself Andy Stockwell. Iron Man defeated this Titanium Man, too, who—as of 2006—was last seen lost in outer space. Given the tenacity of all who have worn this armor, this Titanium Man will no doubt return or yet another one will arise to challenge Iron Man.

The original Titanium Man appeared in the 1966 *The Marvel Super-Heroes* animated TV series and the animated *Iron Man* (1994–1996). But perhaps his most unusual appearance in media is in Paul McCartney and Wings' song "Magneto and Titanium Man" (1976), which also mentions the Crimson Dynamo. —*GM*

Titano
the Super-Ape

K ryptonite meets King Kong, in one skyscraping package—that's Titano the Super-Ape. During the late 1950s, when the various Superman media (TV, newspapers, and the host venue, comic books) incestuously passed ideas back and forth, Titano thumped into view in a 1959 *Superman* newspaper comic-*strip* sequence in which the

mammoth monkey was called "Big Boy." Promptly thereafter, he made his more canonical comic-*book* debut in DC Comics' *Superman* vol. 1 #127 (1959). Otto Binder and Wayne Boring's "Titano the Super-Ape" rolls out "famous intelligent chimp" Toto, hamming it up for a charity event and becoming the "friend for life" of the mistress of ceremonies, reporter Lois Lane. The next day, Toto enters the space race, his orbiting satellite smacked with radiation from colliding uranium and kryptonite meteors. When he returns home, he mutates into a gargantuan gorilla that goes ape for lovely Lois. Superman arrives but is waylaid by Toto's—rechristened "Titano" by Lane—eye-emitted kryptonite beams. In a game of monkey-see monkey-do, Lois gets Titano to don lead-lined glasses to block his kryptonite vision, long enough for Superman to hurl the Super-Ape into the "prehistoric past," where he frolics with dinosaurs. This story was retread in 1966 as "The Chimp Who Made It Big," an episode of Filmation's animated *The New Adventures of Superman*.

Titano occasionally appeared throughout the early to mid-1960s, returned in 1970 and 1978, then wasn't seen again until his nostalgic reintroduction into the Man of Steel's revised continuity in *Superman Annual* vol. 2 #1 (1987). "Monkey Fun," a 1997 episode of the WB's *Superman* animated series, brought the giant ape to television for a new generation of fans. —*ME*

Toad

O ne of Magneto's original Brotherhood of Evil Mutants, the Toad hopped into the Marvel Universe in *X-Men* vol. 1 #4 (1964). An outcast because of his gargoyle-like looks, mutant Mortimer Toynbee welcomes Magneto's vision of a society ruled by mutants and becomes his bootlicking pawn. The Toad is also obsessed with the Brotherhood's Scarlet Witch, a stalker-worthy fixation he would nurture for years.

The Toad was pathetically deferential to the harsh Magneto, even when they were both held captive on another planet by the alien known as the Stranger. Finally buckling under the weight of his master's tyranny, the Toad turned against Magneto and even tried to take his life. The Toad studied and stole advanced technology during a return trip to the Stranger's planet, then came home to Earth to strike against his former enemies, calling himself "the Terrible Toad King" on a short-lived, unsuccessful path of vengeance. The Toad considered becoming a superhero but opted to continue his villainy, confidently stretching his legs by forming his own Brotherhood of Evil Mutants. He eventually returned to his familiar turf of subservience to other supervillains. The Toad also exists in Marvel's reinvented "Ultimate" Universe in the series *Ultimate X-Men* (2001–present).

The Toad's often cloying manner, repellent appearance, and bizarre superpowers are offensive to both "friend" (of whom he has few) and foe. His superhumanly strong legs allow him to leap tremendous distances and lift several tons, and, like his namesake, he frequently crouches. After a time-traveling sojourn on the sentient spaceship Prosh, the Toad gained the abilities to lash his long, prehensile tongue as a weapon and exude from his pores paralysis-inducing mucus; these freakish traits, and his foul body odor, often keep others at arm's length.

Actor Ray Park, under green, wart-encrusted makeup, popularized the Toad in the live-action movie *X-Men* (2000), but that wasn't the mutant's first screen appearance. He and the Brotherhood were seen in an episode of television's animated *Spider-Man and His Amazing Friends* (1981–1986). The cartoon *X-Men: Evolution* (2000–2003) also utilized the Toad, renamed from Toynbee to Todd Tolensky. Toy Biz has produced Toad action figures based upon the comics, movie, and *Evolution* interpretations.

A different supervillain calling himself the Toad, a counterfeiter wearing a frog-head mask, briefly fought the Archie Comics superhero the Black Hood in the mid-1960s. Other frog-like supervillains include the Hulk's enemies the Toad Men and Daredevil's jumping foe the Leap-Frog. —*ME*

Tom Strong's Rogues' Gallery

Tom Strong, created by Alan Moore and Chris Sprouse, served as the flagship title of Moore's America's Best Comics (ABC)—a line launched in 1999 as an imprint of WildStorm Comics. With a strong emphasis on solid storytelling and art, ABC was intended to reinvigorate mainstream superhero comics after a decade rife with grim-and-gritty anti-heroes and marketing gimmicks. As Moore asked in a 2000 *Comics Journal* interview, "Would it be possible to come up with a company that looks like mainstream comics, but was in fact filled with all this quite radical stuff?" Moore initially wrote all of the ABC books, each of which reflected a different aspect of superhero comics. *Tom Strong* is ABC's action-adventure book, though (as is the case with all of ABC's books) it is innovative and stretches the boundaries and expectations of its genre. *Tom Strong* pulls from a broad historical context and spectrum of fictional types. Accordingly, his rogues' gallery reflects the wide range of the book itself.

With an origin story that recalls Doc Savage and Tarzan, *Tom Strong*'s title character is rooted firmly in the pulp fiction of the 1930s. Tom is born and raised on an island in the West Indies and lives among the island's natives for many years. Reminiscent of Philip Wylie's 1930 novel *Gladiator*, Tom develops superhuman strength and near invulnerability through morally questionable experiments conducted by his father. He later emigrates to Millennium City, a futuristic fictional metropolis, and becomes Earth's greatest "science hero." Characters in *Tom Strong* are not known as superheroes or supervillains. Rather, indicative of the book's Victorian and pulp influences, characters are called "science heroes" and "science villains." Born in 1899, Tom embodies the shift from the Victorian to the modern age. Whereas the heroes in *Tom Strong* reflect Victorian optimism toward science and industry, the villains generally reflect *modern* fears and anxieties.

The book's first major storyline (#2–#7) introduces and ties together the core of Tom Strong's rogues' gallery: the Aztechs, Ingrid Weiss, the Modular Man, the Pangaean, and Paul Saveen. Saveen, Tom's arch-nemesis and "Earth's deadliest science-villain," is the most archetypal supervillain in the book. Like Superman's Lex Luthor and Sherlock Holmes' Moriarty, Saveen is the lead hero's doppelgänger—the brilliant, gifted,

AN ICY SHOCK FROM THE PAST!

Tom Strong

MARCH 2004 24

wildstorm.com

DIRECT SALES 02411

$2.95 US $4.50 CAN

PETER HOGAN
CHRIS SPROUSE
KARL STORY
DAVE STEWART
TODD KLEIN

Dr. Permafrost. *Tom Strong* #24 © & ™ America's Best Comics, L.L.C.
COVER ART BY CHRIS SPROUSE.

but often jealous double who is instinctively compelled to choose evil over good. Whereas Moore uses many of Tom's villains to cement the book's pulp and science-fiction genres, he uses Saveen to emphasize the book's epic scope. In issue #13 (2001), Saveen recruits several hundred incarnations of himself from across the space-time continuum to challenge only a few incarnations of Tom. Even after his death, Saveen plagues Tom in one form or another throughout time and space.

While Tom continually looks forward, embracing many aspects of modernity, many of his villains seem intent on stopping or turning back time. In issue #5, Tom encounters the Pangaean, a supernatural spirit of Earth's first supercontinent dating back 300 million years. When the Pangaean realizes that Tom is the modern age's greatest hero, it tries to destroy him so that the future will devolve back into primordial chaos. A similar backward-

ness is seen in a superpowered Nazi femme fatale named Ingrid Weiss, whom Tom fights in Germany during World War II. Ingrid's fervent fascism and racism suggest the Nazi determination to freeze and control history and culture. The Aztechs, a group of South American cyber-terrorists from an alternate Earth, merge ancient culture and futuristic technology in an attempt to seize control of modern-day Earth. Tom's battle against the Aztechs underlines the modern fear of technology out of control. A similar threat is presented by the Modular Man, a self-replicating sentient machine who threatens to overtake Millennium City before Tom transplants him to Venus. Collectively, Tom's villains represent the extremes of chaos and totalitarianism—a tension that Tom constantly tries to mediate and balance.

In his last story arc for *Tom Strong* (#20–#22, 2003), Moore wrote a three-part story based loosely on DC's *Crisis on Infinite Earths*. In one of Tom's many alternate realities, Tom "Stone" actually reforms all the villains who plague Tom Strong in the book's core continuity. Saveen becomes Tom Stone's crime-fighting partner, and several familiar reformed villains form a *heroic* league called the Strongmen of America. Moore uses this alternate reality both to explore many of the basic motivations of villains and to expose superheroes' roles in creating them. Eventually, Tom Stone and Saveen revert to bitter enemies, suggesting an inherent, invariable quality of both heroism and villainy in superhero comics.

Since Moore's departure from *Tom Strong*, the book has focused more on Tom and his supporting cast than on his villains. A few minor villains, such as Permafrost, have been fleshed out, and a few new villains, such as Zodiac and Tengri Khan, have been introduced. But overall, the villains have been less iconic and less coordinated than they were during Moore's tenure on the book. —AB

The Top

The pivoting purloiner called the Top first battled Barry (Flash II) Allen in *The Flash* vol. 1 #122 (1961). Writer John Broome and artist Carmine Infantino's tale introduces penny ante crook

The Flash vol. 2 #222 ©2005 DC Comics.
COVER ART BY HOWARD PORTER AND LIVESAY.

Roscoe Dillon, who twists his childhood fascination with gyroscopes into a career as the Top, a thief who spirals like the toy from which he takes his name. The Top keeps the Fastest Man Alive on his toes with his rapidly revolving, giant-sized "atomic grenade," around which the hero must continue to run to stop it from detonating.

For years Dillon spun back to confront the Flash with his top-like weapons, often teaming with the Flash's Rogues' Gallery. In the 1970s, the Top dated Captain Cold's sister Lisa Snart (aka the Golden Glider), and evolved a form of mind over matter that made him hyper-sensitive to the Flash's superspeed, a vulnerability that proved fatal in *The Flash* vol. 1 #243 (1976).

The Top refused to roll over and play dead, however. Dillon's implacable spirit briefly possessed the bodies of Barry Allen's father, Henry, and later, U.S. senator Thomas O'Neill. In the

wake of the best-selling miniseries *Identity Crisis* (2004–2005), it was revealed that the Top was one of several DC Comics supervillains whose minds had been altered by the Justice League's Zatanna the Magician. Once his memories were restored, the resurrected Dillon—boasting an additional, vertigo-inducing superpower—swore vengeance against Wally (Flash III) West by using his mind-over-matter gifts to return reformed rogues to their previous sinister states, and villain fought villain in a 2005 *Flash* story arc titled "Rogues War." In *Flash* vol. 2 #222 (2005) the Top was killed by Flash-foe Captain Cold, who froze and then shattered Dillon. With his gift for comebacks, however, the Top may yet spin again. —ME

Toxin: *See* **Carnage**

Toyman

Pummeling the Metropolis Marvel with perilous playthings, the Toyman has long been one of Superman's craftiest arch-foes. He springs into view—literally, on a flying pogo stick, hopping out of Superman's butterfingered grasp—in *Action Comics* #64 (1943), in a tale penned by Don Cameron and penciled by Ed Dobrotka. This "publicity-mad as well as money-mad" eccentric is actually Winslow Schott, a tubby, long-maned Gepetto who pulls heists with his sleeping gas–firing mechanical soldiers and explosive-discharging toy truck. When the Toyman endangers nosey reporter Lois Lane with remote-controlled, poison-clawed dolls, Superman zips to her aid in the nick of time and captures the cunning crook. The Toyman vows to return: "How the world will laugh when Superman is defeated by a toy!"

True to his word, the Toyman returned for numerous encounters with Superman through comics' Golden Age (1938–1954), with toy-based weaponry such as flying Superman action figures that detonated on contact, acid-blasting water pistols, razor-sharp pinwheels, and a jumbo jack-in-the-box that catapulted him through the air. Often assisted by flunkies, the Toyman teamed with Lex Luthor and the Prankster as "the Terrible Trio" in *Superman* vol. 1 #88 (1954), but their alliance fizzled.

Despite the camp humor that dominated much of comics' Silver Age (1956–1969), the Toyman was irregularly seen during that period. Filmation Studios, however, dusted him off for a trio of 1966 appearances in its *The New Adventures of Superman* cartoon.

By the 1970s Schott had reformed, and in *Action* #432 (1974) Jack Nimball assumed the toymaker's guise by becoming Toyman II. The physical opposite of Schott, the sprightly Nimball was festooned in a kitschy jester's outfit and appropriated his predecessor's injurious toy gimmicks for a few skirmishes with the Man of Steel. In *Superman* vol. 1 #305 (1976) the original Toyman reclaimed his title, eliminating Nimball with a booby-trapped cuckoo clock. Toyman II's death didn't stop Hanna-Barbera from using him as one of the Legion of Doom in *Challenge of the Super Friends* (1978–1979), with Frank Welker voicing the villain. In the comics, Schott made irregular Toyman appearances, one of the most unusual being *DC Comics Presents* #67 (1984), in which he battled not only the Man of Steel but also the world's most munificent toymaker, Santa Claus.

When all things Superman were overhauled beginning with writer/artist John Byrne's continuity-changing *The Man of Steel* miniseries (1986), the Toyman was also retooled into a darker, more dangerous interpretation. "Toys in the Attic" in *Superman* vol. 2 #13 (1988) (re)introduced Winslow P. Schott, a successful toy manufacturer driven mad after being put out of business when his company was acquired by Lex Luthor's LexCorp. As the Toyman, the vengeful Schott unsuccessfully targeted Luthor for death with a lethal toy arsenal, and in later tales allied with the criminal organization Intergang and even co-starred in a 1996 one-shot, *Superman/Toyman*. Schott has been transformed in the twenty-first century into one of DC Comics' creepiest menaces—a registered pedophile, his traditional fascination with children has adopted psychotic implications. A repulsive sight in shaded granny-glasses and close-cropped hair, the Toyman committed his most heinous act in *Lex Luthor: Man of Steel* #4 (2005): a Timothy McVeigh–like bombing that struck, among other businesses, a children's daycare.

Superman vol. 2 #177 (2002) introduced a teenage genius named Hiro Okamura, a Japanese whiz kid who flirted with crime with his high-tech gadgets. In the mid-2000s Okamura, nicknamed "Toyman," has been on the straight and narrow, under contract by Batman to design crime-fighting weapons.

The Toyman was parodied as Quackerjack, a recurring foe played by Michael Bell on the Disney cartoon *Darkwing Duck* (1991–1995). Sherman Hemsley, best known as television's upwardly mobile dry cleaner George Jefferson, played a live-action—and light-hearted—Toyman in the "Season's Greedings" episode of ABC's *Lois & Clark: The New Adventures of Superman* (1993–1997). The WB's animated *Superman* series (1996–2000) included a pair of appearances of a new Toyman, radically redesigned to resemble a marionette; Bud Cort provided the cartoon villain's voice. Despite the Super-foe's appearances in comics and on television, success has escaped the Toyman in one venue that seems obvious given his modus operandi: toys. No Toyman action figures have been produced as of the mid-2000s. —*ME*

The Trickster

In folklore, a trickster is a creature, sometimes sly, sometimes silly, that violates the rules; Loki is a trickster, and so is Bugs Bunny. In *Flash*lore, the Trickster similarly bends the laws of nature and of man, always for profit and often to pester, and has done so for two generations of Scarlet Speedsters.

The movers and shakers behind the lore of the Silver Age (1956–1969) Flash, writer John Broome and artist Carmine Infantino, rolled out DC Comics' Trickster in *The Flash* vol. 1 #113 (1960). As teased on Infantino and inker Joe Giella's eye-popping cover, this newest of the Fastest Man Alive's rapidly expanding Rogues' Gallery defies logic as he eludes the Flash by running on air. This costumed crook has no superpowers, but instead gains his light-footedness from his "Airwalker Shoes," offering the ultimate in getaways. He learned this trick during his days as the youngest member of a family of circus aerialists, the Flying Jesses, but with a name like his—James Jesse—is it any wonder that he would turn to crime, especially after growing obsessed with the exploits of his infamous "reverse namesake"? Intoxicated by

The Flash vol. 1 #152 ©1965 DC Comics.
COVER ART BY CARMINE INFANTINO AND MURPHY ANDERSON.

the thrill of thievery after using his Airwalkers to conduct armed robberies—of in-flight planes!—the Trickster, the Flash's most garishly garbed foe (an orange, yellow, blue, and black vertically striped outfit with a domino mask and a cape), darts through a Central City stealing spree until tripped up by the Sultan of Speed.

The thrill of the chase was the Trickster's primary appeal. *Flash* covers from the Trickster's subsequent appearances depicted the Fastest Man Alive always a couple of steps behind Jesse, trailing him by running on telephone wires, or being repelled away from the mocking villain as the Trickster scooted away on a tricycle. An occasional member of both the Flash's Rogues' Gallery and the Secret Society of Super-Villains, the Trickster migrated to Hollywood after the Flash died in *Crisis on Infinite Earths* #8 (1985), and after a few tussles with Blue Devil applied his gimmickry to a movie special-effects career. In the real world, a

Joker-like Trickster popped up in two episodes of CBS's live-action drama *The Flash* (1990–1991)—the only Flash villain to appear in costume on the show—with *Star Wars*' Mark Hamill having the time of his life in the role. Hamill returned to the role in 2005 to voice the Trickster on the animated series *Justice League Unlimited* (2004–present).

An altercation with the demon Neron gave comics' Trickster a taste of hell in the crossover *Underworld Unleashed* (1995), inspiring him to clean up his act and become a Federal Bureau of Investigation informant, helping bust criminals with insider information. By the mid-2000s, however, it seemed as if Jesse was returning to his old tricks.

The Flash III, who followed in the Silver Age speedster's footsteps, had his first run-in with the all-new Trickster in *The Flash* vol. 2 #183 (2002). Spiky-haired wild child Axel Walker survived his parents' divorce with a mistrust of people—his credo is to trick others first, before they get the chance to trick you. Axel ripped off the Trickster's costume, trading in his Air Jordans for Jesse's Airwalkers to become the new Trickster. An expert hacker and gamer with an inability to distinguish fantasy from reality, the Trickster chased after Flash's organized Rogues, ready to sign up, and while at first disregarded by the more experienced supervillains he soon became one of the gang. Wearing an updated version of the original Trickster's uniform loaded with Flash-confounding gimmicks like itching powder and liquid-gel snares, Walker is wreaking havoc in the Flash's Keystone City, and loving every minute of it! —*ME*

Trigon

A powerful other-dimensional demon, Trigon has bedeviled the DC Comics Universe—and the Teen Titans in particular—since his first appearance in *The New Teen Titans* #2 (1980) in a Marv Wolfman–penned and George Pérez–rendered story. Clad in a white cape, boots, and a loincloth, Trigon has bright red skin, four eyes, small antlers, and sharp, pointed teeth. As the manifestation of evil, he has the power to drain souls; manipulate matter; travel through time, space, and other dimensions; fire force beams from his eyes; command legions of demons; and grow to hundreds of feet tall.

Trigon was born to a demon-worshipping woman on a dying world, and by the age of six, he had destroyed his race and his homeworld. At age thirty, he ruled his entire dimension and millions of worlds, but he wanted more. Desiring a child to rule by his side, he broke through to Earth's dimension, took the form of a handsome human, and fathered a child with a woman named Arella. The daughter that was born was Raven, but Arella fled with her to the mystical other-dimensional community known as Azarath, whose sorcerers were keeping Trigon at bay. There, Raven was taught to use her powers to heal and help others, and to rebel against the demonic blood within her.

Feeling too strongly the call of her father, Raven fled Azarath and came to Earth, reassembling the Teen Titans group to fight Trigon. Arella aided the Titans and they were eventually able to banish Trigon to a Nether-verse; Arella stayed behind to guard its dimensional doorway.

Over time, Raven eventually began to succumb to her evil ancestry, even as Trigon escaped to destroy the souls of his dimension and Azarath. Trigon assaulted Earth, transforming it into a literal hell, until the Teen Titans—along with the souls of those from Azarath—were able to find a way to destroy him forever. The Azarathian souls were tainted by Trigon, however, and caused later destruction on Earth. Raven became evil again, planting "Trigon seeds" in several of the Titans' allies and forcing them to confront the Titans. They were defeated, and Raven was given a new body.

Recently, the Trigon-worshipping Church of Blood manipulated Raven, and tiny hordes of demons that resemble Trigon have been shown in a demonic dimension. Whether this implies the return of the Titans' greatest foe has yet to be revealed.

In the animated *Teen Titans* TV show (2003–2006), Trigon is shown to be the demonic other-dimensional father of Raven as well. In the series' fourth season, he finally broke through to Earth to attack the Titans, along with his foot soldier Slade. A Trigon toy figure was released in 2004 from Bandai. —*AM*

TV Toon Terrors: Beyond Saturday Morning

The Saturday-morning cartoon shows that dominated broadcast networks ABC, CBS, and NBC throughout the 1960s and 1970s, earning ratings of more than 20 million viewers, began to decline in the mid-1980s. The rise of first-run syndicated animated programs, the increasing popularity of home video, and the emergence of cable and satellite TV—which began to replace the networks as the one-stop-shopping-place for all things cartoon—contributed to this shift.

Early 1980s shows like *He-Man and the Masters of the Universe* (1983–1985) and *G.I. Joe* (1983–1986) began the trend of packaging new animation into syndication. (During the 1970s, syndicated cartoons that aired during the afternoon were reruns of shows mostly produced for Saturday morning.) Like generations before them, children sat glued to their television sets as He-Man battled the evil Skeletor, "real American hero" G.I. Joe defended the states against Cobra Commander, and King Features' comic-strip heroes the Phantom, Flash Gordon, Mandrake the Magician, and Lothar teamed to protect Earth against the evil machinations of world dominator Ming the Merciless on *Defenders of the Earth* (1986–1987). The bionic-powered Bennett family regularly faced off against the evil Dr. Scarab on *The Bionic Six* (1987). *The Adventures of the Galaxy Rangers* (1986–1989) showcased a team of futuristic guardians of planet Earth who continually met up with space bandits and intergalactic menaces like Captain Kidd, the Disney-esque evil Queen of the Crown, and crime boss Bappo.

The feline-human hybrids *Thundercats* (1985–1987) fought the magical Mumm-Ra and his evil mutants, Luna and her band of Lunatics, and a variety of "Third Earthers," including Ooze, Tashi, Grune the Destroyer, Mad Bubbler, Mud Hog, Inflamor, and the Crabmen. Even short-lived hero teams on shows like *The Centurions* (1986)

and *The Inhumanoids* (1986) faced recurring villains in Dr. Terror and his Doom Drones and Blackthorne Shore and his subterranean Inhumanoids.

Amidst these fondly remembered syndicated toons lie a staple of classic superheroes who helped keep Saturday morning alive on various network TV shows, fighting a bevy of world-class supervillains (and some long-forgotten made-for-TV bad guys) on *Super Friends* (which had started on ABC in 1973 and proved popular through the mid-1980s, albeit with various title changes), *Spider-Man and His Amazing Friends* (NBC, 1981–1984), and *Kid Super-Power Hour with Shazam!* (NBC, 1981–1982). At the end of the 1980s, as part of his 50th anniversary celebration, the Man of Steel gave a brief but stellar performance in the Ruby-Spears–produced *Superman* (CBS, 1988–1989), facing off against long-time adversaries Lex Luthor (and his Defendroids), the Prankster, General Zod, and Wild Sharkk.

Still, afternoon syndicated cartoons continued a competitive edge over their Saturday-morning counterparts and the 1990s saw a resurgence of animated superhero shows. The critically acclaimed "Dark Deco"–style *Batman: The Animated Series* (1992–1995, later followed by its continuation, *The Adventures of Batman & Robin*) showcased many Batman comic-book villains, including the Joker (voiced by Mark Hamill), Catwoman (Adrienne Barbeau), Clayface, Two-Face, the Mad Hatter (Roddy McDowell), Ra's al Ghul, and Talia. The breakthrough of the show was the introduction of the Joker's girlfriend, Harley Quinn, but other revamped or original villains included Baby Doll, Roxy Rocket, Red Claw, Lock-up, the sinister computer HARDAC, Calendar Girl (a variation on the comics' Calendar Man), Maxie Zeus, the Clock King, and the Cluemaster. (The success of *Batman: The Animated Series* has kept Batman and his rogues' gallery in near-perpetual television view with the cartoons *Batman Beyond*, 1999–2001, and *The Batman*, 2004–present.)

The Man of Steel received a similar animated treatment in the fledgling WB network's *Superman* (1996–2000), with Lex Luthor (Clancy Brown), Metallo (Malcolm McDowell), the Toyman (Bud Cort), and Darkseid (Michael Ironside) running amok,

along with villains created specifically for the show: Livewire, Luminus, and the Preserver.

Along with Batman and Superman, Marvel's *X-Men* (1992–1997) began its long run in the early 1990s, with villains such as Magneto, the Sentinels, the Morlocks, Kang the Conqueror, Silver Samurai, Red Skull, Mr. Sinister, Apocalypse, and Lady Deathstrike beautifully rendered and true to their comic-book roots. Marvel's web-spinner debuted with a brand-new show in *Spider-Man* (1994–1998), which included key villains from the spider-pantheon, including the Green Goblin, Dr. Octopus, the Lizard, the Scorpion, the Rhino, Mysterio, Venom, Carnage, the Shocker, the Vulture, the Chameleon, the Kingpin, and the Hobgoblin. Two Marvel series were combined in syndication for *The Marvel Action Hour* (1994–1996), with *Fantastic Four* and *Iron Man* sharing the screen. *Fantastic Four* saw the likes of Puppet Master, Krang, Galactus, Dr. Doom. Mole Man, Annihilus, Hydro-Man, Juggernaut, the Skrulls, and Ego the Living Planet, to name a few, while Iron Man encountered Mandarin, Blizzard, Whirlwind, Modok, the Living Laser, Fin Fang Foom, Madame Masque, Titanium Man, Crimson Dynamo, and the Grey Gargoyle.

The 1990s also saw heroes and villains collide in *Jim Lee's WildC.A.T.S* (1994–1995) as the prehistoric alien race, the Daemonites, fought for control of the universe. In *Phantom 2040* (1994–1996), the purple-clad, skull-ringed hero battled environmental villains in a futuristic Metropia ravaged by corrupt corporations and international terrorists with destructive ecological agendas.

Lighter fare included New England Comics' big blue hero *The Tick* (1994–1997), who bounced onto the scene with his dozens of memorable comedic villains in tow. Animated characters met live-action guest stars in the galactic talk show *Space Ghost Coast-to-Coast* (1994–2003), on which the supervillainous insectoid Zorak, the cat-like pirate Brak, and heat-inducing Moltar stole the stage.

Disney's first hero-oriented cartoon, *Darkwing Duck* (1991–1995), introduced parodies of established supervillains, such as Negaduck (superhero

Darkwing Duck's evil counterpart), the "Lord of Electricity" Megavolt (a parody of the Spider-Man villain Electro), the "Master of Plants" Dr. Bushroot (likely inspired by DC's the Floronic Man, with hints of Poison Ivy), Quackerjack, a demented court jester obsessed with toys (a cross between DC baddies the Joker and Toyman), and the watery Liquidator (in celebration of Marvel's Hydro-Man). The superheroic duck stood alongside another unlikely hero, a video game–playing hedgehog, as the *Adventures of Sonic the Hedgehog* debuted in 1993. Loaded with *Tiny Toons*–like slapstick humor, the speedy blue animal delighted in stopping the evil Dr. Ivo Robotnik and his fleet of vicious robots from taking over the planet Mobius. The show morphed into the Saturday-morning program *Sonic the Hedgehog* (1993–1995), with Jim Cummings voicing the role of Dr. Robotnik.

Another popular, villain-rich series was the Canadian import *ReBoot* (1994–2002), the first TV series produced entirely with computer animation, and seen on ABC and in syndication. The show's action primarily occurred in Mainframe, a computer on the Internet, where a band of heroes fought the ruthless supervillains the Darth Vader-esque Megabyte and the evil queen Hexadecimal.

Cable TV networks Disney Channel, Nickelodeon, and Cartoon Network formed the triumvirate of cartoon supremacy in the 2000s. Airing cartoons 24/7, cable has "changed the programming paradigm" for the broadcast networks, notes children's television expert Brian O'Neil in *Animation World* magazine: network Saturday-morning cartoons only exist on ABC Kids, FOX Kids, and Kids' WB. In this new climate, supervillains dominate action-adventure, humor, anime, and superhero shows in the forms of either brand-new characters or edgier reincarnations of past favorites.

Franchise-friendly superhero series based on best-selling comic books portrayed dark, grim, and gritty supervillains and pushed the envelope with the hero-villain relationships, with shows like *Justice League Unlimited* (2004–present) presenting allied villains—like the diabolical Legion of Doom—banding together to usurp established political systems and destroy the heroes. *Teen Titans* (2003–2006) reinvigorated existing comic-book villains, with new takes on the evil-hearted

Slade, Terra, Brother Blood, Trigon, and the Brain, the latter of whom stepped up as leader of the Brotherhood of Evil. The evil crimelord Shredder joined Mousers, Foot Soldiers, and an array of miscreants and monsters in the pumped-up *Teenage Mutant Ninja Turtles* (2003–present). And series like *Static Shock!* (2000–2004), winner of the Humanitas Prize in 2003, examined real-life villainy in the issues faced by today's teens, including peer pressure, gangs, and survival in an ethnically diverse urban neighborhood—but the streetwise teen hero Static still encountered his share of costumed criminals, like the flaming Hotstreak, Slipstream, Replay, and Ebon, the illusive leader of the Breed.

As they embrace their villains, some 2000s shows celebrate animation "firsts": *Justice League* marks the first time in more than fifteen years that DC Comics' heavy-hitter superheroes have banded together in an animated television series since uniting in *Super Friends*, and *Static Shock!* earns credit for being the first animated series centered on an African-American superhero and an urban supporting cast. With the help of Mainframe Entertainment (of *ReBoot* fame) and writer/executive producer Brian Michael Bendis, *Spider-Man: The Series* (2003) broke away from traditional animation techniques, using computer aided 3-D modeling in conjunction with traditional 2-D animation styles for enhanced fight scenes. As usual, Spidey wrests with concealing his secret identity while wrangling a host of foes, a mix of comic-book favorites (albeit slightly updated) like Electro, the Lizard, and Kraven the Hunter, and brand-new villains such as Talon (voiced by the rapper Eve).

Pint-sized heroines and action adventurers also take on their share of supervillains. The kindergarten *Powerpuff Girls* (1998–2004) battled Mojo Jojo and other infiltrators of Townsville. In *Totally Spies!* (2001–present), developed by French animation studio Marathon, a teenaged trio of *Charlie's Angels*–like international agents attempt to circumvent sociopathic villains with bizarre personality disorders, such as Max Exterminus, Sunny Day, Myrna Beesbottom, Triple Threat, Macker the Safecracker, Frankie Dude, Helga Von Gugen, and Inga Bittersweet. Laced with a hip, comedic element, these villains' plans revolve around their twisted obsessions and their desire to convince the world to buy into their demented worldview.

Cheerleading-captain-turned-crime-fighter *Kim Possible* (2002–2005), and ten-year-old rebels in *Codename: Kids Next Door* (2002–present) similarly battle grotesque, satiric, and outright evil world dominators while dealing with the trials and tribulations of childhood and adolescence. Anchored by Kim's arch-enemy and most recurring thorn, mad scientist Dr. Drakken, *Kim Possible*'s rogues' gallery includes the likes of the smart and sadistic femme fatale Shego, multibillionaire villain Señor Senior Sr. (originally voiced by Ricardo Montalban), the eccentric English Lord and monkey-obsessed Lord Monkey Fist, and Amy Hall, a disgraced former geneticist obsessed with Beanie Baby–type collectable dolls who breeds living mutants to supplement her doll collection. Supervillains are so insidious, they even have managed to sneak into comedy cartoons: on *SpongeBob SquarePants* (1999–present) Man Ray battles Mermaid Man and Barnacle Boy, SpongeBob's favorite TV heroes, and Plankton covets the secret Crabby Patty recipe.

In this mix, shows like *Samurai Jack* (2001–2004) and *American Dragon: Drake Long* (2005–present) portray villainy against a backdrop of martial arts, magic, and mysticism. In the action-heavy *Max Steel* (1999–2001), diabolical Psycho and Vitriol combated nanite-charged superspy Max Steel, simultaneously parlayed into a line of action figures from Mattel. Many of these 2000s shows were either nominated for or garnered Emmy Awards (*Samurai Jack*, for example, which scooped up an Emmy for Best Animated Television Series in 2004), receiving accolades for their smart dialogue, fluid animation, and engaging, well-written characters.

With these and other programs, Cartoon Network in particular has made attempts to attract viewers outside its core audience of young children. The network's Saturday-evening cartoon block Toonami is dedicated to reruns of teen-oriented anime from Japan, with its darker, supernatural themes found in shows like *Duel Masters* and *Naruto*. With the comic-book world developing villain-centric titles like *Villains United* (2005), one wonders if it's only a matter of time before villain-centric programming makes its way to television. —*GM*

Two-Face

Harvey Kent had the world on a string. Introduced in *Detective Comics* #66 (1942) in a story by Bill Finger and Bob Kane, Gotham City's youngest district attorney had great things predicted for his future. He was engaged to an adoring young woman named Gilda, and was so handsome he was nicknamed "Apollo."

A champion of law and justice, it was thought that Kent's prosecution of gangster "Boss" Moroni would be his greatest blow yet to the criminal underworld of Gotham City. But when Kent proved Moroni was present at a crime scene through the discovery of a two-faced silver dollar Moroni carried as a good luck charm, the crime boss became enraged and threw a vial of acid into Kent's face. The acid was prevented from totally disfiguring Kent by the actions of Batman, who was testifying against Moroni, and who was able to deflect the trajectory of the acid vial. Only the left side of Kent's face was disfigured, turned into a mass of sagging, decayed flesh—but that proved sufficient. Kent, driven mad by the incident, disfigured one of the faces of Moroni's double-faced silver dollar and became a criminal, calling himself Two-Face.

Consonant with his new persona, Two-Face adopted the motif of duality for all his crimes, basing them all around the number two, such as robbing a messenger riding a double-decker bus and holding up the patrons of a movie theater viewing a double feature. And, when faced with a crucial decision, such as killing a captured Batman or letting him live, Two-Face flips his two-headed coin, letting whichever side lands face up determine his decision, the unscarred face representing "good," the scarred face representing "evil." Eventually, "Apollo" Kent's face was restored by a brilliant plastic surgeon, bringing an end to the career of Two-Face, if only briefly.

For a time, the appearances of Two-Face were variations on a theme. Three times it appeared that Harvey Kent had resumed his criminal career as Two-Face, but he was being framed, the first instance occurring in *Batman* #50 (1948–1949), when district attorney's butler Wilkins masqueraded as Two-Face. (At this point, Kent's last name was changed to "Dent" to eliminate any conflict or confusion with Clark Kent, the secret identity of Superman, although Michael L. Fleisher, in his 1976 tome *The Encyclopedia of Comic Book Heroes,* vol. 1: *Batman,* ascribes this change to a "chronicler's error.") Then Paul Sloane, an actor playing Harvey Dent in a television recreation of the Two-Face story, was disfigured when real acid was substituted for colored water in a recreation of "Boss" Moroni's trial, and he resumed Two-Face's criminal career. This story, "The New Crimes of Two-Face" (*Batman* #68, 1951–1952), is also of historical interest, for when it was reprinted in *Batman Annual* #3 (1962), the disfiguring sequence was redrawn to show a klieg light exploding in Sloane's face, rather than portraying the "imitable behavior" of throwing acid, which the Comics Code, adopted in 1954, prohibited. Lastly, in *Detective Comics* #187 (1952), theater manager George Blake disguises himself as Two-Face, but is exposed by Batman, who realizes that Blake had disfigured the wrong side of his face with makeup.

Finally, in *Batman* #81 (1954), the inevitable happened. Dent's plastic surgery was shattered in an explosion, restoring his visage to that of Two-Face—forever. Dent is tempted to resume his former life of crime, but leaves the final decision to his two-headed coin. When the scarred side lands face up, Dent's decision is irrevocably made. Two-Face's return, however, was short-lived; this issue was his last appearance for over a decade. Perhaps thought too freakish to be featured in new stories after the institution of the Comics Code, Two-Face's next appearance was not until *World's Finest Comics* #173, in 1968. He returned to the *Batman* title with issue #234 in 1971. Since then, Harvey Dent has committed one crime after another as Two-Face, and has time after time been incarcerated at Arkham Asylum in Gotham City by Batman.

Of all Batman's bizarre foes, Two-Face is one of the few for whom Batman harbors genuine sympathy, for he realizes Two-Face, though mad, is not evil, and his madness is not of his own making. Whenever they meet, Batman refers to Two-Face only as "Harvey," perhaps an attempt to remind Two-Face of the friendship they once shared.

Sometimes variations to the basic Two-Face story are grafted onto the character's legend, for bet-

Batman #234 ©1971 DC Comics.
COVER ART BY NEAL ADAMS.

ter or for worse. One 1976 story attempted to convince readers that Harvey Dent was not the target of "Boss" Moroni's acid-throwing spree, while a 1996 story tells readers that Harvey Dent was subjected to abuse as a child, making his already-damaged psyche that much more prone to fall into Two-Face's madness. A woman claiming to be Two-Face's daughter, Duella Dent, appeared in DC comics in the 1970s, but rarely has been seen since.

Interestingly, in 1946, a second Two-Face was created. In the *Batman* syndicated comic strip for Sunday, June 23, 1946, an actor named Harvey Apollo was disfigured in circumstances similar to those of Harvey Dent's. This story, which is not considered part of the *Batman* comic book continuity, ran until August 18, 1946, ending with Two-Face's tragic death.

Is imitation the sincerest form of flattery? Chester Gould, creator of comic strip lawman *Dick*

Dick Tracy's Rogues' Gallery

Chester Gould's comic strip *Dick Tracy*, which originated in 1931, and its hard-edged, deformed criminals inspired creator Bob Kane's vision of the rogues' gallery of Batman (first seen in 1939), as well as other supervillains.

- **Big Boy**, debuting in 1931, was a rotund gangster in the Al Capone mold, a template followed by many comic-book crimelords including Batman's Boss Anthony Zucco (*Detective Comics* #38, 1940) and Boss Rupert Thorne (*Detective* #469, 1977).
- **The Blank**, first seen in 1937, was a gangster formerly known as Frank Redrum ("Murder" spelled backward) who lost his facial features from a gunshot. The Blank's closest imitator, Steve Ditko's faceless anti-*hero* the Question, debuted in 1967.
- **Flattop**, the square-headed killer for hire first seen in 1943, is without a doubt Dick Tracy's most famous felon—in fact, fans mourned the character's demise in 1944, and cartoonist Gould eventually introduced Flattop's look-alike son. Spider-Man foe Hammerhead, the flat-headed mobster who uses steel-skull as a battering ram, strongly resembles Flattop; Hammerhead bowed 1972.
- **The Mole**, a ghastly ganglord with mole-like facial features, used his ability to burrow with his hands to form an underground getaway labyrinth when first seen in 1941. Twenty years later, Marvel's similarly grotesque Mole Man retreated to his subterranean kingdom in *Fantastic Four* #1 (1961).
- Plastic Man's 1980s' enemy Lowbrow, aka I.Q. Small, was a takeoff of **the Brow**, the bad guy with the crumpled forehead. Another foe of "Plas" was Brickface (real name: Terrence Cotta), a nod to the wrinkle-pussed Nazi spy **Pruneface**.
- In the vein of Dick Tracy's rogues' gallery comes **Jigsaw**, arch-nemesis of the Punisher, who debuted in 1972. Originally an enforcer for the Maggia, handsome Billy Russo, aka "Billy the Beaut," was horrifically disfigured when the Punisher booted him face-first through a window.

Tracy, introduced in 1967 a character, half of whose face was disfigured, under the name Haf-n-Haf. Despite this similarity, students of Gould's work do not feel Gould was imitating Two-Face, claiming that Gould, to avoid charges of unoriginality, would not have used this character if he had been aware of the older *Batman* villain.

The original character of Two-Face, despite these Two-Face imposters, is kept fresh by constant interaction with Batman and his supporting cast. When the character of Dick Grayson became a teenager and a younger boy, Jason Todd, became the second Robin, Todd carried a grudge against Two-Face for having killed his father, a small-time criminal. Jason had the opportunity to kill Two-Face, but chose justice over revenge.

Despite having such narrow parameters for his stories, Two-Face stays as current as the calendar. The villain was a vital supporting character in Frank Miller's ground-breaking miniseries *Batman: The Dark Knight Returns* (1986), evolving a complex plan around the twin World Trade Centers. He attempted to steal for ransom the Constitution of the United States, "the second-most important document in American history," in 1987, the 200th anniversary of its writing, and in 2000 he tried to take over Gotham City during a spell of Y2K paranoia. There seem to be no end of permutations to Two-Face's schemes, and Batman's most tragic enemy seems set to devil the Dark Knight until at least the twenty-second century.

Two-Face continues to appear in the 2000s, both in the comic books and in media adaptations. Throughout the 1990s Richard Moll voiced Two-Face in several episodes of *Batman: the Animated Series* (1992–1995) and its continuations; in the cartoons, the villain's scarred skin hue was altered from the comics' purple to light blue. Tommy Lee Jones played Two-Face in the film *Batman Forever* (1995), in a performance that perhaps was a little over the top in showcasing the character's insanity. He characteristically supplied himself with two molls: Sugar, a "good girl" portrayed by Drew Barrymore, and Spice, a "bad girl" performed by Debi Mazar.

This media exposure garnered an enthusiastic following for Two-Face, and there's been no stopping since, neither to his comic-book appearances, nor to his merchandising. These include a 1989 action figure from Toy Biz with a scarred coin accessory; several figures based on the version of the character from *Batman: The Animated Series*; a *Batman Forever* action figure in 1995 in Jones' likeness, with a "Turbo-Charge Cannon" accessory; a 2005 figure by Kia Asamiya, imported from Japan and limited to 10,000 copies; and, also in 2005, an action figure based on artist Tim Sale's version of the character from the *Batman: The Long Halloween* series.

Two-Face continues to oppose Batman, despite the risk that he may eventually defeat the Dark Knight, and come in first. —*MWB*

The Ultra-Humanite

Lex Luthor prototype the Ultra-Humanite was the first recurring supervillain to challenge Superman during comics' Golden Age (1938–1954). A hairless mad scientist with a crippled body, the Ultra-Humanite (sometimes shortened to "Ultra") was envisioned by the Man of Steel's co-creators, writer Jerry Siegel and artist Joe Shuster, as an evil counterpart to the hero, harkening back to the pair's original 1933 vision of Superman as a bald bad guy. First seen in *Action Comics* #13 (1939), the Ultra-Humanite devotes his "tremendous brain" to world domination, and realizes to achieve such a goal he must first eliminate the Metropolis Marvel. His electrical weapon fails to vanquish the hero, but he doggedly keeps trying, appearing in *Action* six times in nine months, with schemes including a biological "purple plague" and a deadly "atomic disintegrator."

The Ultra-Humanite's most successful anti-Superman weapon was evasion, as he ducked both death and the Man of Steel in *Action* #20 (1940) by transferring his mind into the body of Hollywood ingénue Dolores Winter. Not content to be DC Comics' first transvestite supervillain, Ultra skirted capture by diving into a volcano in issue #21, and he was shunted into limbo by the premiere of Luthor two issues later, who grabbed the baleful baton of baldheaded badness in Metropolis.

The door to limbo is revolving, as countless buried-but-unearthed supervillains have shown. The Ultra-Humanite worked "her" way back into comics in the early 1980s in the "Mr. and Mrs. Superman" feature (the adventures of the Golden Age, or "Earth-Two," Man of Steel and Lois Lane) in *Superman Family*, taking the form of "Ultra-Ant," a gargantuan insect. He then relocated his brain into the form in which he is most famously known, a mutated albino gorilla, reorganizing the Secret Society of Super-Villains in 1981 and fighting the Justice Society of America (JSA) and the Justice League of America. Writer Roy Thomas frequently used the Ultra-Humanite in the mid-1980s as a JSA adversary in the pages of *All-Star Squadron*, a series set during DC's Golden Age (in which the villain wielded the strength-inducing Powerstone, an artifact used by the Golden Age Luthor), and in the then-present day in *Infinity, Inc.*, the title starring the JSA's progeny, although post–*Crisis on Infinite Earths* (1985–1986) continuity rewritings have altered some of these appearances.

The 1993 miniseries *The Golden Age*, set in the years immediately following World War II, disclosed that the Ultra-Humanite had transferred his brain into the body of the superhero Americommando. After decades of mind-swapping and malevolence, Ultra met his demise in the pages of *JSA* in the 2002 storyline "Stealing Thunder." Occupying the body of Justice Society hanger-on Johnny Thunder to usurp the might of Johnny's "genie," Thunderbolt, the Ultra-Humanite was executed by the Crimson Avenger II in retribution for killing the hero's predecessor, the original Crimson Avenger.

Death didn't stop the Ultra-Humanite from appearing, in his white-gorilla form, in episodes of the animated television series *Justice League* (2001–2004), at the insistence of Warner Bros. animator James Tucker, a self-professed DC Comics fanboy. In his TV incarnation, voiced by Ian Buchanan, Ultra, despite his grotesque appearance, was an urbane mastermind with a passion for classical music. —*ME*

Ultron

A "child" like Ultron is the nightmare of every "father." This sentient, sinister robot was constructed by scientist Henry Pym, the size-changing superhero alternately known as Ant-Man, Giant-Man, Goliath, and Yellowjacket. A flashback sequence in *The Avengers* vol. 1 #58 (1968), written by Roy Thomas and illustrated by John Buscema, discloses Pym's greatest technological achievement, doomed to be his utmost failure: his creation of an android possessing artificial intelligence. Dubbed Ultron-1, this automaton rebels against its creator and attempts to murder Pym with energy blasts: "Your destruction is inevitable, father … you cannot resist me … !" Yet Ultron spares Pym as his creator lay prostrate: "It would be far too simple … not worthy of my consummate genius!" The renegade robot erases Pym's memory of its existence—although the scientist's recollections of his creation of his malevolent brainchild were restored—and initiates an Oedipal war against the Avenger.

When Ultron first appeared four months earlier in *Avengers* #54, however, his connection to Pym had yet to be revealed. The robot was veiled under the guise of the Crimson Cowl, a presumably human mastermind who orchestrated the union of a quintet of supervillains—Klaw, Whirlwind, the Melter, the Black Knight, and Radioactive Man—as

the new Masters of Evil, directing them in combat against Marvel's mightiest super-team. Taking the name Ultron-5, having upgraded itself from Pym's original programming, in *Avengers* #57 the robot attacked Pym and his teammates through a synthetic "son" of its own: the Vision, an android possessing total mastery of its density. Programmed to destroy Pym and the Avengers, the Vision soon overrode Ultron's design and obliterated the malevolent machine, although Ultron's "evilly smiling head" went missing after an explosion.

Ultron in fact survived that skirmish and has routinely enhanced itself into a nigh-unstoppable threat to Pym and the Avengers. In some of its incarnations its outer shell has been forged of adamantium, the same indestructible metal from which X-Man Wolverine's skeleton and retractable were created. Ultron commands tremendous super-speed and strength, and fires through its eyes and palms concussive bolts capable of paralyzing even the thunder god Thor. Fueled by intense hatred and bereft of compassion, Ultron can interface with virtually any computer, and with its "encephalo beams" exercise subliminal control of humans.

Ultron envisions itself as the progenitor of a new digital order. The Vision was its first attempt to fashion an "extended family." Ultron later created two "female" androids: Jocasta, which, like the Vision, turned against "her" creator and joined the Avengers; and a "mate," Alkhema the War Toy.

One of the most heralded Marvel Comics storylines involving this metallic monster was "Ultron Unlimited," serialized through *Avengers* vol. 3 #19–#22 (1998), in which Ultron annihilated the entire population of the Baltic nation of Slorenia, then commanded hundreds of hive-minded Ultron duplicates into battle against the Avengers. Ultron, with a steely voice provided by actor John Stocker, appeared in six episodes of FOX's animated *Avengers* series (1999–2000). —*ME*

Underworld Supervillains

What greater villain could there be than the devil himself? The devil is an archetypal figure in scripture and Western literature, beginning with his appearances in the Bible. In his *Divine Comedy* (1308–1321), the poet Dante Alighieri depicted Satan as a monstrous, three-headed giant entrapped in the lowest circle of the "Inferno."

The devil's role as tempter of humankind is central to the Faust myth, in which the elderly scholar Dr. Faust sells his soul to Mephistopheles (a name used either for Satan or another devil) to gain greater knowledge. The two most influential versions of the story are Christopher Marlowe's play *Doctor Faustus* (circa 1593, adapted into a graphic novel by Oscar Zarate in 1986) and Johann Wolfgang von Goethe's two-part drama *Faust* (1808, 1832; adapted into comics in *Classics Illustrated* #167, 1962).

In *Paradise Lost* (1667), the English poet John Milton portrayed Satan as a tragic anti-hero who preferred ruling in hell to serving God in heaven.

Comic-book writers have followed the examples set by these classic works in their own portrayals of hell, underworld demons, and the devil. For example, in their *Faust* comics series (1989–1997), writer David Quinn and artist Tim Vigil created a contemporary version of the classic tale. Marvel's evil sorcerer Belasco (from *Ka-Zar the Savage* #11, 1982), who resembles a horned devil, once ruled an underground realm that he claimed inspired Dante's depiction of hell.

Over the years Marvel Comics has tended not to identify its devil figures specifically as the Judeo-Christian Satan. Marvel's principal surrogate for Satan is Mephisto (introduced in *Silver Surfer* #3, 1968). Mephisto was eventually established as the "Devil" who transformed Johnny Blaze into the Ghost Rider by bonding him with the demon Zarathos (who first appeared in *Marvel Spotlight* #5, 1972). As for Daimon Hellstrom, the "Son of Satan," Marvel later identified his father as a lesser demon named Marduk Kurios. In *Daredevil* #270 (1989) writer Ann Nocenti and artist John Romita, Jr. gave Mephisto a son, Blackheart, who seeks to overthrow his father. Mephisto also has a daughter, Mephista (from *Doctor Strange* #6, 1988).

Marvel's other obvious substitute for Satan is the demon Satannish (who first appeared in *Doctor Strange* #174, 1968), who grants mortals such as

the Sons of Satannish (from *Doctor Strange* #175, 1968) mystical power in exchange for their souls.

Writer Steve Gerber co-created his own stand-in for Satan, the horned demon Thog the Nether-Spawn, ruler of the hell dimension Sominus, as an adversary for the Man-Thing in *Adventure into Fear* #11 (1972).

Marvel has also made use of underworld figures from ancient mythologies such as Hela, the Norse goddess of death. One of the leading enemies of Marvel's Thor and Hercules is Pluto, the ancient Greeks' and Romans' god of the underworld, who, when Stan Lee and Jack Kirby introduced him in *Thor* #127 (1966), posed as a movie-studio head. Perhaps coincidentally, under his Greek name of Hades, this god was also the main villain of Disney's animated *Hercules* (1997), played by James Woods in the manner of a glad-handing but ruthless Hollywood executive. Another of Thor's enemies is the Egyptian death god Seth (starting in *Thor* #240, 1975). Conan the Barbarian's creator Robert E. Howard gave a similar name to Set, a dark "elder god" in the form of a serpent who is worshipped by evil sorcerers.

Marvel writers and artists have also created their own demons. Among these is Chthon, a demonic "elder god" (who first appeared in *Avengers* #187, 1979), who created the sinister book of magic called the Darkhold. Another demonic entity is D'Spayre (created by Chris Claremont and John Byrne in *Marvel Team-Up* #68, 1978), who infuses despair into mortals. Claremont also co-created a race of demons, the N'garai, who first appeared in *Giant-Size Dracula* #2 (1974).

DC Comics likewise has a history of creating demons. In *Justice League of America* #10 (1962), by writer Gardner Fox and artist Mike Sekowsky, the sorcerer Felix Faust freed the primeval Demons Three: Abnegazar, Rath and Ghast. In a Spectre story in *Showcase* #61 (1966), Fox and artist Murphy Anderson introduced Shathan the Eternal, the ruler of a sinister cosmos called Dis, in a clear analogue to Satan and hell. The ghastly Nekron (from *Tales of the Green Lantern Corps* #2, 1981) rules the Land of the Unliving, a realm where spirits of the dead wait before being sent to heaven or hell.

Starting in the 1980s, though, DC has explicitly presented its variation of the Judeo-Christian version of hell and its underworld menaces. The first being to be condemned to DC's hell was the First of the Fallen (introduced in *Hellblazer* #42, 1991), who was eventually supplanted as ruler by Lucifer, but who has become the archenemy of DC's supernatural investigator John Constantine.

British writer Neil Gaiman was apparently following Milton's lead in conceiving his updated, anti-heroic version of Lucifer in *Sandman* #4 (1989), who has since become the star of his own comic-book series (2000–present) for DC's Vertigo line. Having wearied of ruling hell, Lucifer has created his own universe instead.

Among the "archdukes" of DC's hell are Belial, the "Father of Lies" (from *The Demon* vol. 1 #2, 1990) who is the father of both Merlin and Etrigan the Demon, the character created by Jack Kirby; Beelzebub, the "Lord of Flies" (from *Sandman* #4, 1989), who is an adversary of Kid Eternity; and Nergal, a long-time enemy of John Constantine (from *Hellblazer* #6, 1988).

The demon prince Neron endowed various supervillains with increased power in exchange for their souls in DC's *Underworld Unleashed* (1995–1996). Other demons of DC's hell include Abaddon the Destroyer, Asteroth, Azazel the Abomination, and hell's enforcers, Agony and Ecstasy.

Vulnerable to supernatural forces, Superman has contended against the half-demonic siblings Blaze (from *Action Comics* #655, 1990) and her brother Lord Satanus (from *Adventures of Superman* #493, 1992), who proved to be the evil children of Shazam, the wizard who mentors the original Captain Marvel. DC has even portrayed Islam's counterpart to Satan, Iblis, as the menace of the *JLA Annual* in 2000.

Demons and dark figures exist in comics outside the Marvel and DC Universes, as well. The title character of Todd McFarlane's *Spawn* (1992–present) made a Faustian bargain to serve the demon Malebolgia, ruler of hell, but later slew him. Another of Spawn's foes is the minor demon Clown, who transforms into the monstrous Violator (who first manifested in *Spawn* #2, 1992).

Chaos! Comics!' character Lady Death (who debuted in *Evil Ernie* #1, 1991) was once an innocent young girl. Through the machinations of her enemy Lucifer, she died, became the ruler of hell, and for centuries sought to wipe out all life on Earth before finally forsaking her genocidal quest.

Demons even infest Japanese comics and animation. The heroine of the 1999 manga series *Chrono Crusade*, which was adapted into anime in 2003–2004, is sixteen-year-old Rosette Christopher, who lives in 1920s Brooklyn and belongs to the Magdalene Order of nuns, who exorcise demons by shooting them with special "gospel bullets." Rosette's partner Chrono is himself a demon, and their greatest enemy is the demon Aion, who captured her brother Joshua.

According to *Devilman* (created by Go Nagai as a manga series in 1972, and adapted into anime three times, in 1972–1973 and then in 1987 and 1990), demons rule Earth before the coming of humankind. Now Satan intends to lead the demons in bringing about Armageddon. But a teenager, Akira Fudo, takes on the power of the demon Amon, thus becoming Satan's adversary, Devilman.

There are an extraordinary number of other examples of devils and demons in comics from around the world, far too many to list in this entry, including the devil's appearances in Foolbert Sturgeon's 1969 underground comic *The New Adventures of Jesus*, in writer Garth Ennis's *Preacher Special: Saint of Killers* (1996), and in Bill Sienkiewicz's *Stray Toasters* (1989); as the childlike title character of Harvey Comics' *Hot Stuff* (1957–1994); and as Philip, the Ruler of Heck, who has been punishing minor sins in Scott Adams' strip *Dilbert* starting in 1989.

The devil has continued to appear as a villain in prose fiction, including Stephen Vincent Benet's short story "The Devil and Daniel Webster" (1937; in film in 1941), Nikos Kazantzakis' novel *The Last Temptation of Christ* (1960; in film in 1988), and Stephen King's *Needful Things* (1991; in film in 1993).

In modern times devils also show up on film and television. Walt Disney's most powerful portrait of evil is the colossal demon Chernobog in the concluding segment of *Fantasia* (1940). The devil was a powerful off-camera presence in his two biggest movie hits, *Rosemary's Baby* (1968) and *The Exorcist* (1973). Novelist and filmmaker Clive Barker created his own versions of devilish characters, the Cenobites, led by Pinhead, in the *Hellraiser* movies (beginning in 1988). The devil appeared in various episodes of the original *Twilight Zone* (1959–1964), such as "The Howling Man" (1960), and turned up briefly as the witch Angelique's master Diabolos on *Dark Shadows* (1966–1971).

There is also a tradition of treating devils as comedic figures, dating back to medieval drama. Modern versions include Mr. Applegate in the musical comedy *Damn Yankees* (1955; in film in 1958); the devil in the movie *Bedazzled* (1967, remade in 2000); the "Evil Genius" in Terry Gilliam's film *Time Bandits* (1981); Darryl Van Horne in John Updike's novel *The Witches of Eastwick* (1984), played by Jack Nicholson in the film (1987); the title demon in Tim Burton's movie *Beetlejuice* (1988); and the ludicrous Satan of television's animated *South Park* (1997–present).

In other words, in one form or another, the devil and his underworld minions have pervaded the popular culture. —*PS*

Vampire Villains: *See* **Blood-Sucking Bad Guys (and Gals)** *and* **Monster Supervillains**

Vandal Savage

" I have seen empires bloom and wither and die," intones the deathless conqueror Vandal Savage in *DC One Million* #1 (1998). "And, periodically, I have chosen to rule the Earth." In Vandal Savage, countless superheroes have found an entrenched evil evocative of Lucifer and as old as humanity itself. Founder of the history-manipulating Illuminati and the author of the fall of Atlantis, Savage has played many pivotal roles in history: an ancient Sumerian king; the Egyptian pharaohs Khafre and Cheops; Julius Caesar; Genghis Khan; Vlad Dracul the Impaler; Jack the Ripper; and Josef Stalin. Savage has also worked behind the scenes for tyrants and conquerors such as Napoleon, Bismarck, and Hitler.

The creation of science-fiction writer Alfred Bester (author of the seminal 1956 novel *The Stars My Destination*) and original Golden Age Green Lantern artist Martin Nodell in *Green Lantern* vol. 1 #10 (1943), Vandal Savage (originally Vandar Adg) was born some 50,000 years ago; overcome by mysterious meteorite radiation, he gains immortality, superhuman intellect, strength, and endurance, and the ability to access other dimensions. To maintain these magical pow-

ers, Savage must periodically drink his enemies' blood, and he later harvests transplant organs from his descendants.

In the 1940s, Savage used the Axis powers to abet his own global domination plans. He tricked the U.S. government into appointing him America's war labor chief, only to run afoul of the original Green Lantern. Savage later co-founded the Injustice Society of the World, one of the earliest supervillain teams, which attacked the Justice Society of America in *All Star Comics* #37 (1947). Though Savage failed, he later got the JSA investigated by the U.S. Congress for subversive activities, thereby disbanding the era's premiere superhero cadre—and single-handedly ending the Golden Age of comics (as revealed in *JLA: Year One* #2, 1998).

To maintain his suddenly waning powers, Savage tricked the original Flash (Jay Garrick) and Flash II (Barry Allen) into recovering the original meteor that created him (*The Flash*, vol. 1 #215, 1972). Savage subsequently sought world conquest through drug trafficking, only to be thwarted regularly by Wally West, the third Flash throughout the late 1980s and early 1990s. Over the years, Savage also tangled with Superman, Wonder Woman, various Justice League of America members, the Justice Society (revived in 1991 specifically to deal with Savage), Resurrection Man, and the Teen Titans. Despite numerous defeats, Savage lives on until the 853rd century or later, amid such trophies as the Holy Grail (Savage claims to have started the Grail myth), a signed copy of *Mein Kampf*, and even Pandora's box (*DC Universe Villains Secret Files* #1, 1999). Savage's daughter Scandal, a hard-edged combatant wearing wrist-mounted "Lamentation Blades," was introduced in *Villains United* #1 (2005).

Savage finally reached a mass audience in 2002 via several episodes of the Cartoon Network's popular *Justice League* animated television series (2001–2004). Voiced by *Static Shock!* and *Kim Possible* veteran Phil Morris, Savage exudes an air of menace and mystery and has become a key Justice League TV villain, though his "ancient immortal" aspect has given way to a more Blofeld-esque persona, including Nehru-style apparel. Thus reinvented for television, a very long future may indeed await the immortal Vandal Savage. —*MAM*

Venom

In many ways, Venom is the quintessential supervillain of comics' "grim and gritty" era of the 1980s. His grotesque appearance and violent character—a stronger, darker, more driven version Spider-Man—is an amped-up take on the darker view of superheroes that emerged in the wake of *Watchmen* and *Dark Knight*. And yet as bad as he is, Eddie (Venom) Brock is a wildly popular character who has teamed with many heroes and starred in his own series from time to time. Cunning and powerful, Venom sees himself as a hero who is trying to protect the innocent—he's even been known to champion the homeless of San Francisco. It's this duality—brute force and moral awareness, however twisted—that has given him a place in Spidey's all-time rogues' gallery.

Venom's origin also plays to the strengths of Marvel Comics' convoluted continuity, going back four years before his first appearance. His story has two beginnings. One is that of Eddie Brock, an ambitious reporter for the *Daily Bugle* who was fired in a scandal after his big story—the identity of a villain named Sin-Eater—turned out to be wrong. He blamed his downfall on Peter Parker, aka Spider-Man.

Meanwhile, Spider-Man had gone off to the interdimensional Secret War and returned with a new black costume, in *Marvel Super Heroes Secret Wars* #8 (1984). The costume turned out to be a powerful and evil alien symbiote, and after removing it, Spider-Man abandoned it. The symbiote also sought vengeance against Spider-Man, and was drawn to Brock, who was about to kill himself. The demented duo then bonded in a quest to see Spider-Man dead.

Venom first appeared as the Brock/Symbiote character in *The Amazing Spider-Man* vol. 1 #298 (1988), by writer David Michelinie and artist Todd McFarlane, but his origin wasn't revealed until issue #300, in which he and Spidey had the first of many battles. Venom quickly caught on as a fan favorite, getting numerous return appearances and his own miniseries (the first of many) in 1993. Perhaps the best-known Venom story is 1993's "Maximum Carnage," a fourteen-issue crossover epic in which Venom and Spider-Man teamed up to defeat Carnage, an even more savage version of Venom.

In recent years, the symbiote has abandoned Brock as his host, and has been given to inhabiting many different people to suit its purposes, including a woman and a crime boss. Mac Gargan, better known as Spidey's foe the Scorpion, united with the Venom symbiote to become the new Venom in a 2005 *Marvel Knights: Spider-Man* story arc.

Venom's original creative team is the subject of some confusion. Michelinie came up with the idea for the villain, and had planted several clues in issues preceding the character's debut in #298. It was McFarlane, however, who gave Venom his signature look of a gaping maw, a bank of razor-sharp teeth, and a long, serpentine tongue, extrapolating from *Secret Wars* artist Mike Zeck's original design for Spider-Man's black costume. An alternate version of the character, Ultimate Venom, has appeared in the Brian Michael Bendis–penned pages of *Ultimate Spider-Man* (2000–present). At the hands of artist Mark Bagley, Ultimate Venom became even more garish and long-tongued than in days past.

Given his popularity, it's no surprise that Venom has appeared in almost every media, including the FOX Kids *Spider-Man* cartoon (1994–1998), voiced by Hank Azaria and collected as the DVD *The Venom Saga*, and numerous role-playing games and video games, including *Venom-Spider-Man: Separation Anxiety*. He also makes a terrific action figure (particularly the early 1990s "Talking Venom" from Toy Biz, which gave mothers nightmares by saying, "I want to eat your brains"). But Venom will perhaps achieve his greatest notoriety in the Sam Raimi–directed *Spider-Man 3*, with *That '70s Show* actor Topher Grace in the role. —*HM*

The Ventriloquist

W ho's in charge here? With Batman's odd foe the Ventriloquist, it's never easy to tell.

Created by co-writers Alan Grant and John Wagner and artist Norm Breyfogle and first seen in *Detective Comics* #583 (1988), Arnold Wesker is a nebbish crime-family heir who manifests his repressed anger—seething since he witnessed his mother's gangland execution years earlier—through his ventriloquist's dummy, Scarface. A puppet version of an Edward G. Robinson–like Prohibition-era mobster in a pinstriped suit and fedora, Scarface remorselessly butchers rival racketeers with a working miniature Tommy gun. Drawing inspiration from a long history of fictional deadly dummies, including the movies *The Great Gabbo* (1929) and *Magic* (1978), Grant and Wagner (and later scribes) adroitly keep readers guessing as to whether the schizophrenic Wesker is actually puppeting Scarface, or if the dummy supernaturally has a life of its own.

Real-life ventriloquists have difficulty pronouncing the letter "B," a fact played for laughs in Ventriloquist tales, in which Scarface calls the Dark Knight "Gatman." A regular inmate of Arkham Asylum for the Criminally Insane, Wesker becomes psychotic when separated from Scarface.

The Ventriloquist's stature in the Dark Knight's mythos was cemented when the villain and his dummy were featured in three episodes of television's *Batman: The Animated Series* (1992–1995), beginning with 1993's "Read My Lips"; George Dzundra played both roles, and Kenner released a tie-in Ventriloquist/Scarface action figure. "The Big Dummy" brought Scarface and the

Detective Comics #808 ©2005 DC Comics.
COVER ART BY DAVID LAPHAM.

Ventriloquist (voiced by Dan Castellaneta) back to animation in 2004 on the WB's animated *The Batman* (2004–present). —*ME*

Vermin

T hroughout his tormented life the repulsive Vermin has been surrounded by rats. Created by writer J. M. DeMatteis and artist Mike Zeck, traumatized young Edward Whelan is a street urchin, scurrying from his sexually abusive father. Two late-twentieth-century Nazi criminals, Baron Zemo II and Arnim Zola, make Whelan a human guinea pig in their perverse genetic experiments, turning him into the cannibalistic Vermin, a 6-feet-tall, fanged and furred rodent-man with superhuman strength and agility and a feral instinct of self-preservation. Engineered to attack their foe Cap-

Peter Parker, the Spectacular Spider-Man #131 ©1987 Marvel Comics.
COVER ART BY MIKE ZECK AND BOB MCLEOD.

tain America, Vermin sics an army of obedient rats on the Star-Spangled Sentinel. Zeck's cover to *Captain America* #272 (1982), Vermin's first appearance, evokes memories of the 1971 horror film *Willard*, with the hero being eaten alive by rats—but Cap crushes the vermin of all sizes.

The mentally ill Vermin is childlike in thought and open to suggestion, yet when cornered or threatened will strike with lethal force with his razor-sharp teeth and claws. Vermin's most famous storyline was "Kraven's Last Hunt," DeMatteis and Zeck's six-part 1987 Spider-Man opus, in which yet another manipulator—Kraven the Hunter—used the rat-man in his personal vendetta against the wall-crawler. DeMatteis teamed with artist Sal Buscema to produce "The Child Within" in *The Spectacular Spider-Man* #178–#184 (1991–1992), in which Vermin

attempted to kill his father but was netted into another gambit against Spidey, this time by the Green Goblin II. Whelan's psyche struggled for dominance over Vermin's savagery, and with the help of psychologist Dr. Ashley Kafka he nearly succeeded in purging his rodent mutation.

Yet tragedy and creative whims reverted Whelan to Vermin, and in the 2000s he has scampered in and out of the limelight, in scrapes with Wolverine and the Punisher. When not spreading pestilence throughout the Marvel Universe, Vermin is caged at Ravencroft, the maximum-security asylum for deranged supervillains. —*ME*

Vertigo Villains

Vertigo, an imprint of DC Comics, was launched in 1993 as a way to consolidate many of DC's horror and dark-fantasy books under one recognizable banner. Each of the books chosen for inclusion in the Vertigo line carried a "Suggested for Mature Readers" label for several years, but the features that most clearly distinguished Vertigo books from other DC-universe books were tone, atmosphere, and a sophisticated literary quality.

In the 1980s, DC editor Karen Berger recruited several British writers to revive dormant and long-forgotten characters in fresh, innovative ways. Alan Moore began writing *Swamp Thing* in 1983 and quickly drew critical attention both within and outside of the comics industry. *Swamp Thing*'s popularity led to several similarly successful experiments in the late 1980s. The established books pulled under the Vertigo umbrella in 1993 were *Animal Man, Swamp Thing, Hellblazer, The Sandman, Doom Patrol*, and *Shade, the Changing Man*. Additional ongoing series launched within the year included *Kid Eternity, Sandman Mystery Theatre*, and *Black Orchid*. Each of these series features a protagonist who at one time had been part of DC's main universe, and several of them brought with them established palettes of villains and rogues.

Since many of Vertigo's first books are supernatural, a number of the line's original villains are also supernatural. Perhaps the most prototypical villain is Anton Arcane, the mad scientist turned demon who has plagued Swamp Thing in various incarnations throughout the character's history. The Sandman's rogues' gallery pulls from a broad spectrum of myth, folklore, and literature. Morpheus' most dangerous enemies are plucked from Norse mythology (Loki), fairy tales (the Cuckoo), and Shakespearean drama (Puck). John Constantine, the protagonist of *Hellblazer*, is locked in an unending struggle with the First of the Fallen, the biblical villain also known as Satan. The main villain in *Shade, the Changing Man* is the American Scream, the living embodiment of collective American madness.

Often, traditional superhero rogues' galleries are inverted in Vertigo books. Before they officially became Vertigo books, both *Doom Patrol* and *Animal Man* were dramatically overhauled by writer Grant Morrison. In *Animal Man*, a book featuring a character who had once been a member of a superhero team called the Forgotten Heroes, Morrison used second-tier villains Psycho-Pirate and Mirror Master in clever, inventive ways, much as he used Animal Man himself. Doom Patrol, a historically significant team of outcast heroes reminiscent of Marvel's X-Men, once had an established, familiar lineup of rogues that Morrison altered drastically during his tenure on the book. The Brotherhood of Evil was replaced by the Brotherhood of Dada, a reference to an early twentieth-century avant-garde art movement in Europe. Surreal villains such as the Scissormen (pulled from the German children's book *Der Struwwelpeter*), the Beard Hunter, and the Men from N.O.W.H.E.R.E. surfaced to torment the misfits and oddballs who comprised the Doom Patrol. Morrison's run set the intelligent, surrealistic tone that would characterize most of Vertigo's books from the very beginning of the line.

Later superhero comics from Vertigo reflect the type of psychological complexity that Morrison introduced. *The Scarab* and *Enigma*, two early miniseries patterned on superhero comics, are more about the process of self-discovery than about inconsequential fights with costumed supervillains. *Sandman Mystery Theatre* features a number of pulp-noir villains whose names sound like Dick Tracy rogues (the Tarantula, the Face, the Brute, the Vamp, Dr. Death), but the book is more a love story than an adventure comic.

Although many of Vertigo's early villains are rooted in horror and fantasy, the variety of Vertigo villains quickly expanded as the imprint's range of genres expanded. This shift is most clearly seen in a series of one-shot books released in 1995 under the subheading "Vertigo Voices." In the Voices books, the main characters are also the villains. *The Eaters* features a family of cannibals on a road trip across the U.S.A. *Tainted* is a noir-ish psychodrama about a murderer who ends up mutilating himself in a horrific way. In *Face*, writer Peter Milligan speculates on what might happen if a millionaire art fanatic hired a plastic surgeon to turn his face into a Picasso work. Each of these stories is set in the "real" world, and each features realistic forms of evil and madness. Similar patterns are found in current series such as Brian Azzarello's *100 Bullets*, a "real-world" revenge drama in which good and evil are subjective and ambiguous. Even a concept book such as Brian K. Vaughan's *Y: The Last Man*, which is in the mid-2000s one of Vertigo's most popular and widely acclaimed titles, is guided by a hypothetical realism that exposes the uglier, more sinister sides of human nature.

In Vertigo books, the lines between good and evil, between sanity and madness, are blurred and broken down to such an extent that it is often hard to determine who the villains are. In fact, many of the books star heroes who might in fact be called villains in different circumstances. One of Vertigo's ongoing books, *Lucifer*, stars the familiar biblical antagonist who originally acted as a foil to Morpheus in Neil Gaiman's *Sandman* series. In two of Vertigo's longest-running series, Grant Morrison's *The Invisibles* and Garth Ennis and Steve Dillon's *Preacher*, the villains are extensive semi-fascist organizations led by deformed, tragicomic characters. The Grail, a clandestine cult organization dedicated to protecting the last descendant of the Son of God in *Preacher*, proves to be both incompetent and obscene. In *The Invisibles*, cells of revolutionary anarchists battle against forces of order and conformity (symbolized by the authoritarian Sir Miles and the impish, sadistic Mr. Quimper). Heroism and villainy resist expectations and traditional representations in these stories.

In a 1996 "On the Ledge" column, Karen Berger wrote, "It's been three and a half years since Vertigo first launched, and what began as a line of horror

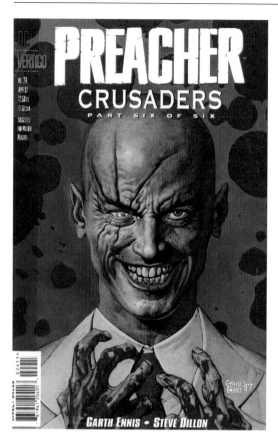

Starr. *Preacher* #24 ©1997 DC Comics.
COVER ART BY GLENN FABRY.

things—harmless diversions that provide children with a creative way to explore and focus their imaginations. But children have vivid imaginations, and the little figurines they use to enact their fantasies frequently turn against them in their dreams and fancies. Clowns and dolls often create an early fear factor in humans that lasts well into adulthood, and many supervillains exploit this fear when they create their criminal identities.

Supervillains from the toy box have their origin in the concept of the "carnival," a period of excessive celebration (such as Mardi Gras) prior to Lent in the Christian tradition. In 1940, a Russian writer and theorist named Mikhail Bakhtin wrote a dissertation entitled *Raselais and His World* in which he applied the concept of the carnival to the social arena. According to Bakhtin, carnival is not just associated with festivals of costumes and revelry, but also with social class. Carnival festivities provide a period of time when social laws and norms are put on hiatus. During carnival, all classes of society are equalized, reducing the power of the upper class and elevating the power of the working class. This period when commoners are valued more than the aristocracy might be especially dangerous and troubling to millionaire playboys and authority figures whose are responsible for maintaining social order.

The idea of the carnival is crucial to understanding supervillains who dress up in bright costumes, face paint, and red noses. In a curious historical confluence, the year Bakhtin wrote *Rabelais* is also the year that the Joker made his first appearance in *Batman* #1 (Spring 1940). The Joker, the "Clown Prince of Crime," taps into deep-rooted collective fears about clowns, fools, and jesters. His actions are guided purely by madness and excess. Liberated from social norms and mores, he lacks any sense of conscience or repression. The Joker's one goal is the complete, unbridled pursuit of sensory satisfaction, and he usually finds this satisfaction in murder and chaos. He is the full embodiment of Austrian psychoanalyst Sigmund Freud's concept of the "id."

Most supervillains represent the concept of the id (in relation to superheroes' superego), but villains from the toy box take this role to an extreme. They merge chaos and disorder with childhood fantasies to create a truly frightening image of

and dark fantasy comics imbued with a real-world sensibility has gradually expanded to include a much broader spectrum of material, reflecting an eclectic range of attitudes and points of view." Berger's assessment remains true in the mid-2000s. Whatever their genre, Vertigo books more often focus on the *human* than the *super*human. Accordingly, whether a book is a war drama or an urban romance, its threats and villains are more internal than external—more psychological than physical. —*AB*

Villains from the Toy Box

Most children encounter clowns, dolls, puppets, marionettes, and various other toys during their youth. Toys are usually considered play-uncontrollable, infantile madness. The toy-box motif has made its way into a wide variety of popular cultural media, including the clown villain from Steven King's *It* (brought to TV in miniseries form in 1990), Chucky from the movie franchise *Child's Play* (which began in 1988), the title villains from cult classic movie *Killer Klowns from Outer Space* (1988), the murderer in the film *Saw* (2005) who dresses as a marionette and rides a tricycle during part of the movie, and a roomful of "possessed" toys (particularly the clown doll) in the classic horror film *Poltergeist* (1982). The Insane Clown Posse, a hip-hop duo, use clown identities in their public appearances, and their live shows are characterized by the chaotic frenzy their name suggests.

One of the oldest and most revered forms of the toy-box motif is a British puppet show called "Punch and Judy." Made popular to contemporary audiences through Neil Gaiman and Dave McKean's graphic novel *The Tragical Comedy or Comical Tragedy of Mr. Punch* (1994), Punch and Judy actually date back to the Commedia dell'arte tradition in sixteenth-century Italy. In the Punch and Judy story, after Mr. Punch murders his wife and child, he tricks and kills every single authority figure who tries to bring him to justice. The horror of Punch's murderous, maniacal rampage is enhanced by the fact that the story is enacted with hand puppets and dolls.

The toy-box motif in comics dates back to the origins of the form. In Winsor McKay's *Little Nemo in Slumberland*, a popular comic strip that began in 1905, Nemo's adventures were often complicated by a pesky, troublesome imp named Flip who looked like a clown and accompanied Nemo through Slumberland. This tradition continued when supervillains emerged to plague superheroes in comic books in the early 1940s. The Joker was followed by a slew of villains based on dolls and clowns. The Dummy, so named because he resembled a ventriloquist's dummy, appeared in *Leading Comics* #1 (1942) to fight the Golden Age Vigilante. The Dummy was actually inspired by a wooden puppet named Charlie McCarthy who frequented films and radio in the 1930s and 1940s. The Dummy serves as a prototype for the more contemporary Scarface, the 1920s-style gangster puppet who is controlled by the Batman villain Ventriloquist.

In addition to the Dummy, several toy-box villains surfaced during the early age of comic books to harass the growing number of superheroes. The Harlequin fought the Golden Age Green Lantern (Alan Scott) before reforming and actually marrying him. DC has introduced several villains named Harlequin, including a woman named Duela Dent (aka "The Joker's Daughter"), who fought and later joined the Teen Titans in the 1970s and 1980s. Another Golden Age Green Lantern villain, the Fool, looked like Pinocchio and used toy inventions to play dangerous pranks on Green Lantern and his supporting cast. The Prankster, a gap-toothed practical joker named Oswald Loomis, used trick toys such as squirting flowers and pop guns to harass Superman. The Prankster was once called "Superman's most annoying foe," suggesting the general silliness and harmlessness of the Golden Age's villain contingent.

As comics matured, toy-box villains were updated for a more modern audience. The Prankster was recast as a children's television show host who went on a crime spree after his show was canceled. Punch and Jewelee, professional puppeteers who wore harlequin costumes and fought Captain Atom, joined a covert government organization called the Suicide Squad before reforming, marrying, and retiring to the suburbs to raise their children. The Jester, a former actor turned criminal, sought media and public attention by staging a series of intricate toy-related crimes that also drew the attention of Daredevil. Rag Doll, a circus contortionist who fought the Justice Society of America during the Golden Age, was succeeded in the modern age by his son. The modern Rag Doll, a much darker reflection of his father, artificially altered every joint in his body so that he might have the flexibility and contortion abilities that his father had naturally. Despite his grotesque backstory, the Rag Doll joined the Secret Six, who fought against a reunited society of supervillains in the 2005 miniseries *Villains United*.

One of the most popular contemporary examples of harlequin-type villains first appeared in animated form before making the transition to comics. Dr. Harleen Quinzel worked as a psychotherapist at Arkham Asylum before going insane and adopting the new identity Harley Quinn. Harley troubled Batman for several years in *Bat-*

man: *The Animated Series* and *The New Batman Adventures* (1992–1999) before she was introduced into comics continuity in *Batman: Harley Quinn* (1999). Another clown-like villain who has appeared in several media incarnations is Clown, the darker, more sinister and grotesque version of Joker from writer/artist Todd McFarlane's *Spawn*.

The Toyman, once a member of the Legion of Doom in the 1970s cartoon *Super Friends*, was updated in the post–*Crisis on Infinite Earths* DC continuity. The Toyman was recast as a former British toymaker named Winslow Percival Schott who, after being fired from his job in London, moved to Metropolis to seek revenge on the man he blamed for his misfortunes: Lex Luthor. In 1996, Toyman was updated again for *Superman: The Animated Series*—this time as the son of toymaker Winslow Schott, who dresses as a diminutive grinning doll, turns his warehouse headquarters into a giant dollhouse, and seeks revenge on the those responsible for the imprisonment and death of his father. This embodiment of the Toyman is the creepiest, most sadistic and maniacal version to date. Other villains who adopt toys and games as the basis for their identities are frequent Justice League villains the Royal Flush Gang and *Astro City* villain group the Chessmen.

Perhaps the most self-referential, postmodern versions of villains from the toy box are toys based on villains based on toys. Action figures patterned on comics-based villains have been popular since the mid-1970s, beginning with the 8-inch-tall Joker poseable figure from Mego's World's Greatest Super Heroes line. The Joker has been cast as an action figure dozens of times, including a high-quality marionette produced by DC Direct in 2003. Harley Quinn and Clown have also appeared numerous times in three-dimension form. —AB

Villains of Mecha Anime

Perhaps one of the most popular icons of anime (the term for Japanese animation) and manga is the giant robot, or *mecha*. Ironically, the term "mecha" refers to any vehicle or ship featured, but

it has become affixed to giant robotic fighting machines. Mecha can be of any size or shape, but the majority are humanoid shaped, resembling high-tech suits of armor, equipped with a wide variety of weapons.

Giant robots are featured in both the manga and original 1960s anime for *Astro Boy*, but *Gigantor* (in Japan, *Tetsujin-28 go*) was the first anime to feature a giant robot as a major character. It would not be until the 1970s with Go Nagai's *Mazinger Z* that the main elements of the mecha genre would be introduced: the stalwart teenage hero, his loyal but concerned girlfriend, his one-of-a-kind giant robot, the super-secret base of operations, and the truly evil villain—sometimes human, sometimes not—who would send countless creations of his own to wreak havoc on the hero in a diabolical plan to rule Earth.

Unfortunately, the mecha anime that followed *Mazinger* recycled the formula to the point of staleness. In 1979 director Yoshiyuki Tomino took the mecha genre in a fresh direction with his series *Mobile Suit Gundam*.

Set nearly two hundred years in the future, *Gundam* chronicles a devastating civil war between Earth and a rebellious group of space colonies. Much of the fighting is done with machines called "Mobile Suits." The anime was the first to combine mecha with a hard science-fiction feel, resulting in a very believable series. For his villains, Tomino created two major characters who, despite being human and lacking true superpowers, would set the standard for other villains of mecha animation: Gihren Zabi and Drake Luft.

Gihren Zabi is *Gundam*'s true villain. The eldest son of Degwin Sodo Zabi, Gihren is the supreme military commander of the Zeon forces (the group of colonies who began the war against the Earth Federation). A highly intelligent man in his mid-thirties, Gihren has no superpowers to speak of … but he was the ultimate mastermind behind the war that had wiped out nearly half of the human race—around four to five *billion* people. Tomino patterned this arch-villain after the major dictators of the twentieth century: Hitler, Stalin, and Mussolini. As with all megalomaniacs, Gihren has the ability to rally the people, and he believes that God had chosen the people of Zeon to lead humanity into a new age (after getting rid of those pesky earthbound Federation types, of course). Gihren is assassinated by his sister Kycilia at the end of *Gundam*.

A "descendant" of Gihren is Drake Luft from Tomino's 1983 series *Aura Battler Dunbine*. A fascinating anime that blends sword and sorcery with mecha, *Dunbine* takes place in the fantasy world of Byston Well (but later moves to Earth). Drake begins as the ruler of the small province of Ah, but his ambition for power leads him to bring in two people from Earth to create "aura machines" and "Aura Battlers." These robotic weapons allow Drake to conquer most of Byston Well and even Earth (referred to as "Upper Earth"). Only the brave rebel army of Neal Given can halt Drake's plans, but not before many lives are sacrificed.

The most unique villain in mecha animation has to be Char Aznable of *Mobile Suit Gundam* (1979). Char is Zeon's ace pilot, and with his silver mask and helmet, red outfit, and urbane personality, he is called the Red Comet. Throughout the television series, he proves to be quite the foe for *Gundam*'s hero, Amuro Rey. Char's skills as a pilot are due to the fact that he is a NewType—a human possessing a heightened state of awareness, intuition, and ESP.

Char is closer to an anti-hero, cut from the cloth of Gully Foyle from Alfred Bester's *The Stars My Destination* (1956). While he is fighting for Zeon, he is also secretly plotting to kill the members of the Zabi family to take revenge. At the end of *Gundam*, Char disappears—but emerges as a *hero* in the 1985 series *Zeta Gundam*. Under the alias "Quattro Bagina," he fights against the Titans, a vicious and corrupt army created by the Federation. Char even meets—and fights alongside—his old enemy, Amuro Rey. At the end of *Zeta*, Char disappears again. In the 1988 film *Char's Counterattack*, Char returns, this time as a villain. Still seeking the independence of the colonies from Earth, Char decides that desperate measures are needed—namely, crashing asteroids into the planet to trigger a nuclear winter and wipe out all life on the planet. Once again, he and Amuro cross paths, but at the film's conclusion, both men sacrifice themselves to save Earth.

Other popular mecha villains would emerge over the years, such as Khyron from *Macross*

(1982), Paptimus Scirocco from *Zeta Gundam* (1985), the Magnificent Ten from *Giant Robo* (1992–1998), and even characters bearing a resemblance to Char—Zechs Marquis from *Gundam Wing* (1995–1996) and Rau Le Creuset of *Gundam Seed*—but no mecha villain has matched Char in popularity, either in Japan or America. In the world of mecha anime, Char Aznable truly stands alone. —*MM*

Violator

Violator, also known as Clown, is the arch-nemesis of Spawn, a superhero created by writer/illustrator Todd McFarlane in 1992. *Spawn* is the flagship title of Image Comics, a company formed when several prominent artists working at Marvel Comics left to form their own line based primarily on creator control and ownership. *Spawn* is perhaps the best example of the grim-and-gritty tone that dominated mainstream superhero comics in the late 1980s and much of the 1990s.

The title character of *Spawn* is Al Simmons, a covert government assassin who, after he is murdered by a fellow government operative, returns to Earth as a Hellspawn. The primary mission of a Hellspawn, an agent of the demon Malebolgia, is to recruit enough damned souls on Earth for the forces of hell to wage a final war on heaven. The Violator, a demon servant of Malebolgia, is assigned to keep an eye on Spawn and guide him in the right direction. As Violator tells Spawn in issue #4, "I'm not here to game-play. I'm here to keep you in line—make sure you don't stray." In the 1997 live-action film, Violator tells Spawn to "just think of me as your guardian angel … the Clown from Hell."

On Earth, Violator chooses to appear in the form of the Clown—an obese, grotesque character almost as disturbing as his demonic Violator form. Guided by the jealousy of Al Simmons' promotion to Hellspawn, Clown tries to provoke Spawn instead of guarding and guiding him. As Violator, he goes on a murderous rampage through New York's mob underworld in an attempt to pull Spawn into direct combat. This strategy succeeds, but it eventually gets Clown into trouble. Malebolgia

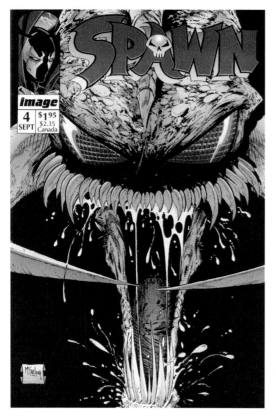

Spawn #4 © & ™ 1992 Todd McFarlane.
COVER ART BY TODD MCFARLANE.

arc called "A Thousand Clowns" (issues #134–#138), Clown possesses the body of fellow Spawn enemy Jason Wynn, recruits a legion of disciples, and orchestrates a chaotic riot in New York City before Spawn is able to stop him.

As Todd McFarlane has ventured into several different media outlets since 1992, Clown and Violator have made appearances in numerous two- and three-dimensional forms. One of the highlights of the 1997 live-action *Spawn* film, directed by Mark A. Z. Dippé is John Leguizamo's portrayal of Clown. The film version of Clown, like his comics counterpart, is simultaneously comical and menacing. His flatulence, cursing, and general obscenity are all effectively enhanced in the live-action format. Clown was also featured prominently in the HBO *Spawn* animated series (1997–1999), which stayed much closer to the comics than the movie in terms of tone and continuity. In the animated series, which ran three seasons, Clown is appropriately dark and sinister. In each of Spawn's forays beyond comic books, Violator/Clown has appeared as the primary villain. The first series of McFarlane Toys' long-running action figure line featured both Violator and Clown figures, and Violator/Clown has also been the villain of several video games. While crimelord Lukas, with his brutish right-hand man Barabbas, is the first villain in McFarlane's newest television venture, *Spawn: The Animation* (2006–present) from DPS/Film Roman, one might suspect that the Violator will find a home there as well.

Like Spawn himself, Clown is partially derivative of other recognizable comic book characters. If Spawn is an amalgam of dark superheroes like Batman and anti-heroes like the Punisher, then Clown offers a modern twist on the Joker, the "Clown Prince of Crime" in the Batman mythos. Whereas Joker is tall and somewhat dignified even in madness, Clown is short, fat, crude. He is a comic figure—a type of incompetent fool or court jester—but he is also extremely horrific and dangerous, both to Spawn and to humanity. —*AB*

breaks up the fight, punishes Clown for his incompetence, and strips his Violator form and powers from him.

Violator's demotion doesn't prove to be much of a deterrence, however. In the first issue of *Violator* (1994), a three-issue miniseries written by Alan Moore and illustrated by Bart Sears, Clown indicates that he hasn't changed much despite his limitations: "Maybe I don't look like a demon outta hell no more, but that don't mean I ain't thinkin' like one!" In this miniseries, Moore also reveals that Violator is one of five demonic siblings called the Phlebiac Brothers. In addition to his troubles with Spawn, Violator also has to cope with his role as the family embarrassment. Clown has emerged numerous times to provoke Spawn throughout the long-running comics series. Although he has reclaimed his Violator form from time to time, he chooses to appear as Clown most often. In a story

Viper

The terrorist and mercenary known as Viper first appeared as Madame Hydra, created by writer/artist Jim Steranko, in *Captain America* vol. 1 #110 (1969). (She is not to be confused with the later supervillain Madame Hydra VI, who debuted in *Nick Fury vs. SHIELD* #3, 1988.) An orphaned child, the future Viper suffered an accident that permanently scared the right side of her face. She turned to crime to support herself and became a mercenary, then enlisted as one of the first female recruits into the subversive organization Hydra.

Under the name Madame Hydra she headed up Hydra's New York operations, where she encountered and battled Captain America. In *Captain America* #157 (1973), writer Steve Englehart introduced a male costumed villain named the Viper, who later joined the supervillain team the Serpent Squad. In issue #180 (1974) Madame Hydra, no longer a member of Hydra, murdered the original Viper, took over his alias, and reorganized the Serpent Squad.

The new Viper followed a nihilist philosophy, believing in nothing. In her most spectacular terrorist act, she tried to crash the SHIELD Heli-carrier into the U.S. Capitol (*Marvel Team-Up* vol. 1 #85, 1979), eerily foreshadowing the September 11, 2001, attacks by more than two decades.

A brilliant criminal strategist trained in various martial arts, the Viper is a skilled markswoman and bullwhip wielder. She is also extremely knowledgeable in the properties and uses of toxins, poisons, and snake venoms (hence her identity), often creating her own poisons that she dispenses through her fangs or through poisoned lipstick. She has been known to carry a set of lethal, snake venom–tipped darts.

Viper is a frequent partner of the Silver Samurai, although their various criminal activities often take them in different directions. She has clashed with several costumed heroes, including the original Spider-Woman and the Black Widow. The villainess has a tangled history with Wolverine, whom she manipulated into marrying her, and then later divorced. Since then the Viper has affiliated herself with the Inner Circle of the infamous Hellfire Club. —*GM*

Vulture

Swooping into writer Stan Lee and artist Steve Ditko's *The Amazing Spider-Man* vol. 1 #2 (1963), the avaricious Vulture was the wall-crawler's first costumed foe (the Chameleon, the supervillain in issue #1, wore a mask, not a costume). No spring chicken, Adrian Toomes, the bald, beak-nosed, and sinewy senior partner of an electronics company, turns to crime once his conniving associate swindles his corporate profits. Donning an electromagnetic flying harness of his own design, the resentful Toomes accouters himself in a jade-hued, feathered outfit, and as the Vulture he vengefully strikes against his former colleague. Relishing the gifts of flight and enhanced strength afforded him by his harness, he becomes an airborne cat burglar, gliding silently from Manhattan rooftops and filching valuables from nescient prey. Spider-Man swings into his path, and after initially being beaten by the fluttering thief the web-slinger clips the Vulture's wings with a handheld apparatus that negates Toomes' anti-gravity device.

Amazing Spider-Man #2's "Duel to the Death with the Vulture!" marked the first time Peter Parker—the friendly neighborhood superhero's youthful alter ego—secretly snapped photos of himself in action against the supervillains he encountered. Borrowing from his Aunt May a camera that belonged to his late Uncle Ben, Peter sold his exclusive aerial photos of the Vulture to publisher J. Jonah Jameson, beginning a long-standing relationship between the two.

The Vulture returned in issue #7, having modified his flying harness but being trounced once again by Spider-Man. He joined Dr. Octopus, Sandman, Electro, Kraven the Hunter, and Mysterio as the original Sinister Six in *Amazing Spider-Man Annual* #1 (1964), and was soon caged by the wall-crawler.

In *Amazing Spider-Man* #48 (1967), the imprisoned Toomes violated the cardinal rule of penitentiary conduct—never confide in your cellmate—and, believing he was on his deathbed, told fellow con Blackie Drago the location of his hidden Vulture ensemble, having Drago vow to take wing to exact revenge upon Spider-Man. Drago had other ideas—lining his pockets through aerial thievery—but once he busted out of jail and became the new Vulture, he inevitably found himself in Spidey's sights. After a brief crime spree as the Vulture II, Drago was challenged by Toomes himself, fully recovered and back in the air, who defeated the usurper and reclaimed his Vulture mantle.

A third Vulture briefly appeared in the mid-1970s—Dr. Clifton Shallot, a university professor and bio-mutation scientist to whose body the Vulture uniform melded. The Vulturions, thieves who appropriated Toomes' technology, tried to take over the villain's roost in 1985. Yet Adrian Toomes, the one true Vulture, has bested all comers to resume his perch as one of Spidey's most retaliatory enemies, attacking the hero numerous times over the decades with his ability to soar at nearly 100 mph to heights of over 11,000 feet. Like the predator from which he takes his name, the Vulture will not rest until he picks apart Spider-Man's carcass.

The Vulture was played by Paul Soles (also the voice of Spidey) in the animated cartoon *Spider-Man* (1967–1970) and by Eddie (*Green Acres*) Albert in the 1994–1998 Spidey toon. Scott McNeil voiced a parallel-world Vulture in three episodes of FOX Kids' *Spider-Man Unlimited* (1999–2001). *—ME*

Weather Wizard

A blowhard in both powers and personality, the Weather Wizard stormed into the life of the Fastest Man Alive in *The Flash* vol. 1 #110 (1959–1960). In "Challenge of the Weather Wizard!" by writer John Broome and penciler Carmine Infantino, low-rent crook Mark Mardon is on the lam and seeks refuge at the laboratory of his estranged brother Clyde, whom he finds dead. Mardon discovers that his scientist brother was developing a weather-control device—a wand—and follows Clyde's notes to complete the project. Donning ostentatious green gear, Mardon, as the Weather Wizard, wreaks meteorological mayhem with his Weather Wand, threatening lives and property by creating a flash flood that is stopped, appropriately enough, by the Flash II, who whirls his arms into a super-windmill to force back the torrent.

The Weather Wizard's weapon enables him to, with a mere gesture, project "eolic energy," creating from nothingness any climactic pattern he can imagine, from tornadoes to electrical storms to blizzards. He can minimize his inclement attacks—causing a curtain of rain to envelop the Flash, for example—or cast broad meteorological patterns, such as blanketing a town with snow. With the power of the elements in his very hand, Weather Wizard has been known to be quite boastful. Mar-

don was not among Flash's assembled rogues' gallery during their earliest unions (but joined them later), instead pummeling Kid Flash and the Elongated Man (in *Flash* #130, 1962) and Batman and Robin (*Detective Comics* #353, 1966) with his weather assaults, as well as the Flash, whom he fought with a hurricane's ire in numerous vengeful return bouts. Weather Wizard even stormed onto television in 1979, in the campy live-action *Legends of the Superheroes* NBC special, with comedian Jeff Altman hamming it up in the role.

When the Flash died in *Crisis on Infinite Earths* #8 (1985), Mardon temporarily retired, but later resumed his weather warfare against the Scarlet Speedster's successor, the third Flash. Weather Wizard and four other Flash foes died and were given a new, soulless lease on "life" in *Underworld Unleashed* #1 (1995), but their humanity was later restored by the fleet-footed hero they so frequently battled. In the 2000s the Weather Wizard, sporting a sleek new costume of olive and gold, has become a regular member of the Flash's Rogues' Gallery, confessing in *Flash* vol. 2 #220 (2005) that he, like the biblical Cain, had actually killed his sibling Clyde, a retroactive alteration of the villain's origin.

The Weather Wizard made animated-television appearances in a 1997 episode of the WB's *Superman*, guest-starring the Flash, with real-life comic-book fan Miguel Ferrer voicing the villain; and in the 2003 "Hereafter" episode of the Cartoon Network's *Justice League* (2001–2004), voiced by Corey Burton. —*ME*

Wendigo

Because few places are as friendly to juxtapositions of folklore and pop culture as the four-color comics page, ancient American Indian tales of evil spirits such as the Wendigo provide the perfect fodder for supervillainy. Although the horror writer Algernon Blackwood's classic 1907 tale "The Wendigo" is frequently cited as the birthplace of the creature, far older Inuit lore describes a 15-feet-tall flesh-eating creature of the Minnesota north woods known as Witigo, Witiko, Wee-Tee-Go, or Wendigo, all of which translate roughly to "the evil spirit that devours mankind," or even "cannibal" among various Great Lakes Indian tribes. According to many tribal myths, a human being who resorts to cannibalism finds himself magically transformed into a Wendigo, a large hairy snow-creature with glowing eyes, giant yellow fangs, a grotesquely long tongue—and an insatiable hunger for human flesh. Other tribes posited that any man or woman guilty of entering a pact with an evil spirit might be changed into a Wendigo, thereafter lurking in the woods, awaiting victims to murder.

While the Wendigo may have served the Algonquins and other tribes as a cultural alarum concerning the evils of cannibalism, it has also treated the readership of Marvel Comics to more than three decades of entertainment. Introduced by writer Steve Englehart and penciler Herb Trimpe in *The Incredible Hulk* vol. 2 #162 (1973) as a shaggy, ravenous, superstrong adversary for the Hulk during the Bigfoot-obsessed 1970s, the role of Marvel's Wendigo is played initially by a hapless French Canadian named Paul Cartier.

A Francophone named George Baptiste was the next to be transformed—Cartier gets better—battling the Hulk in the two-part saga that introduced future X-Men superstar Wolverine in the landmark *Incredible Hulk* #180–#181 (1974). In the early 1980s Francois Lartigue served as the next unwilling iteration of the hungry were-beast, attacking the Hulk and Alpha Flight's Sasquatch before being cured by Alpha Flight's mystic healer Shaman. In the

early 1990s, guided by the pencils and prose of fan phenom Todd McFarlane, a fourth and (as of 2006) unidentified individual later served as a vessel for the Wendigo spirit, which Spider-Man and Wolverine discovered has been framed for child-murder in a small town in British Columbia.

Although the Wendigo was conceived as a denizen of the backwoods, the creature has done battle with Marvel's good guys in the concrete jungles of New York City. Various Wendigos seemed to proliferate greatly over the years, bringing their fangs and talons to bear against Wolverine, Captain Marvel, the Hulk, Alpha Flight, and Wild Thing. A Wendigo once even teamed up with erstwhile Ghost Rider John Blaze (in *Blaze* #4, 1994)!

While Marvel's take on the Wendigo legend transcended the comics page in 1998 by becoming an action figure, it has by no means supplanted the original folklore that engendered it; the underlying Indian legends continue to inspire twenty-first-century pop cultural reinterpretations, such as writer-director Larry Fessenden's horror film *Wendigo* (2001). Regardless of how many two-legged snacks succeed in evading the Wendigo's maw, the creature's future seems assured. —*MAM*

Whiplash

The mercenary Whiplash, the Iron Man villain who has assumed two identities throughout his career, was introduced in a Stan Lee–scripted and Gene Colan–penciled story in *Tales of Suspense* #97 (1968). A part-time hitman for the Maggia crime syndicate, he creates a steel-fiber whip capable of penetrating virtually any substance, and in his Whiplash identity takes on Iron Man.

Several years later, in *Iron Man* #62 (1973), the villain was established as Mark Scott, aka Mark Scarliotti, research head of Stark Industries Cincinnati. After serving time at Ryker's Island Prison and having his identity revealed to the authorities, the washed-up Whiplash reinvented himself as Blacklash. As a freelance mercenary for the Maggia, Blacklash often came head to head with criminals of organized crime, various miscreants, and his arch-rival Iron Man. Wearing a steel-mesh battle-suit, he displayed strong hand-to-hand combat and an adept control of his numerous whips, including one that converted into a nunchaku and could be extended into a pole for vaulting.

Blacklash also battled Spider-Man (in team-ups with Iron Man) in *Marvel Team-Up* vol. 1 #72 (1978) and #145 (1984), the Thing in *Marvel Two-in-One* #96 (1983), and a solo web-slinger in *Amazing Spider-Man* #319 (1989). Writer Kurt Busiek and artist Sean Chen brought the character back as Whiplash in *Iron Man* vol. 3 #8 (1998), with a new costume that some reviewers have likened to an S&M look. A version of Blacklash, renamed Backlash, appeared in the *Iron Man* animated television series (1994–1996). —*GM*

White Queen

Having been aimed primarily at adolescent male audiences for decades, superhero comic books are replete with provocative images of the female form. One of the most iconic of these is the White Queen, aka Emma Frost, a key villainess in Marvel Comics' X-Men franchise. One of the central leadership figures of the centuries-old evil organization known as the Hellfire Club, the White Queen is the creation of the writer/artist team of Christ Claremont and John Byrne first seen in *X-Men* vol. 1 #129 (1980), who patterned her costume—essentially a white lace-up teddy, skimpy underwear, thigh-high stocking-like boots, and a white cape, all of which complements her striking ash-blond hair—after the black "Queen of Sin" outfit worn by Diana

Rigg in the classic 1960s British television spy series *The Avengers*. According to Byrne, the name "Emma Frost" is an homage to Rigg's memorable character, Emma Peel.

Born to old Boston money, the brilliant Emma Frost first begins manifesting mutant powers during her early teens; her powers include telepathy and the ability to make her skin diamond-hard, though the use of the latter power shuts down her psionic talents. Thanks to her keen mind, her mutant gifts, and her family fortune, Frost reaches the top of the

Emma Frost, the White Queen (Finola Hughes), and Banshee (Jeremy Ratchford) from the Fox television pilot *Generation X* (1996).

business world while still a very young woman, thereby attracting the attention of the Lords Cardinal of the Inner Circle of the Hellfire Club, who extend to her a rare invitation to join their world-dominating ranks. She quickly accepts the Hellfire Club's offer—as well as its rather extreme wardrobe requirements—to become the White Queen of the Inner Circle's chess-based hierarchy.

Although immersed in the pursuit of the Hellfire Club's global political and economic agenda, Ms. Frost presents a relatively innocuous face to the public at large. Indeed, as chairwoman of the board, chief executive officer, and majority stockholder of Frost International, a large transportation and electronics corporation—as well as headmistress and chairwoman of the board of trustees of the exclusive Massachusetts Academy prep school—Frost seems to be one of the proverbial pillars of American society. Little does anyone outside the Hellfire Club suspect that matriculating at her school are the teenage supervillains-in-training known as the Hellions (*New Mutants* #16, 1984), who clash with the X-Men and the New Mutants on numerous occasions.

Frost's actions are never entirely evil, however; in one of her earliest adventures as the White Queen, in 1987, she helped to prevent Dr. Steven Lang's Sentinel robots from wiping out every mutant on Earth. She was later rendered even more sympathetic by the tragedies she endured, most notably the murder of her Hellion students by the time-traveling Trevor Fitzroy, aka Chronomancer, a powerful adversary of the Hellfire Club who nearly succeeded in killing Frost as well. By 1994, Frost's Hellions were replaced by a new group of superpowered students known as Generation X, though they eventually disbanded along with their prep school.

Moved by the genocide committed against the mutants of the nation of Genosha by Cassandra Nova's Sentinels, Frost eventually became a member of the X-Men, having come to see the "good-guy" mutant team as an attractive alternative to the bleak, world-beating ethos of the Hellfire Club (*X-Men* vol. 2 #115, 2001). Free for now from the Inner Circle, Emma Frost demonstrates the transcendent power of hope over villainy.

The White Queen's look hugely influenced the generations of lingerie-clad, dominatrix-styled female heroes and villains that followed. The character has even migrated from the comics back into the medium that inspired her: voiced by Susan Silo, the White Queen appeared in the animated *Pryde of the X-Men,* a television series pilot that was aired in 1988 in syndication and was subsequently released on VHS; and in the live-action FOX teen-mutant dramatic pilot *Generation X* (1996), in which Finola Hughes donned the White Queen's combat-ready lingerie. —*MAM*

Wizard I

Tibet—the one-stop shopping source for superheroes and supervillains craving mastery of occult or martial arts—was where "W. I. Zard" (William Asmodeus Zard) studied to become DC Comics' wicked Wizard. First seen in the Justice Society of America (JSA) serial "The Wiles of the Wizard!" in *All Star Comics* #34 (1947), written by Gardner Fox and drawn by several artists including Irwin Hasen and Joe Kubert, the Wizard is garbed like a stage magician—a tuxedo, cape, top hat, and magic wand. An accomplished illusionist, having mastered hypnotism under the tutelage of a Tibetan monk he later slays, the deceitful Wizard mistrusts the JSA, believing their altruism to be a façade, and dares them to stop a quintet of his crimes. When thwarted by the JSA, he appears to leap to his doom.

But this is merely an illusion. The Wizard returned as a founder of the Injustice Society of the World (issue #34, 1947) and made another outing (again partnered with other villains) before vanishing as the final curtain was drawn on comics' Golden Age (1938–1954). Writer Fox revived him in *Justice League of America* (JLA) #21's (1963) landmark JLA/JSA crossover "Crisis on Earth-One," this time as one of the Crime Champions, working with the Fiddler and the Icicle. Rarely a solo villain, the Wizard regularly appeared in the *Secret Society of Super-Villains* series (1976–1978) and conjured chaos in several JLA/JSA team-ups. Author Neil Gaiman used the character in his original *Books of Magic* miniseries (1990–1991), and as an occasional player in DC's

Vertigo imprint the Wizard's misadventures became more supernatural in scope, with his perverted soul at one time being imprisoned within the cloak of the bizarre hero Ragman. Never one to remain out of the limelight for long, in 2005 the Wizard joined forces with Lex Luthor's Society in the pages of *Villains United*.

The Wizard was not the first supervillain to use this name, nor was he the last. *Top-Notch Comics* #1 (1939), from MLJ Publications (Archie Comics), offered the Wizard, the "man with the Super Brain" who started as a Mandrake the Magician imitation but later gained a superhero costume and a sidekick (Roy the Super Boy)—but when revived in *Fly-Man* #33 (1965) had acquired mystical powers and used them for crime. A black-hooded instigator called the Wizard (played by Leonard Penn) with a remote control that stopped machinery and vehicles was the adversary in Columbia Pictures' movie serial *Batman and Robin* (1949). Marvel Comics' Wizard became a regular foe of the Fantastic Four starting in 1962, and DC introduced a second Wizard, a devilish persona of Robby Reed, in the 1980s version of its "Dial H for Hero" concept. —*ME*

Wizard II

The Human Torch found himself the "Prisoner of the Wizard" in his solo series in *Strange Tales* #102 (1962), written by Stan Lee and Larry Lieber with artist Jack Kirby. An unnamed scientist/magician grows jaded of his technological achievements and selects the path most commonly chosen by those of a megalomaniacal malaise: supervillainy. This knave known only as the Wizard traps the Torch, the youngest member of the Fantastic Four (FF), then dons a costume that simulates the flaming hero's superpowers, using them to create chaos. The Torch escapes and extinguishes the Wizard's plans, earning the villain's hatred.

The non-costumed Wizard was a recurring Torch foe in *Strange Tales*, but in *Fantastic Four* #36 (1965) first donned the uniform he has worn since: a purple armored bodysuit with a jumbo, egg-shaped helmet. In this Lee/Kirby adventure, the high-tech Wizard attacked the entire FF with an

FF of his own: the Frightful Four, the Wizard's superteam comprised of Paste-Pot Pete (with whom he had partnered in *Strange Tales*), the Sandman, and Madam Medusa (aka Medusa of the Inhumans).

Since then, the Wizard has remained one of the Marvel Universe's most constant and cunning threats, tackling everyone from the Avengers to Spider-Man. His primary weapons are his anti-gravity discs, which he uses for flight; he also wields his discs against heroes, making them weightless. The Wizard's power gloves emit energy blasts that rival Iron Man's repulsor rays, and over the years he has employed everything from giant robots to nuclear bombs in his war against justice. Ron Perlman voiced the Wizard in a 1994 *Fantastic Four* cartoon, which inspired a Wizard action figure from manufacturer Toy Biz. —*ME*

The Wrecking Crew

Although the purveyors of wanton violence have little prestige among super–bad guys, villains who smash things nevertheless possess an evergreen working-class appeal. Thus did the Wrecking Crew—jointly created by Stan Lee, Jack Kirby, Len Wein, Chris Claremont, and Sal Buscema—become the quintessential 1970s "blue collar" Marvel Comics supervillain group. This garage band of mayhem was founded by a convicted robber known as the Wrecker (Dirk Garthwaite), an antisocial former demolition company laborer who can raze buildings and challenge gods, thanks to a 4-feet-long iron crowbar powered by stolen Norse magicks (*Thor* vol. 1 #148–#150, 1968). After the Wrecker escapes from Ryker's Island with three fellow inmates (*Defenders* vol. 1 #17–#19, 1974–1975), he recovers his confiscated crowbar, only to experience a freak lightning strike that transforms his confederates into thematically simpatico supervillains: the armored juggernaut known as Bulldozer (Henry Camp); the ham-fisted pummeler called Piledriver (Brian Philip Calusky); and the wrecking ball–wielding Thunderball (Dr.

Earthquaking Supervillains

Countless supervillains have attempted to conquer Earth, but others have literally *shaken* it:

- **Vibraman**, originating in *T.H.U.N.D.E.R. Agents* #3 (1965), was a blind supervillain who used his sonic "Vibragun" cannon to extort a fortune before being buried in a cave-in.

- **Major Disaster** first employed his "Stress-Null Beam Ray Machine" in *Green Lantern* vol. 2 #43 (1966), creating catastrophic events such as seismic tremors, landslides, windstorms, and meteor showers.

- **Vortex**, who soared over San Francisco on an airborne scooter, possessed a ray gun that manipulated centrifugal force to create calamites in the tradition of Major Disaster's device, and fought Supergirl in the early 1970s.

- **Quakemaster**, a purple-costumed supervillain with a large yellow "Q" chest emblem, initially rattled Batman with his super-jackhammer in 1977. Preceding Quakemaster in print was Marvel Comics' similarly equipped **Piledriver,** one of the Wrecking Crew, who debuted in 1968.

- **Avalanche**, a Greek mutant named Dominic Petros, first plied his ability to produce earth-rumbling vibrations as one of the Brotherhood of Evil Mutants in *X-Men* vol. 1 #141 (1981). As a solo supervillain Avalanche once dug up the familiar plot of threatening to sink California into the ocean.

- **Shakedown**, a tremor-creating supervillain for hire, was one of the Masters of Disasters in *Batman and the Outsiders* #9 (1984); his teammates were the icy Coldsnap, the combustive Heatstroke, the water-controlling New Wave, and the mistress of air currents, Windfall.

- **Vibro** was originally a geologist named Professor Vibereaux who was swallowed alive into a chasm and emerged with the power to create tremors, as readers of *Iron Man* #186 (1984) discovered.

- **Earthquake** has continued the tradition of planet-shakers in the new millennium; this supervillain first rumbled through Metropolis in *Superman: The Man of Steel* #110 (2001).

Eliot Franklin, the team's only arguably "white collar" member).

Under the Wrecker's leadership, the quartet has demanded enormous ransoms in exchange for not demolishing New York City skyscrapers and engaged in nuclear blackmail before being temporarily recaptured by Dr. Strange, the Hulk, Nighthawk, and Luke Cage. From the 1970s through the early 1990s, the Wrecking Crew was out of stir for clashes with such superheroes as Captain America, Iron Fist, Thor, Spider-Man and Spider-Woman II, the Avengers, Iron Man, Hercules, Excalibur, Code: Blue, and even the ectoplasmically powered Ghost Rider. Brawlers at heart, members of the Wrecking Crew clearly have little compunction about getting sideways with one another or with other supervillains, such as Venom.

The Wrecking Crew finally transcended their "street level" status when they were transported across the universe by the mysterious entity known as the Beyonder to participate in a gigantic heroes-versus-villains battle royale in *Marvel Super Heroes Secret Wars* #1–#12 (1984–1985). But the Crew's newfound cosmic stature didn't last; they were back on Earth and in prison within the year, courtesy of Spider-Man and Spider-Woman II.

Freed yet again and re-powered by Doomsday Man, in the late 1990s the Wrecking Crew attacked the Statue of Liberty, only to be thwarted by the young Thunderbolts superteam; they later took over the extradimensional realm of Polemachus, until its legitimate sovereigns Arkon and Thundra, along with the Avengers, booted them out and re-imprisoned them. Though they languished behind bars in the mid-2000s, the Wrecking Crew waits patiently, in Ralph Kramden–like fashion, for yet another opportunity to seize the day. —*MAM*

The Yellow Claw

A paranoid America believed that Communists lurked behind every corner during the cold war, but their invasion of the U.S. was largely limited to fiction—including comic books. Writer Al Feldstein and artist Joe Maneely introduced Marvel (then Atlas) Comics' Asian mastermind Tzing Jao, aka the Yellow Claw, in *Yellow Claw* #1 (1956), one of the earliest instances of a supervillain being awarded his own comics series. In the vein of Sax Rohmer's Fu Manchu and Flash Gordon's arch-foe Ming the Merciless, the Yellow Claw is sworn to displace Western culture with his own familial hierarchy. Rendered in the classic yet politically incorrect interpretation of the dreaded "Yellow Peril" with jaundiced skin, pointy ears, claw-like fingers, and the obligatory "Fu Manchu" goatee, the Yellow Claw has lived for at least a century and half, his longevity the result of an herbal elixir. Unforgiving and unrepentant, the Yellow Claw shows no regard for anyone other than his sole living relative, his grandniece Suwan, who stands opposed to his machinations.

Throughout his four-issue series the Yellow Claw exploited science and sorcery to initiate insidious plots (three per issue) against America, allying with Communist Chinese soldiers and Nazi war criminals, and casting illusions to sway the weak-minded. The bane of his existence was

Strange Tales #161 ©1967 Marvel Comics.
COVER ART BY JIM STERANKO.

The Supervillain Book

Asian-American FBI agent Jimmy Woo, who, to the Claw's displeasure, was Suwan's lover. Writer Feldstein, a carryover from the intensely graphic EC Comics of the 1950s, felt restrained by the newly implemented Comics Code and vacated *Yellow Claw* after issue #1 (returning to EC to edit *MAD*), Maneely departing with him, and writer/artist Jack Kirby took over for the remainder of the run.

Resurrected by writer/artist Jim Steranko in the Nick Fury, Agent of S.H.I.E.L.D. story in *Strange Tales* #161 (1967), the Yellow Claw now fronted a network of uniformed anti-American operatives, their jumpsuits emblematized with a yellow oval claw icon. Although it was revealed that this Yellow Claw was a robot proxy, Steranko had successfully integrated the menace into the Marvel Universe, bolstered by agent Wu's reemergence as a S.H.I.E.L.D. agent. The real Yellow Claw returned in *Captain America* #164 (1973), and his cold war–era villainy galvanized a group of 1950s superheroes into action in *What If?* vol. 1 #9 (1978). The Yellow Claw has appeared occasionally since, battling Iron Man, Nova, and the Avengers with mutated monsters, cyborgs, and his will-nullifying "id paralyzer." His grandniece Suwan, has died. —*ME*

Zombie Priest

When a comic book's heroes are underworld gangsters, its villains are bound to be extraordinarily evil. In *The Goon,* this sort of superlative villainy is precisely what the Zombie Priest provides. *The Goon*, created by writer/artist Eric Powell and published by Dark Horse Comics, is an amalgam of various periods and genres of comics. The book is part humor, part mystery, part action, and part horror. One of the series' staple gags occurs when Goon's partner, a character named Frankie, yells "Knife to the eye!"—a direct reference to the war on comics' content that Dr. Fredric Wertham launched with his 1954 book *Seduction of the Innocent. The Goon* is apparently set in the 1930s, but contemporary technology and popular culture references pervade the series. The book offers a unique mixture of familiar comics elements, and its feature villain reflects the complexity of the book as a whole.

The Zombie Priest (also known as "the Nameless One") is loosely patterned on a traveling southern preacher, but he is also a mad scientist, a witch doctor, and a voodoo priest who dabbles in monstrous reanimation of dead creatures. The Priest's past is murky, but bits and pieces of his history have been revealed over the course of the series. A short story in *The Goon* #14 (2005)

The Goon #14 2005 © & ™ Eric Powell.
COVER ART BY ERIC POWEL

revealed that the Priest is an ancient manifestation of evil whose destiny is tied to his archetypal nemesis, the Goon. Before the Zombie Priest settled in Goon's city, he traveled from town to town corrupting local populations. In one of these towns, the Priest subverted the authority of the sheriff and gradually killed off the town's populace only to revive them later as zombies. The sheriff (now known as Buzzard) survived the attack, but the Priest cursed him with a cruel, horrible fate.

As of early 2006 the Zombie Priest has set up his headquarters on Lonely Street in Goon's hometown. Despite Goon's repeated attempts to defend his own turf against rival gang leaders, the Priest appears to be cultivating an army of the undead to wage a final war against humanity. —AB

Zorak

No supervillain has come closer to defeating Space Ghost than the lethal locust Zorak. With a robotic minion named Titanor in his thrall, Zorak, resembling a human-sized praying mantis, issues "The Challenge" to Space Ghost in an episode of the Hanna-Barbera cartoon *Space Ghost and Dino Boy* cartoon (1966–1968) originally aired October 29, 1966. Space Ghost is pummeled by the mechanical warrior until discovering that the insidious Zorak has substituted his power bands with neutered duplicates. His energies restored, Space Ghost junkheaps Titanor, but Zorak slinks away.

Animation voice great Don Messick played Zorak in his 1960s television appearances, in which he bedeviled the cloaked champion with weapons manufactured (such as his Matter Intensifier) and organic (his razor-sharp claws and mandibles). For his frequent but unsuccessful attempts to conquer planets, Zorak served a stretch on Gaolworld (Comico's 1987 *Space Ghost* one-shot comic book by Mark Evanier and Steve Rude). He was later imprisoned on Space Ghost's own Ghost Planet, from which he was paroled to become the bandleader (of the Original Way Outs) on the animation/live-action hybrid *Space Ghost: Coast to Coast* (1994–2004), a talk-show parody on cable television. Zorak loathed and insulted the heroic host, only to be belted by a blast from

Space Ghost's power bands in response to each barb. Zorak's evil knew no bounds: "My favorite episode of *The Golden Girls* is the one where they all took contaminated Geritol and died," he once cackled, his voice provided by actor C. Martin Croker, but when informed there was no such program he replied, "Well, there *should* have been!" In the early 2000s an action figure of Zorak was produced as one of several tie-ins to the show.

Zorak's camaraderie with fellow Space Ghost rogue Brak earned him a supporting-cast slot on the Cartoon Network's *The Brak Show* (2000–2003), a suburban-based sitcom in which child-aged Zorak and Brak were playmates. Writer Joe Kelly and artist Ariel Olivetti overhauled Zorak in DC Comics' miniseries prequel to the 1966 Space Ghost cartoons, *Space Ghost* (2005), reimagining him as a gruesome, multi-armed insectoid. Zorak, leader of a hive-like swarm of planet pillagers, allied with Space Ghost's former military commander in an attempt to end the crusader's career just as it was starting, and engaged in a gory duel with the hero, remarking, "Inside, all men are soft," while spearing Space Ghost's abdomen. Whether portrayed as spine-chilling or funny bone–tickling, Zorak stands supreme as Space Ghost's arch-nemesis. —ME

Zurg

Evil Emperor Zurg is the "arch nemesis of Buzz Lightyear"—it says so right on his box. In the Disney-Pixar computer-generated movie *Toy Story 2* (1999), Zurg, voiced by screenwriter/director Andrew Stanton, is, in the film's reality, a supervillain action figure that attempts to "Destroy Buzz Lightyear!" when swashbuckling spaceman figure Lightyear (Tim Allen) launches a rescue mission to liberate Woody the cowboy doll (Tom Hanks) from a money-grubbing toy collector. Cloaked in royal purples, blues, and reds, with a horned helmet and flowing cape, Zurg unapologetically parodies *Star Wars*' Darth Vader, even with Zurg claiming to be Lightyear's father, as Vader did to Luke Skywalker in *The Empire Strikes Back* (1980).

Buzz Lightyear of Star Command (2000–2001), a 62-episode cartoon series, continued the hero's adventures outside of *Toy Story*. Elevated from walk-on status to the show's chief adversary, Emperor Zurg, now voiced by Wayne Knight, was revealed to be not only Lightyear's nemesis but the enemy of the intergalactic network called the Galactic Alliance and its peace-keeping force, Star Command. From his battleship Zurg initiated, in almost every episode, a Machiavellian plot that required the intervention of Lightyear: Zurg cloned Star Command members, displaced planets to other dimensions, mutated vegetables with his "Transdibulator," and transformed Lightyear's allies into beasts, snarling such phrases as "Vengeance shall be mine, Lightyear!" and "Come to me, my prey!"

Zurg skirmishes with his arch-foe in the attractions "Buzz Lightyear's Space Ranger Spin" and "Buzz Lightyear's Astro Blasters" at various Disney theme parks. He has been manufactured in a variety of merchandising from candy dispensers to, coming full circle with his original "form," an action figure. —*ME*

How to Build a Supervillain:
The Resources

PERIODICALS AND FANZINES

Alter Ego. Published monthly by TwoMorrows Publishing, 10407 Bedfordtown Drive, Raleigh, NC 27614. www.twomorrows.com

Anime Insider. Published monthly by Wizard Entertainment, 151 Wells Avenue, Congers, NY 10920-2064. www.wizarduniverse.com

Animerica. Published monthly by Viz Communications, 655 Bryant Street, San Francisco, CA 94107. www.animerica-mag.com

BACK ISSUE. Published bimonthly by TwoMorrows Publishing, 10407 Bedfordtown Drive, Raleigh, NC 27614. www.twomorrows.com

Comic Book Artist. Published by Top Shelf Productions, P.O. Box 1282, Marietta, GA 30061-1282. www.topshelfcomix.com

Comic Shop News. Published weekly by Comic Shop News, Inc., 2770 Carillon Crossing, Marietta, GA 30066. wwwcsnsider.com. Available at comic-book shops nationwide or through Diamond Distributors.

Comics Interview. Published by Fictioneer Books, Ltd., 52 Trillium Lane, Screamer Mountain, Clayton, GA 30525.

The Comics Journal. Published monthly by Fantagraphics Books, 7563 Lake City Way NE, Seattle, Washington, 98115. www.tcj.com

International Journal of Comic Art. Published twice yearly by John A. Lent, 669 Ferne Blvd., Drexel Hill, PA 19026.

The Jack Kirby Collector. Published quarterly by TwoMorrows Publishing, 10407 Bedfordtown Drive, Raleigh, NC 27614. www.twomorrows.com

Manga Max. Published by Titans Magazines. 42-44 Dolben Street. London SE1 OUP England.

Newtype USA. Published by A.D. Vision, Inc., P.O. Box 631607, Houston, TX 77263. www.newtype-usa.com

Protoculture Addicts. Published monthly by Protoculture, P.O. Box 1433, Station B, Montreal, Quebec, Canada H3B 3L2. www.protoculture-mag.com

Wizard: The Comics Magazine. Published monthly by Wizard Entertainment, 151 Wells Avenue, Congers, NY 10920-2064. www.wizarduniverse.com

NONFICTION WORKS

Anime and Manga

Baricordi, Andrea, et al. Translated from the Italian by Adeline D'Opera and presented by Claude J. Pelletier. *Anime: A Guide to Japanese Animation (1958–1988).* Montreal: Protoculture, 2000.

Clements, Jonathan, and Helen McCarthy. *The Anime Encyclopedia: A Guide to Japanese Animation since 1917.* Berkeley, CA: Stone Bridge Press, 2001.

Gravett, Paul. *Manga: Sixty Years of Japanese Comics.* New York: Harper Collins, 2004.

Kinsella, Sharon. *Adult Manga: Culture and Power in Contemporary Japanese Society.* Honolulu: University of Hawaii Press, 2000.

Ledoux, Trish, and Doug Ranney. *The Complete Anime Guide,* 2nd ed. Issaquah, WA: Tiger Mountain Press, 1997.

McCarthy, Helen. *The Anime Movie Guide: Movie-by-Movie Guide to Japanese Animation*. Woodstock, NY: The Overlook Press, 1997.

Patten, Fred. "TV Animation in Japan." *Fanfare* (May 1980).

Poitras, Gilles. *The Anime Companion: What's Japanese in Japanese Animation?* Berkeley, CA: Stone Bridge Press, 1998.

_____. *Anime Essentials: Everything a Fan Needs to Know*. Berkeley, CA: Stone Bridge Press, 2001.

Schodt, Frederik L. *Manga! Manga! The World of Japanese Comics*. Tokyo and New York: Kodansha International, 1983.

_____. *Dreamland Japan: Writings on Modern Manga*. Berkeley, CA: Stone Bridge Press, 1996.

Comic Book Academia and History

Benton, Mike. *The Comic Book in America: An Illustrated History*, 2nd ed. Dallas, TX: Taylor Publishing Company, 1993.

_____. *Masters of Imagination: The Comic Book Artists Hall of Fame*. Dallas, TX: Taylor Publishing Company, 1994.

Bridwell, E. Nelson. *Batman: From the Thirties to the Seventies*. New York: Bonanza Books, 1971.

_____. *Superman: From the Thirties to the Seventies*. New York: Bonanza Books, 1971.

Chinn, Mike. *Writing and Illustrating the Graphic Novel: Everything You Need to Create Great Graphic Works*. Hauppauge, NY: Barrons, 2004.

Daniels, Les. *Comix: A History of Comic Books in America*. New York: Bonanza Books, 1971.

DC Comics. *Fifty Who Made DC Great*. New York: DC Comics, 1985.

Duin, Steve, and Mike Richardson. *Comics Between the Panels*. Milwaukie, OR: Dark Horse Comics, Inc., 1998.

Eury, Michael. *The Justice League Companion*. Raleigh, NC: TwoMorrows, 2005.

Feiffer, Jules. *The Great Comic Book Heroes*. 1965. Reprint, Seattle, WA: Fantagraphics Books, 2003.

Goulart, Ron. *Great History of Comic Books*. Chicago: Contemporary Books, 1986.

_____, ed. *The Encyclopedia of American Comics*. New York: Facts on File, 1990.

_____. *Over 50 Years of American Comic Books*. Lincolnwood, IL: Publications International, 1991.

Harvey, Robert C. *The Art of the Comic Book: An Aesthetic History*. Jackson: University Press of Mississippi, 1996.

Horn, Maurice, ed. *The World Encyclopedia of Comics*. 7 vols. Broomall, PA: Chelsea House, 1999.

Jones, Gerard. *Men of Tomorrow: Geeks, Gangsters, and the Birth of the Comic Book*. New York: Basic Books, 2004.

Kunzle, David. *The Early Comic Strip*. Berkeley: University of California Press, 1973.

Lee, Stan, and George Mail. *Excelsior! The Amazing Life of Stan Lee*. New York: Fireside, 2002.

Overstreet, Robert M. *The Overstreet Comic Book Price Guide*, 35th ed. Timonium, MD: Gemstone Publishing, Inc., 2005.

Sanderson, Peter. *Marvel Universe*. New York: Harry Abrams, 1996.

Savage, William W., Jr. *Comic Books and America, 1945–1954*. Norman: University of Oklahoma Press, 1990.

Simon, Joe, and Jim Simon. *The Comic Book Makers*. New York: Crestwood Publications, 1990.

Spiegelman, Art, and Chip Kidd. *Jack Cole and Plastic Man: Forms Stretched to Their Limits!* San Francisco: Chronicle Books, 2001.

Steranko, James. *The Steranko History of Comics*. 2 vols. Reading, PA: Supergraphics, 1970, 1972.

Thomas, Roy. *The All-Star Companion,* Vol. 1. Raleigh, NC: TwoMorrows, 2004.

Wiater, Staley, and Stephen R. Bissette. *Comic Book Rebels: Conversations with the Creators of the New Comics*. New York: Donald I. Fine, 1993.

Wright, Bradford. *Comic Book Nation: The Transformation of Youth Culture in America*. Baltimore: Johns Hopkins University Press, 2001.

Superhero and Supervillain Wit and Wisdom

Beatty, Scott. *Batman: The Ultimate Guide to the Dark Knight*. New York: Dorling Kindersley, 2001.

_____. *JLA: The Ultimate Guide to the Justice League of America*. New York: Dorling Kindersley, 2002.

_____. *Superman: The Ultimate Guide to the Man of Steel*. New York: Dorling Kindersley, 2002.

_____. *Wonder Woman: The Ultimate Guide to the Amazon Princess*. New York: Dorling Kindersley, 2003.

_____. *Catwoman: The Visual Guide to the Feline Fatale*. New York: Dorling Kindersley, 2004.

Benton, Mike. *Superhero Comics of the Silver Age: The Illustrated History.* Dallas, TX: Taylor Publishing Company, 1991.

_____. *Superhero Comics of the Golden Age: The Illustrated History.* Dallas, TX: Taylor Publishing Company, 1992.

Bongco, Mila. *Reading Comics: Language, Culture, and the Concept of the Superhero in Comic Books.* New York: Garland, 2000.

Colón, Suzan. *Catwoman: The Life and Times of a Feline Fatale.* San Francisco: Chronicle, 2003.

Coogan, Peter. *Superhero: The Secret History of a Genre.* Introduction by Denny O'Neil. Austin, TX: MonkeyBrain Press, 2006.

_____. "The Secret Origin of the Superhero: The Emergence of the Superhero Genre in America from Daniel Boone to Batman." Doctoral dissertation, East Lansing, MI: Michigan State University, American Studies Department, 2002.

Cooke, Jon B., ed. *The T.H.U.N.D.E.R. Agents Companion.* Raleigh, NC: TwoMorrows, 2005.

Daniels, Les. *DC Comics: Sixty Years of the World's Favorite Comic Book Heroes.* Boston: Little, Brown, 1995.

_____. *Marvel: Five Fabulous Decades of the World's Greatest Comics.* Special collector's edition. Introduction by Stan Lee. New York: Harry Abrams, 1995.

_____. *Superman: The Complete History: The Life and Times of the Man of Steel.* San Francisco: Chronicle Books, 1998.

_____. *Batman: The Complete History: The Life and Times of the Dark Knight.* San Francisco: Chronicle Books, 1999.

_____. *Wonder Woman: The Life and Times of the Amazon Princess: The Complete History.* San Francisco: Chronicle Books, 2000.

DeFalco, Tom. *Spider-Man: The Ultimate Guide.* New York: Dorling Kindersley, 2001.

_____. *Hulk: The Incredible Guide.* New York: Dorling Kindersley, 2003.

_____. *Fantastic Four: The Ultimate Guide.* New York: Dorling Kindersley, 2005.

_____. *The Avengers: The Ultimate Guide.* New York: Dorling Kindersley, 2005.

Dougall, Alastair, senior ed. *The DC Comics Encyclopedia.* New York: Dorling Kindersley, 2004.

Eury, Michael. *Captain Action: The Original Super-Hero Action Figure.* Raleigh, NC: TwoMorrows, 2003.

Fingeroth, Danny. *Superman on the Couch: What Superheroes Really Tell Us about Ourselves and Our Society.* New York: Continuum, 2004.

Fleisher, Michael L. *The Encyclopedia of Comic Book Heroes: Volume 1: Batman.* New York: Macmillan, 1976.

_____. *The Encyclopedia of Comic Book Heroes: Volume 2: Wonder Woman.* New York: Macmillan, 1976.

_____. *The Encyclopedia of Comic Book Heroes: Volume 3: The Great Superman Book.* New York: Macmillan, 1978.

Howe, Sean, ed. *Give Our Regards to the Atom Smashers!* New York: Pantheon Books, 2004.

Jacobs, Will, and Gerard Jones. *The Comic Book Heroes: From the Silver Age to the Present.* New York: Crown, 1985.

Johnston, Ollie, and Frank Thomas. *The Disney Villain.* New York: Hyperion, 1993.

Klock, Geoff. *How to Read Superhero Comics and Why.* New York: Continuum, 2002.

Lee, Stan. *Bring on the Bad Guys: Origins of the Marvel Comics Villains.* New York: Fireside Books, 1976.

Marvel Comics. *Marvel Encyclopedia.* New York: Marvel Comics, 2002.

Misiroglu, Gina, ed. *The Superhero Book: The Ultimate Encyclopedia of Comic-Book Icons and Hollywood Heroes.* Detroit, MI: Visible Ink Press, 2004.

Morris, Tom, and Matt Morris, eds. *Superheroes and Philosophy: Truth, Justice, and the Socratic Way.* Chicago: Open Court, 2005.

The Rough Guide to James Bond. London: Rough Guides, 2002. Distributed by Penguin Books Ltd., London.

The Rough Guide to Superheroes. London: Rough Guides, 2004. Distributed by Penguin Books Ltd., London.

Sanderson, Peter. *Ultimate X-Men.* New York: Dorling Kindersley, 2000.

DOCUMENTARIES AND FILMS

Comic Book Superheroes: Unmasked. Directed by Stephen Kroopnick. 100 min. Produced by Triage Entertainment for The History Channel, 2003. Documentary.

The Many Faces of Catwoman. Directed by Jeffrey Lerner. 30 min. Produced by New Wave Entertainment for the Warner Home Video DVD release of *Catwoman*, 2005. Documentary.

WEB SITES

AC Comics. www.accomics.com

Anime News Network. www.animenewsnetwork.com

Anime Web Turnpike. www.anipike.com

Animefringe. www.animefringe.com

Animation World Network. www.awn.com

Captain Planet. www.turner.com/planet

Comic Book Resources. www.ComicBookResources.com

Comic Shop News. www.dreamsville.com/CSN/

Dark Horse Comics. www.darkhorse.com

DC Comics. www.dccomics.com

Diamond Comics. www.diamondcomics.com

Don Markstein's Toonpedia. www.toonpedia.com

The Grand Comics Database Project. www.comics.org

The Holloway Pages. www.home.comcast.net/~cjh5801a/Pulp.htm

The Internet Movie Database. www.imdb.com

Lambiek Comiclopedia. www.lambiek.net

Marvel Comics. www.marvel.com

The Online World of Anime and Manga. www.ex.org

Silver Bullet Comic Books. www.silverbulletcomicbooks.com

Spawn. www.spawn.com

World Famous Comics. www.worldfamouscomics.com

ORGANIZATIONS AND FAN CLUBS

The Comics Arts Conference is a conference designed to bring together comics scholars, practitioners, critics, and historians who wish to promote or engage in serious study of the medium, and to do so in a forum that includes the public. Affiliated with the Comic-Con International, the CAC homepage can be found at www.hsu.edu/faculty/duncanr/cac_page.htm

Photo and Illustration Credits

The following materials are reprinted with permission:

DARK HORSE comics are published by Dark Horse Comics, Inc. Dark Horse Comics®& the Dark Horse logo are registered trademarks of Dark Horse Comics, Inc. THE MASK™ © Dark Horse Comics, Inc. MADMAN™ © Mike Allred. THE GOON™ © Eric Powell. HELLBOY™ © Mike Mignola.

E-MAN™ & © 2006 Joe Staton/First Comics. All rights reserved.

Original JOKER cover art to *BACK ISSUE* #3 (Two-Morrows Publications, 2004) reprinted by permission of Brian Bolland.

JUDGE DEATH: 2000 AD, Judge Dredd & Judge Death™ & © 2006 Rebellion A/S. www.2000 adonline.com. All rights reserved.

RASPUTIN: Mike Mignola's Hellboy and related characters™ & © 2006 Mike Mignola.

SHREDDER © 2006 Mirage Studios, Inc. Teenage Mutant Ninja Turtles and the Shredder are trademarks of Mirage Studios, Inc. All rights reserved.

SKELETOR © 1983/1984 Entertainment Rights PLC. All rights reserved. He-Man and the Masters of the Universe and other character names are trademarks of Mattel, Inc.

SPAWN and all related characters © &™ 2006 Todd McFarlane. All rights reserved.

T.H.U.N.D.E.R. AGENTS, UNDERSEA AGENT, and all related characters © &™ 2006 John Carbonaro. All rights reserved.

ZOLTAR and all related BATTLE OF THE PLANETS® characters © 2006 Sandy Frank Entertainment. All rights reserved. *Battle of the Planets Artbook* vol. 1 © 2004 Top Cow Productions, Inc.

TV and Film Stills Credits

p. 8: Paramount/The Kobal Collection; p. 32: 20th Century Fox/Greenway/The Kobal Collection; p. 44: The Kobal Collection/EON/UA; p. 67: Warner Bros./The Kobal Collection; p. 87: Hanna-Barbera Productions Inc./DC Comics; p. 88: Lucasfilm/20th Century Fox/The Kobal Collection; p. 97: New Horizons/Constantin Film Produktion GmbH/Marvel Entertainment Group; p. 104: Marvel/Sony Pictures/The Kobal Collection; p. 105: New Line/The Kobal Collection; p. 138: Warner Bros./DC Comics/The Kobal Collection; p. 147: Columbia/Marvel/The Kobal Collection; p. 179: 20th Century Fox/The Kobal Collection; p. 189: Paramount/The Kobal Collection; p. 202: 20th Century Fox/Marvel Entertainment/The Kobal Collection/Nels Israelson; p. 222: 20th Century Fox/Marvel Entertainment/The Kobal Collection/Nels Israelson; p. 233: Saban/Toei/The Kobal Collection; p. 235: Universal/The Kobal Collection; p. 261: 20th Century Fox/Marvel Entertainment/The Kobal Collection/Nels Israelson; p. 275: Warner Bros./DC Comics; p. 280: Warner Bros./The Kobal Collection/Christine Loss; p. 290: Warner Bros./DC Comics; p. 299: Warner Bros./The Kobal Collection/Ralph Nelson Jr.; p. 314: Warner Bros./DC Comics; p. 317: Saban International/Fox Children's Network, Inc./Marvel Entertainment Group; p. 334: The Kobal Collection/Warner Bros. TV; p. 355: Disney/Pixar/The Kobal Collection; p. 401: New World Entertainment/Fox/Marvel Productions, Ltd.

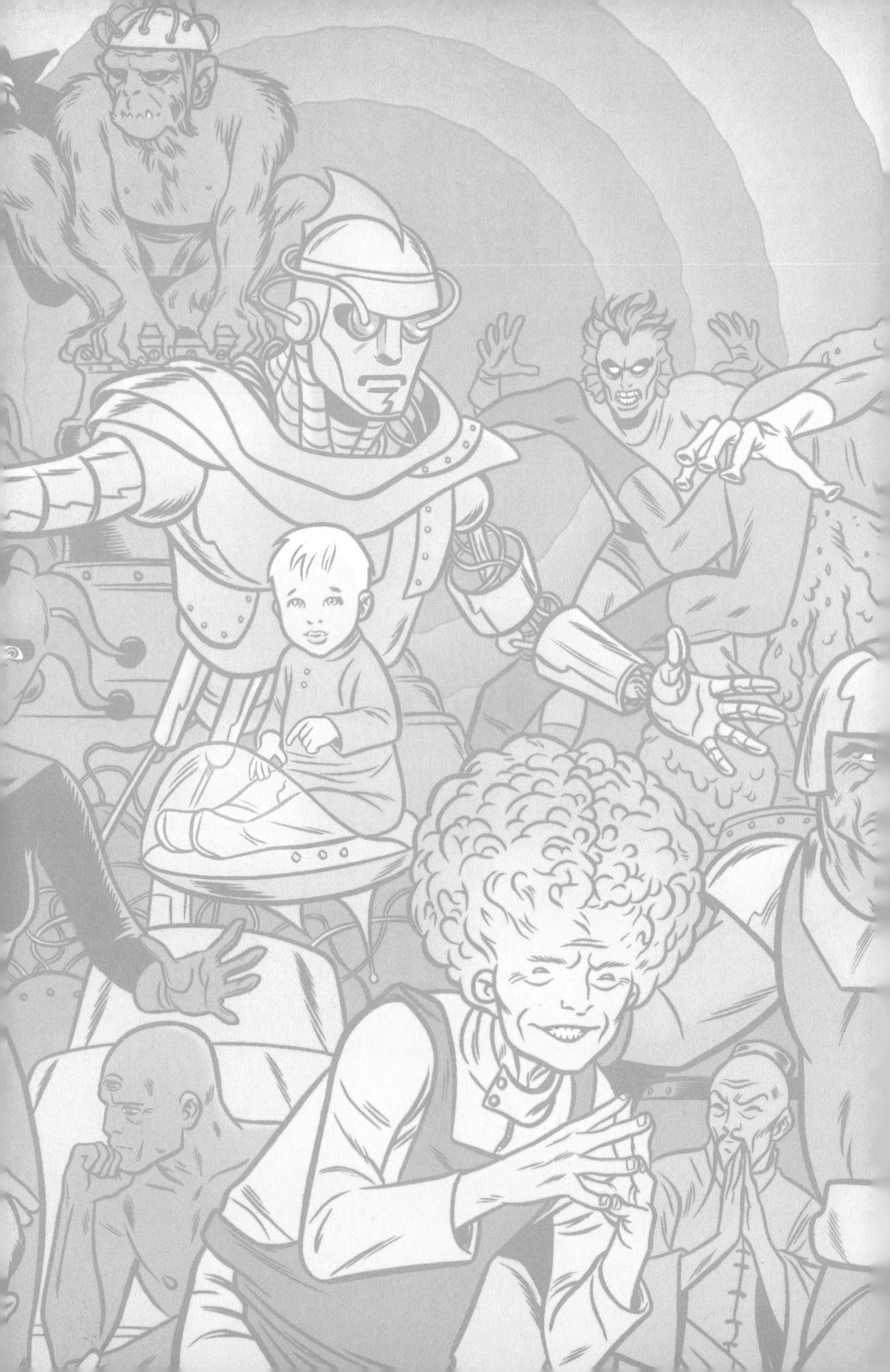

The Ultimate Supervillain Locater:
The Index

Boldface refers to page numbers on which main entries appear.

B

C

G

H

The Supervillain Book

K

L

M

The Supervillain Book

X

Y

Z

EPIC HEROES FOR AN EPIC AGE

With more than 150 full-color illustrations, including dozens of classic comics covers, *The Superhero Book* is the ultimate A-to-Z compendium of everyone's favorite super-heroes and their mythology, sidekicks, villains, love interests, superpowers, and modus operandi. Almost 300 entries cover the best-loved and historically significant comic-book, movie, television, and super-heroes of fiction—mainstream and coun-terculture, famous and forgotten, best and worst. Star-studded contributors include Michael Eury, Andy Mangels, Michael A. Martin, Adam McGovern, Marc McKenzie, Frank Plowright, and David Roach.

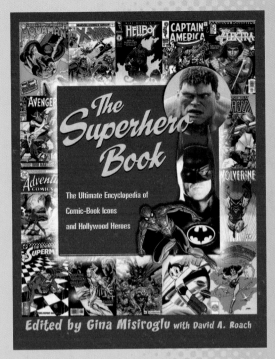

CRITICS RAVE, LEGENDS EXCLAIM

"This is a reference of Superheroic pro-portions that introduces the hundreds of comic-book heroes that have peopled the mythology of the twentieth century. An important addition to any library."

—Will Eisner, comic-book legend, creator of the Spirit

"... excellent compendium of comic book superheroes ...."

—*Choice*

"Being a 'super-hero' book rather than a 'comic book' book, it includes plenty of non-comics entries ... Happily, it has both a contents page and an index."

—*Comic Buyer's Guide*

"Here's an 'ultimate' encyclopedia that lives up to its billing."

—*Atlanta Journal-Constitution*

"*The Superhero Book: The Ultimate Encyclopedia of Comic-Book Icons and Hollywood Heroes* bills itself as 'the first comprehensive work to profile main-stream and counterculture, famous and

forgotten, best and worst superheroes from all companies and in all media ... ' and it lives up to the billing. Edited by Gina Misiroglu along with David Roach, the book includes a wide array of charac-ters, events and themes that have popu-lated the four-color world of superheroes. While it misses the Brownies (hey, they had super powers!), it's got just about every other major and many minor char-acter or set of characters in it, along with plenty of interesting observations. This is a great reference book and it's also fun for a casual read."

—*Scoop*'s Best Publications About Comics for 2005

"It definitely fills a much-needed niche in the growing lore of the genre and will be a welcome addition to the collection of any fan of spectacular superhero sagas. Excelsior!"

—Stan Lee, comic-book legend, inventor of the modern superhero

MORE...

"This book is alive with detail, generous with comic book cover reproductions, comprehensive, colorful, accurate, and, most of all, entertaining. It wants to cover as much ground as possible, and cover it right. The impressive thing is, it succeeds ... This encyclopedia is inspiring, and as a reference tool it is going to get a lot of use."

—*Silver Bullet Comics*

"A wonderful book with the BANG POW enthusiasm that ultimately helps to explain the lasting appeal of the world of superheroes. This book will be treasured by anyone who digs a good superhero comic book as much as I do."

—Michael Allred, creator of *Madman, The Atomics, Red Rocket 7,* and *X-Statix*

"An awesome project! A collection of facts, figures, and trivia from the Golden and Silver Ages of superhero comics. A must for comic historians and fans of all stripes!"

—Dick Giordano, legendary inker and illustrator, and former DC Comics editorial director

"You'll discover lots of fun details and history about some of your favorite superheroes in their comic-book, film, and TV incarnations."

—Amanda Conner, comic-book illustrator and co-creator of *The Pro* and *Gatecrasher*

"To me, the abstraction of the comics pages and on to motion pictures is what takes us back to times before, and to the present. This is a well-stated work."

—Mart Nodell, creator of the Green Lantern

"*The Superhero Book* will be fun to browse through, checking out entries at random—it's that reader-friendly. But I think it will have a more serious use as a valuable reference work for scholars and anyone else genuinely interested in popular culture."

—Dennis O'Neil, comic-book writer and editor

"This is a book I've been waiting for—an easy-to-use and entertaining reference book filled with comic books' greatest characters."

—Jerry Ordway, comic-book penciler, inker, and writer

"A wonder-filled collection of who's who and what's what in comicdom!"

—Julius Schwartz, legendary editor, DC Comics, 1944–1986

"Finally, a quick reference for a *Jeopardy* game show or a smart remark at a comic-book convention—Who would not want to know which superheroine had an invisible airplane? Or if Wolverine can pass security on U.S. airlines? Seriously, *The Superhero Book* is interesting for comparing ancient mythology with the new and a handy reference for artists and writers in creating new characters and using the old."

—Marie Severin, fifty-year veteran of the comic-book industry

"This colossal encyclopedia of all things superhero could not have come at a better time. With a slew of comic-book movies each year, kids are more interested than ever in anything to do with these heroes ... It is a must-buy for comic readers interested in knowing the early roots and conceptions of comic-book heroes."

—*School Library Journal*